CW00350824

JOHN S. BECKETT
The Man and the Music

In memory of, and in gratitude to, John Beckett

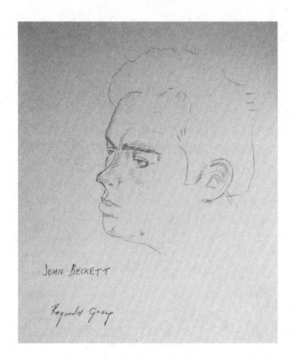

JOHN BECKETT

Reginald Gray

JOHN S. BECKETT
The Man and the Music

CHARLES GANNON

THE LILLIPUT PRESS
DUBLIN

First published in 2016 by
THE LILLIPUT PRESS
62–63 Sitric Road, Arbour Hill,
Dublin 7, Ireland
www.lilliputpress.ie

A CIP record for this title is available
from The British Library.

ISBN 978 1 84351 665 1

Set in 12 pt on 14 pt Perpetua by Marsha Swan
Printed in Spain by GraphyCems

Frontispiece: pencil sketch of John Beckett by Reginald Gray, 1952.
(Courtesy of Reginald Gray)

Contents

Illustrations

Foreword

John Stewart Beckett, who was born in Dublin in 1927 and died in London on his eightieth birthday, was a musician of powerful intellect, unswerving purpose and utter commitment in his performances and interpretations.

On an international level, he is remembered as a brilliant harpsichordist and interpreter of Bach's music, and as the conductor of the ground-breaking Renaissance music group Musica Reservata, based in London. Less well known are his compositions of *avant-garde* music for many BBC Third Programme radio plays, his expert playing of other instruments – piano, organ, lute, viol, recorder – his conducting of a wide range of music from early to modern, and his deep interest in folk music and certain types of jazz. He was a cousin of the famous writer Samuel Beckett and wrote music for some of Samuel's works: a mime, a radio play and readings from three of his novels.

John's great legacy to his native land was as a pioneer and innovator in the cause of early music in Ireland. I first met him after he had returned to Dublin from London around 1972 and it was not long afterwards that he conceived the idea of presenting an annual series devoted to Bach's cantatas. I was then manager of the New Irish Chamber Orchestra and I was gratified when he started to discuss his plan with me in detail. Written communication from John was always difficult to decipher as his handwriting resembled Chinese characters sloping backwards!

The choice of St Ann's Church, Dawson Street, Dublin, as the venue was sealed when he discovered that the building was completed in 1723, the same year that Bach became Cantor in St Thomas's Church in Leipzig. An auspicious link was established from the outset.

The first series took place in 1973 and it was apparent immediately that here was something new and very special. John conveyed energy, sincerity, freshness;

but above all, a magisterial authority as to how the cantatas should be performed. He was direct, he was blunt. Diplomacy was not exactly a Beckett trait, but his honesty and the conviction of his vision opened our ears, our minds and our hearts to this wonderful music. Even his initials, J.S.B., seemed to be confirmation that the spirit of Bach was embodied in John's burly and forceful figure.

Those of us who were privileged to take part in, and who were present at John's Bach performances, were touched by an experience that has influenced and affected us ever since. Many current developments in early music in Ireland can trace their origins in John Beckett's endeavours, not only on the concert platform, but also in his classes in the Royal Irish Academy of Music.

One of John's most significant and far-reaching actions was to persuade the Board of Arthur Guinness & Company to fund one of their employees, Cathal Gannon, to make harpsichords on a full-time basis. Cathal produced a succession of fine single- and double-manual harpsichords, which were rapidly acquired by performers in Ireland and the UK. John himself owned and played a double-manual Guinness Gannon instrument.

John Beckett's cantata series ran from 1973 to 1983, during which time well over fifty cantatas were revealed – and I use that word advisedly. The concerts achieved almost a cult following. It was not only in Dublin that these performances were admired. Nicholas Anderson, a BBC music producer, finding that many Bach cantatas were not in the BBC's archives, came to Dublin several times to help fill those gaps, by recording a number of concerts from the series. This happy association culminated in an invitation from the BBC for John, soloists, choir and orchestra to give an all-Bach concert – two major cantatas and two sinfonias – in the Royal Albert Hall, as part of the 1979 Henry Wood Promenade Concerts.

John revered the music of many composers other than Bach – Monteverdi, Purcell, Haydn, Mozart (though a little more grudgingly as he felt Mozart did not write such good development sections), Schubert, Chopin, Brahms, Fauré and, above all, Mahler. He also cherished an ambition – unfortunately not realized – to conduct a concert consisting entirely of Strauss waltzes.

He had intensely strong musical dislikes. The works of Handel and Vivaldi were anathema to him. *Messiah* was consigned to outer darkness and he once told me that the only worthwhile piece in it, the recitative 'Thy rebuke has broken his heart' must have been written by someone else, as it was too good for Handel!

Vivaldi fared even worse. It was, in John's view, an artistic tragedy that Bach stumbled across some Vivaldi scores in the library at Weimar. Even a hint of Italianate style in a Bach movement would produce a sorrowful shake of the head and an expression of regret for what he called 'Bach's Vivaldi mode'.

Not surprisingly, born into such a literary family, John had a striking flow of language. His commentaries were sculptured with total clarity and economy. Many people came to his cantata series not only for the music, but also to enjoy John's pithy and idiosyncratic introductions. His aphorisms were many and incisive. One example must suffice: exhorting the choir for better diction, he told them, 'I want to feel the spittle of your consonants on my chin!'

In view of the close friendship between John Beckett and Cathal Gannon, it is singularly appropriate that Cathal's son, Charles Gannon, has written John's biography. For so doing Charles deserves our warmest gratitude and felicitations. A devoted labour of scholarship and research, it vividly and elegantly brings alive a fascinating and sometimes infuriating musical personality. It is an indispensable account of the career of a formidable Irish musician, who made a seminal and vibrant contribution to Irish musical life. I trust that this book will reach the largest possible number of people who, having read it, will give thanks for the insights that John Beckett brought to his art, especially to Bach, whose music he loved and served so well.

Lindsay Armstrong, September 2015

Author's Introduction

Many years ago I showed a sample of John Beckett's handwriting to a graphologist. She was perplexed – never had she seen anything like it before. Unaquainted with John, she pronounced him to be a highly individualistic person. And indeed he was. The bold slashes that form the letters suggest defiance, and the illegibility reflects the man's character: complex and difficult to fathom. Overall, though, the handwriting – like the man himself – is, and was, unconventional.

As handwriting can tell us much about a person's personality, I have included examples of its development in this account. John was a larger-than-life person, whom people either loved or loathed. Outwardly he could be gruff and confrontational, though inwardly he was often soft and perhaps lacking in confidence. John was also self-deprecating and is known to have destroyed all the music that he composed.

Although he was a fine musician, a competent composer and a successful conductor, John was never truly famous, and his name, sadly, is in danger of being forgotten. Perhaps a reason for this was his propensity to stick to his firmly-held theories about the interpretation of music and its performance, despite the criticism of others. Once again, the word 'unconventional' comes to mind.

So why did I choose to write a biography of a composer who condemned the music he composed, a musician whose outward grumpiness and set ideas almost ensured that he would never be famous, and a conductor whose rudimentary technique was tolerated, though often ridiculed? The answer is simply because he was so unconventional and interesting. His background, the people he mixed with, his relationship with his cousin Samuel, the events in his life, his ideas, his likes and dislikes, and the things that he said and wrote all warrant an account of this extraordinary and unique character. Another important reason for writing this book is to record how he and his friend Michael Morrow changed our perception of how medieval and early Renaissance music might have been performed, through the somewhat controversial performances of their early music group, Musica Reservata (again, like John, now almost forgotten).

Apart from these general comments and a few others scattered throughout the text, I have resisted the temptation of trying to analyze John's character. Instead, I have simply presented the facts and opinions of others so that the reader may come to his or her own conclusions.

Readers will notice that I have referred to my subject by his first name rather than his surname – the latter a device commonly used in biographies. This is because of the personal connection mentioned by Lindsay Armstrong in his Foreword. John had a profound influence on my father's successful career as a harpsichord-maker, hence the wording of the dedication at the beginning of this book. Although I knew John since boyhood and later studied music with him, I did not know him well. Indeed, few people did.

This account was written over a period of eight years, in my spare time. For two of those years, I put the project aside because of illness and other commitments. This, in fact, proved to be fortuitous, for in late 2014 a file of correspondence between John and the Director of Music in Radio Éireann, dating from the early 1950s, was unexpectedly discovered in the RTÉ Document Archives. The material answered many questions and removed a certain amount of speculation concerning dates and events.

Writing this book has been like assembling a huge jigsaw puzzle, the pieces of which I had to find somehow or other. Many of the pieces are undoubtedly still missing and may never be found – especially those stored in the memories of people who have taken them to their graves. However, I was fortunate enough to interview some individuals in the nick of time, before they died. Hence, this biography is assembled from fragments of information taken from many sources, not all of which were accurate or complete. Missing information was often found in the most unexpected places. Anecdotal detail, so essential in a good biography, is missing from some sections simply because it was not available. In these instances, the reader must be satisfied with an account of what John was doing at those particular times.

As author, I must take full responsibility for any mistakes, omissions and inaccuracies in the text, although every effort has been made to ensure that all the information is as accurate as possible. It must be stressed that the Appendices at the end of the book make no claim to be exhaustive; as many events in John's life were not documented in printed form, it is quite possible that some material has been omitted.

Acknowledgments

Without anecdotes and insights into a person's character and daily life, the biography of a musician can be a dull, academic list of incidents and achievements. As John tended to be a rather private person and was inclined to compartmentalize his life, many people only knew him slightly. For example, when he went to work for the BBC in his latter years, few of his colleagues knew anything about what he had done before then. So, to learn as much as possible about John during every stage of his life, it was necessary to interview as many people as possible (in Ireland, the UK and abroad) who knew him at different times. Unfortunately, several people who could probably have given me valuable information are now deceased, and so there are periods of John's life that cannot be documented fully. The best authority on John's life was John himself, but sadly I was denied the chance of interviewing him (which he probably would not have countenanced), owing to his sudden death. Indeed, I had been contemplating the possibility of writing his biography when I learned of his passing away, which, despite the fact that I did not know him particularly well, upset me greatly. During a telephone conversation with the late Morris ('Sunny') Sinclair, I was warned that writing a biography of John would be a very difficult undertaking; bearing this in mind, I approached the challenge with a certain amount of trepidation.

The person who probably knew John best of all, and for the longest period, was his good friend Seán O'Leary, a fellow Irishman, who lives in the UK and who met John and Michael Morrow in Hampstead when their early music group Musica Reservata began to perform in public. Without Seán's tireless help and encouragement, the writing of this book would have been almost impossible. I am also most grateful to his gracious and late wife Odile for her kind hospitality when I was invited to their home in Reading. I must also thank Patrick and Melanie Cuming, who live in Wraysbury, Middlesex, for introducing me to Seán, for having recounted their experiences with John to me, and for their kind hospitality at home. The person who initially encouraged me to attempt a biography of John was his relative, the flautist Edward Beckett; I am grateful to him for all his information and contacts. Rose Hilton, the daughter of John's late partner Ruth Hilton (née David) has kindly supplied me with information and corrections. I am also very grateful to Prof. Barra Boydell, who provided me with some information and corrected a selection of passages dealing with music.

I must thank several people who were kind enough to contribute generously to the funding of this publication: Brian Dalton on behalf of RTÉ, Deborah Kelleher on behalf of the Royal Irish Academy of Music, Dublin, Edward Beckett, Joseph Brennan, David Goldberg, Margaret Quigley, Billy Reid, Hugh Tattan, John Whelan and Alison Young. My thanks also to Antony Farrell of The Lilliput Press for his enthusiastic commitment to publish this work, and to his very patient and understanding editor, Djinn von Noorden.

Those who must be sincerely thanked for their help and information are as follows.

In Ireland: Carol Acton, David Agnew, Lindsay Armstrong, Janet Ashe, Gerald Barry, the late Mrs Mary Boydell, David Carmody, James Cavanagh, the late Brendan Chawke, Eithne Clarke, Paul Conway, Aleck Crichton, Michael Dervan, Marion Doherty, Mirette Dowling, Rhoda Draper, Brigid Ferguson, Patrick Fitzgerald, Christopher Fitz-Simon, Alan Geraghty, Peter Hamilton, Anthony and Carmel Harrison, Aidan Higgins and Alannah Hopkin, James, Ross and Mary Kelly, the late David Lane, Máire Larchet, Éamonn Lawlor, David Lee, Ray Lynott, Geraldine Malone, Hiromi Mooney, Kathleen Moran, Caroline Murphy, the late Colm Murray, Doireann Ní Bhriain, Anthony OBrien, Honor O Brolchain, Prionnsias Ó Duinn, Pat O'Kelly, the late Venetia O'Sullivan, Derek Paine, Joyce and Irwin Pearson, Richard Pine, Malcolm and Susan Proud, David and Gerry Pullman, Margaret Quigley, Andrew and Jenny Robinson, Aiden Scanlon, Killian Schürmann, Dan Shields, the late Deirdre Sinclair (Hamilton), Vera Škrabánek, Gillian Smith, Adrian Somerfield, David Sowby, Junette Stronge, Sydney Stokes, Brian Studdert, Kilda Taylor, Tim Thurston, Thérèse Timmoney, Bláthnaid Uí Chatháin (née Ní Annracháin), Mary Wheatley, Rosalind Whittaker, Mary Willis; Alison Young, Thelma Clinton and Rosaleen Cox of Aravon Preparatory School, Bray, Co. Wicklow; Caitríona Honohan, Contemporary Music Centre, Dublin; Laura Gilsenan, Feis Ceoil Association; staff of the General Register Office, Dublin; Eibhlin Colgan (née Roche) and Deirdre McParland of the Guinness Archive Department, Diageo Ireland;

Andrew Moore, Library Assistant, and Niamh MacNally, Assistant Curator, Prints and Drawings, National Gallery of Ireland; staff of National Irish Visual Arts Library, National College of Art; Colette O'Flaherty and Frances Clarke, National Library of Ireland; Lawrence White, Royal Irish Academy; Philip Shields, Royal Irish Academy of Music; the staff of the Radio and Television Archives, RTÉ; staff of the *RTÉ Guide*; staff of the RTÉ Stills Library; Tina Byrne, Michael Talty and Brian Lynch, RTÉ Document Archives; Nancy Crisp and Sally Gibbs, St Columba's College; Ellen O'Flaherty, Assistant Librarian, and Aisling Lockhart, Reading Room Services Executive, Manuscript and Archives Research Library, Trinity College Dublin; Sharon Sutton, Digital Resources and Imaging Service, Trinity College Dublin, and staff of the Ussher Multimedia Library, Trinity College Dublin.

In Northern Ireland: Norman Lush, Robin McKinney, Billy Reid (widower of Irené Sandford).

In the UK: Nicholas Anderson, Jantina Barker (née Norman), Clifford Bartlett, Edward Beckett, Christina Burstin, David Cairns, John Calder, Patrick and Melanie Cuming, Mark Deller, David Fletcher, Professor Trevor Herbert, Jill Higgins, Professor K.T. Hoppen, Adrian Jack, the late Arthur Johnson, Judy Jordan, James Knowlson (biographer of Samuel Beckett), Patrick Lambert, Harold Lester, Priscilla (Skylla) and Oengus MacNamara, Jeremy Montagu, Hedy Morrow, Roland Morrow, Christopher Nobbs, Frida and Vic Robinson, Tom Sutcliffe, Bernard Thomas, Mark Windisch, Theo Wyatt; Joanna Attree of the BBC Archives; Monica Thapar and Louise North of the BBC Written Archives; Dr Mark Nixon of the Beckett International Foundation, University of Reading; staff of the British Library Newspapers department, Colindale; staff of the British Library Sound Archives and reading rooms, St Pancras; Linda Nicol, Permissions Manager, Cambridge University Press; Martin Cullingford, editor of *Gramophone* online; Mimi Waitzman, Deputy Keeper of Musical Instruments, The Horniman Museum and Gardens; Libby Rice, Archivist of the London Symphony Orchestra; Elaine Andrews of Morley College, London; Joanna Marston and Lisa of Rosica Colin Ltd, London; Andrew Morris, Library Assistant, Royal Academy of Music Library; Chris Bornet and Paul Collen, Curatorial and Administrative Assistant, Centre for Performance History, Royal College of Music; and Christopher Bastock, Gallery Records, Tate Library and Archive.

Elsewhere: Professor Jeremy N. Timmis, Adelaide (Australia); Emer Buckley, Virginie Desrante at the Conservatoire de Paris, and Reginald Gray (France);

Beate Luszeit of the Schlosspark Theater, Berlin; the late Michael Richter, Werner Schürmann, Siobhán Yeats (Germany); the late Morris ('Sunny') Sinclair, (Switzerland), and Lois More Overbeck (USA).

Finally, I must thank my cousins Anne and John O'Brien for having put me up and put up with me when I stayed with them several times in their delightful home in Ealing, when doing research in London and Reading.

Permissions:

BBC copyright material reproduced courtesy of the British Broadcasting Corporation. All rights reserved; Edward Beckett; Eithne Clarke; excerpts from certain of Samuel Beckett's letters to John Beckett of 18 February 1974*; 7 March 1974*; 11 May 1975*; 27 July 1976*; 15 May 1977 (x3)*; 19 January 1978*; 30 September 1983*; 26 November 1983*; 14 March 1984*; 27 March 1986*; 5 December 1987*; 26 July 1989*; 16 October 1989*; 16 November 1956* and 7 May 1957*, reproduced by kind permission of the Estate of Samuel Beckett c/o Rosica Colin Limited, London; Beckett International Foundation, The University of Reading; Guinness Archive Department, Diageo Ireland; Aidan Higgins and Alannah Hopkin; *The Irish Times*; James L. Kelly; King's College London Archives; *The Letters of Samuel Beckett* 'The Estate of Samuel Beckett 2014, Introduction, translations, and notes' George Craig, Martha Dow Fehsenfeld, Dan Gunn, and Lois More Overbeck published by Cambridge University Press, reproduced with permission; Deirdre McParland, Guinness Archive, Diageo Ireland; The National Portrait Gallery, London; quotations from letters from Samuel Beckett reprinted by permission of the publisher from *No Author Better Served: The Correspondence of Samuel Beckett and Alan Schneider*, edited by Maurice Harmon, pp. 13, 122, Cambridge, Mass: Harvard University Press; Beckett material copyright © 1998 by the Estate of Samuel Beckett; Schneider material copyright © 1998 by the Trustees of Boston College; Introduction and editorial matter copyright © 1998 by the President and Fellows of Harvard College.

* © The Estate of Samuel Beckett.

Preface

Never had I attended such an unusual funeral. Sitting on a hard pew in Lewisham Crematorium, I closed my eyes, blocking out the ecclesiastical images before me – the stained-glass windows, flowers and brass crucifix – and allowed the unearthly wailing and sobbing of a Japanese flute, the *shakuhachi*, engulf me. The small group of people sat motionless and silent; apart from a general introduction from John's relative, the flautist Edward Beckett, and the brief announcements for each piece given by Patrick Cuming, no words were spoken. The first recorded mournful piece, written in the distinctive Japanese semitonic penta-scale – was Buddhist music for the rite of the dead; the second piece, *Kokū* (Sky), one of the three oldest pieces written for *shakuhachi*, was more intense. During the third, which John had not requested, the coffin descended and, after a signal from Edward, we all left and walked out into the weak February sunshine, wondering why a man who had wallowed in the music of composers like Purcell, Bach, Haydn, Schubert and Mahler had chosen to depart from this world to the stark, lonely strains of an end-blown wooden flute. It was John who had devised this programme of no words and no religion shortly before his death, which had occurred on the morning of his eightieth birthday.

The vague feeling of unease that I had experienced in the crematorium now vanished as we introduced ourselves to one another and learned that John's ashes would remain here along with Ruth's. I approached Edward Beckett and asked him if I should consider writing a biography of John. Without hesitation he said yes. Therefore I was happy to be driven to John's little house in Azof Street, Greenwich, where he himself had requested we drink a glass of Irish whiskey (or whatever took our fancy) and have a bite to eat in his honour. There I was introduced to various people who had known John over the years, and who were willing to speak to me about him.

Curious, I now delved into the past, finding the hidden pieces of a large, complicated jigsaw. Bit by bit I began to piece together the main events of his interesting and rewarding life: the latter years in his home at Greenwich following the loss of his twin sister Ann and, before that, the tragic death of his beloved partner Ruth David; his spell of work as a producer in BBC Radio 3, his ten-year stint of conducting Bach cantatas at St Ann's Church, Dawson Street in Dublin; the years of performing, conducting and teaching in Ireland; his involvement in the early music group Musica Reservata, which dated back to the late 1950s; the recordings made for the Third Programme and the incidental music he wrote for various experimental BBC radio dramas; the serious car accident of 1961; three years of struggle in Dublin in the early 1950s; a year and a half spent in Paris with his cousin Samuel; his study of composition at the Royal College of Music and harpsichord at Morley College, London; encouragement from the composer E.J. Moeran; his general and musical education at St Columba's College in the outskirts of Dublin; his first school, Aravon Preparatory School in Bray, County Wicklow, and the family home in Greystones. I finally arrived at the beginning of the story when, travelling by train from Reading to London, I read a transcript of two interviews with John that Samuel Beckett's biographer, James Knowlson, had recorded in the early 1990s. In one of them, John had stated that when he and his sister had been born, the family was living 'in a little house called "Red Cottage" at Sandyford, just outside Dundrum.'

PART ONE

Dublin, London, Paris and Dublin 1927–1953

One

1927–33

Travelling southwards from Dublin city towards Enniskerry in County Wicklow during the mid 1920s, one would have passed through the village of Dundrum and come to a fork in the road.[1] The left fork led you past St Mary's Roman Catholic church to the small, tranquil village of Sandyford: a short stretch of road lined by houses, a few small shops and, on the right, Flavin's pub (originally Sandyford House). This contained a grocery shop on one side of a partition. A little farther onwards was a crossroads known as Sandyford Cross. To the left, a narrow, twisty road led to Leopardstown and on to Foxrock, where Samuel Beckett and his parents lived. The turn to the right ended at a junction with the Sandyford Road, where, situated at the foot of the Dublin mountains, there was a collection of shops in a two-storey stone building, a section of the old Pale nearby, and, a short distance down the Blackglen Road, a hand-operated petrol pump, a pub in a downstairs room of a little house (later to become the well-known Lamb Doyle's), and a butcher's shop with an abattoir behind.

Straight ahead lay the Kilgobbin road; the first house on the left, approached through a lych gate surmounted by a pitched roof of orange-red tiles and double wooden doors, was the Red Cottage, built on land that had originally been part of the grounds of Mount Eagle House, the next dwelling along the road. Although the front garden of the Red Cottage was small, the avenue was wide enough to accommodate a car. There was also a back garden. The house, an attractive bungalow, had a porch in the centre and windows on either side; there were orange tiles on the roof and beside the house was a garage.[2]

The Red Cottage was the home of Gerald and Peggy Beckett and their young son Peter Gordon Stewart, who had been born in 1922 when they had lived at Sydenham Place in nearby Dundrum.[3] The Becketts were Irish Protestants descended from French Huguenot *émigrés*, who had in times past become wealthy through the family weaving business.[4] Gerald Gordon Beckett, a medical doctor, was the son of William Frank and Frances (Fannie) Beckett (née Crothers), and was born in 1886. Gerald's father William had been a master builder and had been living in Prince William Terrace, Grand Canal Street, at the time of Gerald's birth.[5] William's brother James (from whom the composer Walter Beckett was descended) was in partnership with him for a while. William and James constructed many important buildings in Dublin, including the Adelaide Hospital, the National Library of Ireland and the National Museum in Kildare Street.[6] William was also actively involved in public life: he was a member of the Pembroke Urban District Council, acting as chairman both of the Council and its various committees, and was chairman of the Old Age Pensions Committee.[7]

Fannie Crothers, William's wife, was extremely musical. She wrote songs, adapted pieces for piano and set poems to music. Her son Gerald, who was very fond of her, had a book of piano duets which he played with his mother; her favourite piece was called *Robinetta*. A bound manuscript of the songs that she composed included a setting of Alfred, Lord Tennyson's poem, 'Crossing the Bar' – the only music that Samuel Beckett was allowed to play in the house after his father died.[8]

Gerald Beckett had four siblings: William (father of Samuel and Frank Beckett), James, Henry Herbert, Howard and Frances (known to all as 'Cissie'). Gerald studied medicine in Trinity College, Dublin, where he and his brother James were leading swimmers. He played water polo, was a good rugby player and played for Ireland at least twice. His faded jersey was kept at home for many years as a reminder of his achievements. However, he was not interested in being competitive. A mischievous individual with a dry sense of humour, he was fond of pronouncing life to be 'an infectious disease of matter' – a phrase taken from Thomas Mann's novel, *The Magic Mountain*. He often referred to one of his Trinity professors, H.O. White, as T. Hee White. He was quiet and thoughtful, with many interests: a committed Darwinian, he was totally irreligious. He was interested in science, was a great admirer of H.G. Wells and had 'a fresh directness of being'.

Most importantly, for our story, Gerald was musical. He was a very good pianist and sight-reader; the sort of person who could go to a cinema, hear a song, then come home and play it on the piano. He enjoyed all sorts of music, except jazz.[9] He was fond of Gilbert and Sullivan's music and often played it on the piano to entertain his colleagues and friends.[10]

During World War I Gerald served as a doctor in the Royal Army Medical Corps, and was stationed for a while in West Africa. Two photographs taken of him at this period exist: one shows a handsome young man with a moustache, dressed smartly in army uniform, and the other depicts a dishevelled individual with dark tousled hair and bags under the eyes, wearing an open-necked shirt.[11]

In January 1918, when Gerald returned to Dublin and was living in Herbert Park, Ballsbridge, he married Margaret Robinson Collen, daughter of Joseph Collen, a well-known and important builder and contractor.[12] Originally from Armagh in Northern Ireland, Joseph was then living in Homestead, an imposing house on Sandyford Road, between Dundrum and Sandyford.[13] The couple probably met because of Gerald's father's business connections; the very prestigious Collen Bros had a small office at 5 Clanwilliam Place, a turning off Grand Canal Street, where William Beckett lived.

Although the family was involved in building from the early 1800s, Collen Bros had formally opened for business as building contractors in 1867, in Portadown, Northern Ireland. Important contracts followed, such as churches of various demoninations, the Royal Dublin Society buildings in Ballsbridge, the reconstruction of Kylemore Castle (later Abbey) in County Galway, Killarney House, the asylum in Portrane, County Dublin, and even the Cavan and Leitrim Railway. The Collen brothers soon became established members of the social elite in Victorian and Edwardian Ireland.[14]

Gerald Beckett's wife Margaret, known as Peggy, had been born in Ashton Villa, Portadown, County Armagh, in 1892. Her mother was Hannah Maria Collen, née Stewart.[15] Peggy had a brother and two sisters: William Stewart, Hannah Sophia (Sophie, known variously as 'Jack' and 'Toshie'), who remained unmarried and who would later live in the Red Cottage,[16] and Mary Elizabeth (Molly) Heron, mother of the sculptress Hilary Heron. Molly in fact would later live in Mount Eagle House, next door to the Beckett home. Molly's method of decorating her rather dilapidated house was rather unorthodox: curtains were hung on walls instead of windows, her hallway was adorned with samples of tweed, and newspaper cuttings (one of which depicted a naked woman) were pasted on the ceiling. Apart from her daughter Hilary, who became well known for her work in wood and stone, Molly had three other children: Barney, Roderick (Roddy) and William (Billy).[17]

Molly Heron had quite extraordinary handwriting. Hilary was a person of note: she became a founder of the Exhibition of Living Art, a member of the Radio Éireann authority, and looked after the aged and ill. Hilary sculpted Molly and Sophie's plain but elegant tombstones, which can be seen in the graveyard of the ruined Kilgobbin Church nearby.[18]

Now married, Gerald set about studying and sat his Diploma of Public Health examination. During this time, he and Peggy lived for about a year and a half in 'a marvellous little thatched cottage' on Portmarnock golf links by the sea in north County Dublin. For Gerald it was an idyllic period of study and golf.[19] Later they moved to Sydenham Place in Dundrum and from there to Sandyford; both places were within easy reach of the Collen family home on Sandyford Road.

Unlike Gerald, Peggy was religious and worshipped in the Church of Ireland church a few miles farther south at Kilternan, another small village on the road to Enniskerry. She was completely unmusical but was artistic; she liked to paint and loved gardening. Although she was barely literate and more or less uneducable, she had terrific feeling, was childlike in nature and was naturally attractive. She was also the sort of person whom children loved and felt at ease with, despite the fact that she later acquired a reputation for being domineering.[20]

Peggy, now in her mid thirties, found herself pregnant in 1926 and on 5 February 1927 gave birth to a daughter, Ann Margaret, in 87 Lower Baggot Street at ten o'clock in the morning. Ten minutes later Ann's twin brother was born: John Stewart (Stewart after Peggy's mother's maiden name). The children were christened in Kilternan church and the births were registered in April of that year.[21]

Young John was blessed with rude health but Ann was not so lucky. At the tender age of three or four a kitchen knife fell and pierced her foot,[22] causing what was then called 'blood poisoning'. As a result she became very ill, and she later recalled, 'I was practically dead at the time.' The affliction was debilitating and she remained thin. It was advised that her leg be amputated from above the knee and the operation was finally done when she was about thirteen years of age. She improved, but was for ever dependent on a prosthetic leg.[23]

John remembered nothing of living in the Red Cottage, but we can imagine him playing in the garden and breathing the fresh country air. He may well have crossed the sandy ford, which was located between their house and St Mary's church, scrambled about in the Moreen woods, ambled down Beech Walk, a long avenue of trees that led to Moreen House (an old mansion with ramshackle gate-lodges and lots of weeds), walked along the right-of-way path to the old look-out turret and remains of the Pale wall near the junction with Sandyford Road, and hopped over the stepping-stones of a mountain stream nearby to survey three old cottages – two of them in ruins – and a field of furze.[24]

Gerald's father William died in February 1930.[25] John had met his grandfather but remembered very little about him apart from his appearance (stocky and bearded) and the fact that he had a parrot in a cage at his home in Herbert Park, Donnybrook.[26] The mourners at William's large funeral at Mount Jerome

Cemetery included many of the Becketts and members of the Collen family.[27] Gerald benefitted greatly from his father's will, for four houses in upmarket Pembroke Park, one in Moyne Road, one in Merrion Road and one in Harold's Cross Road had been left to him. Houses had, in fact, been left to all his brothers and to his sister Frances. According to *The Irish Times*, William, who was 'prominently identified with the building industry ... left property in England and the Irish Free State valued at £23,191 18s 3d.'[28]

Probate of William's will was granted to his first son, William (Bill) – father of Frank and Samuel Beckett – and he was left 'certain rent charges, and premises known as Estate Cottage'.[29] James Beckett (John's uncle Jim), had been left 'house property' in Grand Canal Street and a house in Moyne Road; *The Irish Times* referred to him as 'the former international footballer and well-known swimmer'.[30] Although he had been a rugby player, captain and referee, had played water polo in the Pembroke Swimming Club and represented Ireland at water polo for twenty-five years, he suffered a similar fate as Ann, though even worse: both his legs had had to be amputated due to a serious illness. John recollected that he was 'incredibly brave and dignified'.[31]

Jim, who was more rotund and more heavily built than his brother Gerald, trained as a doctor but worked as a freelance anaesthetist all his life; he did some hospital work but the bulk of his work was with dentists. He had a good reputation and meticulously recorded all the cases in which the anaesthetic had gone wrong, noting the reasons why.[32]

Uncle Jim rented a house in Sutton, near Howth, which had a garden that sloped down to a sandy beach. John, Ann, their parents and presumably Peter used to visit Jim's house, spending the whole day there and finishing with supper. Their father would doubtless have taught them to swim when they were on the beach. Uncle Jim was very generous and touching. He had a 'Becketty sort of humour' and liked to use phrases such as 'striking the iron before it freezes'. Jim would have finished his days in a public ward in a long-term geriatric hospital, were it not for Samuel Beckett's help and generosity. Samuel kept him out of hospital and at home until he died, blind and with both legs amputated.[33]

William's third son, Henry Herbert (known as Harry), was deceased by this stage. His widow's name was Katharine Victoria and they had a son, John William George Beckett, who went to live in South Africa. Harry had been a bit of a mystery – he had been looked down upon by his brothers and was rarely spoken about in the family. Samuel Beckett, who thought that he had met him once, described him as thin and not like the other brothers. At the time of Harry's father's death, his widow Katharine received seven premises in trust, with the remainder for her son John.[34]

Five premises were left to William's youngest son, Howard, born circa 1894. John found him a 'very strange person'. He had huge bushy eyebrows and was nicknamed 'the Kraken' after the legendary sea monsters. 'I met him as a child but he was rather frightening, without intending to be, but he was so odd I was rather daunted by him – but I believe my father was fond of him,' John explained. He was also known as 'Poyntz' and 'Eyebrows Beckett'. He had been in the Ambulance Corps during World War I, was an excellent chess player and managed to beat José Raúl Capablanca y Graupera, the Cuban world chess champion of the 1920s, when he came to Dublin for an exhibition match. Unmarried for a long time, he lived at home with his parents. He eventually married and he and his wife, Enid, had a son named Roger.[35]

William left his daughter Frances (known as Fanny or Cissie) six premises in his will. John's father Gerald was very fond of Cissie; like him she was musical and loved the piano music of Chopin, Mozart and Beethoven. She could play a vast amount of Irish and English songs and was very good at picking out popular music-hall songs. A high-spirited woman, she was also a talented artist and attended The Dublin Metropolitan School of Art, where she was taught to paint by Walter Osborne and William Orpen. In the summer of 1904 she secured her parents' approval to go to Paris with two friends, Dorothy and Beatrice Elvery (Lady Beatrice Glenavy), in order to perfect her skill at drawing. Back in Dublin she continued her study of art and mixed with the likes of Estella Solomons, Bea and William Orpen, Oliver St John Gogarty and a flamboyant and charming Jewish art dealer, William A. Sinclair, known familiarly as 'the Boss'. Two years later and contrary to the wishes of her family, she married the penniless Boss and moved to a tiny cottage in Howth with him. She and William had three daughters: Peggy (with whom her cousin Samuel later became infatuated), Sally, Deirdre, Nancy (who would marry Ralph Cusack – more of him anon), and a son, Morris,[36] known as 'Sunny'.[37] After World War I the family moved to Kassel in Germany from where William Sinclair shipped antiques and paintings to his twin brother Henry in Dublin, who successfully sold them from the family shop in Nassau Street.[38] The Boss's son Morris, who lived in Dublin during the 1940s and played the violin, found John's father Gerald jovial, kind and friendly; Gerald often accompanied him on the piano.[39] John Beckett and Morris would become very close in later years.

At some stage after sitting the Diploma of Public Health examination, John's father Gerald applied for and was appointed County Medical Officer of Health for County Wicklow.[40] As it was known that he was a Protestant and had been in the British Army, he had taken the precaution of applying for the same post in Southampton. Gerald was acutely aware of the fact that tuberculosis was rampant in Ireland and that sanatoria were needed rather than workhouses, which he was determined to have closed.[41] Although he was a medical doctor, he had found it difficult to cope with people suffering and so must have been delighted with this appointment, especially as he preferred administrative to clinical work. In fact, as Gerald had a scientific turn of mind, he might have chosen a different career; his father, however, had insisted that he become a doctor.[42] His new job was based in Rathdrum, County Wicklow, which was quite a distance from the family home in Sandyford. Although it would have made sense to move to Rathdrum, his wife Peggy did not want to do so as she preferred to live as close as possible to Dublin. A compromise was reached and in 1933 a fine house befitting a Medical Officer was purchased[43] – undoubtedly with some of the welcome proceeds of the property left to Gerald by his father – in the fashionable seaside town of Greystones in Wicklow. Close to Bray and the Dublin border, the town was connected to the capital by rail.[44] Things were looking up for Gerald and his wife.

Two

1933–40

'Greystones,' the Irish writer Aidan Higgins wrote in his novel *Dog Days*, quoting an acerbic remark made by his father, was a 'seaside resort where Protestants come to die'. The harbour, the beach, the railway line, the hump-backed bridge at the train station, the nearby tunnels and the walks along the cliffs of Bray Head, the seagulls, the dogs, the Railway and Grand Hotels are vividly depicted in Aidan's humorous and quirky account. He knew Greystones well as he and his family moved there later and lived near the Becketts' home.[1]

Aidan's father was not far off the mark. Although there was a refreshing mix of people who came on holidays from Dublin and other parts of the country during the summer months, Greystones in the winter was very much the bastion of well-off, middle-class retired Protestants who lived there all year round.[2] South of the little town's impressive bay is a long, straight sandy beach and on the other side of the railway line, a road, the small town centre and the Burnaby housing estate. So far, so good: a typical Irish seaside resort of no great distinction, but step into the Burnaby Estate and you enter a different world. Here, situated along leafy roads and avenues are exclusive and individually-designed houses. One is suddenly struck by the Englishness and cosiness of this well-ordered neighbourhood, where the inhabitants must have distinguished, at one time (and perhaps even now), between 'them' (the Irish Roman Catholics) outside and 'us' (the Protestants) inside. The estate was not unlike parts of the upmarket village of Foxrock where Samuel Beckett's parents lived, though the houses there were much grander than those in Greystones.

The house that Gerald had bought for himself and his family was situated in the Burnaby Estate, on the junction of Portland and Saint Vincent's Road.[3] The

pink-tiled roof featured several gables with windows, prompting a neighbour to
refer to it as 'the house of seven gables'.⁴ John disliked its name, Drummany, as it
reminded him of the word 'mammy' – the Irish way of pronouncing 'mummy'.⁵
It is possible that the family may have employed a cook. The children had a
nanny: May Harper, a teenage girl from a remote village in County Wexford,
looked after John and Ann. She stayed with the family until about 1944, when
she married Paddy Synnott from Newtownmountkennedy, County Wicklow.
The family was very fond of the couple and remained in touch with them until
they died.⁶

Although John said very little about his childhood, he must have been happy
here. His father, who drove to Rathdrum every day to work, was now earning a
good wage and must have had enough money to support his wife and three children. John and Ann had unlimited access to the beach, where they could romp
around on the sand and swim in the sea, especially in the summer. When older,
they spent most of their spare time swimming either in the sea off the beach
or in the harbour, where the really brave and hardy children dived off the back
of the wall. They also challenged each other to swimming races and dived into
what was known as the 'little dock', which, when filled with water, was quite
deep. The harbour was a simpler affair at this period, without the remains of the
Kish lighthouse at the end.

The children were amused at their father's clever nicknames for the local
people; Gerald called one man Joseph of Arimathea because he had been
observed carrying 'a bit of wood over his shoulder or something', as Ann recalled
later. Gerald loved Wicklow, walking in the mountains, and he also enjoyed
working with the local people. Ann recollected how some of the old people
in Rathdrum had remembered him in those days and said, 'Ah, he was a great
doctor'. They used to look forward to him coming to the schools. Norman Lush
(who would later teach John mathematics at college) remembers that, when he
was nine, Dr Beckett arrived to examine all the pupils.⁷ Gerald was one of the
people responsible for helping to set up the structure of the health service and
then the dispensary services in the relatively new Irish Free State. He was well
suited to this job as he was fair-minded and well respected. (One of the first
things he helped to establish were sanatoria for the treatment of tuberculosis.)

Gerald's working day began at half past seven and finished at around six in
the evening when he returned to the family home for 'high tea'. On summer
evenings, it was his habit to go to the Greystones golf course for a game, accompanied by John and Ann, who went just for the sheer pleasure of being with him,
as John remembered: 'He was a man whom it was a pleasure to be with, to be
near. I can think of a myriad of little incidents. Sitting on a beach perhaps of an

afternoon, little things – a great pleasure to remember.' Gerald did not play golf competitively though he was an excellent player with a scratch handicap. He liked to go to the first nine holes in the golf links where he could 'knock a ball about for a few hours'. Despite his relaxed attitude to the game, he became Captain at Greystones for a time.

Gerald also played in Croney Golf Club, near Bray, where there was a big house with grounds and a swimming pool in which John and Ann were allowed to swim. The club was patronized by well-to-do people. Although Gerald felt that he was not one of them, 'he was a person who inspired respect of a human kind and he was made Captain,' John explained:

> Somebody applied to join the club: a gentleman called Segal, I remember, and the only reason I remember was that it was a funny name because I thought it was odd being called 'Seagull' – for that was what I thought it was. But there was trouble over this because the Committee wouldn't accept this man because he was Jewish and I remember my father resigned over this matter, which I am, again, proud of.

Gerald used to read the London *Times* and regularly sent little Ann to the golf links in Greystones in order to fetch the previous day's copy so that he could do the crossword. 'He got into the knack of the chap who wrote the crossword,' Ann remembered.[8]

John recollected how his father used to take a month off work for a summer holiday. He did not need entertainment of any sort – he was 'perfectly happy to sit in the sun and watch the tide go out and come in again, [then] swim for an hour or so, all day really, and we often would [sit or swim] with him.' John did not remember him talking very much but he did remember 'the felicity of the man in the summer sun beside the sea.'

An event that occurred in June 1933 that John would probably not have remembered was the death of Samuel Beckett's father, Bill, from a massive heart attack. When Gerald Beckett went to the funeral and met Bill's widow May at the door of their Foxrock home, Cooldrinagh, he cheerfully greeted her with, 'Well May, Willie's got it over with!'[9] May's reaction is not recorded but can be imagined. Bill was buried in Redford cemetery, on the opposite side of the bay from Greystones harbour. In September of that year, Bill's will went through probate: the executors were May, Frank, Samuel and Bill's brother Gerald. The family was amused that Gerald was chosen, for he was known as the brother who had the least concern for the value of money: his method of financing his children's education was to sell off the property left to him by his father, piece by piece. In the end, Samuel Beckett's brother Frank took over the management of Bill's estate, leaving Gerald a trustee in name only.[10]

John's schooling began when he was eight years of age. 'I think it's a dreadful age to send a child to school,' he commented later.[11] In 1935 he was sent, along with his brother Peter (who had started three years previously), to Aravon Preparatory School,[12] then situated between Meath Road and Sidmonton Road near Bray town centre. The school had been founded in 1862 when it was called The Bray School, and over the years it grew in size with the acquisition of new land and buildings. The name Aravon was derived from Novara (from Novara Road, an extension of Sidmonton Road), spelt backwards. Like the Burnaby Estate in Greystones, Aravon was like a little piece of England placed in Ireland, for once ensconced in this Protestant school, Ireland and the Irish almost ceased to exist.[13] John did not like his boarding school and complained that he was 'very miserable' there. Whenever there was an opportunity he took off on his bicycle and went for long rides in the countryside.[14] His misery was not helped by the fact that his brother did not want to have anything to do with him at school – something that John resented for the rest of his life. Because Peter was four years older, John never knew him very well: 'He was just that degree ahead of me.' After 1936 Peter was sent to Epsom College in England as the fees were reduced for doctors' sons. When John got to know Peter a little later, he discovered that he 'was a very nice person'. Peter went on to study medicine at Trinity College in Dublin, worked at psychiatry at the Mayo Clinic in Rochester, Minnesota, USA, and then, on his subsequent return to Dublin, became Head of Health Sciences at Trinity College.[15]

Although John said almost nothing about his education, it is not too difficult to ascertain the cause of his misery at school. Several factors would have contributed to it: the sudden change from a blissfully relaxed and sheltered life at home to the rough and tumble of a boys' boarding school; sport, which young John disliked (he later pronounced rugby to be 'a brutal game, a bully's game'[16]); and the tyrannical headmaster, Arthur B. Craig (known as 'A.B.C.' or simply 'the Boss').

Mr Craig, an old Aravonian, had been headmaster from 1924. He had done service in World War I and had studied for a history degree in Oxford. According to *The Aravon Story* by Charles Mansfield, he:

> single-handed and without financial endowments set to work to bring Aravon up to date and in line with the standards set by the Incorporated Association of Preparatory Schools, of which he was soon a member. Above all, Craig was responsible for an example of manliness and straightness, which inspired the boys with his own high standards of what a Christian gentleman should be.[17]

There were about five teachers in the school, plus a so-called matron, 'a decent spinster of uncertain age'.

The education that John received here was essentially what one would have encountered in any British prep school of that period, with special emphasis on English history and the glories of the British Empire: during geography lessons the pupils were made to draw maps of the world with special drawing pens and mark various parts of the Empire on them in red. The boys took little interest in things Irish or Roman Catholic – these fell under the general heading of 'Shinner', the derogatory term used for Sinn Féin. On Armistice Day they gathered below the Honours List, sang 'Oh Valiant Hearts' and listened to Mr Craig reading the names of Old Aravonians who had died during the Great War.

Other subjects included English, French, Latin (but not Irish), history, scripture and music. Every boy dreaded mathematics because this subject was taught by the irascible Craig, who shouted at, slapped and beat the boys with a cane when he lost his temper. The only sport in which John participated was swimming; David Sowby remembers the final of a race between him and John in the Cove on the sea front where the boys were taken to swim.

Once a week Canon Scott from Christ Church in Bray came to the school to give the boys a pep talk. 'By then he was old and shaky, and was in the habit of inserting the sounds "Er ay" into virtually every sentence. We were so busy counting the number of times he said "Er ay" that we never took in a word of his homily,' recollects David Sowby in his amusing account, *Memories of Aravon 1936–40*. On Sundays, full-time boarders donned Eton jackets, collars and straw boaters and were marched off to the church in the morning. From time to time there were exeats when the boys could be collected by their parents after church and brought home or into Bray for a meal and then returned to the school at about five o'clock. David Sowby remembers Dr Gerald Beckett arriving in his white and silver Vauxhall car to collect John. On other Sundays, Mr Craig brought the boys for a walk up Bray Head. When they reached the top and Greystones came into sight, Mr Craig used to proclaim that they were viewing 'the Promised Land'.[18] John presumably spent any spare time he could find reading boys' books such as *The Wind in the Willows*,[19] for later he would become a voracious reader.

Each day at school began with prayers, 'beginning with one of the drearier hymns lurking in the Church of Ireland hymn book. "Breathe on me, breath of God" made frequent appearances, sung to a most lugubrious tune. A passage from the Bible was [then] read by one of the older boys.' Also in the mornings there was physical training, led by Sergeant Major Hastings, 'a dapper little man with a red face, white hair and a white waxed moustache' and his son Frank, known as the Sergeant Minor. Frank was tall, had red hair, sported a bushy red moustache and was said to have served in the Irish Army. Both were togged out in immaculate white clothes and shoes. According to David Sowby's account:

The school gym had a gallery at one end, where the Sergeant Major stood and shouted orders to us to perform various exercises. Frank cruised round the ranks, waiting for his father to yell, 'Frank, bash that boy', whereupon Frank would lash out with a gym shoe he carried around with him.

Every year there was a picnic on the Silver Strand, near Wicklow town – an event that was always announced after morning prayers. Great excitement ensued as the boys got ready and changed into suitable clothing. Amazingly, the weather was always good for these picnics.[20] The Silver Strand remained one of John's favourite beaches.[21]

Both David Lane and David Sowby remember John and one of the teachers, Mr O'Shaughnessy, playing a four-hand arrangement of the Overture to Mozart's opera *The Magic Flute* on the piano. John had begun to learn the piano at around this time, though whether he was taught at school or privately is not known. In fact, David Sowby does not remember John playing the piano until he was eleven.[22] 'Like many another musical child, I was set to the piano at about the age of eight, and, like many another, I couldn't be torn away from playing by the hour, by the day – even by the night. As it turned out, however, it was music that absorbed me – not the instrument's music,' said John in 1969 at the beginning of a BBC Radio 3 programme devoted to him called *Studio Portrait: John Beckett*.[23]

When he had mastered the piano in the years that followed, he and his father spent many happy hours together playing duets. Together they played arrangements of Haydn's symphonies and quartets, Beethoven symphonies and, what they loved best, arrangements for four hands of Mozart's late quartets. John, who clearly remembered the oblong volumes with blue bindings, commented that they were beautifully and sensibly arranged – they were not 'filled in with octaves and things' and that the four parts of the score were assigned to the four instruments. 'We took great delight in them,' he said. When in June 1936 Samuel Beckett came to Dublin for a summer holiday, he joined Gerald and the family in Greystones to play duets, though John stated that he was never a very good pianist. The two men used to sit down at the piano, which was situated in the large dining room, and play for hours:

> My father didn't really approve of Sam's playing because he used to play the bass part, but the catch is that the bass player controls the sustaining pedal which must catch sound at the right moment and even more important [he] must release it at the right moment otherwise you get a shambles, and Sam didn't understand that. This used to offend my father – not that he said anything about it. ... [Sam] had no pretentions, he loved playing, he loved music; and also to play piano duets with someone you like, that you are in sympathy with, is a very pleasurable activity.

John also remembered a tattered volume of Mozart symphonies, which was the property of a public library in Kassel, Germany. Samuel had 'borrowed' it when he had been with the Sinclairs years previously and had brought it to Dublin in his luggage. Samuel and Gerald played these arrangements and then later, when he was able, John and his father. Much later Gerald and John 'dipped into the miraculous piano duets of Schubert'.[24]

One person who remembers hearing John practising the piano some three years later was the young Christopher Fitz-Simon, whose grandparents rented a seaside bungalow named Arc-en-Ciel in Greystones for the summer. When Christopher tired of playing in the garden, he used to ask permission to see Mrs Beckett, though it was really the parakeets and canaries in her garden aviary that he wanted to see. He remembered how Peggy Beckett wore long, filmy dresses of petunia, mauve or lilac, gossamer scarves, and how her fingernails were painted in the same colours. While admiring the birds, Christopher could hear John inside the house constantly practising on the piano, the sound mixing with the song of the birds. Occasionally he saw Samuel sitting in a deck-chair in the garden, reading a book or writing.[25]

Samuel's other form of relaxation in Greystones during that summer of 1936 was swimming. Because of his slim build and the type of swimming costume that he wore, John thought he looked like an insect in the water. Gerald, who was a firmly-built man with a fine body, 'swam like a seal'.[26] John, who also adored swimming and was generally happier in the water than he was out of it,[27] recollected that, during the summer, 'we spent more time in the water at Greystones ... than we did on the land'.

The young Gerald frequently went to music halls and had a huge repertoire of songs that he would often sing in the car. One of them, a musical tongue-twister, went as follows:

> Swim Sam, swim,
> Show them you're some swimmer
> You know how the swan swam
> Swim just as the swan swam
> Six sharp sharks...

As well as being amused at Samuel's appearance when he swam, Gerald used to call him the 'frog footman' because of the way he walked with his feet turned outwards. The children were certainly not in awe of Samuel; for them he was somebody who came to visit them from time to time and who never seemed to work.[28]

A great treat for the children was the annual pantomime at the Gaiety Theatre in Dublin. When making their way there at the beginning of January 1938 they were attracted by the cries of a newsboy and stopped to buy a paper, in which they read of the stabbing of Samuel Beckett by a pimp in Paris.[29] Naturally, the incident caused a great deal of concern in the family. Fortunately Samuel recovered quickly and was able to return to Dublin in July and November of that year.

In July Samuel's mother May rented a two-storey house at Greystones harbour from which she could see the cemetery where her husband had been buried. Whenever she stayed here, she sent formal invitations to the Beckett children to join her for tea. John recollected that it was 'rather heavy going' – cucumber sandwiches, tea, cakes and so forth – but the occasions were calm and pleasant. In retrospect, he realized that this was a 'very charming thing to do'. For John, she was an awe-inspiring lady dressed in black, whose presence was rather forbidding, though she could be generous and kind. Ann shared John's feelings about her: she found May severe, overbearing and definite in the way she spoke, though, at the same time, she was exciting – there was warmth from her as well. The local children loved May's house and often persuaded Ann to bring them because of two great attractions: a couple of 'scary' Kerry Blue dogs, and an enormous jar of bull's-eyes, which May distributed among them. When Ann got one stuck in her windpipe and began choking, May caught her by the feet, turned her upside down and walloped her on the back until the sweet became dislodged. 'The other kids were fierce impressed by this rapid treatment,' Ann recalled.[30]

May liked to take four o'clock tea in the lounge of the Grand Hotel, Greystones (later named the La Touche) with other ladies. Often present at these afternoon teas were the writer Anthony Cronin and his mother and the painter priest Father Jack Hanlon with his mother.[31]

It was possibly in November 1938 when, after a walk, Ann and her mother returned to the house and heard music: Samuel and her father were sitting beside each other at the piano, 'all sort of tucked together playing a duet' in a totally relaxed way. Ann recollected that both men had great affection for each other and that 'there was a lovely feeling of warmth which surrounded them both when they were together.'[32]

Samuel was back in Dublin again in August of the following year: the family home in Foxrock, Cooldrinagh, had been sold and his mother was having a new house built nearby. Named 'New Place' when it was completed, it overlooked the Dublin mountains.[33] Samuel joined May in her house in Greystones, which was livened up by visits from his brother Frank, his wife Jean and their baby Caroline, and May's sisters Mollie Roe and Sheila Page. Sheila's two daughters and John and Ann Beckett were often in the house. Samuel swam with John and Ann, walked the dogs along the beach and, once again, played piano duets with Gerald.[34] Like his father, John had fallen in love with Wicklow; he and Ann often explored the surrounding countryside on bicycles until war broke out in September of 1939.[35] Samuel returned to France and the family would not see him for the next few years.

John's first composition, December 1939, with an inscription written by John F. Larchet.
(Courtesy of the late Deirdre Sinclair.)

At the age of twelve, John, who had inherited his father's musical ear, felt competent enough to try his hand at composition. His first attempt has survived: a simple piece of nineteen bars with a repeated first section. It is dated 5 December 1939 and bears an inscription at the bottom right: 'Young Beckett (11 [*sic*] years old). 9/12/39. This is really very promising. Work hard and you will be a good composer some day. J.F. Larchet.'[36] John F. Larchet (1884–1967) had been appointed to the staff of the Royal Irish Academy of Music in 1920, where he succeeded his teacher Michele Esposito as senior professor of composition, harmony and counterpoint. He was also Professor of Music at University College, Dublin and was known to be an excellent teacher of standard harmony and counterpoint. In fact, John's relative Walter Beckett had studied with him.[37] It was obvious that the young John was talented: he had mastered the piano in a very short space of time and was able to compose a piece of music after just four years of study. Larchet's assessment must have been terrific encouragement for him and was probably instrumental in convincing him that he could become a composer.

Although school reports for John's period in Aravon have not survived, it seems safe to surmise that he had done well, and it was now time for him to leave prep school and move on. His father decided to send him to St Columba's College in Whitechurch, at the foot of the Dublin Mountains. Because of the distance from Greystones, John would once again stay there as a boarder.

Three

1940–43

A Church of Ireland college, St Columba's was the obvious choice for people living in the Dublin area who had sent their sons to Aravon. Named after the Irish missionary, it was founded at Stackallan House, County Meath, in 1843. In 1849 it moved to its present 150-acre site on the slopes of the Dublin Mountains. In a letter to an old friend in 2006, John wrote:

> I went to school at St Columba's College, so beautifully perched on the brow of Kilmashogue, with a marvellous view over Dublin Bay, to Howth and, to the north, in fine weather, looking over the city to the Mourne Mountains. It was a good school and I was happy there, especially through being in the hands of our wonderful music master Joe Groocock, whom I came to revere and love, as I still do. [1]

William Sewell, one of the founders, believed that young people should be educated in beautiful and spacious surroundings. The original house on the grounds is Georgian, and around it the school buildings are grouped: the Warden's House, the Big Schoolroom, the Argyle Building, the cloisters (on one side of a quad) and the chapel. The latter, with its unusual vaulted roof and wooden beams, stained-glass windows and great bell (also used as a fire alarm), was designed by the eminent Victorian architect William Butterfield. [2]

Although officially Anglican, St Columba's was unusual in that it was liberal and welcomed all creeds: even in John's day there were a couple of Sikh students wearing turbans, and one Roman Catholic. Rugby matches were played not only with other Protestant colleges but with Catholic schools such as Belvedere College and Clongowes. Irish was taught, and indeed St Columba's had been the first college to produce a grammar of the Irish language. The College during

John's time housed around 150 boys, all boarders, who were grouped together in houses which, from time to time, moved from one building to another. Sports included rugby, cricket, lawn tennis, boxing, Eton Fives and hockey. There was an athletic club, a literary society, a debating society, a printing club, a photographic club, a natural history society, a metal-working club, and a college farm where students could study farming and even beekeeping.[3]

John started in St Columba's at the beginning of Michaelmas term 1940, when he was placed in the Junior House (he later moved to Glen) and in class IVa, which was for bright boys who had done well in the Common Entrance examination (which John had sat at Aravon).[4] At the same time, David Sowby – whose father was Warden (headmaster) – and Robin McKinney entered the College. Although they were not all in the same form, they remembered John clearly. One of the first things that happened at the beginning of term was a test for the chapel choir: young Robin passed the test but whether John did or not, Robin cannot remember – he suspects that he did not. Both he and John were entered for the entrance Lefroy Music Scholarship and astonishingly Robin won it and John came second. Robin believed that the 27-year-old Precentor or music director, Joseph Groocock, who had adjudicated them, had made a mistake as John was 'immeasurably a better musician' than he.[5]

Delighted with his new surroundings and now more at ease with his schoolmates – though he still tended to keep to himself – John settled down to the study of English, Irish, Latin, French (taught by Mr D.H. NcNeil), history (which now included Irish history), geography, mathematics (taught by a nineteen-year-old Mr Norman Lush), science (with Mr George Lodge), divinity or religious education (taught either by the chaplain or the Warden), art (Mr Brian Boydell) and music (Mr Groocock). Under the progressive guidance of Warden Sowby, who saw the need to integrate the College more into the new Irish state than it had heretofore been, the Irish language was taught in accordance with the rules of the Department of Education, which also made it possible to sit for the Intermediate and Leaving Certificate examinations, both of which required a pass in Irish and other specified subjects, including English. The students were therefore encouraged to study the language so that they could pass the Intermediate Certificate, then allowed to drop it if they chose to do so. However, their parents had to pay extra to make up for the College's loss of £15–20 per boy, given to the College by the government as an incentive to study the language. If pupils wished to continue, they could (and most did) stay to sit the Leaving Certificate examination.

Since all pupils coming from Aravon and similar schools had not studied Irish before, they had to learn it in a hurry. They were lucky to have Mr W.H. (Harry)

Lush, brother of Norman, as their teacher. A fluent speaker of the language and an inspiring teacher, his technique was to encourage the boys to learn a great deal of Irish poetry and four or five stories by heart; his philosophy was that if they got stuck in an examination, they could throw in some poetry as it was sure to impress the examiners. Harry, who accepted that for many of the pupils Irish was a bore and a chore, was able to bring new boys up to Intermediate Certificate standard in the short space of just two years. A remark stating that 'Harry Lush will get you through exams but you won't learn any Irish' was incorrect. Interestingly, John was one of the many boys who enjoyed learning Irish and a few Irish tunes from Mr Lush.[6]

Although Anthony Cronin, in his biography of Samuel Beckett, described John at this period as being a dark, brooding boy,[7] Adrian Somerfield, who entered St Columba's a year later, remembered John as a friendly, amiable and 'jolly-looking' lad.[8] Norman Lush, the mathematics teacher, found John a studious boy with a quiet voice, 'extremely pleasant' and not at all argumentative or boisterous like the other lads. He was plump, with black hair, easy-going, and had all the appearances of having been thoroughly spoilt at home. As he showed so little interest in sport, his Glen housemaster Dr Sandham Willis did not force him to play any of the usual games. Instead, he made him don sports clothes and sent him off on 'cross-country' runs to the back gate of the College and back – a dash of about 150 yards. One day, as John was walking back from his 'run', he bumped into the Warden. 'Have you been out on a cross-country run, Beckett?' Sowby asked. 'Yes Sir,' replied John.

Although the classrooms were centrally heated, the College, including the dormitories, was icy cold in winter owing to the shortage of fuel and electricity during the war years or 'Emergency', as this period was called in Ireland. Every morning the Glen boys were obliged to take a cold shower; hot showers were available in the afternoon for the rugby players and at night for the whole house. The food served in the dining hall was good and wholesome, with lamb, mutton and pork from the school farm.[9] These difficult years of shortages encouraged the College, which in those days was a long way from Dublin's city centre, to be a self-contained community.[10]

The boys attended services in the chapel twice a day – according to the College statute, every boy was obliged to attend chapel, no matter what their religion was. Although the chapel was divided by a wooden screen in John's time, it was much the same as it is now; on the left wall there was a large memorial listing the names of Old Columbans who had been killed during World War I. However, there was no gallery and the console of the organ was in the main part of the chapel where only the pipes are now, on the right.[11]

This, then, was the organ played by the Precentor, Joe Groocock and some of the boys who studied music with him. David Sowby remembers how Joe, who was a jovial man with a sense of humour and who inspired a love of music in many of the boys, used to play an improvisation on the final hymn tune as everyone processed out of chapel after the Sunday evening service, and often cunningly wove in a little of the latest popular song. Boys and masters would then rush back into the chapel for an informal organ recital. 'The most favoured had the privilege of sitting beside Joe and turning the page when he gave a brisk nod,' David recollected. Joe also composed and produced musical comedies for the boys to perform at the end of term, of which the best known, *Jack and Jill and the Drainpipe*, has been revived many times since.

Joseph Groocock was born in November 1913, in Croydon near London; soon afterwards the family moved to Rugby. He attended St Michael's College, Tenbury Wells, as a choral scholar, was a pupil at St Edward's School, Oxford (where David Sowby's father taught him), and later read classics and music at Christ Church, Oxford. At first he had read Divinity at Oxford, and was sponsored by a friend of the family who had offered to pay his fees on condition that he study Divinity, but had given this up after a while. From his father he inherited an exceptional aural ability and an unshakeable belief that students should practise taking musical dictation, as he considered this to be essential training for composers who must write down what they hear in their imagination. He was an outstanding accompanist and excelled in improvising at the keyboard.

Joe came to Ireland in 1935 to teach music at St Columba's and soon afterwards married Rhoda Houston, who came from Belfast. Over the next few years Rhoda gave birth to five children. The family lived in one half of a farmhouse that had been divided in two: Delmaine Cottage, near Tibradden and a short distance from the College. Joe and Rhoda were in the habit of inviting the music students to afternoon tea on Sundays, which the boys loved. Although Joe's background was church music, he was not a religious man;[12] nonetheless he did compose Hymn 560, *Alone with none but thee my God*, attributed to St Columba and commonly sung to the tune *Emain Macha*. The hymn, which Adrian Somerfield remembers singing, is included in the new Church Hymnal under the title *Tibradden*.[13]

Joe wrote many songs and sonatas in an idiom that evoked England in the 1930s. A great admirer of Bach, many of his compositions were influenced by him and he wrote several canons, preludes and fugues. The website of the Contemporary Music Centre, Ireland, lists almost eighty of his compositions, which include a completion of Bach's *The Art of Fugue* for organ. Later in life, Joe lectured in the music department of Trinity College, the Royal Irish Academy of Music and the Dublin Institute of Technology Conservatory of Music and Drama.[14] His wife Rhoda died tragically in 1962 and he married Dorene Droste, with whom he had two more children.

John studied piano with Joe in a tiny cubicle in the Kennedy Memorial Building (named after a former Senior Prefect), which was built a year after John arrived; a couple of photographs of a chubby John, seated at an upright piano and smiling into the camera, were taken by Robin McKinney at around this time. Robin remembers playing Mozart symphonies with John, in piano duet arrangements.[15] John was greatly impressed by Mr Groocock, and Joe quickly realized how incredibly talented his young pupil was; he later told his daughter Jenny that John was the first really gifted pupil that he ever had.[16] Joe was still praising him many years later when he was a lecturer in Trinity College; he told a story of how he had proposed to give him a lesson in writing music in the style of Brahms and how John had said, 'What do we need a lesson for? Let's just do it!' In John's mind, there was no need to have a lesson; as he was already familiar with the composer's music, all he had to do was sit down and compose some music in his style.[17]

Robin, John and another classmate named Tom Lancaster played the organ at services in the chapel. Robin cannot remember John improvising on the instrument and was unaware that he was composing music in his spare time. Practice on the organ at that time was limited to one hour per week owing to the shortage of electricity during the war years. Because of this, a piano was placed in the chapel and often used instead of the organ. Robin, who was religious as a boy, noticed that John did not show much interest in religion while in college.[18] Adrian Somerfield realized how intensely interested John was in music – his tuck box contained little or no food but was instead filled with manuscript paper, which was difficult to obtain during the Emergency. So keen was John to study music that an arrangement was made whereby he received extra lessons from Mr Groocock in lieu of time devoted to sport.[19]

John and Robin were two of the boys who were regularly invited to the Groococks' home for afternoon tea, to play music, sing madrigals and, in the summer, help chop back the trees. Joe later told his daughter Jenny that when John was fourteen, he wrote his first fugue while standing against a tallboy in the house.[20] Although not in John's form, Adrian Somerfield knew that John was composing and remembered a fugue – probably this first attempt. As Adrian and his parents spent their summer holidays in Greystones, he often saw John and his sister Ann swimming together there.

John, possibly encouraged by Joe Groocock, must have decided to leave school early in order to concentrate on music.[21] Instead of staying for the customary five years and sitting the Leaving Certificate examination, he left abruptly at the end of the 1943 Michaelmas term. The terse entry in *The Columban* for December of that year reads: 'J.S. Beckett (1940):– Glen. Remove. Lefroy Music Scholarship 1940. School Certificate'.[22] Glen was the name of the house, Remove was the name of the form or school year, and the School Certificate was the examination set by the Oxford and Cambridge Joint Board, which was taken one year after the Intermediate Certificate. Thus, at the age of sixteen, John finished his eight-year spell of formal education, ready to face the world and devote the rest of his life to what he loved best of all: music.

Four

1943—45

John's progress under Joe Groocock, whom he admired just short of idolatry, must have been remarkable, for in December 1943 he won the Coulson Exhibition in Organ and Piano. This scholarship was awarded by the Royal Irish Academy of Music in Westland Row, Dublin, for the academic year 1944—5. His success was duly noted in *The Columban*.[1]

Although John undoubtedly would have spent most of his time studying, composing and practising, he would have devoted some of his time to reading. From around 1942 he had been enjoying the exploits of Bertie Wooster, Jeeves and company in P.G. Wodehouse's novels. He was fond of quoting passages from these stories in later life.[2] He also began to socialize a little.

By now Aidan Higgins and his family, who had moved from Celbridge, were living in a bungalow on Kinlen Road, on the edge of the Burnaby Estate, in Greystones.[3] When John met Aidan, he loaned him four books; one of them was Samuel Beckett's novel, *Murphy*.[4] Written and first published in 1938, John had read it as a boy. Although he had not understood it (and probably had failed to find any humour in it), he was 'amazed' by it.[5]

The three other books made no impression on the young Aidan, who was the same age as John, but *Murphy* 'raised the hair on [his] head'. *Murphy*, he claimed, 'was the business'. When John's mother discovered that he liked the book so much, she advised him to visit the composer Walter Beckett in Donnybrook, who gave him a copy of Samuel's *More Pricks than Kicks*, which he had no intention of reading, discreetly wrapped in a brown paper parcel.

Aidan then wrote a fan letter to Samuel, but John told him that it was no use posting it as he never replied to his mail. Surprisingly, he did – but Aidan was unable to read his letter because of the illegible handwriting. Peggy, John's mother, managed to decipher it; Samuel's message was 'Despair young and never look back.'[6] Aidan, who would become a very able and successful writer, met Samuel in London some years later. He and John became good friends at this period and kept in touch for several years.

The first composition of John's to be played in public was *A Short Overture for Orchestra*. It was performed by the Dublin Orchestral Players and conducted by Brian Boydell on 23 May 1944 in the Metropolitan Hall, Lower Abbey Street.[7] Although the hall was large and the acoustics were good, the building tended to be dusty and dirty. The seats were tiered and there was a balcony with a wrought-iron balustrade. As there was no proper concert hall in Dublin then, the Metropolitan Hall was often used for performances of classical music. It also was the venue for the annual competitive music festival known as the Feis Ceoil.[8]

The Dublin Orchestral Players had been founded in 1939, and had been conducted by Havelock Nelson, who had subsequently left for Belfast. It was now conducted by the young, energetic and enthusiastic Brian Boydell (1917–2000), who was then teaching art in St Columba's. He would go on to establish himself as the foremost Irish composer of his generation and an ardent advocate for public music education. He became Professor of Music at Trinity College Dublin in 1962 and a noted musicologist.[9]

One advantage of directing the Dublin Orchestral Players, which was usually referred to by its initials, DOP, was that Brian was able to have his own works publicly performed. Brian was aware of the limitations of this amateur orchestra and conceded that some of the performances must have been 'undoubtedly dire'. If Dubliners wanted to hear live orchestral music at that time, the DOP was all they had because the Radio Éireann orchestra played for most of the time in a studio that was situated in a part of the General Post Office building, facing Henry Street. Brian believed that the DOP made up in enthusiasm for what they might have lost in perfection.[10] However the standard must have been deemed good enough for broadcasting, for the second half of this particular concert went out live on air.

The leader of the DOP on the 23 May was John's cousin Morris Sinclair ('Maurice' on the programme). The cellists included Morris's sister Nancy and Betty Sullivan; on percussion was a certain Charles Acton, later music critic of *The Irish Times*. The evening of music started with John F. Larchet's arrangement of the Irish National Anthem (standard procedure at the time), followed by Mozart's Overture to *Il Seraglio*. After this came the first performance in Dublin of J.S. Bach's Brandenburg Concerto No. 5 in D major, with Claude Biggs (piano), Nancie Lord (violin) and Doris Cleary (flute) as soloists. The first half of the concert ended with an arrangement by Michele Esposito of *Wachet auf* ('Sleepers Awake') from Bach's Cantata No. 160.

The second half began with John's Overture, which the programme notes described as follows: 'This overture is constructed as a Sonata movement. The character of the main fast section, with its light tripping tune and syncopated accompanying figure contrasting with a broad sweeping melody, is gradually developed in the slow introduction, which is in fact the germ from which the whole overture grows.' Next came Schubert's Symphony No. 4 in C minor (the 'Tragic') and the concert concluded with the first performance of Brian Boydell's *Satirical Suite: The House of Cards*, op. 18a.[11]

'Quidnunc', the pseudonym used by the author of *An Irishman's Diary* in *The Irish Times* had written some days previously:

> Another composer is John Beckett. Setting eyes on John Beckett during rehearsal this department believed John Beckett to be somebody's young brother, in for the fun of the thing. He shrunk [*sic*] behind the piano, keeping out of the way. But Beckett, in fact, has composed an overture, which will be performed at the concert. He is seventeen years of age, comes from Greystones, and is a son of Dr Gerald Beckett. I think it is probable that I have seen the composer, in recent years, in short trousers on the beach – Burnaby end. He is shy with information. In reply to a question, he said: 'I only wrote the Overture – I didn't compose it.' But the Overture sounds good.[12]

Advance information was also printed in the *Evening Mail*. A regular article entitled *Jottings*, written by 'A Man About Town', included a section on the forthcoming concert: 'Start of a Career: Yet another first performance at the concert will be the first work by John Beckett to be given in public. It is an overture (literally and otherwise; the composer is not yet 19, and left St. Columba's College only a few months ago).[13]

A member of the audience on 23 May was Adrian Somerfield from St Columba's; he and other pupils were allowed to go to the DOP concerts in the Metropolitan Hall, no doubt thanks to their art teacher, Brian Boydell. Adrian confesses that John's Overture was 'a bit beyond' him – he remembered that it contained quite a lot of drumming.[14]

On the following day, the *Evening Herald* made mention of the work but offered no comment, as did the *Evening Mail* and the *Irish Press*. The *Irish Independent*, in an article entitled 'Local Composers' Work Performed', devoted a paragraph to Brian Boydell's work (ending with 'Why the composer wishes to perpetuate such a clangour, and apparently take pleasure in it, is beyond me') and went on to say: 'An overture by John Beckett had no particular merit, and its main idea is reiterated until interest is lost.'[15] *The Irish Times*, although brief, was more understanding, encouraging and positive: 'A short overture for orchestra, presented for the first time, suggests that the youthful composer, John Beckett, has quite a promising future. He shows good understanding of orchestration and grouping.'[16] The July edition of *The Columban* noted the concert thus: 'We congratulate: J.S. Beckett (O.C.) on the performance of his Overture by the Dublin Orchestral Players in the Metropolitan Hall on the night of May 23rd.'[17]

It would be interesting to know what people thought of young John's music; it is quite possible that Brian Boydell thought little of it. (John had a poor opinion of Brian's music.)[18] In all probability the amount of people in Ireland at this time who would have appreciated and understood the type of music produced by contemporary composers such as Boydell and Beckett was very limited. Indeed, the general attitude towards British and Anglo-Irish intellectuals was quite hostile. Boydell admitted that at one time he had levelled arrogant and tactless criticisms at Dublin musical life, believing that his musical background was broader than that of his fellow composers.[19] Small wonder then at the non-committal or critical reviews in the national press towards Brian and John's music. At the same time it must be remembered that Boydell's *Satirical Suite* was a playful work brimming over with good humour, whereas Beckett's Overture would have been a more serious, introspective composition. The Metropolitan Hall audience, amazed by John's youth and seeing him before them taking a bow, undoubtedly would have applauded loudly, but his brief moment of exultation may have quickly given way to frustration and annoyance on reading such indifferent notices – but then again the Anglo-Irish community would have considered *The Irish Times*, with its favourable comment, the only newspaper worth reading.

John and Brian were not the only composers in Ireland at the time. Denis Donoghue, then music critic of *The Irish Times*, believed that the majority of Irish composers of that period tended to fall into 'the trap of folk-music', a trap that John would, in general, tend to avoid.[20] Another composer who suffered from the same accusation was E.J. Moeran, an English composer of Anglo-Irish descent, who spent much of his time in Ireland and who was to become an important figure in John's life. By this time the Radio Éireann orchestra had performed Moeran's *Scherzo* twice in 1942, and his *Lyric Movement for strings* and *Spring Nocturne* in 1944.[21]

John, who by now was taking his music very seriously, submitted three songs to the Feis Ceoil during the summer of 1944. These may have been settings of poems by Emily Dickinson (his favourite poet), Emily Brontë and Thomas Hardy. John was fond of Hardy's poem *In Time of 'The Breaking of Nations'* but his father had mocked it; the line 'only a man harrowing clods' became a catchword between them.[22] It so happened that E.J. Moeran, of whom John had not heard at the time, was adjudicating the competition. John claimed that he was 'very pleased to receive the news from the Feis Ceoil office subsequently that the songs had won the first prize.'[23] In fact, John was wrong: the Belgian Staf Gebruers, who was organist, *carillonneur* and choirmaster of St Colman's Cathedral in Cobh, County Cork, won first prize for Original Song in the Composers' Competitions that year.[24] John may have been thinking of the Fitzgerald Organ Trophy that he definitely won at the Feis Ceoil the following year. Nonetheless, Moeran was impressed by John's songs and a week or two later wrote him a letter, in which he said that he thought the songs showed talent and that he would like to meet him. Speaking on a BBC Radio 3 programme devoted to E.J. Moeran many years later, John recollected:

> I can see him now – I was expecting to find a distinguished-looking chap, you know, artistic and all – but in actual fact he looked like the sort of figure you'd find in a cattle fair in Kerry: the old raincoat and the rather battered general dress, the face and the stick and ... he would have fitted in absolutely in the streets in the markets along the quays perfectly easily. His face was a ruddy complexion, a rather battered face with a kind of visionary blue eyes looking out of it, and his hair greyish (and black also), brushed straight back from his head.
>
> We sat down and we got talking about music a little; he told me that he was composing the *Sinfonietta* at the time. I was trying to write a string quartet movement and I showed him this, and he was saying how difficult it was to write well for string quartet; as he put it, 'What you must remember is that you're not writing for four string players – you're writing for sixteen strings' – I remember a remark he made about it.[25]

Ernest John Moeran was born near Hounslow, west of London, in 1894; he learnt to play the violin and piano and, beginning in 1913, studied music with the Irish composer Charles Villiers Stanford at the Royal College of Music in London. Moeran had come to Dublin in March 1944, where the first performance of his Violin Concerto had been given in the Capitol Theatre. He then went to Kenmare, where he abandoned work on his Cello Sonata and recommenced work on his Cello Concerto. In early May he was in Cork, adjudicating for the Feis Ceoil and then, after a brief stay in Dublin and Waterford, he returned to Kenmare, where he worked on his *Sinfonietta*.[26]

John explained to Moeran that he was about to study for a year in the Royal Irish Academy of Music and that his hope was to go to the Royal College of Music in London afterwards. Moeran, convinced of John's capabilities and realizing how difficult it might be for him to be accepted in the Royal College of Music, decided to help.

Moeran introduced John to his fiancée, the cellist Peers Coetmore, who was the inspiration for his Cello Sonata and Concerto. John noticed the strange relationship between them. When all three of them were together in the County Wicklow village of Enniskerry, Moeran suddenly announced that he wanted to see somebody at the end of the village. He went off downhill on his stick and returned after 'just about enough time to have a good stiff drink'. Even though John hardly knew Moeran or his fiancée, he sensed an 'edginess' about what was happening that afternoon.[27]

Apart from these incidents – the loaning of *Murphy* to Aidan Higgins, the performance of John's Overture in May and the meeting with E.J. Moeran in the summer, we know little else of what John was doing for the first half of this year. What we do know is that he started his year-long study at the Royal Irish Academy of Music, Dublin, in September 1944, at the beginning of term. The purpose of this was to work towards a Bachelor of Music degree, though students had to sit the exams for such extern degrees not in the Royal Irish Academy of Music, but in nearby Trinity College.[28]

It so happened that John's cousin Morris Sinclair was studying in the Academy at the same time; they both studied piano and harmony, which was compulsory.[29] John was given lessons in piano and composition by John F. Larchet,[30] and learned to play the organ from Thomas Weaving.[31] He would have encountered Brian Boydell once again here, for he was appointed Professor of Singing at the Academy during the year.

Unfortunately there is little else to say about this period of John's study other than the fact that he won the Coulson Academy Scholarship sometime in 1944 and the Fitzgerald Organ Trophy at the Feis Ceoil before July 1945.[32]

Five

1945–47

E.J. Moeran had not forgotten his promise to John. With the ending of war in May 1945 it was possible for him to use his connections with the Royal College of Music in order to help John be accepted as a pupil. Entrance to the College was difficult at that time as a great number of talented musicians were returning home from the forces and places were being reserved for them. Moeran wrote to the Director, Sir George Dyson, recommending that John be considered for a place.[1] John was contacted and informed that he would have to submit some of his compositional work and attend an interview. On 13 August he wrote the following letter to Brian Boydell:

Dear Mr Boydell,

As you know, I am trying to get into the R.C.M. for next term. I was to have gone over for the entrance exam. on July 25th, but was not able to get my pass-port in time. Instead, they want me to bring some of my work over for an interview in the first week of September.

I started work on a new quartet for strings as soon as I heard of this, and will have two of the three movements finished for the interview. The point is that I want, if at all possible to hear them tried over on the four instruments before september [sic]. And so I write to ask whether you might know of anybody who would be willing to spend an hour or so, before Sept 1st trying over the movements. They would not of course commit themselves to any sort of performance whatever. I just must hear the distribution, as it will sound in practice.

I hope that you dont [sic] mind me writing to you like this; but as it is very important to me, and as there is not much time left, you seem the only chance!

Please let me know as soon as you can, so that if there is any chance [?and] I can get everything ready in time.

        Yours

        John Beckett.[2]

Letter written to Brian Boydell by John Beckett, aged 18. (Courtesy of Digital Resources and Imaging Services, Trinity College Library, Dublin.)

This clumsily-worded letter was written in a cursive and rather elongated hand, so different from the almost illegible angular style (often dubbed 'Chinese') that he developed later in life. The careful handwriting, yet artless style of writing, suggests an awkward teenager struggling to be confident but requiring help and reassurance. Unfortunately we do not know whether John succeeded in having his music performed, but luckily for him he was accepted by the College. He believed that without Moeran's help, it would not have been possible.[3]

Moeran, who was by now married to Peers Coetmore, lived in 55 Belsize Lane, in Hampstead, home to many of London's intellectuals, artists, literati and musicians.[4] Moeran was very kind to John and they saw each other occasionally in London during John's three-year stay. Moeran brought him to concerts and an 'important' rehearsal of Sibelius's Symphony No. 1, a work that John came to love, even though he realized that it was not the composer's best work. Moeran also gave him tapes of his own quartets.[5] When he and Peers moved to Swiss Cottage in 1946, they showed John the one-roomed building in the garden where Moeran composed his music.[6]

The London that greeted John when he arrived in September 1945 was in ruins; rubble was being removed and buildings were being repaired and rebuilt. Luckily the Royal College of Music was still intact, for it was situated in the non-industrial and non-commercial district of South Kensington, which had, on the whole, been spared the worst of the bombing.[7]

John began his first term of study on 17 September 1945; his subject was composition and his instrument was organ. John had two composition teachers during his time at the College: the well-known British composer Edmund Rubbra and Dr R.O. Morris.[8]

Rubbra, born in Northampton in 1901, had been a pupil of Cyril Scott and then Gustav Holst, first at the University of Reading and then at the Royal College of Music, where he had studied with John's other composition teacher, R.O. Morris. By the time John started to study with him, he had moved out of his formative stage and into a more personal harmonic style. A 'traditional' progressive, he neither sought to discover new sounds nor wished to extend the breadth of aural frontiers; instead he exploited the existing ones in greater depth.[9]

Helping students to write a Theme and Variations was the practice of composition teachers of Rubbra's generation. Rubbra encouraged his students to delve into the theme very carefully and thoroughly. He did not alter a note of the music but added ties, suspensions and passing notes, and made each part more contrapuntal, more of itself. When one variation was completed to Rubbra's satisfaction, the student moved on to the next, and each variation was subjected to the same contrapuntal analysis. Rubbra's habit was to improve the variations

by improvising at the piano, humming in his strange nasal voice. The more music
the student composed, the more encouragement and suggestions Rubra offered.
He was very open-minded.[10]

John's other teacher, Dr Reginald Owen Morris, a professor of counterpoint
and composition, was born in 1886 and had studied music at the Royal College
of Music. The first of his several students' textbooks, *Contrapuntal Technique in
the 16th Century*, had a lasting influence on teaching in the UK and elsewhere. By
the time Morris started to teach John he had stopped composing, either because
of the lack of public response or because he had nothing to say. As his music had
not been experimental, it had been unfashionable; however, it did reflect the
man. He never spoke of his own music and few people knew that for many years
he was a regular contributor of crossword puzzles to *The Times*.[11]

John, therefore, studied composition with two men who, although highly
respected and very professional, were fundamentally conservative in their
outlook and used fairly traditional methods of teaching. John would have fully
mastered the techniques and would certainly have gained a thorough understanding of counterpoint. But, in the light of what was to come, the fact that R.O.
Morris had given up composing and had turned to devising crossword puzzles
may have set John thinking. Could this have been a turning point for him? Did he
begin to ask himself if there was any point in devoting his energy to composition?

John's organ teacher was Dr George Thalben-Ball, who was born in Australia
in 1896. A leading performer, he was an international recitalist for more than
fifty years. He, like Morris, had studied at the Royal College of Music and, at the
age of sixteen, had become a Fellow of the Royal College of Organists (of which
he later became President). He was also a member of the BBC music department from 1939 to 1946, which may have been helpful to John.[12]

John studied orchestration and theory (the latter for the whole of his final
year) with Dr Gordon Jacob. Born in 1895, he had studied under Stanford and
Howells in the Royal College of Music. As well as being a teacher and composer,
he wrote a textbook on scoring and transcription, entitled *Orchestral Technique*;
he also wrote *How to Read a Score* and *The Composer and his Art*. John did acquire
a good knowledge of the art of orchestration.[13]

In addition, John also had piano lessons, perhaps for only one term, with
Basil C. Allchin and viola lessons, also for one term, with John Yewe Dyer.[14]
Dyer was remembered chiefly for his thankless task of trying to teach first-study
pianists to play the second-study viola, and for his caring and painstaking tuition.
Many of the best players in the College were his pupils.[15]

John was a 'paying student' – though it is more likely that his father was
paying – for three terms from September 1945; in midsummer 1946 he was

awarded the K.B. Stuart Prize of £3 3s 0d.[16] The July edition of *The Columban* congratulated him on being awarded the Open Scholarship for Composition at the Royal College of Music[17] and, under the heading 'Examinations in the School of Music', noted 'Preliminary Examination for Mus. B. J.S. Beckett (1940)'. John had evidently travelled back to Dublin to sit this exam.[18]

Back in Greystones he would have played piano duets with his father. A friend of his father, David Owen Williams, who lived in the Burnaby Estate and worked in the Guinness Brewery, also used to come to the house to play piano duets with Gerald. Mr Williams had served with the British Army in Germany. 'At the end of the war he discovered a house which had been owned by some German chappy, and which had in it all the Bach cantata scores – and he couldn't resist swiping them! So he had them packed up and he brought them back to Ireland as kind of war booty, and it's a rather civilized war booty!' reported John, on whom the music made a huge impression.[19]

It is most likely that John spent all his summer holidays in Ireland during his period of study in London and, possibly influenced by Moeran or the Gaelic scholar Robin Flower, he began travelling to the west coast. Flower and others had written of the Blasket Islands and had encouraged some of the Islanders to write about their unique traditions and way of life. John may well have been acquainted with the works of the three principal writers: *An Old Woman's Reflections* by Peig Sayers, *Twenty Years A-Growing* by Muiris Ó Súilleabháin and *The Islandman* by Tomás Ó Criomhthain (Crohan). During this period he travelled to Dingle and the tiny village of Dunquin at the end of the Dingle Peninsula, and made journeys across the rough sea in flimsy currachs to and from the wild and windswept Blasket Islands.[20] What he witnessed there was the end of an era, for the islanders, whose safety could no longer be guaranteed by the Irish government, were finally evacuated to the mainland towards the end of 1953.[21]

Here John would have savoured the experience of living with the locals in their rough stone cottages, sitting by the turf (peat) fires and absorbing the richness of their native language, though one wonders how much he could understand with his limited Intermediate Certificate Irish. Some of the Islanders would have spoken heavily-accented English, but not all. John also travelled around County Mayo with his father.[22]

All this was a far cry from the cosy, sophisticated life enjoyed by Irish Protestants at the time; now John was thrown in among rustic Roman Catholics whose strong, unquestioning faith was part of their everyday life. Their language was peppered with pious expressions, such as *buíochas le Dia* (thanks be to God) and *le cúnamh Dé* (with the help of God). Churches – and pubs – were never far away and the parish priest was regarded as a figure of authority, to be feared and respected. The traditional music, which interested John greatly, consisted of lively dance tunes or slow airs played in a distinctive rough style on a fiddle or melodeon, with sometimes the rhythm beaten on a *bodhrán*, a simple vertical hand-held frame drum covered on one side with goatskin. Also there were songs, sung by a solo man or woman in the traditional and highly ornamented *sean nós* ('old custom') style. Bagpipes, particularly the Irish version known as *uilleann* ('elbow') pipes were also used, but might not have been available on the islands. Food was basic, consisting mostly of bacon, cabbage and potatoes and, if no bacon or cabbage was available, then just potatoes. Women, whose married life was harsh and consisted of a series of almost uninterrupted pregnancies, wore shawls and, in old age, smoked clay pipes like the men. John's experiences in the harsh conditions of rural Ireland would have a profound effect on him now and in later life.

On 26 October, 1946, the following notice was printed in Saturday's edition of *The Irish Times*, under the heading 'Song Recital in Dublin': 'First performances in this country of works by the Finnish composer Kilpinen, and the young Irishman, John Beckett, will be given in a song recital by the Carmel Lang string trio in the Gresham Hotel, Dublin, on Monday night next [28 October]. A new song cycle by Mr Boydell will also be performed, as well as works by Brahms and Taniev.'[23]

At this period, it was the habit of Brian Boydell to rent a room in a Dublin hotel (with financial help from his father) for the performance of chamber music, in much the same manner as a painter or sculptor might display work in a one-man show.[24] In this recital, Brian himself was the singer, accompanied by Joe Groocock. The first performance of John's *Three Songs* (1946) – *Had I the Heaven's Embroidered Cloths* (W.B. Yeats), *Strike Churl* (G.M. Hopkins), *Peace, O my stricken Lute!* (Peter Abelard) took place in the second half of the concert.[25]

Unfortunately Joseph O'Neill, music critic for the *Irish Independent*, made little comment on Beckett's songs, but opined that the most impressive of the three was Abelard's *Peace, O my stricken Lute!*[26] Criticism came from the *Irish Press*: 'G. O'B' wrote, 'It was hard to understand how Yeats's poem "Had I The Heaven's Embroidered Cloths" could have inspired such a discordant accompaniment' but the reviewer had nothing to say about the other two songs.[27] All the newspaper reviewers praised Joe Groocock's piano accompaniments.[28] John could hardly have been present at the recital, for he would have returned to his studies in London in September.

John's *Cycle of Three Songs* was performed once again by Boydell and Groocock at the opening meeting of the Dublin Musical Club at the Royal Irish Academy of Music 'by kind permission of the Governors' on Tuesday 5 November, along with various other items. Unfortunately, as this was not a public concert, no music critics were invited and no reviews were written to tell us about the reception of the songs.[29]

John continued his studies at the Royal College of Music in London and during the summer break of 1947 sat his Bachelor of Music examinations in Trinity College Dublin. He obtained his degree at the Commencement held on Wednesday 2 July. Three days later, *The Columban* was proud to print an extract from an article in *The Irish Times*, written by 'Nichevo' (the pseudonym – a Russian word meaning 'nothing' – of the editor, R.M. Smyllie). Entitled 'A Musical Family', it read:

> Professor George Hewson has been having a busy time of late coping with the demands of the Beckett family. During the week I noticed Mr. W[alter] K. Beckett received the degree of Doctor of Music in Dublin University, while, at the same time, Mr. J.S. Beckett became a Bachelor of Music. The new Doctor, who at one time was organist of Kilkenny Cathedral, is the Music Critic of the *Irish Times*, and a musician of outstanding ability. His young kinsman – he is no near relative – is a son of Doctor 'Gerry' Beckett of Greystones, Medical Officer of Health for Co. Wicklow. He is only 20 years of age. Since leaving St. Columba's College he has been devoting most of his time to the study of music. A couple of years ago he jumped into prominence by winning a competition prize at the Dublin Feis Ceoil, and I remember at the time how E.J. Moeran, who is not usually lavish in the bestowal of his encomiums, told me that this young man had a big future ahead of him. All the Becketts are musical, but, so far, none of them has reached the standard already achieved by young John. My congratulations to him and his popular family.[30]

It would appear that John did not spend the summer at the family home in Greystones: he had moved to a rented flat in a large Georgian house, number one, on the corner of Fitzwilliam Square in Dublin. Also living in the same house (and possibly in the same flat) was the noted landscape, figure and portrait artist Nano Reid.[31] She was born in 1900 and had studied in the Dublin Metropolitan School of Art along with Hilda Roberts (who would later paint a portrait of John). Another fellow student had been the Dutch-born Hilda van Stockum, who described Nano as a 'fierce redhead', who 'stared with green eyes behind spectacles. She was uncompromising, blunt and desperately looking for truth'.

Nano was also extremely critical of the church and commerce. It is tempting to suppose that she exerted a strong influence on the young John, who either had or soon would turn his back on religion. Nano's style of painting was anything but conventional; much of her work was chunky and executed in a vigorous manner.[32]

Nano would not have been surprised or shocked by the fact that John was sharing the flat with a young lady – in fact, she may have been responsible for the arrangement. The young lady, born Vera K.H. Stapley on 19 December 1913 in Hackney, London[33] and now thirty-three years old (like Nano, she constantly lied about her age), had already been divorced twice. In 1933 she had married Eric L'e Smith at St George's Church, Hanover Square, London[34] and, in 1940, following her divorce from Eric, had married the cinematographer Douglas Slocombe (more correctly Ralph D.V. Slocombe) in Hampstead, Middlesex.[35] Douglas had been born in the same year as her, on 10 February 1913.[36] After she had left Douglas, Vera had come to Dublin from London in pursuit of a new lover, a man named John Peel. Her mother, whose maiden name was Evelyn May Peters, was born in 1894[37] and, like her daughter, had married twice. Her first husband was Frederick W.G. Stapley, whom she married in Hackney sometime between July and September 1913, when she was already pregnant with Vera.[38] Her second husband was Frederick Nielson, who married her in St George's Church, Hanover Square.[39]

It has been assumed that John and Vera were in a relationship at this time and living together, though evidence suggests that a proper romantic relationship between them may not have begun until about three years later, when John Peel had probably left Vera.[40] One wonders how John's parents reacted to this arrangement. John's father was an easy-going individual, but Peggy Beckett was a religious woman and would most likely have taken exception to her son consorting with a twice-divorced woman who was several years his senior. According to John, his mother had 'volcanic feelings' and he and Ann used to have 'frightful quarrels' with her in their teens.[41] Also, it must be remembered that many ordinary Dubliners at that time would have been scandalized at the thoughts of a young man from such a good background sharing accommodation with a divorced English woman, even though artistic, literary and musical people were considered a race apart. In any event, if there was a serious relationship at this early stage, it would seem that Vera did not accompany John when he went to Paris during the autumn of 1948.

A person whom John would certainly have met at this period was Ireland's most notorious writer, playwright, poet and drunkard, Brendan Behan. John may have met him through the composer and music critic, Frederick May, whom he would have known at the time. A Musical Director at the Abbey Theatre, May had studied with Larchet at the Royal Irish Academy of Music and had continued at the Royal College of Music in London with Ralph Vaughan Williams and Gordon Jacob. He wrote his finest work, the String Quartet in C minor, when he returned to Dublin in 1936. Some sixteen years older than John, he introduced him to the music of Mahler, playing some of the composer's works for him on the piano.[42]

In addition to being a fine pianist and composer, Frederick May was something of an aesthete – he dressed immaculately and wore white cotton gloves – and was homosexual. Despite the fact that Frederick was Protestant, was frustrated at not being British and was tormented by his nationality, he fell in love with Brendan Behan long before he had been released from prison at the Curragh Camp in September, 1946. (Brendan had had his parole extended to January 1947, when a general amnesty for political prisoners was announced.) As Brendan had been condemned to a fourteen-year prison sentence for his youthful anti-British exploits, Frederick's infatuation for him was difficult to fathom.[43]

Amazingly, John and Brendan got on very well together; despite their differences, they both admired each other and 'got on like a house on fire'.[44] John, who would have heard all about Brendan, would not have been too surprised by his views and would have been interested to discover that Brendan was enormously proud of being a member of the working class.[45] Brendan's outlandish behaviour, hilarious impersonations and rough sense of humour would have made John laugh heartily. Brendan had been a house painter, 'a very bad one', as Aidan Higgins was later to comment. 'The screams of Peggy Beckett in Greystones. Behan painted the living-room ceiling. Painted my eye. Scattered shit.'[46] Aidan's acerbic assessment of Behan was, 'a dilution of (or rather, a lower class) Rimbaud – but lacking that one's genius and carpet bag.'[47] Apparently John and Brendan went on a holiday together; it is believed that they might have gone to Salzburg, but when, nobody seems to know.[48] Having met the native Irish on the west coast of Ireland and now wallowing in the company of such an outspoken Nationalist and IRA member, John's perception of his own upbringing was being challenged. Although more or less reformed by now, Brendan would have expressed his hatred of the British establishment but respect for the British people. As Protestant Irish Nationalists with strong anti-British feelings existed at that time, John (and his sister Ann) might easily have been persuaded to adopt such a stance. Although John would later spend much of his life in London, his anti-British feelings were noticed by some.[49] He was no worshipper of the royal family and generally dropped the term 'Royal' from noted establishments, such as the Royal Irish Academy of Music and the Royal College of Music.

Brendan was in the habit of visiting the whimsical sculptor and set designer Desmond MacNamara at his studio-cum-apartment on the top floor of the Monument Cafe in fashionable Grafton Street. Anyone who was vaguely artistic was welcome to join the bohemian acquaintances of Desmond (generally known as 'Mac') and his first wife Beverlie ('Bev') Hooberman. All sorts of people turned up at the studio in Grafton Street, including the physicist Erwin Schrödinger, who was a colleague of Einstein's and a refugee in Dublin from Nazi Germany.[50] Schrödinger, who was a very cultivated man, a writer of poetry and a ferocious womanizer, had an affair with Frederick May's sister, Sheila, who was an actress. Although married to David Greene, a brilliant academic, she had a baby girl with Schrödinger. David accepted the situation but later he and Sheila separated. Interestingly, David then married John's cousin, Hilary Heron.[51]

As a young man, Desmond had attended the National College of Art, where he studied sculpture. He also became involved with a progressive theatre group. Mac made a precarious living making papier-mâché sculpture and props for the Abbey and Gate theatres. Bearded and benign, he later moved to London, where wrote articles for the *New Statesman* and a biography of Eamon de Valera[52] among other books. He also became a literary critic and a lecturer in art. A vegetarian all his life, he was careful of everything he ate and drank. Although dignified and well-mannered, he was, like Behan, revengeful when crossed. He had an encyclopaedic mind, a terrific memory and was a great raconteur of anecdotes, which he constantly embroidered. He was regarded as a central figure in Dublin cultural life.

It is possible that Brendan Behan might have brought John to Mac's hospitable Grafton Street studio. Other visitors included the American writer, J.P. Donleavy and Gainor Crist, the model for the central character in his infamous book, *The Ginger Man*. John undoubtedly would have met these individuals but it seems that he never became involved with them.[53]

It was the habit for those who had gathered in Mac's studio to adjourn to McDaid's pub in nearby Harry Street, off Grafton Street. Although it became Dublin's leading literary pub, anybody and everybody drank there. After closing time, hardened revellers then proceeded to the so-called Catacombs, a warren of basement rooms under one of the Georgian houses in Fitzwilliam Place, a stone's throw from John's flat in Upper Fitzwilliam Street, where the drinking continued into the small hours. John would have been acquainted with both places but it appears that he frequented neither; if he had money to spare for drink, he would have joined his fellow musicians for a pint of Guinness in Kennedy's pub just across the road from the Academy of Music, as John would have called it. This was the pub that had been frequented by his cousin Samuel, and which features in his early novels. John, now only twenty years of age, had not yet become a hardened drinker.[54]

Six

1948–50

A s if John were not busy enough at the Royal College of Music in London, he found time to teach musical theory at the James Ching Piano School,[1] which had been established in 1946. The premises was a three-storey house with a large basement in 8 Hollycroft Avenue, Hampstead. Samuel James Ching was a concert pianist, teacher and author of books on piano technique. He had been born in 1900 in Croydon, Surrey, and died in 1961. He composed music and played in the Henry Wood Promenade Concerts at the Queen's Hall in London. Like John, he loved Bach's music, which suited his small hands. He set up the James Ching Professional Service and became interested in developing an improved piano technique as he was concerned about the problem of pianists developing tendonitis, and wrote a book on the subject. He wrote another on the effect of nerves on piano performance.

James bought the large house in Hampstead in 1945 and the Piano School was launched at the beginning of the following year in a blaze of publicity. He enrolled students of all ages, planned lectures, and arranged students' concerts. The rooms were equipped with upright pianos and two grand pianos were put in the basement. Although this was undoubtedly the high point of Ching's career, the promise of a successful school never really materialized. In 1948, the Town and Country Planning Act decreed that Hollycroft Avenue be designated for residential use only and the school was forced to close. Unfortunately, we do not know exactly when John taught at the school and for how long – we can only surmise that he must have worked there sometime between 1946 and 1948.[2]

John also found time to study the harpsichord with Gertrud Wertheim at Morley College, situated south of the Thames near Waterloo train station.

Speaking on the BBC Radio 3 *Studio Portrait* programme, John said: 'When I came from Dublin to London to study composition, I had never seen a harpsichord. At Morley College I met Gertrud Wertheim and took harpsichord lessons from her, since when I have ceaselessly tried to play it well. It does not break my heart but entices and delights me.' The breaking of John's heart refers to his confession that trying to master Chopin's F minor *Ballade* had resulted in frustration.[3]

An entry in the 1947-8 syllabi at Morley College mentions that Mrs Gertrud Wertheim taught harpsichord on Mondays and that the fees were sixty shillings for twelve twenty-minute lessons. These were to be paid for in advance and were arranged directly with the tutor. As her name did not appear in the following year's syllabli, and was not in the card index of staff either, it can be concluded that her stay at the college was brief.[4]

A German pianist, harpsichordist, music editor and composer, Wertheim had been born in 1867. She had studied at the Royal College of Music and had been a student of the legendary Wanda Landowska, for whom John developed great respect. In *Early Birds*, a BBC Radio 3 programme broadcast in 1988, John reverently told listeners that Landowska had been trained as a concert pianist and that she had decided to dedicate herself to the harpsichord. The harpsichord that she played, made specially for her by the firm of Pleyel in Paris, had an iron frame, to which thick strings were attached at high tension. Playing early music in a decidedly romantic manner, she was no seeker after unattainable authenticity, as John said.[5]

Presumably Gertrud Wertheim played on a more traditional type of harpsichord at Morley College; John later wrote, 'I studied the harpsichord and made a special study of late seventeenth- and eighteenth-century music'.[6] It is tempting to suppose that Gertrud's Germanic temperament and manner of playing might have encouraged John to perform on the harpsichord and organ in a rather 'relentless' style – a criticism often applied later to John's keyboard playing – but it is more likely that this was John's idiosyncrasy and that Gertrud had inherited Landowska's free, colourful and romantic style.

John happened to attend Morley College at an interesting period. Michael (later Sir Michael) Tippett was director of music. The noted editor of music for the recorder, Walter Bergmann (1902–1988) played harpsichord for him and also for the famous counter-tenor Alfred Deller. Deller became a soloist largely due to Tippett, who had heard him sing and had recognized the unique beauty of his voice.

Deller and Tippett collaborated on many musical projects at Morley College from 1944 onwards, particularly their vigorous revival of the music of Henry Purcell, who had been, up to this point, overshadowed by Handel.

Tippett realized Purcell songs (i.e., filled out the harmonies from the 'figured' bass or *basso continuo*), such as 'Sweeter than Roses' and 'Music for a While', which were sung by Deller to harpsichord accompaniment played by Bergmann. The first recording Deller and Bergmann ever made was of the second of these two songs.[7]

While attending his harpsichord lessons with Gertrud Wertheim, John must surely have been aware of these exciting developments in Morley College and certainly must have heard and met Tippett, Bergmann and Deller there, for he would later accompany the singer in Dublin. Thus, John was exposed to what we nowadays refer to as 'early' music and one can guess that his lifelong love affair with the music of Henry Purcell, with its bold harmonies and scrunching discords, began at around this time.

On 30 March 1948 John was, surprisingly, back in Dublin, attending a preliminary meeting of what was then called the National Music Association, shortly to be renamed the Music Association of Ireland. Not only was John listed as being a member of the new Association, but he was also a sponsor. Members (some of them sponsors) included Brian Boydell, Edgar M. Deale, Aloys Fleischmann, Joseph Groocock, Victor Leeson, Frederick May, Olive Lyall Smith and Dorothy Stokes.[8] Although John's input was, for the time being at least, almost non-existent, he was passionately behind all the aims of the Association.

At around the same time, in early April, John was one of ten signatories attached to a letter of protest sent to the editor of the *Radio Review* over a review, written by John O'Donovan, of a studio concert given by the Radio Éireann Orchestra, conducted by Jean Martinon. O'Donovan had written: 'The concert ended with a performance of the Symphony in G minor by Roussel. At least, that is how the announcer described it.'

The letter to the editor of the *Radio Review* began:

> Dear Sir, – We, the undersigned, have decided to utter a solemn protest against your action in permitting an individual like J. O'D. to run riot in your columns and masquerade as a music critic. There are certain unwritten canons of decency and good taste which reputable journalists, like the rest of us, feel bound to observe, but of these your contributor seems never to have heard.

The signatories, John, Brian Boydell, James Delany, Brendan L. Dunne, Aloys Fleischmann, Madeleine Larchet, Nancie Lord, Frederick May, Michael McMullin and Dorothy Stokes, voiced their strong opinion that this was:

not a criticism at all, but a most grossly insulting libel, for which your contributor
is as obviously incapable of feeling any shame as he is of taking his duties seri-
ously. This Symphony was first performed by the Boston Symphony Orchestra under
Koussewitsky, and is regarded as a serious work of art both in America and on the
Continent. If your critic would read a few standard works of musical reference
before he next attempts to review a concert, he would at least be able to avoid
making such a pitiable exhibition of himself in future.

John O'Donovan 'was immensely tickled by his fan mail, so much so that
he willingly accepted my invitation out to coffee and biscuits,' wrote the staff
reporter of the *Radio Review*. 'I am not in the least surprised to find ten people
who say that it is bad taste for a critic to express his opinions as honestly as he
can,' O'Donovan wrote:

I didn't insult Roussel. I have the highest respect for anyone who could write such
a fine work as his G minor Symphony. But I did think the performance of the work
left something to be desired … No: I will keep my nose out of standard works of
musical reference when making up my mind about any performance. … If these
ten boys and girls base their opinions on Grove's Dictionary, that is their look out.[9]

John completed his studies in the Royal College of Music, after six terms, on
17 July 1948. He had thrived in the College; as well as studying assiduously he
had played tuned percussion (piano, celeste, xylophone, glockenspiel and so
forth) in the orchestra when the students had given concerts there.[10] In 1946 he
had won a scholarship worth £60 and another, worth the same amount, in the
following year; he now had won the Julian Lyttelton travelling scholarship for
study in Paris, worth £120.[11]

John was back in Dublin in August, at the same time as his cousin Samuel.
Writing to his friend Georges Duthuit in France, Samuel described how John,
an 'obsessive bear of a man', played his song settings of Shelley and Blake's
poems on the piano. As John was not a singer, he whistled the vocal line. He
then performed piano reductions of his quartet and his concerto for flute and
strings. Samuel went on to describe John as:

bellowing, no joke … he left us without a word, about turn towards I well know
what deserted side streets, I have done that, let him do it better than I could, and
the rest, he will come over to France, get on my nerves, well, willingly enough
– if I am there, but we will have to disappear somewhere, in Paris or outside it.[12]

According to Samuel's nephew Edward Beckett, none of the music mentioned 'survived the determined destruction' of his compositions. It seems that the only survival, treasured by his cousin Deirdre Sinclair, was the youthful composition mentioned in an earlier chapter.[13]

When John arrived in the French capital on a swelteringly hot night in late September, at the Gare Saint-Lazare, Samuel was there to meet him. As neither of them had enough money for a taxi, they lugged John's heavy cases down into the Métro and emerged at Montparnasse, where they walked along the boulevard Raspail to the apartment where Henri and Josette Hayden lived.[14] Samuel had met this couple in the village of Roussillon in the Vaucluse region during the war. Henri was a Polish-born French painter and his young wife Josette was French. Samuel's lifelong friendship with the couple began when he discovered that he and Henri shared an interest in painting and he started to play chess with him.[15]

John did not stay with the Haydens in their apartment but was accommodated in their *chambre de bonne* or maid's room. Samuel had told Josette about John's arrival and had asked her to rent this room to him. 'Nobody in their senses would ever live in the thing except some poor devil of a maid,' reported John, 'but it was absolutely thrilling for me – I couldn't believe it.' (John's cousin Morris Sinclair and his wife Mimi stayed there for a while after they were married.)

Every evening, with the sun setting before him, John used to walk along the rue de Vaugirard, and occasionally he visited Samuel and his partner Suzanne Deschevaux-Dumesnil at their apartment in the rue des Favorites, nearby. The name Vaugirard (in Old French, *Val Girard*), which Samuel explained meant 'the valley of Gerald', reminded him of John's father. John was delighted to know that his father meant so much to him. On one such visit, Samuel told him about the district when he first came to live in it in 1938, and described an old man who had goats and who used to walk around the back streets selling shoes made from their skins.[16] Samuel showed John some photographs, one of which was of Samuel's parents Bill and May walking along the promenade at St Germain-en-Laye. Samuel said to him, 'My mother gave me that photograph and in giving it to me she said, "We were so happy then."' John was very touched by this. Realizing that Samuel was busy writing (he was then working on *En attendant Godot*), John took care not to pester him.

As John was trying to survive on the small amount of money from his scholarship, he was often impecunious and occasionally had to ask Samuel for some cash, even though he was hard up as well. John was ashamed to admit that he got himself into 'frightful scrapes', though fortunately 'not very bad ones'. Samuel was very kind to him. John remembered Samuel's apartment, which was on the seventh floor of a building, and also the lift that brought him up to it. It was a 'funny place', rather small and constricted. There was a kitchen off the tall main room, in which Samuel's writing desk stood in front of the window, and a stairway led to a little sleeping area, which was 'within the space of a kind of balustrade'. Samuel slept there on a single bed; John remembered seeing him lying on it when he was ill. John could only assume that there was another bedroom where Suzanne slept.[17]

Suzanne was a good pianist and knew quite a number of musicians. During the 1920s she had studied at the Ecole Normale de Musique with the distinguished pianist and composer Isidor Philipp, who was of Hungarian descent, and who had studied at the Conservatoire de Paris under various teachers including Camille Saint-Saëns (whose music John disliked). When John expressed his admiration for Gabriel Fauré, she dismissed him with the words, '*Il est pompeux!*' ('he's pompous!'). John sensed that, although she was always civil and kind to him, she did not have the slightest bit of interest in him at all.[18] Speaking to James Knowlson in 1991, John said that he felt that Samuel and Suzanne's level of existence together was one to which he could not possibly attain and that he was never part of it. 'I speak as if I knew Samuel intimately,' John continued. 'I never knew Samuel intimately at all. I knew him … from my childhood and he's a presence and a very congenial one, and one I have always loved and absolutely accepted. I loved his affection for my father and as I got to know [his] work I came to revere him.'[19]

No doubt John's interest in James Joyce was aroused by conversations with Samuel, who had known and helped Joyce in many ways. As John possessed an early edition of *Ulysses*, which he religiously read many times during his life, it is quite possible that he bought it in Paris, for it was banned in Ireland. John venerated Joyce as much as he venerated Samuel, though Samuel was still a relatively obscure writer at this stage – fame would come in early 1953 with the first French production of *En attendant Godot*, later to be translated as *Waiting for Godot*.

It so happened that Desmond MacNamara was also in Paris at this time. He visited John in his tiny *chambre de bonne* and noted some type of complicated arrangement for letting down the keys by means of a string. Another guest, though hardly such a welcome one, was the irrepressible and inescapable Brendan Behan, who had arrived in Paris at around the same time as John. Positioned between the rue de Vaugirard and the boulevard Saint-Michel, John's room was within Brendan's familiar beat. Much to John's annoyance, Brendan invited himself to stay and John, being Irish, did not have the heart to turn him down.[20] Because of the restricted amount of space, Brendan had to make do with sleeping *under* John's bed[21] – a situation that Morris Sinclair, who was also in Paris at the same time (along with Hilary Heron),[22] found 'absolutely plausible'.[23] Brendan, who was drinking regularly but not as heavily as he would do later, would have slept soundly anywhere, bed or no bed. Brendan stayed there for some time and, in his usual manner, helped himself to whatever was available. Eventually John managed to shift him out and on to somebody else.[24] Luckily for Samuel Beckett, Brendan did not manage to contact him during this visit; Samuel would have to forgo the dubious pleasure of meeting this fellow Irishman until 1952. One can only surmise that John might have helped Samuel avoid him, knowing full well that he would not have relished such an intrusion. When the two eventually did meet at 6.30 in the morning, Brendan made so much noise that Samuel was obliged to get out of bed and admit him to his apartment in the rue des Favorites. Samuel soon wearied of his endless anecdotes and, like John, managed to pass him on.[25]

John did not stay in the Haydens' cramped *chambre de bonne* for all of his time in Paris; he eventually moved to a small room, which he liked very much, in the old Grand Hôtel des Principautés unies off the rue Vaugirard, which he described as 'a wonderfully run-down place ... it was the same as it must have been since the Revolution. The old lady who ran it was a very kindly old lady and she put up with me,' John recollected:

> I used to get behind with the rent and I hired a piano and I didn't keep up the payments, and I'm ashamed of myself. Anyway it was a real mess and I'm not very proud of it all. One pouring wet night, there was a knock at the door and here was Samuel, soaked to the skin. My father had written to him to say that they were worried about me because they hadn't heard from me for I don't know how long – I'd decided to let things go a bit – and I thought to myself, 'You should be ashamed of yourself that that man walks down here to see you because your father writes to him.'

John admitted that he 'was young and stupid' and 'not a very admirable sort of person', which fits in with Samuel's rather unsympathetic description of him.[26]

John had the company of his two cousins, Morris Sinclair and Hilary Heron, for a while. Hilary was in Paris on a scholarship, studying art – and racing around the city on a motorbike. Samuel Beckett and Desmond MacNamara helped her after she had been injured in an accident and thrown off her motorbike.[27]

One would assume that John had come to Paris in order to study at the Paris Conservatoire; having won the travelling scholarship, it would have been the most obvious thing to do. However, he did not and one wonders why not. Had he failed to impress his composition teachers in London or had he lost his nerve? The Paris Conservatoire has no record of his attendance;[28] when asked by James Knowlson if he had studied there, he said no, hesitated, explained that he was 'just on a travelling scholarship' from the Royal College of Music, and did not elaborate.[29] However, he did have private lessons with Nadia Boulanger, with whom all aspiring composers studied at that period.[30] Born in Paris in 1887, she entered the Paris Conservatoire at the age of ten. She studied organ with Alexandre Guilmant and Louis Vierne, and composition with Gabriel Fauré and Charles-Marie Widor. Her sister Lili, who was six years her junior, was one of her first composition students. By 1948, Nadia had become director of the American Conservatory in Fontainebleau, though she gave private tuition in her family apartment at 36, rue Baliu in Paris.[31] What her opinion of John's music was is anybody's guess, for John appears to have told only a couple of people about his lessons with her. The fact that he wrote relatively little 'serious' music after his year and a half in Paris and that he was so reluctant to talk about his lessons with Nadia suggests that something might have dampened John's burning desire to become a composer. 'I did have a little talent as a composer as a boy,' John told James Knowlson in 1992:

> I wrote stuff naturally but then I began to get into the world of experimental, *avant-garde* music and I began to be quite unable to operate in it, and I am very glad I found it; so I gave up composition in any serious way as quite a young man. I don't think it's possible to write good music any more. I honestly, seriously don't. And I came to feel that long ago.[32]

Not only had John's teacher in London, Dr Reginald Owen Morris, stopped composing but Nadia Boulanger had almost stopped composing by the time she gave John lessons. She told Gabriel Fauré, 'If there is one thing of which I am certain, it is that I wrote useless music.'[33] One wonders if she also said this to John. Although crazy about Béla Bartók, John had become apprehensive or scared of the *avant-garde* scene, and was not prepared to accept any of the *avant-garde* composers of the fifties.[34]

Morris Sinclair remembered that, in order to make ends meet, John got a job at teaching English in a *lycée* in the western suburb of Saint Germain-en-Laye. He used to travel there on the SNCF train from the Gare Saint-Lazare. He relished this journey, which brought him through the countryside that his beloved French Impressionists had painted. He must have been impressed by Saint Germain-en-Laye, the wealthiest suburb of Paris, with its elegant tree-lined streets, its upmarket residential districts and its fine château.[35] One can assume that John, who had been studying French from the age of eight, acquired a fair degree of fluency in the language during his stay in Paris.

Although he had not used his time well there, John enjoyed his stay in Paris. Living so close to where Samuel lived, he would have frequented the same restaurants and cafés such as the Coupole, the Select and the Dome, and, funds permitting, would have savoured French cuisine, though one suspects that he probably survived for most of the time on bread, cheese and wine. Samuel, who had a reputation for being hospitable to Irish visitors, would have shown him around, and most probably would have introduced him to the capital's fleshpots and seedier parts of the city.[36] Reading between the lines, one has the distinct feeling that John may have spent most of his stay having a good time, revelling in the company of his cousins, visiting the various museums and art galleries, listening to music and soaking up French culture, which he adored. He took a liking to the local popular music, especially the songs of the hugely popular *chanteur* Georges Brassens (1921–1981), whose many CDs John bought in later life. Brassens, whose lyrics were written in French *argot*, composed some 250 songs, 200 of which were recorded. John also liked the songs sung by Jacques Brel (1929–78) and he would have heard the legendary Edith Piaf. He loved the comic films of Jacques Tati, which he probably saw for the first time in Paris.[37] If he had watched Tati's zany 1949 film, *Jour de Fête*, he may have noticed the very brief appearance of an elderly man, introduced by the narrator as 'old Godot'. Perhaps Samuel had watched this film too.

Eventually the time and the money ran out and he had to bid Paris farewell and return to Dublin, where, it seems, his father was ill. He would return to Paris and France many times in the years to come.

Seven

1950

Home from Paris with his formal musical studies completed and no regular employment, John now attached himself to Dublin's bohemian set, drifting from one place to another, in search of company and conversation. John probably spent much of his time playing in private gatherings, teaching a little, composing, devouring music and literature and, most importantly, making new acquaintances. One of these was Aleck Crichton, who had been born in 1918. As a boy, he had often met W.B. Yeats at his parents' home in Fitzwilliam Square when the poet had been invited to tea. John probably shared his love of Yeats's poetry with Aleck. In 1946 Aleck had returned to Ireland after wartime service with the Irish Guards and was now managing the family business, the Jameson whiskey firm, in Dublin's Smithfield. John would later develop a strong liking for whiskey.[1]

Oenone Venetia Carew, daughter of Sir Thomas and Lady Phyllis Carew of Haccombe House in Devon, was another one of the many people John met at this time, when she was in Dublin with her family. A school friend of hers, who lived in Greystones, brought her to meet John, as she knew that both Oenone and John were interested in music. Oenone remembered being driven to a derelict rented cottage somewhere in County Wicklow.

John, who had wildly overestimated Oenone's musical abilities, showed her some songs (presumably his own) and asked her what she thought of them. As Oenone was unable to read both his highly unusual handwriting and the music, she felt 'completely discombobulated' and was unable to say anything. She also recollected that there was no mention of Vera, who seemed not to be there. Morris Sinclair, however, remembered Vera living with John in the cottage.[2]

Because of Oenone's interest in music, she was approached by Radio Éireann and asked to present a programme. Her half-hour show, which consisted of favourite opera records, was aptly named *Opera Box*, and she broadcast using the radio name Carey Kent.[3]

John must have met Oenone's future husband, John O'Sullivan, at around the same time; they soon became good friends and fellow musicians. O'Sullivan, like Beckett, was Irish, but unlike him had come from a Roman Catholic background. Two years older than Beckett, he had been born in Bermondsey in London. As music had come naturally to him, he attended Trinity College of Music, where his principal teacher was the harpsichordist and organist Charles Spinks. Spinks was adept in improvising at the keyboard, a skill that the young O'Sullivan would acquire from him. In time he would become a master of the art.

On the outbreak of war, the O'Sullivan family moved to Dublin. John continued his music studies at the School of Music in Chatham Street. By the age of eighteen he was organist at St Joseph's Church, Glasthule, a job that he came to loathe. One Sunday morning, he disguised the music-hall song *Oh, I do like to be beside the seaside* as a voluntary recessional for the amusement of the more musically-aware members of the congregation. This would become O'Sullivan's 'theme tune' for many years to come – he regularly played it on the harpsichord at unexpected moments for what the Irish call 'divilment'. Despite his sense of humour – he collected limericks and, like Beckett, relished P.G. Wodehouse's novels – he found it difficult to relate to people and, over the years, increasingly turned to alcohol as a means of escape. He was at his wittiest after a few drinks.

O'Sullivan, who was an accountant, presented music programmes on Radio Éireann in his spare time. When playing some early choral music on the radio, he asked the broadcaster Seán Mac Réamoinn whose 'nice voice' he had heard over the airwaves and was told that it was Oenone Carew's. They were introduced and five years later they married. Oenone then changed her name to Venetia.[4]

The people whom John had befriended in Dublin before he set off for Paris would inevitably have introduced him to the well-known horticulturalist and connoisseur of music and the arts, Ralph Cusack. He and his Russian wife Kira lived in Uplands, a period mansion set in several acres of land in Annamoe, a small village near Roundwood in Wicklow. Ralph was famous for his hospitality and his violent temper. He was liberal and progressive in his outlook; his politics were left-wing and he was a pacifist. He painted pictures than nobody dared to criticize, and was a member of the White Stag artists' group (which included

Brian Boydell), as well as the Dublin Society of Painters. He grew exotic plants and sold flower bulbs, and worked as a designer and painter of stage sets. He later wrote an extraordinary surrealist book, partly autobiographical, called *Cadenza*. He had once invited the Griller Quartet from England to play Bloch's string quartet at his previous home in Portmarnock; this had been at a period when Bloch's music was virtually unknown in Ireland.[5]

The one item everyone remembered in his home in Wicklow was an enormous horn gramophone that could play several records consecutively. Musicians were regularly invited to the house to play for him and his friends; the Boydells went there, and Brendan Behan and the writer Anthony Cronin were regular visitors. John and Vera Slocombe, who seem to have been together again in early 1950, took to visiting the household for Ralph's musical evenings.[6]

According to Desmond MacNamara's second wife, Priscilla, Mac had met Vera at Ralph Cusack's house in County Wicklow, where she was staying. Following the break up of her marriage and the ending of her affair with John Peel, she was feeling suicidal. Mac brought her to his new home, a mews at the rear of number 35 Baggot Street, in Dublin's city centre. At around the same time, Mac's present wife Beverlie bought herself a small car, which she never learned to drive. Nothing daunted, she decided to drive Mac, Vera and John out to Ralph's house in Wicklow for what must have been a children's party, for they had balloons in the car. Mac sat beside Beverlie (possibly with his eyes closed for most of the journey because of her appalling driving), and John and Vera shared the back seat. As Bev had almost managed to drive the car into a canal in Dublin, it came as no great surprise to them when she lost control of the vehicle – fortunately on an empty road – and it overturned. In doing so, Vera fell into John's lap and, according to Priscilla, that was how the romance started.[7]

We must assume, therefore, that Vera probably moved in shortly afterwards with John, living with him in the cottage in Wicklow. John's mother could hardly have approved of this and we can imagine the arguments that must have taken place. If John had not turned his back on religion before this, he surely must have done so now.

Vera had been a fashion model and it is believed that a photograph of her made it to the front cover of *Vogue* magazine.[8] However, as the models featured on the front cover were rarely named, attempts to identify her have proved to be fruitless although a superb black-and-white screen-printed photograph of her taken by the Navarra studio at 274 Oxford Street exists, presumably for distribution and autographing.[9] Vera was a lively, excitable and explosive young woman, whose hair was sometimes dyed red, and always styled short and absolutely straight. Some people found her very attractive and sexy. She had certain traits in common with Ralph Cusack, who, we have noted, could be rather fiery. One had to be careful about what one said to her and it was necessary to be on one's guard in her presence – many people found her quite odd.[10] She was inclined to go off the deep end with conversation, babbling on and forgetting what she had said previously.[11] Morris Sinclair considered her 'sparkling', but 'as dumb as they come'. He remembered that she had a hot temper and that she and John often had arguments.[12] She had a great feeling for fashion and clothing,[13] and was a good dressmaker. Although she was not musical, she liked listening to music.[14] She was quite ahead of her time in her attitude to many things. Priscilla MacNamara remembered her running about and climbing a tree, wearing nothing but a fisherman's pullover, though normally she dressed very flamboyantly.[15] She was a terrific cook and loved Mediterranean cuisine, which was not popular in the 1950s.[16] She surely would have introduced John to two of the things he liked best in life: garlic and olives *with* the stones – never pitted.[17] However, a trait of hers that must have irritated John intensely was her untidiness. John was by nature fastidiously tidy; everything had to be in its proper place and he was known to move an object, such as a pot, a quarter of an inch so that it was just in exactly the right spot.[18]

Vera was also incredibly brave. While married to Douglas Slocombe, who had been just a stills photographer up to that point, she, Douglas and another couple, Herbert and Rosa Kline, had gone to Poland in 1939 to film the lights going out in Europe, which was then on the brink of war. Some of the shots were incorporated into the film *Lights Out in Europe*, directed by Herbert in 1940. They were in Poland when the Germans invaded in September. Letters written to her mother from Warsaw, in a train from Vilnius to Riga, then from Riga itself, described in graphic detail the trauma of fleeing the country. The journey, which normally would have taken three and a half hours, took twenty-six hours to complete; the return journey, during which they were miraculously saved from being bombed to death by the presence of another train beside theirs, lasted thirty-six. They arrived in Warsaw just as the station was being bombed. Eventually they boarded a train for Brest-Litovsk, which was hit by a bomb. When Vera, Douglas and their friends sheltered under the train, a second bomb fell within ten feet of them, and a third found them flat on their faces in a ditch. The raid continued for almost fifteen minutes, after which they took their luggage and went to some nearby woods, where they hid while the bombs continued to fall. They decided to abandon the train and continued their journey in farm carts. They finally made it to Vilnius and safety. Writing to Vera's mother Evelyn from the Hotel de Roma in Riga, Douglas reported:

Vera certainly has been through some terrifying experiences in Poland, enough to last her throughout this war I imagine. Anyway, she certainly bore up wonderfully. Lying under the wheels of a train, on the floors of railway carriages and in ditches while bombs are exploding within seven yards and planes are swooping down and mowing people down like blades of grass with their machine-guns is not the best kind of fare for a young girl. Particularly when this goes on for ten days without a single night's rest. Still, most of the danger is over now I believe and I hope to have her safe home soon. Many is the time I cursed myself for having brought her with me, but she doesn't seem to care.[19]

Mary Boydell is one of the people who remembered that John seemed to have no particular job or regular source of income at this time.[20] This is not surprising considering that there was very little work to be found in Dublin then and that many people found themselves unemployed. However, Fachtna Ó hAnnracháin, the Music Director of Radio Éireann wrote to John on 11 January 1950 to confirm an arrangement made during an unrecorded previous conversation:

[…] when it was agreed that you would compose an orchestral score, in the form of an Irish Rhapsody or Suite lasting 15-20 minutes, for Radio Eireann, and let us have the completed score not later than February 15th 1950, such work to be regarded as a commissioned composition which would be paid for by Radio Eireann at the rate of £1 per minute of music provided that the finished work was acceptable to the Director of Broadcasting.[21]

John responded with a terse, formal note typed on the family letterhead:

Dear Sir,
*   I have received your letter of the 11th of January, and*
*   I agree to accept the conditions stated therein.*
*   I look forward to hearing from you at your convenience,*
*   About any possible rehearsal with the Cór Radio Eireann.*
*   Yours sincerely,*
*   J.S. Beckett[22]*

However, John was unable to complete the work on time; in an undated hand-written note, written at some time before the deadline, he explained: 'Dear Mr O'Hanrachain, I regret to say that I find myself unable to finish the 'Rhapsody for Orchestra' on which I have been working, by the date you mentioned.'[23] John had decided that O'Hanrachain was the spelling of the Music Director's name; either he could not decipher the signature or his knowledge of Irish orthography was poor.

Having got his foot in Radio Éireann's door, he wrote another letter to Ó hAnnracháin shortly afterwards and enclosed some of his songs:

Dear Mr O'Hanrachain,

I am enclosing with this, four sets of songs. As you will notice, only two of them are for the same type of voice, namely the Walter de la Mare set with piano, and the Shelly [sic] set. The de la Mare set with string quartet is technically and musically the simplest and would possibly proove [sic] suitable for inclusion in a quartet recital. The Brontë poems were only recently completed, and I have not as yet had the opportunity of hearing them. I would be glad if it were possible to do so.

I have written to the publishers concerned about copyright difficulties and hope to hear from them soon. [24]

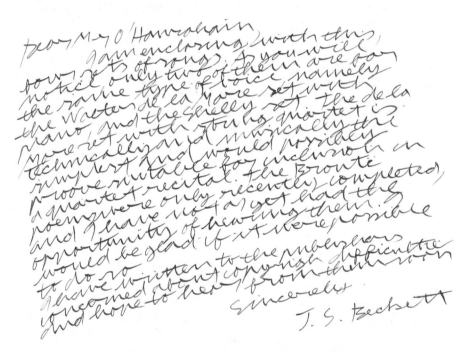

Letter written by John Beckett to Fachtna Ó hAnnracháin, Music Director of Radio Éireann, early 1950. (Courtesy of RTÉ Document Archives.)

Ó hAnnracháin acknowledged this letter and the scores of his songs: *Three poems* by Walter de la Mare, for tenor voice and piano, *Three fairy poems*, also by de la Mare, for soprano voice and string quartet, *Two poems* by Shelley for tenor voice and piano, and *Four Poems* by Emily Brontë, for mezzo-soprano voice and piano. [25]

In his next handwritten letter to Ó hAnnracháin, John wondered if there was any possibility of a performance. [26] Ó hAnnracháin responded by informing

John that the songs had been given to the singer Tomás Ó Súilleabháin, who expressed an interest in singing some of them; he thought that they could make up an interesting programme with the three others that Brian Boydell had sung in 1946: 'Had I the Heaven's Embroidered Cloths' (W.B.Yeats), 'Strike Churl' (G.M. Hopkins), and 'Peace, O my stricken Lute!' (Peter Abelard), all for baritone and piano.[27] John was 'very glad to hear that Tomás Ó Súilleabháin would like to sing some of [his] songs' and promptly posted the scores to Radio Éireann.[28] A date in July was promised for the broadcast, arrangements were made regarding copyright, and it was decided that Tomás Ó Súilleabháin would sing the three songs composed in 1946 and the Emily Brontë poems that John had set to music, though only three of the four submitted seem to have been performed.[29]

In his quest for music and literature, John often visited the National Library of Ireland, where one day he bumped into a soft-spoken young man with a refined English accent, named Michael Morrow – or to give him his full name, Norman Michael MacNamara Morrow. They conversed about music and the arts, and so impressed was Michael by John that he invited him to his home on Strand Road, Merrion, overlooking Dublin bay. As his mother was not there at the time, Michael asked his seventeen-year-old sister Brigid to cook a meal, which she dutifully did. Later she was persuaded to sing some songs by John Dowland, which Michael accompanied on his lute. Although John thought she was a good singer, she was very embarrassed at having to perform in front of him. She found John rather strange but concluded that he was a nice person with a 'kind streak'. John would have noticed Michael's paintings and musical instruments about the house (including a ukulele banjo, which he also played),[30] and he undoubtedly would have been impressed by Michael's wonderful store of out-of-the-way knowledge. Michael used to say of himself, 'I'm not well read but I'm curiously read'.[31] This chance meeting would, in time, alter the course of both young men's lives.

Michael, who unfortunately suffered from Christmas Disease, a form of haemophilia, spent much of his time at home in bed and, later in life, in hospital. He had been born to Larry and Léonie Morrow in London, on 2 October 1929. His father worked at first as a journalist in Fleet Street, and later was employed by the BBC.

Michael's formal education began when he was sent to St Andrew's school in Clyde Road, Dublin. As he was bullied by the other boys, his parents decided to educate him at home. His father procured suitable books for him to read and employed a nun from Sandymount to teach him calligraphy as his handwriting was atrocious. Michael thus became very well educated in the arts; his father complimented him and said that he had a better brain than he had – and Larry was known to have a very good brain. Larry only knew a little about everything, but gave the impression that he knew more, whereas Michael was much deeper. Regarded as being the weakling in his family, everything was done for him by either his mother or his sister.

In 1941 Larry began working in Radio Éireann, at their headquarters over the General Post Office in Henry Street, Dublin. One is tempted to think that he may have been instrumental in getting John Beckett work in the station, but in fact Larry never met him.

Between 1946 and 1947, Michael, his father, mother and sister were in London, where Michael attended the Hammersmith School of Art. He loved his time there but his enjoyment was cut short when the family decided to return to Dublin, where they lived in a flat in Fitzwilliam Square, just around the corner from where John and Vera were living in Upper Fitzwilliam Street. Michael continued his studies at the National College of Art in Dublin, but when the family (minus Larry) moved back to Belfast, he attended the Belfast College of Art, which he loathed. After about six months he decided to escape. He cycled all the way back to Dublin, found accommodation with a friend and returned to the National College of Art. One of his classmates was Beatrice ffrench-Salkeld, who became a good friend of his and later married Brendan Behan. Michael also befriended John ffrench, whose work was exhibited with Beatrice and Michael's. John lived at Castleffrench, near Ballinasloe, in the West of Ireland. As Michael had developed an interest in ornithology and falconry he spent periods at Castleffrench, where he painted, played music and hawked.

Michael eventually left his friend's house to rejoin his mother, his father and his sister, who were by now back in the flat in Fitzwilliam Square. They lived here for a year or two and then moved, without Larry, to the house by the sea at Merrion.[32]

From now on, John, Michael and Brigid kept in regular contact. Brian Boydell's wife Mary was very fond of Michael;[33] Michael liked Brendan Behan, but Brendan did not care much for him. Michael was also friendly with Beatrice ffrench-Salkeld's father, Cecil, who was an artist. At this time, Michael was more interested in art than music.[34]

At some time during the year, Joe Groocock became ill and John stepped in to take his place teaching music at St Columba's College. David Lee, who attended the college between 1948 and 1953, clearly remembered John's lessons on the organ and piano. David had never met anyone with such strong views and such a forceful personality; he was struck by John's prejudices and snobbishness. Even at the age of twenty-three, John had developed his life-long hatred for the music of Handel, Vivaldi, Corelli and Bruckner. Although he must have realized the importance of the first three of these composers' works in the development of Baroque music, as an influence on German music and on his beloved J.S. Bach in particular, he dismissed their music as rubbish simply because he regarded it as second rate and inferior to Bach's. As John was determined to steer David away from the music written by these composers, David cursed him bitterly.[35] During the lessons, John and David played various bits and pieces, including music by Debussy and Schubert, and a little early music.

David found John's method of teaching very trying; if he played a wrong note, John would stop him and get him to play it again correctly. Although David thought that John played the organ in a rather 'relentless' manner, his playing nonetheless made a tremendous impression on him, and he believed that John's influence on him was the most important in his life. Joe went sick again two years later and David received more lessons from him. When he requested further tuition and John did not respond, he concluded that he was a reluctant teacher. David noticed that he was very self-centred; his manner was sharp and he was capable of making withering remarks.

John's style of playing, accurately described by David as 'relentless',[36] seems to have been an expression of himself and his personality. He had a strong, forthright sense of rhythm that could not be deterred, and even his facial expression, when seated at the keyboard, often assumed the look of grim determination. John O'Sullivan, on the other hand, had a delightfully gentle approach, and was able to make to make a beautiful sound on any instrument. And yet, when playing Romantic music on the piano, John Beckett was capable of being flexible with the tempo and make the instrument sing, especially when accompanying singers.[37]

The programme of poems set to music by John and sung by the baritone Tomás Ó Súilleabháin was broadcast on Radio Éireann at 9.30 pm on Sunday, 23 July 1950.[38] Shortly before the programme was broadcast, Fachtna Ó hAnnracháin received a pencilled note from somebody in Radio Éireann to inform him that there was not enough music to fill the allocated twenty minutes. 'He hasn't got another song but he has some very charming piano pieces for children written in the modern idiom which he plays very well indeed. Might he play them on Sunday to fill up the time? Miss Rhoda Coghill will vouch for the excellence of his playing.' Ó hAnnracháin wrote at the bottom of the note, 'The piano pieces may certainly be included but in one way it spoils the idea of the programme.'[39] After the programme, a wry comment was entered on an internal 'Report on

Programmes as Broadcast' document: '"Eye hath not seen and ear hath not heard nor can the mind of man conceive" the things that must take place before John Beckett's music is committed to paper. With apologies to St Paul.' The Radio Éireann employee was wise enough to leave the document unsigned.[40] However, somebody else wrote that John had played some short pieces as well as his own compositions, and added, 'Very modern – well written for the piano. Very good technique. Songs interesting & should be heard again.'[41] Despite the praise, it seems that John was already proving to be a difficult person to work with.

Eight
1950

John must have returned to Dublin at the beginning of 1950 on account of his father's health, which presumably deteriorated during the year. He died in Sir Patrick Dun's Hospital on 3 September of heart failure, aged only sixty-three.[1] The funeral took place two days later at St Patrick's Church, Greystones and his coffin was taken to Redford Cemetery, where Gerald's brother Bill had been buried – indeed, Bill's widow May had died during the previous month. According to *The Irish Times*, the chief mourners at Gerald's funeral were John's mother Peggy, Dr Peter Beckett, John and Ann, Dr Jim Beckett (Gerald's brother) and Howard Beckett.[2]

John, who treasured such wonderful memories of his father, was greatly saddened by his loss. Many years later, in England, when listening with a friend to a four-hand piano arrangement of Beethoven's Piano Trio No. 2 in E flat major, written in homage to Haydn, John said, 'That was the last piece of music I played with my father,' then broke down and wept.[3]

With Gerald gone and Peter and John no longer living in the large house in Greystones, John's mother Peggy decided to sell Drummany and have a new and smaller house built nearby. A single-storey bungalow was built on New Road; Aidan Higgins suggested that it be called Field Place, since the land on which it was built had been fields and because the poet Shelley had been born in Field Place, near Horsham. Samuel's brother Frank was of great help during the construction of the house, coming every fortnight to check with the builder that everything was in order. John's sister Ann helped her mother design the garden, which Peggy laid out as if she were painting a picture, adding splashes of colour with flowers. Ann did the dirty work with digging and compost, and together they created a 'smashing' garden. Ann was at that time training to be an occupational therapist in England, where she learned crafts such as woodwork, leatherwork, weaving and spinning. When back in Greystones, she taught her mother how to spin. Ann and Peggy set up a 'little weaving place' in the back yard, where the two ladies derived endless pleasure from dyeing, spinning and weaving.[4]

Now that John's mother had inherited Gerald's money and from now on controlled the purse strings, it would have been prudent for John to toe the line and behave as an obedient son should do, but he chose to do otherwise. As John undoubtedly would have shown no inclination to part from Vera and was unable to find himself a steady job, his mother may well have decided not to support him from the time John and Vera began to live together. If so, this may explain why John was virtually penniless from this period onwards.

If John really detested Corelli's music at this period, then the following letter to Arthur Duff, Radio Éireann's Balance and Control Officer (and also a composer), is quite surprising. Nonetheless, if John was desperate to earn money, he would have played any type of music. Dated 14 September 1950, and bearing his parents' home address in Greystones, it began:

> Sir,
>
> I recently acquired an edition of the parts of the "Twelve Sonatas for Two Violins with a Bass". Opera Prima, by Arcangelo Corelli; published by John Walsh in London about 1713. I have just finished preparing an edition for performance from these parts.
>
> As you may know, the harpsichord in the museum has been recently repaired, and is now in very good condition.
>
> In view of this fact, I would like to suggest that I myself, harpsichord continuo; Francois dAlbert, and William Shanahan, violins; and Betty Sullivan, 'cello; (all of whom I have approached, and all of whom are interested) should be asked to do a broadcast of these sonatas.
>
> Taking into consideration the difficulties of moving the harpsichord, this could be done most simply, directly from the Metropolitan Hall, while the instrument is there for the [Bach] B minor mass.
>
> Alternatively the sonatas could be recorded there during that time. In this event it would be possible to record three seperate [sic] programmes with three sonatas in each.
>
> I shall be glad to hear from you about this at your convenience.
>
> Yours sincerely,
>
> J.S. Beckett[5]

The harpsichord mentioned by John was the eighteenth-century Ferdinand Weber instrument, which had been moved from the National Museum to the Metropolitan Hall in Dublin's city centre for an upcoming concert. Arthur Duff replied a week later and informed John that it would not be possible to consider a broadcast of the Corelli sonatas at the end of the month, but that Radio Éireann might record one programme of three sonatas during the first week of October.[6] John leapt at the opportunity, responding on the following day with a suggested list of three sonatas: 'Sonata in G major, Op. 1, No. 9 (Duration 6 mins.), Sonata in D minor, Op. 1, No. 11 (Duration 4½ mins.), Sonata in D major, Op. 1, No. 12 (Duration 6½ mins.). These, with announcements, would make a well balanced programme of 20 minutes.'[7]

However, John had to put these plans to one side for the moment, as an important musical event, which would firmly establish him as a keyboard performer of note in Dublin, was about to take place. The event was a festival marking the bicentenary of Johann Sebastian Bach's death, organized by Mrs Lyall Smith of the Music Association of Ireland. It began with a performance of his B minor Mass in the Metropolitan Hall on 29 September 1950. This was a big event for Dubliners then, and it was remembered and spoken of for a long time afterwards. At the beginning of the previous year, the MAI had failed to start up a series of concerts involving the Radio Éireann Symphony Orchestra, which had been restricted to playing in its dedicated concert studio at the Phoenix Hall in Dame Court since 1948. Radio Éireann now realized the importance of the upcoming bicentenary concert and decided to allow its orchestra to perform in the Mass. The regular orchestra was augmented by two trumpets in D, played by George Eskdale and Bramwell Wiggins of the London Symphony Orchestra, and joined by two choirs, the Culwick Choral Society and Cór Radio Éireann. The soloists were Margaret Field-Hyde (soprano), Anne Wood (contralto), Ronald Bristol (tenor) and Owen Brannigan (bass). The *basso continuo* was performed by John playing the Ferdinand Weber harpsichord, which had been made in Dublin in around 1768.[8] The instrument was on loan from the National Museum and had not been played in public for the past twenty-five years. As it could not be tuned up to modern pitch, John had to transpose all the music up a semitone to C minor.[9] The large ensemble was conducted by Otto Matzerath, who came from Karlsruhe in Germany and was a conductor of the Radio Symphony Orchestra of Frankfurt.[10]

By way of advance publicity, *The Irish Times* of 21 September described John playing the harpsichord in the National Museum:

> At the keyboard, John Beckett impassively permitted the instrument and himself to be photographed, rippling from time to time through the plangent gaiety of a Scarlatti sonata with a delicacy of touch and feeling that belied his

bulk. The music and the setting obviously demanded wigs and knee-breeches; but Mr. Beckett wore a sombre lounge suit.

Brilliant Musician

John Beckett, who has written the harpsichord part for next Friday's performance of the "B Minor" from the figured harmonies appended by Bach to the original score, belongs to a Dublin family well-known in the professions and the arts. His cousin, Samuel Beckett, was a close friend of the late James Joyce in Paris and has written a number of Joycean novels on Dublin which enjoy an esoteric distinction among a selective readership.

[…] He told me that he is looking forward enthusiastically to his part in the Bach concert on Friday week, as he prefers the harpsichord to all keyboard instruments – a favouritism only to be expected from an inheritor of the Landowska tradition.[11]

Photographs that include Otto Matzerath and Brian Boydell, still exist. In them, John appears as a handsome young man, stocky in build though not yet fat, with a good head of black hair. Desmond MacNamara's son Oengus always had the impression 'that he was old before his time'.[12] His performance in such a long work was something of a *tour de force*. A great deal of preparation was needed for the realization of the *basso continuo*, which features in every number, and had to be transposed into a different key. From here on it would be John's practice to produce his own written realizations, which were thick with chords, and which he expected other musicians to use. Nowadays his style would be considered to be old-fashioned.[13]

The festival proper started on Monday 25 September with a lecture given by Joe Groocock on the B minor Mass in 16 Saint Stephen's Green at 8 pm. The Mass itself was performed, to great acclaim and presumably to a packed house, at the Metropolitan Hall, Lower Abbey Street, at 7.15 pm on the Friday. Part I was broadcast by Radio Éireann live and Part II went out on the following evening. It was, according to *The Irish Times* music critic Charles Acton, writing in 1973, 'the most moving performance of [the B minor Mass] of my whole lifetime, and performed with a degree of authenticity then very rare'.[14] However, a review of the concert, printed in *The Irish Times* on the day after its performance was somewhat guarded:

> This monumental work of Bach's involves so many players and singers and presents so many difficulties, both in the performance itself and also in the organisation of the concert, that the Association must be congratulated upon a successful venture. Of the standard of the performance, it may fairly be said that, if one judges by professional achievements, it was mediocre; if one compares it with amateur performances, it was magnificent.[15]

John himself remembered the performance 'as a great occasion – though in no sense 'baroque'! The harpsichord was not in good condition – how could it have been after a century and a half? But that it was being used again, and that I was playing it, was most exciting.'[16]

This festival of six events was what really put the MAI on the map. Bach cantatas, conducted by Joe Groocock, were performed at the Methodist Centenary Church in Saint Stephen's Green, a lecture was given by Brian Boydell on *The Cantatas and Orchestral Works of J.S. Bach* at 16 Saint Stephen's Green, and more cantatas were performed in the Metropolitan Hall, where they were conducted by Sixten Eckerberg, and also in the Methodist Centenary Church, this time conducted by Sylvia Fannin.[17] No doubt John would have attended all these concerts and lectures, but it seems that he was not involved in any of the other performances.

On 6 October, John received a short letter from the National Museum of Ireland stating that the authorities there were willing to allow him to play the Weber harpsichord and Radio Éireann to record the proposed programme of Corelli sonatas.[18] After John had forwarded this note to Radio Éireann,[19] he wrote again to Fachtna Ó hAnnracháin with another idea for a programme of Bach cantatas.[20] Ó hAnnracháin thanked John for his letter and wrote:

> *I fear it would not be possible to arrange a broadcast of your suggested programme unless you yourself could organise an instrumental group which we should like to hear before confirming an engagement. Please let us know if you decide to go ahead... P.S. What about that composition you were to do for us? Could you let me know when we may expect to receive the scores from you.'[21]*

One wonders if the postscript refers to the composition that John was unable to finish by the deadline set earlier in the year.

By 9 November, Ó hAnnracháin had good news for John: the Corelli sonatas would be recorded in the National Museum on the 18th of the month,[22] and John and the three other musicians (François d'Albert, William Shanahan and Betty Sullivan) would be paid £5 each.[23] The programme was broadcast on 2 February 1951.[24] John had obviously been impressed by young Betty Sullivan's playing and, as she was happy to perform with him, the two became inseparable whenever *basso continuo* was needed for Baroque music in Dublin.

Coming so soon after his own father's death, John would have been saddened to hear of the death of his friend and mentor, E.J. Moeran, who died suddenly of a cerebral haemorrhage on 1 December, at the age of fifty-five, and was found in the River Kenmare. Moeran had left behind about two dozen orchestral and chamber music works, as well as songs, choral pieces and a number of piano miniatures. Unfortunately he had not achieved the status of a great composer because of his early death; at fifty-five he was just beginning to produce some of his greatest pieces, such as his Cello Sonata and Symphony in G minor.[25] For many years his music was only performed occasionally, but thankfully it is now played more often.

Nine

1951

Early in January 1951 John came up with another suggested programme for Radio Éireann: a Sonata in G major for flute, violin, cello and harpsichord by Bach, and a Sonata in C minor by Joachim Quantz for the same combination of instruments.[1] Fachtna Ó hAnnracháin acknowledged his letter and stated that the Music Department was interested in his suggestion.[2] Permission was requested to record the thirty-minute programme in the Music Room of the National Museum on 20 January, and was duly granted.[3]

John then wrote to Fachtna Ó hAnnracháin with more ideas for programmes, which included one that featured three sonatas by Pergolesi, and another with two piano trios by Haydn.[4] The Pergolesi sonatas were recorded on 10 February in the National Museum,[5] but seem never to have been broadcast, and the Haydn trios, which featured Trio No. 7 in A major and Trio No. 4 in E major, were broadcast on 7 May 1951, entitled *Monday Recital – Dublin Harpsichord Ensemble*.[6]

Thanks to John's success with the Bach B minor Mass, he was now accepted as a performer of note in Dublin and from now on his name begins to appear in the national press. On 26 January 1951, a notice appeared in *The Irish Times* stating that 'the Series of Public Lectures by John Beckett entitled "A Survey of Western Music from the 6th to the 20th century" will be resumed at the [Royal Irish] Academy [of Music] on Wednesday next, 31st January, at 8 pm, and will be continued on successive Wednesdays until 7th March, inclusive.'[7] Michael Morrow's sister Brigid, who admits that by this time she was smitten by John, attended these lectures. It appears that she was not the only young lady who fancied John; as he treated her just as a friend and as no relationship developed, Brigid concluded (probably correctly) that he must have preferred older women.[8]

Another young lady who would have been aware of John's presence at the Academy and who had attended the performance of the Bach B minor Mass, was the young Carol Little, who was about to marry Charles Acton. He had become music critic of *The Irish Times* because Joe Groocock had been offered the job and had turned it down. During the 1950s, Carol played in the Dublin Orchestral Players and was on the staff of the Academy, teaching the violin. Originally her teacher was Nancie Lord; later she transferred to Jaroslav Vaneček. She found John likable but formidable. She realized that the only other person who could play the harpsichord as well as John at that time was John O'Sullivan, whom she found an odd sort of person – so much so that she wondered what harpsichords did to people! She regarded John Beckett as a clever man, though she was bothered by his relentless manner of playing and found his speeds too fast. According to her, John had 'the greatest respect' for her husband and that they were 'friendly combatants'. The Actons, however, were not on visiting terms with John.[9]

In May 1951, an advertisement appeared in *The Irish Times*. Under the heading 'Education, Tuitions', it read, 'Lessons in Piano, Organ, Harmony and Counterpoint, Composition, and the History and Appreciation of Music. For details, write to John Beckett, Mus.Bac., 5 Lower Hatch street, Dublin'. Although he may have given piano lessons in his flat, he was available to teach students at their homes or in a church where there was an organ. However, it seems that he was able to attract very few students.[10]

Number 5 Lower Hatch Street was a Georgian house that John and Vera now shared with the writer Anthony Cronin. There was much interest among the Dublin literati at the time about an extract from Samuel Beckett's novel *Watt*, which had been published in the January edition of *Envoy* magazine, edited by John Ryan. Anthony remembered talking about Samuel Beckett with John, the painter Seán O'Sullivan, Arland Ussher, Ralph Cusack and Nancy Sinclair at Ralph's house in Wicklow.[11]

Desmond MacNamara and his new partner, Priscilla Seare, known by everyone as Skylla, used to come to John and Vera's flat in Lower Hatch Street for a bath as they did not possess one at the mews in Baggot Street. They noticed that Anthony Cronin and the artist Patrick Swift were not particularly enamoured of Vera. It seems that several people were hostile towards her.[12] When, on one occasion, the poet Patrick Kavanagh (whom John disliked) approached Vera in the flat and managed to coax her to give him the last two pounds that she possessed, John exploded when he discovered what had happened. He confronted Patrick and demanded that he return the money, which he did. In her dotty, scatterbrained manner, Vera had a notion that Patrick Kavanagh, whom she was fond of, was somehow connected with County Cavan.[13]

Brian Boydell's wife Mary remembered John and Vera during this period. She was fond of John and his sister Ann but was wary of Vera. John, she thought, was very bright and full of original ideas – he was ahead of his time. However, for such a young man, he had a remarkably 'short fuse'. Brian made allowances for his strong opinions and the fact that John disliked his music, and appreciated his talent; according to Mary, the two men got on very well together.[14]

One advantage of sharing a house with Anthony Cronin was that Anthony, who was the associate editor of a literary magazine named *The Bell – A Survey of Irish Life*, could offer John the possibility earning a little money by writing articles for it. Originally edited by the writer Seán Ó Faoláin, the magazine was now edited by Peadar O'Donnell, a former republican revolutionary. It appeared monthly and ran from October 1940 to December 1954. It contained articles on various topics written by regular contributors such as Anthony Cronin, James Plunkett, Mary Beckett, Seán Ó Faoláin, Benedict Kiely, John Montague and Maurice Craig. Either John asked Anthony if he could write some articles on music or else he was invited to do so because of the connection. Either way, he had become the *de facto* music editor for the magazine by the end of the year.[15] The first of nine articles written by him, submitted over a period of nineteen months, appeared in the edition dated 2 May 1951. Simply entitled 'Music, by John Beckett', it began:

> In the course of the last few weeks I have heard two large-scale orchestral works, the significance of which, in relation to Irish music, and to modern art music, seems to me to be of particular interest. They are the tone poem 'With the Wild Geese' of Sir Hamilton Harty, and the violin concerto of E.J. Moeran. In this article I propose to try to assess the significance of the achievement of these two works in relation to Irish music, and to modern art music; and to record, and I hope to justify my belief in the negative and redundant nature of that achievement.

John went on to pose the question, 'What is meant by the term "Irish music"?' In the course of answering his own question, he stated that the folk composer 'is isolated and ignorant'. Folk music, he stated, 'is the only national music; the folk music of Ireland is the only Irish music.'[16]

His article in the June edition of the magazine was a review of recent concerts and broadcasts, 'music which has been representative of a long period of composition dating from the 16th to the 20th century'.[17]

The July edition included his review of two Mozart operas performed by Hamburg State Opera: *Don Giovanni* and *Così fan tutte*, and a letter written to the editor by Aloys Fleischmann, Professor of Music at University College Cork, who was well-known for stating his opinions in published letters written to editors.

Sir, – A new, and in some respects a welcome note has been sounded by Mr. John Beckett in the May issue of *The Bell*. ... Mr. Beckett, however, is not content to be a prophet, or a pioneer. He must needs be an iconoclast, too, as extreme in his way as the most doctrinaire exponent of the school which preaches no salvation but through the folk idiom. ... No Marxist could be more relentless or more sweeping in his denunciation of everyone who does not toe the party line. If membership of the twelve note school is the important criterion in assessing compostion, one may assume that in dealing with the English scene the work of Britten and Rawsthorne would be classed as 'redundant', while Elizabeth Lutyens would rank as a harbinger to the new millenium.[18]

Readers must have waited with bated breath for John's riposte in the following edition, but nothing of the sort appeared; he ignored Fleischmann's criticisms and once again wrote another review of recent concerts.[19] In the May 1952 edition, he added his comments to the debate on whether a concert hall should be built in Dublin or not and ruminated on the state of musical education in Ireland and suggested improvements. In his opinion, there was no serious instruction in music in schools around the country; better qualified teachers from abroad, such as Jaroslav Vaneček (who was Czech) and Francis Engel (who was Swiss), were needed. He concluded this article with: 'Not only a National Concert Hall, but a National Music, is unthinkable in the long run, without such beginnings'.[20] In his final article, which appeared in the November edition of 1952, he reviewed a new book published by the Cork University Press, entitled *Music in Ireland: a Symposium*, edited by Aloys Fleischmann and with a foreword by Sir Arnold Bax. The most important conclusion that John drew from it was that the 'pall of musical apathy which has shrouded this country for so long must be lifted at two points simultaneously.' Afraid that too much emphasis might be put on nationalism in music in a National School of Music within a country that was so conscious of its nationality, John concluded, 'The function of a National School of Music must be to orientate its students to the great achievements of twentieth century western music and to enable them, eventually, to contribute to that achievement in terms of their own society.'[21]

One is struck by John's depth of knowledge concerning the music and the performances that he had heard, his pertinent remarks and cogent arguments, and the fact that he was not afraid to express his opinions, no matter what the consequences might be. Even E.J. Moeran, lately deceased, had not escaped his criticism. Considering that he was only in his early twenties, this was certainly a case of an old head on young shoulders – and also a great deal of bravery considering that many of the established musical people in the country were a good deal older than he was. Although his attitude towards Matzerath might be considered callous, especially as John owed his recent success in the Bach B minor Mass directly to him, he was right to criticize him for applying a romantic style to music of an earlier era. This was typical of that period, when performers and orchestras played only in a romantic style, replete with heavy vibrato and *portamenti*. John, like Brian Boydell, was ahead of his time and was aware even then of a growing interest in playing early music in an authentic manner, and would battle against this anachronistic trend of contemporary orchestras for many years to come.

Radio Éireann's Music Director, Fachtna Ó hAnnracháin, returned from sick leave at the end of May 1951 to find another letter from John on his desk. The contents, yet another detailed list of more suggested programmes in which John and his friends were prepared to participate,[22] must have come as no great surprise to Ó hAnnracháin, though one may wonder how he reacted to the twenty-four-year-old Beckett's quite determined attempt to plan Radio Éireann's output of 'serious' music. However, judging by Ó hAnnracháin's courteous replies to John's frequent missives and the fact that he often accepted his suggestions, he seems to have appreciated John's help in providing suitable music for the station to broadcast.

John now suggested 'two more programmes of piano trios by Joseph Haydn', which Doris Cleary, François d'Albert, Betty Sullivan and he would be willing to play.[23] Ó hAnnracháin's reply was brief and to the point: 'We shall endeavour to find a place for the two programmes of Piano Trios by Joseph Haydn.' However, he was kind enough to add, 'It may be possible to fit in, at a later date, one or more of the programmes of piano duets which you have suggested. We shall let you know in due course if it is possible to do this.'[24] The programme of Haydn Trios was broadcast in July; the listener was treated to two trios – one of them for flute, cello and piano – and Mozart's Adagio in B minor for piano.[25] Later in July, a programme devised by John, entitled *Schubert Piano Duets: John Beckett and Seán Lynch* was broadcast.[26]

At the Adults' Summer School in Drogheda on 4 August 1951, two dozen members of the Adult Education Association – an organization sponsored by the Dublin trade union movement – met up, and lectures were given at Drogheda Grammar School the following week. Participants included 'Mr. John Beckett on Music; Mr. Liam Carlin on Visual Arts; Mr. Henry Wheeler on Archaeology; Mr. David Greene on Literature; Mr. D. Nevin, Research Officer,

Irish T.U.C., on "The Economic Outlook for Ireland"; and Dr. J. Chubb, T.C.D., on European Co-operation'.[27]

John was still in contact with Aidan Higgins, who was living in Greystones. He now put Higgins in touch with an acquaintance of his, the writer Arland Ussher. Like John, Ussher was interested in Yeats and Joyce (his book *Three Great Irishmen*, on Shaw, Yeats and Joyce, was published the following year).[28] Aidan wrote to him in September, mentioning that he had been referred to him by John.[29] Soon afterwards, John informed Aidan that Ussher and Samuel Beckett were friends. 'I like his books more than I can say,' Aidan wrote to Ussher, 'probably because I like Joyce so much, but Sam's obsession about insanity rather frightens me. He used to cross-examine Ann Beckett closely but discreetly about her first-hand experience of lunatics. Why?'[30]

In October John wrote to Fachtna Ó hAnnracháin from Lower Hatch Street with a new proposal: two programmes of music by Corelli, played by William Shanahan and François d'Albert (violins), David Lane (oboe), Betty Sullivan (cello) and himself on a harpsichord newly purchased by Radio Éireann.[31] Although Ó hAnnracháin responded cautiously,[32] the programme was accepted and broadcast in the evening of 11 February in the following year.[33] 'Nice programme – the general effect was rather stiff & the tempos too rigidly kept. Harpsichord sounded well' was the comment entered on a 'Report on Programmes as Broadcast' form.[34]

Dubliners were treated to a rare taste of early music in November when the counter-tenor Alfred Deller, whom John would have met at Morley College in London, and who was a friend of the Boydells, came to Dublin with the English lutenist Desmond Dupré to give a recital at the Gresham Hotel, under the auspices of the Irish Musical Arts Society. Deller sang lute songs by the sixteenth-century composer John Dowland (who at the time was believed to be Irish rather than English). Included were 'I saw my Lady Weep' and 'Sorrow Stay'. The lute was heard as a solo instrument in two groups of pieces. John accompanied Deller on a piano for a group of songs by Henry Purcell, as the Weber harpsichord had been returned to the museum by now.[35] Members of the audience, which must have included the Boydells and Michael Morrow, would have noticed Deller's unusual hand gestures when singing, as if he were painting a picture in the air.[36]

We next find John performing music by the dreaded Handel, this time on an organ. The event was a production of the composer's oratorio *Samson*, given in the Rupert Guinness Memorial Hall on 6 and 7 December by the St James's Gate Musical Society, directed by the young Victor Leeson, a member of the Guinness Brewery staff. Like him, all the singers worked for the famous brewing company.[37] Joseph O'Neill, writing for the *Irish Independent*, was not entirely happy with the choir, but he reported that there was 'general competence in the playing' of the orchestra, led by Peggy Roche.[38]

Ten

1952

John began the year with another letter to Radio Éireann's Music Director, Fachtna Ó hAnnracháin. This time it was to offer a proposed programme of songs from Berlioz's *Neuf Mélodies Irlandaises*, Opus 2. Having explained that missing items of the work could be obtained in Paris, and concluding his detailed letter with, 'I will be glad to hear your opinion in these matters',[1] one could be forgiven for believing that John, in fact, was Radio Éireann's Director of Music, and that he was seeking approval from a subordinate. Nonetheless, Ó hAnnracháin welcomed the idea; he wrote to the Director, Service du Prêt de la Bibliothèque Nationale in Paris the following day[2] to see if he could secure copies of the missing numbers.[3]

John had the opportunity of playing a harpsichord in public once again in January, when he performed on the new Dolmetsch instrument owned by Radio Éireann in a Scarlatti Suite arranged by Vincenzo Tomassini (1878–1950). The concert, which also featured the Radio Éireann Symphony Orchestra, took place on 22 January in the Phoenix Hall. According to a review in *The Irish Times*, the Scarlatti suite 'had a specially charming and gracious performance, with great clarity in the texture, and beautiful and sensitive moulding of the phrases'.[4] On the following day, John gave a short talk on 'Beethoven's Sketch Books' on the Radio Éireann programme *Music Magazine*, presented by John O'Donovan. John spoke again on the topic two weeks later on the same programme.[5]

In mid February, John's arrangement of William Butler Yeats's poem, 'Had I the Heaven's Embroidered Cloths' (first performed in 1946) was sung by Frederick Fuller, baritone, accompanied by Daniel Kelly, along with songs by Edgar Deale, Frederick May and Brian Boydell, at a concert given in the Aberdeen Hall at the Gresham Hotel.[6]

A few days later, John sent Fachtna Ó hAnnracháin a long typed letter containing more information about Berlioz's *Neuf Mélodies Irlandaises*. One particular paragraph, which somebody – probably Ó hAnnracháin – has marked with an encompassing bracket and a large X, makes for interesting reading:

> *I would be most interested in writing the announcements for all the broadcasts of serious music each week, and would be able to commence doing so as soon as is convenient to you. I have noticed that in three consecutive weeks, recently, there were ten, eleven, and twelve, such broadcasts, respectively. On the basis of these figures I would suggest a regular weekly fee of £3.[7]*

Fortunately for him, Ó hAnnracháin responded favourably to this latest proposal.[8] On the same day, Ó hAnnracháin sent a note to the Deputy Director, P.G. O'Raghallaigh: 'I should like to try him out on the programme notes for the two main Orchestral Concerts each week for £2.0.0. but then I feel that if we get good notes for all programmes of serious music for £3 per week that this would be a far better return for our money.'[9]

John was in luck; Ó hAnnracháin wrote to him in March that Radio Éireann would pay him 'a fee of £3 per week for suitable programme notes for all programmes of serious music each week, both live and recorded', starting the following month.[10]

One day in the spring of this year, the young artist Reginald Gray was walking down Grafton Street with his then girlfriend Celia, daughter of the *avant-garde* artist Cecil ffrench-Salkeld, and was introduced to John for the first time. Reginald, who was a friend of Michael Morrow's and was living in the ffrench Salkeld household, had heard of John. Reginald found him 'a most determined sort of person'. Shortly afterwards, Michael, who was teaching Reginald and Celia to play the recorder, turned up at Cecil's house with John. Cecil's charming German wife Irma made tea for them all, and Reginald did a quick drawing of John in the downstairs sitting room. Afterwards, Reginald handed him his sketchbook, which contained many other drawings. John turned over the pages to look at them. Although he made no comment on the sketch of himself, his overall assessment of Reginald's work was something along the lines of 'quite good'.[11]

Soon after his first encounter with John, Reginald was sitting alone in the Robert Roberts coffee house in Grafton Street (a favourite haunt of actors, musicians and literati), when John walked in and joined him at the table. Reginald brought up the subject of Olivier Messiaen because some months earlier he had been listening to the BBC Third Programme and had been over-whelmed by the French composer's long work for solo piano, *Vingt Regards sur l'Enfant-Jésus*. John knew the work and seemed a bit surprised that Reginald, a young painter, should be acquainted with such an *avant-garde* composer of mystical music. Interestingly, John (who either then or later came to despise this composer's works) made no comment about the music. Ever since then Reginald has nearly always painted to the accompaniment of music by Messiaen and the Russian composer Alfred Schnittke.[12]

Towards the end of April, John once again played the harpsichord on Radio Éireann: the *Wednesday Recital* programme featured John's Dublin Harpsichord Ensemble playing music by Handel, Frescobaldi and Bach.[13] The following programme that evening was a discussion, which included John, who was described in *The Irish Times* as 'a composer and broadcaster on musical matters'. Entitled *The Arts and the State*, it focussed on the question of State assistance for the Arts. Edgar Deale was the chairman and the other speakers were the writer Seán Ó Faoláin and Samuel Beckett's close friend and confidant, Thomas MacGreevy, who was by this time Director of the National Gallery in Dublin.[14]

In May, John was involved in another concert held in the Rupert Guinness Hall with the St James's Gate Musical Society, under the enthusiastic direc-tion of Victor Leeson. The music performed was the 'Peasant Cantata' by Bach, then *Hiawatha's Wedding Feast* and *The Death of Minnehaha* by Samuel Coleridge-Taylor.[15] The hall was crowded for the occasion and Joseph O'Neill of the *Irish Independent* was fulsome in his praise for the production, despite a few small hitches here and there.[16]

The next concert in which John was involved was an evening of Elizabethan music, with Alfred Deller, in the Dining Hall of Trinity College, towards the end of May. This also featured the College Singers, conducted by Stewart Cross. It had been hoped that Michael Morrow, 'the only accessible lutenist' could have accompanied Alfred Deller, but he was abroad, in Munich, Paris and Florence (where he shared a *pension* with his friend John ffrench). Instead, John accompa-nied him on 'the nearest equivalent instrument', the virginals,[17] which was most probably loaned by Peter Schwarz, a Trinity College graduate who later went to America. 'Alfred Deller gave a polished performance of two large groups of songs,' reported *The Irish Times*. 'He included in his first group Dowland's amaz-ingly lovely "Flow My Tears". This song, which enjoyed great popularity in the early years of the seventeenth century, has lost none of its magic, though it is no longer in the fashion. The singer made the most of its mournful phrases, and was artistically accompanied by John Beckett.'[18] In addition John played some solo keyboard music by the Elizabethan composers John Bull, Giles Farnaby and Martin Peerson.[19]

One of John's piano pupils at around this time was the young Theo Hoppen (now Professor K.T. Hoppen of the University of Hull), who came with his parents from Germany to Dublin in 1947 when he was five. The family lived in Pembroke Road during the early 1950s. Theo's mother engaged John to teach her son the piano and paid him for two one-hour lessons a week. Realizing that John was not well off and never a figure of fashion, Mrs Hoppen took pity on him: she mothered him, gave him sandwiches when she thought he could do with them and, when he expressed a wish to hear Wagner's great cycle of operas, *Der Ring des Nibelungen*, she gave him about £50 in order to make the trip to Bayreuth, which he possibly made during the summer. Professor Hoppen recollects how he had been 'taught the piano at home in Dublin by a charming, unpractical, shambolic young man,' who bribed him 'with unselfconscious directness and biscuits.'

Professor Hoppen has very fond memories of John and his lessons. According to him, 'He was a thoroughly nice and sweet man'. He considered John to be a 'super' teacher. He noted that John did not talk down to children or treat them like adults; teaching music was a 'pleasant but serious business'. According to Theo, 'He cut his style to suit the person he was teaching and pitched it right.' He was quite different from Theo's previous teacher, an unpleasant individual from the country with a cigarette stuck in his mouth. John did not make Theo play the 'usual boring stuff', but made him play pieces by Kodály and so forth. He even played some of his own compositions, which Theo found very modern. Although the music left him 'completely baffled', he politely complimented John on his work. John also showed him some pictures by the Swiss painter Paul Klee, his favourite artist. Professor Hoppen also remembers John's extraordinary angular and almost illegible handwriting, and John gave him some music by Schubert that incorporated 'his trademark scrawl'.

John's attitude towards young Theo was quite different from his attitude to the fifteen-year-old David Lee. It was a trait of John's to be more tolerant with children and musicians of limited abilities than people who had the slightest tendency towards precociousness or professionalism.

Another thing that Professor Hoppen remembered was the fact that John lived in an 'appallingly untidy' flat in Baggot Street.[20] This flat was situated in the main part of house number 35. Desmond MacNamara and his partner

Skylla had lived in the mews from January to March 1951, when they had left for London. Skylla remembered being in the mews when Vera called her a 'suburban housewife'. Incensed, Skylla threw the contents of a teapot, which she was holding in her hand, at her. Despite the incident, they managed to remain on good terms.[21]

Mary Boydell also remembered John and Vera's flat, which she described as 'horrible'.[22] Venetia O'Sullivan recollected how John O'Sullivan used to call on John Beckett, whose habit was to get up at any time of the day, and play piano duets with him when he was often still dressed in his pyjamas.[23] Michael Morrow's sister Brigid recalled seeing a ladder there with several cats sitting on the steps. Vera, she said, tried to make pea soup in a pressure cooker on one occasion and, not surprisingly, it ended up all over the kitchen.[24]

It was from this flat that John wrote another long letter to Fachtna Ó hAnnracháin in mid June. In his letter, John outlined the details of a *Wednesday Recital* programme to be broadcast on 16 July: details of three proposed recitals, each one featuring a recorder sonata, a violin sonata and a harpsichord suite by Handel, all to be performed by the Dublin Harpsichord Ensemble with Peter Schwarz on recorder; a suggested series of six programmes, to be introduced by John, of the 'remarkable and little-heard music' contained in the complete set of the *Anthologie Sonore* records that he had found in the Radio Éireann Gramophone Library; and finally he mentioned that he had been preparing a thirty-minute recital of harpsichord sonatas by Domenico Scarlatti, which he asked to be included in one of the station's programmes.[25]

Fachtna Ó hAnnracháin was glad to inform John that an audition 'with Mr. Schwarz on Friday last was successful.' Because of this, he was positive about the three proposed programmes of music by Handel and suggested that they be longer.[26]

Another letter from John arrived on Mr Ó hAnnracháin's desk on 14 July:

> Tomas O'Suillebhain [sic] and I have prepared a series of three programmes designed to illustrate Gabriel Faure's development as a song writer. The first consists of early songs, the second of songs from the middle period of his life, and the third of two important late song cycles. The programmes could be introduced by something more than the usual introductory script, which I would write myself and for which I have allowed time.'

A list of songs by Fauré followed.[27]

As there is a gap in the correspondence between John and Radio Éireann during the month of August, we can only surmise that John might have been in

Bayreuth enjoying Wagner's four great operas, *Das Rheingold, Die Walküre, Siegfried* and *Götterdämmerung*, which together make up the famous *Ring*. The Bayreuth Festival was now at the beginning of its rebirth after struggling through World War II and Nazism. Winifred Wagner, the composer's English-born daughter-in-law had been removed from authority at the Festival because of her political affiliations and had been replaced by her two sons. The lack of money was obvious to everyone, for the brothers' semi-abstract productions were set on almost empty stages, with few props, simple costumes and elaborate lighting. Despite this, we are probably safe in presuming that John thoroughly enjoyed the experience.[28]

Michael Morrow, who had won the Henry Higgins Travelling Scholarship when studying in the National College of Art, and who had then spent a year in Munich, Florence and Paris, returned to Dublin in September with a new friend. This was the sculptor and singer Werner Schürmann, whom he had met in Munich. Werner had come to Dublin in the vague hope that he might get a teaching job in the National College of Art. For the first six weeks he stayed at the Morrows' home on Strand Road in Merrion. After this he moved to County Galway, where he lived with Michael's friend John ffrench in Ballinasloe, returning to Dublin only on a few occasions for brief periods. During the following year he returned to the capital, where after a two-week stay at the Morrows' home, he settled down in a house on Monkstown Road and remained there until he returned to Germany that October.

Michael, whom Werner regarded as being very gifted as a painter, was well acquainted with the intellectual scene of the time and through him Werner met John Beckett and John O'Sullivan, who took him to concert rehearsals. (A bust of John Beckett, which Werner sculpted at around this time, was one of the works on view at the Living Art Exhibition in August 1954.) Werner's 'very small octavino spinet', which he had brought with him, was used as a continuo instrument when they played with recorders and strings in Peter Schwarz's rooms in Trinity College.[29] Brigid Morrow remembers playing the bass recorder at these sessions. On one such occasion, John Beckett glared at her as only her top notes were sounding. Much to her embarrassment, she discovered that she had left her cleaning rod in the instrument. After this incident, John often said to her mischievously, 'Have you got your cleaner in the right place?' John's remarks could be quite sharp: when Brigid failed to play a passage correctly, he 'cut her in half' by saying, 'Brigid is taking umbrage', a phrase that she always remembered and associated with him.[30]

At around this time Werner and John met my father Cathal Gannon, who had managed to make a harpsichord in a tiny glass conservatory at the back of his modest dwelling in the not very fashionable Dublin suburb of Rialto. John O'Sullivan, who seems to have met Cathal at some earlier period, might have brought John and Werner to see the instrument.

Cathal's harpsichord had been based on one housed in the Benton Fletcher Collection of London, then in Chelsea, but he had examined the modern Dolmetsch harpsichord belonging to Radio Éireann and, influenced by what he saw, decided to alter the structure and stringing of his instrument. As the result had been disappointing, he had consigned it to a spare bedroom, where he may have reluctantly shown it to his guests. Unfortunately, the instrument would stay there for a few years until Cathal undid the so-called 'improvements' and restored it to a more authentic copy of the original. What the three men thought of the harpsichord in 1952 – if indeed they saw it at all – is not recorded, though they seem to have had a good impression of the maker. The instrument would not be played in public until 1959 and that, it would seem, was due to John Beckett's insistence.[31]

John wrote Fachtna Ó hAnnracháin another letter on 25 August suggesting that 'my present weekly fee of £3 should be increased to the more adequate sum of £5.'[32] Ó hAnnracháin wrote, 'unfortunately it would not be possible for us to pay you £5 per week as you request, for the present at any rate.'[33] John responded, 'I regret that it is not possible to increase my weekly fee for writing music programme scripts to £5; a sum, I would emphasise, that is only reasonable for the work involved.'[34] One can imagine John's feeling of disappointment – or more likely anger – on learning that his weekly fee would not be increased.

John discovered from Ó hAnnracháin that the first of the proposed Fauré programmes would be broadcast on 21 October. Dismayed, he wrote to him, 'I presume that this is the first of the series of three programmes on Faure's songs which I planned in detail and submitted to you. If this is so, would it be possible to record them all before I go away on 7th. October? We are ready to do this at any time. I will wait untill [sic] I hear from you before completing and returning the advance notification form.'[35]

After a radio broadcast entitled 'Music in Ireland: A Book Talk by John Beckett' towards the end of September,[36] John made what must have been his Dublin debut as a conductor. As there are no records of him conducting the students' orchestra at the Royal College of Music (though, of course, he may have), it is anybody's guess as to where or when he studied conducting – or if he ever studied it at all. Because of his rather rudimentary skill in the art, it may be concluded that he might have had little or no formal training. Eschewing the use of a baton, his technique was simply to beat the time with his right hand and arm, in a vigorous downward motion (which became known as 'the chop') and making an occasional gesture with his left. The work he now conducted, on 29 September, was – rather bizarrely – Gilbert and Sullivan's comic opera *Patience*, staged in the Rupert Guinness Hall by the St James's Gate Musical Society. Victor Leeson, who was responsible for the production, and who obviously had entrusted John with the job of conducting it, played the part of the 'Fleshy Poet', Bunthorne. John would have been familiar with this type of music thanks to his father, who after the Wicklow County Council meetings used to sit down at the piano and play pieces by Gilbert and Sullivan for his colleagues.[37] According to a very favourable review in *The Irish Times*, 'Victor Leeson … saw to it that the traditional Savoy style was preserved, and the dialogue, business and songs followed very faithfully in the familiar lines. … John Beckett conducted and got excellent results from his orchestra, well led by Arthur Short.' John had plenty of opportunities to get master this new skill, as the production ran for a week.[38]

The three programmes featuring the songs of Gabriel Fauré, sung by Tomás Ó Súilleabháin and accompanied by John on piano, must have been pre-recorded as requested, for John was away from 5 October to 10 November and the programmes were broadcast on 21 and 28 October, and on 4 November.[39] Carol Acton remembered Ó Súilleabháin as a fine singer with a gentle voice; he was much in demand. He was also considered to be one of the most important champions of contemporary Irish music at the time.[40]

At the beginning of December, John complained to Fachtna Ó hAnnracháin:

> I was asked to write scripts for the Saturday night Irish Concerts, and the Tuesday afternoon Light Orchestra concerts, both of which rarely contain serious music; and now you wish me to write a script for the enclosed programme of dance music. I would like to suggest that before I agree to continue writing scripts for light programmes such as those I have mentioned, the terms of our original agreement should be revised.[41]

Ó hAnnracháin replied:

> In view of the representations you have made therein it will not be necessary for you to write scripts for programmes of Irish dance music. I must point out, however, that we expect you to continue to write scripts for the other programmes as hitherto. As I mentioned in an earlier letter I am hopeful of being able to offer you a higher fee in the next financial year, but I fear no increase can take place before this.[42]

The year ended with John giving a short radio talk, entitled 'A Musical Holiday', on John O'Donovan's evening programme, *Music Magazine*. The other contributors were Joe Groocock, who spoke about *A Victorian Best Seller* and Mosco Carner, whose talk was entitled *The Art of Toscanini*.[43] Carner later became a noted musicologist and a biographer of Puccini.[44]

Eleven

1953

Towards the end of January 1953, Aidan Higgins wrote to Arland Ussher:

The Resident Beckett continues to surprise us. J's mother, who has been threat-ening to "take up" painting, with increasing energy, for some time, <u>has</u>. The results are most unexpected. So far she has painted three landscapes, in guache [sic], on thick cartridge paper. The first was just about what one would expect. The following two, anything but that. Though no Primitive, she is very remote from the conventional garden-roller of suburban opinion:— a Very Powerful Eye. She makes baskets for a hobby and also works the — whatsit — the-mediaeval-wooden-stand-for-making-cloth [sic].

The morose Bach- Fauré- Klee- Yeats- Kafka-addicted son, last week subjected to recordings of his own Songs, written while he was yet in Columba's, has been so taken a-back by their unexpected all-round excellence (he is not conceited, far from it), that he as put aside all thoughts of even the most tentative--- yes. Sam has bowed before his music. The Songs are from Yeats ("do not tread on my dreams"), Shelley ("A Dirge"-), and others.

> *My mother groan'd, my father wept;*
> *Into the dangerous world I leapt...*[1]

A programme devoted to John's music, 'New Songs by Irish Composers (Second Series): No. 1, John Beckett', was broadcast a month later; the singer was Arthur Moyse, tenor.[2] In February a concert of choral works was given at the Rupert Guinness Hall, accompanied on piano by John, and in some of the items, by him and John O'Sullivan. Apart from excerpts from Handel's *Samson* and the Wedding Feast section of Coleridge Taylor's *Hiawatha*, much of the music consisted of arrangements of folk songs. According to Joseph O'Neill of the *Irish Independent*, 'the "Bill" song from Kern's "Showboat" was most effective, but accompanist John Beckett was dealing with music quite out of his sphere in these numbers'.[3]

On the very next day, a midday concert given in the Graduates' Memorial Building in Trinity College offered a varied programme given by John on piano and Shirley Pollard on viola. It included a sonata for unaccompanied viola by Hindemith, *Grotesques* for piano, composed and performed by John, and W.F. Bach's Sonata in C minor for viola and piano.[4] John and Peter Schwarz had origi- nated the idea of these lunchtime chamber music concerts in Trinity College some years previously, perhaps as early as 1950.[5]

At around the same time, John wrote again to Fachtna Ó hAnnracháin about his weekly fee, outlining a list of pieces recently performed by the Radio Éireann Light Orchestra (including *Tunes from 'Call Me Madam'* by Irving Berlin, *Faith can Move Mountains* by Merril and *You Belong to Me* by Pee Wee King), which were clearly beneath his dignity. He then went on to suggest two new programmes, the first performed by his Dublin Harpsichord Ensemble and featuring music by John Dowland, and the second, of early music by Nicolas Carlton and Thomas Tomkins, which he and John O'Sullivan would play as a piano duet, then *Cinq Pièces Faciles pour Piano à Quatre Mains* by Igor Stravinsky. Finally he mentioned that he was preparing a performance of the Lamentations of Jeremiah by Thomas Tallis and a setting of the Lamentations for five voices by Robert White, which would take place in Trinity College Chapel in March. 'It occurred to me that you might care to record one or both of these works for broadcasting near to Easter time. If you are interested perhaps you would send a representative along to the performance.' Written at the top of the letter, in a different hand, is 'Spoken to Mr Beckett today' and, under John's address (still in Lower Baggot Street) is, 'Arranged with Mr. O Farachain to increase Mr. Beckett's fee to £5 per week from 20/2/53'.[6]

At some time before 31 March, John applied for the post of Assistant Music Director in Radio Éireann. The official application form makes for inter- esting reading: female applicants are reminded that they must be 'unmarried or widows'. John's personal details are typed on and between the dotted lines and his address is entered as 35 Lower Baggot Street, Dublin. His educational qualifications are 'Music scholarship to St Columba's College, Rathfarnham. Scholarships to the R.I.A.M. Scholarships to Royal College of Music, London. Prizes in composition and organ playing won while at R.C.M. Travelling schol- arship from R.C.M.' His professional qualifications are 'Bachelor of Music of Trinity College, Dublin' and his professional experience reads 'Teaching musical theory at the James Ching Piano School, London. Teaching English at a Lycee in France. Assistant music master at St Columba's College. Lecturing, and private teaching. Extensive experience as concert and radio performer; conductor [*sic*]; organist; and [crossed out] composer; and writer on music.' After 'Administrative or Executive Experience (if any)', John typed 'Only that necessary to organise small and fairly large musical ensembles.' He admitted that his knowledge of Irish was 'Very limited', that French was the only other language that he knew, and he finally stated that his present occupation was 'Professional Musician, Teacher, performer, composer, and writer.' A handwritten note at the top right of the form reads, 'Temperament + Characteristics known to us'. It comes as no great surprise that John did not get the job.[7]

John was still unhappy about the type of scripts that he was being asked to write for Radio Éireann. On 25 May he wrote again to Fachtna Ó hAnnracháin:

> *I spoke to Mr Reedy [recte Reidy, better known as Seán Ó Riada] the other day about my scripts for broadcasts of light music a few of which I have been writing at your request. ... I understand from him that you wish me to do scripts for such broadcasts of light music.*
>
> *I regret that I am not prepared to do this. I consider it outside the terms of our original agreement as quoted above. In future, from Saturday next 30th May, I will write scripts only for those programmes which may reasonably be considered to include serious music.*

He also informed Ó hAnnracháin that he had decided to change the name of his group, the Dublin Harpsichord Ensemble to Musica da Camera. 'It... describes our aims more precisely as we hope to include medieval, late 18th century, and contemporary music in our programme.'[8]

John's friend Werner Schürmann was auditioned successfully by Radio Éireann early in June[9] and a programme of popular sixteenth-century German songs arranged for organ and lute was broadcast later in the month. The group, now Musica da Camera, consisted of Werner, John on organ and drum, and Michael Morrow on lute and recorder.[10]

In the middle of July, Radio Éireann broadcast a talk by John entitled 'The Neo-Classicism of Stravinsky'. As an example of how programmes of a diverse nature were thrown together on Ireland's one and only radio station, the preceding programme was *Country Journal*.[11] In *Radio Review*, an article published in the *Irish Independent* on 18 July, Maxwell Sweeney had this to say:

> The opening of the Stravinsky talk, however, was rather up in the stratosphere and somewhat "off-putting" for the average listener. If you persevered you

would have found that talk – and its illustrations – interesting, but difficult. Mr. Beckett's problem was that of many an expert – he was too far over the heads of many members of his potential audience and frightened them.[12]

Starting on 21 July, four important twenty-minute programmes, which had required a great deal of careful research and planning, were broadcast on Radio Éireann. Written, devised and presented by John, and featuring John Bilton (tenor) and Michael Morrow on lute and recorder, they were entitled *John Dowland's Achievement as a Song Writer*.[13] Although RTÉ possesses no archival recordings of these programmes, we know the contents, thanks to a document kept in the RTÉ Document Archives. The details had been sent by John in a letter to Margaret Pigott, the Assistant for Vocal Programmes, at the end of May, and Fachtna Ó hAnnracháin had written to John, 'we shall do our best to fit in the four programmes designed to illustrate John Dowland's achievement as a song writer.'[14] What these programmes sounded like is anybody's guess, but a young man named Seán O'Leary, who would become a long-time friend of John's in the UK, heard one of these programmes and was impressed. Seán, who had been born near Castleisland, County Kerry, was on holidays in Galway in July 1953. One evening he listened to a radio programme about John Dowland, a composer of whom he had never heard, presented by somebody named John Beckett, who he did not know was related to Samuel. He came to the conclusion that John was 'a remarkable chap – very cultured', and declared that the programme was a revelation for him. At least somebody appreciated the broadcast, as there was no comment about the programmes in any of the Irish newspapers.[15]

Towards the end of July John was suddenly and unexpectedly deprived of his job of scriptwriter for Radio Éireann's announcements and the weekly £5 that he was earning. Undoubtedly incensed, he wrote to the then Minister for Posts and Telegraphs, Erskine Childers, who was responsible for broadcasting in Ireland (and later became president of Ireland):

> In May of last year I was engaged by Radio Eireann to write scripts for all broadcasts of serious music. I was paid a weekly fee of £3. This was later increased to £5. Owing to Mr. Reedy's recent appointment as Assistant Music Director this work has been relegated to Dr. [Arthur] Duff. The cessation of this regular income has brought about a state of financial affairs such as will make it necessary for me to leave Ireland in the near future, and seek employment elsewhere.
>
> It was not my intention to bother you or anyone else with what I regarded as a personal inconvenience. I write to you now, however, at the suggestion of the Director of Music at Radio Eireann, Mr O'Hanrahain.
>
> […]I am, I think, the only person in the country trained in the technique of

playing the harpsichord, and in the style of interpretation for the performance of the music written for it. I have given many broadcasts and other performances with the Dublin Harpsichord Ensemble in the last three years and can claim an intimate acquaintance with the whole of the chamber music repetoire [sic]. I have recently been wondering whether some post could be created at Radio Eireann which would include the playing of the harpsichord, and the supervision of broadcasts of chamber music and of talks on the subject.[16]

Details of programme 3 of John Dowland's Achievement as a Song Writer (August 1953), written by John Beckett on a Radio Éireann Artistes Engagement Form and transcribed in a clearer hand. (Courtesy of RTÉ Document Archives.)

After receiving a curt reply from the Secretary for the Minister of State,[17] John soon heard from the Director of Broadcasting, Maurice Gorham, who regretted that that Radio Éireann could find no regular job for him.[18] However, John continued to work for the station; in August he provided programme notes, which were read by Brendan Burke, for a broadcast of Ravel's *L'Enfant et les Sortilèges*.[19]

As well as doing occasional work for Radio Éireann, John had now got himself involved in the new Pike Theatre Club, founded by Alan Simpson and his wife Carolyn Swift[20]– probably due to the encouragement of Michael Morrow, who was designing the scenery. His sister Brigid was helping to make the costumes.[21] Alan Simpson was then developing a reputation as one of the most innovative directors in Irish theatre. On 29 August the *Irish Times*'s regular column, *An Irishman's Diary*, reported that 'Three generations of workers in the field of Irish drama were represented at the pleasantly informal little party which was given last Thursday evening to celebrate the completion of the Pike Theatre Club.' The Pike had appointed an advisory panel, which included John, the actor Cyril Cusack, the playwright Denis Johnston, the poet Valentin Iremonger, and the painter Tom Nisbet. The article mentioned that many people hoped that the new theatre would give Ireland its first performance of Samuel Beckett's play *Waiting for Godot*, 'which has aroused lively controversy in Paris.'[22] Alan and Carolyn probably hoped that John's presence on the advisory panel would influence his now famous cousin. However, because of protracted negotiations and endless delays connected with the first London production, which Samuel did not want to be anticipated by a production in Dublin, it was some considerable time before the Pike could stage it. (The play was finally performed at the Pike on 28 October 1955.) The tiny theatre, a converted mews in Herbert Lane, opened its doors on 15 September with the posthumous world premiere of G.K. Chesterton's *The Surprise*. In the following year, the theatre famously produced Brendan Behan's play *The Quare Fellow*.[23]

During this period, Brigid Morrow, who had left school aged eighteen, had an office job, which she hated, at Proprietaries Ltd, close to Kingsbridge (now Heuston) railway station. As John's partner Vera took pity on her and wanted to find her something better, she checked the advertisements in the London *Times*, which she bought every day, for a suitable job. One day she telephoned Brigid and asked her to call in on the way home. Brigid did as she was told and cycled to the flat in Baggot Street, where Vera showed her an advertisement for an *au pair* girl that was needed for a family in French Morocco. Brigid applied for the job and, after a hiccup caused by a postal strike, finally got it.[24]

More broadcasts on Radio Éireann followed: in *Wednesday Recital* on 2 September, John's Musica da Camera group played music by Bartók, Mozart and Telemann. The Bartók work was Eight Pieces from *Mikrokosmos*, which John performed on the piano; he played Mozart's *Adagio in C major for Glass Harmonica* K.356 on a celeste; and the group performed Telemann's Sonata in C minor for oboe continuo, for which John played harpsichord continuo.[25]

In two programmes, broadcast in late September and mid October, Alfred Deller sang to John's harpsichord accompaniment.[26] Five programmes, broadcast in early September, then later in October and in early November, featured the six Sonatas for Violin and Harpsichord by Bach, which were played by John on harpsichord, François d'Albert on violin, and Betty Sullivan on cello.[27]

However, John only heard two of these Bach sonatas, broadcast on the first programme of this series, for by 9 October he and Vera had packed up and moved to London, where they lived in 8 Reid Street, N1. John wrote to a Miss McGreevey in Radio Éireann:

> *Greetings from the unfashionable but cheap wastes of Islington. You may remember some recordings that Francois d'Albert, Betty Sullivan, and myself made of the Six Bach Violin Sonatas. Two of them were broadcast before I left, I think, could you let me know, a little in advance if possible, when the other four are being done. I want to use them as testimonials here.[28]*

Werner Schürmann, who returned to Germany in October, stopped off in London and met John at this flat in Islington.[29] The reason for John and Vera's sudden departure was John's lack of a regular income from Radio Éireann. Although John had clocked up an impressive list of achievements between 1951 and 1953 and seemed to have carved out something of a niche for himself in Dublin's musical scene, he now had no regular employment. Jobs were almost impossible to find in Dublin at the time – the war years had left Ireland poor and lacking in job opportunities and many people were leaving to seek work abroad.[30] Aidan Higgins had left for London the previous year, where he worked in Ponds Cosmetic Factory in Perivale and then in an extrusion mouldings plant near the Great North Road; he later worked in Wall's ice cream factory.[31] 'I was trying to make a living in Dublin,' recollected John many years later, 'but couldn't make anything of it, there's no mystery about that.' He and Vera left for London, 'penniless as hell, having a very tough time'. It must have been difficult for John to make the decision to leave, for he was very fond of Ireland.[32]

By 6 December John and Vera had moved to another address: Studio House, 1 Hampstead Hill Gardens, from where he wrote to Radio Éireann's Music Director Fachtna Ó hAnnracháin:

I have just been appointed as music master at a London School. In order to have my salary assessed by the Ministry of Education it is necessary for me to have docu-mentary evidence of my previous experience as a professional musician. Could you please let me have, at your early convenience, a note containing details of my work at Radio Eireann during the last two years and more.[33]

Ó hAnnracháin thanked him for his letter and asked him what he wanted him to put in the note.[34] John supplied the details in a terse letter[35] and Ó hAnnracháin responded with the following document, dated 16 December:

To Whom It May Concern.
This is to confirm,
(1) that Mr. John Beckett was employed by Radio Éireann to write announcers' scripts for all broadcasts of serious music from 6th April, 1952, to 27th June, 1953.
(2) that he wrote and broadcast talks on various musical subjects in recent years;
(3) that he directed and gave broadcasts from time to time with the Dublin Harpsichord Ensemble, and,
(4) that some of his compositions have been broadcast from Radio Éireann.[36]

Towards the end of the month, W.T. Davies, the Chief Education Officer attached to the City Borough of East Ham Education Committee, wrote to Ó hAnnracháin to enquire whether John had been employed by Radio Éireann on a full-time or part-time basis, and to ask how many hours a week he had been engaged if he had been employed part-time.[37] Ó hAnnracháin explained that John 'was paid a weekly fee in respect of the scripts he prepared for all our broadcasts of serious music,' but as he was not on the staff of Radio Éireann, he could not say how many hours he had spent on the work each week.[38]

John's friend Michael Morrow had decided to stay in Dublin for the time being. When his sister Brigid set off for French Morocco in October, she had to break her journey in London. John met her there and brought her to the station for the next part of her journey, which was to Paris. Before she left, he took what-ever little money he had out of his pocket and saying, 'This is all I have,' gave her £1, which Brigid thought was very kind of him, considering that he was always broke. Michael sat at home for a month or so, idle, until he decided that he would have to make some money. Following in John's footsteps, he finally left for London.[39]

PART TWO

London 1954–1971

Twelve

1954–55

W hen Michael arrived in London, he headed immediately, as John had done, for bohemian Hampstead, where he found accommodation in a flat at 18A Belsize Lane, close to the Royal Free Hospital. The house – a solid, three-storey affair with a basement and attic – was also home to Jill Damaris Anders, who was born in South Africa and would later marry John's friend Aidan Higgins. She lived in the third-floor flat, which included three rooms in the attic and overlooked the quiet road.[1]

Like Michael, all that John and Vera could afford in this part of London was a flat; the fact that apartments were readily available is evidenced by the number of different addresses at which they would live over the coming few years. Although John's appointment as 'music master' was confirmed[2] and he had some form of regular income, it would seem that the reason why they were on the move so often was simply because they could not afford the rent and had to find somewhere cheaper to live.

In their present flat at 1 Hampstead Hill Gardens, they were close to shops and public transport, and also within easy walking distance of famous landmarks and historic buildings such as Hampstead Heath, Kenwood House, Constable's house, Burgh House, Keats's home, Fenton Grove and, most importantly for John, Fenton House, where there was a collection of important harpsichords on which he could practise and play. In fact, John had started practising on the instruments from 8 November 1953; the dates on which he played and the amounts that he paid, ranging from 2s 0d to 3s 0d, though mostly 2s 6d, were recorded in a book by Eileen Jackson, the curator at the time. His name, now written in capitals, and in its distinctive angular or 'Chinese' style, appears five times between 8 November and early December. The signatures in the book read like a virtual *Who's Who* of budding early music revivalists resident in England at that time.[3]

John met the recorder player John Sothcott in Fenton House, where they played Baroque sonatas for harpsichord and recorder. As they got on so well together, they decided to form a duo.[4] Born on the Isle of Wight and a student of Edgar Wouncher, John Sothcott had started to study the violin in Morley College, where Walter Bergmann encouraged him to take up the recorder.[5] He was a forthcoming and direct person; he was slightly rebellious, his reactions were not commonplace and he was refreshingly unconventional.[6] John thought highly of him and his playing: 'To put it briefly,' John once wrote, 'he plays the recorder about as well as it can be played.'[7] John Sothcott, who was nicknamed 'devilish' on account of his dexterity on the instrument, admired John Beckett, and regarded him as being the finest harpsichord player with whom he had ever worked, but thought that he was slightly uptight and 'buttoned-up about his approach to music'.[8] In Sothcott's opinion, John was 'a very good exponent of the treble viol and an excellent recorder player'. As well as being musical colleagues, they became good friends and spent many convivial evenings together.[9]

Another person whom John met sometime in 1954 was the musician Harold Lester; Harold cannot remember exactly when or how he met John but he remembers how he brought him to classes for contemporary ballet, where he improvised an accompaniment on the piano. Harold was born in 1931 and studied at the Royal College of Music between 1949 and 1952. He invited John to his house and introduced him to his new wife. Both Harold and his wife were very fond of John; in time Harold came to have tremendous respect for him and to regard him as an old and very dear friend. He noted John's interest in litera-ture, poetry and painting, and his tastes, which were eclectic. Harold found Vera rather eccentric – it seemed as if she lived in a world of her own. He knew about John's friendship with Brendan Behan, but never met the man.[10]

At some time during this period, John and Michael worked in Forte's Monaco restaurant in Piccadilly Circus, which was famous for its musical foun-tain.[11] Both Brigid Morrow and Mary Boydell, who visited John and Michael in London, came to the restaurant; Mary remembered having a meal with John there.[12] John and Michael entertained the diners by operating the fountains for fifteen minutes every hour, in time to recorded ballet music by Delibes and other composers, for the grand sum of £12 per week. To do this, they had to climb up a narrow staircase to a tiny, cramped room, where they operated a set of levers that controlled both the jets of water and their colours, which were changed by means of coloured lights. As can be imagined, the tempo of this operation was necessarily slow. Michael found that, with practice, he could spray the customers, though his excuse was that he had been 'distracted'. He remembered with amusement how, several years later, his marriage certificate read, 'Occupation: Musical Fountain Operator'.[13]

The recorder player Theo Wyatt, who met John and Michael at this time, probably through Ken (Cecil) Kenworthy of the Oriel Consort, remembers how John filled in the time during the intervals by arranging chorale preludes for recorders from Bach's *Orgelbüchlein* (the Little Organ Book), which Schott published in 1959. The Oriel Consort, with which Theo played then, was recruited to play through them and approve John's breath marks. 'The experience of reading his extraordinary handwriting, so closely approximating to cuneiform, was not easily forgotten,' recalls Theo, who taught at Morley College and remained a friend and musical colleague of John's for many years.[14]

Michael spent his time, when not operating the fountain, transcribing old music from a variety of sources found in libraries and museums in London. When in Dublin, he had studied many important manuscripts in Marsh's Library and Trinity College, especially ones of lute music. As he had become particularly interested in music of the thirteenth century and onwards, he had to grapple with and teach himself modal rhythm, and also the intricate and often ambiguous systems of notation, such as the Petronian, Philippe de Vitri's *Ars Nova* and the cumbersome Italian *Ars Nova* or *Trecento* systems used during the middle ages. In addition, he had to learn lute tablature and tackle the vexed question of so-called *musica ficta* (the sharpening or flattening of notes in modal music). Thus equipped, he was able to transcribe pieces from the original sources and write them in modern notation.[15] Eventually John would acknowledge that Michael, over the years, had become 'a formidable musicologist and scholar (at, or beyond, the forefront of the field)' but stressed that, despite the fact that he did perform in public, he was 'emphatically *not* an executant performer' (John's emphasis).[16]

Although John had ceased working for Radio Éireann, he had not forgotten about the station and now saw a possible opportunity for earning a little more money. He wrote to Fachtna Ó hAnnracháin in February 1954, informing him that he would be in Ireland for a couple of weeks in April. As he had been 'working on a series of four programmes devoted to the harpsichord works of Francois Couperin le Grand', each lasting thirty minutes, he proposed that they be recorded during his stay.[17] Ó hAnnracháin suggested that the programmes be reduced to fifteen minutes;[18] John, who was not happy with this, replied, '15 minutes is rather less than the minimum time for what I had planned. Could

we compromise with 20? If you insist on 15 minutes I will alter my original idea
and leave out the script. ... I would suggest a fee of £8 for each programme.'[19]
Ó hAnnracháin's reply was short and to the point:

> Thank you for your letter of the 21st February. The programme space is very limited
> and our stock of recording tapes insufficient to allow us to pre-record everything
> we would like. I would prefer to arrange the four half-hour programmes if possible,
> but as matters now stand it may not be possible even to take four quarter-hour ones.
> If we succeed in arranging anything, I shall write again.[20]

He did not write again, and that was the end of the matter.

After this disappointment, John must have realized that the only course of
action was to approach the BBC Third Programme (now Radio 3) and offer the
station four programmes on John Dowland – something along the lines of what
had been broadcast on Radio Éireann. The Third Programme was the ideal radio
station for such a series. Although regarded by many as 'elitist' and 'highbrow'
at the time – 'if a programme appealed to two people rather than two million,
it was worth doing' was the official attitude – it nonetheless was liberal in that
it encouraged new music, new writers, and broadcast (despite its limited hours
of air time, from six to midnight) a certain amount of *avant-garde* experimental
drama and material that had never been broadcast before.[21]

John now wrote to John Davenport of the Third Programme from a new
address: 16 Ellerdale Road,[22] near Michael's flat. They seem to have moved here
in around May 1954, perhaps after the short stay in Dublin.

Using the same tactics that he had employed when dealing with Radio Éireann,
John explained to Mr Davenport that he wished to read four twenty-minute
illustrated talks on Dowland's songs, the scripts for which he had enclosed. He
stated that Alfred Deller was 'most interested' to sing; 'He is the only person
I can bear to hear singing these songs,' he wrote. He also stipulated that he be
accompanied by Desmond Dupré. As an afterthought, he concluded: 'I have also
done a talk on the neoclassicism of Stravinsky. Would this interest?'[23]

The first indications of interest by the BBC are revealed in an undated note
from John Davenport to his colleague Dr Roger Fiske of the Talks Department:

> This man Beckett is an extraordinarily good musician. Clark has his file. I hope this
> suggestion may interest you.

> Denis [?]: These are the scripts I spoke to you about. They don't pretend to be
> contributions to learning. The thing is, are they sound statements of what is gener-
> ally known of Dowland? Roger.

> *Roger: I have read these scripts with great interest and agree with what you say. But I wonder whether Third would agree to placing four concerts by Deller and Dupré ....*
> *Perhaps three would be a more suitable number, and the idea could be put up after the nine 'English Lutenist' programmes have been repeated in May and June. Denis.*[24]

Despite the initial show of interest, the Third Programme moved infuriatingly slowly and nothing more was done about these programmes until the following year. John probably realized that getting himself on the radio in England was not as easy as it had been in Ireland – in England the standard was higher and there was more competition. A lot of patience would be needed.

In May, John approached the BBC once again, this time requesting an application for an audition of both himself and John Sothcott. In his letter to Norman Carrell, the music booking manager, John invited him or a representative to a concert in Fenton House and enclosed a programme.[25] This took place on Saturday 12 June and featured himself on harpsichord and John Sothcott on recorder; they played sonatas by Telemann and Haydn.[26] This was the first Beckett–Sothcott public recital remembered by John Sothcott, and it was followed by several others in various venues in and around London.[27] Mr Carrell sent John his regrets and asked him to fill out an Application Form for Audition.[28] On the form, John mentioned that his last three concerts were the recital at Fenton House, an organ recital of Bach Preludes and Fugues that he had given in March at All Saints Church, Forest Gate, and a piano recital of music by Mozart and Bartók in Trinity College, Dublin. This time, John wrote from 10 Strathray Gardens, off Eaton Avenue, near the Swiss Cottage tube station.[29]

On 15 June, Roger Fiske wrote to John, asking him to come in for a microphone test and told him that nothing could be done about the Dowland programmes until 'well into 1955'.[30] John, now writing from 24 Parliament Hill, adjacent to Hampstead Heath, replied to him on the following day to accept the invitation and took the liberty of enclosing two additional scripts, one on *l'Enfant et les Sortilèges*. In addition, he made some suggestions for future programmes, such as the aforementioned opera by Ravel, Stravinsky's *Histoire du Soldat*, Bartók's *Music for Strings, Piano, Celeste and Percussion*, and the *Petite Sinfonie Concertante* by Frank Martin. 'The Stravinsky talk is intended to be provocative but unpedantic,' John wrote; 'It should have an effect with the illustrations which I have chosen most carefully.'[31]

At the request of Alfred Deller, John began editing some songs from Henry Purcell's *Orpheus Britannicus* and wrote to Desmond Osland of the Third Programme, offering a series of four to six programmes of Purcell songs, which Deller would sing, and recorder sonatas by Telemann (also edited by John), which

he and John Sothcott would play.[32] John continued to apply pressure on Roger
Fiske; the microphone test was held in October and was successful. It transpired that if John were to read his own script for the Dowland programmes and
others, he would have to audition as an actor with the drama department, which
presumed joining equity, 'a very over-crowded profession', as Roger explained.[33]

Brimming over with ideas and obviously impatient with the slowness of
the BBC's reaction, John wrote to Roger in November, now from 35 South
Hill Park (an elegant house near Hampstead Heath), offering him a draft of 'a
study of the Irish actress Harriet Smithson who [be]came Berlioz's first wife ...
Musically I am, not a blind, but an enthousiastic Berliozian', he added, using one
of his occasional and curious misspellings. He also mentioned the Purcell songs
that he had sent to Desmond Osland, presumably in the hope that Roger might
be able to expedite matters.[34]

Friends of John's at around this time in Hampstead were the journalist
John Willett and his wife Anne, who lived in Volta House, Windmill Hill, close
to Fenton House. John Willett, who wrote an anonymous article on Bertolt
Brecht for the *Times Literary Supplement* in 1956, went on to become a leading
expert on Brecht, editing and translating the playwright's work into English.
John and Anne were extremely hospitable, and their ramshackle mansion was
regularly filled with important and well-known musicians, artists, performers,
poets, publishers and critics, with whom John would have mixed. Despite
John Willett's well-off background, he dressed shabbily and was on occasions
mistaken for a workman. He was interested in music, played the cello and had
studied stage design.[35] He also drew very well and made interesting Christmas
cards, which John collected, along with his cartoons. Although Willett was no
fan of Samuel Beckett, John suggested that they meet, but Willett backed out of
the arrangement, saying, 'No, no, no – he's far too intelligent!'[36]

Another one of John's good friends, whom he encountered during this
early period, was the composer and flautist Fritz Spiegl, who was a year older
than John and distantly related to his idol, Gustav Mahler. Spiegl, who had a
good sense of humour, was born in Austria, near the border with Hungary, and
became famous for composing the theme music for the BBC series *Z-Cars* and
the Radio 4 *UK Theme*, which incorporated traditional British melodies and
which was played each morning at the start of transmission, until 2006.[37]

Bizarre though it may seem, John was now working in a paint factory, though
whether he still retained his job of music teacher is not clear. This, as can be
imagined, turned out to be something of a disaster. Apparently he was put in

charge of a paint-mixing machine that once went haywire and spewed paint all over the place.[38] Aidan Higgins wrote to Arland Ussher, 'Beckett works in a paint factory now. Seems to find it hard going. Have quarreled [*sic*] with Vera and rarely see them. Michael Morrow lives precariously in and out of hospital and hopes.'[39]

After a successful audition on 25 March 1955, programmes one and two of the series originally called *The Songs of John Dowland*, produced by Roger Fiske, were finally recorded on 31 March, and three and four on 2 April. John received a fee of ninety-five guineas. A reworking of the four programmes that John had devised for Radio Éireann, he now had the luxury of having Dowland's lute songs performed by Alfred Deller and Desmond Dupré. The programmes, renamed *John Dowland's Song Books*, were broadcast between 14 April and 3 May 1955.[40] 'He got just under £100 for four BBC talks,' Aidan Higgins reported to Arland Ussher. 'No more paint factories.'[41] Unfortunately, the recordings were not archived but the typed scripts for all the programmes have survived and are kept at the BBC Written Archives in Caversham, Reading.

John's research for these four programmes was careful and thorough, and he produced scripts that were interesting, enlightening and lacking in stuffiness. For those who remember the sound of John's voice, it is easy to imagine John reading them because of his style of writing. The series began:

> William Shakespeare was born, as all the world knows, at Stratford on Avon in 1564. The circumstances of John Dowland's birth are less exactly, and perhaps less widely known. The year was 1563. The place is conjectural. It has been said that it was the borough of Westminster. There is, however, some, though only some evidence that it may have been Ireland.

Throughout the four programmes, John outlined the main events in Dowland's life, stressed how had been considered 'the greatest performer on and composer for the lute of his day', and introduced selected pieces from his four books of songs – one of which was featured in each of the four programmes. In addition, John devoted a couple of paragraphs in the first programme to a description of the lute, mentioning that it was of ancient Arabic origin and first known in the west during the time of the Crusades. As in the Radio Éireann broadcasts, each of the four programmes dealt with Dowland's four books of *Songs or Ayres*. The final programme included the famous song *In Darkness Let Me Dwell*, performed not only by Deller and Dupré, but also by Harry Danks and Robert Donington on viols.[42]

As the public's reaction to these programmes has not been recorded it is impossible to judge what people made of them, but it is safe to assume that

John had put his knowledge to good use and caught his listeners' imagination at a time when few people appreciated the beauty of this precious, often melancholy, but wonderful music. The authorities in the Third Programme must have been duly impressed, for, from now on, John would become a fairly regular performer and broadcaster on the station.

Thirteen

1955–56

In early April John was in Dublin, presumably with Vera. In a letter to Roger Fiske, John wrote, 'I heard the first of the Dowland programmes in Ireland. It was at least not as chokingly embarrassing as I suppose one expects one's first recorded talk to be. I hope the others went over the air satisfactorily.'

This letter, in fact, was written from Genoa, where John and Vera were staying between May and July. 'While I was in Dublin I was offered an opportunity of spending a holiday in Italy where I have never been before, which I could not resist,' John explained. 'So here I am, having a useless, sunny and most pleasant time. How good it is actually to hear no music for a while. I packed the scores of ten Mozart Quartets and Mahler's 9th, and I bathe in them every day, or is it the sea?'[1] In one of his letters to Arland Ussher, Aidan Higgins mentions John 'and his woman' in Genoa, though in the context of vacancies with the Berlitz School.[2] It is therefore possible that John had deliberately covered up his true purpose for travelling to Italy when writing to Roger Fiske; because of his meagre earnings, John could hardly have afforded a holiday in Italy with Vera. Seán O'Leary, who had heard one of John's Radio Éireann programmes on Dowland, was quite certain that John had taught in the Berlitz School 'somewhere just outside of Genoa'.[3]

In mid July Aidan Higgins wrote to Arland Ussher, 'John Beckett is back from Genoa with Vera, is promised a repeat programme of his Dowland on the Third: fifty percent is £50. And also talks of going to the West.' The second sentence refers to plans that were being made for him and 'the South African bird' (his girlfriend Jill Damaris Anders) to travel to the West of Ireland and visit the Aran Islands.[4] John and Vera did join them on the trip to the islands, for in an article entitled *A Wet Exposed Place*, printed on 5 January 1980 in *The Irish Times*, Aidan wrote:

> We sailed for the islands on a grand blue day. On Inishere you taught Orla Kundsen to make brass rubbings from headstones sunken in sand in the twelfth-century cemetery. We ate mackerel, always hungry. Sarah O'Donnell remembered John Beckett as a lad, always hungry. Ah, Jahn, she said, emitting her high laugh. My mother and his girl friend were there before us, sunbathing. The sun shone every day for a week, the wind blew, we were ravenous.[5]

Later in the aforementioned letter to Arland Ussher, Aidan mentioned that Samuel Beckett's *Waiting for Godot* would open on 3 August at the Arts Theatre Club in London: 'Self and mews woman [probably Philomena Rafferty] and South African and a homosexual go to opening night. Vera presented herself at the Arts, saying she was Mrs Sloecombe [*sic*] from Paris, and asked for details of the production.' In July, Aidan was sceptical about the play's success: 'The rights were bought by a gentleman whose name means nothing to me, some years ago, and it is generally supposed not to go down very well.'[6] It is quite probable that John benefitted from *Godot*'s success in a roundabout way, for, from now on, the fact that he was related to the famous Samuel Beckett would have been remembered by many. John, however, never drew attention to this.

By the end of September, John and Vera were living in 21 Tanza Road, off Parliament Hill, close to Hampstead Heath. From here he wrote to Roger Fiske, enclosing a script on the subject of Mozart's son, Franz Xaver Mozart. 'My idea is that it should be used as an introduction to four programmes, each including music by him'. He admitted that this was not 'great or even very considerable art, but merely that all the works I have chosen can stand on their own musical feet.'[7] At the beginning of November, Roger proposed that a chamber music recital of works by Leopold and Franz Xaver Mozart be broadcast in the following year. As the BBC had no music by these composers in its library, he suggested that the better of the two violin sonatas by Franz Xaver should be performed, along with six of his songs, plus some chamber music by Mozart's father, Leopold, which he invited John to choose.[8]

At around this time, the young Sadlers Wells-trained dancer, Deryk Mendel was performing a clown routine in a cabaret in Paris. As he was asked to contribute another item for the following programme, he wrote to several authors, including Samuel Beckett, and asked them if they would write a short scenario for him. After Samuel's partner Suzanne had seen him perform, Samuel sent

Mendel a script named *Acte sans paroles* (*Act without Words*). In it, the actor, who is thrown on to the stage at the beginning and is thrown back again each time he tries to make an exit, finds himself in a desert, where he unsuccessfully tries to grasp a small carafe of water, which is suspended from the flies and is always out of reach, despite the actor's attempts to climb on to cubes and up a knotted rope. As Deryk liked to work with music and as Samuel wanted to help his cousin, John was invited to go to Paris for a week in order to compose an accompaniment for the mime.[9]

John met Deryk in October and read through Samuel's text. They talked about it and set about working together, without Samuel, in a large rehearsal room off the boulevard de Clichy in Montmartre. John watched as Deryk made the sort of movements that the script demanded and jotted down approximate timings for them. John thought that Mendel was a 'nice little man', a good mime artist, and that he took his work very seriously.

After a week, John returned to London and wrote the music for a small ensemble of piano (which he would play), xylophone and percussion based on his notes, his memory and close study of the stage directions. It was not a continuous score because of the silences needed — indeed, John felt that the silences were more powerful than the music. The final version, which lasted about twenty minutes, consisted of a prelude followed by segments of music. John explained:

> The music ... was all based on this kind of kaleidoscopic variation of a small number of ideas, with the ring of the xylophone and the harsher side drum ... all very brittle sounds, you see. They weren't in any sonata, developmental sense, pieces of music. They were just accompaniments to movements and equivalent in a kind of way to what I felt and we both felt. It was needed in terms of the energy of the movement, you see, so sometimes slow, sometimes fast and then we'd just stop. I didn't end the thing; it just stopped... [10]

John showed the text, and perhaps played the music, to Aidan Higgins, for Aidan later wrote to Arland Ussher that John had done 'a sort of ballet for Paris clown-dancer Moendel (spell) [*recte* Mendel], Jew queer, for which John did the music; and hopes for production soon, here or in Paris. John showed it to me, but have to admit I didn't care greatly for it, not that I cared for the play in print.'[11]

On 26 November Aidan married Jill Damaris Anders,[12] the South African who lived in the same house as Michael Morrow at 18A Belsize Lane. John played the organ at their wedding at the Church of St Thomas More, Swiss Cottage.[13] Aidan, who lived in Notting Hill Gate,[14] had visited Michael at Mile End Hospital the previous year and had been introduced to Jill by him.[15] Michael had been encouraged to make overtures to Jill but was not interested.[16] Michael suggested that Aidan come to a party at Belsize Lane and there Aidan met Jill again and became friends with her. Aidan remembered how there had been dancing in a very confined space and how he and Michael had sat back on a spare bed to smoke Balkan Sobranie and to drink slivovitz, which had been supplied by the Yugoslav Embassy, where Jill worked. After the marriage, Aidan moved into 18A Belsize Lane with Jill.[17]

Samuel Beckett did not attend the premiere of *Waiting for Godot* on 3 August. He was later persuaded to come to London to see the play following its transfer to the Criterion Theatre, Piccadilly, in September; this was after he had taken a brief holiday in Zurich in October with James Joyce's son, Giorgio, and had visited Joyce's haunts. He stayed at the Regent Palace Hotel, where John dined with him on mackerel, their favourite dish. In November, John and Vera dined with Samuel's friend A. J. Leventhal (known to everyone as 'Con') in London.[18]

Aidan Higgins met Samuel Beckett in London at the beginning of December. Samuel had found the time to go to Godalming in Surrey, where he had stayed with his cousin, Sheila Page, and returned to London with Peter Woodthorpe, the actor who played Estragon in *Godot*, and Ethna MacCarthy, with whom Samuel had fallen madly in love when he was at Trinity College Dublin in the 1920s. John had also met Ethna.[19]

Aidan's meeting with Samuel took place when he and his wife Jill joined John and Vera, who were now living on Haverstock Hill, Hampstead, for a supper consisting of a silverside of beef, done quite rare. Aidan was extremely nervous – so much so that he retched into the wash-hand basin in the bathroom – but Samuel was polite, courteous and considerate. After the meal, Samuel sat beside Aidan and presented him with a signed copy of *Textes pour rien*, even though he knew that Aidan did not understand French.[20]

On the following evening, Aidan, Jill, John, Vera, Michael Morrow and Samuel went by trolley bus to Collins Music Hall in Islington, where the young Chaplin had once performed. During the journey, Samuel divided his attentions between the two women, resisting Vera's attempts to monopolize him. At one point in the show, a nude chorus girl was pushed across the stage on a bicycle and a comedian gave a long and hilarious rapid-patter monologue on what the world needed: castor oil. It reminded Aidan very much of Lucky's monologue in *Waiting for Godot*. In a letter to Arland Ussher, Aidan described how they had 'heard a piece from a man called Dooley, which might have been written for Sam, delivered apparently blind drunk, a sort of tract on misery. Sam spoke to him

afterwards; he said his real name was Ffrench. The meditations of condemned
brutes. The dark spoil of glitter.'[21] The only person who was not in stitches
laughing was Samuel. However, when the comedian entered the bar afterwards
and everyone offered him their congratulations, Samuel politely offered his.[22]

By early 1956 John and Vera were living in 54 Belsize Park Gardens. All of a
sudden, plans for the broadcast of John's programmes of music by Leopold and
Franz Xaver Mozart took shape. He received fifteen guineas for devising the
two programmes[23] and a further forty-five (increased from forty guineas), as
an overall payment. Not only did he devise the programme, wrote Roger Fiske
on the official Talks Booking Requisition, but he also 'found the music, which
needed a great deal of research'. The recording session, which included approximately twenty-five minutes of script, took place in the BBC Concert Hall studio
on 14 February, just one day before the broadcast on the Third Programme. This
first programme included some chamber music by F.X. Mozart, performed by
David Martin (violin) and Iris Loveridge (piano), and songs sung by Wilfrid
Brown (tenor), accompanied by Charles Spinks (piano).[24] Unfortunately there
is no archive recording of this programme but the script does survive. In care-
fully-worded sentences, characteristic of John's style, he tells the sad story of
Mozart's second surviving son, whose life was lived under the shadow of his
famous father. Franz Xaver was also dogged with a lack of success, despite his
brilliance at the keyboard and ability to compose; at best he was known as a
salon virtuoso. However, the musical examples proved that the young Franz
Xaver wrote charming piano pieces, chamber music and songs that should not
be dismissed or consigned to oblivion.[25]

    The second programme, broadcast on the 18th, was a recital of music by
Leopold and F.X. Mozart, (Wolfgang Amadeus's father and son) with Charles
Spinks playing both piano and harpsichord, and with Florence Hoorton playing
the cello. Leopold Mozart's Trio in A was performed, along with F.X. Mozart's
Six Songs, *An Emma* ('To Emma'), Op. 24 and Sonata in E, Op. 19.[26] Although
this second programme was not archived, another programme of F.X. Mozart's
Sonata in E and the Six Songs was made in 1968, though using different musi-
cians, and a recording of it has survived.[27]

    Directly after the two programmes were recorded in mid February, John
travelled over to Paris for another session with Deryk Mendel, playing the
music that he had written for *Acte sans paroles* on a piano, 'in order to see how it
fitted'. Various adjustments were made, with passages being either lengthened
or shortened.[28]

In March, John received the following curt note from Harry Croft-Jackson, the BBC Music programme organiser:

Dear Mr Beckett,

Thank you for letting us see the score of your 'Two Songs from Orpheus Britannicus by Henry Purcell'. We regret to have to tell you that we are not prepared to promote performance of this work on our National Programmes – Light Programme, Home Service, or Third Programme...[29]

Considering the amount of work that he had lovingly applied to the editing of these now well-known and often-performed songs, John must have been bitterly disappointed to receive this communication. However, he was not to be put off and undoubtedly he would have resolved to renew his efforts at a later date.

By the end of April, John was happy to hear that something was being done about his proposed programme on Harriet Smithson and wrote to Roger Fiske to say that he was glad that she was 'to get a look in'.[30] Indeed, John seems to have had very little work from the BBC during the year – what exactly he was doing from day to day is something of a mystery. It is quite possible that he, Michael Morrow and John Sothcott were by now playing together and discussing medieval and early Renaissance music in various Hampstead coffee bars, as John Sothcott remembers.[31] Michael, who had become somewhat dissatisfied by the rather lugubrious and reverential performances on gramophone records and the Third Programme of such old music, as he called it (the term 'early music' had not yet been coined), was turning his attention to European folk and non-European folk and art music, in which medieval traditions of singing and playing had been preserved. He remembered listening to a Balkan singer at a festival of folk music and noting the singer's perfect intonation, his perfect fourths and fifths, very wide major seconds and dissonant wide major thirds. This, he concluded, was how a thirteenth-century motet must have sounded.

Like John, Michael was also aware that many of the instruments used in medieval and Renaissance music had been brought to Europe from the east as a result of the Crusades, trade through Constantinople and the Moorish occupation of Spain. As a result of this, eastern performance practices had been almost certainly imported into Europe. In addition, Michael (and others) believed that voice production might also have been eastern and folk-like; in European religious paintings, angels were frequently depicted singing with tightened throats and mouths barely open. John, who was also interested in folk music and the relationship between it and 'old' music, would have been aware of this. Both he and Michael would have known that the people of the medieval and early Renaissance periods wore colourful clothes, ate spicy food and enjoyed sharp contrasts in their paintings – the latter being reflected in the sharp distinction of parts favoured in medieval music. Sharp contrasts were also experienced in people's emotions. Town centres were noisy with cart wheels, the cries of hawkers and performances by itinerant musicians, who sang lustily and played loud outdoor instruments such as bagpipes and shawms.

Michael's aim was to perform this old music in something like the vigorous style in which he believed it would have been played originally, though he was constantly aware that any attempt to perform this music in a definitive 'authentic' manner was next to impossible. The main barrier to this was the earliest extant written music, the notation of which was too vague to give any real clue as to how it was to be performed. Instruments were never specified and the notation tended, at best, to be ambiguous. As composers wrote for the present and not for posterity, and as contemporary musicians were well acquainted with the style of performance of the period, there was no need to write down everything. At first Michael studied what was available in modern editions and then, when he became dissatisfied with this, he turned to the original manuscripts and transcribed them.[32] Michael, John Beckett, John Sothcott and the counter-tenor Grayston Burgess (known to everyone as Donald) often played and rehearsed either in Michael's flat or in a nearby converted chapel at 17 Holly Mount, Hampstead, which was owned by two friends, Heinz and Ruth Liebrecht.[33] At first, using what instruments they had, they played some of the musical examples printed in Volume One of *The Historical Anthology of Music*, edited by Archibald T. Davison and Willi Apel, and first published in 1949.[34] As time went by, reproductions of historical instruments were procured and the number of musicians increased, until the group famously known as Musica Reservata appeared on the scene.

Fourteen

1956–57

A t around this time John met the cellist Christopher Bunting, for in June and September 1956, recitals of music for cello and harpsichord, played by Christopher and John, were broadcast on Radio Éireann.[1] Bunting, who became a soloist of renown both on cello and piano, and also a teacher, composer and conductor, was born in 1924 and, like John, lived in Hampstead. He had studied with Maurice Eisenberg in the USA and Pablo Casals in France. Over the years, he and John became good friends.[2]

John must have spent some time in Dublin during the year, for on 30 September Radio Éireann broadcast 'Mozart's Son: an illustrated talk by John Beckett on his research into the life of Franz Xaver Mozart.' One wonders if the BBC knew about this – possibly the same script was used. The forty-five-minute programme featured Jaroslav Vaneček on violin, Rhona Marshall on piano and Michael Ledwith, tenor.[3] The *Irish Independent* later commented that 'John Beckett, in another feature of musical interest, "Mozart's Son", attracted interest because he was talking about a little-known character linked to a famous one, and had his programme well illustrated with music from Jaroslav Vaneček ... and Michael Ledwith.'[4] Like the Third Programme, a second programme of music by Mozart's father and son was broadcast in October, using the same performers but with the addition of Maurice Meulien on cello. For this programme, John played the harpsichord.[5]

On the same day, John wrote to his friend James Plunkett from his previous address at Studio House, 1 Hampstead Hill Gardens. John had encountered Plunkett (*nom-de-plume* of the writer James Plunkett Kelly, born in 1920) as far back as 1952, when he featured on a *Music Magazine* radio programme with John and wrote on music in *The Bell* magazine in the same year.[6] They had become good friends and now corresponded from time to time. A modest, gentle and compassionate person, Plunkett was a man of many parts. He had studied music, played the violin and viola, and he regularly invited John to the family home in Terenure to play quartets. The other musicians were James's wife Valerie, who played viola and piano, and either (or both) Kevin Roche from Radio Éireann and Betty Sullivan on cello. These musical gatherings had been held in the Plunketts' house from 1954 or earlier.[7]

As well as being a musician, James Plunkett had been a trade union official in the Workers' Union of Ireland, and had worked in Radio Éireann; in time he would become an Executive Producer and Head of Features in RTÉ Television, positions that would prove to be advantageous to John. He wrote short stories and plays, and would later become famous as the author of the novel *Strumpet City*. He would also be a member of the prestigious Irish Association of Artists, Aosdána.[8]

John wrote to James about his programme on Harriet Smithson:

> *My dear James,*
>
> *I got my Smithson script back from [the Irish writer Francis] MacManus today, despised and rejected, as the man said. He thinks it too 'third programme', too 'austere', too 'forgetful of the needs of Irish audiences.' He suggests that I should do an imaginative treatment of the material bringing out all the 'potent romantic drama' in the story. Even if I felt I had the necessary literary skill to to [do] this I would have no inclination to, for, as I said in a note to him, whether as author, listener, viewer or reader, I prefer biographical fact to biographical fancy. I see and appreciate his point, but I am not the type.*
>
> *I enclose MOLLOY and MALONE DIES. Also, believe it or not, VILE BODIES [by Evelyn Waugh]. I would be most interested in your views of the two former oeuvres.*[9]

James read his script and offered him his advice. Writing shortly afterwards from a different address, 7 Pembridge Crescent, London W11, John begged James's forgiveness for not having replied to his long and interesting letter about the script, adding:

> *I have replied to Macmanus declining to dramatise the thing. … Your offer to tart the script up for me touches me farther than anything else, I know how much work would be involved; but I am not that type either. As I have just said in a letter I have just written to Kevin [Roche]: either this programme is presented as the sober talk based on authentic documents (unearthed, I may irrelevantly plead, after months of research) I have written, or not at all. With careful casting of voices I believe it*

would be effective and even interesting to even your listeners. (Though I left out the last 'even' to Kevin.)[10]

In an *Irish Times* column entitled 'A Letter from Paris', Desmond F. Ryan had written in August:

It is sad to hear that Beckett's mime, "Thirst," with music by his cousin, John Beckett, and his new play, "Fin du Jeu" (or possibly "Fin de Partie"; at any rate, roughly speaking, "The End-Game"), will not after all be put on in the Festival de l'Avant-Garde on the roof of Corbusier's Cité Radieuse at Marseilles this month, but will have to wait for the Paris season.'[11]

The 'Thirst' mime was, of course, *Acte sans paroles*, which had at an early stage been provisionally titled *Soif* ('Thirst'). John rehearsed his music with Deryk Mendel in Paris in November: 'A very complicated thing to rehearse with all the ropes and the cues and the blocks and the glass ... and in retrospect I can't actually quite remember how on earth it was done but it was,' John recollected. Jocelyn Herbert had designed the tree used in the mime, which, according to the directions, is lowered during the piece; later its palms close, depriving the actor of shade and then its single bough folds downwards, depriving him of the opportunity to attach a rope to it. Samuel was interested in how it worked as it was quite complicated. John also attended several rehearsals of *Fin de partie* (*Endgame*) both in the theatre and the bar of the Théâtre de l'Oeuvre, rue de Clichy, where it was believed that an agreement had been made with the director, Lucien Beer, to stage both the play and mime the following January. While there, John met the actor, Jean Martin (whom he thought was a nice man and a fine actor) and the producer Roger Blin, who was also acting in the production. John found Blin 'very unapproachable – I couldn't get anywhere near him at all.' Because of John's attendance at so many of the rehearsals, he became more familiar with the French version of *Fin de partie* than with its English version, *Endgame*. Unlike *Acte sans paroles*, John was not involved in *Fin de partie*. 'Being a rather retiring sort of person, I didn't regard it as my mission to be involved at all so I was sitting at the back sopping it all up,' he explained.[12]

While in France John took the opportunity to travel down to Bern in Switzerland to see an important exhibition of works by Paul Klee at the Kunstmuseum, which ran from 11 August to 4 November. It was 'One of the most magnificent exhibitions I have ever seen in my life,' John reported. He kept the catalogue of the exhibition and remained a fan of Klee for the rest of his life. Samuel was also interested in Paul Klee and later owned one of his pictures, which he gave to John when they met for the fourth last time.[13]

In January of 1957 the theatre in Paris where Samuel Beckett's *Fin de partie* and *Acte sans paroles* were to be given their world premiere suddenly backed out of its engagements in order to stage a commercial play that had financial backing. Because of this, Samuel offered his mime to Alan Simpson of the Pike Theatre for the Dublin Festival in May. In a letter to Simpson, Samuel informed him that John's music was not yet ready and that John was supposed to come to Paris at the end of the month to complete it. However, Samuel doubted that John's original music would be suitable for the Pike's tiny stage and the actor, Dermot Kelly. John wrote to Alan Simpson in mid January, explaining that he preferred to 'complete the work in terms of the [stage] dimension we originally had at our disposal, and likely will have again, in Paris, and of the type of movement envisaged by Mendel and me. Your stage is, of course, much too small to provide the one, and, having seen him as Vladimir [in *Waiting for Godot*], I do not think that Dermot Kelly would be able to reproduce the other.'[14]

John completed his music in mid February[15] and the premiere of *Fin de partie* and *Acte sans paroles* finally took place not in Paris but in the Royal Court Theatre, Sloane Square, in London on 3 April 1957 during a 'French Fortnight'. The theatre's artistic director, George Devine, had heard about Samuel Beckett's problems with the productions in Paris and had rushed over to see the plays and offer to have them performed at his theatre in London. John met Devine but thought 'he was rather a bore ... Rather paternal sort of fellow, I thought. Calm, with a pipe in his mouth.'

As the first night gala performance was to be performed in front of the French Ambassador, his wife and other important dignitaries, along with thirteen French critics and several English ones, it was a very tense affair and the actors were understandably on edge. It was customary at the time to precede theatre performances with the National Anthem, and so John was asked to write a piece of music that incorporated the melodies of *God Save the Queen* and the *Marseillaise*, which he played on the piano. 'National anthems embarrass me, you see,' John admitted, 'and these versions didn't embarrass me. They were just... slightly surreal.' John considered his arrangements of the pieces, which were played separately, to be 'rather good... It was a comic attempt, a slightly bizarre... harmonization of them,' but the audience thought otherwise.[16] An amusing description of the reaction to John's music appeared in *The Irish Times*:

> In his two new plays, which had their world first showing in London last night, Mr. Samuel Beckett has abandoned the hope, the fellow-feeling and the humour which were the saving charm of the otherwise desolate "Waiting for Godot", and has given us the plain nightmare. The evening began memorably. Seated in our places we became aware that the dissonant, off-key noise coming from Mr. John

Beckett, a relative, at the piano, was the "Marseillaise". All rose, and listened with barely controlled hilarity to a rendering more *avant-garde* than the elder Mr. Beckett at his best. The same deception brought us to our feet again in the midst of "God Save the Queen", played in the manner of a Beethoven sonata. This was too much. At the end the house broke into laughter, and then into sustained applause. Mr. Beckett bowed, with a bewildered expression, and disappeared.

On this appallingly false note the curtain rose on Mr. Samuel Beckett's deeply serious portrait of human decay, "Fin de Partie".

The unnamed critic thought little of *Fin de partie*, which was performed in its original French, and the mime *Acte sans paroles*, 'which might have been subtitled "Out of Reach – or, A Child's Guide to the Symbolist Drama". There was no comedy in this either... It was done terribly slowly to repetitive, percussion music that was *avant-garde* in 1931.'[17] The music was performed by John, once again on the piano, Jimmy (T.G.) Clubb on the xylophone and Jeremy Montagu on the side drum. John and Jeremy remembered an incident during rehearsals when Jimmy did a *glissando* on the xylophone, 'skidded off the end' of the instrument and hit a hot water pipe that ran around the inside of the pit. It made a 'most fantastic noise, a tremendous shrill reverberating kind of cry in the theatre,' John recollected. He raised a hand and cried, 'Keep it in!' and so the sound of the water pipe was incorporated into the music, which the musicians were instructed to play *fortissimo* throughout, with occasional crescendos. (He informed Jeremy Montagu that not all his music was like that.)[18]

Another incident that John remembered in connection with this production, which could not have happened on that first night as Samuel had flown back to Paris, was of Samuel and himself, along with some of the musicians and actors, going up to the restaurant on the top floor of the theatre for supper. Samuel was not allowed in because he was wearing a polo-necked pullover and did not have a tie.[19] Writing to Barney Rosset in New York from Paris, Samuel admitted that he had sneaked away from London before the premiere. He reported that the mime had gone well and mentioned to both Barney and Arland Ussher in Dublin that John had done a fine job with the music.[20] Samuel also wrote to his friend, the American theatre director Alan Schneider, 'We "created" *Fin de partie* and mime at Royal Court and played from April 1st to 6th. The press was hostile. A fine article from [Sir Harold] Hobson. We go on here at the end of the month at the Studio des Champs-Elysées. Much advance hostility in the air, and the papers, here, which I do not understand, but rather welcome.'[21]

Acte sans paroles was performed when *Fin de partie* moved to the Studio des Champs-Elysées in Paris (on the fifth floor of the Théâtre des Champs-Elysées) though John was not involved as a recording of his music was played over loudspeakers;[22] however he did remember performing the music for the mime when the production was staged in Berlin later in the year.[23]

Back in January of 1957, John had written to James Plunkett from 7 Pembridge Crescent, London W11:

> *My dear James,*
>
> *Thanks for the books. On seeing the parcel I thought, for a confused early morning moment, that Macmanus had changed his mind in a four volume letter. By the way they are doing my Harriet Smithson script on the Third at the beginning of March.*
>
> *Did you hear ALL THAT FALL. I did, and, though I found much of the production unconvincing, thought it a thing of beauty and, shall we say, a joy. The sound effects were claustrophobic where they should have been open, echoing; and Mary O'Farrell lacked that sense of habitual panic which so becomes Sam's creatures. But the thought of Minney, who would have been 50, "girding up her lovely little loins, and waiting for the change", is glorious. The piece was full of such good things.*
>
> *I don't see how you could possibly do it on R.E. [Radio Éireann] Surely it embodies that most henious of blasphemies, disgust.*[24]

John's progamme about Harriet Smithson was indeed broadcast on the BBC Third Programme, on 6 March 1957. Entitled *My Ophelia* and featuring the actors Hugh Manning, Sheila Raynor and Raymond Nemorin, it was narrated by John and illustrated with music on gramophone records.[25] Earlier, Roger Fiske (the producer) had written to John: 'I think your new script is most successful and you will read with a wry, disbelieving smile, that I think it is much improved in its shortened form.' It was agreed that the actors should not use French or Irish accents, and the fees were increased from forty to forty-five guineas.[26]

The script for this forty-five-minute programme ran to twenty-six pages, though there were some last-minute cuts and changes. The central character, Smithson, was dear to John's heart as she was born in County Clare, Ireland. John began by outlining her early life and how she started her acting career in Drury Lane Theatre, London; the three actors read contemporary critics' descriptions of her acting style and appearance. John went on to describe how she played the part of Ophelia in Shakespeare's play *Hamlet* to great acclaim at the Odéon theatre, Paris, in 1827. The young Hector Berlioz, who was in the audience, was captivated by her. It was his passion for her that inspired him to write his great work, the *Symphonie Fantastique*, which John now discussed, along with *Lélio, ou le Retour à la Vie*, composed in 1831 in Rome. When both works were performed at the Salle du Conservatoire in Paris, Harriet attended the concert. Berlioz had himself presented to her afterwards, 'when he declared his love to her in, we may be sure, most passionate terms. His joy when she confessed herself ready to accept his proposal of marriage was unbounded.' However, she was alarmed by his ardour and dithered until Berlioz pressurized her into marrying him in 1833. In a section omitted from the broadcast, John described Berlioz's attempt to pay off his wife's pressing debts and the birth of their son Louis. Gradually the relationship between Berlioz and his wife deteriorated and she became intensely jealous of any woman that he chanced to meet. She began to drink and the marriage came to an end in 1844, when Berlioz left and went to live with the singer Marie Recio. A moving letter written to her son in French, full of mistakes, was read in the original language by Sheila Raynor, who took the part of Harriet. The programme ended with the death of Harriet at Montmartre in 1854, and Berlioz's journey to the priest's house by cab, passing the Odéon theatre, where, twenty-six years previously, 'he had seen there, for the first time, his Ophelia'.

This sensitive account of Smithson's tragic life, illustrated with a minimum amount of music, was well constructed and, although concise, was full of John's usual attention to detail. [27]

In November of the previous year, Samuel Beckett had hinted to John Morris of the Third Programme that he would be prepared to do something for the station, 'possibly with my cousin John Beckett of whom I spoke to you'. [28] In May of this year, Samuel wrote to Donald McWhinnie, the BBC Assistant Head of Drama (Sound), 'I suggested to John that he might do some music for a published text, the end of Part I of Molloy for example', and suggested various passages to be included. [29] About a week later, McWhinnie reported to Samuel, 'Your cousin telephoned the other day and we are going to meet and have a meal when he gets back from Dublin. I think we ought to look very carefully at your suggestion of doing a section of 'Molloy' with special music – I think the result might be extremely interesting.' [30] By the 19 August the necessary arrangements were made for the broadcast of a solo reading of selected passages from Molloy by the actor Patrick Magee. [31]

At around this time, however, a cautionary note written by Bernard Keeffe, a conductor who worked in the Music Department stated that 'Our only knowledge of John Beckett as a composer is based on two songs with piano accompaniment which he has submitted recently. They were rejected as being somewhat less than competent. Music Department cannot, therefore, recommend his use as a composer of incidental music without substantial evidence of his talent in this direction.' [32]

Despite this, the plans went ahead and by the beginning of September John was able to report from his mother's house, Field Place, in Greystones, 'The music for 'Molloy' is under way, and has turned out, as I thought it would to be scored for three trumpets, three trombones (two tenors and one bass) and three solo double basses.' He also requested the Philip Jones Brass Ensemble – 'They play excellently together and specialize in this rather tricky dissonant sort of stuff' – and they were booked.[33] Writing to Samuel in November, Donald McWhinnie reported, 'Spent the day with John Beckett yesterday. We went over the music on the piano with Magee. It sounds very exciting. I also introduced him to John Gibson and I hope that in due course there may be a possibility of his writing some incidental music for other programmes.'[34]

It seems that John went to Russia at some time during the summer of this year,[35] possibly as a delegate for a cultural exchange programme. He may have been a guest of the Soviet Cultural Relations Society (VOKS); as his friend James Plunkett and five other *Bell* 'under-writers' had been invited on a 'Cultural Mission' to the Soviet Union in 1955, James may have encouraged John, who had also written for *The Bell*, to join another such group this year.[36] John's intense interest in Russian icons – the darker and older the better – may have begun at this period. Somehow he managed to acquire a small and much cherished collection of them, which he often proudly displayed to his friends. The primitive aspect of these sacred works appealed to him greatly. He was always interested in the art and architecture of various out-of-the-way countries.[37]

In September John was in Berlin for three weeks looking after his music for the *Acte sans paroles* mime, which was performed by the Schiller Theater company along with *Endspiel* (the German translation of *Fin de partie*), in the Schlosspark Theater.[38]

Writing towards the end of December to Alan Schneider in New York about a production of his play *Endgame*, Samuel Beckett mentioned that he would ask John to write a setting of Clov's song, with words written not by Samuel himself but by James Thomson (1700–1748). John however offered words and music, in triple time, from a music hall verse.[39]

The music that John had composed for the reading of Samuel's *Molloy* was conducted by Berthold Goldschmidt and recorded at the beginning of December. Articles about this forthcoming programme, to be broadcast on the tenth of the month, and a twenty-minute reading of *From an Abandoned Work* (then unpublished) on 14 December, appeared in *The Times* and *The Irish Times*.[40] The latter half of Part One of *Molloy*, in which the crippled Molloy reflects on his situation and ultimate deliverance from the dark forest in which he has been wandering, had been translated by Patrick Bowles, in collaboration with the author. Approved by Samuel, Patrick Magee's harsh, gravelly voice – or rather, in this case, a barely audible rasp produced at the back of the throat – was ideal for this bleak, though often humorous text, which was delivered by Magee in a monotonous drone, totally devoid of inflection: the correct delivery, surely, for a text written as one very long paragraph. John was full of praise for Magee's delivery.[41] His extraordinary and highly dissonant music complemented the stark reading; it began with a short burst of aggressively urgent, staccato wind music, performed by the Philip Jones Brass Ensemble. The spoken passages that included those in which Molloy complains of the pain in his leg and his asthma, were punctuated by more segments of angry, discordant music (one of them being a solo on a trombone), which came crashing in during pauses in the monologue. The overall effect was electrifying and a deliberate feeling of discomfort and tension was palpable.[42] Samuel was very pleased with the music and wrote to his friend Con Leventhal to say that it was remarkable. He used the same word to describe Patrick Magee's performance when writing to Alan Schneider.[43] When John wrote to Samuel, he mentioned that if he had to write the music again, he would do it differently. He also met Donald McWhinnie to discuss commercial recordings, but nothing came of this. However, John and Patrick Magee did make private recordings of the readings from *Molloy* and *From an Abandoned Work*, which were sent to Samuel in Paris at the beginning of the new year.[44]

Fifteen
1958–60

Early in the new year plans were being made to record another reading by Magee, this time from Samuel's next novel, *Malone Dies*; in mid February Donald McWhinnie requested permission to ask John to write music for it. A couple of days later he wrote to Samuel suggesting passages that might be read, and reported that he had spoken to John about the music and that John had been 'very excited'. A discussion about the selected passages followed and John was officially commissioned to write approximately twelve minutes of incidental music on 26 March.[1]

News of John's extraordinary music must have been circulated among the staff of the Third Programme even before *Molloy* was broadcast, for the producer John Gibson contacted John, now living at 18A Belsize Lane, Hampstead, asking him for incidental music for *The Ballad of the Northern Wastes*, a play by the German writer Wolfgang Weyrauch.[2] On the day when *Molloy* was broadcast, John was formally commissioned to compose about seven minutes of music for Weyrauch's play, which would be broadcast in February.[3]

Shortly after the play's broadcast, John Gibson requested permission to use John for music that needed to be composed for *Pantagleize*, a farce written in 1929 by the prolific Belgian playwright Michel de Ghelderode; John's fee would be about £123.[4] John had by now succeeded in getting himself well established within the BBC. He later remarked:

I built up a lot of contacts with Radio 3 drama producers ... the poor saps used to think that what I did was good! ... I used to enjoy it because for radio, you see, you can use ensembles which would be out of the question for any sane concert oratorio, and you can also balance them in any way you like, piano

accordions and all sorts of things. I used harps in one of them I remember ...
you can get wonderful effects. I used to make some money out of it. I enjoyed
doing it – they were reasonably effective. The question about whether the music
was worth the paper it was written on was quite another matter.[5]

In March Samuel Beckett was writing a stage monologue for Patrick Magee.
As it featured a tape recorder, the mechanics of which he was unfamiliar, he
asked John to send him an instruction manual, though he also asked Donald
McWhinnie to supply the same if John could not find one. The play, of course,
would later be named *Krapp's Last Tape*. He was also working on the proposed
reading from *Malone Dies* for the Third Programme. The sections to be included
were discussed with Donald McWhinnie, John and Patrick Magee. Samuel
wanted to exclude the character Sapo from the readings, but was persuaded to
include him by Donald, John and Patrick.[6]

John was back in Dublin to play the continuo for Bach's *Saint Matthew Passion*
in the St Francis Xavier Hall on 22 March. The work was performed by the St
James's Gate Music Society, conducted by Victor Leeson. Although successful, it
was not flawless, as *The Irish Times* pointed out:

> The two continuos were provided by John O'Sullivan at a very well managed
> electronic organ and by Betty Sullivan (cello) and John Beckett (piano). At first
> sight one started various mutters about Radio Eireann and their harpsichord.
> But the piano had been suitably "harpsichordized" so that it was almost indistin-
> guishable in John Beckett's hands. Since he emigrated, his playing seems to have
> matured greatly and his realisation was a real joy throughout (and, of course, in
> perfect accord).[7]

The 'harpsichordization' of the piano was achieved by affixing drawing pins
to the hammers – a strange compromise considering that John's acquaintance,
Cathal Gannon, and the national radio station, Radio Éireann, both owned harpsichords that could have been used. John's ambivalent attitude towards playing
in large religious works such as this one is summed up in a remark that he made
to James Knowlson many years later: 'I was based in London then – I used to
go and do the Passion. I'd go inside of a week and I'd come back again with a
cheque in my pocket.'[8]

John, in fact, may have stayed in Dublin for more than a week on this occasion, for at around this period he and Vera lived for a while in the faded Victorian
splendour of Woodtown House at the foot of the Dublin Mountains, not far
from St Columba's College.[9] Set in its own grounds and with a farmyard and

gardens behind, this once fine house was owned by Arnold Marsh, former head-master of Newton School, Waterford, and his wife, the artist Hilda Roberts. John and Vera were given a basement flat in the house, which was divided into apartments and rented to various artistic people.[10] John's friend, the singer and sculptor Werner Schürmann had been living in Woodtown Park since 1956;[11] Hilda later did pencil sketches of Werner's wife Gerda Frömel and John's cousin Samuel.[12] A striking portrait of John, painted in oils by Hilda, is still kept in the house by her daughter, Eithne Clarke.[13]

John and Vera were in the habit of visiting Joe Groocock any time they came to Dublin. Joe did not take to Vera at all. Joe's daughter Jenny remembers Vera clearly. She made Jenny her very first dress; Jenny recollects that it was as beautiful inside as it was outside. Up until that time, Jenny and her sisters had to make do with pass-me-downs, but she now had a dress all of her own. Jenny thought Vera an extraordinary lady. She found John devastatingly handsome: her childhood memory of him was a 'gorgeous, benign and yet dangerous character' whose big brown eyes bored into her. She can remember him sitting in the kitchen, chatting to her mother or playing duets with her father. Joe was fond enough of John to put up with Vera, though Jenny now feels that John revered Joe more than Joe appreciated John.[14]

By now plans were well on the way for the recording of Patrick Magee's readings from *Malone Dies*, which would be broadcast on the Third Programme on 18 June.[15] Samuel had chosen the sequence of passages and Donald McWhinnie had written to him to say that 'Magee is not unnaturally overcome by the monologues and I fear it will give him many sleepless nights.' John's music would be performed on harmonica, two mandolines, a tuba, a cello and a double bass.[16] In a letter to Arland Ussher, Aidan Higgins asked, 'Did you hear any of John B's background music (I can't put it plainer) to Sam's radio work? And if so what do you think of it? He seems to be a man with great potentials. I hope he is not forced to go back into the paint factory.'[17] He had written in a previous letter, 'That John Beckett has begun to produce now that it seemed impossible, and is mentioned in OBSERVER radio column.' He also mentioned that Michael Morrow, who was 'still working on the fountains', would be 'marrying a German girl'.[18]

John Gibson now confirmed that he wanted twelve minutes of music for *Pantagleize*, which would be scored for seven instruments: two violins, one trumpet, one trombone, one piano and two percussion players. Ironically, the man who had questioned John's talent at composing, Bernard Keeffe, was due to conduct the *ad hoc* ensemble of seven players. The recording session took place in the middle of April at the Maida Vale studios. He also conducted the music for *Malone Dies*. John wrote the music for *Pantagleize* in five days and completed it just one day before it was recorded on the 11th.[19] The play was broadcast on the Third Programme shortly afterwards.[20]

John did not have to wait long for another commission: in July he was asked to compose more incidental music, this time for a radio play by David Paul, *Remember Who You Are*, described as 'a cautionary comedy' illustrating the 'career and catastrophe of the Heavisides family'. John completed the music, scored for recorder, two violins, one trombone, one piano and two percussion players, by 19 July and the programme went out on air four days later.[21]

Now that John was regarded as an established composer of *avant-garde* music, albeit in a minor capacity, it is not surprising that he was introduced, at around this period, to a young lady named Melanie Daiken, aged about thirteen, who was composing her own music. Her father, Leslie Herbert Daiken (born Yodaiken), who introduced her to John, had been one of Samuel Beckett's students at Trinity College in Dublin. A devotee of Samuel, Leslie helped him in several ways, such as trying to find a publisher for his book *Watt*. He became an Irish writer and journalist, who, as well as producing a great deal of articles in various magazines, wrote poems and books about Ireland. He was an expert on children's toys and games, and had published several books on the subject. He was a good friend of Michael Morrow's; although he knew John, he did not get on with him particularly well. As John was a stickler for truth and doing things the right way, and as Leslie was always inclined to exaggerate, John found him rather over the top and something of an embarrassment.

His daughter Melanie played her compositions for John on the piano; John was impressed by what he heard and gave her great encouragement. She went on to study composition and piano at the Royal Academy of Music under Hugh Wood and Vivian Langrish. Sadly, Melanie's father died young. Melanie was eighteen at the time and about to take up a scholarship to study composition at the Paris Conservatoire with Olivier Messiaen, and also piano with Yvonne Loriod, Messiaen's second wife. She spent two years in Paris, between 1966 and 1968, where she met both Samuel and John Beckett. John disliked Messiaen intensely, calling him a 'manic Papist' and his music 'Papist crap'. John later asked Melanie: 'What did he teach you? He couldn't have taught you anything!'[22]

By November 1958 John and Vera had moved to No. 1A, Frognal Mansions, close to the centre of Hampstead. John and Vera had a ground-floor apartment in this unusual five-storey building, constructed of red brick and white stone, at the top of a hilly road. John may have known that the contralto Kathleen Ferrier had once lived in the building. As they would stay here until 1965, their nomadic lifestyle had effectively come to an end. Those who visited them at Frognal over the next few years included John's old friends from Dublin, the MacNamaras – Desmond, Priscilla and their son Oengus, who later became an actor. John and Vera rarely visited the MacNamaras at their home in nearby Woodchurch Road; they either met at Michael Morrow's or in the apartment at Frognal. Oengus regarded John as being delightful company.

John became very fat during this period. Oengus's explanation for this was simple: he ate very well and took very little exercise. He was fond of having long meals with Michael Morrow, eating garlicky sausages, spicy food and the like, despite the fact that Michael preferred simple meals. No spices were to be found in the Morrow kitchen – Michael was happy to eat basic meals like potatoes and lamb.[23]

John wrote to Roger Fiske at the BBC in November, enclosing a script based on a lecture that Michael Morrow had given to the Lute Society, entitled *Claudin de Sermisy and the Paris Chanson*, in the hope that a radio programme, or a series of radio programmes, might be made about de Sermisy, who was one of the most renowned composers of *chansons* in the sixteenth century. Another letter, in large, shaky handwriting, was posted to Roger on the following day from Michael Morrow. In it, he suggested that his talk would make one introductory programme lasting about an hour, which could be followed by three half-hour programmes of music.[24]

Towards the end of November, the world premiere of *Bloomsday*, Alan McClelland's adaptation of James Joyce's famous book *Ulysses*, was staged at the Oxford Playhouse by the University Experimental Theatre Club. The play, which featured incidental music composed by John, had been banned in Ireland by the Bishop of Dublin and sixteen cuts in the text had been imposed by the Lord Chamberlain. Despite the cuts and the limitations of adaptation, McClelland remained, on the whole, faithful to the book; so faithful, reported *The Irish Times*, 'that some of the critics called it an "Under Milk Wood" version of "Ulysses". Certainly, because of its essentially episodic nature and its use of a Narrator, the play did have a distinct if superficial Dylan Thomas flavour; but it was much more dramatic.' The production 'was greeted rapturously by the large first-night audience, but moved the local and national Press critics only to cautious enthusiasm.' It was a pity that the play could not have been staged in Ireland and acted by a Dublin company, which would have done full justice to 'the marvellous Joycean language and [would have] felt more relaxed in settings as familiar as Davy Byrne's [pub] and Westland Row Station.'[25]

Meantime, things were happening again in the BBC: Roger Fiske wrote to

Michael Morrow, thanking him for the Claudin de Sermisy script and expressing an interest in the project, and by the end of December the Third Programme had decided to make a forty-five minute programme during the following year.[26] John was commissioned to write seven minutes of music for six viols, two piccolos, one lute and two percussion players for another play, *The Bow and the Beads* by the poet D.S. Savage, and an request came from Donald McWhinnie for ten minutes of music for a reading from Samuel's novel *The Unnamable.*[27]

The recording of the music and speech for *The Unnamable* took place on 17 January: once again, Patrick Magee read the selection of passages and John's music was conducted by Bernard Keeffe.[28] According to a memo sent by David McWhinnie, John 'attended the actual rehearsal and recording of the music and gave very helpful advice. He was also present for a whole day of the programme rehearsal and again I found his advice invaluable.' This advice earned John an extra eight guineas.[29] The reading was preceded by a talk by Anthony Cronin, who, unlike many reviewers of Samuel Beckett's work, saw him as a simple man whose 'expressions have been made unnecessarily esoteric by people who have mis-read his intense Irishness.'[30] (The reading itself preceded the publication of Samuel's book in London by John Calder.)[31] Although Samuel considered the broadcast to be excellent, he did complain of mistakes in the rhythm and inter-pretation, and found that John's music had not always been in the correct place.[32]

The programme followed the same pattern as the reading from *Molloy*, in which John's music was purposely aggressive, though in this production his music was more tortured, in keeping with the feeling of hopelessness evoked by the text. The introduction, which consisted of short, sharp high-pitched chords played on the strings, with a solo played high on a cello, was spooky: in general the music was discordant, with long held notes, harmonics and deliber-ately rough playing from the ensemble. Very forceful and aggressive cello solos, which were intentionally played out of tune, featured at certain points.[33] Writing later to Aidan Higgins, Samuel said that John 'did some good screeches for the <u>Unnamable</u> reading.'[34] Higgins, however, did not care much for this programme; later in the year he wrote to Arland Ussher:

> Back to Beckett. What's your opinion of the Unmentionable? It gave me nothing, or is this South Africa speaking through me? I missed the earth and the sky, not to mention men and women, between them — I mean men and women between earth and sky. All one got was a noise like indigestion with no stomach to account for it, no mind to think of it, no nothing to remember it-- or words to that effect. MALONE is still the best.'[35]

On 15 March 1959 John was back in Dublin, playing the continuo for Bach's *Saint Matthew Passion*, but this time on a real harpsichord. Either John or Victor Leeson, the conductor of the St James's Gate Musical Society had remembered that Cathal Gannon had made an instrument in the early fifties. John tried it out at Cathal's home, found it quite satisfactory, and the harpsichord was borrowed for the occasion.[36] Many years later, John remembered the instrument as being 'sturdily made'. It had 'a lively sound, and was a pleasure to play. The performance was thoroughly and musically prepared in a general atmosphere of wholehearted dedication, as was anything that Victor [Leeson] tackled. He was, until his death, a much valued friend.'[37] The concert was hailed as a great success, despite the small audience.[38] The performance was in two parts: the first in the afternoon, when Roy Hickman sang the part of Christus, and the second in the evening, when a twenty-nine-year-old William Young sang the same part. His wife Alison remembers that Hickman had not realized that he was needed in the evening and had booked an early flight home. Victor Leeson therefore approached William, a semi-professional bass baritone who worked in an insurance company, and asked him if he could sing in the second half.[39] John would have occasion to work with him again some thirteen years later.

Unfortunately, the *Claudin de Sermisy and the Paris Chanson* programme turned out to be something of a disaster.[40] Listening to a recording of it now, the programme comes across as extremely academic, lifeless and dull, though it must be remembered that this was the style of broadcasting favoured in the late 1950s on the Third Programme. What one hears is Michael Morrow giving a very learned talk, lasting forty minutes, on the various arrangements of Claudin de Sermisy's *chansons*, with musical illustrations played in a rather subdued manner. As the programme progresses, he becomes fatigued (probably because of his ill health) and begins to hesitate and trip over his words. Listeners at the time would have been puzzled by a gap in the middle of the programme.[41] This was due, Roger Fiske later explained to Michael, to a change of shift in the room where the tapes were being played, 'and the new chap got the impression that the last reel was on the machine. The result was that when it ended there was no second machine set up with the second reel on it, and it took them a minute or two to find this.'[42] This was hardly a good start for the group that would soon emerge as Musica Reservata.

In early May John was commissioned to write eight minutes of music for *The Voice of Shem*: passages from *Finnegans Wake* by James Joyce, freely adapted by Mary Manning. The cast included Patrick Magee and Cyril Cusack.[43] The programme was broadcast on the Third Programme in the evening of 27 May, the same day that another programme involving John went out in the morning, on the Home Service. This was a programme of music by Telemann and John himself, played by John on harpsichord and John Sothcott on descant and treble recorder. The music that John had composed (specially for John Sothcott), was his *Wedding March* for descant recorder and harpsichord.[44]

Shortly afterwards Aidan Higgins wrote to Arland Ussher: 'We get odd cuttings showing the progress made by the talented cousin John. Music for the Finnegans Wake extract. And Third Programme emission from his side-kick Morrow. Married Morrow. Despite your snarls.'[45] The 'Third Programme emission' probably refers to the recent *Claudin de Sermisy* programme; 'Despite your snarls' refers to Ussher's objection to Michael marrying his girlfriend Hedy Pelc. She came from an Austrian Jewish family that had moved to England in 1938. Hedy lived in Hampstead, and she and Michael had met through a mutual friend who mended guitars. After they were married, they shared the flat with John and Vera in Frognal.[46] It appears that on Michael's wedding night, John got up out of bed and went to the kitchen for a drink. Michael appeared and the two men sat down to discuss some interesting musical topic for several hours, oblivious of their respective partners.[47] Hedy said that she could well believe this story, which John related to a friend. Sharing the flat with John and Vera was not successful and although Hedy always liked John and found him an impressive figure, she only 'sort of got on with him'. She thought that Vera was very talented and beautiful, but never 'clicked' with her or knew what 'she was on about'. After they moved out of John and Vera's flat, they lived in 26 Belsize Square for a while and then moved to 9 Aberdare Gardens, Hampstead, where they remained for many years.[48]

In November John was commissioned to write some incidental music for Alfred Jarry's play *Ubu Roi*, translated by Barbara Wright. The script editor was Barbara Bray, a young widow with two daughters, who was a former companion of Donald McWhinnie, and who at this time had started an affair with Samuel Beckett. The play would be broadcast in February of the following year.[49] According to a review in *The Times*, John 'provided music of unusual but appropriately grotesque ugliness'.[50] Hot on the heels of this, another commission materialized at the beginning of December: original incidental music and settings of ballads for singers and an orchestra for *Come All You Gallant Poachers*, a ballad opera by H.A.L. Craig and Dominic Behan (brother of Brendan Behan). John protested at the fee of sixty guineas, saying that it seemed 'considerably too low'. He demanded ninety guineas but accepted eighty.[51] The opera, which was about convicts punished by transportation to Australia, was broadcast on the Third Programme at the beginning of the following year.[52]

An event that had been scheduled for the end of January – although a modest enough affair – was to be a turning point for John and Michael Morrow and a milestone in the performance of early music: the first formal public concert given by their new group, Musica Reservata.

Sixteen
1960

The denizens of Hampstead who thought they might doze through an evening of pleasant medieval music in the elegant and peaceful surroundings of Fenton House on 30 January 1960 were in for a bit of a surprise, especially when they discovered that the members of the new group, Musica Reservata, included Francis Baines on hurdy-gurdy and bagpipes, and Jeremy Montagu on percussion. The other members were Grayston Burgess, counter-tenor, Eric Halfpenny, early cross flute, John Sothcott, recorder, June Baines, tenor viol, John on tenor viol and regal (a small, portable reed organ), and Michael Morrow, lute.[1]

Because this was a local event and therefore not reviewed in the national press, we have no contemporary account of how the concert was received. However, based on later recordings of the pieces that were performed that evening, we can guess that the audience must have been taken unawares by the opening four-teenth-century dance music, an anonymous *Saltarello*, in which Jeremy Montagu would have walloped a drum and one of the tenor viol players would have played a vigorous melody in a loud, rough manner. The next three items by Guillaume Dufay for voice and two instruments — *Bon jour, bon mois* ('Good day, good month'), a *rondeau* in praise of living a good life, *Vostre bruit* ('Your fame') and *Vergine bella* ('Beautiful Virgin') — were more gentle and may have put some of the listeners to sleep. If so, they were rudely awoken by the fourteenth-century anonymous *Estampie* dance music that followed: more deafening drumming and a shrill, fast melody played on a descant recorder by John Sothcott. The rest of the first half consisted of pieces by John Dunstable, Dufay, Johannes Ockeghem and Gilles Binchois — his *Files a marier* ('Maids still to wed'), a light-hearted warning to young girls about the troubles that attend married life.

The second half included a composition by the blind Italian composer Francesco Landini, *Gram piant' agli occhi* ('Tears pour from my eyes'), a sad and gentle *ballata*, said to be the finest composition of the age. Musica Reservata would perform this piece many times during the coming years. The recital ended on a grim note: *Ad mortem festinamus* ('We hasten towards death'), a dance by an anonymous Spanish composer of the fourteenth century. One has the feeling that John or Michael might have chosen this as the final item with a certain sense of morbid glee.[2]

Although John did not conduct the group that evening, as he would do later, he would doubtless have succeeded in infusing into the music the raw energy and earthiness for which he became famous. The harsh quality of sound, which would become such a distinguishing feature of Musica Reservata's performances, fits in perfectly with John's penchant for composing rough, discordant *avant-garde* music for the Third Programme's experimental dramas. Michael Morrow's aim, like John, was intonation and articulation. He also wanted a series of sounds characteristic of each period and country. If it all sounded the same, he declared, then one had lost the battle. According to him, the sounds sprang from two things: the instruments (although it was impossible to know how they sounded in a number of cases) and, what became increasingly important to him, the language of the country at the particular time when the music was composed.[3]

The group, as we have discovered, did not suddenly appear on that evening in January 1960 – it had been slowly evolving over the previous few years. The first concert by the group that Michael could remember was a performance for The Fellowship of the White Boar, later renamed The Richard III Society. Brian Galpin of the Galpin Society had asked Michael and his group to play some music for them after the chairman's speech. However, the audience had paid no attention as they were too busy eating and drinking.[4] Michael had refused an invitation from the BBC for a broadcast, preferring to wait until they got the sound right.[5]

Much has been written about the disputed meaning of the term *musica reservata*. The *New Grove Dictionary of Music and Musicians* explains that Michael gave his group this name because he considered it to be most unlikely that any performance of early music, no matter how carefully it was researched, could be a true reproduction of the original sounds.[6] According to Michael, the name sounded suitably pompous and summed up the problems encountered when performing early music.[7]

The instruments that Musica Reservata used at first were not entirely appropriate; for example, they had to make do with Baroque-style recorders before reproductions of earlier types became available; the instruments used during the middle ages and Renaissance were louder and stronger than their Baroque equivalents. In this first concert in January, Jeremy Montagu played on jazz tom-toms, a modern tambourine and a triangle.[8]

The astringent sound world of Musica Reservata was, and still is, an acquired taste. However, the audience was appreciative enough to encourage them to play in public again and develop the group. During the early years, their perfor-mances were not perfect; there would have been a certain amount of strug-gling with unfamiliar instruments, and it would be a while before the singers mastered the art of singing at full belt with tightened throats (the 'Reservata clamp'), using the precise intonation that Michael demanded. He was lucky to find performers who were prepared to sing and play music in the manner that he had requested and to take suggestions and carry them out very seriously.

It was at around this period when a fellow Irishman, Seán O'Leary, met Michael Morrow and, through him, John Beckett. (The reader may remember that Seán had heard one of John's John Dowland programmes on Radio Éireann when he was in Galway in 1953, a time when very little classical music was to be heard in that part of the country.)

Seán was born near Castleisland, County Kerry in 1932. He studied at Galway University, where his subjects were Greek, Latin, Irish, science and mathematics. He was a brilliant mathematician and obtained a degree in the subject.

He moved to England in 1955, where he worked at computer software, then in its infancy. When he got a job at teaching mathematics at Kynaston Technical School in St John's Wood near Hampstead, he moved to Greencroft Gardens, the road behind Michael Morrow's house – the two back gardens backed on to each other. Although they lived in such close proximity, Seán did not actually meet Michael until he was introduced to him by the wife of Peter Walsh, one of his colleagues at the school. Peter's wife was Beverlie Hooberman – the very same Bev who had been Desmond MacNamara's first wife. She soon was to become Peter's ex-wife, as they were separating when Seán and Michael met.

Seán found Michael a special and quite an extraordinary person; he was scholarly despite his lack of a formal education. Although he only performed moderately well on the lute, there were very few people at the time who knew as much about the instrument as he did. Michael, like the house in which he lived, was very disorganized. He was constantly busy researching music and telephoning people at odd hours for information. He once asked Seán to deci-pher some medieval Italian, in dialect, which Seán knew nothing about. Seán met all sorts of people in his home and although Michael was gregarious and sociable, he was a little uneasy in company. When Seán met him first, he did not drink at all, though later he began to drink moderately. He was a heavy smoker by this time and some time afterwards he developed a liking for snuff.

Michael's haemophilia upset things constantly – it was not unusual for him to start bleeding for no particular reason and to be rushed off to hospital (usually St Thomas' Hospital) for a blood transfusion – though later, when a technique of isolating the element that he required was developed, all that was needed was an injection. He had also begun to suffer from arthritis, for which he should have been taking aspirin; however, because of the haemophilia, he was unable to do so. He was in pain for most of the time and only played in Musica Reservata when he was well enough.

Seán thinks that he must have met John in Michael's house, probably at a rehearsal. He also believes that John was teaching music or coaching at evening classes and conducting at music courses at the time. At this early stage, John looked up to Michael for inspiration and instruction; Michael did the research on the repertoire, while John increasingly became concerned with developing the performances and Musica Reservata's style of playing. Michael's enthusiasm for folk music from different parts of the world, often inspired by the pioneering work of A.L. Lloyd, (a key figure in the revival of folk music during the 1950s and sixties), rubbed off on John. John and Michael had many discussions, often heated, about music and how to perform it. Seán noted that although both men were quite different as regards personality, they got on well together and both had an influence on each other. This would change over the coming years, owing to their different ways of working, different approaches and different backgrounds. One big difference between the two men was that John was very punctual, whereas Michael rarely had his work completed on time. This would later lead to a great deal of friction and frustration.

As Seán became better acquainted with John, he realized that he had an enormous number of friends of various kinds. Seán felt that he was a terrific teacher: he never studied music formally, but thanks to John and Michael, he learned to appreciate and listen to it. There was no condescension and John was not patronizing. What Seán liked enormously was that 'he'd get it straight, but he'd get it straight in the right form and the right terms'. John was equally appreciative of what Seán had to offer and learned much from him.

Naturally, Seán met Vera, whom he regarded as a talented painter. He was conscious of the age difference, which was perhaps not so significant at this point in John's life (he was now in his thirties), but became more so a decade or more later, though she was always a very energetic and vital person. He noted that Vera was very supportive of John and although she had a feeling for music but did not share John's intense love of it, she did respond well to some of it. Seán was one of the many people who witnessed Vera's explosive manner and her frequent rows with John and others. Often she and John were not on speaking terms. Seán remembers how Hedy, Michael's wife (for whom John did not much care) always wanted to run away when Vera was around.[9]

Despite the eccentricities of both Michael and John, Seán became an inseparable friend of them both and would remain a very close companion of John's for the rest of his life.

Seventeen
1960–61

Aconcert given by some of the members of Musica Reservata (Grayston Burgess, John Sothcott, Daphne Webb on cello, Theo Wyatt on recorder and John at the harpsichord) took place at Hampstead Parish Church on 23 April, 'by kind permission of the Vicar'. Theo can remember the concert, which included music by Telemann, Bach, Jean Baptiste l'Oeillet (Loeillet as we now spell the name), 'Monteverde' (as John spelt Monteverdi then), Sweelinck and Purcell.[1] A more ambitious concert of medieval music, performed by the entire group, took place at 17 Holly Mount, Hampstead (the converted church owned by Heinz and Ruth Liebrecht), on 26 May. In addition to the musicians used in January were John Whitworth, counter-tenor, Alan Lumsden, sackbut (an early form of the trombone), Joan Rimmer, psaltery (a type of zither), and Guy Oldham on bowed monochord and cymbala (a set of bells). As in January, John just played the treble viol.[2]

Admission to this concert was by invitation and one of the people John had asked was the eminent British musicologist Thurston Dart. Thurston regretted that he could not come and wrote, 'Good luck to you all. Make the music sound *robust* now and then – so often one hears it as though everyone were wearing kidgloves.'[3]

Seán O'Leary remembers the Liebrechts, who hosted the concert. Michael Morrow was very fond of them and they were sympathetic towards him and the group. Heinz was a successful businessman and Ruth was very much a mother figure to Michael.[4]

John began to teach harpsichord at evening extramural classes in Belmont Primary School, which was attached to Chiswick Polytechnic (closed in 1982

and now replaced by the Arts Educational School).[5] Belmont School was situated near Turnham Green and close to the old Chiswick Empire, a well-known
theatre and music hall that had closed during the previous year. The evening
classes were run by Brian Richardson, whose innovative idea was to use good
performers as teachers. Francis Baines taught there, Peter Crozier was the piano
teacher and David Fletcher led the recorder classes.

John taught on a harpsichord made by Robert Goble and Son, which Goble
senior, and then his son Andrea, tuned and maintained. One of John's students
was a vivacious young redhead named Christina Gates (now Burstin), who
admits to having become very fond of him. As well as giving his students harpsichord lessons, John encouraged them to sing; Valerie Baulard, for example,
was persuaded to sing songs by Fauré. Christina remembers how enthusiastic
John was, and how compassionate he was towards the odder and more eccentric students. She noted that 'there was no snobbery'. He was also very patient,
though he gave up trying to teach Christina musical theory, which she could not
master. Most of his students were women. It appears that many of the women's
husbands became irate when their wives spoke so fondly about John.

Christina remembers how J.B., as she always called him, wrote out realizations of *basso continuo* for her to play. He liked performing cantatas by Telemann
and always chose a singer with a 'white' voice – such as Christina – to sing them,
as he did not approve of 'wobbly operatic singers' for music like this. John and
Christina went to Fenton House together to perform on the period instruments.
As the house was far more peaceful than the school, he took the opportunity to
get Christina to sing to his accompaniment; sometimes he asked her to sing the
same song a dozen or so times. John also helped Christina by providing accompaniments when she went to work in a Roman Catholic school afterwards as a
piano teacher. Vera, who knew about Christina, rebuked John by saying, 'Why
did you choose a little Catholic?'

A rumour at the time suggested that John and Christina were engaged to be
married, but this was untrue. John liked Christina's voice and both got on very
well together.[6] However, the fact that Vera regarded Christina as a rival is vividly
illustrated by the following story told by the musician, arranger and editor
Clifford Bartlett, who knew John well enough to write an obituary of him. After
one of the Chiswick viol classes, Clifford, John and Christina adjourned to a
nearby pub and sat down to enjoy a drink together. Vera arrived, ordered a glass
of beer and promptly poured it over Christina's head. As Clifford remarked, this
could have been charitably interpreted as being an accident, but the replenish-
ment, which he bought for her, and which once again was poured over Christina,
certainly was not.[7]

An example of John Beckett's realization of Henry Purcell's basso continuo for his song Love's Pow'r in my Heart, *Z. 395, written by John. (Author's collection.)*

Christina remembers the shock she received when the first glass was poured over her, and also the annoyance of having a new jumper ruined; perhaps she was too upset to remember being doused by the second glass.[8] Both Seán O'Leary and Michael Morrow's sister Brigid had noticed John's fondness for the ladies and heard about affairs that must have infuriated Vera.[9]

Christina remembers an occasion when she and John turned up at a concert in central London, expecting to hear music by Mozart, only to discover that the orchestra was about to play music by a composer that John disliked – perhaps Alban Berg. He stormed out, Christina managed to get her money refunded, and they walked all the way home to Chiswick, stopping at various pubs, where John drank pints of Guinness, followed by triple whiskeys.[10]

David Fletcher, who was an amateur musician and was enthusiastic about recorders, first met John and Michael at a party. The two men had been on holidays and brought back some instruments from 'middle Europe', which David thought was very exciting. He then met John at the evening classes at Chiswick. John formed a consort of viols there, which consisted of 'fairly old ladies' who wore 'William Morris-patterned' clothes. David remembers a concert in which his recorder group played with the viol consort – they were extremely good. He also remembers John's 'amazing' realizations of Purcell's music.[11]

Another Musica Reservata concert of medieval music was given at the beginning of November, this time in the Horniman Museum at Forest Hill, near Greenwich. The choice of this venue, a museum of natural history, cultural arte-facts and musical instruments, was made by the group's percussionist Jeremy Montagu, who worked as curator of the musical instruments there in 1960. By now, Jeremy had made his own reproductions of medieval percussion instru-ments and played them publicly for the first time in this concert. Jeremy, who lived not far away, brought his wife and young daughter, then about four years of age, to the concert. Every time the little girl cried, 'Mummy, haven't they finished yet?' Michael or John cut a couple of items from the programme.[12]

The music played that evening included an exotic-sounding song called *Kalenda maya* ('Calends of May') composed by the Provençal troubadour Raimbaut de Vaqueiras (fl. 1180–1207), which became a favourite of the group. It would be played often in their concerts and was sung in a suitably raucous manner.[13]

At around this time, Michael Morrow began working for the Encyclopaedia Britannica as music editor, a post that he held until the end of the sixties.

According to Aidan Higgins, Michael had 'a good job with E. Brittanica [*sic*] which he can perform at home. Jill met Mrs M. in the bus and she described his salary as fat.'[14] Michael commissioned A.L. Lloyd to write an article for the encyclopaedia about folk music. Michael, John and Seán O'Leary became friendly with Lloyd and once went to his home with a Ferguson tape recorder, where they spent a 'fantastic evening recording stuff'. Seán regarded Lloyd as 'an extraordinary chap'; he had a room full of tapes of folk music that he had recorded and collected from all over the world, and which he knew 'inside out'. During the 1960s he made a series of half-hour radio programmes about folk music for the BBC.[15]

1961 began with a BBC memorandum sent, by Michael Bakewell, Script Editor, Drama (Sound) to Martin Esslin, Assistant Head of Drama (Sound), explaining that he and his colleagues wanted to produce another programme involving both John and Samuel Beckett. Just a few days earlier, Samuel had written to John about his 'words music idea', and informed him that he could get them commissioned if he wished.[16] This proposal would eventually become Samuel's radio play, *Words and Music*.

Early in the morning on 4 March John was in Ireland, driving home from Cork in a Mini Minor, having played Haydn string quartets with some friends. His friends had invited him to stay overnight but he was anxious to return home as he was using his mother's car. At 4 am he fell asleep at the wheel and hit a wall in Little Bray, crashed the car and was badly injured. It was fortunate (and somewhat ironic) that he had crashed into the wall of a local policeman's house: the policeman telephoned for an ambulance to bring John to nearby St Columcille's Hospital in Loughlinstown. If this had not happened he might have lain in the car for hours and bled to death. Both of John's arms had been broken, and his hip and ankle were badly damaged.[17]

Aidan Higgins reported the accident to his friend Arland Ussher:

John Beckett was in a car-smash on Sunday morning about four am, fell asleep after playing quartets all night, woke up as he was going into the wall, braced his arms and one leg on the brake (the worst thing he could have done), smashed into the wall at about 50 mph, breaking both arms and one leg. Is suspended from pulleys in St Columcille's Hospital on the Shankill Road. They are a most unfortunate family. He will need all his courage to come out of this, and even then will be crippled for life. He was about to start work on the music of a new radioplay with Sam, who is finishing the text now. It is a most bloody unfortunate accident — he will require 3 operations, then the leg will be broken again, reset, operated on again.[18]

So serious was the case that the doctor in charge of John, who was about to go on holidays, cancelled his leave in order to attend to him.[19]

Everyone who knew John, including members of the Beckett family, were shocked to hear this terrible news, and it was feared that he would never be able to play a keyboard instrument again.[20] Even Samuel was prepared to cancel his forthcoming wedding to Suzanne in Folkestone in order to come to Ireland and be with John, Peggy and Ann. He telephoned Peggy, who assured him that nothing could be gained by his coming to Dublin; she and Ann persuaded him to stay in England.

Because of the seriousness of his injuries, John was hospitalized for five months.[21] Michael Morrow's sister Brigid, newly married to David Ferguson, came to visit him with her husband. She described him as looking 'like a puppet' because of the way he was strung up in the bed.[22] Werner Schürmann rigged up a device on which a book could be placed at the correct height and angle.[23]

During his time in hospital, he read many books, including the works of Thomas Mann. John's friend Seán O'Leary was surprised to discover this as John generally disliked novels.[24] Ann wrote to Samuel regularly to keep him informed of John's progress. At the beginning of April, Samuel wrote to Barbara Bray, 'He is much more comfortable but has to face another operation this week, X-ray having shown that union is not satisfactory and will not give perfect movement. Appears he has taken it very well.' Samuel told Barney Rosset that John was 'all bust up to hell, arms and legs, but life not in danger.'[25] Towards the end of the month, Samuel reported to Barbara that John was to have had an arm pinned some days previously, but that, as yet, there was no news. This was to reset his arm. He told Donald and Sheila Page that other operations would be necessary: 'pinning, resetting and such horrors. He seems to be taking it all very calmly.'[26]

John told his friend Theo Wyatt that his greatest pleasure during this period of inactivity was to lie in bed with a volume of Haydn string quartet scores and to listen to them in his head, with all the repeats.[27] Later, my father loaned him a clavichord, which was placed on a table (or Werner's contraption), for him to practise without disturbing the other patients.[28] Unsurprisingly, he gave the nurses a hard time and frequently used the four-letter word although the matron was able to handle him; she tried to persuade him to say 'fish hooks' or 'sugar' instead of the usual expletives.[29]

In the meantime other Musica Reservata concerts took place in London, some of their programmes bearing John's name as, presumably, they had been printed before the car accident. A 'Concert of music by Musica Reservata' was hosted by the Hampstead Music Club at Fenton House on 27 April, in which Daphne Webb filled in for John playing a rebec.[30] Michael Morrow had seen her crossing the road carrying a cello at her home in Belsize Square and asked her if she could play in the concert.[31]

Another Musica Reservata concert was given in the Chelsea School of Art in May.[32] By this time, John had not recovered as well as had been hoped; an operation to pin the bones in one of his arms had failed and he was still hospitalized. Samuel planned to visit him during the month but in fact did not.[33] (Aidan Higgins reported that 'the operation on John B's arms was not successful. Sam was to come in early June but says he can't face it.'[34]) Instead, he decided, after being prompted by Michael Bakewell of the BBC, to involve John in the composition of some music for the new radio play (*Words and Music*), which might have the effect of giving him something to do and cheering him up.[35] At the end of July P.H. Newby, Controller of the Third Programme, wrote to John, wishing him a speedy recovery: 'I just wanted you to know you were in our minds, that we were looking forward to hearing you were active once more, and that, when you next come to London, I should very much like to meet you.'[36] John's courteous reply of 1 August reveals that Samuel had written to John concerning the proposed radio play earlier in the year.[37]

Martin Esslin, the BBC drama producer, wrote to John in the middle of August, wondering when they might receive his music. 'We don't want to hurry you unduly,' he wrote. 'On the other hand we are so eager and anxious to broadcast this work that we would, of course, be glad to have it as soon as it is at all possible.'[38] Samuel's radio play, which he finally completed in November and sent to John in December, was innovative in that it treated music as an autonomous character rather than an accompaniment or mood setter. When John received the text of the play, his comment to Michael Bakewell was, 'Most most beautiful. Most moving'.[39]

In the play, 'Words' (or Joe as the character is called) and 'Music' (Bob) are two servants of Croak, an old man who asks them for contributions on the themes of love and age. It has been stated that this work was a collaboration between Samuel and John but this is incorrect: John stated very clearly that Samuel sent him the script and that he wrote the music independently.[40] Although John had, by now, plenty of experience at composing incidental music for the BBC Third Programme's dramas, he realized that this work for Samuel, whom he regarded as being a great writer, was a serious matter and that he would have to write music that was worthy of the play, though he felt it was 'perfectly impossible to do'. 'In fact, it was distressing,' John told James Knowlson:

> I did it. I wrote something as I would have done for any other thing but I realized after that, that this must not go on, that it's quite out of the question. [It] had to stop because I didn't believe in my music as significant creative music. And

I don't and I haven't ever since, and there's no great mystery about it at all. It seems to me a perfectly intelligible and indeed honourable decision.

Although Samuel found his work remarkable, John declared that Samuel did not know what he was talking about and that *he* knew what he was talking about, as he knew perfectly well what was involved in writing music. He knew if it could be done or not and did not regard this as being a 'neurotic' view. In fact, he never heard any music that he considered good enough for Samuel's plays, no matter who composed it. He even criticized Samuel for giving him his loyalty, which he felt he should not have done.[41] His sister Ann was aware that John always ran down his own music and that he could not possibly do justice to Samuel's work. She was inclined to agree with him on the latter point, realizing that nobody could as it was on a 'different plane'.[42]

According to John Calder, the publisher of Samuel's novels and an acquaintance of John's since the 1950s, John was quite philosophical about his accident and being in hospital for so long.[43] He was finally discharged in October in order to convalesce. Vera proposed that he stay with her in the south of Dublin, in a little house named Dolphin Cottage, situated in picturesque Coliemore Harbour and overlooking Dalkey Island. He happily agreed, but his mother objected strongly as they were still unmarried and as she wanted to look after John herself. Brigid Ferguson remembers how insistent and domineering Peggy could be.[44] As she put so much pressure on John to marry Vera and make an honest woman of her,[45] they agreed to marry so that she would have no claim over him at all.[46] Accordingly, the wedding banns were published in *The Irish Times* on 13 and 21 October:

> To: R. V. H. DOWNEY, LL.B., Registrar of Marriages for the District of Dublin. I, JOHN BECKETT, of Loughlinstown Hospital, Dublin, give Notice of my Intended Marriage to VERA SLOCOMBE, of 5 Haigh Terrace, Dun Laoire. Dated this 10th day of October, 1961.[47]

Notification of the low-key ceremony, also in *The Irish Times*, was short and to the point:

> Mr. J.S. Beckett and Miss V. Slocombe
> The marriage arranged between John Beckett, younger son of the late Dr. G.P.G. Beckett, and Mrs. M.R. Beckett, of Greystones, Co. Wicklow, and Vera Slocombe, only daughter of Mrs. Evelyn Nielson of London, took place in Dublin on Monday 23rd October.[48]

Samuel Beckett was very pleased to learn of the 'good news'.[49] One positive advantage of being married was John's entitlement to money for his hospital bills, which he could claim from the national health service.[50]

John wrote to Michael Bakewell from Dolphin Cottage at the end of November:

> *Just a note to say that I hope this finds you in the pink (if not in the red) as it leaves*
> *me. In other words to tell you that I am out of hospital. My, to use the clinical term,*
> *multiple fractures, have in fact mended very much better than at first appeared*
> *possible. I am stumbling around, Malone-like, with one stick only, and hope to be*
> *able to discard even that in about a month's time. Another hope is that I shall be*
> *back in London by January or a pessimistick [sic] latest February. A whole year for*
> *ressurection [sic].*
>
> *Also, of course, to say that if the services of my muse are any use to you they are,*
> *thanks be to your man (as the natives say here) at your disposal once again...*[51]

When Aidan Higgins and his wife Jill came to Dublin at around this period, they visited John and Vera at Dolphin Cottage. They took their children along and had a wonderful evening listening to music by Mahler. Although she described Vera as 'a ball of fire – impossible', she knew her well and regarded her as a very good artist – so much so that she purchased some of her paintings.[52]

Harold Lester, who came to Dublin some time after John had been discharged from hospital, noticed that John had become gentler after his accident. He went with John to Greystones to meet Ann and Peggy, who had just had a hip operation. He was amused to see the three of them limping together – Ann with her prosthetic leg, her mother with her new hip joint and John unsteady on his legs – and compared the halting progress to a scene in one of Samuel's plays.[53]

During this period of recuperation in Dublin, John was given the opportunity to present four half-hour programmes called *Personal Choice* on Radio Éireann, which were broadcast in November and December.[54] The year ended with him playing harpsichord continuo with the Radio Éireann Symphony Orchestra under Tibor Paul at the Phoenix Hall on 22 December. The music critic for *The Irish Times*, Charles Acton, wrote:

> We started admirably with Corelli's Christmas concerto. It was a stylish and
> enjoyable performance and particularly notable for the superlative harpsichord
> continuo of John Beckett. His recovery from his accident is as welcome as his
> playing; if only Radio Eireann would retain him in Ireland as harpsichordist.'[55]

Eighteen
1962–63

Writing to Martin Esslin of the BBC on 8 February from Dolphin Cottage, John informed him that he had now 'completed a score for my cousin, Samuel Beckett's Radio Script, for which he tentatively suggests the title: Words and Music. I will be crossing back to London during the first week in March, to take up work and life there again.'[1] A little later, Samuel wrote from his cottage in Ussy to his friend Alan Schneider: 'John Beckett has done his music for *Words & Music* (BBC). No idea yet what he has done, but have full confidence.'[2]

During John's hospitalization and recuperation, John Sothcott had taught his recorder consort class at Belmont Primary School, Chiswick. Mark Windisch, a pupil who lived nearby, enjoyed the classes and found Sothcott a 'nice, gentle soul', but when John returned to London in March and took the class soon afterwards, Mark was immediately struck by his new teacher's electrifying personality. John was an inspirational teacher with very high standards. Those who could stand the pressure stayed and they formed a very competent group.[3]

In January David Thomson of Features, BBC, had notified his colleagues that John had 'at last written to say that he is returning to London and is fit to start work again. As he has been out of action so long I promised to remind as many people as possible of his availability for composing incidental music.'[4] By 22 May, when John was back in Frognal, he received a commission from producer Michael Bakewell to compose about nine minutes of music for a radio play by the British dramatist, poet and novelist Bernard Kops entitled *Home Sweet Honeycomb*, to be recorded in June for the Third Programme. Kops was a working-class Jewish man and his writings were predominantly about Jewishness, the isolation of the Jewish people and death. This play was about the execution of people who are not prepared to relinquish their individuality.

By 6 June John had completed the music, which lasted about four minutes longer than requested (the fee was adjusted accordingly). It was recorded at Farringdon Memorial Hall in London and was played by eleven musicians on two flutes (both doubling piccolo), two E flat clarinets, two trumpets, one bass tuba, percussion (three players), and one double bass. The *ad hoc* ensemble was conducted by John himself, and the play was broadcast in July.[5]

John's introductory music is scored for percussion and wind band, beginning with a march rhythm played on a drum. When the wind band enters, there is liberal use of the cymbals. The following musical interludes are played on xylophone and drum, again in march rhythm, and, later, on trumpet and xylophone.[6]

The dialogue and music for *Words and Music* were recorded in two sessions, the first on 5 July and the second on 10 September; interestingly, Samuel was not present during the recordings. The part of Words was spoken by Patrick Magee and Croak was played by Felix Felton. The play lasted almost twenty-eight minutes and the music, which totalled twelve minutes in all, was played by an *ad hoc* orchestra of twelve musicians, conducted by John. Martin Esslin later wrote, 'This is an extremely difficult operation, as the play (which is not 15' but 30' duration) is one of the most intricate merges of sound and music we have ever undertaken.'[7] Samuel wrote to Barbara Bray that Magee seemed pleased with *Words and Music* 'but has to re record the songs. John objecting that he [had] sung too well!'[8] Once the entire production had been recorded, John was pleased with the results.[9]

John used to visit his friend Theo Wyatt at home, where they and others played Haydn quartets and Beethoven's Opus 1 piano trios. Theo remembers how John played the viola like a viol, on his lap – the most comfortable way to play it after his accident. Theo considered John's piano playing to be 'brilliant'. What stood out in his memory, however, was the incredible speed at which he turned over the pages of music:

> There would be a lightning flash of a hand, a crack like a pistol shot and he would be on the next page. ... In the early sixties I had built a massive sand-filled corner enclosure with a powerful 12" speaker designed by Wharfdale and installed it in my music room. ... John had borrowed a 78 r.pm set of Mahler's *Symphony of a Thousand* recorded in Holland before the war and wanted to hear it on this equipment. We turned the sound up as loud as we thought was possible without inviting a visit from the police but still John was not satisfied He looked

as though he would have got inside the speaker if he could. He obviously was hoping to be overwhelmed by the sound as he might have been with a thousand musicians in the Concertgebouw. The work lasts around an hour and I spent the evening turning over records every four minutes.

John joined Theo's Oriel Consort for a concert at the Mary Ward Settlement, in Tavistock Place, London. The programme included the six-part *Passamezzo Pavan* by Peter Philips which they played, at John's insistence, at a speed that Theo would now regard as twice what the composer intended: 'He always knew exactly what he wanted and would accept nothing less. But his manner and his way of putting his demands had a most unusual, circumlocutory politeness which together with his precise diction made him sometimes seem like a character from Jane Austen or Trollope.'[10]

In September, John spent some time in Spain and France (where he missed seeing Samuel in Paris).[11] During the following month, when Samuel was in London rehearsing his play *Happy Days* at the Royal Court Theatre, he visited John and Vera in Hampstead. He found John limping more than he had been given to believe. John showed him his *Words and Music* score.[12] John and Ann then went to see the English premiere of *Happy Days*, starring Brenda Bruce, at the beginning of November, which John liked very much. He, Ann and Samuel lunched with John Calder and his wife. (Samuel often stayed with the Calders when he was in London).[13]

On 11 November *A Taste of Madeleine* by the Greek playwright Kay Cicellis, for which John had been commissioned to compose incidental music for piano in June, was broadcast on the Third Programme.[14] *Words and Music* was broadcast on the same station two days later. 'Beckett's new play,' enthused the producer Michael Bakewell in the *Radio Times*, 'written as a text for music for his cousin John Beckett, is a fresh exploration of the possibilities of radio.' He stated that the play's theme, a common one in Beckett's writing, was that of the master and the servant and the power of each over the other. Words and Music (Joe and Bob) are the servants of the tyrant Croak, who comes to their cell every night, demanding that they improvise on themes that he barks at them, such as 'love' and 'age'. This they do individually and, with some conflict of wills, together. When they falter, Croak thumps the floor with a massive club. 'Words and Music are Croak's "balms", his "comforts", but his pleasure in their art is masochistic: the themes on which he broods and which his servants painstakingly re-create bring him only anguish and suffering over memories of lost love, old age and a face whose features continually haunt him.'[15]

In keeping with the strangeness of the play, John's unsettling music sounds quite disembodied, as if it is being played from a loudspeaker – there is a deliberate lack of 'presence'. The short segments of dissonant music are played by a group of twelve musicians on strings, brass, vibraphone and percussion. When Words tries to sing with Music, we hear a tortured melody played on a cello, accompanied by the vibraphone. John did not take Samuel's directions too literally: for example, the opening direction for the orchestra to tune up is rendered as a discordant cluster of notes tunelessly played by the strings.[16] A short review of the play, which appeared in *The Times* on 17 November, was favourable. The writer, who stated that it was not difficult to be engaged by this new radio play, described it as a fantasy. 'Mr. Patrick Magee, as the inventive servant, and Mr. Felix Felton, as the downcast tyrant, gave macabre and eloquent performances. *Words and Music* offered the same suggestion of echoing distances and haunting depths as *Godot*,' the article concluded.[17]

Despite the fact that Samuel thought highly of John's music at the time, John himself became diffident about his score and decided to withdraw it soon after its French production (*Paroles et musique*) some ten years later. As a result of this, it was not possible to broadcast the play until 1987 when the American composer Morton Feldman wrote new music for it.[18]

On 26 November members of Musica Reservata were recorded in BBC Broadcasting House playing about seventeen minutes of music, chosen and arranged by John and Michael Morrow, for Jean Morris's play *The Heretic*, set in Sussex during the reign of Mary Tudor. The producer was Michael Bakewell. The programme was broadcast on the BBC Home Service in December. The music included a French Pavan played on the harpsichord by John.[19]

1963 began with three programmes for children on Radio Éireann, *Music Can Tell*, which John presented in January.[20] During the same month, John was commissioned to write incidental music for Michel de Ghelderode's play *Lord Halewyn*,[21] which was broadcast in January on the Third Programme and produced by H.B. Fortuin. A review printed in *The Times* praised the production and its atmospheric sound effects. 'Mr. John Beckett supplied a song of enchantment with little seductive magic in its melody, and numerous appropriate but markedly dissonant fanfares.'[22]

Shortly afterwards John was commissioned to write some more music, this time for John Bakewell's production of *Spring '71*,[23] a radio play, broadcast on the Third Programme in March. This was based on Arthur Adamov's stage play concerning the Paris Revolution of 1871. John received forty-five guineas for approximately nine minutes of music.[24]

Later in the month, Terence Tiller of the BBC had a long conversation with Michael Morrow about the fourteenth-century satirical poem by Gervais du Bus, *Le Roman de Fauvel*, which incorporated music such as motets by Philippe de Vitry. Terence wrote to a colleague, convinced that translating the verse excerpts, which he was willing to do, and transcribing the music, which Michael would undertake, would be 'a major project of the greatest interest and importance, and that a really memorable programme could emerge.' Little did he realize how difficult it would be to complete this project.[25]

That April in Dublin John met his friend Cathal Gannon, who had by now made his second harpsichord. This was based on an instrument discovered in Townley Hall, near Drogheda, County Louth, when Trinity College acquired the house and grounds some years previously. This original harpsichord, made in 1772 by Jacob Kirckman, was in such poor condition that it was later sent by Trinity College to Morley's of Lewisham, where it was restored, though not in a particularly sympathetic manner. John, who obviously had played Cathal's new instrument and was so taken by his skills and the fact that he had made a faithful copy of an historical instrument, decided on a course of action. He made an appointment to see his father's friend, David Owen Williams, who was now the Assistant Managing Director of the Guinness Brewery, where Cathal worked. He remembered waiting in a room near his office before being admitted. He put it to Williams that Cathal could be better employed making harpsichords, which could be sold or donated to interested institutions or individuals. As a result, the Guinness Brewery could become a patron of the arts. According to John, Mr Williams was 'very sympathetic' to the idea. Following more discussion of the matter at a high level, the brewery furnished Cathal with a large workshop in a quiet part of the complex, where he set about constructing a number of instruments during the following year. Thanks to John's foresight, Cathal became a well-known and much respected harpsichord builder and restorer of antique pianos.[26]

The original Kirckman harpsichord, which had arrived back in Dublin after its renovation, was inaugurated at a concert given in Trinity College in May. John played the harpsichord, John Sothcott the recorder, Daphne Webb the cello continuo and the soprano was Barbara Elsy. The audience was treated to two of Telemann's cantatas, his Sontata in D minor for recorder and continuo, Bach's Partita in B minor, BWV 831, *Greensleeves to a Ground* by an anonymous seventeenth-century composer, and John's *Three Pieces for Descant Recorder and Harpsichord*. Charles Acton, writing in *The Irish Times*, praised these pieces composed by John and continued:

> The climax of the evening was undoubtedly the Partita. I have never heard Bach [played] on the harpsichord with as complete authority, authenticity, musician-liness and sense of scale. We not only heard an aural treatise on how this great work should be played but it was a deep emotional and artistic experience. This, one felt, was how the Old Man himself would have played it, and made me hope that we may soon hear John Beckett giving a solo recital on this instrument.[27]

Patrick Cuming's brother Michael, who studied in Trinity College between 1959 and 1963 remembers attending this concert. John was a kind of 'absent figure' in Trinity College; everyone Michael met talked about him and was influenced by him. John, he soon discovered, did not suffer fools gladly and his views were very strong. He was aware of how much John loved the writings of James Joyce. Michael also met the harpsichordist John O'Sullivan in Davy Byrne's pub, and also David Lee. He went to David's lodgings, and was amused by his imitations of John Beckett.[28]

The first 'major' concert to be given by Musica Reservata took place in the Wigmore Hall, London on 26 June. It was a curious programme of medieval, Renaissance and contemporary music. The rather rigid formality required that John wear a suit, in which he was noticeably uncomfortable. He asked his friend and pupil Christina Gates how he looked. 'Like a penguin,' she replied.[29]

The group, comprising Jantina Noorman, mezzo-soprano, John Sothcott, recorder, Daphne Webb, tenor rebec, John Whitworth, counter-tenor, John Beckett, treble viol and Michael Morrow, lute, began the concert with a selection of medieval songs and dances, starting with Raimbault de Vaqueiras's lively *Kalenda maya* ('The calends of May'). The rest of part one consisted of contemporary music: the Elizabethan Singers, conductor Louis Halsey, sang pieces by Adrian Cruft (1921–87) and Bernard Naylor (1907–86), and then Malcolm Williamson gave the first performance of his Piano Sonata No. 4, specially commissioned for the concert.

The second part of the concert began with a selection of fourteenth-century French and Italian songs and dances, played by Musica Reservata. After Olivier Messiaen's *Neumes Rythmiques*, performed on the piano by Malcolm Williamson, the concert ended with some French *chansons* of the fifteenth and sixteenth centuries.[30]

Praise for this concert was cautious. David Cairns, the music critic, journalist and leading authority on the life of Berlioz, had this to say in *The Financial
Times*, after he had dealt with the contemporary music:

> Musica Reservata performed their music with vivacity and assurance. Par
> ticularly notable was a shrill but sweet and devilishly agile little recorder, played
> by John Sothcott. Jantina Noorman sang, and accompanied herself on the porta
> tive organ.[31]

Jantina Noorman, whose extraordinary voice soon became the most distinguishing feature of Musica Reservata, was the group's latest acquisition. She
was born in the the Netherlands; after the war the family moved to the USA,
where she attended the University of Illinois, and obtained a Bachelor and
Master degree in Music Education with a major in voice. Like John and Michael,
she was interested in folk music. She was also a member of the Collegium
Musicum, founded by George Hunter, a group dedicated to the performance
of medieval music.

Jantina had attended a concert given by Alfred Deller in St Louis, Missouri in
1959 and had met him at a reception afterwards. She gave him a copy of a record
of music by Machaut that she had recorded with the Collegium Musicum. She
made contact with Margaret Ritchie, a soprano who had worked with Alfred
Deller and Benjamin Britten, and handled the advertising for her first summer
school for singers in Oxford, which took place in 1960.

Jantina came to England to attend the course; the singers were accompanied
by David Barker, to whom she became engaged. John and Michael Morrow,
who had both heard Jantina's LP of music by Machaut, were at the course and,
having been introduced to her, invited her out to lunch. She declined their invitation to join Musica Reservata as she had to return to the States in order to
continue her work as a teacher at the University of Eastern Illinois.

Jantina married David Barker in 1961 and, as she had decided to live in
England permanently, wrote to John and Michael to say that she could join
Musica Reservata. She had a very good impression of the two men and found
them both easy and wonderful to work with. Michael was very explicit about
the way she should sing – something that John admired. Michael explained to
her that the voice should sound like the instruments used to accompany the
singer. When he accompanied her on the bagpipes, her voice needed to be loud.
However, when she sang with a crumhorn, he requested her to sing differently.
She therefore was endowed with an enormous palette of vocal colours, ranging
from her well-known 'barking' sound to a soft, lyrical tone. She was aware of the
controversy caused by the group's later performances and the criticism of her

voice sounding like that of a 'fishwife'. Once, when her husband David attended one of the concerts and Jantina began to sing, two women sitting behind him exclaimed, 'She sounds just like a man!'

Jantina was allowed to have her say – discussion and a flexibility of performance practice were encouraged. However, she did not pay too much attention to the English translations. Once, when she discovered what the words of a very bawdy song meant, she said that she couldn't possibly sing it, and so John Whitworth sang it instead.

Jantina occasionally had meals with Michael and when they were on tour there was a certain amount of socializing. Of John she had this to say, 'He was a tremendous influence in my musical career and a dear, dear friend. He was always so enthusiastic and encouraging and there was never a moment when we didn't appreciate, respect and love each other's performances.'[32]

Nineteen
1963–64

The first Stour Music festival in Kent was held during the summer of 1963. Founded during the previous year by John's acquaintance, counter-tenor Alfred Deller, it was devoted to early music though initially it included exhibitions of paintings. This first festival lasted just one day (Saturday 29 June) and consisted of a talk on early instruments by Francis Baines in Chilham Castle, a Bach concert in St Mary's Church, Chilham, and a concert of sixteenth- and seventeenth-century music given at Olantigh by the Deller Consort, the Jaye Consort of Viols and the Kalmar Chamber Orchestra.[1] John Sothcott, who regarded John as being an excellent player of the recorder, remembered them both performing in the Bach concert. Together they played recorders in the Brandenburg Concerto No. 4, Cantata 106 (*Actus Tragicus*) and the *Magnificat* in D major, BWV 243.[2]

By now, Desmond MacNamara and his wife Skylla were living in Woodchurch Road, Hampstead, not far from where John and Michael lived. Seán O'Leary remembers an occasion when he and John took Desmond and Skylla out to lunch, a meal that was accompanied by generous helpings of drink. During the meal, John got into a heated argument with Mac and made an authoritative statement about Wagner's music. He then tried to remember J.M. Synge's last poem and said to Seán: 'I can't remember this f—ing poem – can you recite it?' When Seán said that he could not, John then turned to Mac and, on discovering that he was not acquainted with the poem, exclaimed, 'Jesus Christ! Holy God! How come you don't have a copy of it?' Seán, who owned a book of poetry by Synge, was urged to telephone his wife Odile in order to get the poem for John. Seán told her where the book was; she fetched it, read the poem over the phone and Seán wrote it down.[3]

>I read about the Blaskets and Dunquin,
>The Wicklow towns and fair days I've been in,
>I read of Galway, Mayo, Aranmore,
>And men with kelp along a wintry shore.
>Then I remembered that that 'I' was I,
>And I'd a filthy job – to waste and die.[4]

Back in June, John had been commissioned by Michael Bakewell to write music for another radio play by Bernard Kops, this time *The Lemmings*.[5] The music, scored for one flute, one piccolo, two vibraphones, one violin, one viola, one double bass and percussion, which lasted about fifteen minutes before editing and was conducted by John, was recorded at the Maida Vale studios in July. The production was recorded in August and broadcast on the Third Programme.[6]

This disturbing 'new play for radio', a haunting allegory of conformity and mass destruction, a theme commonly encountered in Kops's writings, is about the drowning of people, like lemmings, in the sea. As in *Home Sweet Honeycomb*, an anonymous male voice addresses a crowd, over a loudspeaker, though this time on a beach. The people do as they are bid and enter the water in an organized manner. A working-class family, then a rich family arrive late and, although they decide to make their own plans, they too end up walking into the sea.

John's opening music, scored for flute and vibraphone, is chilling and very atmospheric. When the music finishes, we hear outdoor seaside effects, then two popular songs, 'I do like to be beside the seaside' and 'There is a happy land far, far away'. After this comes an announcement over the loudspeaker: 'Mass immersion will take place at eleven o'clock precisely.' Music on two flutes, a vibraphone and drum is played at the conclusion of this section, and the strings are heard further into the play. The music adds an unearthly, spooky effect to the strange story as it unfolds.[7]

During the summer John was in Dublin, where he was recorded playing music by Bach on Cathal Gannon's first harpsichord at his home in Rialto. A friend of Cathal's, Arthur Agnew, who had bought himself a tape recorder, taped John and a record was produced. Unfortunately Cathal accidentally damaged his copy of the record and subsequently threw it away, then Arthur, at a later period, mislaid the tape. John had only a vague memory of this in 1998 but did remember that he and Werner Schürmann had made recordings of Mahler songs in a studio over Frederick May's music shop in Saint Stephen's Green. Werner sent a copy of this record to his mother in Germany.[8]

On 16 August John was commissioned to write incidental music for *Fando and Lis*,[9] an 'absurdist' play by Fernando Arrabal, who was born in 1932 in Spain and later moved to France, where he wrote in French. When John had finished writing the music in early September, the producer John Tydeman wrote to thank John and said that 'The music fitted in absolutely splendidly with the slightly strange action.'[10] The play was broadcast on the Third Programme in October and repeated in the following month.[11]

In September, John was recorded playing Bach's Partita No. 4 in D major for harpsichord. This was broadcast on the BBC Home Service at 9.20 am on 2 October.[12] Seán O'Leary remembers the huge amount of time and effort that John devoted to the practising of this Partita and others that were recorded.[13] The music critic of *The Irish Times*, Charles Acton, wrote to John from Dublin to express his congratulations:

> *Dear John,*
>
> *May we now thank you for Wednesday's broadcast? Even at that hour of the morning it was a memorable experience. If I may say so, it is so exciting to hear a harpsichord performance with such a complete insight into Bach's intentions and phrasing, such an ideal use of the classical instrument without frills. I think Carol had some reservations about the triplet semiquavers in the allemande but the point was too subtle for my ears and we both admired your treatment of repeats (especially this allemande) and your ornaments and your beautiful feeling for rhythm.*
>
> *I hear rumours that if R.E. [Radio Éireann] could be persuaded to produce even a meagre appointment you could be persuaded to return home. I do not expect that any agitation would be effective, but if it had your blessing I would like to try any small agitation possible?[14]*

Unfortunately we do not have John's reply to Acton's kind remarks, if indeed he did reply. Acton could be harsh on musicians and singers when writing for the newspaper, but was encouraging and helpful when he corresponded with them, which he did often.[15]

Bach's Partita in B minor, BWV 831, which John had performed in Dublin earlier in the year, was broadcast on Radio Éireann on 14 November, and a recording of John playing the Partita No. 6 in E minor, BWV 830 would be broadcast on the BBC Home Service's programme *Music at Night* in November 1966.[16]

The following anecdote may serve to illustrate John's sensitive nature. When his friend Seán O'Leary once used the expression 'playing it by ear' while talking to some people in John's presence, John poured scorn on the phrase. Seán's retort was, 'You never play it by ear!' Misinterpreting what Seán meant, John took this remark very badly and continually referred to it for some time afterwards. He believed that Seán thought that he was 'bounded by the bar lines' and was too rigid in his performance of music. Seán told him that he did not mean this at all and explained that the phrase meant doing things in a disorderly and unplanned manner, in complete contrast to John. Although he admitted that he was not disorderly, John still felt that Seán might have been criticizing him. It was a long time before he let the matter drop. Seán noticed that he never forgot what other people said about him and that he often repeated what they had said, especially if they were words of criticism.[17]

Determined to be employed by the BBC as a conductor, and urged by Stephen Plaistow to submit tapes of Radio Éireann recordings before making a decision about 'more ambitious conducting projects' for him,[18] John procured a tape of Mozart's Mass in C, K. 317 ('Coronation'), which he had conducted at a public performance on 25 October in Dublin,[19] and submitted it to the BBC. The work, which was performed by 'A Radio Éireann Symphony Orchestra Group', the St James's Gate Choral Society, the bass William Young and other soloists, had been broadcast on Radio Éireann in December along with music by Haydn and Mozart.[20] In an undated letter to the Assistant to the Chief Assistant, Stephen Plaistow wrote:

> John Beckett writes to be considered by us as a conductor, besides as a solo harpsichordist and continuo player. He wants to conduct Haydn, especially Symphonies Nos. 43, 47 and 51. Herewith a tape of him conducting the Radio Eireann Symphony Orchestra and the St James's Gate Choral Society in a performance of Mozart's Coronation Mass, K317. In a letter to me Beckett says; "the orchestra was the least good third of the Radio Eireann Symphony Orchestra (the other two thirds were at the Wexford Festival at the time); the choir was entirely amateur; of the soloists only the soprano was chosen by me; the performance was recorded straight through at a public concert". But he doesn't want to make excuses. I'd be grateful if the tape could be included in an Artists' Committee Playback session.[21]

The BASF tape was received on 5 December[22] and if John had read the report on the playback session he would have been shocked, for at the top of the page, somebody had written 'NO'.

> Mr Lam. This abysmal performance of K317 could give little idea of the conductor's gifts. He keeps everything together, allowing for obviously terrible performers, but there is nothing to suggest that Beckett is a sensitive conductor. Having a noted a tendency to drive on aggressively in his otherwise impressive harpsichord playing, I would certainly not recommend our accepting him without more convincing evidence of his musicality when directing performers.

Mr Middlemiss. Securing a good ensemble always and his tempi are sensible, when the chorus don't run away with it. He can accompany, we know. But, if he is to be judged on this, as he has asked to be, he cannot communicate much spirit to the players or discrimination to the chorus. A strong beat is a strong beat to them and it is nothing more – and little else matters. Apart from the first mentioned considerations it is impossible to judge.

Mr Walsworth. This tape really told me nothing but that Beckett managed to keep his forces more or less together. He accompanied the singers well but judging from the awful sounds emitted by the choir and orchestra, it would be difficult to judge how much was happy chance, and how much design. I would prefer to await further evidence of his powers.[23]

The failure of this venture must have been a blow to John, but it probably strengthened his resolve to do better and to be accepted as a respected conductor, which is indeed what came to pass.

Some time in 1964 John was employed as a freelance keyboard and tuned percussion player with the London Symphony Orchestra for two years or more. This was thanks to Harold Lester, who also worked for the orchestra and put a lot of work in John's way. Harold remembers how John did not fit in with the musicians, who would ask, 'who is this strange person?'[24] Playing with the orchestra during this period (1964 to 1966) meant that John rehearsed and performed under many famous conductors including Istvan Kertesz, Georg Solti, Antal Dorati, Lorin Maazel, Pierre Monteux, Aaron Copland, Colin Davis, Norman del Mar, George Hurst, Gennadi Rozhdestvensky and Seiji Ozawa.[25]

The new year began with a thirty-minute programme of recorder and harpsichord music played by John, John Sothcott and Daphne Webb on the BBC Home Service's evening programme, *Music at Night*, in January.[26] Then in February, Musica Reservata performed in a concert of early Italian and French music in the Hamilton Room at the College of St Mark and St John, Chelsea.[27] Seán O'Leary attended rehearsals for this concert and others that were held in schools and halls at the time. Although they tended to be shambolic, there was an air of adventure about them and everyone was happy to be there and to be involved. Seán remembers that Vera and her mother often attended the concerts; although Vera could be critical at times, she was very supportive.[28]

Samuel came to London to rehearse his new production, *Play*, at the National Theatre in March. When John met him at a Lyons Corner House, he was fuming because the theatre's director Kenneth Tynan had objected strongly to the almost unintelligibly fast dialogue that Samuel wanted in his play and, as he would not allow it in his theatre, there had been a row. John had never seen Samuel in such a state before. However, George Devine, the director, stood his ground and said that the dialogue had to be spoken at that speed and that was the way it was done.[29]

During the same month, a demonstration tape of music played by Musica Reservata, conducted by Michael Morrow, was submitted to the BBC but by May the reports were inconclusive and it was proposed that the BBC should wait until the *Roman de Fauvel* programme was broadcast before reaching a decision about the ensemble. This project was floundering; Terence Tiller had written to Michael the previous December to say that he was having great trouble in obtaining a text and a transcription.[30]

At this stage, Tom Sutcliffe, an enthusiastic twenty-year-old tenor and student of English literature from Magdalen College, Oxford, met Michael through Don Smithers, an American trumpeter and cornett player who had worked for Noah Greenberg and the New York Pro Musica. Don, who was a larger-than-life character with a glass eye and who became an authority on the Baroque trumpet, had recently played at a concert in Trinity College, Oxford, in which Tom had sung. A very gifted musician, Don had not only played his cornett but had performed on other instruments such as crumhorns – a practice soon to be adopted by Musica Reservata and later by David Munrow.

Don brought Tom to Michael's home in Aberdare Gardens (he would have met John at around this time or a later). Tom, who knew little about Irish people, noted that neither John nor Michael spoke with Irish accents, because, as he realized, they were Protestants. He sensed that both of them felt very alienated living in London and that, like most Irish people at that time, they disliked the English. He figured that they must be sympathetic to the British Labour Party, as the Conservatives were connected with everything that they did not approve of in Ireland. Although Tom was a singer, Michael was not interested in his singing for various reasons, one of which was the fact that he already had Grayston Burgess. For the time being, Tom was happy to be a friend of Michael's until he was appointed manager of Musica Reservata in 1965.[31]

John, who went to Dublin in May, played three of Bach's solo harpsichord Partitas, Nos 6 in E minor, 5 in G major and 4 in D major at a recital in the Royal College of Physicians, Kildare Street. 'This should be an outstanding experience,' proclaimed *The Irish Times* in its listing of forthcoming events.[32] John wrote the programme notes, in which he described these works and stated that he would play all the marked repeats: 'I observe all these repeats. It is a question of scale of form and of tonality.'[33] However, Charles Acton, in his *Irish Times* review, wrote that a repeat should be 'something more than an exact, carbon-copy repetition' and criticized John for not changing the decorations or registration in some of the Partitas. However, John was given full marks for the repeats in the *Allemande* of Partita No. 4, judged by Acton to be 'an absolutely brilliant example of virtuoso decorative variation at its most flowery and authentic'. John's fault-less and seemingly effortless technique was praised, as well as his superb sense of phrasing. Charles Acton concluded, 'I felt that Bach would have found here a performance and a player after his own heart.'[34] A critic in another Dublin newspaper thought that some of the quick movements were played 'rather too fast', though John's virtuosity and dedicated authority were warmly praised.[35]

Bernard Thomas, who would later play in Musica Reservata and who now was in his teens, remembers attending this concert with his teacher David Lee, who probably introduced him to John. As Bernard knew that John had a repu-tation for being rather uncompromising, he was surprised at his conservative manner of playing, which was greeted very well. When applauded at the end, John said, in what sounded like a slightly contemptuous manner, that he did not see any point in playing little bits and pieces by way of an encore, and would rather go off to enjoy a pint of Smithwicks. Bernard's impression of John was that he was rather austere; he had become something of a mythical figure in Dublin. Later John and Michael Morrow would invite Bernard to join Musica Reservata, which he did, playing early wind instruments such as the recorder, flute, crumhorn, rackett, rauschpfeife and shawm.[36]

On 3 June John appeared for fifteen minutes on Ireland's national televi-sion station, Telefís Éireann, playing harpsichord pieces by Henry Purcell, on the *Music Room* programme. Viewers were introduced to him in the pages of the *RTV Guide* and mention was made that he was a cousin of Samuel Beckett.[37] John would probably have used the station's Dolmetsch harpsichord for the programme. Rhoda Draper, who worked as a production assistant in the Telefís Éireann studios, remembered how a mirror was rigged up directly over the keyboard so that the camera could look straight down at John's hands. The tech-nicians altered the camera's scans so that the image was not upside down and back to front. Rhoda was enthusiastic about early music and would become a friend and pupil of John's later.[38] John appeared again, on another televised *Music Room* programme on 17 June, this time playing a recital of music by Mozart and Haydn on the harpsichord. The Mozart music was written when the composer was aged five and the Haydn music consisted of three movements from the composer's Sonata No. 1 in C.[39]

While in Dublin John was recorded playing Bach's Partita No. 6 in E minor for Radio Éireann, which was broadcast in July. In the summary of radio programmes printed in the *RTV Guide* it was stated that, 'A perfectionist in most things, but certainly where Bach is concerned, Beckett has devoted about a year's spare time to practising this work. Listeners may be sure that it will be played not only with loving conviction but also with complete authenticity of style.'[40]

Meanwhile, back in London, Basil Lam of the BBC had decided to offer Musica Reservata a 'test date', when the group would be assessed for future broadcasts.[41]

A young Gillian Smith, the daughter of Olive Lyall Smith, remembered seeing John playing the piano and celeste in the London Symphony Orchestra when she and her mother journeyed from Dublin to Scotland for the Edinburgh Festival in August. Gillian was intrigued as her mother knew John from the famous performance of Bach's B minor Mass that she had helped organize in Dublin back in 1950.[42]

John was back in Ireland immediately afterwards, this time teaching students to play the recorder at a large house named An Grianán (The Sunny Place) in the village of Termonfechin in County Louth, near Drogheda. The eighteenth-century house was owned by the Irish Countrywomen's Association and was used as an adult education centre. An article written by Ina Condon for the Farm Home Pages of *The Irish Farmers' Journal*, described how 'Mr. John Beckett taught the students how to play the recorder, and Mr. J. Groocock, who directed the course, had a supply on hand at 14/6d. each'.[43]

John continued to teach the recorder to beginners at An Grianán every August and became a recorder and later viol tutor there when the Irish Recorder Course, founded by Theo and Kitty Wyatt in 1969, held its annual week-long course during the same month.[44]

John was back in Ireland in October during the Wexford Opera Festival to give a recital of Bach music played by himself and his young cousin once removed, Edward Beckett. Edward was the son of Frank Beckett, Samuel's brother, who had died tragically of cancer in September 1954. Edward, who had studied the flute for one year in Dublin under André Prieur and had taken a sabbatical year at the Paris Conservatoire, had decided that he wanted to become a professional musician rather than following in his father's footsteps and studying engineering. Samuel and Suzanne had looked after him during his studies at the Conservatoire and had introduced him to their friends.[45]

Although Edward had not yet fully completed his studies, the recital, organized by the Wexford Fringe Committee and held in White's Barn, turned out to be very successful. In Charles Acton's review in *The Irish Times*, entitled 'Accomplished and erudite Bach recital', he mentioned that this was the audience's first opportunity to hear Edward playing and another welcome opportunity of hearing John playing 'Cathal Gannon's beautiful harpsichord'. In spite of inadequate publicity outside Wexford, there was a surprisingly good attendance.[46]

Charles Acton wrote to John soon afterwards to reiterate his appreciation of the recital. 'First of all may I thank you for the pleasure you gave me at Wexford with Edward, in case my notice did not make it plain', he began. He continued:

> The other thing was the possibility that you would return home to Ireland if it were possible to keep most of the wolf from the door. That is something that many of us would try hard to make possible. I have in the past tried to make some people in R.E. see that they would be doing something important if they were to try to persuade you to come back by offering you all the R.T.E.S.O. orchestra keyboard work ... If you are considering returning I would be very glad indeed to try hard to work on people in R.E. at the highest level than I have before.

He told John that the Royal Irish Academy of Music would soon acquire a harpsichord, and suggested that he apply for a position of harpsichord teacher there.[47]

John played the French Suite No. 5 again early in the following month, this time on BBC Third Music.[48] This programme and a recital of secular choral music of the thirteenth and fourteenth centuries with Musica Reservata, recorded at Maida Vale later in the month, brought the year 1964 to a close.[49]

Twenty
1965

By now, John and Vera had left Frognal and were living in Brampton House, Church Street, situated in a delightfully old-world corner of the London suburb of Chiswick. Leading down to the River Thames, this short but picturesque street contains a Roman Catholic church, the bells of which irritated Vera. The house, a small two-storey addition to Ferry House, is near the entrance to Fuller's Brewery and The Old Burlington pub.[1]

Living in Chiswick was advantageous for both John and Vera: John was still conducting his evening classes at Belmont School and Vera worked in Gunnersbury Museum nearby, where she was a costume expert.[2]

Although John was in Chiswick in late January, he was back in Dublin by 5 February inaugurating a 'magnificent library of 120 classical recordings' acquired by the Dublin Gramophone Society. A newspaper article reported that 'Mr. Beckett, who chose sonatas by Beethoven and Brahms and a Fantasie for violin and piano by Schubert, came specially from London for the occasion.' Included was a photograph of a portly Mr Beckett attired in a suit and tie, surrounded by four female members of the Society, all gazing with intense interest at a record of music performed by Yehudi Menuhin, held in John's right hand. The collection of records had belonged to the late Maurice Nesbitt, who had been a member of the Society for many years.[3]

John spent his time in Ireland at the family home in Greystones. Before he had left Chiswick, he had written to his friend Cathal Gannon, who by now was working on a harpsichord that would soon be finished and donated by the Guinness Brewery to the Royal Irish Academy of Music. With obvious excitement he wrote, 'May I come and try it? Is it at the Brewery? I am coming over to Dublin next week, and might be able to come along on Monday afternoon.'[4]

While in Dublin, John probably visited his Uncle Howard, who was by now gravely ill in the Adelaide Hospital, and his Uncle Jim, who had had one of his legs amputated in an effort to check his diabetes. Jim's eyes were deteriorating rapidly and his arms had been so badly affected by a muscular disease that he was unable to hobble around on crutches.[5]

John made three Radio Éireann broadcasts between February and March.[6] In April he was the guest artist at the Culwick Society's spring concert held at the Aberdeen Hall of the Gresham Hotel in Dublin.[7] Always fussy about the height of chair that he needed to play the harpsichord, he persuaded Cathal Gannon, on whose harpsichord he was performing, to bring one of his own chairs to the hotel. 'He fancied the height being the right thing and I had to walk all the way down O'Connell Street with the chair under my arm and back,' recollected Cathal with perhaps a small amount of exaggeration.[8]

Charles Acton reviewed the concert in *The Irish Times*:

> As the soloist was John Beckett the enjoyment and the musical excitement were inevitable … On Cathal Gannon's harpsichord he played this French Suite with the love and joy that seem to come only from his playing. Repeats were there of course and exquisitely devised and varied decorations. Once more I felt that the Old Man himself would not have done it differently. The Scarlatti sonatas sound more straightforward in their reading, but then their virtuoso, extrovert style leaves less to the player's initiative, though Mr. Beckett made them the music of a virtuoso and showed us so much of fascinating interest.[9]

The new Guinness-Gannon harpsichord was formally handed over to the Royal Irish Academy of Music by Lord Moyne, vice-chairman of the Guinness Brewery, at a special reception held in the Brewery on 12 April. John, who played pieces by Bach and Scarlatti on the instrument after the lunch and speeches, was photographed and featured in a couple of the Irish national news-papers.[10] Formally dressed in a dark suit and tie, he looks uncomfortable among the dignitaries as he sits at the harpsichord, unsmiling. Also in one of the photo-graphs is myself, aged ten, looking somewhat in awe at this giant of a man, who had by now become very fat.[11] At the end of his letter to my father in January, he had been kind enough to send his greetings to him, my mother and me with the words, 'Warmest regards, and to Margaret and Charles. John.'[12] Such genuinely heartfelt words were often used to close John's letters to his friends; lurking within the larger-than-life, tense and often gruff exterior was a warmth and friendliness that occasionally emerged, providing the conditions were right. Interestingly, it is from around this period onwards that most people's memo-ries of John begin (or at least become clearer).

John was back in London by May, when a concert of medieval and early Renaissance secular music was given by Musica Reservata in the Conway Hall, Red Lion Square, Holborn, in which John played viol and virginals, Michael Morrow the lute, Desmond Dupré the viol and lute and Jeremy Montagu percussion.[13] In the audience that evening were Ruth David, a viola player who knew some of the musicians, and her daughter Rose.[14]

In an article entitled 'Cheerful Medieval Music – From Our Music Critic', a reviewer in *The Times* had this to say about the concert at the Conway Hall:

> They began with an *Estampida* by Vaqueiras that sounded like a very wild party indeed. Some French dances of the same type involved two bearded gentlemen who looked sobriety incarnate while one of them sustained feats of frenzied agility on the recorder and the other battered a military drum as if convinced that eventually he must succeed in bringing down the ceiling, and perhaps the walls too, of Conway Hall. My ears yielded before the bricks and mortar did; shortly afterwards this bombardment mercifully ceased.[15]

Tom Sutcliffe, who had helped organize this concert, was appointed manager of the group shortly afterwards. Up until now he had only served as a 'useful dogsbody'. Although he was never paid anything by Michael for what he did, Tom threw himself willingly into the management of the group. For him, it was an education to work with Michael and John.[16]

In early June John and Vera were with Samuel in Paris when Edward Beckett finally completed his studies at the Conservatoire and was awarded two *premier prix* for flute and chamber music. John was sitting beside Samuel and 'When it was announced that Edward had got his *premier prix*, Samuel turned to me and said with the utmost fervour, "Thank God". I never heard him invoke the name of God before for anything but he did it with great intensity over Edward,' reported John.[17]

John and Edward were in Dublin later in the month for a short Bach festival organized by the St James's Gate Musical Society. The first of three concerts took place at the Rupert Guinness Hall with the Irish Chamber Orchestra and the Guinness Choir, conducted by Victor Leeson.[18] In the second concert, an organ trio sonata by Bach, BWV 525, which John had arranged as a trio sonata for flute, violin and continuo, was performed by Edward Beckett, John Ronayne, John and Betty Sullivan.[19] Another, BWV 527, which John had arranged for two violins and continuo, was also played. Charles Acton praised Betty Sullivan's continuo cello playing, which was:

> [...] always exactly right and in place, and with just the same rhythmic precision as John Beckett's. His, of course, is wonderful to hear. It is, perhaps, more than

anything else the quality that lifts his Bach playing right away from the ordinary run. It is something that one must respond to; physically, mentally, emotionally. And where he led, throughout the evening, his companions followed with him.[20]

The Irish harpsichordist, organist and pianist David Lee, whom John had taught at St Columba's College when he was fifteen, reappeared around this period. David, although greatly influenced by John, was not exactly enamoured of him. He remembered that John had jokingly but tactlessly referred to the *Agnus Dei* (Lamb of God) section of Bach's B minor Mass, which had been performed in St Andrew's Church, as 'pig's trotters', which David thought was rather thoughtless as Roman Catholics might well have been within earshot. John knew what he wanted and demanded the utmost out of everyone; nevertheless he was not unkind or unpleasant. David drank with John and John O'Sullivan at the Red Bank Restaurant, opposite the *Irish Times* offices in D'Olier Street. When John ordered a brandy and the waiter asked him what type he wanted, he replied, 'A *large* one'. He was well known for handing a barman a slip of paper with the words 'hot stout' written on it.

David remembers that John adored the music of Fauré and, of course, Mahler, though he only liked the latter's third, fourth, sixth and ninth symphonies – not the second and eighth. During a very long interval of a performance of Bach's *Saint Matthew Passion*, in which David was playing the continuo, they repaired to his flat in Leeson Street, where they listened to the whole of Mahler's ninth symphony. John's verdict on Mahler's third symphony was, 'It's just a masterpiece'.[21]

John was back at Chiswick in early July from where he wrote to Cathal Gannon to say that, when in Dublin, he had spoken to Tibor Paul (principal conductor of the Radio Éireann Symphony Orchestra and director of music in both Radio Éireann and Telefís Éireann). Tibor wanted John to use the harpsichord that Cathal had made for the Royal Irish Academy of Music for a concert of music to be performed at the American Embassy in September. He also said 'that he intended buying a new harpsichord for RE [Radio Éireann]. He asked me if I thought he should get one of yours. I said he should. He said he would.' Thus started a train of events that would eventually end with Cathal making a harpsichord for Radio Éireann.[22]

At the end of the month, John accepted a commission to write incidental harpsichord music for *The Plain Dealer* by the Restoration dramatist William Wycherley.[23] Produced by John Tydeman, it was adapted for radio by Raymond Raikes. For this production, John composed a series of short pieces written in a twentieth-century style with, occasionally, a slight nod in the direction of

Elizabethan music.[24] The music was completed and accepted on 10 August, and John received thirty guineas for it. The play, starring Flora Robson, Patrick Allen, Jill Bennett, Prunella Scales, Penelope Lee and Michael Spice, was broadcast on the BBC Third Programme in October.[25]

John went to Dublin in September, where he practised on the Royal Irish Academy of Music instrument for the concert at the American Embassy. 'The instrument sounds magnificent in the resonant room and is a pleasant and an excit[e]ment to play,' John scrawled on a piece of paper, which he posted to Cathal. Cathal tuned it 'under great difficulties' before the concert,[26] which included Bach's Harpsichord Concerto in E major, BWV 1053.[27] Charles Acton, in his review 'Music in candle-light setting', wrote: 'John Beckett was the soloist in the Sebastian Bach concerto, the most serious part of the evening, and he discoursed the music with all his accustomed authority and in the slow movement all Bach's beauty.'[28] On the following day, the writer of 'An Irishman's Diary' commented that 'the sound was warm, rich, and at the same time delicate, and once again the 18th century was recaptured, especially in the Number 2 Bach Harpsichord concerto, with John Beckett, the soloist, looking more like Orson Wells than ever.'[29]

John, who now was anxious to procure a harpsichord for himself, wrote to his father's friend, David Owen Williams, the director in the Guinness Brewery :

> *Dear Owen,*
>
> *I have at present no harpsichord, nor have ever had one of my own.*
>
> *With the increasing amount of work I am being asked to do it is becoming more than ever essential that I should acquire one.*
>
> *I would rather posess [sic] an instrument of Cathal Gannon's, than one by any other maker. I see no likelihood of my ever being able to afford a large, double-manual instrument; I would, however, be very content with a single manual instrument with two 8 foot stops, and one four foot.*
>
> *Would it be possible for Cathal to make me such an instrument, as and when, of course, it fitted in with his and your commitments? How much would an instrument of this kind cost?[30]*

Despite Mr Williams's noncommittal response, John lost no time and typed a letter to Cathal in a fever of excitement – a typical trait of John's when he had got an idea into his head:

> *Dear Cathal,*
>
> *If it is agreeable to the powerful powers that be and to you of course! [added by hand] that you should make a harpsichord for me, what I would like (I mean*

what, at the £500 you quote, I could possibly afford) would be a single manual
instrument with three stops: one 4 foot, and two 8 foot; the two 8 foots differing a
little, but not too much in tone.

I would not want a felt damped stop.

I would not like the keys covered in celluloid.

I would like a plain, unpainted wooden case.

Could this be done for £500? Could you start on it at the same time as the RE
one? If so, when could it be ready? I could put down £250 now, and would find
the remainder later.

If the thing is a possibility, I would like you to go ahead. As I said to Owen
Williams in another letter, I need an instrument NOW. I have more recitals and
broadcasts than ever to prepare, and no instrument to work on — pathetic and silly.
So the sooner the whole thing can be put in train the better. Let me know when
what is decided.

Wish I had enough money for a two manual machine, but haven't, nor ever
will have.[31]

Having reached the bottom of the page, John concluded his letter with his
signature, written sideways in the left margin, extending almost from the bottom
to the top of the paper. Cathal responded and John wrote to him again nine days
later with more specifications, ending: 'I am writing to Owen Williams to the
above effect. If he (the Brewery) agrees, I would like you to start wrok I mean
work on the instrument as soon as possible. I can send you (them) a cheque for
250 stinking smackers whenever you (they) like.[32]

Believing that money would talk (even though he possessed so little of it),
John steamed ahead, despite the Brewery's indecision; no doubt the Board of
Directors was reluctant to sell an instrument for such a small sum. John was
determined to get a harpsichord and get one he finally did, at his own price,
though he would have to wait until 1967 for it to be finished.

Twenty-One
1965–66

In early October 1965 John was playing the celeste in the London Symphony Orchestra when John Ogdon was performing Michael Tippett's Piano Concerto, conducted by Colin Davis. When prolonged applause brought John Ogdon back on to the stage, he caught John and embraced him. Seán O'Leary, who recounted this story, believes that John would not have cared for Tippett's music – he would have preferred the other works in the concert: Berlioz's *Symphonie Fantastique* and Elgar's *Cockaigne Overture*.[1]

Also in the same month, John received commissions to write up to twenty minutes of incidental music for Alfred Jarry's play *Ubu Cocu* (*Ubu Cuckolded*),[2] to be performed by an eight-piece orchestra, and eleven minutes of music for Euripides's tragedy *Electra*,[3] translated by David Thompson. John composed fifteen minutes of music for the latter, which meant that his fee was augmented. The producer, John Tydeman, wrote to John and thanked him for his 'magnificent music'. 'Once again a delighted customer. I was amazed at how smoothly all went with the chorus and more than pleased. The music fitted in well with the production and especially assisted the climax at the end.'[4] The music was recorded towards the end of November and John was paid eighty-five guineas the following month.[5]

By the beginning of November a solution had been found to the making of a cheap harpsichord for John: Lord Moyne agreed that Cathal Gannon should make three harpsichords concurrently, 'as by doing so they can be made a good deal cheaper'. Mr Williams wrote to John to say that Cathal would make him a harpsichord for £500.[6] Delighted, John wrote to Cathal:

I had a letter from Owen Williams yesterday to say that it has been decided that I
can have a simple double-manual harpsichord from you for a price of £500; £250
to be paid down, which I happily can manage, and the remainder to be paid over
a period of three years, which I hope I can not too unhappily manage also. I am
thrilled – a word I don't remember often using.

 BUT, having thought the project over, as you must have done, are YOU agree-
able also? It seems to me terribly cheap for such an instrument. I fear that I may be
exploiting your great skill, and your friendship. If you have any such feeling please
tell me. If you think the price too little, which it is – too inadequately little for
your work and time, say so now. I mean that seriously.[7]

Writing from Brampton House on 20 November with more instructions for
the design of his harpsichord, John complained, 'I have been nearly capsized with
work this last three weeks – a lot of playing, and two scores to write and record
for the BBC.' The two scores refer to the music for Jarry's *Ubu Cocu* (completed
and delivered by 1 December) and *Electra* (recorded at the end of November).[8]

John arrived back in Dublin just as his friend Cathal had finished renovating
the Kirckman harpsichord owned by Trinity College, which had been restored
by Morley's of Lewisham in 1963. The instrument had been sent to Cathal in
the Guinness Brewery, where he had been working on it from the beginning
of the month.[9] A young man named Anthony OBrien was brought to see the
instrument by David Lee. David had been endeavouring, 'rather unsuccessfully',
to teach Anthony to play the harpsichord, and Anthony sang in his choir at St
Bartholomew's Church in Clyde Road, Dublin. Anthony had met Cathal briefly
at a party hosted by Brian and Mary Boydell, and vaguely knew that John was
related to both Samuel and Edward Beckett. Other than that, he knew nothing
about John, who was now about to test the restored harpsichord.

David and Anthony duly admired the instrument while awaiting John's arrival.
Then, as Anthony recalled:

In shambled this extraordinary, more-or-less spherical bear of a man with enormous brown eyes, who plonked himself down in front of the harpsichord, and
with no further ado launched into Purcell's *A New Ground*, (one of the few pieces
I ever managed to play). I don't remember much else – just this mesmerizing
man and an unforgettable piece of music. But I do remember the expression of
delight on John's face as he played the instrument, and much rolling of the eyes
– an expression I'd get to know well a couple of decades later.[10]

On Sunday 28 November Musica Reservata gave a concert at Balliol College
in Oxford for the Balliol College Musical Society. In the concert, John played
the viol and harpsichord, and David Munrow played the crumhorn.[11] This

appears to be the first time that Munrow, who would later found the Early Music Consort of London, played with Musica Reservata.

Alfred Jarry's 'paraphysical extravaganza', *Ubu Cocu,* was broadcast in December on the BBC Third Programme, using the incidental music that John had written. The play had been translated by Cyril Connolly and the producer was Martin Esslin. John's music was played on two piccolos, two trumpets, two tubas and percussion.[12]

The *Roman de Fauvel* programme, which initially had been planned back in March 1963,[13] had finally been recorded in November and was broadcast the following month on the Third Programme.[14] It was produced by Terence Tiller, who had finally obtained the books and translations for the programme and had written the script by the end of March.[15] The music interpolated into this fourteenth-century satirical poem, named after a fawn-coloured stallion, was performed by Musica Reservata;[16] the narrator was Denis Goacher and the part of Fauvel was played by Victor Lucas.[17]

The earliest recording of Musica Reservata performing is this BBC Archive programme. Commenting on it in 1995 on the BBC Radio 3 programme *Mining the Archive,* Christopher Page remarked that it would have sounded to people back in 1965 exactly the way it sounds to us now, since, ever since the group ceased to exist, we have developed the type of tastes and styles against which Michael Morrow wanted to react. Nobody, he said, would perform the music now as they did then; for example, he had not heard crumhorns played by a professional ensemble in medieval music for the best part of twenty years. There was nothing romantic about the way Michael performed such music. Michael's message was that he did not know what the music sounded like in the fourteenth century; whatever it sounded like, it certainly did not sound like nineteenth-century music and 'by God he was going to make it sound different'. One of the items was played twice as fast as it would be performed today. The singers used a very bright tone colour, the phrasing was chunky and the pieces ended with no hint of a *ritardando*. Christopher regarded Michael as a visionary who loved medieval and Renaissance music as if later music did not exist. He realized that the inspiration that he derived from music of many parts of the world other than western Europe was provocative.[18]

The new year, 1966, began with a recording for the BBC on another of Cathal Gannon's harpsichords, which had been on display in Harrods during a 'Charm of Ireland' promotion. As the instrument had been neglected and had been over-voiced by a piano tuner, Cathal had to fly to London on 4 January and work on it during the following day in Broadcasting House. Unfortunately, it is not known what John played on the instrument. However, the anecdote illustrates the high regard that John had for Cathal's instruments – he obviously had declined to use whatever instrument the BBC had offered him and had insisted on using Cathal's, thereby putting Cathal to a certain amount of trouble and the Guinness Brewery to a certain amount of expense.[19]

A month later, John, Edward Beckett and Samuel performed music to accompany Jack MacGowran reading passages from Samuel's works (*Malone Dies*, *Watt*, *From an Abandoned Work*, *Molloy*, *Endgame*, *The Unnamable*, and *Echo's Bones*) for Claddagh Records, at the Pye Studios in Edgware Road. The theme from the slow movement of Schubert's *Death and the Maiden* Quartet in D minor was played before and after the readings; Edward played the first violin part on his flute and John played the rest of the parts on an old harmonium hired from Impossibles Ltd, a supplier of unusual theatrical items. Samuel's contribution was to strike a simple dinner gong in between the readings, in order to separate them.[20] John remembered how Samuel had struck the gong with 'terrific concentration' just to get the right type of sound that one would hear from a distant corridor upstairs. He also remembered how he had arranged to meet Samuel at the studio near Marble Arch in Edgware Road. 'I am usually punctual,' he told James Knowlson:

> and I expected to find Sam there, and I said to the attendant at the door that I was expecting Mr Beckett here, had anybody been looking for me, and he said, 'Yes, an elderly gentleman was enquiring after you,' and I felt surprised by that. I never thought of Samuel as an elderly gentleman – well, he was only fifty-nine really.[21]

John travelled back to Dublin and was there on 10 February when he and Harold Lester gave a concert of Schubert piano duets in the Rupert Guinness Hall. Charles Acton proclaimed it to be 'a splendid evening'.[22]

On the evening of the following day, *Electra*, the play that John had written music for, was broadcast on the Third Programme. *The Times* was ecstatic about the production: 'John Beckett's music, which was reminiscent of Weill's jazz themes and jaunty military airs, balanced the tensions of the text and built the dramatic structure into forms of strength and clarity. This is surely a production that will be pulled out of archives for repeated broadcasts during the next decade.' The programme was repeated shortly afterwards, once in 1967 and again in 1968.[23]

At the beginning of March, John and Betty Sullivan played first continuo for Bach's *Saint Matthew Passion* in the Royal Dublin Society, Ballsbridge. The Saint James's Gate Musical Society, conducted by Victor Leeson, performed the work, with members of the Radio Éireann Symphony Orchestra in the double orchestra. Peter Bamber was the Evangelist and a bass singer whom John would use frequently in the future, William Young, sang the part of Christus. Another up-and-coming singer, the mezzo-soprano Bernadette Greevy, whom John would also use many times, also sang.[24]

It was probably at around this time that John composed music for a short George Morrison film, *Irish Rising: 1916*. This would have been screened in 1966, when the fiftieth anniversary of the Easter Rising was commemorated. A mere seventeen minutes long, it dealt with the events leading to the failed rising and its consequences, using contemporary footage and stills. Two segments of music used in the film were composed by Seán Ó Riada and the rest (mostly short snatches) were by John. At least one of these was used in Morrison's film *Éamon de Valera – Portrait of a Statesman*. Much of the music, used to accompany shots of Kilmainham Gaol, sounds suitably menacing.[25]

John told Seán O'Leary what he considered to be an embarrassing anecdote concerning himself and Leonard Bernstein, who had come to England to conduct the London Symphony Orchestra in a performance of Mahler's Ninth Symphony on 24 April. John was playing the glockenspiel, which enters some six or seven minutes into the first movement. During the rehearsal, John diligently counted all the rests and came in bang on time. Surprised, Bernstein stopped the orchestra and announced that in all the time he had been conducting the work, this was the first time ever that the glockenspiel had come in on time, and with that went over to John and embraced him.[26] However, it should be noted that none of the present members of the orchestra can remember this incident[27] and nor can Harold Lester, who played regularly with the LSO. According to Harold, John thought that Bernstein's interpretation of Mahler was the best. He was terrific to work under during rehearsals, but played to the gallery during the performances – a trait that John did not approve of.[28]

At around this time, a young Arthur Johnson had graduated in music from Edinburgh and had found a job in the Hampstead studio of Saga Records, which was then a leader in the marketing of cut-price LPs. When he had mastered the operation of an Ampex tape machine, Stan Horobin, who was both engineer and tape editor, came to him one day with instructions to go to the audition room and continue playing back a tape about which Arthur knew nothing. It turned out to be the first edit of a harpsichord recording by John. He had been invited to listen to the tape and either pass it for publication or to request certain alterations.

Evidently John and Stan had managed to cross swords at some point and the tape editor wanted to have no more to do with 'the recalcitrant Irishman'. Arthur therefore found himself opening a door and being confronted by a glowering visage, 'a terrifying experience and one I will never forget'. However, he did what he could and the two men parted on reasonably amicable terms.

Arthur was unable to remember what was on the tape, 'apart from hiss, which was quite prevalent in those days'.[29] The record, in fact, was of Scarlatti sonatas played by John, which was released soon afterwards on the Saga Pan label. Entitled *Scarlatti Sonatas for Harpsichord played by John Beckett*, the cover was predominantly pink and orange in colour, with a rather psychedelic depiction of a bearded gentleman (vaguely resembling one of the Beatles on their *Yellow Submarine* album) playing a harpsichord in which can be seen musical notes and the faces of various composers. On the record, John played on a two-manual harpsichord made by Robert Goble – the one he used in Belmont School, Chiswick. The most well-known piece on the disc was Kk 492 in D major. Marked *presto*, it was certainly played presto and also with great precision. All in all, the music was well performed. The only quibble is that the harpsichord's lute stop tends to snarl a little too much, especially in the lower register.[30] The facts that the LP was not reviewed in the pages of *The Gramophone*, that the label was not exactly prestigious and that John was greatly outshone by other harpsichordists in the UK probably contributed to the obscurity of this disc and its moderate success. On hearing the record at the time of writing, Arthur commented on John's lively approach to the sonatas, almost without exception – the E major Kk 264 and D minor Kk 517 works being splendid examples of such interpretation. Although he could have wished for some more slow pieces, he now could appreciate the quality of John's musicianship as well as his virtuosity.[31]

Another person who regarded this record highly was Mark Windisch; listening to it got him interested in Scarlatti. Mark has seldom heard a musician immersing himself or herself in the drama of each piece as John did.[32] On the other hand, a person who had reservations about this recording was Michael Dervan, who many years later would become music critic for *The Irish Times*. There were certain aspects about the LP that he liked and others that he disliked. For him, John was the 'world's most rigid harpsichordist' and 'an annoying performer because he had an idea in his head and he stuck to it, come hell or high water.' Michael acknowledges that John was a fine musician on many levels, but believes that he effectively narrowed his expressive and communicative range as a harpsichordist, which resulted in his not having the successful career he probably deserved. John was able to indulge in his whims when playing solo as he was not obliged to bend to anybody else's will, whereas when he worked with an orchestra, a singer or a choir, there were other people's intentions to be taken into account. Indeed, it was a point in his favour that he could work differently with different people.[33]

Undoubtedly impressed by the recent *Roman de Fauvel* programme, the BBC now started recording three recitals given by Musica Reservata during the summer. The first, *Music in Venice*, introduced by Michael Morrow (who also played the lute), was recorded at Maida Vale in June and broadcast three days later on the Third Programme.[34]

The next programme was *Early Renaissance Music*, recorded and broadcast in July. Like the previous one, it was produced by Basil Lam and was directed and introduced by Michael Morrow. In this programme, the group performed three Spanish songs, English pieces for the virginals, German songs, French *chansons* and dances, Italian *frottole* and dances, and a madrigal.[35]

The third programme was a recording of Jacob Obrecht's *Missa Fortuna Desperata* and *chansons* by Antoine Busnois, in which John conducted and played the regal. This was recorded in July but not broadcast until June of the following year. Breaking new ground, this experimental performance included ornamented solo sections, a reconstructed keyboard part, and a totally unconventional harsh choral tone, which the group would use again.[36]

John was back in Dublin in August; on the 19th, he, Edward Beckett and Betty Sullivan performed Bach's Sonata in B minor for flute, obbligato harpsichord and cello continuo at a lunchtime recital in Trinity College. 'PMD.' of *The Irish Times* regarded the Bach sonata as the centrepiece of the concert and the musical climax of that particular series of lunchtime concerts.[37]

On the 8 September a recording took place in the BBC's Maida Vale Studios of Spanish Music between 1500 and 1550, which was performed by Musica Reservata and produced by Basil Lam.[38] By now a new player had joined the group: Ruth David, who played the treble rebec.[39] In 1947 she had married the artist Roger Hilton, a pioneer of abstract art in post-war Britain, with whom she had had two children, Matthew and Rose. The couple divorced in 1963.

Ruth Catherine David had been born on 30 July 1921 in Winchester, Hampshire, and had gone to the Royal Academy of Music to study the viola as a principal instrument; she also played the violin, became a sub-professor and later worked with the violinist Max Rostal. A freelance musician since the end of World War II, she played with the Philomusica of London and worked with many other leading orchestras, including the New Philharmonia and the London Mozart Players. She was a member of the Esterházy String Trio and became a professor of viola at Morley College, London. A very respected musician, she played with the likes of Yehudi Menuhin and Pablo Casals. Like most musicians she always did some teaching: she taught individuals at home and at Maidstone, Kent on Saturdays.[40]

As everyone spoke well of Ruth – her warm and pleasant nature, her shrewdness and strength of character – it was not surprising that John fell for her, despite the fact that she was six years his senior. Indeed, John, who was at heart an extremely modest and self-deprecating person, and was inclined to say 'I can't do this' and 'I can't do that',[41] may have been happy to be in the company of a woman who was older than he – somebody who could encourage and mother him. The fact that he and Ruth had gone through rocky relationships might have drawn them together. John's irascible and confrontational nature, gruffness and increasing inclination to turn to alcohol for relaxation and solace may have been partly due to Vera, whose fiery temper and heated arguments he must have faced endlessly. The fact that he had been flirting with other women could indicate that his patience might have been sorely tested. Certainly, Ruth would have discovered John's complex character fairly quickly. John once told his good friend Seán O'Leary that Ruth had said that he was like 'a person going through life dragging two grand pianos behind him', which John readily acknowledged as being true. Seán felt that this encapsulated John's personality perfectly.[42]

Twenty-Two
1966–67

O n 20 September 1966 a new Guinness-Gannon harpsichord was formally handed over to Radio Telefís Éireann (RTÉ) at a special evening reception at the Guinness Brewery. After the ceremony, music by Henry Purcell was performed by John, Betty Sullivan and Frank Patterson,[1] a twenty-three-year-old tenor from Clonmel, County Tipperary, who had won all the major awards at the Feis Ceoil a couple of years previously after just two years of study. He was now becoming well known in both Ireland and America.[2]

John was back in London at the end of the month, when he received a commission from David Thomson of the BBC to write incidental music for an adaptation for radio of F.C. Ball's novel *A Grotto for Miss Maynier*.[3]

Frank Patterson, John, Betty Sullivan and Edward Beckett teamed up as the John Beckett Ensemble for a concert of music by Purcell, Bach and Telemann in the Examination Hall of Trinity College early in December.[4] It is interesting to note what Charles Acton's wife Carol had to say about this concert:

> The second half was made up of two fine Telemann cantatas separated by a selection of pieces from the Anna Magdalena Notebook. These pieces were interesting in John Beckett's hands – dignified, as with [Rosalyn] Tureck, but often unvarying in timbre (the last two minuets) and indeed almost relentless in drive but with a sure and certain feel for rhythmic uprightness and an innate sense of where to decorate and ornament that is comforting. How Mr. Beckett enjoyed the return of the G major minuet! Some weak notes on the instrument weakened the treble of the G major march.
>
> The cantatas were most satisfying. Firstly, this group is a specialist group who know *what* to do and how to do it. John Beckett himself is obviously their

inspiration and their maestro, but Betty Sullivan is a born continuo player, and they have been very lucky to acquire Frank Patterson as their singer.[5]

It was to John's immense advantage at this time that the one music critic who mattered in Ireland (Charles Acton), writing in the country's most respected newspaper, praised his music-making almost unreservedly. Carol, on the other hand, was prepared to be more objective. She accurately describes John's style, which was accepted at the time but would soon go out of fashion in the wake of further study into the authentic performance of early music.

1967 began with an hour-long BBC Third Programme on 24 January on the Scottish Songs of J.C. Bach. This was an illustrated talk by Roger Fiske, with musical examples played by John on square piano and harpsichord, James Galway and Christopher Hyde-Smith on flutes and Tess Miller on oboe, with Margaret Kingsley, soprano and Duncan Robertson, tenor. Also taking part was the Amici Quartet. This interesting programme included first performances of music by Geminiani and J.C. Bach. At the beginning of the programme, Duncan Robertson sang a popular song, *She rose and let me in*, with harpsichord and cello continuo, and then Geminiani's arrangement of the same song, with an elaborate introduction played on the harpsichord, strings and two flutes. Various other examples followed, including songs arranged by J.C. Bach and Haydn.[6]

A review of an LP that had been recorded the previous year now appeared in *The Gramophone* magazine. Entitled *Music of the Early Renaissance: John Dunstable and his contemporaries*, it was issued on the Vox and FSM Turnabout labels. The music, a mixture of gentle and lively secular pieces and peaceful, contemplative sacred works, including plainchant, was sung by Grayston Burgess's Purcell Consort of Voices and performed by six members of Musica Reservata.[7] Although Roger Fiske, who knew John through working with him in the BBC, commended the record and wrote in *The Gramophone* that the instruments had 'a vitalizing effect at all times', he never once mentioned Musica Reservata, even though the name of the group and a list of those taking part were clearly printed on the cover. The balance and the quality of sound was deemed to be good, the record was cheap (15s.) and it was 'admirably designed to convert unbelievers to the joys of early Renaissance music'.[8] Peter Dickinson, writing about this 'lively record' in *Music and Musicians*, recommended the disc.[9] Hans Heimler, in *Records and Recording*, was less enthusiastic and wrote: 'A recording of Dunstable's music and that of his contemporaries is not only highly desirable, but it presents a great challenge. Unfortunately the challenge has not been fully met in this recording. ... the performance [of '*O rosa bella*'] by Grayston Burgess and the recorders and viols of … Musica Reservata is badly balanced and sounds plodding despite a too-brisk tempo.'[10] Overall, the performances on the disc were rather low key and perhaps sound a little dated to the modern ear. This was, as it were, Musica Reservata's gentle entry into the world of commercial recordings.[11]

In February, John and three fellow musicians joined the RTÉ Quartet in the National Gallery, Dublin, for a mixed programme of music from the *Fitzwilliam Virginal Book* (which John played on RTÉ's new Guinness-Gannon harpsichord), Purcell's Trio Sonatas in A and G minor, and Beethoven's Quartet No. 7 in F, Op. 59, No. 1.[12] Charles Acton declared that the harpsichord pieces were 'excellently chosen and, of course, excellently played. Mr. Beckett not only graced the music most becomingly, but always allowed the divisions to declare their true character. The Byrd Fantasia was particularly rewarding, and so sensitively performed.' John loved anything from the *Fitzwilliam Virginal Book* and would become well known in Ireland for his performances of pieces from this collection. He was particularly fond of the works of William Byrd. John was not involved in the Beethoven work, which was played by the new RTÉ Quartet. Indeed, it has been said that John did not care too much for Beethoven's music, though, as we shall see, he was prepared to play it.[13]

By now, John's friend Werner Schürmann was living in a house that he had built for himself on about two acres of ground purchased from Arnold Marsh, the owner of Woodtown Park, at the foot of the Dublin Mountains. He, his wife Gerda and their two boys, Wenzel and Mauritz, had moved there the previous Christmas. I can remember being in this very modern and unusual house, with windows and glass doors facing inwards towards a central courtyard. I had been brought by my father, who was tuning an old piano that Werner had bought: while he tuned, I played with the two boys. I can also remember an occasion when John Beckett, John O'Sullivan and Werner, as thick as thieves, derived great merriment from some doggerel, probably written by John O'Sullivan, set to (what seemed to me) very strange-sounding music, which could only have been written by John Beckett. I have a hazy recollection of seeing the music, neatly written on large sheets of manuscript paper, with the words scrawled, in John's inimitable handwriting, under the notes. The song, which was about an elephant, concluded with the words, 'So they cut it into slices / And gave it to the cat'.[14]

In February, a record of Beethoven and Hummel's works for mandoline and keyboard, *The Classical Mandoline*, played by Hugo D'Alton and John appeared. Like the record of Scarlatti music produced in the previous year, this one was also on the Saga label.[15] Mark Windisch believes that John acquitted himself brilliantly on this record, though criticizes the way the instruments were miked.[16]

A review of the disc in *The Times* discusses the music and commends D'Alton's performance but makes no comment on John's playing.[17] Oddly the reviewer fails to mention that John plays a fortepiano made by Hugh Gough; although the keyboard parts of the Beethoven work mentioned above and his Sonatina in C minor of 1795 are clearly marked *cembalo* (harpsichord) in the manuscript, the style of writing and the use of dynamic markings would indicate a forte-piano – and hence John's choice of instrument. Julian Budden in *The Gramophone* complained that the fortepiano had a 'steely shallow sound' that did not blend too successfully with the mandoline. Although he cared little for the Hummel Sonatina in C major, he enjoyed the Beethoven works and regarded the playing as being of a very high order.[18]

John was back in London early in April, conducting the choir of Musica Reservata in choral music by the Tudor English composer Robert White at the Church of St George the Martyr, Queen Square. The music, which included White's *O praise God in his holiness*, *Lord who shall dwell in thy tabernacle* and his five-part setting of *The Lamentations of Jeremiah*, was broadcast on the BBC Third Programme on 19 July.[19] Not only did John and Michael insist on the choir singing in what they believed was the correct style, with harsh, uncompro-mising voices (the 'modified shout'), but they also sang using contemporary English pronunciation.[20] Once again they threw caution to the wind, casting aside received precepts of performing English church music and caring little for what anyone else thought.[21] As Christopher Page stated on Radio 3's *Mining the Archive* programme in 1995, the recording still stands today as an extraordinarily imaginative, provocative and penetrating performance.[22] The opening of *The Lamentations of Jeremiah* is gutsy: the all-male choir sings with perfect intonation and ensemble, and the basses are rich and powerful. A great deal of rehearsal and an insistence on the highest of standards from the singers must have been neces-sary for such a faultless recording of this wonderful music, which, according to the editors of *Tudor Church Music*, attains the level of Byrd and Tallis.[23] However, not everybody liked John and Michael's approach; reviewing a new recording of White's *Lamentations* and other works by the Scuola di Chiesa in the May 1968 edition of *The Musical Times*, the author was relieved that the conductor, John Hoban, did not share John's belief that dynamic nuance, subtlety of phrasing and the blending of voices had no place in music of this period.[24]

In April, F.C. Ball's adaptation for radio of his novel *A Grotto for Miss Maynier* (a story of the strange relationship between a solitary old lady and her garden boy) was broadcast on BBC Radio 3 with John's incidental music. John had received ninety guineas for the music, which had been recorded in March. *The Times* described the play as being 'delicate, compassionate, full of strange atmosphere evoked partly by John Beckett's music but mostly by the text and acting – there are beautiful performances from Nigel Anthony and Miriam Margolyes.'[25]

St Patrick's Hall in Dublin Castle was the venue for a televised concert during the same month, *The Music of Swift's Dublin*. This was one of a series of programmes to mark the tercentenary year of the birth of Jonathan Swift (1667–1745) and, according to its producer James Plunkett, its audience included 'over one hundred eminent scholars from all over the world' who were visiting Dublin for the Swift Symposium week. The programme was introduced by a lively Professor Brian Boydell; the music (which was arranged by John) included pieces by Handel, John Gay, Matthew Dubourg, Carolan, Geminiani, a *Cantata in Satire of the Italian style* by Jonathan Swift and the Rev. John Echlin, a Purcell Trio Sonata, and a suite of airs and dances from *The Castle Balls and Publick Assemblies in Dublin composed by the best Masters*. By today's standards, the black-and-white television coverage looks crude and amateurish, but it allows us to see the performers in action. Brian Boydell's almost forced jollity contrasts sharply with John's grim expression and the attitude of the other players, who all play or sing with great concentration and earnestness. An occasional and unchanging shot of the audience reveals a hall full of mildly interested dignitaries and academics, who applaud without too much enthusiasm.[26] Charles Acton, who was at the event, complained that the programme was too long: 'It would have been quite long enough had it all been great music played to a primarily musical gathering.'[27] However, the programme was deemed to be important enough to be repeated in an edited version in November and transmitted on the BBC some time afterwards.

A couple of days after *The Music of Swift's Dublin* was shown, John, on harpsichord, and Daphne Webb, on cello continuo, accompanied Frank Patterson in a programme of music by Henry Purcell that was broadcast on the BBC Third Programme. Frank sang several songs, including 'If music be the food of love', 'Fairest isle' and 'Ah! how sweet it is to love', and John played some solo harpsichord pieces, including *Sefauchi's farewell* and *A new ground*.[28]

Musica Reservata's status as a specialized group performing early music for a small but interested band of followers was about to change when a large-scale concert was staged in the Queen Elizabeth Hall on 2 July 1967 and broadcast live on the BBC Third Programme. Utilizing thirty-five players, and a bewildering collection of musical instruments, the concert would eventually become known as the group's South Bank debut concert.[29]

Twenty-Three
1967

The South Bank concert was managed by Tom Sutcliffe, who, thanks to his vigorous promotion and selling of advertising space in a cheaply-produced but handsome programme, managed to sell all 1100 seats for the concert. As the new Queen Elizabeth Hall had been opened by the Queen in March of that year, it was an ideal venue for the concert as everyone was interested to be there.[1]

The singers that evening were Jantina Noorman, mezzo-soprano, Grayston Burgess, John Whitworth and Tom Sutcliffe, counter-tenors, Geoffrey Shaw, baritone and John Frost, bass. The twenty-four musicians included Ruth David, John Sothcott, David Munrow, John O'Sullivan, Harold Lester, Christopher Hogwood, Desmond Dupré and Michael Morrow. John was the conductor of this formidable ensemble.

The first half consisted of music of the Italian Renaissance, starting with Monteverdi's arresting *Toccata* from his opera *Orfeo*, and featuring other pieces by the same composer. In addition, there was music by Massaino, Giovanni Gabrieli, Marenzio, Malvezzi and Cavalieri. The second half consisted of secular vocal and instrumental music from thirteenth and fourteenth-century France and early sixteenth-century Spain, and included the familiar *Kalenda maya* by de Vaqueiras and *Tant con je vivray* ('As long as I live') by de la Halle. According to the programme notes, 'the performance will attempt to recreate some of the musical colours and textures that contemporary audiences would have expected: sounds that today are seldom even approached because of the constant obtrusion of modern and inappropriate mannerisms of interpretation.' The handsome booklet included biographies of many of the main performers and an introduction to the group.[2]

One can imagine the sense of excitement generated in the packed hall on that Sunday evening in London. Enthusiastic reviews appeared in several of the newspapers over the next couple of days. 'What impressed most,' said *The Daily Telegraph*, 'was the tremendous vitality of the performances and the variety of the vocal and instrumental textures. These could only be achieved by accomplished singers and players and by an enlightened conductor, John Beckett.'[3] *The Guardian* reported that, 'Under John Beckett's firm unobtrusive direction, the most complicated pieces maintained their impetus and sense of direction.'[4] Another review, entitled *Renaissance top of the pops*, continued, '...one appreciated the musical genuineness regenerated by Messrs. Michael Morrow and John Beckett, and could only quibble that the non-musical conventions of conductors, bow ties and facial reserve, were in conflict with the music's ambiance. But the music won with its sharp fresh sounds which buzz in the head afterwards.'[5]

Nicholas Anderson, who attended some of the Musica Reservata concerts in the Queen Elizabeth Hall and who may have been at this debut recital, remembers how the group suddenly became the talk of the town:

> People who were interested in early music found Musica Reservata very exciting, and I think I would still find it exciting because of that one thing about John, that was as attractive as it was absolutely distinctive and, I would say, unique: John had a sort of primitive side to him, a kind of earthiness, which he introduced to the music.

He remembers the 'buzz' after the performance of the Monteverdi *Toccata* and the terrific applause, which went on and on until a very grumpy-looking Beckett came out of the wings, stood on the podium, glared at everybody, did the type of bow that he could most easily get away with, and then disappeared again:

> John appeared to loathe audiences. Of course we now know that he didn't really – that was his manner. But all that was fun to teenagers like myself, and this was all exciting. This was a new kind of music that wasn't just coat tails and bow ties and absolute anonymity, which I'd been used to from my childhood days ... With John you had a feeling that you were hearing this sort of music for the first time, and that John was the first person to conduct it. And that John also had a kind of hot line somewhere, in a direction where nobody else seemed to have it. [6]

Parallels had been drawn between this performance of early music and pop music with reason – any young person who had been listening to the Rolling Stones or the Beatles would have been fascinated by the sounds that they heard at the concert and would doubtless have taken to this music.

As regards John's seeming grumpiness, Tom Sutcliffe observed that he and Michael Morrow did not believe in trying to ingratiate themselves with the public; both were idealists in the sense that people were supposed to enjoy what they were listening to without either of them making any special effort to make them feel welcome. He also pointed out that little skill was needed to conduct the ensemble, especially as John insisted on such a rigid, unvarying beat; all he needed to do was get everyone started and keep them together. Overall, Tom felt that the standard of playing that evening was very high and that the concert worked extremely well.[7]

David Cairns, who reported the 'capacity house' in *The Financial Times*, was a little more cautious in his praise, though he found that the sackbuts, cornetts, crumhorns, chitarrone and the other instruments were played with 'admirable fluency and with good intonation (once the main snag in "authentic" concerts of old music); only the recorders caused me any discomfort in this respect … the biggest one of all – an interminable thing like a telegraph pole in the act of falling – was to all appearances inaudible.'[8]

Favourable comments were printed in the August edition of *Recorder and Music Review*: 'One can only praise in the highest terms the devotion and organisation that brought this evening into being and add the hope that encouraged by such phenomenal success, Musica Reservata will find ways and means of becoming a regular concert-giving group.'[9]

Speaking on BBC Radio 3 in 1998, Anthony Rooley remembered how John and Michael's performances had sent shivers down people's spines:

Officially, Morrow was the musical director and scholar and Beckett was the conductor and keyboard player, but in practice they were fire and brimstone, and you never knew who would be which. Their working relationship was symbiotic to an extraordinary degree and the abrasive love-hate partnership was very much part of the incredible contribution these two made. I've never met two people more ardently, passionately in love with music making, and they imparted this passion generously to all the singers and players who worked for them. The list of musicians who did work under [them] is long; almost everyone who was anyone in early music through the seventies and most of the eighties, had at least a passing relationship with Morrow and Beckett. Many didn't stay for long; the working conditions and demands were more than most had stomach for, but – wow! – their influence was wide and all-permeating. Erratic, irascible, rude, wrong-headed, contrasting with devotion, passion, endearing, delightful – and you never knew which side of the coin would be up. Rehearsals were a nightmare. I've seen grown men come out of a session almost in tears and certainly voiceless, but coming back for more. I've seen hardened brass players waiting meekly for hours till it was their turn to play a sackbut drone. I've seen the utter state of chaos of parts and scores only moments before a rehearsal was to begin, and I've seen the obstinate Beckett unmoved by the bizarre difficulties of a fifteenth-century organ score and play it nimbly, like one in a dream. Morrow's playing on the lute had to be seen to be believed – you certainly couldn't hear it … Many associate Musica Reservata with an array of wacky instruments but both Morrow and Beckett were but jelly when it came to the human voice – but it had to be the right human voice. Not for them the received tradition of Deller, let alone the enormously popular wobble, fashionable in operatic circles, their aim was, like a laser beam before its time, to cut through received opinions and standards, and have the human voice produce a direct, cutting edge sound that went straight to the base of the spine and shot from there to alpha rhythms at the back of the head, like the release of *kundalini* energy in yoga – the serpent must wake. These men didn't need flower power pot, though one of them [Michael] was seriously into snuff, for their high came with high-energy direction of the human voice.'[10]

This, better than anything, describes vividly the relationship between John and Michael at the time and the often chaotic atmosphere that they generated around themselves.

Michael Morrow's obituary in *Early Music* summed up the July debut concert as 'an unforgettable occasion when we felt that early music had at last taken off in London.' Musica Reservata had stepped into the limelight and John had finally become recognized in the UK and abroad as a respected, if somewhat grumpy, conductor of early music.[11]

There was little time to wallow in the euphoria caused by the success of Musica Reservata's concert in the Queen Elizabeth Hall; later in July the first of two programmes featuring John playing pieces from *The Fitzwilliam Virginal Book* was broadcast on the BBC Third Programme,[12] then the recital of choral music by Robert White (mentioned earlier), sung by the Musica Reservata Choir, conducted by John.[13] Around the same time John was heard twice on RTÉ Radio playing harpsichord music by William Byrd.[14] Before the end of the month, the BBC was recording German music of the Renaissance period, performed by Musica Reservata,[15] and also incidental music for flute and harp written by John for *The Good Natur'd Man*, a radio programme featuring Felix Felton as Oliver Goldsmith, which was broadcast towards the end of August.[16]

Despite the fact that *The Good Natur'd Man* had been broadcast, John had not been paid for his work. Writing to David Thomson of the BBC from Edinburgh at the end of the month, where he was serving 'three weeks operatic sentence', he complained, 'I have not been commissioned, and therefore run not the slightest risk of being paid for my Oliver Goldsmith arrangements. Some secretariel [*sic*] slip-up I suppose. Could you get things moving as speedily as possible? As, alas, nearly always, I need the stinking money.' David returned from his holidays to find John's letter and was horrified to discover that no contract had been drawn up. The very next day John was offered twenty guineas.[17]

John's 'sentence' in Edinburgh was his involvement at the annual Festival's production of Haydn's *L'Anima del filosofo* (*Orfeo ed Euridice*) at the King's Theatre, in which the part of Euridice was sung by Joan Sutherland. Six performances were staged between 25 August and 9 September. As he was unable to teach at the recorder course in An Grianán, Termonfeckin because of this, he asked his friend Theo Wyatt to deputize for him. Theo remembers that John had accepted this more lucrative and attractive engagement, which involved accompanying Joan Sutherland's arias on the harpsichord.[18]

In September a letter was written by Francis Grubb of the Recording and Concert Agency to William Glock, the Controller of Music at the BBC, about the possibility of including Musica Reservata in one of the Henry Wood Promenade Concerts during the following year. Writing on behalf of Michael Morrow, Grubb emphasized the amount of attention the debut South Bank concert had attracted in July: the hall had been completely sold out and 'the young and enthusiastic audience applauded heartily, demanding encores'. In another letter he added:

> I have had the pleasure during recent months of presenting the 'Reservata' to the recording companies and even I have been surprised by the immediate response which a tape recording of the group has produced. 1968 is going to be a very busy year for Michael Morrow and his artists, and its crowning glory would be an appearance at the Royal Albert Hall.[19]

He followed this with a telephone call in the middle of the month, but to no avail – Mr Glock sent a memo to his secretary: 'Daphne, will you please say 1969? Sorry we can't fit them in this time. W.G.'[20]

Frank was correct in predicting that the following year would be a busy one for Musica Reservata, for all of a sudden there was a veritable explosion of radio and commercial recordings. Starting in October 1967, a new record appeared of medieval music performed by the Jaye Consort, led by Francis Baines, with members of Musica Reservata. This was *Medieval Vocal and Instrumental Works*, issued on the Pye Golden Guinea label. Malcolm MacDonald of *The Gramophone* found this record of mainly anonymous songs and dances to be of 'endless fascination'; among all the imaginative and courageous performances that he had heard of such music, none was equal to those of this new disc, which he found fresh and enjoyable.[21]

John's most ambitious project to date was broadcast on 19 October as part of the BBC Radio 3 *Interpretations on Record* series: a talk on Mahler's Ninth Symphony, with recorded musical illustrations.[22] This programme was produced at a time when Mahler's music was not so well known. As the BBC did not have one of the recordings of Mahler's Ninth that John wanted to use (probably the Columbia Philharmonic Orchestra's performance of 1961, conducted by Bruno Walter), he had to borrow it from a friend.[23] Although the recordings sound poor and rather scratchy by today's standards, John's presentation and analysis of the material is masterly, evidencing the depth of his knowledge of Mahler's music and his ability to make sound judgments on the recordings available at the time.

In the programme, John compared seven recordings: Bruno Walter and the Vienna Philharmonic Orchestra (1938), Bruno Walter and the Columbia Philharmonic Orchestra (1961), Paul Kletzi and the Israel Philharmonic Orchestra, Jascha Horenstein and the Vienna Symphony Orchestra, Otto Klemperer and the New Philharmonic Orchestra, Sir John Barbirolli and the Berlin Philharmonic Orchestra, and Leopold Ludwig and the London Symphony Orchestra. He did not clearly state which recording he considered to be the best – each one had its merits and drawbacks. However, it is obvious that he favoured the two Bruno Walter recordings as regards different sections of the various movements, though neither recording pleased him entirely.[24]

John received another invitation from the BBC for incidental music in November: a radio adaptation of Sophocles's *Oedipus Rex*. Approval was sought by John Tydeman for John to compose music for a maximum of twelve musicians: 'the same number as John used in his highly successful music for "Electra". I have always found John Beckett a splendid interpreter of both my own and the author's intentions, and an added advantage (perhaps) in this case is that we are using the W.B.Yeats translation and John is an Irishman!'[25] The play, translated as *Oedipus the King*, was broadcast in March of the following year.[26]

Meanwhile, in a letter to John at The Guardship, Church Street, written on 14 November 1967, H.B. Fortuin commissioned John to write seven minutes of music for Sandro Key-Åberg's play *O*, which would be recorded in January of the following year.[27]

'The Guardship' refers to John and Vera's new residence in Church Street. Just across the road from Brampton House, this extraordinary building had a ship's female figurehead attached to the left-hand upper window, a ship's wheel at the bottom of the central window (formerly a door), an anchor hanging from a triangular-shaped metal bracket between the two windows, and 'Guardship' painted on a board underneath.[28] When John and Vera moved there, a mezzanine floor that was approached by a steep wooden staircase had housed a coopers' workshop. Here everything had been preserved – tools, leather aprons and so forth – under a thick layer of dust. As well as this, steps led down from the ground floor to tunnels, resembling catacombs, that led underground to Fuller's Brewery, situated a short distance away on the opposite side of the road, and also down to the river.[29]

John and Vera lived on the upper storey where there was (and still is) a large room right up to the pitched roof, with skylights, which was excellent for rehearsing and playing music. Although interesting, it was not a very practical house as the ceilings were high and it was cold.[30]

John's friends Vic and Frida Robinson, (Vic had been involved with Musica Reservata at some stage), remember playing music with John in the large upstairs room. They and some other musicians had volunteered to be guinea pigs for John, who was trying out some music. Frida recollects playing some of Bach's Brandenburg Concertos with him. She also remembers listening to a recording of Mahler's Fifth Symphony at top volume in the house. She remembers how John's views were 'incredibly strong and unchanging – they were set in stone, really'.[31]

Tom Sutcliffe remembers going to John and Vera's home at The Guardship for meals. He found John a ponderous yet intriguing man: big in person and big in personality, like an Old Testament figure. Tom was quite impressed by him and at the time believed everything that was said about the correctness of his approach, though later he began to feel a little uncomfortable about what he and Michael were actually trying to do in Musica Reservata. Although one could shout at Michael, one did not dare shout at John as it was too risky and he could retaliate.[32]

The new harpsichord that John had waited patiently for finally arrived at The Guardship 'on schedule, and safe and sounding' on 15 November. He wrote to David Owen Williams at the Guinness Brewery, 'I would like to thank you, and all others concerned, for overcoming what I imagined would be the formidable difficulties of transportation and customs formalities with such magical ease and efficiency – and good will. Truly thank you.'[33] John remembered that it was shipped to him in a specially made case. 'It was all practically a miracle,' he said many years later, 'a large miracle for me to get the thing, and I'm very proud to have [had] it.'[34]

Shortly afterwards, John wrote to his friend James Plunkett, who was now working in RTÉ Television, with a request for some new programmes:

Is there any chance of Telefís Eireann offering me and Frank (with, as I said, Betty) a Purcell prog. or two, or so, in January? I think Frank sings Purcell marvellously, to the point where he will create new standards of listening to the songs — and several ruthlessly discerning people here, who have heard him, agree with me. The Big Brother Corporation [BBC] is very impressed with him. In fact, I personally believe that he is going to be a distinguished sinfer [recte singer] (my tyling [recte typing] — hell — again). It would be very good for him to be asked to work in Jan. — he and Eily are hiving [recte having] a toughish time living in Paris on not much money, while he studies with Janine Micheau.[35]

Luckily for John, James was able to help and did devise four programmes of music by Henry Purcell, as we shall see.

Twenty-Four
1968

The year began with a recording of Thomas Tallis's *Lamentations* and two of his motets, *Miserere Nostri* and *Salve Intermerata Virgo* in the Church of St George the Martyr, Queen Square. Like White's *Lamentations of Jeremiah*, this Latin church music was sung by the Musica Reservata Choir, conducted by John and with Harold Lester on organ.[1]

Also in January, John's music for *Oedipus Rex* was recorded, using a piccolo, two oboes, a cor anglais, three trumpets, three trombones, two percussionists, three cellos and a double bass.[2] On the twelfth of the month, *O* by Sandro Key-Åberg, 'seventeen "Speakies" translated from the Swedish by Brian Rothwell with music by John Beckett', was broadcast on the newly-named BBC Radio 3. A handwritten note at the bottom of an internal document reads, 'Check that music was composed at length commissioned (approx 7') and if so, pay 2nd ½ [i.e., the second half of the fee].'[3] Obviously the BBC people had become wise to John's habit of writing more music than requested and then demanding a revised fee.[4]

Within a very short time, John had accepted another commission to compose five minutes of music for Gerard McLarnon's play *The Chinese Jig*, to be produced by Christopher Holme. The music, recorded in March, was scored for a piccolo and flute, an E flat and bass clarinet, a tuba, a piano accordion and percussion. As well as his own music, an arrangement by him of Handel's *Dead March* from *Saul* was included.[5]

In the middle of February, John played two pieces for harpsichord by William Byrd, and Frank Patterson, accompanied by John on harpsichord and Betty Sullivan on cello, performed songs by Henry Purcell on a Radio 4 *Music at*

Night programme. Frank sang some of the Purcell songs that he would become famous for (at least in Ireland): 'On the brow of Richmond Hill', 'Music for a while', 'Since from my dear Astrea's sight', 'What a sad fate is mine', 'I'll sail upon the dog star', and 'If music be the food of Love' (first and second settings). It was this broadcast that brought Frank to the attention of the Philips Record Company. He was quickly placed under contract and six albums were recorded in the space of three years.[6]

John returned to Dublin when his mother Peggy died on 17 March at St Michael's Nursing home, Dun Laoghaire.[7] Samuel, who had always been very fond of her, had been writing to her while she was ill. When he was told about her death, he flew over to Dublin on the following day. John and Ann probably met him at the airport, where Ann remembered the 'terrible hoo-ha' that occurred in his effort to avoid the press knowing that he was there. Ann remembered being amazed that there was such a fuss as it had not dawned on her 'what a wonderful thing his work was at that time'. As there was no room for him in Peggy's house, he was put up in the Grand Hotel in Greystones. John remembered going to collect him from the hotel, which was half a mile from the house, and noticing that the place smelt curiously of fresh hay. Samuel spent the few days in Greystones and Killiney with members of his family.

The funeral service was held in St Patrick's Church, Greystones, on 19 March and Peggy was buried in nearby Redford Cemetery. During the wake at Field Place, Samuel was discovered sitting at the kitchen table with his head bowed and a hanging wall clock, which Peggy had bought at an auction, ticking noisily behind him. As Ann realized that something was bothering him, she said nothing until he looked up and said, 'Look, I can't go on with this clock – you'll have to stop the clock.' (It was at this period when Samuel was listening intently to sounds such as footsteps, resulting in his play *Footfalls*.) After the funeral, Ann gave John his mother's clock, which he kept for the rest of his life.

For Ann, Samuel's presence in the family home felt so different from when he used to visit them when they were young. John remembered that, on the day after the funeral, Samuel discovered some fruit juice on the breakfast table, which he decided to drink. Having swallowed a couple of mouthfuls of it he smacked his lips and said, 'Cuts through the morning scum!' A day or two later he flew back to Paris.[8]

Back in London, John was commissioned to write music for another play: this time fifteen minutes' worth for David Paul's *Poor Mrs Machiavelli*, produced by David Thomson.[9] The music was performed by John on harpsichord and James Blades on vibraphone, and was recorded in May.[10] The play, a 'domestic crisis', which was broadcast in June, is set in Florence during the Renaissance period.[11]

After John, Vera, Morris Sinclair and his wife Mimi had gone in Paris at the beginning of May to visit Samuel and see a major retrospective of Henri Hayden's paintings, which was opened by André Malraux at the Musée National d'Art Moderne,[12] John and Vera returned to London, where a new Musica Reservata record, *A Florentine Festival*, was recorded at Kingsway Hall, Holborn (home of the West London Mission of the Methodist Church and well known for the intrusive subterranean rumblings, courtesy of the London Underground). More of the music would be recorded in August. Bernard Thomas, now a new member of the group, was invited to the sessions by Michael Morrow so that he could get an idea of what they were doing. He remembers that they were 'rather wonderful'.[13]

The record was later released on the Argo and Decca labels. Conducted by John, the singers included Jantina Noorman, Grayston Burgess, Nigel Rogers and John Frost (baritone). Apart from the usual quota of anonymous composers, the music included works by Monteverdi (a rousing performance of his opening *Toccata* from *Orfeo*), Luca Marenzio, Bartolomeo Tromboncino and other Italian composers.[14] The LP, full of interesting and lively music that accompanied the spectacular *intermedii* or interval acts of a play performed during the nuptial celebrations of the Grand Duke Ferdinand of Florence and Maria of Lorraine in 1589, received a favourable review from Denis Arnold in *The Gramophone*, who thought that this type of unemotional music suited Musica Reservata perfectly. It was well recorded and balanced, with, fortunately, no intrusive rumblings from the London Underground.[15] The music on side two of the LP was written for private entertainment and was a little more earthy.

The disc was later released as the second CD of a two-CD boxed set, the first of which was, ironically, *Ecco la Primavera – Florentine Music of the 14th century*, performed by David Munrow's group, the Early Music Consort of London. Listeners would have been able to compare the different styles of the two groups, and note that Munrow's interpretation was the sweeter of the two.[16]

Also recorded in March was a disc that would later become very successful: *Music from the time of Christopher Columbus*. This was the first of several LPs to be recorded by Philips. The person responsible for setting up the session, booking the people and the location was David Cairns, who, as well as being a writer and journalist, worked for Philips at the time.[17] David met John through Francis Grubb, who, according to Tom Sutcliffe, 'fixed' the recordings with Philips.[18] David, who would get to know John better over the years, came to regard him as being a 'wonderful man'. He thought it odd the way he revered Bach and yet hated Handel. He also met Michael Morrow, whom he regarded as being quite eccentric but a pioneer. David found him a chaotic individual – the music to be performed was never quite ready. This was something that John was already beginning to find quite irksome. To David, Jantina Noorman's voice 'sounded like a medieval oboe'.

As well as being at this recording, David would be present at the various other Musica Reservata recordings over the years, which always took place in London – either in Wembley Town Hall (where most of the recordings were made), Watford or Walthamstow (which was the best venue for large-scale works). Because of the Dutch way of doing things, according to which the producer was required to learn 'all the electronic techniques', David did not produce any of these recordings; like the *Christopher Columbus* recording, he merely organized them as regards sessions, locations and people.[19]

Although *Music from the time of Christopher Columbus* became so successful later, the reviews (which appeared early in the following year), were mixed. Denis Arnold in *The Gramophone* was cautious; for him there was no control of nuance, no sense of phrasing and no delicacy. However, he found the Cabezón pieces for keyboard attractive: 'John Beckett plays them straightforwardly, perhaps a shade too much so, and whether it is the recorded sound, the instrument or his actual touch, the result is distinctly more agreeable than on some of his earlier record-ings.'[20] Charles Cudworth, in *Records and Recording*, wrote: 'the odd assortment of sounds which comes from this particular disc is not necessarily everyone's cup of tea, or even stoup of wine... All in all, a most memorable, out-of-the-way treasure trove, robustly sung and played, and brilliantly recorded in stereo.'[21]

At around this time, the HMV series of records, entitled *Music of the Court Homes and Cities of England* was released. The first one, featuring various artists, concentrated on music performed at the Chapel Royal. One of the tracks featured John playing John Bull's galliard *Saint Thomas Wake* and on another, Purcell's Trio Sonata No. 10 in A major, Z 799, edited by John and performed by him on harpsichord, Ruth David and Roderick Skeaping on violins, and Desmond Dupré on viola da gamba. Denis Arnold, writing in *The Gramophone*, thought that the Purcell sonata sounded the least adequately performed item on the disc, believing that it was the lack of vibrato that made the strings sound a little harsh.[22]

The second disc, devoted to the music played at Hampton Court, in which Musica Reservata performed pieces by William Cornyshe, Albarte and Henry VIII, appeared a little later. The same reviewer in *The Gramophone* thought that the group performed the 'Consort' piece by Henry VIII in a 'virile' manner, that they played the dances (by Albarte and an anonymous composer) with 'immense panache' and that the cornett playing sounded 'smooth and voice-like'.[23] In *Records and Recording*, Peter Dennison believed that the selection of music on this record was more successful than the first. 'Cornyshe's piece demonstrates a highly advanced use of imitation, and both the early and middle consort pieces are given with a relishing freshness and drive by Musica Reservata.'[24]

The third record of the series, *Composers of Whitehall Palace and Wilton House*, contained music by William Lawes, edited by John and performed by him on organ with Ruth David and Roderick Skeaping, violins, and Desmond Dupré on viola da gamba. A dance suite by Henry Lawes, also edited by John, was performed by him on the harpsichord, with Ruth and Desmond on their respective instruments. Denis Arnold of *The Gramophone* found the harsh sound of the violins hard to stomach.[25]

On the fourth disc, *Composers of Greenwich House and Ingatestone House*, which appeared at the same time, John played William Byrd's *Pavana Bray* on the harpsichord and he, Desmond, Ruth and Roderick played a suite by Coprario, which John had edited.[26] Included on the fifth record, which was favourably reviewed in *Records and Recording*, John played a short piece on the virginals – William Byrd's *The Queens Almain*.[27] On the sixth in the series, *Composers of Chichester and Worcester*, which was reviewed in the August edition of *The Gramophone*, John played Tomkins's *Worcester brauls* on the harpsichord, which Denis Arnold thought suited John's style better than more delicate pieces did.[28]

A disc variously (and confusingly) known as *At the Court of Henry VIII*, *To Entertain a King*, *Music to Entertain a King* and *Music to Entertain Henry VIII*, which was shared once again with Grayston Burgess's group the Purcell Consort, now appeared. The pieces on this LP played by Musica Reservata included instrumental works by anonymous composers of the period. As before, the voices in the items sung by Grayston Burgess's group are a good deal less harsh than those in Morrow's – one wonders what John and Michael thought of the singing. Like *A Florentine Festival*, this record serves as an excellent introduction to early music.[29] Once again, Denis Arnold, writing in *The Gramophone*, wished for an occasional touch of emotional extravagance.[30]

Twenty-Five
1968—69

John wrote to James Plunkett in April, informing him that he had completed all the scores and was copying the parts for four television programmes of music by Purcell that were being prepared. He wanted to know about rehearsal arrangements and begged him to 'ask and pay Cathal Gannon to look over the RE Gannon instrument we are using – it tends to have nothing done to it for months and months, in the normal run of events, and is sure to need touching up. You also, of course, haven't forgotten that it must be tuned each day.' This is typical of the precise instructions that John often included in his letters. He also informed James that he, Vera and Ann were off to Paris for a week, at Samuel's invitation, and would be back in London by early May. He finished with, 'What news of your London trip? Remember you are all welcome, and workably welcome here.'[1]

John, Ann, Vera and also Morris Sinclair's sister Deirdre set off on the holiday to France – and Switzerland – on the morning that this letter was written. They drove in a little Mini and stayed, when in Paris, in an apartment belonging to Frank Patterson; Deirdre remembered seeing a list of singing practices hanging on a wall.

They visited Samuel at his little house at Ussy. He was apologetic about offering them nothing from his garden, saying that anything he planted in it would immediately die. When driving to Chartres, a stone flew up and broke the windscreen of the car. They stopped at the 'nearest hostelry' to get help, and because it was a Sunday and nobody was available, they had a 'happy day at the hostelry'. When driving, Ann sat in front with John, who at one stage began to doze off. Ann took over and 'saved the day'. They then travelled down to the

German-speaking part of Switzerland, where they saw bears in the zoo at Bern, and went to the picturesque medieval town of Gruyères, where John would have probably purchased some of the famous cheese made in the region.[2] It seems that they also met up with Ralph Cusack in Geneva while they were in Switzerland. He had lost his wife in January, when she had taken her own life by swallowing an overdose of sleeping pills.[3]

Over two days towards the end of May 1968, *The Golden Age*, the four programmes of music and songs by Purcell that James Plunkett had produced at John's request, were recorded by RTÉ Television in Dublin. The music was played by Hugh Maguire and Iona Brown on violins, Edward Beckett on flute, John on harpsichord, Betty Sullivan on cello, and the songs were sung by Frank Patterson.[4]

One of the songs was *What a sad fate is mine*, a haunting tune on a simple ground bass. According to David Clark, John had stretched Purcellian harmonies to the utmost in his realization of the accompaniment. 'The sound engineer came over to look at the score, because he thought there must be a mistake (I suspect he had heard consecutive sevenths). "You stick to your job; I'll stick to mine", commented John tartly.'[5]

John's latest programme of music by Franz Xaver Mozart was broadcast on Radio 3 in mid June. This included the young Mozart's Sonata in E major (played by Hugh Maguire, violin and Viola Tunnard, fortepiano) and six of his songs, sung by Frank Patterson and accompanied by John on the fortepiano.[6] On the day when this programme was broadcast, John was commissioned by Martin Esslin to compose music for *Ubu Enchained*, another play by Alfred Jarry. The music, for bass tuba, clarinet and percussion (which John directed) and a 'pub style' piano (which he played), was composed and accepted a month later.[7]

In August, a review written by Denis Arnold appeared in *The Gramophone* for another record of music performed by the Purcell Consort of Voices and Musica Reservata: *Metaphysical Tobacco*. Arnold was on the whole pleased with the disc and praised John's solo harpsichord playing of John Bull's virtuoso arrangement of Dowland's *Captain Digorie Pipers Galliard*.[8] A favourable review, written by Watkins Shaw, appeared in the *Musical Times* in October.[9]

Another large-scale concert was given by Musica Reservata on 15 September in the Queen Elizabeth Hall: this one was grandly entitled *The Hundred Years War and the Age of Chivalry in France*. It was recorded by the BBC and broadcast the following month as *Music of the 100 years' war*.[10] As before, John conducted this concert of French and English music composed between 1337 and 1453, but this time he also played the organ. The thirteen musicians included Ruth David on rebec, Michael Morrow on lute, and Bernard Thomas on shawm and crumhorn.[11] Bernard came to like John very much. John, he soon discovered, enjoyed life, loved going to France, ate lots of French food and appreciated the French way of life. Bernard was also fond of Michael and got to know him very well.[12]

The singers on the evening of the *Hundred Years War* concert included Simon Woolf, a boy treble, who sang Dufay's *Magnam me gentes* to the satisfaction of Dominic Gill of *The Financial Times*.[13] David Cairns, writing in the *New Statesman*, enthused about Musica Reservata's recent successes, noting the professionalism and the fact that the instruments were played in tune. He concluded: '…the noise they make has an exhilarating harshness, brilliance and ferocity. Medieval music is the highbrow pop.'[14] A decision had been made by Philips back in April to record this music for an LP towards the end of the month.[15]

Michael Nyman, writing in the *Spectator*, noted with interest that the BBC would be juxtaposing the music of Guillaume Dufay and Peter Maxwell Davies in the following month's *Invitation Concert*, which was recorded on 3 October and broadcast on BBC Radio 3 a few days later.[16] A selection of Dufay's secular music was performed by Musica Reservata, conducted once again by John, and some of the composer's keyboard settings, taken from the Buxheimer Orgelbuch, were played by him on a chamber organ. The programme was favourably reviewed in *The Listener* by John's former teacher Edmund Rubbra, who thought that such a juxtaposition of early and modern music was very illuminating.[17]

As we have noted, Michael was disorganized and the music to be rehearsed for performances like this was often not ready on time. John, who by now was conducting the group on a fairly regular basis and was more business-like, expected everything to be ready and used to say, 'Tell me when it's ready and then I'll come back'.[18] On one occasion, all the players had to waste time on a first rehearsal because of the lack of music and, because of the resulting exasperation, a rift began to appear in the relationship between John and Michael.[19] Michael felt that John should have been more involved in the preparation and production of the music, but John, who was indeed capable of discovering old manuscripts in libraries and transcribing the music into modern notation, just wanted to have the music handed to him – probably because he was busy and had other things to do.[20]

The next concert to be given by the group took place soon afterwards on the final evening of the Hexham Abbey Festival in Northumberland, where they performed French and English music ranging from the thirteenth to the fifteenth century.[21]

By November, another Musica Reservata record had been issued, this time on the Delysé label: *French Court Music of the Thirteenth Century*. This interesting collection of trouvère and troubadour songs, interspersed with invigorating dances, was quite exhilarating, as noted in *Records and Recording* and by Denis

Arnold in *The Gramophone*. John, as well as conducting, played the citole (a type of wire-strung lute), drum and organetto.[22] 'This is a record which explains those packed houses on the South Bank for mediaeval music concerts,' wrote Denis Arnold. 'It would be thin blood indeed which did not warm to the vitality of the very first piece Kalenda maya, played and sung with such spirit, and more likely than not you may find yourself whistling snatches of a Royal Estampie before long.'[23] 'One of the surest winners of the collection is an *estampie* played simply, but with marvellous verve, on John Sothcott's recorder and John Beckett's drum', wrote Christopher Butchers in *Records and Recording*. 'Michael Morrow's theories of authentic performance are quite immaterial to the enjoyment of the end-product in this disc: it is difficult to conceive of a more captivating or imaginative account of pre-Machaut music.' When it was reissued in early 1973 and reviewed again (in a rather facetious manner) in *Records and Recording*, Charles Cudworth opined that the record was 'a splendid example of its kind, performed with gusto and recorded with great care.'[24]

In Ireland, Michael Dervan, who was excited by the development of early music, first became aware of John Beckett through Musica Reservata records like this one. He considered the group to be unique; the music had a raw, uncompromising quality and the sound of the singing was unlike anything that one would hear anywhere else. For him, it was interesting to hear something that was so much outside the norms of twentieth-century classical music singing.[25]

Once again, the Queen Elizabeth Hall was the venue for the next Musica Reservata concert, recorded live by the BBC and broadcast the following year in April. Dedicated solely to music by Henry Purcell, it included his incidental music to *Abdelazer or The Moor's Revenge*, the Chacony in G minor, the song *If ever I more riches did desire*, and *Great Parent, Hail!* (his ode in commemoration of the centenary of Trinity College, Dublin). For this music, John conducted the group along with the Wandsworth School Boys' Choir, the soprano Valerie Hill, Jantina Noorman, Grayston Burgess, Nigel Rogers, Edgar Fleet, and the baritone Geoffrey Shaw.[26] Despite the fact that this was the type of music that John relished, he conducted the singers and players in the wooden manner that he had been using for much earlier music and, by today's standards, at rather slow speeds. Although the music was well performed and sung, most of the newspaper critics were disappointed in the manner in which it was played and surprised at John's dry, uncommitted style of interpretation.[27]

Tom Sutcliffe was one of the people who regarded this concert as being rather unsuccessful and blamed this on John's limited (and possibly not fully developed) conducting technique and the fact that he tended to be a not very expressive or communicative person. Although John was always very particular about precision in playing, and playing exactly on the beat, he either lacked the ability to make his musicians relax and perform Purcell's theatrical music in a more expressive and lively manner or else he simply did not want them to play it that way, believing that rigidness was a feature of music of this period. Tom felt that he was not a Restoration figure; he was more attuned to the eighteenth century and to the more Germanic (and perhaps rigid) music of Bach. And yet curiously, John was quite capable of wallowing in and performing Romantic music with all its *rallentandi*, *crescendi*, *diminuendi*, long lines and lyrical phrasing.

Another possible reason for the failure of this concert was that Musica Reservata was not yet connected with Baroque music in the eyes of the public. It is interesting to note that Michael Morrow had nothing to do with it; this was the first time, in fact, that John had the group entirely to himself.[28]

By December, *Music from the time of Christopher Columbus*, which had been recorded in March, was released. This was the group's most successful record; until fairly recently a CD version was widely available. A Dutch reviewer in *De Groene Amsterdammer* was ecstatic with the new record and, unsurprisingly, singled out Jantina Noorman as 'the star of this ensemble of stars'. As well as conducting the ensemble, John also played the organ, the harpsichord and the tenor viol.[29] In the following year, the prestigious and oldest Dutch music prize, the Edison Award, was awarded to John in connection with this record on the *Grand Gala du Disque 1969* television show, though it is not clear if John actually appeared on television or not. An elaborate certificate preserved in King's College London grandly states: '*Bij de viering van het Grand Gala du Disque 1969 is de internationale onderscheiding Edison 1968/1969 toegekend aan* John Beckett *voor de bijzondere fonografische prestatie welke geleverd werd met* Musik aus der Zeit Christoph Columbus', which can be loosely translated as 'The Edison 1968/1969 international award has been awarded to *John Beckett* at the celebration of the Grand Gala du Disque 1969 for the special phonographic performance, *Music from the time of Christopher Columbus*.'[30]

The next live concert in which John performed also lacked sparkle, though in this case it was no fault of his. This was Handel's *Messiah* given by Our Lady's Choral Society and the RTÉ Symphony Orchestra in the National Stadium, Dublin. 'Like last year,' Charles Acton wrote in *The Irish Times*, 'it was conducted by Aloys Fleischmann, but this time the results were far less happy.'[31]

This busy and fruitful year ended with another large-scale concert in the Queen Elizabeth Hall: *A Renaissance Christmas* on 29 December. The eighteen musicians (including David Munrow and Christopher Hogwood) and six soloists were joined by the Choir of Musica Reservata with boys from Wandsworth School.[32] The failure of the Purcell concert did not deter the group's followers and the hall was full on this occasion. Ronald Crichton, writing in *The Financial Times*, mentioned that the occasion was informal, with free programmes being offered to the audience. After some 'deep-frozen' carols and a long motet, *Factor orbis* by Obrecht, sung with 'dogged roughness' by the choir, the ice was broken by a group of lively dance-songs for voices and instruments. Included were groups of short anonymous instrumental dances, which were useful for giving the singers a rest.[33]

1969 began with two more Musica Reservata concerts, this time in the smaller Purcell Room on the South Bank. The first was a programme entirely devoted to the music, mostly secular, of Guillaume Dufay.[34] This was well received by the critics. John both conducted and played the organ.[35]

The second concert was entitled 'Music of the time of Boccaccio's Decameron', recorded by the BBC and broadcast later in the year as 'Italian music of the 14th and 15th centuries'.[36] In a programme of archive recordings on BBC Radio 3 many years later, Anthony Rooley played a decorated organ version of Landini's *Che pen' è quest' al cor* ('What heartache is this to my heart'), which had been performed in this concert by John in a 'particularly nimble style', as Rooley described it. Anthony remembered how the narrow stage in the Purcell Room afforded barely enough room for the array of instruments and singers, though he noted that normally only four or five musicians played at a time.[37]

Shortly afterwards, the group assembled in Wembley Town Hall to record a new Philips LP based on the music performed in this second concert. As well as conducting, John also played the organ and the drum.[38]

On 17 March, Saint Patrick's day, John presented a programme on Radio 3 entitled *Studio Portrait*, in which he introduced his personal choice of music, played by himself on a 'small organ' and a harpsichord. The half-hour-long programme had been recorded in February at Maida Vale. The acoustic in Studio 2 was quite reverberant and John's delivery was rather formal, in keeping with the standards of the time. In the programme, John performed some early works on the organ, three pieces from *The Fitzwilliam Virginal Book* and two by Purcell on the harpsichord, and the Gigue from Bach's Partita No. 6 in E minor, BWV 830, 'played, as I believe it should be, with each written bar of 4/2 treated as 4 bars of fast 6/8'. The programme, in which John played dexterously, concluded with Scarlatti's Sonata in G major, K. 146.[39]

Twenty-Six
1969

In April 1969 John's ambition to conduct Bach's cantatas using professional forces finally came to fruition when he was engaged to conduct the 'Musica Reservata Orchestra', the 'Musica Reservata Choir', Wandsworth School Boys' Choir and soloists Grayston Burgess, Nigel Rogers and John Noble (bass) in Cantata 103, *Ihr werdet weinen und heulen* ('Ye shall weep and lament') and Cantata 12, *Weinen, Klagen, Sorgen, Zagen* ('Weeping, wailing, fretting, fearing') in the Concert Hall, Broadcasting House, for a performance that would be broadcast on BBC Radio 3 later in the month.[1] This was the beginning of a series of cantatas that started in London and would continue some years later in Dublin. Although John privately regarded the content of most religious music as nonsense, his admiration for Bach and the beauty of his music overcame his personal belief, and therefore the fact that he had now embarked on a committed path of conducting Bach's religious *oeuvre* did not bother him unduly.[2]

The same forces were used for another recording of Bach cantatas, this time numbers 167, *Ihr Menschen, rühmet Gottes Liebe* ('Ye mortals, extol God's love') and 30, *Freue dich, erlöste Schar* ('Rejoice, O ransomed throng' – John's favourite), at the Maida Vale studios on 17 April, though this time the singers were the soprano Hazel Holt, Grayston Burgess, Nigel Rogers and John Noble. Harold Lester provided the continuo.[3]

After a Musica Reservata concert of music by Dufay in the Victoria and Albert Museum in May[4] and a BBC recording for *This Week's Composers* of Purcell's harpsichord suites,[5] John played the piano solo part in Anton Webern's *Concerto for Nine Instruments* Op. 24 (1934) with the London Symphony Orchestra as part of the *Crossroads of the Twentieth Century* series with the conductor Pierre Boulez.

Writing in the *Early Music Review* in 2007, Clifford Bartlett, who attended
the concert and witnessed John performing this complex twelve-tone music,
claimed that he could not 'recognise the feeling in the sound, but he looked
utterly involved'.[6]

John must have gone to Dublin at around this time for the production of a
documentary film, *Portrait of a Poet: W.B. Yeats*, which was shown first on RTÉ
television's *Telefís Scoile* (Television for Schools) slot during the afternoon on 5
June. The film was shot in Dublin and Sligo; it used archive stills, was narrated
by Pádraic Ó Néill, was produced by James Plunkett and featured incidental
music composed by John. The film, which was repeated once each year until
1972, focused on the places where Yeats had lived and worked, the people who
had influenced his life, his work in politics, the National Theatre and the Irish
Literary Revival, and, of course, his poetry.[7]

John's music for this programme was performed mainly on harp, flute, oboe,
xylophone and harpsichord. Most of the music is typically astringent and rather
stark, though a few bars played on the harpsichord at one section is relatively
lyrical. The folk-like music composed for the closing credits is rather unsettling
at first because it sounds as though it has been written in two unrelated keys.
However, the melody and accompaniment gradually converge and the piece
ends on a major chord.[8]

John did not see the programme, for he had written to James Plunkett
towards the end of May, 'How did the Yeats music fit and contribute in the end?
Could you arrange a showing when I am next in Dublin?' What John has to say
in the rest of his letter is interesting, for he had been reading Plunkett's new
novel, *Strumpet City*:

> *Dear Jimmie,*
>
>   *I finished STRUMPET CITY yesterday. I very much enjoyed it. It moved me
> to the brink of tears several times. Miss Gilchrist's death is a fist in the face
> indeed. It seemed to me excellently organised, balanced and focussed. I think it will
> have as great or an even greater success than Lusty progjollywellnosticated for it.
> Congratulations.*
>
>   *Would you give this volume of Emily Dickinson's poetry to your cousin – the
> poet – I can't recollect his christian name – Boland [John Boland]. We spoke of
> her the night of your party, and he quoted her as one who needs her. As I do. Give
> him the enclosed letter too...* [10]

James thanked John for his remarks about *Strumpet City*. 'I'm glad you liked it
and found it moving – a change from Mr. Coalheaver of the Obscurer.' He gave
the book of Emily Dickinson's poetry to John Boland, 'who is beside himself

(where else could he be) with delight and overwhelmed by your generosity…'
He also told John about some of the difficulties that he had had with the opening
music for the Yeats programme, though everything else had 'worked fine'. He
mentioned that 'the people who previewed the film liked the music very much',
and promised a showing of it when John came to Dublin the next time.[11]

We have outlined the main events of a considerable chunk of John's life with,
unfortunately, only a few glimpses of the man himself. John lived his life for
music, literature and the arts, and when relaxing with friends talked volubly
about these subjects, but it seems that he rarely spoke about himself. If he did,
most of those who knew him at this period have forgotten what he said.

However, one significant event in John's private life occurred at some stage
during 1969: the beginnings of the break-up of his marriage to Vera. John
had told his friend Seán O'Leary that life with her was becoming impossible.
Although John had met the recently divorced Ruth David in 1963 and had probably started a relationship with her in 1966 at around the time she joined Musica
Reservata,[12] he and those he knew managed to keep this secret from Vera.

Another recording of Bach cantatas for the BBC took place at St Andrew's
elegant church in Holborn. Produced, as before, by Michael Hall, the same
orchestra and choir were used. The two cantatas performed on this occasion
were No. 71, *Gott ist mein König* ('God is my King') and 119, *Preise, Jerusalem, den
Herrn* ('Praise the Lord, O Jerusalem').[13] These recordings, enhanced by the
favourable acoustics of the church, were excellent and must have impressed the
BBC officials. The programme was broadcast in September.

The opening of the first cantata is magnificent; John conducts the phrase *Gott
ist mein König* at a sprightlier pace than the following phrases in this first choral
number, as if to emphasize the faithful's exuberance. The rest of the items in
the cantata are taken at stately speeds, a little slower than one would probably
perform them nowadays. The performance is very polished, professional and self-
assured, with only a slightly uncertain start at the beginning of the final chorus.

The opening of *Preise, Jerusalem, den Herrn*, written as a French *ouverture*, is
hugely impressive – one can imagine John conducting it with his right hand
chopping the rhythm through the air. The cantata concludes with a typically
solid, slow-moving Lutheran chorus, which, like the previous cantata, starts a
little hesitantly.[14] John did have a problem starting movements, a fact remembered clearly by the musicians whom he conducted later in Dublin. The
problem seems to have been that his signals were often unclear; he did not
trust his musicians when it came to starting a piece, and he had a habit of

rehearsing starts again and again if he was worried about them, which made the musicians anxious.[15]

Using the same forces, Bach's cantatas No. 10, *Meine Seel' erhebt den Herren* ('My soul doth magnify the Lord') and No. 147, *Herz und Mund und Tat und Leben* ('Heart and mouth and deed and life'), were recorded two days later at the same location for a broadcast that was aired on 27 July.[16]

The pleasure that John had derived from conducting these cantatas can be judged from a letter that he wrote to the producer, Michael Hall in August:

> *I greatly enjoyed preparing, rehearsing and recording this last batch of Bach Cantatas. I would like to thank you again for giving us the opportunity of doing so... I am pleased with the orchestra in the Cantatas. I feel that as a chamber orchestra we are trying, with encouraging success to do something nobody else is seriously attempting.*[17]

Thanks to the pressure that had been put on William Glock of the BBC by Francis Grubb,[18] Musica Reservata was finally featured in one of the Henry Wood Promenade Concerts, along with the BBC Symphony Orchestra conducted by Charles Groves, on 6 August 1969 in the Royal Albert Hall. The group performed early fifteenth-century French music, much of it anonymous, though including works by Dufay.[19] Conducted by John, they played in the first half of the concert and, surely to John's horror, the orchestra performed Messiaen's Turangalila Symphony in the second. Although both halves were received enthusiastically by the audience, the hall was not full. Reviewers in both *The Times* and the *Arts Guardian* were surprised at the unusual combination of old and new (William Mann of the former thought it seemed foolhardy to programme them together) and both agreed that the delicate music performed by Musica Reservata could hardly be heard in such a large venue.[20] Michael Morrow considered this to be the group's most catastrophic performance. He doubted that people in the first row were able to hear them, though of course they could be heard clearly on the live radio broadcast.[21]

A couple of days later, the group made a BBC recording of thirteenth-century polytextual motets, which had been selected and adapted by Michael Morrow.[22] In September, John conducted Musica Reservata in a concert of sixteenth-century dance music from France, the Netherlands, Germany, Poland and Italy, at the Queen Elizabeth Hall. Entitled *16th century Dance Music*, it was recorded by the BBC and broadcast as *A Renaissance Entertainment* in early October.[23] Although it was well received by both the public and the press, a reviewer in *The Times* thought that the concert, although enjoyable, was too long.[24]

By the beginning of October, a new Philips record of Purcell songs had appeared. They were sung by Frank Patterson, with continuo played by John on harpsichord and Adam Skeaping on bass viola da gamba. John chose the songs and realized the thorough bass.[25] David Cairns, who was present at the recording sessions, believes that these were the best realizations of Purcell's music that he had heard. He remembers the 'dramas' that occurred when they were recording in Bishopsgate Hall; because there were noisy building works in the next street, they had to move to the Conway Hall in Red Lion Square, Holborn.[26] Charles Acton, writing in *The Irish Times*, was puzzled that Philips had not organized any advance publicity for this record in Ireland but that 'he [Frank Patterson] has benefitted enormously from his association with such a musical scholar and superb stylist as John Beckett.'[27] One of the songs was *What a sad fate is mine*, in which Purcell's harmonies were most certainly stretched to their limit in John's realization, as David Clark had noted.[28]

John himself described the rehearsals for this record, held in Cathal Gannon's workshop in the Guinness Brewery on one of his harpsichords, as 'a big event and a kind of low high watermark with my career … We used to go at night because it was quiet and the place was empty, and we'd go in there at about eleven and rehearse till two or three or four in the morning sometimes.' He vividly remembered the smell of hops and the fact that the harpsichord made for him by Cathal smelt of hops, which he loved. 'We used to go to the place where the workers could get draught Guinness on tap, and we'd get a pint or so when we got thirsty – I remember that too: that was very pleasant … We should all have it in the house, don't you think? It should be on tap like North Sea gas!'[29]

John was back in Dublin towards the end of October to conduct eighteenth-century music that he had realized for an RTÉ Television programme called *The Dancing Master*, in which Iain Montague recreated the atmosphere of the eighteenth-century ballroom and demonstrated in a specially created ballet what a twentieth-century choreographer could do using eighteenth-century styles of dance.[30]

In the middle of November, Musica Reservata gave concerts of French and Italian music (including works by Machaut, Dufay and Landini) in St Paul's Church, Birmingham, and the Great Hall of Durham Castle. Ruth travelled with John and played the rebec in both concerts.[31]

John now turned his attention to Purcell – this time for two Radio 3 programmes in a series devoted to the composer's music. They were recorded at the end of November and the beginning of December, and the music, which included incidental music, songs, sacred songs and anthems, were performed by the Musica Reservata Orchestra and Choir, with the Wandsworth School Boys' Choir.[32]

John then conducted a major concert of music by Praetorius, the Gabrielis, Monteverdi, Morenzio and other Italian composers at the Queen Elizabeth Hall on 16 December. A large line-up of twenty-six musicians (including Ruth, Betty Sullivan, David Munrow, Anthony Rooley, Christopher Hogwood and Harold Lester), various singers, and the Wandsworth School Boys' Choir was used. The concert began with Monteverdi's toccata-overture to *Orfeo* – the same piece that had been used to start the group's debut concert two years previously, and included large-scale motets by Praetorius.[33] Although the reviews in *The Times*, the *Daily Telegraph* and *The Listener* were enthusiastic, Gillian Widdicombe in *The Financial Times* was not so pleased. She found the musical content 'hollow and not all well prepared'. According to her, the 'ensemble was often shabby', the 'balance was uneasy' and the solo singing

> on the feeble, uncommunicative side. John Beckett's conducting does not add much to the performances (as distinct from rehearsals, of course) for he simply pumps four with one hand and prods entries rather erratically with the other. Most groups of this kind now prefer to dispense with such services in order to take more notice of each other; perhaps this one should, too.[34]

Michael Nyman was of a different opinion. Writing in the *Daily Telegraph* in August 2006, he admitted to being besotted with the group. He had gone to this concert in order to review them for *The Spectator* and now wrote:

> They were performing motets by the early 17th century German composer Michael Praetorius, who is usually known for a bunch of poppy dance arrangements called Terpsichore. These, by contrast, were massive choral, orchestral works – just thrilling.
>
> Musica Reservata were so different from other early musicians at the time. They were conducted by John Beckett – Samuel Beckett's cousin – and run by a brilliant Irish self-trained musician called Michael Morrow. He was a rough bear of a man with a huge walrus moustache – far from most clean-cut, Oxbridge, polite classical musicians.
>
> I tried to put across my visceral excitement in my review. It was a sheer, bloody-minded shock to the system to find that early music could have the same kind of vitality and heavy-duty effect on your musical senses as Stravinsky, Stockhausen or Steve Reich.[35]

After a hitch concerning the Wandsworth School Boys' Choir, which was quickly resolved, a BBC recording of the concert, entitled *The First Venetian School*, was made and broadcast in January of the following year.[36]

The year ended with John and Ann travelling with James and Valerie Plunkett to Vienna, where they celebrated Christmas, the new year or both.[37]

Twenty-Seven

1970

M usica Reservata should have travelled to Dublin to record two programmes and perform in their concert at Trinity College in early February 1970. However, this had to be postponed until May because RTÉ, which was co-operating in the relatively expensive operation of bringing the group to Dublin, was now on strike, and could not make a planned television programme about the group.[1] Instead, Musica Reservata was scheduled to do a BBC recording of music by Walter Frye, the early Renaissance English composer. The programme, which was broadcast in April, consisted of Frye's Mass *Flos regalis*, two *chansons* and an *Ave regina coelorum*.[2]

The next event was another concert at the Queen Elizabeth Hall in March, this time devoted to the chamber music of Henry Purcell.[3] One would have thought that John might have learned a lesson or two from his last attempted public concert of music by Purcell, but apparently he had not; reviews in *The Times* and *The Financial Times* were far from enthusiastic.[4]

By April, the group's latest Philips LP, *Music from the time of Boccaccio's Decameron* had appeared. Writing in *The Gramophone* about this record, Roger Fiske praised John for his skill on the organ: 'He plays with the total efficiency of an automaton, which is no doubt his intention, and again he may be right.'[5] One critic attributed the harsh sounds and a preference for outlandishness rather than musicality in the music to John instead of both Michael and John.[6]

Musica Reservata returned to the Queen Elizabeth Hall in May for a concert of medieval music of the thirteenth, fourteenth and fifteenth centuries[7] just four days before they performed in Trinity College, Dublin. Charles Acton prepared his readers for the great event with his own advance publicity:

Musica Reservata are appearing this week on Saturday in the Examination Hall of Trinity College in a public concert. Those who think that medieval music is too rarefied, or exotic, or esoteric, or likely to seem "a little bloodless like the hooting of owls" (as Anna Russell described the madrigal) will find the verve and professionalism of this group extremely refreshing. It might also be borne in mind that there are probably areas common to this medieval music and music of the Irish tradition, which are waiting to be explored.[8]

Barra Boydell, the son of TCD Professor Brian Boydell, was partially involved in this venture, in that he encouraged his father to bring the group to Dublin on this one and only occasion. In his early twenties at the time, Barra idolized Musica Reservata; the group was a huge influence on his perception and approach to early music. He remembers that he always rushed out to buy each of their LPs when they appeared and he encouraged his friends to listen to them. In a state of excitement, he now tramped around the city, putting up posters for the upcoming concert.[9]

The programme that Musica Reservata played in the Examination Hall that Saturday was the same programme of medieval music that they had played in the Queen Elizabeth Hall, though this time they called it *Music from the Court of Burgundy*. Charles Acton noted that, of the fifteen members of the group, three were Dubliners: John Beckett (conductor and small drum), Bernard Thomas (rauschpfeife and crumhorn), and Michael Morrow, the musical director (who did not perform). He was disappointed that no information was given about the instruments or the music. The thirteenth-century secular music (mostly French) made the greatest impact on him, partly because it seemed less strange and more direct in its appeal. He derived great satisfaction from four items by Landini, but found that the fifteenth-century Burgundian music sounded too much like the ancestry from which Renaissance music evolved.[10]

Barra Boydell, who had been extremely impressed by the group and this concert, has noted that what Michael Morrow did with Musica Reservata was hugely important for its time, in that it taught people to approach early music as a totally different sound world to the more recent, familiar repertoire. The harsh singing of Jantina Noorman might or might not (he suspected more 'not' than 'might') have reflected early singing styles, except perhaps in some geographically and chronologically limited contexts, but the important thing was that it had got people away from the modern-trained voice approach and made them reconsider the sound world. (When he saw Jantina Noorman, he was slightly surprised to discover that she looked more like a Dutch *huisvrouw* than the sexy-voiced singer that he had imagined.) As for the group's instrumentation, research since then has contributed further knowledge and understanding of what instruments were available where, when and in what social contexts.

Andrew Robinson had by now formed an early music group called the Consort of Saint Sepulchre; one of the members was his wife Jenny (daughter of Joe Groocock), who played the recorder. Barra now joined the consort, and fired by his enthusiasm for crumhorns and medieval music, they strove to emulate the sound of Musica Reservata.[11] When they had gone to the concert in Trinity College, they had been a little disappointed in the group's presentation. John had sat with his back to the audience and banged his drum, and the other musicians, who looked very grim, played to his beat. By contrast, when performing in their own Consort, they put a great deal of energy into their performances in an effort to 'sell' the music.[12] Their friend Anthony OBrien, who thought that Jantina Noorman sang 'unforgettably', noted that Ruth David 'played a rebec that looked like a pencil box'.[13]

Another member of the Consort of Saint Sepulchre, Honor O Brolchain (Carmody) attended the concert that night. She had never heard Musica Reservata before and found the experience quite amazing; after it, she and her colleagues realized what their direction should be. She had first encountered John at the age of ten, when she had been brought to a harpsichord recital given by him at the Hibernian Hotel in Dawson Street in 1959. Because of this, John immediately became a hero for her.[14]

Just before the concert in Trinity College, the group had performed in Coláiste Mhuire, Dublin city centre, for the two RTÉ television programmes that were to be broadcast in the following year. In fact only one programme, devoted to French and English music, seems to have been transmitted.[15]

After recording some arrangements of madrigals from *The Fitzwilliam Virginal Book* at the beginning of June for a Radio 3 broadcast later in the month,[16] John travelled to Belfast, where he conducted a concert of music by Purcell, Bach and – surprisingly – Vivaldi, at the King's Hall Complex in Balmoral. A review appeared in *The Irish Times*, entitled 'Orchestral programme tedious'. It ended: 'A strong and somewhat humourless performance of Bach's Suite in C Major was the most satisfactory work in this colourless programme.'[17]

John and Vera formally separated in June, intending to divorce at some time in the near future.[18] One can only imagine Vera's reaction when she learned of John's liaison with Ruth David and discovered that he and Ruth were now living together in a small terraced house in Azof Street, Greenwich,[19] which Ruth had bought sometime after August 1969. When Ruth had telephoned Seán

O'Leary to tell him that she and John were moving to Azof Street, Seán felt that
Ruth anticipated a violent reaction from Vera, which would have given her some
concern. Seán, who had heard of the decision before Vera, did not meet Vera
but learned how she had 'gone haywire at various people and friends'. When
it became clear that Michael Morrow, who was very close to her, had known
about John's relationship with Ruth, she was furious and frightened the life
out of him. John had been unfaithful to Vera before and had had brief flings
with younger women. Vera had not been too bothered by these flings; Ruth,
being an older and more formidable person, was seen as more of a threat to
her marriage.[20] Michael Morrow would hardly have been sympathetic to John's
worsening relationship with Vera and his leaving her for Ruth,[21] and if this were
the case, it could have begun to sour the long friendship between the two men.

In July John wrote to his friends James and Valerie Plunkett in Ireland to
explain the situation.

> Dear Jimmy and Valerie – I am writing to tell you that Vera and I have seperated
> [sic] – about a month ago now. Things have been getting more and more nearly
> impossible between us for the last two years or so; a break became inevitable, and
> we made it. Don't think it has been done without self-searching, without a sense of
> responsibility, without pain. I feel dreadful at leaving her alone, but know that I had
> to. I am in touch with Vera, and will always support her in whatever ways remain.
>
> I am living with Ruth David. I have known her for several years. Between us
> there has always been a growing and I think deep harmony of feelings and interests
> which we feel now we must try to live our lives in terms of.
>
> I dont know what you will think of me – of us – but whatever it is know that
> I love you both deeply and forever.
>
> Young Valerie wrote to Vera and me the other day asking if she could stay for a
> few days with a friend at the end of August. I am writing to say that of course they
> could stay with Vera at the Guardship, or here – and explain.[22]

As the break-up was acrimonious[23] John would have wished to distance
himself from Vera, for he later told his friend Seán O'Leary, 'We would have
killed each other'.[24] After they separated, John paid Vera an allowance. Deirdre
Sinclair's son Roland Morrow wondered if John had had pangs of guilt. Vera,
who was very disappointed and who never recovered from John's leaving
her, said some very derogatory things about Ruth and was rude to her. John
remained the love of her life.

Some years afterwards, Vera came to Ireland and lived in Salthill, just outside
Galway, and then in Monkstown, in the south of Dublin. Despite the fact that she
spoke very little French and had misconceptions about France, she eventually

bought a house in Rasiguères, west of Perpignan and near the border with Spain, in the vague hope that she might coax John back to her. Another attraction that she thought might lure John there was the fact that Moura Lympany, the pianist, played there. She also bought a house in the Jura, at Saint-Amour. This was near where Morris ('Sunny') Sinclair lived at the time. Vera drove John's little Fiat 500 Estate to Saint-Amour, even though she could not drive. Whenever she took it out of her garage, the local people fled. Sunny eventually drove it back to England for her.[25]

We next find John in France – in the Loire Valley, to be precise. He journeyed there with Michael Morrow and Musica Reservata to give a concert of Renaissance French vocal music on 15 July at the Collégiale Saint-Martin de Trôo and another, possibly following the same programme, on the next day at the Abbaye de Fontevraud.[26]

A couple of days later, the group played a concert of French and English music of both the thirteenth and fifteenth centuries, and also Italian music of the fourteenth century, at Carpentras in the Provence-Alpes-Côte d'Azur region, as part of the Festival Vaison-Carpentras. A photograph of John, looking somewhat perplexed and wearing a dark suit with no tie, together with other members of the group, appeared in a local newspaper. Another photograph showed the entire group performing in a cathedral. The accompanying review described how the concert was planned to take place outdoors but, because of the Mistral that began to blow in the Rhône valley, they were offered the use of the Théâtre du Palais, the Cathédrale or l'Arc Municipal. They opted for the Cathédrale, to which a large crowd flocked. The event was hailed as '*un merveilleux concert*'.[27]

Towards the end of June, John wrote to James Plunkett, outlining a rather bizarre scheme that he and Ruth had in mind.

Dear Jimmy,

Ruth and I are applying to rent a marvellous house which stands on the river near here – early 18th century – quiet – with six rooms – plenty for music and everything else.

It is owned by the MORDEN COLLEGE ESTATE – a property owning trust in Blackheath, long-established and honourable.

They have asked us to supply the names of two 'substantial people' who know us both well. I have given your name – and they will be writing to you. Hope its [sic] not too late to say I hope you wont [sic] mind.

*If you can find anything good to say of me __AND__ my work — do. Also mention
Ruth — if you will. I have explained openly to them that I am seperated [sic] from
Vera, and am living with Ruth...*

*Ruth and I are delighted that you would like us to be with you on September
4th. She will be coming to Dublin on the 3rd. Could we stay at the cottage from
the 3rd until the 7th? How much we would love to I will not try to say.*

*Sorry for this whirl of events — just write simply to your man with your thumbs
I hope uppish.*[28]

It is anybody's guess as to why they wanted to rent a house when Ruth
already had one.

At the beginning of the following month, Musica Reservata performed a
concert of music by Machaut, Dufay and Dunstable in the Sainte-Chapelle, Paris,
as part of the Festival Estival. A review, written by Roger Tellart, described
John as '*le chef John Beckett qui dissimule des trésors d'érudition et de délicatesse sous
un flegme très britannique et qui, à l'occasion, sait tenir efficacement les percussions...*'
('the conductor John Beckett, who hides his treasures of erudition and refinement under a very British impassivity and who, on this occasion, knows how to
play percussion effectively...').[29]

While John was in Paris, James Plunkett replied to his last letter:

Dear John,

*Put your man on to me and I'll such a tail unfurl of honour, necessity, worthi-
ness and uncompromising genius that there won't be a dry eye left in the length
and breath (stet) of Morden College...*

*The cottage is booked for you both for September 3rd to 7th but I hope to see
you [for] rehearsals before that — 27th August or thereabouts — isn't it? I'll check
with Kevin Roche.*

Valerie and I and the boys will be on holidays in the cottage...[30]

Although James did write a character reference for John, nothing came of
the Morden College Estate venture.[31] John replied to James's letter about two
weeks later. Once again his spelling — or perhaps his typing — was careless.

*Tnaks [sic] for your live lovely letter. Tnaks [sic] — how are you — anyway you
know what I meant to mean.*

*The housing estate chappie is giving every indication that he is going to cast us
into outer darkness because we are not married at the moment — had to tell him as
he wants separate Banker's references — none of his bloody buisness [sic] as far as
I'm concerned — Ruth doesn't agree just to uncomplicatedly complicate matters. So
you probably wont [sic] hear from him at all. However (whatever that means) I'm*

going to see him double chinned face to face on Turdsday to try to persuade him to
take us seriously — so perhaps you may hear from him after all.

I'll be in wholly Ireland from 25th for the OFF THE BEATEN BEETHOVEN
programmes. Ruth comes over on 3rd — I'll meet her and we'll go to the Cottage
that evening if we may — more thanks than the word will convey for it.

I'll be staying at Ann's until 3rd. Give me a ring if I dont [sic] see you 324256.
What are the arrangements for 4th? Ruth is bringing her violin is that alright?
Up Haydn. We both send uor [sic] love to you both. WE'Ld [sic] love to spend an
evening in Prosser's [pub] with you.

We go to Amsterdam on Friday evening — 21st. Then to Bruges in gallant little
Belgium — whence I flay [sic] straight to Dublin.[32]

The trip to Amsterdam refers to a concert of English music performed by
Musica Reservata in the Noordekerk.[33] The group then went to Bruges for the
International Fortnight of Music (part of the Flanders Festival), where they gave
an evening concert entitled *Music of Kings and Queens* at the Memlingmuseum.[34]

John and Ruth stayed in the Plunketts' newly refurbished cottage in County
Wicklow, between the Sugarloaf and Djouce Mountain from 3 to 7 September,
as planned. As soon as they returned, John wrote from Azof Street:

Deaf — I mean Dear Jimmy,
Up betimes this morning and perpetrated the enclosed.
Hope it is in time. Its all Andy's fault if it isn't (though dont [sic] tell him) I
was too pissed on Wednesday afternoon after a most agreeable dallying with him
in Prosser's public bar, to do it...
A pleasant trip over on Thursday. Drove uneventfully down yesterday. Glum to
be back in this monstrous city. I see the slope of D[j]ouce mountain more sharper
[sic] than the other side of the street,
We love and loved it at Paddock Lake and long to be there permanently and
hope to be — please everything. We'll talk further about it when I'm over for the
Synge prog. at the end of April. Ruth will be with me — she is playing in it too.
Love to you both as ever,
John.[35]

Andy refers to the RTÉ television producer Aindréas Ó Gallchóir, and the
enclosed document could have been a script for a centenary concert of words
and music associated with the playwright, writer and poet John Millington
Synge — the 'Synge prog.' mentioned later, and which would take place on
29 April of the following year in the state apartments of Dublin Castle. The
programme had been devised and written by John. The selection of music that

was performed was based on references found in Synge's unpublished notes, and included Synge's own composition, the Melody in F for violin and piano.[36]

This letter, along with the others written to James and his wife Valerie, presents a delightful portrait of a relaxed John mixing with the sort of people with whom he felt totally at ease. 'Up betimes' is a phrase frequently used by Samuel Pepys, whose diary for 1660 had just been published. This new and complete transcription was edited by Robert Latham and William Matthews, and was the first of eleven volumes covering the period 1660 to 1669. John bought all the volumes when they became available over the next thirteen years, and read them avidly.[37] A friend of John's, Christopher Stembridge, who was Professor of Music in Cork University, and who later moved to Cambridge, invited John to see Pepys's library in Magdalene College there. John was delighted to see it. The collection included the original manuscripts of the famous diaries, about which he spoke with great feeling, according to Seán O'Leary. Christopher married a Russian lady and once telephoned John from the Trans Siberian Express. He later moved to Italy, where he edited the works of Girolamo Frescobaldi.[38]

Later in the month, John wrote to James and Valerie again.

> Dear Jimmie and Valerie — we were thinking of you both yesterday afternoon moving out to the cottage again for the weekend — with envy and delight. We hope you found everything there alright. We left it too late when departing to get down to empty the dustbin — and what with all of us washing and swigging over the previous weekend the w[a]ter butt was nearly dry. Has it rained since? Here the sun has been glaring down unblinkingly on these dingy dirty noisy streets since we got back. Though Ann rang last night and said it was raining in Dublin. Dear dirty Dublin — expensive filthy London.
>
> Once again thanks for your kindness and hospitality in that marvellous place.[39]

In October, another Philips record, *16th Century Italian Dance Music* was recorded. Once again, John conducted Musica Reservata, which this time included David Munrow on soprano and alto crumhorns, Ruth on treble rebec and violin, Catherine Mackintosh on tenor viol, and John, Christopher Hogwood and Harold Lester on harpsichord. This very satisfying LP comprises instrumental and vocal music by various anonymous and four relatively obscure composers. It is very well recorded and played, with only a hint of unsteady intonation. Most of the tracks were later incorporated into a CD entitled *16th Century Italian & French Dance Music* — the French music taken from the disc recorded earlier in the year.[40] Although Harold Lester did perform with John on this record, Harold now lost touch with John and never visited him again — something that he very much regretted.[41]

Twenty-Eight
1970–71

In October John, Betty Sullivan, the Irish violinist David Lillis and Frank Patterson appeared on the first of the two RTÉ Television *Anthology* programmes devised by John, entitled 'A Shade Superior to Monsieur Kozeluch'. The unusual title referred to a remark made by Beethoven in 1812 about the Czech composer Jan Antonín Koželuh (Leopold Kozeluch), who arranged some Scottish songs for the publisher Thomson of Edinburgh. Beethoven had written: '*Moi je m'estime encore une fois plus supérieur en ce genre que Monsieur Kozeluch (miserabilis).*' ('I again consider myself more superior in this genre to Monsieur Kozeluch.')[1] In this first programme, Frank sang five traditional Irish airs arranged by Beethoven, accompanied by John, Betty (cello) and David Lillis (violin). In addition, the young Irish pianist John O'Conor played Beethoven's *Polonaise* in C, Op. 89 and *Fantasie* Op. 77. Finally there was a performance of Beethoven's Introduction and Variations on *Ich bin der Schneider Kakadu* ('I am Kakadu the Tailor') by John O'Conor, David Lillis and cellist Coral Bognuda.[2]

The writer of a review in the *Sunday Independent* praised the programme and wondered why Irish artists of this calibre were not featured more often on RTÉ. 'Classical music doesn't have to be difficult or boring for non-enthusiasts, as John Beckett's selection amply proved.'[3]

John wrote to James Plunkett again in mid October. 'Dear Jimmy,' he began, 'It is the most exquisite day here – a pale blue pool of light and warmth – heartbreaking – ahem. I think of you (so would Ruth if she were here – she is playing in a concert in Harlow New Town – whatever segment of this muckheap that is) both up at Coolakeagh – perhaps up at and in the lakes. I hope the day is as here with you.' Coolakeagh was the name of the Plunketts' home near Enniskerry, near Calary Bog. It is clear from this letter that John was pining for his beloved County Wicklow. He then went on to describe a programme of music by Haydn that he had devised; 'I would like to write a script – and also perhaps to speak it – if you consider me presentable enough.' He ended with, 'I had one fan letter about the Beethoven prog – from an Aylesbury Rd. address too. Ahem. Love as ever from both to both. Invoke us with a sup in Prosser's one night.'[4] Aylesbury Road is situated in a rather up-market area not far from the RTÉ studios. John's plan would come to fruition later as two television programmes transmitted in November of the following year.

Musica Reservata was back in the Queen Elizabeth Hall at the end of October with a programme of German and Spanish Music of the early sixteenth century.[5] Gillian Widdicombe, writing in *The Financial Times*, thought that this was one of the group's best concerts for some time, partly because this sort of music suited them better than Purcell and the near Baroque.[6]

The second of the two RTÉ Television programmes devoted to the music of Beethoven was transmitted at the beginning of December. This time the arrangements of Irish traditional airs were sung by Bernadette Greevy. The programme had been recorded in the National Gallery and, like the first one, was produced by Kevin Roche.[7]

Another concert in the Queen Elizabeth Hall featuring Musica Reservata, recorded by the BBC in December, brought the year to a finish. The concert, *Music at Christmas*, which was conducted by John, included large-scale music by Monteverdi, Praetorius and Scheidt.[8] In her review in *The Financial Times*, Gillian Widdicombe praised the group's ability to perform medieval and lusty early Renaissance music, but was less enthusiastic about their efforts to perform works by Monteverdi and later composers. She mentioned that the last time she had written an unfavourable review, she had received a letter of complaint from Michael Morrow.[9] On this note, Harold Lester remembers how, after a well-known music critic had written a bad review of a Musica Reservata concert, John and Michael had lain in wait for him, hiding in a privet hedge somewhere, in order to attack him![10]

In February 1971 John conducted Musica Reservata in a concert of fifteenth and sixteenth-century English music in the Queen Elizabeth Hall. This included music by William Cobbold – John had reconstructed the missing quintus part of Cobbold's piece *New Fashions*. A fairly enthusiastic review, acknowledging the group's popularity owing to its lively and unstuffy rendition of early music, appeared afterwards in *The Guardian*.[11]

In mid March a television programme, *Inis Fáil* (one of the BBC's *Bird's Eye View* series and a joint RTÉ-BBC production) was transmitted simultaneously on RTÉ and BBC 2 on the evening of St Patrick's Day. Essentially a view of Ireland from the air, it was scripted and presented by James Plunkett and had music specially composed and conducted by John. Various quotations were read by T.P. McKenna, Richard Pasco and Sir John Betjeman. It seems that the music had been recorded in January, when John had come to Dublin.[12]

Writing on upcoming television programmes in *The Irish Times*, Ken Gray advised readers to watch it, if possible, 'on a colour set'. 'Though he may be looking at Ireland from up in the sky, Mr. Plunkett's commentary is full of down-to-earth humour,' he remarked; '... it is all worth seeing, and listening to – the commentary, the quotations spoken by among others, T.P. McKenna and the brilliantly apt music composed by John Beckett.'[13]

Music only features in certain parts of this hour-long film. In it, Frank Patterson sings *The Croppy Boy* to a harp accompaniment with astringent military-sounding interjections played on trumpets. Low, growling music evokes the atmosphere of the Rock of Cashel, then dramatic cymbal crashes and discordant trumpets accompany shots of a rough sea. Best of all, Frank Patterson sings a haunting and simply-harmonized arrangement of *The Salley Gardens*. Both the introductory and concluding sections of the arrangement, composed by John and scored for harp and flute, are highly original and effective. The film, which overall is informative and well made, was produced by Edward Mirzoeff, and the music was performed by the RTÉ Symphony Orchestra.[14]

John was in Ireland in March, during the annual Wexford Opera Festival, and gave a harpsichord recital in the Theatre Royal on the 20th.[15] John was now busy 'researching a T.V. programme on Synge and music in preparation for the centenary', as James Plunkett reported to Aidan Higgins. 'He too, at last, is finding London unbearable and wants to get out. I hope he does. The prospects seem fairly good.'[16]

John and Ruth came over to stay in the Plunketts' cottage again in April. 'Dear Jimmy,' John wrote:

We are coming over on April 27th – arriving early that morning off the boat. We'll go and have breakfast with Ann, and then what about collecting the keys? Will we leave it that we will come up to Rockfield Drive before lunch and get them then? We'll do that, unless I hear otherwise.

We stay until the evening of May 6th. Vastly looking forward to being there.

Could we have quartets at Paddock Lake on the night of Friday 30th? I have to be out with Ann on the Saturday night, and a Sunday doesn't suit Valerie. How is she? I hope still better. And you? And the boys? Will you ring Betty and or Kevin [Roche] about the quartets?[17]

Rockfield Drive was James's address in Terenure, Dublin. Paddock Lake refers to a cottage, rented by James's daughter Valerie (referred to by John as 'young Valerie'), which was owned by the Slazengers of Powerscourt House in Enniskerry. It was located near a lake hidden in a forest beside Calary Bog and not far from Djouce Mountain. The previous resident was the journalist and music critic John O'Donovan.[18]

John returned to Greenwich soon after the John Millington Synge centenary concert on 29 April and wrote to Aindréas Ó Gallchóir, 'Sorry not to have had a more talkative sup with you after the Synge thing. I greatly enjoyed the giving of it – and feel we all did, and so did they.' In case the programme might be redone for television, John supplied dates of when he would be free.[19] John enclosed a copy of this letter and sent it to James Plunkett, along with one of his own:

> *Dear Jimmy,*
>   *Returned to our so to speak vomit last night.*
>   *Hope you collected the keys from the Powerscourt Arms alright.*
>   *Marvellous weather here today – hope you have it at Paddock Lake – and it has you.*
>   *I enclose a copy of a letter I am sending off to Andy today – not angling for the thing to be done – let them of course do what they want – but so that he may know at a glance when I am free.*
>   *See you in July – if not before – perhaps here?*[20]

In this letter, one can detect John's increasing dislike for living in grimy London and yearning to live in County Wicklow with his friends, where he could breathe fresh, clean air.

James received another letter from John shortly afterwards, in which he wrote, 'I understand from John O'Donovan that I will not receive a letter of confirmation of the RIAM work until the beginning of June – as their next board of governers [sic] meeting is not until the end of may. I'll let you know as soon as I hear.' It now becomes clear that John had applied for a teaching post in the Royal Irish Academy of Music, and that he intended to move to Ireland. He finished his letter with, 'We are in the throes of rehearsals for a RESERVATA concert at the Elizabeth Hall next Tuesday. So must get on and out to one of them.'[21]

This concert, given in the Queen Elizabeth Hall on 18 May, was a sell-out. This one consisted of thirteenth and fifteenth-century French and English music. According to *The Guardian*, John, who was described as 'almost as immobile as Klemperer', conducted a programme of thirty-three separate pieces, not counting the encores.[22]

John wrote to James and Valerie Plunkett at the end of May.

Dear Jimmy and Valerie,

The RIAM appointment was confirmed yesterday by letter. I have written accepting.

So I'll be in Ireland for good (as I hope) from September.

And staying a lot through the summer. But we'll one or both have to come back to clear things up here – in August probably.

We are coming over to Dublin on July 7th or 8th. I'll be doing the two Haydn programmes for RTE [Haydn in London] from the 10th to the 14th. And a harpsichord recital at the Academy the following week.

Have only booked a single ticket for the first time for years.[23]

In July, Musica Reservata's next disc, *Sixteenth Century French Dance Music*, was recorded. The thirty-three tracks comprised mostly anonymous pieces of music, though the known composers included Claudin de Sermisy, Wolf Heckel, Giovanni Pacoloni, Clemens non Papa, Clement Janequin and Passereau. A large band of musicians was used and, as well as conducting, John played the harpsichord. In fact, three other harpsichordists were used: Melanie Daiken, Christopher Hogwood and Harold Lester.[24] The LP was not released until the end of 1972 and reviews were published in January of the following year. Many of the tracks were later included in the *16th Century Italian & French Dance Music* CD issued by Boston Skyline.[25]

PART THREE

Dublin 1971–1983

Twenty-Nine
1971

The *Irish Times* of 21 July 1971 contained a review by Charles Acton of a harpsichord and organ recital given by John in the Royal Irish Academy of Music on the previous evening. Entitled 'Welcome back to John Beckett', Acton's review read:

> One of the best pieces of Irish musical news for a long time is that John Beckett is returning to Ireland to live and, indeed, is joining the staff of the Royal Irish Academy of Music as professor of harpsichord and piano.
>
> [...] It was particularly rewarding again to hear Mr. Beckett playing the [Bach] D major partita, its greatness making a very satisfying second half. His superb embellishments of the repeats of the Allemande are always a joy to hear and match the serious, devoted, virtuoso artistry of the entire performance and work. Let us hope that all our musical authorities and promoters will make sure that Mr. Beckett has opportunity enough for him not to lose by bringing skill, artistry and scholarship back to his own country.[1]

So John was back on his native turf. John had written to James Plunkett in early July with news of his imminent arrival and arrangements to collect the keys of 'Paddock Lake', the locals' name for the small, simple cottage with which John had fallen in love.[2] A letter to a Miss Williams of the BBC confirms that he and Ruth were living in The Paddock, The Old Long Hill, Kilmacanogue in Wicklow (the official address) by the 26th of the month.[3] Although he would return to London many times during the next few years for concerts and recordings, he had distanced himself from Michael Morrow, with whom he found it increasingly difficult to work, and had turned his back on the sophistication of the great capital to live in a plain, isolated country cottage in Ireland.

John's new home was in 'a most beautiful part of the countryside, which Samuel had known and loved in his youth.'[4] It appears that when James Plunkett's daughter Valerie had vacated the cottage sometime previously, James had approached the Slazenger family and had told them that John was looking for a place to live. Both James's house on the Old Long Hill and John's cottage were let to their occupants on a grace and favour basis, which, luckily for John and Ruth, meant living either rent free or for a very low rent, providing they kept the place in good order.[5]

The cottage was so basic that it lacked most modern conveniences, such as running water. Guests of a sensitive nature were horrified to discover that there was only an outside loo, where they were expected to use a bucket and sheets of newspaper.[6] John, Ruth and their guests ate from crude vessels on a table covered in oilcloth; at breakfast-time this was covered over with news-paper. Water for drinking and washing was fetched in a bucket from the nearby stream,[7] and milk was supplied straight from the cow by a local farmer.[8] The first thing that John did when he moved into the cottage was erect a large aerial so that he could receive BBC Radio 3.[9] Although John was ungainly on his feet, he still was a nimble swimmer and swam regularly in Paddock Lake, hidden inside the nearby forest.[10] Patrick Cuming remembers swimming with him, and John regularly swam with James Plunkett. Aleck Crichton believes that he swam with John in the lake; John, he remembers, used to dive into the water as soon as he woke up each morning.[11] Away from everything and everybody, John was in his element, completely relaxed and laid back, and not the anxious musician that everyone knew.[12]

Ruth did all the hard work as John was not at all domesticated. Venetia O'Sullivan remembered a huge fireplace, in which turf (peat) from the bog was burned, and a good stereo system, on which John played records of music by Mahler and other favourite composers. Venetia, her husband John and their son Rowan used to go to the cottage for summer lunches. On one occasion, when listening to one of Mahler's long works on record, John said to young Rowan, 'Go and get me a milk bottle.' When asked what he wanted the bottle for, he said, 'To pee into' – and that was exactly what he did!

Venetia found John overwhelming. Her husband was a pupil of John's and believed that John was always right, which annoyed her. He later realized, 'when the scales fell from his eyes', as she put it, that John was not *always* right.[13]

Michael Morrow's sister Brigid remembers her visits to John's cottage at The Paddock: she often played music with John, Ruth and other friends, she on the recorder and Ruth on the viola. She and her husband used to visit regularly and brought their children when they were young.[14]

Gerry Pullman, a son of the caretaker of St Columba's College, remembers that when he was about thirteen or fourteen, he stayed in a tent at John's place, catching fish in the stream and swimming in the lake. He was jealous of how well John could swim and also of his generous layer of fat, which meant that he did not feel the cold. He remembers that the cottage was very primitive. He discovered John to be a warm, friendly person and remembers him free-wheeling downhill to Enniskerry in the car without using any petrol.[15]

Gillian Smith knew that Ruth had problems living in this highly impractical cottage and recollected that the leg of the bed had fallen through the rotting floor of the little back room. John, on the other hand, adored the place. For him, it was a marvellous experience living there in the wilds, especially after it had snowed.[16] Gillian liked Ruth. She was tall, big-boned and wore her black hair short. Gillian remembers that some people found her difficult and a 'little prickly'. She was probably conscious of living in a country where British people were not always welcomed, even by the Irish Protestants, some of whom (including John and his sister Ann) tended to be republican. One must remember that the bitter sectarian strife in Northern Ireland was very much in the news during the seventies.

Gillian's husband, Lindsay Armstrong, found John direct and forthright, and certainly not somebody who would suffer fools gladly. He had little inclination for casual conversation – chit-chat was not exactly his style. It would have been ridiculous to make a remark such as, 'The weather's not too good, is it?' As regards his own achievements, John was quite dismissive. Although this went further than modesty, he was not exactly self-effacing. What he had achieved in the field of music was of no importance to him and he simply did not want to talk about it. He rarely mentioned his famous cousin in Lindsay's presence, though he once said something along the lines of 'Sam's really not of this world,' meaning that he was aloof from ordinary people. Lindsay was quite familiar with such an evangelical turn of phrase from his Northern Ireland upbringing, but thought that it sounded strange coming from John.[17]

In August John drove to An Grianán, Termonfeckin, for the first nationally adver-tised recorder course there. As about seventy-five people came, the house was full for the week. John's friend Theo Wyatt, who ran the course, remembers that for the first few years John was the star tutor. His enthusiasm and energy were spectacular: after a full day's coaching and conducting he would retreat with a party of cronies – and no doubt a supply of bottled Guinness – to the Lucy Franks garden house and play six-part Brade dances until the small hours of the morning. His most memorable contribution to these recorder courses was a recital at which he persuaded Seán Keane, the fiddler with The Chieftains, to join him in a programme of virginal music by William Byrd and Giles Farnaby interspersed with Irish traditional jigs and reels. Theo also remembers a master-class John did on Byrd's *The Leaves be Green* in which his analysis of what Byrd was doing at each stage was truly masterly. Theo felt that although the recorder was only a tiny part of John's broad musical world, those who were fortunate enough to have enjoyed his tuition were unlikely to have encountered a more inspiring experience.[18]

Two of the players at the course were Janet Ashe and her friend Sydney Stokes. Janet, now fifty, had decided to learn how to play the recorder in order to mark this phase of her life. John taught them their first notes on the instrument. John's sister Ann was also at the course and in order to get her to play her recorder, he told Janet and Sydney, '*Make* Ann play with you – that's the only way she will play with others.' They all got on well together and became great friends.[19]

There were four or five tutors at the course, including John; two others were Jenny Robinson (Joe Groocock's daughter) and her husband Andrew, both members of the Consort of Saint Sepulchre. Joe had been asked to teach and he had declined, saying that his daughter would instead. Jenny remembers being quite in awe of John and a little scared, even though she greatly admired him; she was nervous if he asked her opinion about something as she felt that she was unable to stand up for herself. She was twenty-two at the time and Andrew was twenty-three.[20]

During the recorder course, Andrew and Jenny played with a woman who had attended John's viol consort class in Belmont Primary School, Chiswick, and told her that they had been frightened to see John Beckett in the audience at one of their recent Saint Sepulchre concerts in the College of Physicians, Dublin. Incredulous, the woman reacted by saying, 'Frightened? Of John?' She just could not imagine (and clearly had never witnessed) a harsh word or look from him. It seemed that everyone had a different impression of him.[21]

A little earlier in the year, Andrew and Jenny had performed music edited by John at Christ Church in the Dublin suburb of Rathgar. These were the two Bach flute sonatas (BWV 1030 in B minor and 1035 in E) that had been played by Edward Beckett, John and Betty Sullivan in Wexford back in 1964. This time, Jenny played the flute and her father Joe Groocock and Andrew played the basso continuo. Andrew and Jenny remember the wonderful ornamentation that John had provided for the slow movements.[22]

On 29 August Musica Reservata performed in St Canice's Cathedral, Kilkenny, but interestingly, John was not involved – the conductor was Howard Williams. On the following day, the group played in the Kleine Zaal Concertgebouw, Amsterdam; Michael Morrow's name is mentioned on the programme but not John's or Ruth's. We can only assume that the recorder course at An Grianán clashed with this tour or that John was busy with other things.[23]

At the beginning of September an advertisement in *The Irish Times* stated that the next term at the Royal Irish Academy of Music would commence on 20 September and that 'Mr. John Beckett will take up duty this term as Teacher of Pianoforte, Harpsichord, Composition and Harmony and Counterpoint.' John's official teaching post had now begun. Employed until 1983, he soon became a well-known figure in the Academy. Fearful of being delayed in traffic, he rose early every morning and drove from County Wicklow into the city, arriving in Westmoreland Street long before he was due to start work.[24]

Ruth was also given a job in the Royal Irish Academy of Music. John O'Donovan wrote to James Plunkett:

> *I suppose John Beckett has told you about the Academy and Ruth's post there too. I had them here at Slievecorragh [O'Donovan's home in County Wicklow] and had to have the place reconsecrated after what he said about Handel. Of course as quick as lightning I riposted with 'And bugger Mahler too.' Whereupon John's neck muscles seemed to give, that great taurine head swung loosely, he made a noise like an old mantelpiece clock about to strike and chimed something about Das Lied von der Erde ... could not listen to it without ... without ... and gathering up Ruth, he left. I'll never be forgiven.*[25]

Musica Reservata was featured on RTÉ Television at the beginning of October in a programme devoted to the group, entitled *The Age of the Troubadours*. The musical inserts had been recorded in May of the previous year in Coláiste Mhuire, Dublin. These videotaped inserts were not introduced by Michael Morrow, who had then been suffering from laryngitis, but by Brian Boydell. This arrangement seems to have caused a certain amount of rancour later.[26] Either the producer or Brian realized that the public might be quite unfamiliar with music of such an early period and had opted for a rather dumbed-down script. A second programme, entitled *Italian Music of the XIV century*, had also been recorded when Musica Reservata had been in Dublin the previous year, but this one seems not to have been transmitted.[27]

John joined Musica Reservata in London to conduct the group's next concert later in the month: sixteenth-century French and Netherlands *chansons* and dances. The audience was appreciative and a couple of good reviews appeared in the newspapers.[28]

At the same time, the first of two television programmes, *Haydn in London*, was transmitted on RTÉ Television. John, the presenter, was quoted in an explanatory article printed in the *RTÉ Guide*: 'I hope to evoke something of the flavour of his life there, from day to day; of the things he saw and commented upon; of the trips he took, and the amusements he enjoyed, of the friends he made, and he made many, and of the few quarrels he had.'[29] Both programmes were recorded in the elegant surroundings of the National Gallery in Dublin; readings were by Aiden Grennell and a number of old pictures and etchings relevant to Haydn's years in London were used.[30]

In between these two programmes, John conducted a recital of medieval and Renaissance music, performed by Musica Reservata, in the VARA-studio in Hilversum, The Netherlands. Originally an acronym for *Vereeniging van Arbeiders Radio Amateurs* (Amateur Radio Workers' Association) when it was first established in 1925, VARA had become an association of television and radio stations in 1957. The free concert took place at 4 pm on Saturday 6 November in a modern studio block to a packed house.[31] A review published in *De Gooi – en Eemlander* a couple of days later stated that the attendance of this particular recital, the first of a new series, broke all records, and described how everyone managed to cram into the studio, some sitting in others' laps and using window sills and stair treads as seats.[32]

John's programme about Synge and Music (recorded over two days in the middle of October) for Radio 3 was broadcast a little later in the month. This was compiled and narrated by John, who recounted the early years during which J.M. Synge strove to be a professional musician. Denys Hawthorne took the part of Synge and the music was performed by a section of the Music Group of London, directed by John, and also by John Kelly, a traditional fiddler.[33]

On 28 November, John typed a letter to my father. Headed 'NO TELEPHONE', it read:

Dear Cathal,

I've had my harpsichord moved over from London. It took 2½ months in the coming. God knows how or where it was stored during that time. As a result it is in to me alarmingly poor shape. Could I ask you if you would come, at your convenience, to do a spot of adjusting? I have a recital and some Radio recordings to prepare, and would be greatly obliged if you could come soon.

I must also explain that Vera and I have seperated [sic], since June 1970. I am living here with Ruth David, from England. We intend to be married when a divorce has been arranged. I would want you and all my friends to know.

If, in the circumstances, you should not wish to see us, I shall understand and

accept, and be very sorry, with no diminution of friendship or respect. If you will
come I will be delighted, and, as I say, most grateful.
    Whatever befalls, dear Cathal, warmest regards and respects to you both.
                                        John.[34]

Knowing that my father was a Roman Catholic and possibly not in favour of divorce, he had taken the precaution of explaining his situation. As a divorce from Vera never materialized, it was unfortunate that Ruth could not marry John. However, they stayed together until she died. Although it is possible that my father did not approve of this at the time, he kept the appointment and examined his harpsichord. Indeed, when he arrived to examine the instrument, John was not there and he chatted volubly with Ruth over what John liked to call a 'dish of tea'.

Using rather formal language, Cathal wrote a report in early December that began, 'Dear Mr Beckett, I regret to have to tell you that your harpsichord is in very poor condition and will need much work to make it playable again.' As the soundboard had risen considerably, he concluded that it had absorbed a great deal of moisture either in transit or storage. He suggested a fee of £50 and stated that he would be willing to start work on the instrument after Christmas. The harpsichord was delivered to his workshop on 28 December and he received a cheque from John during the following January.[35]

To mark the fiftieth anniversary of the Signing of the Treaty in 1921, a special hour-and-a-half-long television documentary, *The State of the Nation*, was shown by RTÉ on 6 December, the actual anniversary date. Assembled from contemporary plans and other archive material, the programme traced the development of Irish politics from the Treaty up to the constitutional settlement with the Chamberlain government just before the outbreak of World War II. It was written by James Plunkett, narrated by Niall Tóibín and produced by Aindréas Ó Gallchóir. John composed the music and conducted the RTÉ Light Orchestra. The film covered the history of Ireland as recorded by newsreel cameramen from December 1921 to the outbreak of war in 1939,[36] and in the opinion of the author of 'An Irishman's Diary' in *The Irish Times*, was 'the finest archivistic documentary of its kind that's been done about Ireland since George Morrison's "Mise Eire".' The author credited John with arranging the score with the perception of an Ó Riada and liked the way in which he had worked in 'a very effective sour version of "Rule Britannia?"'.[37] John's music included short military fanfares, twisted versions of popular Irish marching tunes, sepulchral music for funeral processions, and various snatches of Irish melodies, including *Danny Boy* (the only piece harmonized conventionally).[38]

John conducted another Musica Reservata concert in the Queen Elizabeth Hall on 13 December, entitled 'Monteverdi and his Contemporaries'.[39] Reviews by Gillian Widdicombe in *The Financial Times* and Keith Horner in *The Times* were lukewarm.[40]

The year ended with the recording of two programmes of music by Henry Purcell by the BBC in the Concert Hall of Broadcasting House in London, in which the songs had all been edited by John.[41]

Thirty
1972

B y mid January John's harpsichord was fixed and ready for collection. John came to my father's workshop to try it out before it was transported back to his house, and I recorded him playing three pieces from *The Fitzwilliam Virginal Book* on it.[1] A few days later, my father received the following letter:

> Dear Cathal,
>
> That I should have sat in this room at the foot of Djouce all this most beautiful day practising on your marvellous instrument seems to me to surpass most miracles I have heard of.
>
> I just write to thank you for it.
>
> It is so perfectly adjusted now, that I have the alas I know temporary illusion that I can actually play the harpsichord.
>
> Dont [sic] forget to send me your report and bill on and for what you did.
>
> Warmest regards from us both, and to Margaret and Charles.
>
> > John.[2]

If proof be needed of John's deep appreciation, modesty and warmth of character, this must be it; it is a letter that I have treasured and shall continue to do so. Another letter arrived the following day thanking my father for his documents, which John planned to photocopy and send off 'to the pickford bastards in Deptford' so that he could claim insurance compensation to the amount Cathal had suggested.[3] A month later, John wrote again:

> I heard from PICKBLOODYFORDS yesterday. I cant [sic], it appears, claim anything on my insurance, because, as it sais [sic] somewhere in small print, that I

*didn't read, such a claim had to be made within seven days of delivery. Sorry for us
both. I will be pleased, more than pleased to pay the £50 myself.*[4]

The January edition of *The Gramophone* included a review of a new Musica
Reservata LP entitled *Music from the Court of Burgundy*. Most of the music was by
Guillaume Dufay. Although he was critical of the vocal technique, Denis Arnold
warmly recommended the record to all, encouraging schools and colleges to
purchase it as it would fill a useful gap, and praised John's dexterous playing of
the florid organ piece by an anonymous composer, *Collinetto*.[5] Writing in *Records
and Recording*, Kenneth Long also mentioned the 'deft fingerwork' displayed in
John's playing of the same piece.[6] Charles Acton, reviewing the record a year
and a half later, was also impressed.[7]

John played the harpsichord part of Seán Ó Riada's large-scale orchestral and
choral work *Nomos No. 2*, based on text from the Theban plays by Sophocles, in
a special Ó Riada memorial concert held at the Gaiety Theatre in Dublin on 16
January. The entire concert, which included Ó Riada's popular arrangements of
traditional music performed by Ceoltóirí Chualann in the first half, was broadcast live on radio; the second half, which consisted of *Nomos No. 2*, was shown on
television a couple of days later.[8] William Young, the bass baritone who had sung
the part of Christus in Bach's *Saint Matthew Passion* back in 1959, sang the solo
part. As John was so impressed by William's performance, he later approached
him for the Bach cantatas that he was planning to conduct in 1973.[9]

John played in a solo harpsichord recital in Trinity College in February. It
was the second of three recitals to celebrate the bicentenary of the Trinity
College Kirckman Harpsichord. The programme consisted of eight pieces from
the *Fitzwilliam Virginal Book* (by now almost *de rigueur* in a Beckett recital), five
Scarlatti sonatas and Bach's great Partita No. 6 in E minor, BWV 830.[10] Malcolm
Proud, who would become John's pupil two years later, was at the concert
and found John's interpretation of the Scarlatti sonatas quite exciting.[11] Anthony
OBrien found them 'mesmerizing'.[12]

John's treatment of the final gigue movement of Bach's Partita (performed in
his *Studio Portrait* programme in 1969) intrigued Charles Acton:

> John Beckett explained in a most interesting programme note how he had
> become convinced that Bach used a convention of notation of perfectly logical
> consistency which has misled his successors. Mr. Beckett therefore treats
> each 4-minim bar as four 6/8 bars, forming triplets accordingly. The result is
> certainly to make a jig out of it (which it does not ordinarily sound to be) and
> an entirely suitable finale. His treatment is entirely convincing: let us accept it.[13]

A few days afterwards, John was again playing Bach: this time, the continuo (with Betty Sullivan and John O'Sullivan) of the *Saint John Passion*, with the New Irish Chamber Orchestra conducted by Victor Leeson, at the Royal Dublin Society. The Irish Chamber Orchestra, founded by János Fürst in 1963, had been reformed as the New Irish Chamber Orchestra in 1970, with André Prieur as its principal conductor. John would soon conduct this orchestra and it would play an important part in his life during his present stay in Dublin.[14]

At around this time John and Edward Beckett became involved in the making of a film, made from old photographs taken around the turn of the century by the almost forgotten Robert French. These came from the William Lawrence Collection held in the National Library of Ireland. Directed by Kieran Hickey of BAC Films Ltd, the film was entitled *The Light of Other Days*. The words were taken from Thomas Moore's song *Oft in the Stilly Night*, which was sung by Frank Patterson, accompanied by John on piano. This new film would become very successful; it was shown on television, and a handsome book based on it was published in 1973.[15]

After a couple of Musica Reservata concerts in March,[16] a programme of early English music, recorded by Musica Reservata in November 1970, was broadcast on Radio 3 in April.[17] Shortly afterwards another radio programme, this time of music by Josquin des Prés, was recorded. This would not be broadcast until two years later. As we were able to receive Radio 3 in Dublin, I taped it and listened to pieces such as *'Vive le roy'* ('Long live the king'), *'Mille regretz'* ('A thousand regrets'), *'Faulte d'argent'* ('Lack of money'), *'El Grillo'* ('The cricket'), *'Scaramella'* and *'La déploration de Johan Ockeghem'* ('The lament for Johan Ockeghem') again and again. Although I did find the sound rather harsh, especially in the song *'El Grillo'*, I was fascinated by this programme and it certainly helped me develop an interest in early music.[18]

Shortly afterwards John conducted the Choir of Musica Reservata and the Trinity Boys' Choir, Croydon, in the *Missa super osculetur me* by Orlando Lassus in the Church of St George the Martyr, Queen Square. This was recorded by the BBC, produced by Basil Lam and broadcast on Radio 3 in June.[19] Bernard Thomas remembers a story concerning Basil Lam: apparently he telephoned John and said that he would like him to conduct some music by Handel. John simply said, 'I don't like Handel' and put the phone down. As well as disliking the music of Handel, Vivaldi, Corelli and Bruckner, he also hated anything by Debussy and Ravel: he dismissed the former's music as 'wishy-washy'. However, he did like Fauré and slightly later twentieth-century composers. Bernard could not understand why John was drawn to the tortured, neurotic music of Mahler and not to the austere music of Bruckner. Bernard notes that people's tastes in composers are not what one would necessarily expect and are often at odds with aspects of their personalities.[20]

In all probability, John and Ruth stayed in their house in Azof Street while they were in London, for they had not sold it but had made it available to be rented. They continued to use it any time they stayed in London. They were back in Dublin by the end of April, when they called to my parents' house for a cup of tea.[21] On the following day, John was playing music by Haydn in Trinity College, using a 1809 Broadwood piano that my father had restored. The programme included a piano trio and some songs sung by Frank Patterson.[22]

A few days later John was in the church of Saint-Germain l'Auxerrois in Paris, opposite the Louvre, conducting Musica Reservata in a programme of English and French music. This concert was well received. On the following day they were in the Théâtre de l'Hôtel de Ville at Le Havre, where they played what appears to have been the same programme. Next they were in Dieppe, where they played thirteenth-century French and fourteenth-century Italian music. In the advance publicity for this last concert, somebody had mistakenly printed 'Harpiste John Beckett'.[23]

Towards the end of May, John was in the Queen Elizabeth Hall in London, conducting the group in a concert of sixteenth-century German, Polish and Netherlands *chansons* and dances.[24] The reason for including Polish music was that Michael Morrow had accepted a Polish government bursary for two months in order to study at the Institute of Musicology of Warsaw University towards the end of the previous year.[25]

In June and July, the group recorded a boxed set of two records entitled *The Instruments of the Middle Ages and Renaissance* in the Conway Hall, London. These records (now CDs) were made for the American market and the various instruments were introduced by the distinguished American musical commentator and author Martin Bookspan. Like David Munrow and the Early Music Consort of London's *Instruments of the Middle Ages and Renaissance*, recorded in the following year, the various instruments played by Musica Reservata were divided into various categories, such as bowed strings, plucked strings, percussion and so forth, introduced individually and then played together. The demonstrations ended with a 'concert' of seven items. Cleverly devised and well introduced, it provided an excellent introduction to a wide selection of early instruments.[26]

Another LP was recorded at some time during this year, also in the Conway Hall. *A Concert of Early Music* consisted of an assortment of French, English, Italian and German music ranging from the thirteenth to the late sixteenth centuries. There is a good variety of music on this disc; it is performed well and the sound quality is excellent. Although it was recorded in 1972, it was not released until about 1978 as an LP and then again in 1998 as a CD, both of them on Vanguard Classics.[27]

At the beginning of August, John was conducting two Musica Reservata concerts, both held on the same day, in the Sainte-Chapelle, Paris. Entitled *Hommage à Heinrich Schütz*, the programme celebrated the 300th anniversary of the composer's death and was devoted to his and his contemporaries' music.[28] John must have gritted his teeth when conducting this double dose of music by Schütz, a composer he quite disliked ('too many root positions', he once muttered to Patrick Cuming).[29]

About a week later, the group gave two performances at the Flanders Festival in Bruges. The first, *Medieval French and English Church and Court Music* took place in the Sint-Annakerk on the seventh of the month. The concert in the Memlingmuseum on the following day was of music at the courts of Italy (14th to 16th centuries) and Spain (15th to 16th centuries). The author of an acerbic review published in one of the Belgian newspapers was unimpressed by the sound that the group made.[30]

Towards the end of August John came to our house at Knockmaroon with Ruth to rehearse some music for an RTÉ recording; John used a Longman and Broderip square piano that my father had lovingly restored. I taped him playing one of the works to be broadcast: Haydn's Variations in F minor (1793), a recording that I still have and cherish. In the recording, he caresses the delicate little instrument in a most sensitive manner, teasing out the wonderful music, and trips through the intricate variations with nimble fingers and a delight- fully light touch.[31] Early in the following month the piano was moved over to Knockmaroon House, where another rehearsal took place, this time with Frank Patterson.[32] Two recordings were made, the first of which was broad- cast in February of the following year and consisted of the Variations already mentioned and Haydn's Trio No. 45 in E flat, played by John, Betty Sullivan and Margaret Hayes, violin. Sadly, this programme was not archived.[33] The second, divided into two programmes with a later addition of items sung by the RTÉ Singers, conducted by Hans Waldemar Rosen, was devoted to Haydn's songs and was broadcast towards the end of May, 1973.[34]

At around this period, a new record appeared: *An Elizabethan Evening*. John's contributions were *The Leaves bee Greene* by William Inglott, played on organ, *Amarilli di Julio Romano* by Peter Philips and *Galliarda* by William Byrd, both played on virginals. Although Denis Arnold of *The Gramophone* had mixed views on this disc, he praised John's playing, though he wondered why John had chosen to play the piece by Inglott on an organ.[35]

We find John next in Berlin, conducting Musica Reservata, at the Orangerie in the Schloß Charlottenburg, in a programme of English and German music.[36] A critic, writing in *Die Welt*, opined that the music 'did not entirely please the musical sensibilities of today. But in any case the evening was highly informative.'[37] Afterwards, the group gave concerts and made recordings in Cologne, Hamburg and Berlin and then travelled to Vienna, where, at the beginning of October they performed a concert of music from the time of Christopher Columbus in the Brahms-saal.[38] 'The attempt by a vocal quartet to assume the manner of presentation of Spanish folk music which belongs to the culture of North Africa with its throaty forced expression does not always lead to happy results', wrote a critic in the *Salzburger Nachrichten*.[39]

The fact that John was still conducting abroad and also at home obviously meant that he had to be excused from time to time from his teaching in the Royal Irish Academy of Music. When teaching the harpsichord, he used the instrument that my father had made for the Academy. One of his pupils during this term was Emer Buckley, who had studied piano at the Dublin College of Music, had won major prizes at the Feis Ceoil, and who later left Ireland to live in Rome and then Paris, where she studied with Kenneth Gilbert and became a highly-respected harpsichord player. She wrote:

> My first lessons with John were like having a window opened to reveal a whole new world. I can still remember the excitement I used to feel on the thirty-minute bus ride to the Academy for lessons and practice ... I have the best possible memories of John as a teacher: his sense of humour, his vast culture, his respect for his pupils, his humility. It was so refreshing compared to what I had previously experienced. He encouraged me to ask questions, to travel, to attend courses, and was always keen to hear about my experiences. The occasional bottles of Grappa I brought back from Italy were always welcome too.

Emer's interest in French music, and French harpsichord music in particular, must have been a revelation for John, who had rarely ventured into this field.[40] When somebody first played him an LP of music by Charpentier performed by Musica Antiqua Köln at around this time, he was converted. John explained, 'It was like seeing a ghost'.[41] He would soon delight in the music of François and Louis Couperin, Rameau, Marin Marais and other French composers.

Two other distinguished pupils were the harpsichordist Malcolm Proud (more on him later) and the musician and conductor David Adams, who, after graduating, taught at Wesley College. As he was so tired after working he was in no humour for practising and almost gave up playing the organ for a year. 'The real interest I kept up was harpsichord,' he said. 'I was studying with John Beckett, and that's what I really looked forward to every week.'[42]

Another one of John's harpsichord pupils from around this period was Carmel Harrison. Although she found him tough and demanding, she soon discovered that John was an immensely kind person. He was to have a profound influence on her life – not just in music, but as a person. Interestingly, she thought that he was very spiritual, never guessing that he was actually quite irreligious. She felt that he had a great feeling for things, including music, and had a wonderful sensitivity for phrasing.

Carmel had enjoyed listening to the Consort of Saint Sepulchre and so when an opportunity arose for her to go to London, she went to hear Musica Reservata perform in the Queen Elizabeth Hall. Although many thought that John was quite indifferent to the audience's reaction to the group's concerts, he in fact was interested to hear what one thought of the performances. Because of this, he was annoyed when he discovered that Carmel had been at the concert and had not spoken to him afterwards.

Carmel often adjourned to Kennedy's pub across the road with John and others, where they chatted about everything and anything. She felt that as John was so involved in music, he was not particularly interested in the outside world. Ruth did her best to expand his horizons. Carmel liked Ruth, who often acted as a buffer between him and other people.[43]

Marion Doherty was another harpsichord student of John's. Although she used to dread going to his lessons, she found them very beneficial and learned a great deal from him. She found him to be meticulous; as he would accept nothing but the best, he made her play pieces again and again until she got them absolutely right. She stayed with him for several years and at one stage he taught her to play all six of Bach's solo Partitas for harpsichord.[44]

Another of John's harpsichord students was the composer Gerald Barry. In 1972 he won a composer's competition with a setting of text from Samuel Beckett's short story *Lessness*, which he had written for soprano, alto and full orchestra. This was to be performed by the Dublin Symphony Orchestra at a hall in Ely Place. Beckett's story was partly inspired by the American composer John Cage and the experimental music of the 1960s. Gerald needed permission to use Beckett's text and wrote to his publisher John Calder repeatedly but received no reply. In desperation he asked John, who advised him to write to Samuel directly. This he did and, much to his surprise, immediately received a very gracious reply, granting him permission. On another occasion, Gerald set part of *Waiting for Godot*, also to be performed by soprano, alto and full orchestra, and wrote again to Samuel for permission to use the material. This time he received two prompt replies, one in the morning from Paris and, in the afternoon of the same day, another from Samuel's country house in Ussy, worded slightly differently, both giving permission. He clearly had forgotten that he had written in the morning.

As Gerald had been told that John liked to play music at a strict tempo without *rubato*, and as he was determined that John would like him, he prepared and performed Bach's Partita in D major, BWV 828 for harpsichord in the manner he imagined John would like. The trick worked – John loved Gerald's approach and the two men got on well together. Gerald remembers having a drink with John in Kennedy's pub after one of his lessons. John was horrified to hear that Gerald was going to study with Stockhausen, whose music he completely dismissed. In this sense Gerald said, 'John was a classic crank. He had no time for anything he didn't understand.'[45]

Starting from this term, John led a chamber music class in the Academy on Tuesday evenings. At these classes he taught Andrew Robinson to play continuo on the viol, with hardly a word spoken. Andrew sat to the left of John, who stretched out his hand to give him a part to play, and again to take it back. In this way he accompanied every other participant in the class, singers and instrumentalists. Every shading of the music was clearly shown in John's left hand on the harpsichord, which Andrew doubled on the viol. When John started a viol consort class in the following year, Andrew joined it.

Like Carmel Harrison, Andrew soon realized that although John could be a most affectionate and faithful friend, he could be a bitter opponent with a very sharp tongue. He took some lame ducks under his wing, giving them valuable but (he thought) wasted time repeatedly in his classes. On the other hand he could be scathing towards a new pupil. Andrew heard him ask one, 'Are you doing it that way because you like it, or out of sheer incompetence?' He simply could not resist saying what came into his head. Having been verbally attacked like this, some pupils never returned. A professional opera singer who ventured into the class was chided with, 'There *are* four beats in each bar – do you have a problem with that?' The unfortunate lady was so upset that she had to be taken out for a drink afterwards in order to calm her down. John stretched his students to their limits, but most were grateful to him for what he had taught them and for the fact that he had made them play music that, without his encouragement, they would never have tackled.[46]

Michael Dervan, although not formally a member of the chamber music class, accompanied various students on harpsichord. He, his girlfriend (a violinist) and Christine Cooley, a cellist, performed Purcell's Sonata in G minor. As they all favoured the non-vibrato approach when playing music of this period, John was very satisfied with the violinist and became quite fond of her. Together they played the work at a Trinity College Singers' concert and were reviewed by Charles Acton in *The Irish Times*.

Michael remembers how John always insisted on practising the starts of pieces; it was not unusual for him to do seven or eight starts before he was entirely happy. The music was always rhythmically rigid: it had to be played at a certain speed and that was that. Once, Michael made the mistake of attempting to play the piano part in a Haydn Trio; the music contained some very difficult octave passages. John was merciless and let him know exactly what he thought about his attempt – so much so that Michael decided to stick with the harpsichord, which he found was more manageable. The problem with reading John's harpsichord parts was trying to decipher the almost unreadable handwriting, but Michael eventually got used to it.

He also remembers how strict and sometimes harsh John could be with some of his pupils; many were reduced to nervous wrecks. He could be frustrating, and students sometimes complained that he often sat and played all the time, and gave them little opportunity to do so. Despite this and the fact that he was tough, he was an inspirational nurturer.[47]

Rhoda Draper, who played recorder, sang in the chamber music classes and later joined the viol consort class, had begun by taking harpsichord lessons from John. Although officially a harpsichord student, John soon had her playing recorders and singing songs by Dowland, Purcell and other composers. When Lindsay Armstrong called to the classroom with a message for John, he was perplexed to discover him accompanying her while she sang an aria by Carissimi or some other composer. John then loaned her his viol and taught her to play it. Honor O Brolchain remembers John accepting students for a particular instrument, such as the harpsichord, and switching them shortly afterwards to an easier instrument, such as the viol, probably in an effort not to discourage them or simply to get them to play the viol, which he thought was a good instrument to master.

In the chamber music class Rhoda noticed that while John was prepared to indulge her and other amateurs, he could be quite rude to professional musicians. He often favoured enthusiasm over competence and would produce music that was far too difficult for students like Rhoda, who were amateurs and who could not possibly do it justice; he frequently did this just for the thrill of hearing them 'having a go' at it. For her, John was a complete paradox, who could be modest, laid back and arrogant 'all in the one breath'.

Other students in the chamber music class and occasional class concerts in the Dagg Hall were David and John Milne, Clive Shannon, Patricia Quinn, Una Lawlor, Siobhán Yeats, Loretta Keating, Liam Óg Ó Floinn, who played the uilleann pipes, and the traditional fiddler Nollaig Casey, who was regularly asked to play an unaccompanied slow air. A traditional flute player also performed at the concerts, though he did not attend the class. I can remember being brought to some of the concerts (my father having been summoned to tune the harpsichord), where I heard Carmel Harrison and Clive Shannon playing the harpsichord, Rhoda Draper either singing or playing the recorder, John himself playing the recorder and John Milne singing in his fine bass voice.[48]

Many years later Siobhán Yeats, now living in Germany, remembered singing Purcell's *The Plaint* with John in Dublin in a version involving a violin solo. Although she no longer had the music, she thought it would be nice to perform it with some friends, and so she got in touch with John and asked him if he could send her a copy of the music. He promptly did so, and she still has it: voice plus continuo and the violin part, all as an original written by hand in turquoise ink. Her group duly performed the song, and she was very touched that John went to so much trouble on her behalf.[49]

Many of the students went with John to Kennedy's pub, where he would drink whiskey (occasionally adding a clove of garlic) and come out with outrageous *bons mots*; when one suggested itself, Andrew Robinson recollects, he was powerless to resist uttering it. 'He had unshakeable opinions about everything under the sun, delivered in a ponderous drawl; his voice was rather like the actor Patrick Magee's.' John was also adept with pithy epigrams. The students quickly got the measure of John's likes and dislikes, realizing that he held Handel, Vivaldi and Corelli in extraordinary contempt. A phrase he used of a particular Vivaldi piece was, 'A cliché callously used'. He dismissed Orlando Gibbons as 'the Handel of the seventeenth century'.[50]

Paul Conway, a late student of music, got to know John almost by accident. He had been studying musical theory and harmony under Jean Archibald without learning an instrument. When the rules changed and he was obliged to learn to play an instrument, his teacher suggested that he approach John ('an unusual character' as she described him). Paul remembers his first encounter with John in the Dagg Hall, where he asked him for lessons. John agreed to teach him. At a later stage, when John suggested that he learn to play the recorder, Paul bought a treble and practised his scales and exercises. When he sat for his music diploma examinations, he was astonished when John turned up to play his accompaniment. He and John soon became fast friends; Paul regularly visited him and Ruth at their cottage in Kilmacanogue. He can remember his son Simon sitting on John's lap as he played the harpsichord in the cottage.

Paul also attended the chamber music classes; he listened first and then played. He met Andrew Robinson there and was fascinated by the sound of his bass viol. He asked Andrew and his friend Anthony OBrien to make him a bass, which they did in 1980, and he learned to play it. When he had mastered the instrument, he joined the viol consort sessions on Wednesday evenings.[51]

Thirty-One
1973

At the beginning of the year John called to our house in order to make sure that my father could tune his harpsichord for some upcoming recitals, and to ask if we knew the meaning of various religious feast day Latin names. This request had us searching through encyclopaedias, dictionaries and missals. The 'upcoming recitals' that I had noted in my diary were in fact the first three concerts in a new series of Bach cantatas, which were held in St Ann's Church, Dawson Street, in Dublin's city centre. This explained why John was anxious to discover the meaning of the Latin terms.[1]

The first of these cantata concerts, which were unique in Dublin's musical scene at the time, took place on Sunday 28 January at half past three in the afternoon. There had been much discussion about the time, which had to suit everyone.[2] John now conducted the New Irish Chamber Orchestra, members of the Guinness Choir and, in the first concert, the soloists Bernadette Greevy, contralto, Frank Patterson, tenor and William Young, bass.[3]

The idea of using the Guinness Choir goes back to the performance of Bach's *Saint John Passion* at the Royal Dublin Society during the previous year, when it and the New Irish Chamber Orchestra had been conducted by John's old friend Victor Leeson. Thanks to this connection, John was able to obtain the use of Victor's choir, though the numbers had been reduced to suit the circumstances. One of the singers was Tim Thurston, who had been born in Cambridge but worked in the Guinness Brewery. He had first encountered John conducting a Musica Reservata concert in the Queen Elizabeth Hall and was suitably impressed. Although John was tough on the singers in the Guinness Choir, they were used to this as Victor had been a hard task-master. Tim was so much in awe of John that he just did whatever he was told to do. He quickly realized that John's knowledge and understanding of Bach's music was very deep, and concluded that if members of the choir did not respond, it must have been their fault and not John's.[4]

The orchestra, led by Mary Gallagher, was probably not quite as good as the Musica Reservata orchestra that John had conducted in London, but in time they improved and, under John's strict and often annoyingly pedantic direction, became excellent enough to be acceptable to the BBC.

The items performed in this first concert were Bach's Cantata No. 82, *Ich habe genug* ('It is enough'), the Sinfonia from Cantata No. 42 (John's party piece) and Cantata No. 81, *Jesus schläft, was soll ich hoffen?* ('Jesus sleeps, what hope is there for me?'). William Young sang in the first cantata (scored for solo bass), and, according to an enraptured Charles Acton, sang it superlatively and sensitively. Acton liked the Sinfonia and, in the final cantata, thought that Bernadette Greevy's smooth line and velvety quality were 'lovely'. He concluded his review, 'This whole concert had that character both of dedication and of sensuous and stylistic satisfaction that we associate with John Beckett. The next two Sunday afternoons will be compulsory events for Bach lovers.'[5]

The following concert took place at the same time and venue, on Sunday 4 February. This time the works were Bach's Trio Sonata in G, BWV 525, the songs he contributed to Georg Christian Schemelli's *Gesangbuch* (song book), the Trio Sonata in E minor, BWV 527, and Cantata No. 55, *Ich armer Mensch, ich Sündenknecht* ('I, wretched man, a slave to sin'). The two Trio Sonatas were the works for organ that had been arranged by John.[6]

The third and final concert, on 11 February, consisted of Cantata No. 54, *Widerstehe doch der Sünde* ('Stand steadfast against transgression'), the Sinfonia from Cantata No. 42 (again) and Cantata No. 154, *Mein liebster Jesu ist verloren* ('My dearest Jesus is lost'). In his review, Charles Acton singled out Bernadette Greevy for praise and enjoyed hearing the 'unfamiliar' Sinfonia again. John liked this piece to be played at a stately pace, much slower than the speed that it is played nowadays, though not ponderously slow. For him, the music of the Sinfonia depicted the gentle, evening stroll of Jesus and his disciples alluded to in the title of the work.[7]

Lindsay Armstrong noted many years later that it was immediately apparent that these concerts were something new and very special. Many people came to them not only for the music, but also to hear John's pithy and idiosyncratic introductions.[8] Although John often looked uncomfortable, he quite liked imparting information and knowledge. Colm Tóibín wrote in the *Sunday Independent*:

His introductions were informative but laconic, suggesting that he knew much more. Once the music started, it was magic. On one of those Sundays when I was 18 or 19, I realised that I would never be able to go back to my small town. I had found displacement. I was at home.[9]

Jenny Robinson felt that John's passionate introductions, in which he described Bach's close involvement with the church, were done in Bach's voice rather than his own, given that he was not interested in religion. Andrew remembered that he had no complaint about playing or conducting religious music, as long as it was good.[10]

Honor O Brolchain, one of the members of the Consort of Saint Sepulchre, attended the Bach Cantata concerts whenever she could; for her they were 'absolute revelations'. She was fascinated by what John managed to get out of the singers, considering that they would normally not sing in such a pure musical style – though, of course, they were excellent singers in themselves.[11]

Another person who loved John's Bach Cantata concerts and went religiously to them was Gerald Barry. He feels that John's approach to Bach would have worn well over time. His speeds, Gerald recollects, were more measured than other early music groups of the period; he and his friend Christopher Stembridge often laughed at the speeds taken by other groups and dubbed the phenomenon *Autobahn Mentalität* (motorway mentality). For Gerald, John represented an atmosphere that he treasured. He knew that with John, the music and the listener were safe and in good hands: 'That time in Dublin was special. John and a few others like him had an insight into this music which was really inspiring.'[12]

Tim Thurston remembers John's astonishing passion for Bach and his music; in an unguarded moment he said to Tim, 'Ah, I love this man so much – I would have liked to have smelt his armpits!'[13]

Lindsay Amstrong believed that part of the success of these cantata concerts was due to a great deal of intensive rehearsal with the soloists: Bernadette Greevy used to talk about John coming to her house,[14] Alison Young remembers John rehearsing in Rathfarnham with her husband Bill (as everyone called him), and the soprano Irené Sandford journeyed down from Northern Ireland before the performances. John generally approached Bill before Christmas, when he (a member of the Saint Patrick's Cathedral choir) was at his busiest, singing in various performances of Handel's *Messiah*. 'Do you mind leaving it till after Christmas?' Bill would ask him. 'Oh well, I suppose so,' John would say reluctantly, 'though I'm very anxious to get on with it'. Relaxing in bed on the morning of St Stephen's (Boxing) Day after an exhausting month, the telephone would ring and Alison would hear her husband say, 'Oh, hello John – how are you?' Although John was eager to get the rehearsals started at once, Bill had to gently remind him that it was only St Stephen's Day. John would retort, 'But you did say after Christmas, Bill.' Diaries would be fetched and dates pencilled in.

John spent a good deal of time in the Youngs' house between Christmas and February and became part of Alison and Bill's lives; Alison busied herself supplying him with cups of tea, lunches and so forth. She noticed that his work was meticulous; Bill, who became very fond of John and had a huge regard for him, worked hard and accommodated himself to John's wishes. Alison believes that the highlight of Bill's career was singing the Bach cantatas with John; he was particularly fine in Cantata No. 82, *Ich habe genug* and No. 56, *Ich will den Kreuzstab gerne tragen* ('Gladly shall I bear the cross'), both scored for solo bass; the latter would be performed two years later. As Bill had a sense of humour, was easy to get on with and loved singing Bach's music, John liked working with him. Although Alison found John slightly forbidding and was a little nervous of him, she grew very fond of him. Ruth also came to the house and, on one occasion, when they were throwing a party to celebrate the successful conclusion of one of the annual series of cantata concerts, he brought the composer Frederick May, now a sad, broken individual who, by that time, was confined to various hospitals and institutions in Dublin. It was at parties such as these when John would get drunk. Although he was an intellectual, Alison noticed that he led quite a bohemian lifestyle.

On one occasion, John called to Bill's house for a rehearsal as arranged and was greeted by Alison, who apologized for the fact that Bill had not yet returned home from work. She invited him in, offered to make tea for him, and asked to be excused for a few minutes in order to drive her son to the local church hall. John looked at the young boy wistfully and said, 'Alison, could I not do that for you?' Knowing that he had no children of his own, Alison readily agreed and noted that he looked particularly chuffed as he set off in the car with her son.

On another occasion he arrived in a terrible state – he had lost a treasured bag of pencils. It appeared that he had stopped somewhere, perhaps at a petrol station, placed the bag on the roof of the car for some reason and driven off, unmindful of what he had done. Alison noted his punctuality: he was never late and undoubtedly sat in his car outside the house until the appointed time of his arrival.

Members of the audience attending the Bach cantata concerts noticed how reluctant John was to acknowledge the applause and bow. The procedure was for him and the soloists, having bowed, to walk down a side aisle and go through a door on the right, where they disappeared from sight. At this point the applause stopped and, of course, nothing would induce John to return. Bill approached him about this matter and said, 'John, people really need us to go back out again, but you've got to lead us, because you're the conductor.' Bill suggested that, as he was directly in front of him on the way down, he would turn at the door and usher John back for more applause, within sight of the audience. John agreed to this. When walking down at the end of the first cantata on the following Sunday, Bill heard John saying, 'Don't forget your little trick, Bill!'

For fear of being snowed in up in the mountains of County Wicklow during the cold months of January and February, John would often drive into the city on the Friday before the Bach cantata concert, where he would presumably stay with his sister Ann, and not return until after the concert on Sunday. When there were a couple of inches of snow, he would grumble at the low turnout and mutter about people in Germany happily attending events when there were ten inches of snow on the ground.[15]

Michael Dervan, who wrote John's obituary in *The Irish Times*, described John conducting with a 'trademark style of taut rhythm, strong projection and monumental grandeur'.[16] I noticed a certain amount of heaviness when I first heard a concert of these cantatas in 1975, and frankly found much of the music rather depressing.[17] Gillian Smith, when she later played continuo in these concerts, saw heavy accents and indications to bring particular notes out, marked in John's score in coloured pencil.[18] Andrew Robinson, who would sing in the choir several years later, observed that while, in general, orchestral players prefer to be shown things in the course of rehearsing, John's method was to mark each player's part in great detail, using a soft pencil, before the first rehearsal (having completely erased all previous markings), and then give further instructions verbally.[19] As he would not allow Gillian to play the continuo in any other way than his, Gillian was obliged to play his realizations of the continuo, in which he used very thick chords and which were also difficult to read.

Gillian and Lindsay concluded, after playing in many concerts under John, that what he enjoyed most were the rehearsals. John believed that what he was doing was of paramount importance: he went into great detail and painstakingly strove to get the articulation and ensemble absolutely right. He was tough on the choir, insisting that they sing out, enunciate clearly and convey the sense of the words – he could not abide anything that was in any way wishy-washy. Gillian and Lindsay sometimes felt that when the final rehearsal was over, the concert would often be an anticlimax; it was as if he had put all his energy into the rehearsals and was then drained of it. Members of the audience noticed that he looked quite out of humour when conducting. He often got very cross during the performances and if something went wrong, such as a slight mistake or a bad start, he would glower at the guilty (and terrified) player. Naturally this did not help the morale of the unfortunate performer, who had to continue to the end of the piece. John often felt a crushing sense of disappointment at the end of a concert. Gillian reckoned that he thought that it should have been as good as the final rehearsal, but did not realize that he himself had to go up another notch for that to happen. He seemed to think that if he just did the same as he had done during the rehearsals, then everything would work fine. This, of course, did not allow for the players' adrenalin, which could have been harnessed to turn the performance into something quite wonderful. However, if the players were misdirected or made nervous, the performance would tend to trip up and then he would become very agitated. Unlike many of the players, who normally repaired to a pub in high spirits after a concert, one would have found him on his own, in the depths of depression, morose and not at all talkative. The players and singers often wondered what they had done to upset him, but it was nothing to do with them – it was just John down in the dumps. He rarely praised any of the people involved; only occasionally would he have muttered, 'That was good' to somebody or, 'Oh, it was great to hear that music,' and that was it.

These observations may help explain John's grumpy demeanour at the Musica Reservata concerts in London and his reluctance to acknowledge the audience's applause. He rarely looked pleased when being applauded and, at the Bach cantata concerts often held up the score as if to indicate that the audience should be applauding Bach, not him.

Although John was against religion, Bach's music overcame whatever prejudices he had because of its power and beauty. It was evident that John relished the sonority of the Authorized Version of the Bible, even though he did not believe what was written in it. He was also conscious of the fact that the texts used in Bach's cantatas were written in good German. Lindsay Armstrong points out that John may have believed the concepts of Bach's texts artistically and encouraged the singers to sing them with conviction, even though he did not believe in them theologically. Certainly John's cantata series opened everybody's ears to new music, because at the time most of the cantatas were unknown. [20]

Tim Thurston often had a drink with John in a nearby pub after a concert. All Tim wanted to do was to listen to him talk about music, his love of cats, his love of Purcell and his feeling that one line of Bach was as good as several pages of Handel. He amused John by telling him a story about a bassoonist friend of his who worked in a bank in Nigeria and had taught his African grey parrot to say, 'Handel is an unmitigated hack!' Tim was invited to John and Ruth's cottage for lunch, at which John was kind enough to say, 'There's music in every cell of Tim's body.' [21]

Members of the orchestra jokingly referred to John's idiosyncratic method of conducting as 'the chop' or 'the slash'. Lindsay remembered how mechanical his beat, indicated by slicing his right hand through the air, tended to be. Andrew

Robinson noted that the members of the orchestra saw little nuance in this arm movement, which tended to be extra large. His left hand did very little; only occasionally was it used to indicate a *crescendo* or *decrescendo* or to cue an instrument or group of instruments. Compared to the rehearsals, he was quite inanimate when conducting the performances.[22] In Michael Dervan's opinion, John lacked any conducting technique and simply did not know how to conduct.[23]

On the other hand, Tim Thurston found John's unrelenting and mechanical beat perfect for the chorales, which John correctly identified as congregational music, to be sung and played in a very straightforward manner without *rallentandi*, so that members of the congregation could join in.[24]

All the players were aware of John's anxiousness about starting the orchestra. Gillian remembers Betty Sullivan saying, 'He doesn't trust us to start!' If he was worried about beginning a particular movement, he would do it over and over again at the final rehearsal. The trouble with this was that it made the players worry and wonder if it would be all right or not. He was equally worried, and if there was a problem with starting the orchestra at the very beginning of the concert and it went badly, then he became angry. Sometimes his starts were not altogether clear; it was clear enough in his head but, possibly because of his anxiety, his gestures were very unsure and therefore the pulse was not as obvious as it should have been.

In his attempt to recreate, as best he could, the sound he believed Bach would have heard, John fought an ongoing battle over the use of vibrato, even though modern instruments tuned to modern pitch were always used. Although playing without vibrato was difficult for musicians who had never studied baroque technique, he managed to convince them by sheer power of persuasion and also by reference to Betty Sullivan, who had learned to play the bass viol and who was a great disciple of John's. As a result of this, John was regarded as something of a trailblazer in Ireland.[25]

Towards the end of February John was back in London again, this time conducting Musica Reservata in a programme of fifteenth-century Spanish music in the Queen Elizabeth Hall.[26] He conducted the group again at the beginning of May in Lisbon at the Gulbenkian Foundation.[27] Afterwards, John, Ruth and Cyril Taylor, the manager of the group, toured around Portugal, Spain and France. John sent his friend Seán O'Leary and his wife Odile a postcard of Picasso's *Bullfight* with the message:

> We (Ruth and I) are making a marvellous trip with Cyril Taylor (who is seeing agents) from Lisbon (where we had 3 concerts last week) to Seville – Madrid

— Barcelona — Collioure — Carcassonne — Bordeau — Paris — London, by boat — bus
— train. We send greetings and love to you both — and the children. John & Ruth. [28]

On 22 May he was back in London, conducting Musica Reservata in the
Queen Elizabeth Hall, this time in a programme of fifteenth-century secular
music by Dunstable, Dufay and Josquin. [29] In mid July, John gave a lunchtime
harpsichord recital in St Ann's Church, Dublin, which was attended by the
recently inaugurated President of Ireland, Erskine Childers. He performed five
pieces from the *Fitzwilliam Virginal Book* and ten pieces by Purcell. Charles Acton
was suitably impressed. [30]

On 21 July John played the solo harpsichord part of Bach's Harpsichord
Concerto in E, BWV 1053 and the continuo parts of Bach's Suite No. 3 in
D, BWV 1068, Cantata No. 166 and Suite No. 2 in B minor, BWV 1067 at
the Killarney Bach Festival. Started three years previously by George Manos,
an American professor of Greek descent (then on holiday in Killarney), the
festival had become an important annual event. George Manos conducted the
music, which was performed by the New Irish Chamber Orchestra. [31] Lindsay
Armstrong and Gillian Smith remember this and other recitals at the festival and
the fact that they gave John a lift in their Morris Minor car, the suspension of
which never really recovered after the journeys there and back, for at that time
John weighed somewhere in the region of twenty-two stone. [32]

At around this time John became involved with the Music Association of
Ireland school recitals scheme, which Gillian Smith's mother had set up several
years previously. The idea was that a group of three (a pianist and two other
instrumentalists) would set off in a car and play to the students in three schools
within a radius of about fifty miles, all in one day. John and Betty Sullivan did
quite a number of these, and it is possible that Ruth toured with them as well.
The players had to deal with all sorts of situations and, more importantly, with
children, who could quickly become bored or unruly. [33]

Some years later, when Jenny Robinson and Ruth were booked to go to
Galway for some school recitals, John decided to go with them as their driver.
His reasons for joining them was a passionate longing to see the 'sun go down
on Galway bay' (to quote the words of the song), inhale the whiff of the sea,
imagine where the Aran Islands were if he could not actually see them, and have
a conversation with some of the locals in a pub. He was quite happy to leave the
ladies and go off on his own. [34]

John probably started his viol consort classes, held on Wednesday evenings,
in the Dagg Hall of the Royal Academy of Music, at the start of the new term.
Members included Andrew Robinson, Paul Conway, Douglas and Mary Sealy,
and Honor O Brolchain, who joined a little later. Although Honor felt like an

PART THREE: DUBLIN 1971–1983

outsider, it was a marvellous experience for her, especially as she was already familiar with much of the music. John normally lead the group by playing the top part on his treble viol, though occasionally he played an inner part on the tenor. He was never known to play the bass.

Most of the sessions consisted of sight-reading; there was no preparation or set work. If players lost their place or made mistakes, John's method of correction was to say, 'We'll stop and go back to the beginning'. Every time he did this, the players were sharper and more concentrated. He rarely untangled a difficult section of the music, and believed that if everybody was really concentrating, they would not make mistakes. Generally speaking, his method of forcing concentration on the players was effective. Occasionally he made a mistake and got cross with himself. Honor had the impression that he had not mastered the viol as thoroughly as other instruments, and noticed that he was just as hard on himself as he was on others about starting a piece of music again. Another thing he loved to do, especially with music that he was particularly fond of, was to play a piece again and again; each time it was played, everyone became more relaxed and the performance improved. Honor guessed that he probably worked this way in private. The disadvantage of this approach and not addressing problems in the middle of pieces was that whereas the beginnings and endings might be perfect, tricky sections within them could remain unstable.

After the classes Honor often joined John and the others in Kennedy's pub for a drink and a chat, though Honor was content to just listen to what John had to say. Topics for discussion were generally initiated by him and were often addressed directly to someone whom he considered expert in the area, such as Douglas Sealy. The arts were often a topic of conversation and John was quite likely to discourse on Asian art, pottery, kilns and other things that fascinated him. He could be obsessive, and when he was obsessive about music, Honor felt, it drew out wonderful things.[35]

In October John was back in London, conducting Musica Reservata in a programme of fifteenth- and sixteenth-century English music in the Queen Elizabeth Hall.[36] A couple of days later, he was in Belgium, this time conducting the group in a concert of early English music in the Gothic Hall of the Stadhuis or Hôtel de Ville in Brussels. As well as conducting, John played the organ.[37]

As it turned out, this was John's penultimate engagement with Musica Reservata. Tension between him and Michael had mounted; matters had come to a head and he now wished to opt out. Added to this was John's distrust of the groups's management, which, according to Bernard Thomas, led to a big row. A letter written by John in Dublin on 21 November to his friend Heinz Liebrecht, who was still very much involved with the group, addresses this issue and spells out his firm decision:

> I am convinced that an organisation such as you envisaged that evening, made up of Michael, yourself, a new agent-cum-manager, and me, would not work — certainly not with me as an ingredient. With a new conductor perhaps it will. I have reached this decision without any disrespect to you. It is my hope that with a new conductor, who can work closely and constructively with Michael as I cannot do, a newly adjusted organisation with your financial advice, RESERVATA may go on to perform much new music, and to achieve greater and more profitable successes than heretofore; without so much of the pain and frustration which for me (and, I know, for Michael) tainted too much of our work in the past.[38]

John's final engagement with the group was a concert of English and French music of the thirteenth, fourteenth and fifteenth centuries in St Gabriel's Church, Sunderland as part of the Wearmouth 1300 Festival on 27 November.[39] With this concert, another chapter in John's life came to an end. Shortly afterwards, Ann Manly took over the management of Musica Reservata and Andrew Parrott became the new conductor. The group went on to give many more concerts and to tour other countries including the Netherlands, Belgium, Germany, and, in 1976, Russia and Lithuania, then in the USSR. They made just one more record, *Josquin des Prés*, which was released in 1976, and continued to perform until the 1980s, when the group disbanded.[40]

John's friend Seán O'Leary, who witnessed the deterioration of the relationship between John and Michael, maintains that several factors contributed to the break-up: both men had large personalities and were authoritative in manner,[41] John was businesslike while Michael was a procrastinator,[42] Michael did not approve of John's treatment of Vera, whom he liked[43] and Ruth either wanted John all to herself or had her ideas for his own good.[44] Despite their differences, John never lost his admiration for Michael and often talked about him to Seán and his friends. A favourable judgment of others was often expressed as 'He's up to the Morrow standard.'[45]

Thirty-Two
1974

Severing his ties with London for a while, John settled down to working full time in Dublin. The new year began with three more concerts of Bach cantatas: Nos 166, *Wo gehest du hin?* ('Where goest thou?') and 42, *Am Abend aber desselbigen Sabbats* ('On the Evening of that same Sabbath') – the opening Sinfonia of which had been played twice the previous year; 53, *Schlage doch, gewünschte Stunde* ('Strike my Hour, so long awaited') and 54, *Widerstehe doch der Sünde* ('Stand steadfast against Transgression); and 33, *Allein zu dir, Herr Jesu Christ* ('Alone towards You, Lord Jesus Christ') and 159, *Sehet, wir geh'n hinauf gen Jerusalem* ('Behold! We go up to Jerusalem'). Charles Acton noted a softening in John's approach, resulting in a 'lilt and air in all the music. I felt in each that I was hearing the music as Bach wanted it.'[1]

Sometime during 1974 a German named Michael Richter came to Dublin, where he was employed as a lecturer in Medieval History at University College Dublin. Michael had a late vocation for music and decided that he would like to learn to play the viola. Somebody told him about Ruth David and he began to take lessons from her some time later at John and Ruth's home. John was very encouraging. They got on well together and socialized among a small circle of friends; 'There was lots of drinking,' Michael reported. John and Ruth used to go to Michael's home in Loughlinstown, where he cooked for them – John bluntly declared that he was a better cook than a musician!

When Michael found out about the performances of the Bach cantatas, he expressed the wish to sing in them but John said no. However, he allowed Michael to coach the singers and soloists in German. Michael found that the singers were good students. John once told him about the difficulty in obtaining material to perform, but said that he was happy to copy music 'from the august hand of J.S. Bach'.[2]

On 12 February, Ruth was involved in an accident on the Old Long Hill that led to their cottage in Kilmacanogue, when a coal lorry, which was travelling too fast down the icy road, skidded into her. This resulted in her kneecap being smashed, an operation, and her leg in plaster for several weeks. Unsurprisingly, this caused lifelong changes to her mobility.[3] Samuel heard of the accident and wrote to her from Paris, '[Aunt] Peggy writes you are heavily plastered (!). I hope this is an exaggeration and that none of the damage is of a kind to hamper you seriously or long or to interfere with your playing. It would be good to have good news of you soon.'[4]

Disaster of a more serious nature struck on the following day, when John's brother Peter died of a heart attack, aged fifty-one.[5] As mentioned previously, he had been head of Health Sciences in Trinity College Dublin, having returned home from America, where he had worked at the Mayo Clinic in Rochester, Minnesota. He was buried in St Fintan's Cemetery on the west side of the Hill of Howth. John wrote to Samuel, who received his letter on the 18th. 'If there is something of use to say I'll never find it now,' replied Samuel. 'But perhaps there is something I can do to help with medical expenses? Or towards another car? Or in any other way. Don't hesitate to let me know.'[6] According to James Knowlson's biography of Samuel, *Damned to Fame*, there were many other instances of Samuel's generosity; few writers distributed their money with as much liberality as he did.[7] Peter was survived by his Chinese wife Vicky and an adopted son, who sadly committed suicide some years later.[8]

By now Malcolm Proud had started his harpsichord lessons with John in the Royal Irish Academy of Music. Malcolm had studied piano with Elizabeth Huban, organ with David Lee and later would study under Gustav Leonhardt in Amsterdam. During his lessons in the Dagg Hall, John used to wander around the room while he played, often stopping at a reproduction of a Paul Klee painting, which he would study intently; Malcolm believes it was *Death and Fire*, one of Klee's finest late works. Malcolm worked on several pieces by Bach: the Partita No. 6 in E minor, BWV 830, the Brandenburg Concerto No. 5, and the Concerto for two harpsichords in C major, BWV 1061, which he performed with Emer Buckley in the Academy.

Malcolm found John obsessive and dogmatic about many things. A musical example was the last movement of the aforementioned Partita No. 6 by Bach. Although written in duple rhythm, John was adamant that it should be played in

triple rhythm – in other words, in what generally is considered to be conventional *gigue* rhythm. Charles Acton had discovered this at the Bicentenary
Concert in Trinity College two years previously. Malcolm believes that he may
well have founded his theory (shared by other harpsichordists of the time) on
the fact that there is a *Gigue* by the German composer Froberger which is found
in two seventeenth-century sources: in one it is notated in duplets, and in the
other in triplets. Also Bach's French contemporaries expected their music to
be played *inégal*, rather like a good traditional Irish fiddler might 'swing' the
notes of a reel. Many years later Malcolm and John met in a pub near John's
home in Greenwich for a few whiskeys and he revisited the whole subject, this
time applying the theory to Bach's chorale prelude *Vater unser im Himmelreich*
('Our Father in Heaven'), so that all the notated cross rhythms are eliminated
by 'tripletizing' everything. No doubt he would have turned in his grave had he
heard Malcolm's recordings of Bach's *Gigue* and chorale prelude; Malcolm finds
them far more expressive when played as notated.

Malcolm quickly became aware that John loathed the music of Handel and
Vivaldi; he described Handel as 'oily'. As well as loving Bach, he liked the music
of William Byrd. John also loved Purcell, Scarlatti (Malcolm had his Saga LP
of Scarlatti sonatas), and, of course, he adored Mahler. Malcolm remembers
travelling by bus with the bass John Milne to Enniskerry in County Wicklow,
where John picked them up in his Renault 4 and drove them to his cottage
in Kilmacanogue. There he played them an LP of the completed performing
version of Mahler's Symphony No. 10. To this day Malcolm can still hear in his
head the ending of the first movement as it sounded on that recording. He was
bemused that John considered it a 'privilege' to have to collect water in a bucket
from the stream.[9]

At the beginning of March a George Morrison film, entitled *Two Thousand
Miles of Peril* was shown on RTÉ Television. This was to commemorate the 150th
anniversary of the Royal National Lifeboat Institute. As well as focusing on the
work of the institute, the film included a dramatic reconstruction of a rescue at
sea. John composed the incidental music for it.[10] This film and Kieran Hickey's
The Light of Other Days was shown in the Player-Wills Theatre later in the month; I
went with my parents and, describing *Two Thousand Miles of Peril* in my diary, wrote,
'the rotten music by John Beckett ruined it'. John, true to form, had taken his
cue from shots of a rough, heaving sea and crashing waves to compose yet more
discordant music, which, at the age of nineteen, I was unable to appreciate.[11]

A couple of months later, George Morrison's film *Éamon de Valera – Portrait of
a Statesman*, for which John had composed incidental music, was shown in the
Savoy Cinema for a little over a week.[12] The music was performed by the RTÉ

Symphony Orchestra. Despite John's penchant for dissonance and astringency, it followed in the tradition of Seán Ó Riada's music for Morrison's best-known film *Mise Éire* ('I am Ireland'), released in 1960.[13]

The segments of music that make up the film score make use of Irish folk melody, both real and imagined, though its accompaniment is anything but Irish. Once again, a parody of *Rule Britannia*, played on trumpets and a snare drum, finds its way into the score a couple of times. That John had mastered the art of composing for a full orchestra is very obvious: on a tape of the music discovered in his attic after his death, John can be heard calling out the segment numbers in a highly confident manner.[14]

A rather unusual occasion now took place: a tribute to my father, in which three of his harpsichords were used in a concert of music by Bach. The venue was the Examination Hall in Trinity College. John conducted the New Irish Chamber Orchestra and the harpsichords were played by John O'Sullivan, David Lee and David Ledbetter. As this concert was part of the Dublin Arts Festival, John wrote an introduction to it in the programme booklet. The article concluded: 'In all Mr Gannon's instruments the craftsmanship is masterly, and they are made with a musical and historical sensibility that is, I think, exceptionally perceptive. We are proud to offer our performances this evening as a tribute to his work.'[15]

I was at this concert and can clearly remember the packed hall and the long, enthusiastic applause at the end. John gesticulated towards my father and forced him to his feet in order to take a bow.[16]

John was performing music of quite a different nature a few days later, when he played one of the piano parts in James Wilson's *The Hunting of the Snark* for three evenings at Mount Temple Comprehensive School, Malahide Road. The other pianist was John O'Sullivan. The pianists, a string quartet of players from the RTÉ Light Orchestra, a percussionist and the singers were conducted by Brian Grimson.[17] Brian remembers the two Johns performing the frenetic Rumba Toccata for piano duet in this work. 'The two Johns sat at the piano waiting, like greyhounds in the traps at Shelbourne Park. All I had to do, as conductor, was nod at them and they were off. Every dynamic, every note was gloriously exhilarating. And at the end of it, they just sat impassively, as though they had been playing slow five-finger exercises. What is more, they ended together, which is more than can be said for Horowitz and Toscanini on a very celebrated occasion!'[18]

A recital was given in early April in Trinity College by the newly formed Hesketh Piano Quartet, which comprised Thérèse Timoney, violin, Ruth David,

viola, Betty Sullivan, cello and Gillian Smith, piano. In between works by
Mozart and Brahms, John accompanied Anne Woodworth in Fauré's song cycle
La chanson d'Eve and the two glorious songs for contralto, viola and piano, opus
91 by Brahms, in which Ruth played the viola. For Charles Acton, who normally
associated John with the music of Bach, 'It was an added pleasure to hear, in the
Fauré, [his] gentle sensuous tone and the completely apt fluidity and grace with
which he accompanied and supported the singer.' In the Brahms songs, 'Ruth
David's *obbligato* was sheer joy for some of the loveliest viola tone I have heard
for a long time.'[19]

The next venture was a weekend of Haydn chamber music arranged by the
Carlow Music Club and held in St Patrick's College, Carlow at the beginning of
May. This had been organized by a group of chamber music enthusiasts headed
by a pharmacist named Joseph Foley.[20] Back in January, John, Betty Sullivan
and the violinist Arthur McIvor had come to our house to practise some of
Haydn's delightful piano trios, using the Longman and Broderip square piano
that my father had restored and which John loved to play. Towards the end of
April they returned, this time with Frank Patterson, who sang some Scottish
songs arranged by Haydn. The piano was transported to Carlow, where my
father tuned it.[21] Charles Acton wrote:

> The weekend of three concerts ... was devised by John Beckett, who started
> the proceedings with a vivid introduction stressing the importance of Haydn,
> his bewildering variety and quantity and what Tovey rightly called his inacces-
> sibility thanks to the lack of published scores and records until very recently. ...
> Mr. Beckett also introduced the works with his customary easy learning and
> helpfulness.

He continued, 'Carlow Music Club should be really proud of all this. I hope
they feel encouraged to do it again.'[22]

Happily, they did do it again; in the following year there was a weekend of
Schubert music, and in successive years there would be music by Mozart, then
Beethoven, Brahms, Chopin and, finally, a selection of French composers. Dan
Shields and his wife Kitty, both locals, met John during this first weekend of
Haydn's music. Dan can remember the subsequent concerts, which he attended;
he described John as 'the impresario'. Dan and Kitty became friendly with John
and Ruth, and also with Vicky, the widow of John's brother Peter. John came to
Dan's home in Carlow when he, Ruth and Betty came on school concert tours;
John referred to Dan's large family as 'the tribe'.[23]

As in the previous year, John played continuo for a concert of Bach music,
conducted by George Manos, in the Killarney Bach Festival at the end of July.[24]

At the end of August, he conducted the New Irish Chamber Orchestra in a concert of Bach music in the Kilkenny Arts Festival.[25]

Two Saga records featuring John as harpsichordist was released at around this period: *Elizabethan Heritage*, Volume 1 and 2. Denis Arnold of *Gramophone* praised the first disc (Volume 1) for its variety but found the performances of madrigals disappointing. Best of all, according to Arnold, was 'John Beckett's playing of the keyboard music. I confess his somewhat relentless style is not always to my taste. Here, however, his clear articulation and plain manner of exposition (either his instrument is a true virginal or he chooses to play without changes of registration) sound exactly right for the music.'[26]

In mid September John conducted Haydn's Symphony No. 67, performed by the RTÉ Symphony Orchestra in an orchestral concert broadcast on RTÉ Radio.[27] Used to working in the BBC, which had a radio channel devoted to classical music and the arts, John undoubtedly would have found the levels of professionalism, efficiency and commitment to work lower in RTÉ than what he had been used to. At least one radio producer, Venetia O'Sullivan, found him difficult to work with;[28] another found him 'prickly'. Few people in both radio and television would have appreciated and understood John at that time.[29]

The next big event in John's calendar was, in November, a BBC Invitation Concert in the Examination Hall of Trinity College. Called *A Concert of Music in Ireland during the 17th and 18th centuries*, it was a part of an ambitious series named *Four Centuries of Music in Ireland*, which celebrated fifty years of broadcasting in Northern Ireland. The concert, directed by John, was transmitted later in the month on BBC Radio 4 Northern Ireland. As well as conducting and devising the programme, John played the harpsichord with his Henry Purcell Consort and wrote the programme notes.

The rather lengthy first half of the concert consisted of works by Matthew Dubourg, Thomas Roseingrave, Geminiani, John Echlin, Handel, Carolan and Irish-inspired pieces from *The Fitzwilliam Virginal Book* – some of the material that had been used seven years previously for *The Music of Swift's Dublin* on RTÉ Television. The second half consisted of Purcell's grandly titled *Ode upon the ninth of January, 1694, the first Secular Day since the University of Dublin's Foundation by Queen Elizabeth* (better known as *Great Parent, Hail*), performed by the New Irish Chamber Orchestra, the Choir of Saint Patrick's Cathedral and soloists. As Charles Acton noted, this was not Purcell's greatest music;[30] the execrable libretto was written by the Irish poet Nahum Tate, who also wrote the Christmas carol *While Shepherds watch their Flocks by Night*.[31] Nonetheless, the concert was a success.

On the evening of the first broadcast (just the first half of the concert), my parents and I were in the Dagg Hall attending one of the chamber music class concerts. John played the harpsichord and the recorder, Ruth performed, and Emer Buckley, Carmel Harrison, Rhoda Draper and Clive Shannon also played. Afterwards we returned, with John and Ruth, to our house in order to record and listen to the concert on BBC Radio 4 Northern Ireland, which could not be received up in the Wicklow Mountains. I recorded the second broadcast, of the Purcell Ode, a few days later for them.[32]

The year ended with a trip to Galway at the beginning of December, where the Henry Purcell Consort (John, Betty and the soprano Nora Ring) performed at Leisureland, Salthill.[33]

Thirty-Three

1975

The new year began with a performance of Bach's *Saint Matthew Passion* conducted by Victor Leeson, in which John and Betty Sullivan performed the basso continuo. John was once again able to appreciate how well William Young sang the part of Christus;[1] unlike John, William was a firm believer and was able to sing the arias with great conviction.[2] After the Henry Purcell Consort had given a concert in Kilkenny in mid-February,[3] the traditional Bach cantatas were performed once again in St Ann's Church in Dawson Street. I went to the first concert on 16 February and noticed that it was being recorded by the BBC. John introduced each cantata – Nos. 167, *Ihr Menschen, rühmet Gottes Liebe* ('Ye mortals, extol God's love') and 127, *Herr Jesu Christ, wahr' Mensch und Gott* ('Thou who, a God, as man yet come') – in his inimitable manner.[4] Charles Acton was pleased with the performance: 'All the soloists were in excellent form, their styles unified and knit together by Mr. Beckett's expert direction ... We may look forward eagerly to the next two Sunday afternoons and rejoice that the church was so deservedly full.'[5]

The soprano Irené Sandford sang for the first time in this Bach cantata concert. John had met her in Belfast some time previously when he had done some work for the BBC. He had heard her singing and had told her that he did not have a soprano for the forthcoming Bach cantata series. Although she did not know who John was and how enlightening Bach's music could be, she accepted his invitation to travel to Dublin for the rehearsals. A native of Belfast, Irené had sung in the choir of Belfast Cathedral and had taken lessons from the Welsh teacher Carys Denton, who gave her proper voice training.

In Dublin, Irené found John a demanding conductor. Once, when she told him that she needed to take it easy because of a sore throat, he panicked and got hold of another soprano. Irené's husband Billy Reid often accompanied her when she went to Dublin. Billy remembers that when he stayed in John's cottage, he slept on a narrow camp bed – the narrowest he had ever slept in. He and Irené invited John (and often Ruth) to rehearsals in Belfast, where they stayed in their home in Cherryvalley. It was a large house, and Irené and Billy had just moved into it when John and Ruth came for the first time. As a result, their bedroom and bathroom were still being painted and decorated and the floorboards were bare. On one occasion Billy heard the toilet flushing and saw Ruth emerging from the bathroom, clad only in her underwear. Much to Billy's embarrassment, she stopped to have a conversation with him, seemingly oblivious to her state of undress. Although Billy and Irené found both of them quite unconventional, they liked Ruth very much. John came up to them every year and Billy remembers that at one stage he went through a phase of drinking only Noilly Prat. There was never any problem entertaining either John or Ruth.[6]

I returned to St Ann's the following weekend for the next concert: Cantatas 151, *Süsser Trost, mein Jesus kömmt* ('Sweet comfort, my Jesus comes') and 8, *Liebster Gott, wenn werd ich sterben?* ('Dearest God, when will my death be?') These cantatas were very enjoyable and I could find no fault in the performance. Like the previous concert and the one to follow, this one was also recorded by the BBC. I also attended the third in the series, which included Cantatas 199, *Mein Herze schwimmt in Blut* ('My heart is bathed in blood', which Carol Acton found dull and I monotonous) and 56, *Ich will den Kreuzstab gerne tragen*, sung by William Young. This was hardly more cheerful, thanks to the subject matter ('Gladly shall I bear the cross').[7]

As John knew that I had a large and fairly good reel-to-reel tape recorder and wanted to submit a recording of his Henry Purcell Consort to an agent in the UK, he asked me to record his group and Frank Patterson rehearsing in St Ann's church at the beginning of March. He, Betty Sullivan (on viola da gamba), Arthur McIvor and Thérèse Timoney performed various instrumental pieces by Purcell, and later Frank joined them to sing some of the composer's songs. The recording was moderately successful and although I had placed the microphones far too close to the instruments, John was very pleased and thanked me profusely.[8]

My father and I were at the public concert of this music a couple of evenings later. Although poorly attended it was, according to my diary, a 'marvellous success'.[9] Charles Acton, however, was not quite so enthusiastic as he took issue with John's lack of vibrato. 'In our string playing we try to produce the sort of sound that might have been heard in Purcell's day,' John had written in the Dublin Arts Festival programme booklet:

The most radical difference lies in our use of vibrato ... Vibrato was not an organic part of violin technique as it is today, and its expressive qualities were utilised largely as an occasional ornament. As a result the tone, lacking the shimmer of constant vibrato, was more focused in pitch, and there must have been greater clarity of individual lines in ensembles.

He went on to say that ideally they should have been using seventeenth-century violins, but they were impossible to obtain at that time. Acton counteracted by writing, 'It is not enough to say "No vibrato!" without imposing the other stylistic, technical limitations.' He listed three major factors that were necessary for the authentic reproduction of seventeenth-century string technique: the lack of a chinrest, the correct type of bow and lower string tension. 'Mr. Beckett's friends can remove their chinrests quite easily'. He argued that Baroque convex bows were then 'easily available'. Even without the chinrests and with correct bows and thinner strings, he continued, John's group would find a warmth of tone 'instead of the rather boring deadness we heard last night which was in such total contrast to the completely delicious singing of Frank Patterson'.[10]

Acton was correct in that there *was* a deadness about the string sound. On listening to my recording of the rehearsal afresh, I feel that the music was played a little too cautiously, without enough attack at the beginning of the notes. One gets the feeling that the violinists are holding back in an effort not to drown out the continuo instruments and because of this, the music tends be a little expressionless. In general, the performance needed to be more lively overall and more lush in the slower pieces. Nonetheless, John should not be blamed for this; he had done his best to get the players, who were of course schooled in the modern technique, to play without vibrato (as Purcell's music should indeed be played) but they were obviously uncomfortable doing it.[11]

After two *Music Room* radio programmes in March, in which John performed pieces on the harpsichord from the Dublin Virginals Manuscript,[12] John conducted the New Irish Chamber Orchestra, Our Lady's Choral Society and soloists in a performance of Bach's *Saint John Passion* in Whitefriar Street Church, Dublin over the Easter period. This was the first time, it appears, when John conducted a choir of this size in such a large-scale work, in Ireland. On the whole, Charles Acton applauded the venture enthusiastically.[13] It may have been during a rehearsal for this production when Irené Sandford did not agree with the speed that John was taking for an aria that she was singing. When John explained to her that Christ was going to his crucifixion, she replied that he might indeed be going to his crucifixion but he was not having a nervous breakdown on the way![14]

In April, John went to Carlow again for a weekend of music by Schubert.
It began with John O'Conor playing some of the composer's piano music. As
before, this and the two following concerts were devised and introduced by
John. Saturday's concert was devoted to Schubert's songs, sung by Bernadette
Greevy, who informed the audience that this was her first Schubert recital.
According to Charles Acton, John's playing for Bernadette Greevy 'showed him
as a true partner to a singer, gentle and strong and fully understanding the needs
of both music and singer.'[15]

At some period during the month, John and Ruth spent a day visiting places
in and around Dublin associated with Samuel Beckett, in the company of
Rosemary Pountney, a student of Samuel's work from Oxford University. She
was also an actress and performed in his play *Not I* in Dublin at around this time.
John wrote to his cousin to tell him this and received a card from him in Paris
dated 11 May:

> *Dear John ... That was a great jaunt over the old ground. I wish I had been with
> you ... Back yesterday from Ussy. Larks and cuckoos satisfactory. Swallows few.
> Nightingales it [in] the copse behind the house. Hope your Carlow Schubertiad
> came to pass. I've been shivering through the grim journey again in company of
> Gerald Moore's latest (3 Song Cycles). Accompanistically sensitive I thing [think]
> you might allow ... Love from us both to you both.*

The 'grim journey' referred to Schubert's song cycle, *Die Winterreise*, D. 911.[16]

On Saturday 17 May John, Ruth, André Prieur, the organist Gerard Gillen,
the New Irish Chamber Orchestra, Our Lady's Choral Society and four soloists flew to Italy for a week of concerts. As John insisted that my father come in
order to tune the harpsichords that were to be used, he and I joined them.

On the following Monday, my father and most of the party went off to
Perugia cathedral for a performance of Bach's *Saint John Passion*. In order to
tune the harpsichord, my father had to be locked into the cathedral in Perugia.
He met the sponsor, the influential Signora Buitoni of the famous pasta company
who, as John later told me:

> distinguished herself by having sat through the whole of the *Saint John Passion*
> and I suspect of being bored green, you know. And she was introduced to me
> as conductor afterwards, and her request was that we would play the *Hallelujah
> Chorus* as an encore! So I said we wouldn't! Not only wouldn't, but couldn't
> actually! But she seemed to think it was part of the work or something!

The group returned to Rome on Tuesday and my father and I footed it to
the Basilica of Saint Cecilia to tune the harpsichord for the evening's concert

of music by Bach. By the time the audience arrived and settled down, the place was packed – people were standing, sitting on the floor, and around and behind the altar. The main work in the first half was the fourth Brandenburg Concerto, which brought the house down. Before conducting this, John had silenced the coughing and shuffling of the audience by turning around and glowering at everyone until the cacophony subsided. The second half of the concert consisted of John's favourite piece: the opening Sinfonia of Cantata No. 42 and then the fifth Brandenburg Concerto, brilliantly performed by the orchestra, Gillian Smith on the harpsichord, Thérèse Timoney on violin and Edward Beckett on flute. This was greeted with wild applause and a standing ovation that lasted so long that the orchestra was obliged to repeat the final movement as an encore.

Emer Buckley, who was then living in Rome, joined us and we all set off in a bus for a Sicilian restaurant named La Botticella, where Emer helped us order a delicious meal. Soon the noise of the conversation became louder and louder; many sang songs at the top of their voices, told jokes and laughed uncontrollably. John persuaded the owners of the restaurant to sell him a couple of rustic pots to which he took a fancy. At the end of the meal we were given glasses of liqueur and picture postcards of the restaurant. We applauded the staff and set off towards our hotel in the bus, singing the bawdy Irish song, 'Take her up to Monto', made famous by The Dubliners.

Wednesday was devoted to the choir singing at a Papal audience, on the occasion of the Dublin Diocesan pilgrimage to Rome. Gillian Smith, who was not a member of the choir (nor a Roman Catholic), was so disappointed not to be part of this that she persuaded the choir members to allow her to sing with them. André Prieur, who had come with them to conduct Handel's *Messiah* should have conducted, but as he was not available, John did. At the appointed time, they stood in Saint Peter's square and, rather bizarrely, sang a selection of Bach's Lutheran chorales. Pope Paul VI came along in his popemobile to listen and was so impressed that he leaned down to one of his men and said something to him. When, moments later, an official took John by the arm, he turned around and was astounded to discover that he was being presented with a papal medal. To acknowledge his gratitude, he bowed to the pope, much to everyone's astonishment.

Thursday was spent rehearsing Handel's *Messiah* in the fine and very large Jesuit church of Saint Ignatius. As John was not involved in this ('I'm glad to say that I've managed to avoid the *Messiah* in all my professional life', he told me), he, Ruth and some others went off on a trip to Assisi. Amazingly, John turned up at the performance, which was televised by RAI – Lindsay Armstrong claimed that he hid behind a pillar so that nobody could see him! He either came out of loyalty to the orchestra and the soloists or, on a more practical level, because they were all being driven directly from the church to the airport afterwards for the journey home.[17]

In mid June my parents and I attended an informal concert in King's Hospital School, Palmerstown, in which John conducted his Academy Chamber Orchestra, consisting of students from the Royal Irish Academy of Music. The standard of playing was mediocre and the audience was restless. Afterwards we joined John, Ruth, John O'Sullivan and some friends in the headmaster's house for a drink and a discussion about baroque violins. Despite generous helpings of wine, there was a noticeably tense atmosphere. In order to lighten things up a little, one of the guests encouraged our host to sing, and proffered the piano accompaniment of Handel's *Where'er You Walk* to John Beckett, who looked at it in disbelief and exclaimed, 'Christ!' Unsurprisingly, he refused to play it and so John O'Sullivan was persuaded to do so, even though he was rather tipsy by this stage. As the last couple of bars had been torn off the music, he managed to improvise an ending. When John Beckett asked him how he had managed to fill in the missing notes, he replied carelessly, 'Oh well, it was only Handel!' Mercifully, when the two Johns and Ruth left, the atmosphere became considerably more relaxed.[18]

John was far more at ease at one of his chamber music concerts in the Academy later in the month. Everyone was in a good mood and John was smiling. We all laughed when, during one of the introductions, he unsuccessfully tried to read the words of a song by Purcell, written in his own illegible hand. There was a raffle at the end and John drew out my ticket: I won bath salts and a bottle of eau de cologne.[19]

At around this time John went to an early music summer school at Durham University, where he was one of the main protagonists. There he met Linda Howie, a nurse from Dundee who sang in the Bach Choir in Edinburgh. She was active in the early music scene, though mainly as a recorder and cornett player rather than as a singer. As John loved her insightful performances of his favourite Purcell songs, he was determined to foster her singing career.[20] Some time later, when John and Linda were in a London train or tube station, they saw a very fat man ascending a staircase with great difficulty, puffing and panting. Linda said to John, 'Do you see that man? He's going to be dead within a year — mark my words.' John, who was seriously overweight and knew that his brother had died of a heart attack, took fright at this and decided on rather drastic action: he went on a crash diet. He lost so much weight by starving himself that everyone thought he had some type of terminal illness; his skin turned grey and his clothes, which he did not discard, became increasingly baggy. Although everyone was concerned about him, Malcolm Proud remembers that John's definition of dieting was skipping lunch and then making up for it at dinner.[21]

A friend of Linda's, Jeremy Timmis, had sung with her in Scotland in a chamber choir that was an offshoot of the Bach Choir in Edinburgh. Jeremy came to Ireland, where he later became a professor of genetics in University College Dublin. When he went along as a singer to the chamber music class in the Academy, John asked him, 'What voice are you? Are you a tenor?' 'No,' he replied, 'I'm more like a fiver!' John appreciated the joke and the two men got on well together.[22]

In early August the wife of John's friend Werner Schürmann, sculptor Gerda Frömel, died tragically at the age of forty-four when trying to save her son, whom she believed had got into difficulty when swimming in the sea. My parents went to the funeral at a church and cemetery in the Wicklow Mountains, where there were people and flowers in abundance.[23] John and Ruth in all probability did not attend the funeral, owing to the presence of Michael Morrow, who was still a friend of Werner and Gerda,[24] and who afterwards wrote an obituary in one of the British newspapers.[25] John was very good to Werner's boys, who were extremely upset. He later said to young Killian, 'I can see that you have the eyes of a survivor.'[26]

Shortly afterwards, on the final evening of the annual recorder course in An Grianán, Termonfeckin, my parents and I drove there so that my father could tune the harpsichord for the students' concert. We arrived in time for the evening meal, during which John and Ruth sat beside my parents in the dining room. The concert started at eight with a welcoming speech from Theo Wyatt. The first half, which consisted mostly of recorder groups performing, ended with a large Renaissance wind band, which included what John jokingly called 'sackbones' (modern trombones pretending to be sackbuts). He conducted the players by banging a traditional Irish *bodhrán* or drum. This Renaissance band featured again in the second half, as well as a choir, and John was obliged to accompany a flute player on harpsichord in a sonata by Vivaldi.

After the concert had ended and before John left for home, I was encouraged to try a treble viol. John was anxious for me to learn an instrument properly (I had unsuccessfully played the piano when a boy, had mastered the guitar to a certain degree and could tootle a tune on a recorder), and wished me to become his student at the Academy. John showed me how to hold the instrument and use the bow. I was intrigued and delighted to discover how easy it seemed. My parents told me that if I liked the viol and really wanted to learn to play it, they would buy me one for my twenty-first birthday, which would come early in the following year.[27]

Another George Morrison film, *Look to the Sea*, a Bord Iascaigh Mhara (Irish Fish Board) documentary, with music by John, was screened in the Savoy

Cinema, Dublin, at the end of October. This powerful and beautifully photo-graphed film concentrated on various craft at work on the rough seas around Donegal and north Mayo, from currachs to large trawlers; most of the shots were taken in the worst winter conditions, in force 8 and 9 gales. The film, with commentary by Liam Budhlair, was shown on RTÉ Television early in November of the following year.[28]

1975 finished with an enjoyable recital of music, mostly by Purcell, in the Dagg Hall of the Royal Irish Academy of Music (with *basso continuo* played on harpsichord and 'cello da gamba' – John's term for a cello pretending to be a viola da gamba),[29] three radio programmes entitled *Music for the Christmas Season* (with John on piano, celeste and harpsichord)[30] and a television programme recorded in the National Gallery, *Bernadette sings Johann Sebastian Bach*, in which Bernadette Greevy, accompanied by the New Irish Chamber Orchestra and conducted by John, sang arias by Bach. Recorded in the beautiful surroundings of the main hall, Bernadette looks resplendent in a flowing blue dress with a floral pattern, and John, still portly though not as obese as he once had been, is smartly attired in a black suit, white shirt and black bow tie. He still has a good head of hair. The large, creased pages of John's handwritten manuscript can be seen clearly on the harpsichord's music stand. The final aria that Bernadatte sings, *Erbarme dich, mein Gott* ('Have mercy on me, my God') is from the *Saint Matthew Passion*.[31] Viewers familiar with this last item would have been surprised to discover that the final chord of the aria, which, in Bach's original version is in the minor, had been changed by John to the major. Why John decided to tamper with the great composer's tragic masterpiece is anyone's guess; Lindsay and Gillian Armstrong noticed how John had sharpened the minor thirds in the orchestral and continuo parts.[32] Nonetheless, Bernadette Greevy, speaking of this particular aria in 2000, said 'I think I am most proud of that'.[33]

Although John's elementary skill at conducting is very much in evidence in this television production, the playing is clean, precise and the ensemble is excellent – not one note is out of place. Another programme, with more or less the same forces, with tenor Alexander Young and conducted by André Prieur, was recorded in the same venue and transmitted the following year. John would have studiously avoided this one as it contained items by the dreaded Handel. In all, six programmes were recorded.[34]

Thirty-Four
1976

John performed with the Henry Purcell Consort in Cork in the new year; shortly afterwards he played basso continuo for Haydn's *The Seasons* in the Royal Dublin Society Concert Hall with the New Irish Chamber Orchestra and the Saint James's Gate Musical Society, conducted by Victor Leeson. Instead of a harpsichord, he used a restored square piano loaned for the occasion by my father.[1]

My promised birthday present, a treble viol, had arrived and I was now in possession of a beautiful instrument made by Martin Johnson in Holmbury St Mary, near Dorking, south of London. After several telephone calls to John, an arrangement was made for my first lesson, which would take place at 12.30 pm on Tuesday, 27 January. Though I already knew John as one of my father's friends, I awoke that morning feeling both excited and nervous about encountering John as a teacher. According to my diary, I quickly swallowed a cup of coffee and set off from work, walking briskly down Nassau Street towards Westland Row with my new viol in its case.

Some ten minutes later I entered the fine Georgian doorway of the Royal Irish Academy of Music. Any lofty idea of royalty soon disappeared once inside: the foyer was basic and was presided over by a plainly-dressed woman of uncertain age known to everyone as Nan, who worked as a porter and receptionist. A real Dublin character, she had a vicious sense of humour and always made everyone laugh.[2] John was the first teacher to persuade Nan and the other porters to address him by his first name – he did not like being called 'Mr' and he never used the title 'Dr'.[3]

Probably not noticing his name painted on a board beside his room number, I asked Nan where I might find John Beckett and hurried down a long narrow

corridor to a room on the right, beside the entrance to the Dagg Hall. I found
John playing an upright piano. I seem to remember him being in his shirtsleeves;
he generally wore dark – and usually blue – open-necked, long-sleeved shirts
without a pocket (he hated shirts with pockets) and either grey or dark trousers.
As usual, he was tieless; ties were reluctantly worn for very formal occasions.
John stopped playing almost immediately, greeted me and set up two chairs
in front of a music stand. He then took out his own treble viol and his Francis
Baines tutor, and after a few introductory remarks, we were off.

As I described it in my diary, John began to 'thaw out' during the lesson.
Any trepidation I felt now vanished, and I found him to be a most interesting,
good-humoured, patient and encouraging teacher. As I had been practising on
the instrument at home, the progress that I had made pleased him greatly, for
he was full of praise for what I had already managed to achieve. He declared
that his 'hunch' about me had been correct. He now taught me how to hold the
instrument and bow correctly, and how to use the full length of the bow and
produce a note without any initial rasp or hesitancy. The time flew; suddenly it
was 1.30 pm and the next student arrived. I had found my lesson exciting and
stimulating.[4] Perhaps John's gentle approach towards me was in consideration of
my father's harsh treatment when I had attempted to learn the piano as a child,
which I suspect John knew about. When my father had complained to John that
I had spent my rebellious teenage years listening only to pop music, John had
merely replied, 'Any music is better than no music.'[5]

From then on I looked forward to my weekly Tuesday lessons. He seemed to
be pleased with my progress, for he told Rhoda Draper after my second lesson
that I was 'unnatural'. When I asked her whether this was meant to be a compli-
ment or an insult, she explained that John had declared that 'Charles must have
been born with a viola da gamba between his knees'. However, he was obviously
disappointed to discover that I was a poor sight-reader, and told me that if I
could not master it, I would be better off 'chucking it up and making model
aeroplanes'. I practised diligently at home and, thankfully, gradually improved.
He was unusually patient with me and generally in a good mood when I attended
his lessons. As my sense of rhythm was a little shaky and as I had trouble with
syncopated rhythms at first, John advised me to buy a good metronome.[6]

As the Arts Council was not prepared to subsidize the Bach cantata series
yet again, John simply refused to do them at the beginning of this year.[7] Charles
Acton wondered if he was relying too much on Arts Council money and too
little on box office sales. Although a sizeable audience had built up since the
beginning of the series, which Acton thought might guarantee enough money
for the three concerts, the future of the cantata series now seemed uncertain.[8]

However, the Dublin Arts Festival came to the rescue with a concert in St Ann's Church on 7 March that included Bach's Cantata No. 51, *Jauchzet Gott in allen Landen* ('Rejoice unto God in all lands!') and his Brandenburg Concerto No. 2. The other items on the programme were an assortment of pieces and songs by Henry Purcell and, somewhat astonishingly, Handel's Concerto Grosso in E minor, Opus 6, No. 3. Once again, Charles Acton criticized John's lack of vibrato in the Purcell, which resulted 'in a hard, penetrating, unlovely sound.' Fortunately for Acton, John permitted his strings to use vibrato in the Bach and Handel pieces.[9]

John may well have abandoned his Bach cantata series if it had not been for the timely arrival of Nicholas Anderson of the BBC at around this period. In 1976 he had been appointed as a producer in the Music Division. One of his jobs was to listen to 'foreign tapes', which usually contained performances from European music festivals. These tapes had to be listened to and reported on before a broadcast was sanctioned. He can remember coming across one such foreign tape of Bach cantatas conducted by John Beckett (Dublin was then classed as foreign territory). One of them was BWV 127, *Herr Jesu Christ, wahr' Mensch und Gott* ('Thou who, a God, as man yet come'), which had been performed on 16 February 1975 and was broadcast with BWV 167, *Ihr Menschen, rühmet Gottes Liebe* ('Ye mortals, extol God's love') on 17 March of this year. The cantata was performed, Nicholas thought, with such insight into the music that he went hot-foot to Eleanor Warren, the head of his department, to ask if he might travel to Dublin to set up recordings of more cantatas. His request was granted, his flight booked, his reservation made at the Central Hotel, and the first of many happy and memorable visits to Dublin took place in 1976.

Nicholas thinks that he met John first in the Royal Irish Academy of Music. Initially he was rather intimidated by him but Ruth, whom he also met, proved to be a warm and sympathetic intermediary. The two men gradually formed a firm friendship, despite the fact that they were quite different in character.

Nicholas met very few people in Dublin; it never occurred to John, who was 'absolutely hopeless at any kind of social grace', to introduce him to anyone. John must have assumed that Nicholas did not want to meet anybody. Nevertheless, Nicholas did get to know some members of the orchestra, such as Betty Sullivan, the violinists Thérèse Timoney and Mary Gallagher, the oboist Helmut Seeber and, best of all, the continuo player John O'Sullivan. Nicholas was suitably impressed by the orchestra.

The BBC recordings would be made (with the help of either staff from Belfast or RTÉ sound engineers) between 1977 and 1979 in Saint Ann's Church for the public performances and in the nearby Masonic Hall for secular cantatas not featured in the annual series. Nicholas later wrote, 'John's rehearsal methods have become the source of many a legend, and his delight in the smallest detail, often illuminated with picturesque imagery, enlivened Bach's music for all of us.'[10]

Knowing nothing of John's likes and dislikes at that period, I was astounded to learn, at my Tuesday lunchtime lesson on 16 March, that he had attended the best concert that he had ever been to on the previous evening, when he had gone to the Royal Dublin Society in Ballsbridge to hear the jazz pianist Oscar Peterson and guitarist Joe Pass perform. A short review in *The Irish Times* praised Peterson's solos and Pass's undemonstrative playing (of which undoubtedly John would have approved) and mentioned that there had been no rhythm section, which allowed for subtle, quiet playing.[11]

At around the same time, a record of Bach arias, sung by Bernadette Greevy, and with the New Irish Chamber Orchestra conducted by John, was being made by Claddagh Records in Saint Patrick's Hall of Dublin Castle. Items included John's favourite, the Sinfonia from Cantata No. 42, the jaunty aria *Kommt, ihr angefocht'nen Sünder* ('Come, ye sorely tempted sinners') that had been featured in the previous year's *Bernadette sings Johann Sebastian Bach*, and *Erbarme dich, mein Gott* from the *Saint Matthew Passion*, also in the same programme.[12]

When the record was finally released in September 1980, Charles Acton gave it a glowing review and commented:

> [John] is so deeply committed in his soul to every note and detail of Bach that it comes across throughout, but on that account, one senses, he wants each one of those notes and details to speak for itself without interpretative interference, as though they were the details of a Middle-Eastern rug or the faiences of a mosque.[13]

Writing in 1995, however, Michael Dervan had this to say:

> *Bernadette Greevy sings Bach Arias* ... recorded in 1976 with the New Irish Chamber Orchestra under John Beckett, is a memento not only of Greevy's marmoreal way with Bach, but also of the annual Bach cantata series with John Beckett and N.I.C.O., which were such a much-loved feature of the musical life in Dublin at the time. The incongruities of musical style between Beckett and Greevy still jar, however, and it remains a pity that no choral item was included in the sessions.[14]

Bernadette was much in demand at this period; in early April, a half hour of Brahms *Lieder*, including his beautiful *Zwei Gesänge* (Two Songs), Op. 91 for alto voice, viola and piano, were performed by Bernadette, John and Ruth on RTÉ Radio's *Afternoon Recital*.[15]

At some point John was approached by James Cavanagh, a trumpeter who had just left the Irish Youth Orchestra at the age of twenty-one. He asked John to become the musical director and conductor of a new orchestra for young people, which he and his friend Gerard Keenan, a fellow trumpeter, wanted to form, and which they would call the Dublin Training Orchestra. John was somewhat taken aback at first – 'I think that he thought I was off my rocker,' commented James – but allowed himself to be talked into accepting the position. He soon became very enthusiastic about the venture. Many of the best musicians in the country who were available decided to join, such was the attraction of having John as their conductor. The leader was Patrick Fitzgerald; Robert Houlihan played bassoon, Frank Schaeffer played cello and William Halpin played the flute. As the orchestra was always short of funds and had to rely on patrons for money, it is possible that John took on this extra duty voluntarily. Thanks to James's connections, a priest in the Church of Saint Andrew, Westland Row, kindly allowed the orchestra to practise in the nearby Saint Andrew's School, Pearse Street once a week. The first symphonic work that they and John tackled was the Symphony No. 8 by Antonín Dvořák, which was performed in June to a small audience in the Dagg Hall of the Royal Irish Academy of Music.

James also asked John if he could join the Tuesday evening chamber music classes in the Academy as he had some early Baroque trumpet music for small groups; John was delighted to include him. James held John in the highest regard and soon discovered that behind the 'looks of the big bear' he was gentle and pleasant.[16]

In May John travelled to Downpatrick Secondary School in Northern Ireland to conduct the Ulster Orchestra in a programme of music by J.S. Bach, J.C. Bach and Mozart. Writing in *The Irish Times*, Alfred Burrowes had this to say: 'John Beckett conducted. His Bach was firstly firm, attractive and finally very satisfying, his influence an asset to the evening's music. A disciplined order and virility was attained in the last movement of the Brandenburg No. 4 and I have not heard before an Andante so obviously in full sail.'[17]

Bach was on the agenda again on 17 May, when John conducted the New Irish Chamber Orchestra, Our Lady's Choral Society and soloists in the B minor Mass, in the Pro-Cathedral in Dublin. The concert was repeated in Mullingar and Kilkenny within the same week. Charles Acton wrote:

> John Beckett was in charge and while there were a couple of moments of anxiety, especially at the notorious *et expecto*, what the choir did for him and for their chorus master, Oliver O'Brien, was full of splendour.
>
> Mr. Beckett certainly drove them hard, perhaps too hard in the first two

choruses of the *Credo* – too fast for their comfort or the building's acoustics –
but he and they captured the spirit of the great work wonderfully.[18]

In May John devised a weekend of music by Mozart in Carlow[19] and went
to London, where he attended a triple bill of plays by his cousin Samuel: *Play*,
That time and *Footfalls*, which were performed in the Royal Court Theatre as
part of the Samuel Beckett Festival. The festival, which also included *Endgame*,
formed part of the playwright's seventieth birthday celebrations.[20] John wrote
to Samuel about the plays and Patrick Magee's performance and Samuel replied:

> The Royal Court had finally to sack Magee for drunkenness on stage and the
> understudy took over for the last series of <u>Endgame</u> that closed the season. The
> night you saw the triple bill was thus his last appearance and if he did not react
> as requested it was no doubt because he was asleep.[21]

John played harpsichord in early June, this time in the St Francis Xavier Hall
in Dublin, but in music of a totally different genre. This was the premiere of the
Irish composer John Kinsella's work *A Selected Life – in Memory of Seán Ó Riada*.
This work, for narrator, tenor, choir (the RTÉ Choral Society), strings (the RTÉ
Symphony Orchestra), two harps, harpsichord and bodhrán (David Carmody),
was conducted by Proinnsias Ó Duinn. Charles Acton described the harpsichord
and bodhrán parts as important, but regarded the latter's use as symbolic rather
than musically necessary.[22] The work begins with a highly dramatic orchestral
introduction, after which the harpsichord and then the bodhrán enter. The harpsichord part is inventive: busy passages, fast runs, percussive chordal effects,
spread chords and dissonant clusters of notes are used throughout.[23]

In July, John went to Knockmaroon House to record some piano music for a
documentary film made by Kieran Hickey about the National Library (*Portrait of
a Library*). Temporarily stored in Lord Moyne's ballroom was a new and elegant
harpsichord made by my father for John's student Emer Buckley. Finding a
chaconne by Louis Couperin in a book that my father had left on the instrument,
John spent a considerable amount of time playing it over and over again. It was
obvious that he had fallen in love with French music.[24]

Armed with my recorders and now my treble viol, I attended the week-long
recorder and viol course at An Grianán, Termonfeckin in August, at which John
was tutor for both instruments. It started on a Saturday afternoon, and the
following day John conducted a group that we had nicknamed 'the Nasties': a
motley collection of 'sackbones', dulzaines, cornetts, crumhorns, a gemshorn,
a Breton bombard and Renaissance recorders. John, as on previous occasions,
beat a *bodhrán* to keep the band together. The resulting sound, as can be imagined, was quite a cacophony.

Thankfully, the viol consort classes led by John were more successful and easier on the ear. On the Tuesday evening, everyone assembled in the Kellogg Hall to play powerful Venetian multi-choral music directed by John. A couple of days later we had an evening of games devised by Theo Wyatt. One of these consisted of a tape of forty-eight pieces of music cleverly edited together, which we were asked to identify. John won with a score of seventy-six points. On the final day John led a viol consort class in the afternoon. As a bass player was not available, John hummed the part. He was at the final concert that evening, which finished with unrehearsed performances of Bach's Brandenburg Concertos Nos 4 and 2; the young trumpeter Paddy Scarlett made a heroic but somewhat hit-and-miss attempt at the latter, and was rewarded with congratulations and a handshake from John during our enthusiastic applause.[25]

Bernadette Greevy, who had just returned from touring Finland and Russia, gave a recital in the John Player Theatre in mid October, accompanied by John on piano and, for Brahms's *Zwei Gesänge*, Op. 91, by John on piano and Ruth on viola. Charles Acton's review was favourable; he wrote that Bernadette 'is certainly fortunate with John Beckett. He gave her all she could have wished, with deep feeling and firm support.'[26]

Kieran Hickey's film *Portrait of a Library*, for which John had supplied music on piano and harpsichord, was first shown to an audience of about two hundred people in the small cinema in the basement of the National Gallery towards the end of the month. John and Ruth, my father and I attended both the screening and the reception afterwards.[27] George Morrison's latest film *Look to the Sea*, with John's incidental music, was shown on television in early November, 1976.[28] In December John Kinsella's work *A Selected Life* was broadcast on RTÉ Radio.[29] Writing in the *RTÉ Guide* some years later, John O'Donovan had this to say: 'the instrumentation includes, in graceful acknowledgement of Seán O Riada's well-known preferences, a bodhrán played by David Carmody, with John Beckett presiding with his deceptive glumness over what Thomas Kinsella calls "the stricken harpsichord's soft crash".' This conjures up an accurate picture of John, who often looked grumpy and ill at ease when playing the harpsichord.[30]

The first public concert given by the Dublin Training Orchestra, conducted by John, took place in Coláiste Mhuire, Parnell Square in Dublin in December. The orchestra had appealed for funds in October and now was up and running.[31] The items in the December concert were Mendelssohn's *The Hebrides Overture*, Op. 26, Haydn's Trumpet Concerto in E flat, played by James Cavanagh and Brahms's Symphony No. 2 in D, Op. 73. In my diary I noted how John, who looked well groomed, shuffled on to the stage to loud applause. Although I felt sorry for James Cavanagh, who was undoubtedly nervous and made several mistakes, I was suitably impressed by the performance in general.[32]

The young members of the orchestra felt that they were very privileged to have John as their conductor and musical director, whom they held in high esteem. James Cavanagh remembers how, after the Saturday afternoon rehearsals, John and the musicians used to repair en masse to Peter's Pub in Johnson Place, near the College of Music, where they would spend the rest of the evening. John loved being with the young people; they relished his enthusiasm and the way in which he shared his knowledge and expertise with them all.

John invited James to dinner one cold wintry evening soon after the concert in Coláiste Mhuire. James drove to the Wicklow Mountains and, after having being shown John's 'bath' (Paddock Lake), enjoyed a hearty dinner. Afterwards he, John and Ruth (whom James also liked) spent the rest of the evening in front of a big log fire listening to Mahler symphonies. It was an experience he would never forget.[33]

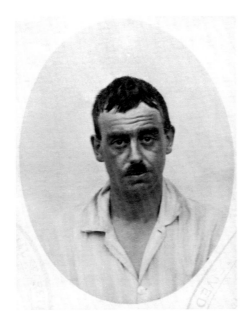

John's father, Gerald Beckett, who served as a
doctor in World War I with the British army.
(Courtesy of the late Deirdre Sinclair)

John with the children's nanny, May Harper, Greystones, April 1933. (Courtesy of Edward Beckett)

The Beckett home on Portland Road, Greystones.

John, aged twelve, at St Columba's College, Whitechurch, Dublin.
(Courtesy of Deirdre Sinclair and Robin McKinney)

John's sister, Ann Beckett.
(Courtesy of the late Deirdre Sinclair)

IV

The composer E. J. Moeran.
(Copyright National Portrait Gallery)

Edmund Rubbra.
(Copyright National Portrait Gallery)

Vera Slocombe, whom John would marry.
(Courtesy of Roland Morrow)

Bronze head of John by Werner Schürmann.
(Courtesy of the Royal Irish Academy of Music)

Michael Morrow. (Courtesy of Seán O'Leary)

Fachtna Ó hAnnracháin, Music Director,
Radio Éireann. (Courtesy of Bláthnaid Uí Chatháin)

Mrs Olive Smith, Brian Boydell, John Beckett (seated)
and the conductor Otto Matzerath in the
National Museum, Dublin. (Courtesy of Gillian Smith)

John Beckett and Otto Matzerath. (Courtesy of Gillian Smith)

Vera and John, with his mother's clock on the wall.
(Courtesy of the late Deirdre Sinclair)

Musica Reservata. Left to right, back row: *Jantina Noorman, Bernard Thomas, Don Smithers, Nigel Rodgers and Roger Groves.* Middle row: *John Beckett (with sunglasses), Ruth David and Grayston Burgess.* Front row: *Edgar Fleet, Daphne Webb, Anthony Rooley, John Sothcott and Desmond Dupré. (Courtesy of King's College London)*

Left to right: *Valerie Kelly, John and Ann Beckett, Valerie and James Plunkett Kelly, Vadim, Ross and James Kelly. Vienna, 1969/70. (Courtesy of James Kelly)*

*Samuel Beckett, John, Edward Beckett Ann and Uncle
Jim's widow, Peggy Beckett. (Courtesy of Edward Beckett)*

Seán O'Leary, 2007.

*Ruth David in the early 1960s.
(Courtesy of Rose Hilton)*

On the Great Wall, China, with Cathal Gannon, Irené Sandford, Gillian Smith, guide,
Lindsay Armstrong and guide. 1980.

Melanie (née Daiken) and Patrick Cuming, 2007.

Adrian Jack, 2007.

Patrick and Jarka Lambert, 2007.

Ruth and John, 1992. (Courtesy of Rose Hilton)

Thirty-Five

1977

In January of 1977 I began to attend John's viol consort classes in the Royal Irish Academy of Music, where we tackled some short pieces by Thomas Weelkes and a pavane by John Jenkins, whose music John relished and played often in these classes. Lacking a bass viol, Christine Cooley played the 'cello da gamba' with us.[1]

Following a repeat of the concert given by the Dublin Training Orchestra in December, this time in Christ Church, Bray,[2] John, the New Irish Chamber Orchestra, the newly-formed Cantata Singers and soloists resumed the Bach Cantata series in St Ann's Church. John asked me to be a 'steward' for the three concerts: my job was to stand just inside the door and make sure that everybody had bought a ticket. Despite the simplicity of the task, John requested me to turn up an hour before the concerts began.[3] The cantatas in the first concert, No. 32: *Liebster Jesu, mein Verlangen* ('Beloved Jesus, my desire') and No. 27: *Wer weiss, wie nahe mir mein Ende?* ('Who knows how near is my end?') were recorded by the BBC. Nicholas Anderson would have made his first appearance as producer of the recordings. In his review, Charles Acton made reference to John's helpful spoken notes and the chamber organ continuo, which was played by John O'Sullivan. He also made mention of the new Cantata Singers and described them as 'an amalgam of many consort enthusiasts'.[4]

The second concert, a week later, consisted of cantatas No. 158, *Der Friede sei mit dir* ('Peace be unto you') and the famous No. 140, *Wachet auf, ruft uns die Stimme* ('Sleepers Awake').[5] The third and final one featured cantatas No. 84, *Ich bin vergnügt mit meinem Glücke* ('I am content in my good fortune') and No. 79, *Gott, der Herr ist Sonn' und Schild* ('The Lord God is a sun and shield').[6] Malcolm Proud, who attended the concert, was greatly taken by the latter work, which is scored for soloists, choir, two French horns (representing the sun and the shield of the title), oboes, strings and continuo. He remembers being overwhelmed by the sound of the horns, especially in the electrifying opening chorus, which John repeated as an encore.[7] The concert was recorded by sound engineers from BBC Northern Ireland and produced by Dr Edgar Boucher. Charles Acton concluded his review, 'As before, the orchestra was NICO and John Beckett conducted and directed all the proceedings with authority and great enthusiasm. One can only thank him and his musicians for these past favours in the lively hope of favours to come.'[8]

During Nicholas's visit to record the first concert, he would have had time to observe John in action. He noticed, for example, that when rehearsing the orchestra and choir, he could be very personal and occasionally quite rude to the musicians and singers. John listened to the recordings made by the BBC but did not always like them; when he muttered something like, 'I do wish you wouldn't sing like that,' Nicholas felt that he would have liked to have thrown everybody out and start again.

Nicholas felt that what made the Bach cantata concerts so good was the nervous tension that John exuded. Every one of the cantatas recorded in Dublin was eventually broadcast on BBC Radio 3 and the recordings helped Nicholas to 'close the gap' in his series of the complete Bach cantatas, some of which were conducted by Paul Steinitz and Nicholas Kraemer in the UK. At that time there were at least fifty of the cantatas that had never been commercially recorded. Although John's performances were closer to Nicholas's heart than Steinitz's, Nicholas had to engage Steinitz out of a sense of fairness. 'I don't know what you see in this Steinitz man – it's all so limp!' John complained. 'Well, John,' Nicholas replied, 'that's hardly the point – you don't know what *I* think about it. The fact is I've got to get these works recorded and I've got to find people who are prepared to do them and who have the time.' 'You could ask me!' John replied. 'I've given you the whole lot to choose from – you can't have every-thing!' said Nicholas in exasperation. 'Why not?' asked John.

On this occasion Nicholas was invited to join John and the musicians at a watering hole within walking distance of St Ann's Church, where 'hot pints' were consumed. Nicholas had no idea what this meant;[9] Malcolm Proud explains that he detested the fad (new at the time) for ice-cold Guinness.[10] John rather frowned on half pints. Nicholas observed that he drank 'generously' after a concert but was always on impeccable form before and during one. He was relieved to have no worries of that kind regarding him.

Ensconced in a pub, John was likely to give vent to some of his opinions, such as his hatred for Vivaldi's music – 'It's just a lot of hot air!' Nicholas surmised that his dislike of Corelli and Vivaldi's music was due to the paucity of counterpoint: he would have found very little serious counterpoint in Corelli's music and not a great deal in the music of Vivaldi. The issue that Nicholas used to take up with John was that when Vivaldi did write counterpoint, it was actually quite good. He pointed out to John that a handful of his concertos are very contrapuntally orientated and come off really well, but John would not countenance this. John loved simple things, but if something simple and pastoral was offered to him, like the music of Vivaldi, he would not accept it. He had some kind of perversity that Nicholas could never fathom. This was always good for entertainment, provided he had not been drinking too much, but for Nicholas it tended to be irrational, unintelligent and just irritating.

With John, things were either black or white. If there was a mutual liking of something, that was fine. Nicholas had never read *Ulysses* at the time, which John found unforgivable. Because he took that attitude, Nicholas refused to read the book. It was always fun for him to find out what pleased John and what did not. If he did not like something, one could try to persuade him to like it over a period of time but it would make absolutely no difference – he simply would not change his opinion. He had a list as long as his arm of people whom he regarded as a complete waste of time.

On the other hand, John had a good sense of humour. He could be wickedly funny – at one time he composed a hilarious limerick about the vicar of St Ann's Church, Samuel G. Poyntz, whom he detested. He also had a wonderful turn of phrase. Once, when both John and Nicholas were listening to some music together, Nicholas put his hand on his heart and murmured, 'Oh, I feel it here!' 'Do you really want to feel it?' asked John, 'I feel it here!' he roared, pointing at his testicles.[11]

Alison Young remembers an incident that happened before one of the cantatas was recorded by Nicholas and his team, who were stationed, as usual, with their equipment in the vestry of St Ann's Church. As Betty Sullivan and her cello had moved and, presumably, the position of the microphone needed to be adjusted, John spoke into it to summon Nicholas but there was dead silence. He repeated what he had said and once again nothing happened. Turning to the orchestra, he commented, 'You know, it's like praying – you're never sure if anybody's listening or not!'[12]

Overall, Nicholas believed John to be hugely talented, inimitable, but in some ways his own worst enemy. He thought that John could very easily have had quite a dazzling career if he had been more flexible and malleable, though perhaps that was not what he wanted. If that was the case, John went further up in his estimation. He felt John should have been more widely recognized than he was[13] – a view shared by the music critic Michael Dervan.[14]

The viol consort classes continued apace; during one of them, John remarked that I had no trouble with the notes but I was not so good at playing the rests. We tackled John Jenkins's beautiful 6-part Pavane No. 2, and by the end of March John decided that we were good enough to perform it in one of the regular concerts in the Dagg Hall.[15]

At the beginning of April, John took part in an illustrated workshop in the Project Arts Centre, Dublin, on the popular music of Shakespeare's time. Entitled *Ayres and Airs*, it involved John on harpsichord and Michael Gavin on traditional Irish flute.[16]

At around this time, Hilary Heron, John's cousin on his mother's side of the family, died. 'She suffered a long and distressing decline from an inoperable tumour on the brain,' wrote John in explanation for one of Samuel's short letters to him. 'She was a dear, humane, strong and very bright person who, from childhood, had been close to my brother Peter.' She had been married to David Greene, who was a professor of ancient Gaelic at Trinity College. 'Thanks for yrs. of May 4th with grievous news, to David & all those to whom she was so dear. Will you be kind enough to send enclosed card to David,' Samuel wrote to John from Paris. 'Sorry you have to leave The Paddock. I know what a wrench it will be. I remember that road well. Often have I trudged it, biked & driven it. I hope the Djouce house comes off.' This referred to an attempted negotiation for another cottage on the slopes of Djouce Mountain that was unsuccessful.[17]

Nicholas Anderson remembers The Paddock in Kilmacanogue; he stayed with John and Ruth for three or four days, probably at around this period or later in the summer. 'John had all that lovely sort of stuff that he always had: nice bedspreads and throws and things all over the place – it was what I call civilized, in that distinctive way that John always cultivated around him,' Nicholas explained. John and Ruth proved to be good hosts and Ruth, who liked cooking, supplied interesting 'pulse-orientated' meals with a good deal of ethnic dishes. There was always an abundance of fruit and fruit juice. Although John liked to eat well, he appreciated simple things such as home-made brown bread and 'dishes' of tea. He used to say, 'Why the hell are you cutting that bread, Ruth? Just let me *have* a piece! Just leave it!' and he would tear it apart. He liked this kind of earthy simplicity.

Nicholas also remembers going for a long walk with John in the Wicklow mountains; the sun was very hot and they lay down in the heather to rest. Nicholas fell asleep and got badly sunburnt on one side of his face.[18]

In May, another programme in the series of Bernadette Greevy in the National Gallery was transmitted on RTÉ Television: in this one she sang five songs by Mahler accompanied by an augmented New Irish Chamber Orchestra, conducted by John. In the programme one can see that John is well able to handle the varying *tempi* of the songs and keep the orchestra in perfect time with Bernadette, who sings beautifully.[19]

In the same month, the Carlow Music Club hosted a weekend of chamber music by Beethoven in Saint Patrick's College; as before, the three concerts were devised and presented by John.[20]

At some time around this period, Dan Shields, whom John had met in Carlow a couple of years previously, visited John and Ruth at The Paddock and slept in the cottage on a camp bed. When reminded of this much later, John swore that he could not have slept there as there was no spare bed. Dan swam in the lake nearby and remembers that there was 'a bit of a flood' caused by a dead sheep that blocked the cottage's water supply. John and Ruth were friendly with their neighbours, the Mulligans, who were farming people. When the aged mother had to be brought into hospital and John asked her bachelor son, 'What are you going to do?', the man answered, 'I suppose I'll have to haul in a woman.' John got great delight in repeating this story to his friends.[21]

Saint Patrick's Cathedral, Dublin was the venue for the next public concert conducted by John, and Mendelssohn's rarely-performed oratorio *St Paul* was the work performed. The event took place towards the end of May. Mirette Dowling's Wicklow Choral Society and soloists sang with the Dublin Training Orchestra.[22] John was very friendly with Mirette, who regularly attended the Bach cantata concerts. Mirette, who had got to know John through Joe Groocock, remembers that he had come to a performance of Fauré's *Requiem* given by her choir in Wicklow.[23] Gillian Smith remembers how determined John was to combine the choir with the Dublin Training Orchestra, a much larger body than the New Irish Chamber Orchestra.[24]

Containing some forty-five movements (including recitatives) and lasting more than two hours, this long work was something of a *tour de force* for everyone. Overall, Charles Acton was pleased with the production; he wrote, 'Now that the Wicklow Choral Society have found their way to Dublin and proved how well they can work with the Training Orchestra, and with the extraordinary gifted and versatile Mr. Beckett, let us hope they will bring other rare works to us.'[25]

In August, John accompanied Bernadette Greevy on piano for an *Afternoon Recital* programme of songs by Gustav Mahler. In the *RTÉ Guide*, John O'Donovan wrote:

> This is a labour of love for both of them. I recall sitting with Bernadette in a pub one evening, she with a robust glass in hand which she was unashamedly enjoying, until I asked her about Mahler. Straight away she became soulfully eloquent and so unmindful of the glass that I trembled for the welfare of her

lovely dress. As for John Beckett, you've only to mention Mahler within ten miles of him and tears well up in his expressive brown eyes.[26]

Also in June, a recital of music for harpsichord and traditional flute was given by John and Michael Gavin in St Columba's College, John's old school.[27] Once again, John was tutor at the recorder course at An Grianán, Termonfeckin in August; his sister Ann was also there, playing the recorder.[28]

On 10 September, a BBC recording was made of Bach's secular cantata No. 208, *Was mir behagt, ist nur die muntre Jagd!* ('The merry hunt is all that I love!') in the Masonic Hall, Molesworth Street, Dublin, not far from St Ann's Church. Nicholas Anderson, who produced the recording, recollected:

> we were in the middle of recording Bach's *Hunt* Cantata (BWV 208) when I noticed, to my horror, that I appeared to have booked only one recorder player – *Sheep may safely graze* requires two. I checked the contracts and sure enough, only one was listed. Sick at heart I could only wait for the moment of truth and, in all probability, a lethal missile from John. When the time arrived for *Sheep may safely graze* I saw John fidgeting and looking a little preoccupied. Then out of his two pockets came each half of a recorder which he assembled and played with characteristic modesty and accomplishment. 'You see, Nicholas, in this f–ing cold church it was the only way to be sure of the tuning.'[29]

More radio programmes followed, including *Let's Sing a Song*, with John accompanying Bernadette Greevy, who sang and gave hints on performance and interpretation,[30] and on 22 November John conducted the first four parts of Bach's *Christmas Oratorio*, which were performed by Our Lady's Choral Society, soloists and the New Irish Chamber Orchestra in the Pro-Cathedral, Dublin. Charles Acton wrote:

> As usual with Mr. Beckett's performances, we had the proper resources, lots of vigour and a deep devotion to Bach. And in contrast to some of his cantata performances, while Mr. Beckett chose good lively speeds that did not flag, he let the music breathe and never drove it hard. Oliver O'Brien had, as always, trained the choir well and Mr. Beckett got excellent singing from them with a splendid distinction between the vigorous passage work of the choruses and the quasi-congregational weight of the chorales.[31]

John conducted the Dublin Training Orchestra in two more concerts, both in December. The first was a fund-raising performance in the Mater Hospital, Dublin, which featured Wagner's prelude to *Die Meistersinger*, Weber's Bassoon Concerto in F (played by Robert Houlihan) and Schubert's Symphony No. 9.[32] The second, which took place in Trinity College and included the Wagner and

Weber works, also featured Haydn's *Missa in tempore belli* sung by the Goethe
Institute Choir and soloists. Charles Acton was not too impressed by the standard of playing in the Wagner prelude: 'Their conductor, John Beckett, should
make plain to them that they must come to rehearsal and concert knowing
their parts and able to play them,' he wrote. He had a better impression of the
Haydn Mass, in which, 'the choir sang with fine tone, real vigour and an excellent dynamic suppleness. With Anne Cant, Alison Browner, Richard Cooper
and William Young as soloists, Mr Beckett made the Mass take its proper place
as the important part of the concert, and one that did real justice both to Haydn
and the choir itself.'[33]

The year finished with John playing pieces from the *Fitzwilliam Virginal Book* on
a spinet at a Christmas party held in a large new house in Newtownmountkennedy,
County Wicklow, owned by his friend Petra Coffey and her husband. I remember
him sitting at the instrument, looking typically glum. Nonetheless, the large
gathering of people enjoyed his recital and also some madrigals and carols that
were sung. In such a convivial atmosphere, John would have been able to relax
after playing, especially when he was invited to help himself to a plentiful supply
of good food and drink.[34]

Thirty-Six
1978

The year began with some more sad news: John's aunt Peggy died in St Vincent's Hospital, Dublin after two years of worsening health. Her husband, John's uncle Jim, had died in 1970. On 19 January Samuel wrote to John: 'Thanks for yrs. of 6th with sad news of Peggy. ... Glad to hear you are settled in your new house. I suppose you pine for Calary. You'll get back one of these days.'[1] The new house refers to a terraced house that John and Ruth had moved into: 4 Parkview Terrace, Dargle Road in Bray. Although small, it was more convenient and comfortable than the cottage near Calary Bog. It was nicknamed 'Patella Villa' because it had been bought with the compensation money that Ruth had received after her knee had been smashed.[2]

One of the people who used to visit John and Ruth in the new house was Mirette Dowling.[3] William Young often went there to rehearse for the Bach cantatas. On his first visit to the new house, Ruth invited him to wash his hands before eating, which he politely declined. When Ruth insisted, he followed her, realizing that she was so excited at having a proper bathroom that she wanted to show it off to him.[4] By now John and Ruth had a cat that everyone knew as Murray, though John told a couple of his friends in Dublin that the name was actually Madrid, pronounced in flamboyant Spanish style with the accent firmly on the final syllable and the Ds almost omitted: Ma-ri. Murray (or Madrid) was a fertile female who regularly gave birth to kittens, for which homes needed to be found.[5] Alison and Bill were often asked if they could take one. When Bill once remarked that the cat might once again be pregnant, John had said, 'Well, I hope so!'[6]

The first of the three Bach cantata concerts took place on 5 February. Just two secular works were performed: the Brandenburg Concerto No. 1 and Cantata

No. 208, *Was mir behagt, ist nur die muntre Jagd!* (the 'Hunt' cantata), which had been recorded the previous September. Charles Acton praised the performance and had this to say about the Brandenburg Concerto:

> I do not think I have ever heard such a spirited, authentic, stylish and entirely enjoyable performance. Mr Beckett put his concertino (Victor Malirsh, Thomas Briggs, Helmut Seeber, Lindsay Armstrong, Patricia Harrison, Mary Gallagher) in a row in front of the ripieno, with Gilbert Berg (bassoon) also in front. This resulted in a new and fresher (and also clearer) balance of sound. Also Mr Beckett had the strings of the NICO using a really baroque style of bowing ... Altogether it was a revelation of what this concerto should sound like and at its most pleasurable.[7]

The second concert consisted of four songs from Schemelli's *Gesangbuch* (Song Book) sung by Irené Sandford, William Young and Frank Patterson, then Cantata No. 21, *Ich hatte viel Bekümmernis* ('My heart was deeply troubled'). Mr Acton was full of praise for the performances and delighted that so many people had turned up to attend the concert, which was recorded by the BBC.[8] On the following day, Nicholas Anderson and his team recorded Cantata No. 99, *Was Gott tut, das ist wohlgetan* ('What God does, that is done well'), and a few days later they recorded Cantata No. 163, *Nur Jedem das Seine* ('To each only his due') using the same singers.[9]

The final concert took place on 19 February. Once again just two works were performed: John's favourite, the Sinfonia from Cantata No. 42 and No. 30, *Freue dich, erlöste Schar* ('Rejoice, O ransomed throng'). Commenting on the first work, Charles Acton wrote:

> One constant feature of the series each year is the playing of the opening sinfonia of Cantata 42, which may well be John Beckett's favourite movement in all Bach. He told us that he and his friends, when working at the cantatas, keep on finding movements 'uniquely beautiful'. This, he said, was certainly one and he pointed out that he had never met it in any concert programme.

Acton praised the performance of Cantata No. 30, recorded by the BBC, and concluded his review: 'As before, the Cantata Singers and NICO were splendid. In spite of the nasty weather, I am most grateful to John Beckett and his friends, who can be the only possible reason for looking forward to such a beastly month of February.'[10]

It was probably on this occasion when John scolded Nicholas for lateness. As we have noted, John was a stickler for timekeeping and was in the habit of arriving at venues much earlier than needed. Nicholas was staying with John and Venetia O'Sullivan, who decided to take him and their children on a drive up the Wicklow Mountains on the Sunday morning as it was a fine wintry day. However, when they got up into the mountains, it began to snow quite heavily and, as a result, they had a difficult journey back to Dublin. As there was little time to spare between their return and then driving to St Ann's for the concert, they arrived late and found John prowling around like a caged tiger. He immediately attacked Venetia for being so irresponsible and Nicholas for being a fool. 'What on earth would have happened if you'd been late?' he asked. 'The concert wouldn't have been recorded!' 'John, it *would*,' replied Nicholas, 'because the sound engineer is here! All I do is make sure that there are no catastrophic mistakes that we need to cover afterwards!' John was very angry, and Venetia was cross with him as she thought that he was making a storm in a teacup.[11]

Following a repeat of the concert given by the Dublin Training Orchestra in early December of the previous year (Wagner's *Meistersinger* overture, Weber's bassoon concerto and Schubert's Symphony No. 9), this time in Christ Church, Bray in March,[12] John went to London. While there, John Calder (the publisher of Samuel Beckett's works) bumped into him in the Hayward Gallery, on the South Bank, which was then hosting a major retrospective exhibition entitled *Dada and Surrealism Reviewed*. One of the items on view was Marcel Duchamp's *Roue de bicyclette: Bicycle wheel*, a bicycle wheel fixed to the top of a simple wooden stool. The original version was created in 1913; this version, one of an edition of eight, dated from 1964 and was signed and numbered. John asked Calder, 'Do you have the authority to turn it?' and, without further ado, went over to rotate the wheel.[13]

John was back in Dublin in April and at the end of the month he conducted two all-Bach concerts in the Examination Hall of Trinity College. This involved the New Irish Chamber Orchestra, Edward Beckett and Madeleine Berkeley, flutes, and Gillian Smith, harpsichord. The first concert, on Saturday 29th, consisted of the Orchestral Suites Nos 2 and 3 (BWV 1067 and 1068) and the Brandenburg Concertos Nos 1 and 3. According to Charles Acton, the hall was packed and a disappointed crowd of people, who could not be admitted, had to forego the pleasure of hearing the music and leave. Apparently a German conductor was to have directed and John was engaged when he 'cried off'. Such was the enthusiasm of the audience that an encore was demanded and, according to my diary, the famous movement known popularly as the *Air on the G string* from the Orchestral Suite No. 3 was played.[14]

Michael Williams reviewed the second concert, which took place on the following evening. This featured the Orchestral Suites Nos. 1 and 4 (BWV 1066 and 1069) and the Brandenburg Concertos Nos 4 and 5. He wrote:

John Beckett's approach to the music last night emphasised its physical size and vigour and never did the controlled violence of the karate chop with which he terminates a movement seem more appropriate. However, he also brought out the intellectual vigour and the amazing creative energy that Bach put into this music.

One can look at a mountain from any one of an infinite number of points, and Beckett's view of Bach, as demonstrated last night, is both coherent and committed ... I came away from Sunday night's concert with a strong feeling of regret at having to miss Saturday night's.[15]

In my diary, I noted that the hall was packed once again. Afterwards we went to the headquarters of the Goethe Institute (who, with the Arts Council, had sponsored the concert), where we accepted generous helpings of food and chatted to John and the musicians.[16]

Another concert involving the Dublin Training Orchestra took place shortly afterwards in St Catherine's Church, Thomas Street in Dublin. The pieces performed this time were Wagner's overture to *Die Meistersinger von Nürnberg*, Elgar's Cello Concerto in E minor, Op. 85 (with soloist Frank Schaeffer) and Schubert's Symphony No. 7 in E, D 729. In a review printed in *The Irish Times*, Carol Acton expressed the view that the Irish Youth Orchestra and some of the country's amateur orchestras had performed better than the Dublin Training Orchestra in St Catherine's Church. She was not very happy about how the orchestra had been trained.[17]

This turned out to be the last concert given by the Dublin Training Orchestra that John conducted; thereafter Prionnsias Ó Duinn was used for the few remaining concerts. James Cavanagh reflects that the orchestra proved to be a useful platform for young soloists like Frank Schaeffer and Robert Houlihan. He firmly believes that the orchestra would probably have lasted longer if they had stuck with the original idea of performing overtures, concertos and symphonies, rather than accompanying choirs and singers. His and his colleagues' lack of administrative skills did not help matters either. He realizes how lucky they were to have John at the time; they all liked him and thought that he was great.[18]

In mid September, two more Bach cantatas were recorded for BBC Radio 3.[19] Shortly afterwards, John arrived at our house to return a tuning fork and drink a cup of tea. We told him that we had passed his cottage in Kilmacanogue the day before and had noticed that it was deserted. He knew about this and was puzzled as to why he had been obliged to leave it so quickly and yet now it was still uninhabited. He told us that it had been a marvellous experience living there in the wilds, especially when it snowed, and that it was a place where he had always wanted to live.

While in our house, John asked my father to fix his mother's clock, which had stopped working. (It was the ticking of this clock that had disturbed Samuel.)[20] My father agreed to repair it and when he removed the dial, which bore a Dublin maker's name, he found it to be a traditional Black Forest clock, complete with its original long pendulum and weights. Cathal fixed it quickly and he and I drove out to Bray a few days later after the viol consort class to return it to John. Ruth opened the door and welcomed us into a tiny but warm living room, which was painted white, simply furnished, and which contained many interesting books arranged on makeshift shelves. The sound of music by Mondonville on period instruments greeted us; this was being broadcast by BBC Radio 3 and played on a neat hi-fi system beside an old rustic fireplace. The place was crude but homely.

John soon appeared, looking tired; Ruth made me sit down while my father proceeded to hang the clock on the wall. While Ruth made a pot of tea, I flicked through a book about Monet. John did not take tea; a large glassful of grapefruit juice quenched his thirst.

My father soon had the clock going. We sat back, drank tea from rough pottery cups and ate delicious bread and butter, covered with a thick dollop of homemade crab-apple jelly. The fire roared; the old clock ticked loudly and five gorgeous kittens, doubtless the offspring of Murray, frolicked around their beautiful mother and wrestled with each other.

Ruth chatted, while John, weary and silent, concentrated on the exquisite Baroque music or gazed fondly at the clock. Occasionally, he broke his silence by laughing heartily at some of my father's jokes. When amused, John was in the habit of smiling, rocking backwards a little as he chuckled and then erupting into open laughter. Knowing that I was interested in the oriental arts, John showed me a prized Japanese tea bowl, which I seem to recollect being dark in colour and typically irregular in shape. He produced books of both Japanese and Chinese art and calligraphy, which I leafed through and admired. What seemed to appeal to John most of all were the sparse, sketchy monochrome ink paintings executed by noted Chinese artists of the past, in which the *xie yi* (capturing of essence) style was perfectly illustrated – in contrast to the more familiar *xie shi* (capturing of detail) style of painting in colour.

Later, before we left, Ruth showed us the cosy kitchen at the back of the house, in which a fine photograph of Gabriel Fauré adorned a wall. She then brought us up the narrow staircase between the front and back rooms to show us the music room upstairs, which housed John's harpsichord, and their bedroom, in which two large brass single beds were lashed together. A bicycle lamp hanging by a string served as a bedside lamp.[21]

John was so delighted to have his clock back and working again that he spoke about it for long and many a day afterwards; whenever he met Cathal, he would report that the clock was still going and working well.[22] Apparently my father loaned him a book, *Black Forest Clocks* by E. John Tyler, which he found delightful. He was probably intrigued by the fact that these simple and afford-able wooden clocks were made by German farmers during the long and dreary winter months, that kitchen bellows could be used to blow dust out of them and that a drop of oil applied with a feather was enough to get them to run again when they stopped. John would have read the legend of a wooden-wheeled clock being brought to the region from Bohemia in around 1640 and copied by the locals, who were expert woodcarvers. It was claimed that the teeth on the wheels of this imported clock were cut with a breadknife – difficult to believe as a saw is needed to do the job accurately.[23]

The simplest things in life gave John the most pleasure. In the Wicklow Mountains he had relished the fresh air, the snow, the scenery and undoubtedly the silence; I can remember him deeply inhaling the aromas of wood, turf and various items of food, such as cheese, of which he was extremely fond.[24]

In November RTÉ Radio broadcast two programmes of music by Schubert to mark the 150th anniversary of the composer's death. The first one, entitled *Schubert's Other Unfinished Symphony*, consisted of the first part of a studio concert given by the RTÉ Concert Orchestra, conducted by John, and Bernadette Greevy singing some of Schubert's songs, accompanied by him. The programme was introduced by John. Listening to it, it is obvious that John is completely at home with this music. His style of delivery is perhaps less pompous and learned than that used in former BBC programmes. One has the impression that his script had been recorded separately and edited in afterwards. This first programme began with the Overture, D591, in the Italian Style. After this, four delightful songs, beautifully sung by Bernadette Greevy, were sensitively accompanied by John on the piano. The programme concluded with a rather laclustre perfor-mance of the Symphony No. 7 in E major.[25]

The second programme, entitled simply *Schubert*, was broadcast a week later and began with the *Entr'acte* in B flat from the Incidental Music to *Rosamunde*. This was followed by five songs, sung once again by Bernadette Greevy. Again, all of these were excellently sung and accompanied by John, especially *Gretchen at the Spinning Wheel*, in which there was plenty of *tempo rubato* and a highly dramatic pause after the words *sein Küss* ('his kiss'). After the pause John began the rippling accompaniment slowly and quietly, then gradually speeded up, indicating that the wheel was spinning again. The final song, *Night and Dreams*, was also superb.[26] The final work in the second programme was the well-known Symphony No. 8, '*the* Unfinished Symphony'.[27]

When playing with John and others at the Wednesday evening viol class shortly afterwards, we were joined by Susan Carolan, Malcolm Proud's girl-friend, with her new bass viol.[28] Malcolm and Susan had met two years previ-ously at one of the chamber music classes in the Academy.[29] Although she had only been playing the viol for a few months, she astounded us all by her virtu-osity. It transpired that she was a viola player. As it was obvious that John wanted her to play more than Cormac Flanagan, who had been playing bass before Susan's arrival, poor Cormac was pushed to one side and only allowed to play a piece one last time before we went on to the next. On that evening, we played through quite a lot of music, including a couple of pavanes by John Jenkins, whose viol music John relished.[30]

When John went to London for a short spell afterwards, my father and a friend of his visited him at his home in Greenwich.[31] He was back by 17 December when he conducted the New Irish Chamber Orchestra in works by Handel, Vivaldi and Bach at the Goethe Institute Christmas concert, which was held in the Examination Hall of Trinity College. Charles Acton was bowled over by the 'sheer vivid, spiriited enthusiasm' of the performance and wrote, 'What an exhilarating conductor he is!'[32]

Thirty-Seven
1979

A Seán Ó Riada tribute concert was held in the Saint Francis Xavier Hall in Dublin at the beginning of 1979. Once again, John played the harpsichord in John Kinsella's work, *A Selected Life*. The concert was recorded by RTÉ and broadcast in September of the following year.[1]

The next engagement was a concert of music by Purcell in the Examination Hall, Trinity College,[2] to which John's loyal fans flocked. The performers were John's Scottish friend Linda Howie, Frank Patterson, Andrew Robinson on bass viola da gamba and John on harpsichord.[3] John was very fond of Linda's interpretation of Purcell and involved her in recitals and recordings over a couple of years.[4] According to Jeremy Timmis, a friend of Linda's, John used to send tapes of the harpsichord and bass viol parts to her in Scotland in preparation for the performances. He also visited her in Edinburgh, where she had a poorly-assembled harpsichord that did not meet with his approval. A talented amateur singer, her natural voice was completely shaped by John. As Linda was instrumental in persuading John to change his diet, which eventually led to his dramatic reduction in weight, John 'reciprocated' by educating her in literary matters, and brought her to plays in the Gate Theatre in Dublin and elsewhere.[5]

The annual series of Bach cantatas began on 4 February with Nos. 133, *Ich freue mich in dir* ('I rejoice in Thee') and 117, *Sei Lob und Ehr' dem höchsten Gut* ('Let there be praise and honour for the highest good'). Acton reported that the church was packed, and that John informed the audience that the BBC was recording all three concerts: 'Mr Beckett also gave us the exciting news that the BBC have invited them to bring across their whole team to London to give the Prom in the Albert Hall on Sunday, July 22nd – a recognition that he and they fully deserve, and it warmed one's heart to hear the vigorous applause that greeted his news.'[6]

Naturally Nicholas Anderson was behind the planned performance at the Henry Wood Promenade concert. Nicholas had sent a memo to the BBC Controller of Music, Robert Ponsonby, asking him if he would consider bringing the New Irish Chamber Orchestra and the Cantata Singers to London for a Prom concert. Ponsonby replied that he would in principle, but that he needed to come to Dublin in order to hear the musicians and singers for himself. He came, stayed in the Hibernian Hotel and attended one of the rehearsals. Nicholas remembers him saying afterwards that he had liked what he had heard. This, in effect, was what had put the wheels in motion. Nicholas's only responsibilities after that were to oversee the costings and write the programme notes.[7]

Three days later, two more cantatas were recorded: Nos. 144, *Nimm, was dein ist, und gehe hin* ('Take what is thine and go away') and 150, *Nach dir, Herr, verlanget mich* ('Unto Thee, O Lord, do I lift up my soul').[8] Nicholas Anderson can remember John introducing him to the latter work, a 'pre-Vivaldi' cantata, which he thought was absolutely marvellous. He said to Nicholas, 'Why couldn't the man go on writing like this, instead of all that bloody violin music?' When Nicholas asked him if he was referring to Vivaldi's influence on Bach, which angered John, his response was merely a growl. Although Nicholas knew what he meant, he did not agree with him.[9]

Cantatas Nos. 86, *Wahrlich, wahrlich, ich sage euch* ('Truly, truly, I say unto you') and 138, *Warum betrübst du dich, mein Herz?* ('Why are you troubled, my heart?') were performed in St Ann's Church on the following Sunday afternoon. Charles Acton did not like what John did with the second movement of the first cantata, which was getting the soprano and alto soloists to sing the chorale verse in unison.[10] The final two cantatas, Nos. 123, *Liebster Immanuel, Herzog der Frommen* ('Dearest Emmanuel, Lord of the righteous') and 177, *Ich ruf' zu dir, Herr Jesu Christ* ('I call to Thee, Lord Jesus Christ') were performed on 18 February, though Nicholas Anderson stayed on to record Cantatas 177 and 174, *Ich liebe den Höchsten von ganzem Gemüte* ('I love the Almighty with all my heart') at the beginning of March.[11]

In March John conducted a performance of Haydn's *Missa Brevis of St John of God,* his Symphony No. 77 in B flat and his *Seven Last Words of Our Saviour on the Cross*, with the New Irish Chamber Orchestra, Our Lady's Choral Society, Mary Sheridan (soprano), Bernadette Greevy, Frank Patterson and William Young, at the Church of the Holy Family, Kill-o'-the-Grange, Dun Laoghaire.[12] This was one of a series of events celebrating the centenary of the Hospitaller Order of Saint John of God in Ireland; Joseph Haydn was associated with the Order throughout his life.[13] Charles Acton praised the performances, saying that in the *Missa Brevis* 'Mr Beckett secured a lightness of touch from the choir which prevented them from seeming too numerous.'[14] A recording was made of the *Missa Brevis* for Network Tapes, distributed by Veritas, and was issued on cassette tape early in the following year; Seoirse Bodley's *Mass of Joy* in honour of St John of God was on side two.[15]

A Czech couple that John befriended at around this time was Vera Škrabánek and her husband Petr, Associate Professor in Community Health in Trinity College. His criticism of modern medical humbug was reflected in his popular book, *Follies and Fallacies of Medicine*. Of great interest to John was the fact that Petr was a world authority of Joyce's *Finnegans Wake* and that he conducted a series of Joycean seminars at University College Dublin (UCD) every year.[16] Vera was also a lecturer in UCD. The couple met John and Ruth through their colleague Michael Richter, who regularly helped the Cantata Singers with their German pronunciation. Michael had told them about John and his cousin Samuel, and had encouraged them to visit John and Ruth. Accordingly, an arrangement was made and John invited them to his home. Vera, who was expecting a grand house like the one in Foxrock in which Samuel had lived, was surprised at the modest scale of the terraced house in Bray, where everything was so simple. They became good friends and either visited each other or went for trips up the mountains together. John and Ruth were very kind to Vera and Petr; when Vera's mother came from Czechoslovakia on a visit, they immediately invited the three of them over to their house.

There was always an abundance of wine in the house in Bray. At one time John went through a phase of drinking Greek *retsina*. When Vera's husband Petr returned from lecturing in Portugal, he brought a five-litre demijohn of red wine, which was shared with John and Ruth one evening at their home in Stillorgan after dinner. They whiled the night away, the two men talking together in one room and the two women in another, and by five o'clock the next morning the wine was all gone. Vera has a vague recollection of John drinking some strong coffee and leaving in his car at about six.[17]

Shortly afterwards John played harpsichord continuo for a production of Bach's *Saint John Passion* with the St Patrick's College choir and orchestra in Maynooth, conducted by Fr Noel Watson.[18] During an interval he was approached and asked how it was going. John merely nodded, then said, 'I feel like a tin can tied to the back of a car at somebody else's wedding!' John, who was not in control, would have been critical of Fr Watson's interpretation of the work and the minimum amount of rehearsal allocated to it.[19]

John then conducted Mendelssohn's *Lauda Sion* and Dvořák's *Stabat Mater* in the Pro-Cathedral, Dublin. This was performed by the RTÉ Concert Orchestra, the Wicklow Choral Society and soloists Violet Twomey, Áine Nic Gabhann, Brendan Cavanagh and William Young.[20] Towards the end of April, John was in Newry, conducting the RTÉ Concert Orchestra again, though this time with Our Lady's Choral Society, in an all-Haydn concert, which included his Symphony No. 77 and *The Seven Last Words of our Saviour on the Cross*.[21]

The reason why John had been asked to conduct the RTÉ Concert Orchestra was because RTÉ was broadening the scope of the orchestra and bringing it to the public in various parts of Dublin and around the country. Accordingly, John conducted the orchestra in a concert of music by Mozart at the beginning of the following month in St Catherine's Church, Thomas Street in Dublin, which was well attended. 'John Beckett's style with Mozart was forthright and energetic', wrote Charles Acton in *The Irish Times*, though he found a lack of elegance in the phrasing of the music.[22]

A week later, another concert of Mozart's music followed in the same venue, featuring the RTÉ Concert Orchestra and this time the soprano Violet Twomey. Charles Acton complained about the reverberation in the church, which had previously been dampened by a carpet, and John's 'very forthright, foursquare readings.'[23] The concert was recorded by RTÉ Radio and broadcast in March of the following year.[24]

In the middle of May, a twenty-five-minute programme of songs by Henry Purcell was broadcast on RTÉ Radio. These were sung by Frank Patterson and Linda Howie, accompanied by John on harpsichord and Andrew Robinson on bass viola da gamba. This delightful programme, introduced by John, began with three songs sung by Frank: 'If Music be the food of Love' (1692), 'I'll sail upon the Dog Star' and 'If Music be the food of Love' (1695). The following two items, the exquisite 'Evening Hymn' and the dramatic 'Blessed Virgin's Expostulation' were sung by Linda. Linda's light voice was perfectly suitable for most of the pieces, though a perceptive listener would have been aware that she was an amateur singer. The programme concluded with a group of three songs: 'There's not a Swain on the Plain', sung by Frank, 'What can we poor Females do?' sung by Linda, and 'Man is for the Woman made' sung by Frank.[25]

Another programme, just fifteen minutes long, that featured Linda and Alison Browner, was also recorded but seems not to have been broadcast. In it, John introduces the items as well as playing the harpsichord. The first item is Purcell's elegy, 'O dive Custos Auriacae domus' ('O God, guardian of the House of Orange'), on the death of Queen Mary, for two voices. The second is a song, 'No, no, Resistance is but vain' and the final duet is 'O the sweet Delights of Love'.[26]

After a weekend of music by Chopin, devised by John and performed by Miceál O'Rourke for the Carlow Music Club,[27] John, Linda Howie and Andrew Robinson gave a lunchtime recital in the Royal Dublin Society, as part of the Festival of Music and Musicians in June. Charles Acton reported that Linda 'has a small and very beautiful voice that would have been much more suitable to Russborough or Carton [House] rather than to the whole of the RDS hall', and that John's selection of pieces from *The Fitzwilliam Virginal Book* were all played 'with a perfection of ornament and rhythm that were immensely pleasing.'[28]

It was probably during this visit of Linda's to Dublin when her children were quite sick and she had to leave them at home in Edinburgh with many misgivings. Because of the problems, she announced to John just before the concert that she would not continue the association. As can be imagined, John was not at all pleased to hear this. He told Linda's friend Jeremy Timmis, 'If I throw up all over the harpsichord [today], you will know why!'[29]

On the following day, John conducted the New Irish Chamber Orchestra in a concert of Mozart and Bach in the Royal Dublin Society. The programme began with two Marches in D (K. 249 and 335/1), which Charles Acton described as 'a splendidly festive start to a festive concert'. The performance ended with Bach's Orchestral Suite No. 3 in D, BWV 1068.[30]

John conducted another concert in the Festival of Music and Musicians at the Royal Dublin Society three days later, on 10 June. As the programme included two works by Vivaldi (or more correctly, five), John could not have been too pleased at the choice of music. However, the first item, played by the New Irish Chamber Orchestra, was Bach's effervescent Brandenburg Concerto No. 4, with the violin played by Thérèse Timoney, and the two recorder parts played by Edward Beckett and Madeleine Berkeley on flutes. Carol Acton, writing in *The Irish Times*, described the performance as 'lively'. Fortunately for John, he did not have to conduct Vivaldi's *Four Seasons*; these were directed by the soloist, Iona Brown.[31] On 24 June, Charles Acton wrote a long letter to John:

Dear John

As you may imagine, I am much disturbed about yesterday, especially as I am deeply shocked that you should not only have spoken obscenely to my wife but confined your obscenities to her.

Moving on to your complaints to me, I would point out that it is not my fault if my colleagues do not attend concerts, but it is theirs and, more, that of the public and of yourself. You and your colleagues could help us all if you would get your

*friends to write frequently to editors complaining about the absence of notices –
editors are strongly influenced by a few letters from readers whose names they do
not know.*

*Next, you stated that I have prevented you from getting further work. I simply
do not believe it. I am continually thankful that here we have not got a situation
like New York's where a Clive Barnes has power. I hope that I may have some influence: I am quite sure (thank goodness) that I have no power – if I had RTE would
not do or would do quite a lot of things.*

*It is sad that you think that I pontificate, because I have no desire to do other
than my job, to attend <u>where invited</u> and express my personal opinion as such. I
do desire to be helpful to everyone – especially to the readers to whom I am above
all responsible.*

Acton then defended his views on the first Mozart concert in St Catherine's
Church, performed by the RTÉ Concert Orchestra, then the second, and
compared them both to the RDS concert with the New Irish Chamber Orchestra,
which, in his opinion was so much better. 'It was only my enormous respect and
admiration for you that prevented me from making a feature of the contrast', he
wrote. He concluded:

*It was sad for me that, yesterday, you would not let me finish a sentence, would not
permit a full discussion of the whole situation, because I think that, if you had, we
could once more have come to an understanding consensus.*

*Please be assured, for the future, that I will continue to do my best for the readers,
for you, for music in Ireland, but please also be assured that any dislike you may
have for my writing gives you no right to blame my wife, let alone to subject her
to the sort of obscenity that no man should address to any woman acquaintance.*[32]

Fortunately we do have John's response to Acton's letter. 'I found your letter
at the RIAM yesterday morning', he began:

*I very much regret that I should have spoken to you and Carol on Saturday after-
noon as you say I did, and horrified that I should have used obscene terms to her
– I was in fact very, inexcusably, drunk and honestly remember very little of what I
said. I spoke to her on the phone yesterday, and she was charitable enough to accept
my unqualified apology – I hope that you may find yourself able to do the same.*

*It is of course both professionally and personally hurtful when work that one
does with all the skill and care at one's command, and considers well done, is
condemned as bad by such perceptive critics as yourselves. One must, however,
endure such verdicts and their consequencs in silence – on this score alone I should
not have spoken to you as I did.*

*I enclose another review of the first of the Mozart concerts in St. Catherine's —
this is more what it felt and sounded like to me. I should add that none of the details
that I was displeased with myself in these performances was mentioned in reviews.*

*To end I would like to say how much I have appreciated your constructive and
kind support over the years.*[33]

The attached review was *Beautiful playing in concert* by Fanny Fehan. In it she
had written:

It is a pleasure to hear an orchestra, which does not shuffle its entries apologeti-
cally, has reliable intonation, and plays everything as if they were familiar with
the music rather than seeing it for the first time. John Beckett who conducted
delighted the orchestra as much as he was delighted by the music.[34]

Acton responded with another lengthy letter:

*Many thanks for telephoning and I trust that your mind is now at rest on that score.
Thank you also for your letter of 26th which I only now have time to reply to — its
first two paragraphs already dealt with by your kindly telephoning.*

*I think that we can both be grateful that the conversation happened, because it
does produce discussion, and I vehemently disagree that performers and critics who
know each other should not converse about their disagreements.*

*That you (or all other real professionals) do your work "with all the skill and
care at your command" goes without saying: otherwise it woud not deserve the
public's hearing or the critic's work. But there are plenty of performances which, for
all that, may seem less pleasing than others. You will be only too familiar with, for
example, the sort of sentimental and thoroughly unstylistic performances of Bach
such as Tibor Paul's and others that still appear even now...*

*That Fanny's opinion of the first Cath's concert corresponded with your feelings
is good, of course, but all critics can and should do no more than express their own
opinions...*

*I hope all this helps and would add just two little things: however reluctant a
critic may be to express an unfavourable opinion of a musician whom he respects
immensely, if he fails to do so when firmly convinced, then any praise that he may
write is totally valueless; I am convinced that all personal exchanges of views
between performers and critics can only help both and music and general...*[35]

This exchange of letters illustrates a side of John's character that so far has
not been discussed: his fondness for alcohol, his unsociable behaviour when
inebriated, his argumentative nature, and his ability to realize his failings and to
offer abject apology when necessary. Although John must have cursed Acton's

reviews from time to time, he realized that he meant well, and that he privately praised and supported him.

John was now busy rehearsing and preparing for the BBC Prom concert, which was scheduled for 22 July. On 15 July John was interviewed by Jeremy Siepmann on Radio 3's programme *Prom Talk*[36] and on the following day, Venetia O'Sullivan talked to him about the forthcoming concert on RTÉ Radio's *Music Magazine*.[37] Then, on 19 July the items to be performed in the Proms were presented to the Irish public in a special concert held in St Ann's Church, Dublin. It was an all-Bach event: the Sinfonia from Cantata No. 174, Cantata No. 21, *Ich hatte viel Bekümmernis* ('My heart was deeply troubled'), the Sinfonia from Cantata No. 42 and Cantata No. 30, *Freue dich, erlöste Schar* ('Rejoice, O ransomed throng').[38] The soloists were Irené Sandford, Frank Patterson and William Young; Bernadette Greevy only sang in one recitative and one aria in the final cantata and because of this, she was rather upset. John was in the habit of choosing the cantatas that he liked without studying the singers, instead of selecting them according to the singers that he had at his disposal. It was therefore not unusual for a singer to have little to do during one Sunday afternoon and then have several demanding arias during the following.[39]

Charles Acton captured everyone's excitement at the prospect of an Irish orchestra performing in the Royal Albert Hall for the first time in his review in *The Irish Times*:

> Whatever about Sunday night at the Albert Hall Prom in London, to which they are borne along on all our good wishes, John Beckett and his friends had a triumphant preview of their programme in St. Ann's last night. We had heard all the items during their customary Sunday afternoons in February, but it all seemed more splendid put together like this and with every available standing space packed.
>
> There is so much more I would like to pick out for praise. More important is the remarkable unanimity among every single performer, welded into a single entity by Mr Beckett's enthusiasm, skill and musical spirit. It is rare indeed for the BBC to honour any foreign team by giving it a Prom to itself. As this honour has come to Ireland and to such an outsdanding team as Mr Beckett's and his friends, may they triumph there indeed![40]

John's Bach contribution to the Prom series was broadcast live on BBC Radio 3 on the 22nd, from 7.30 to 8.20 pm and, after the interval, from 8.40 to 10 pm. In an unusual break with tradition, sponsorship from Allied Irish Banks

Ltd was acknowledged in the *Radio Times*.[41] RTÉ Radio only broadcast Part Two, which was introduced by Christopher Hogwood.[42] Malcolm Ruthven was the presenter on Radio 3. Although the hall was only about half full – some three thousand people turned up – the BBC believed that the concert was well attended considering that most Londoners had never heard of the orchestra before, that it consisted of only Bach cantatas and that it was on a Sunday evening.

There was an enthusiastic round of applause when John appeared, resplendent in a black suit and bow tie. Undestandably, the musicians and singers were all extremely keyed up after all the hard work and rehearsals in Dublin.[43]

Charles Acton, who wrote about the event later, described the opening item, the Sinfonia from Cantata No. 174, as 'a rather sticky start'.[44] (Listening now to a rather indifferent off-air recording, the Sinfonia sounds scrappy and noticeably out of tune – especially the horns. In fact, it took some time for the orchestra and singers to 'warm up' and relax in the unfamiliar surroundings.)

In general, the second half was much better than the first. The familiar Sinfonia to Cantata No. 42 was played confidently and at a lively pace, and Cantata No. 30 went well. The concert was well received and, at its conclusion, the applause was long and loud. Gillian Smith believes that John must have been quite buoyed up by the promenaders and the atmosphere in the hall.[45] Reviews written in *The Financial Times* and *The Daily Telegraph* were laudatory, though Mozelle Moshansky, writing in *The Guardian*, thought little of the performance and John's interpretation.[46]

Nicholas Anderson has a vague recollection of everyone gathering in one of the hall's bars for a well-earned drink afterwards. For him the event had been very exciting, especially at the end of the first cantata. It was his opinion that John felt it was a wonderful recognition of all the hard work that he and everyone else had done. Nicholas remembers that there was a great sense of pride among the soloists. He himself was pleased; he realized that to do what he had done was tantamount to putting his head on the block as there had been no precedent for doing what he had achieved. Only an enlightened head of department would have allowed him to do it. The sad thing was that John, the orchestra and singers were never invited back – something that Nicholas very much regretted.[47]

Although this undoubtedly was the pinnacle of John's conducting career, he would have said little about it beyond 'We all did our best', according to Lindsay Armstrong. Lindsay thinks that he would have felt that his efforts were probably a far cry from those of the early music specialists of the time, considering that his orchestra used modern instruments and played in a modern style.[48] He had certainly done his best with what forces he had at his disposal.

On returning to Ireland, John had another professional engagement with Bernadette Greevy, this time accompanying her on piano at a recital given on 29 July as part of the weekend Robertstown Grand Canal Festa in County Kildare.[49] A month later, the Proms programme was repeated in St Canice's Cathedral, Kilkenny during the Kilkenny Arts Festival. This time however, Alison Browner sang Bernadette Greevy's recitative and Aria in the second cantata.[50]

At some point during the year, Anthony OBrien joined Andrew Robinson in his basement workshop in Marlborough Road, where they made musical instruments. He was encouraged to show John his first viol, 'a bizarre hybrid creature concocted by me with a gourd as the sound box,' he recalls:

> John pronounced it unplayable, but it came with me to the Academy viol class. Once John had accepted that it could be played, however badly, by me, he soon urged me, as he urged everyone, to 'nourish the notes!' And he demonstrated what he meant on his own, more orthodox treble viol. I was too intimidated to say it was all very well telling me to nourish the notes, but at that stage I barely knew how to find them. He insisted that I come to him in the Academy for private lessons to get going properly. So I borrowed Andrew Robinson's Dolmetsch treble, and with much fear and trembling, turned up for my first lesson with John.
>
> I was hardly in the door for my first lesson when he came up to me with a broad grin and said, 'Put that instrument down for the moment. Oh, you've been eating garlic! Wonderful! I hear you like Indian music and food, and I hear you're a very good cook. Can I come to dinner?' And within a week, John and Ruth came to dinner in our house. Quite a few eyebrows were raised about that, as I was seen as a very junior member of the viol community to be hosting the Becketts socially. But in no time we became very good friends, and Ruth taught violin for some time from our house.
>
> John's gift as a teacher was his passion for the music, which was infectious. On one occasion he urged me to get the *Glogaur Liederbuch*, a wonderful collection of about five hundred mostly fifteenth- and very early sixteenth-century three-part instrumental *chansons*. John seemed rather taken aback when I actually bought it (it was expensive). He said he felt rather guilty, but in recompense photocopied the entire thing in three sets of copies on the Academy photocopier. Although edited into modern notation, the score had no barlines. We asked John for suggestions as to how we should count it. He said, 'Just count one, one, one, one, one...'
>
> And during one unforgettable evening, John, Andrew Robinson and I played the entire book, end to end, to the accompaniment of a bottle of Bushmills Black Label whiskey, which was empty at the end of the night. (It was one of the

few occasions I saw John drink neat whiskey without an accompanying clove of garlic crushed in his glass.)[51]

On 9 October, a film on the life and work of John Millington Synge, written and directed by John's friend James Plunkett, was shown on RTÉ Television. The third programme in a series called *Insight: Wits and Dreamers*, this film was entitled *That Solitary Man* and featured a small amount of rather dreary incidental music composed by John for flute and harp, and also for harmonium. The film is interesting; Synge's composition *Melody in F* is performed, a square piano is used and extracts from Synge's plays are enacted or 'rehearsed' outdoors by the actors. Synge's last poem, beginning with the line *I read about the Blaskets and Dunquin* and with which John was familiar, was quoted at the end of the film.[52]

One of John's harpsichord students at around this time was Rosalind Whittaker. She found John an excellent teacher, though he was very demanding and put her under a great deal of pressure. When she played, he used to 'dance' around the room. He asked Rosalind if she had curtains in the room where she kept her harpsichord at home. When she said yes, as it was kept in the dining room, which needed curtains, he stated that curtains did not go with a harpsichord. He then asked her if the room had a carpet, which it did. 'When I told him that I had central heating, he gave up on me,' she reported.[53]

By the beginning of December, John had found a replacement for Linda Howie: a tall, red-haired young Irish lady with a light voice, named Shelagh Best. According to my diary, she sang a Purcell song at a concert in St Columba's College, and afterwards John and she came to our house in Castleknock to return a small harpsichord, made by my father, that had been used in the concert. While Shelagh told us about herself and mentioned that she had tried to get a job in RTÉ, John, who was warming himself in front of the fire, stated bluntly that he would rather clean toilets or work in sewers than be employed in television. Needless to say, he did not approve of me working in the RTÉ television sound department.

My parents persuaded John and Shelagh to stay for supper; before we sat down, they performed the Purcell song that Shelagh had sung at the concert. John praised her highly, for she had taken the bother to learn the song by heart and to travel all the way out to Rathfarnham, knowing that there was a bus strike and that she had no way of getting home to Glasnevin on the north side of the city. John had offered to drive her home, even though it meant travelling in the opposite direction for a considerable distance, then returning to the city centre and heading southwards to Bray. John was quite capable of doing such acts of kindness for those whom he admired.[54]

Thirty-Eight
1980

After John had given a harpsichord recital at the end of January in University College Cork,[1] he conducted the Bach cantatas in St Ann's Church once again in February. Charles Acton gave fulsome praise for the performance of the first two works, No. 57, *Selig ist der Mann* ('Blessed is the man'), and No. 39, *Brich dem Hungrigen dein Brot* ('Deal Thy bread to the hungry'). By now the BBC had filled in their gaps and no more recordings were made.[2]

The second concert included cantatas No. 150, *Nach dir, Herr, verlanget mich* ('Unto Thee, O Lord, do I lift up my soul') and No. 105, *Herr, gehe nicht ins Gericht mit deinem Knecht* ('Enter not into judgment with Thy servant, O Lord'). No. 150, reported Acton, 'is possibly the first Bach ever wrote, according to Mr Beckett's as always immensely helpful introduction.' The second work was 'perhaps written during Bach's first year in Leipzig. It starts with an important chorus beautifully sung by the [Cantata] Singers and sensitively directed by Mr Beckett, including a most delicately handled diminuendo to a lovely pianissimo. … How much we owe to John Beckett and his friends!'[3]

The third and final concert took place a week later and consisted of just one cantata, No. 174, *Ich liebe den Höchsten von ganzem Gemüte* ('I love the Almighty with all my heart'). This was preceded by Bach's Brandenburg Concerto No. 3, with John's transcription of the slow movement from the fourth organ sonata in E minor inserted by way of a second movement. Charles Acton was suitably impressed:

> With scores of cantatas to go … the darkness of February looks like being lightened for many years to come, thanks to John Beckett. I do not seem to have referred yet to his direction as such. That can only be because all the players

and singers and the composer himself are welded by Mr Beckett into such a complete and living unity of music.[4]

Squeezed in between the second and third concerts was a broadcast, on RTÉ Radio, of *Rakastava* by Sibelius, performed by the RTÉ Symphony Orchestra, conducted by John.[5]

The next big event that involved John was a performance of Bach's *Saint Matthew Passion* in Saint Patrick's Cathedral, Dublin, on 30 March. The soloists included Bernadette Greevy, Irené Sandford, Frank Patterson and William Young; the choirs of the Goethe Institute and Saint Patrick's Cathedral sang and the New Irish Chamber Orchestra performed. Charles Acton wrote:

> I predict that, in 40 or 50 years' time, there will be men who will assure their grandchildren that one of the memorable, influential occasions of their lives was the participation, as choristers of St Patrick's Cathedral, in Sunday's deeply-impressive and moving performance of Bach's St Matthew Passion there, in two sessions, Part I in the afternoon, Part II in the evening. When I say that the heart of this performance was John Beckett as conductor, readers will therefore know that it was a performance dedicated to Bach and God; and it should have pleased both.

Acton was full of praise for the performance and all the singers (who, incidentally sang in English) and applauded John for placing Frank Patterson, the Evangelist, in the pulpit to tell the Gospel story and 'elevate it to its rightful place'.[6] Michael Richter at last had the opportunity to sing Bach's music in the Goethe Institute Choir on the day, his birthday, though ironically he had to sing in English rather than his native German. According to him, it was John's choice that the words should be sung in English so that the congregation could follow the story.[7]

In the following month, John was featured on BBC Radio 3's *Early Music Forum*, which was presented by Nicholas Anderson. On the programme, John played a selection of pieces from *The Fitzwilliam Virginal Book*, and the BBC's recording of Bach's Cantata No. 199, *Mein Herze schwimmt in Blut* ('My heart is bathed in blood'), conducted by John, was included.[8]

John was one of the soloists in Frank Martin's 'piquant, delicious and too seldom heard essay exploring the contrasting tones and qualities of piano (Lynda Byrne), harpsichord (John Beckett) and harp (Denise Kelly) as a triple concerto' wrote Charles Acton of a RTÉ Symphony Orchestra concert held in the St Francis Xavier Hall in mid-May. This work, as well as music by Ravel, Stravinsky and Tchaikovsky were conducted by Pierre Colombo.[9]

In June, John and Ruth went on a holiday to the Netherlands, where John bought himself a pair of wooden clogs and wore them for a while. Vera

Škrabánek remembers this clearly. She and Petr had been in Florence and, when they returned to Dublin, John telephoned to invite them to Samuel's play *Happy Days*, which was being performed in the Players Theatre, Trinity College by the Cogitandum Theatre Company, directed by Brendan Ellis.[10] When Vera and Petr arrived at the theatre, they were astounded to discover John happily clumping around in his new clogs. 'John, is this comfortable?' Vera asked. 'It's very comfortable!' he replied. According to Vera, he wore the clogs for a few weeks until Ruth, obviously weary of hearing the constant *clop, clop, clop*, finally said, 'Listen, that's enough!'[11]

John conducted the New Irish Chamber Orchestra in a concert of music by Haydn, Bach and James Wilson, given in the Examination Hall of Trinity College. The concert began with Haydn's rarely performed Symphony No. 1 in D. This was followed by Bach's Cantata No. 202, *Weichet nur betrübte Schatten* ('Begone, dismal shadows'), the 'Wedding Cantata', sung by Irené Sandford – 'a gem', as Charles Acton described it. He also enjoyed Wilson's Harpsichord Concerto, Op. 76, played by Gillian Smith, and the final work, Bach's Orchestral Suite No. 4 in D.[12] Lindsay Armstrong remembers how much John loved Haydn and how there was a little bit of resistance among players in the orchestra when he introduced this composer into the repertoire, as it generally involved extra players and instruments. His dogmatic approach, his insistence on a minimum of vibrato and his stiff manner of conducting would not have endeared the players to him.[13]

On the following evening my father and I drove to the Bank of Ireland headquarters in Baggot Street to attend a reception that marked the beginning of the first Dublin International Organ Festival. This turned out to be a rather stiff and formal event during which everyone stood in the foyer of the building, making polite conversation, sipping wine and nibbling sandwiches. John and Ruth were among the guests. John had little time for the festival and the formalities, and chatted to us while Gerard Gillen made a speech – all he was interested in was the wine. As the evening wore on, he became more jolly and his caustic wit and cynical observations became a cause for much laughter. Also there were John O'Sullivan, David Lee and Professor Brian Boydell.[14]

Two days later I encountered John again, this time in Andrew Robinson's house in Donnybrook, where we had planned an evening of viol consort music. Shortly after I arrived, John appeared in the front garden in his huge pair of Dutch clogs, carrying his treble viol and two bags. As it was raining heavily, he looked wet and down in spirits but perked up when he came in. He told us that he enjoyed 'sloshing about' in his clogs. Because of a change of plan, we piled into Andrew's Volkswagen van and drove to Honor O Brolchain's house nearby.

When everyone was settled, we tuned up and began to play. Our consort must have presented a strange sight: five people playing viols in a kitchen, dressed in an assortment of casual clothing, with John in his unvarnished clogs and me in my wellington boots. However, the music, which was by Ferrabosco, was most enjoyable and we performed it well. Later, John produced the music of Jenkins's Fantasias and Pavanes à 5 and so we proceeded to try several of these.

In the middle of the music, Honor's little boy began to cry and had to be brought to bed. During the interlude we began to talk about Kenneth Grahame's book *The Wind in the Willows*.[15] John's ability to connect with children is recalled by Honor when, on one such evening he arrived at her house for some viol playing and spotted her daughter Isolde, then hardly three years of age, sitting on the sofa. Neither of them said a word, but Honor noticed that 'there was a meeting of souls'.[16]

We returned to the music by Ferrabosco and then to the Jenkins. By now Honor was becoming noticeably tired and so was I, but John pressed on until he called for 'just one more for the road' – a favourite expression of his. We finally stopped by about 11.30 and drank a glass of wine before leaving.[17]

We were to have many evenings like these. There was always a slight feeling of tension when John played with us; he was the one who decided what we would play and the number of times that we would repeat it. Normally, we did not dare to introduce decorations as John always played the music exactly as it was printed, in a rather bland but precise manner. Also we never dared to suggest a piece or a composer that he did not like. If he was in a Jenkins mood for the evening, we just played and talked about Jenkins – it was always clear that he had no intention of changing the music or the topic of conversation. We would generally take a short break for a cup of tea, during which his anxiousness to resume was always obvious. As soon as he sensed that everyone was refreshed, he would say, 'Let's get back to the music now!' I can remember one occasion when we sat around the kitchen table in Andrew's house during one of our breaks, drinking and eating. John spotted the Robinsons' cat, probably an offspring of Murray, and offered it a morsel of the cheese that he was eating. The cat nibbled off a piece and, without further ado, John placed the cheese back in his mouth.[18]

Charles Acton gave much praise to a recital of songs by Purcell sung by Frank Patterson, accompanied by John and Andrew Robinson on harpsichord and bass viol, in Christ Church Cathedral, Dublin at the beginning of July. The songs were interspersed with organ voluntaries by John Blow and Purcell, played on a chamber organ by Peter Sweeney. 'As was to be expected from these artists, the singing and playing were all most stylish and stylistic', Acton commented. I too attended the concert and found it most enjoyable.[19]

In preparation for the New Irish Chamber Orchestra's performance in the Flanders Festival, Bruges in July, John, the choir, the singers and the orchestra performed the planned all-Bach programme at two public concerts in St Ann's Church, Dawson Street a few days earlier.[20] The first concert consisted of two Brandenburg Concertos, Nos. 3 and 1, and two cantatas, No. 174, *Ich liebe den Höchsten von ganzem Gemüte* ('I love the Almighty with all my heart') and No. 79, *Gott der Herr ist Sonn' und Schild* ('The Lord God is a sun and shield'). Although the concert was well attended and much appreciated, Charles Acton had mixed views about it and found fault with some aspects of the performance.[21] He was more enthusiastic about the second concert, held on the following evening. This consisted of three cantatas: No. 150, *Nach dir, Herr, verlanget mich* ('Unto you, O Lord, do I lift up my soul'), No. 151, *Süsser Trost, mein Jesus kömmt* ('Sweet comfort, my Jesus comes') and No. 208, *Was mir behagt, ist nur die muntre Jagd!* ('The merry hunt is all that I love!') 'Last night's concert was as splendid as anyone could wish', Acton wrote. 'One can only hope that the Flanders audience enjoy their performances as much as I did.'[22]

The two concerts in Bruges took place on 26 and 27 July in the Saint Walburga Church.[23] Malcolm Proud, who was now living and studying harpsichord under Gustav Leonhardt in Amsterdam, remembers attending the concerts as he was playing in the International Harpsichord Week competition at the time.[24]

On the day after the second concert, John, a slimmed-down version of the orchestra, Irené Sandford and my father set off on probably what was to be John's most exciting journey in his life: a trip to China. I had been partly responsible for this venture. In 1977 I had gone on holiday to the People's Republic and, while there, had made an amateur cine film. Some time afterwards, Lindsay Armstrong, then the manager of the New Irish Chamber Orchestra, invited me to show my film to him, his wife Gillian Smith and friends at their home.[25] Lindsay then wrote to the Chinese Embassy in London in May 1979, expressing the wish to visit China in 1980. He pointed that a visit by an Irish orchestra would be all the more appropriate in the light of the imminent opening of diplomatic relations between the two countries.

He received no answer until mid May 1980 when, one morning, the telephone rang. An official from the embassy in London simply informed him that they were expected in Beijing on 29 July. Two frantic months of fundraising followed. The plan was to give seven concerts in three cities: Beijing, Chengdu and Xi'an.[26]

Unsurprisingly, John wanted a programme that would include music by Purcell and Bach. In addition, it would feature music by Irish composers Arthur Duff and John F. Larchet, and it was decided that a couple of popular Chinese songs would be sung as encores. Irené was to be the singer and Professor Tao Kiang, who taught Chinese in University College Dublin, selected the popular songs and helped her with the pronunciation. As a harpsichord was needed for the continuo, a small instrument made by my father was borrowed from a friend, and he was invited to come in order to tune and maintain it.[27] What worried John most of all were the obligatory inoculations.

John, the orchestra, Irené and my father arrived in Beijing on 29 July and were greeted by a large welcoming party, which included the first Irish Ambassador to China, John Campbell. They were then introduced to their three guides and interpreters, Mr Liu, Miss Qing and Mr Zhou. They were driven from the airport to the centre of Beijing and brought to the Friendship Hotel, where John and Cathal shared a suite of two bedrooms, a hall and a WC. John related his rather fanciful recollection to me in 1998:

> When we landed at Peking airport and we were taken in a bus, and the bus drove to the kind of hostel place where we were staying, which was terribly, terribly simple – it was like a military barracks, you know (which I liked very much – there were no frills about it whatsoever), and drew up in a kind of earthenware square – no, not tarred or paved at all (there was grass growing in it), and there was a sort of hissing noise – I can remember it distinctly getting off the bus. There was a very loud hissing noise, as if a gas main had suddenly burst and the gas was coming out under great pressure – sort of *SSSSS!* – like that, only very loud. And I didn't know what on earth it was, and I asked one of our minder blokes, and he said these little insects, they're like locusts, which are in the trees, and when the sun comes out on the trees, they all start to make this noise, and when the sun goes off, they STOP! – like that. Fifty thousand of them suddenly STOP! ... But I asked one of the Chinese people what they were and he said ['they're cicadas']. He said the Chinese name, and I said 'What does that mean?' And he said, 'It means the creatures that know what's what.' They know when the sun is shining and they know when the sun's not shining, you know, and they behave accordingly. That's what he told me.[28]

(John may have been aware of Henry James's famous remark, 'never spoil a good story for the sake of the truth'.) As the Friendship Hotel in Beijing would have been a good deal more sophisticated, John was possibly confusing it with another hotel that they stayed in later.

John and Cathal were thrown together, and from then on they shared accommodation throughout the tour. After the tour, John remarked on how they had sweated, slept, snored, joked and farted together; they had become, he added with a mischievous grin, 'farting friends'.[29]

In the evening, they were treated by the Ministry of Culture to a Peking roast duck banquet. Speeches were made and their host spoke warmly of the recently established diplomatic relations between Ireland and China.

They were up at half past six on the following morning; having breakfasted an hour later, they were brought to see the Great Wall of China and one of the nearby Ming Tombs.

The orchestra began rehearsing at eight o'clock in the morning of the following day – as Lindsay Armstrong wrote in *The Irish Times*, 'the earliest known rehearsal in the history of the NICO.' This first concert started with a selection of music by Henry Purcell, which was undoubtedly quite unfamiliar to the Chinese. The audience was noisier than what the orchestra was used to – a fact commented on by both Lindsay and John. John reported:

> The concerts were all much the same in that the venue was usually a very large hall full of people who, I certainly had the impression, had been detailed off by the party [cadres] that they must come to this recital, though they didn't partic- ularly want to. They made a terrific noise all the time and they were getting up, you know, to get ice creams and have a pee and doing this all the time, and talking to themselves and so on. I just didn't know how to deal with this and then I real- ized the only thing was to just fire ahead. ... When I at first was worried about it, I spoke to the Chinese blokes who were managing this stage and I said 'we're not going to be heard if that's going to go on in the next concert,' and he said 'well, you should be amplified – we should amplify the band.' And I had said no to that for the first concert, but I said yes to it subsequently. But there was no other way of doing it – you wouldn't have heard us at all!³⁰

The first half of the concert ended with Bach's 'Wedding Cantata', BWV 202, sung by Irené. The second half of the concert began with Mozart's *Divertimento* in D, K. 136. Next in the programme were the Irish composers: Arthur Duff and John F. Larchet. The Larchet work was *The Dirge of Ossian* and *MacAnanty's Reel*. The Duff was the *Irish Suite* for strings. Irené Sandford, who wore a dazzling green gown for the occasion, then sang four Irish folk songs. These were greeted with enthusiastic applause. After singing her two Chinese songs as encores, she was presented with such a large floral bouquet (known as a *hua lan*, 'flower basket') that it was necessary for two Chinese girls to present it to her. This was an over-the-top gesture typical of the period.

On the following day, everyone enjoyed a lazy two-hour cruise around the lake of the Summer Palace in one of two covered barges pulled by a motor boat, and were serenaded by Chinese student musicians, who played on traditional instruments. Some members of the Irish orchestra played Irish music for the students. For Cathal, this was an idyllic way to celebrate his seventieth birthday.

The next day the orchestra was brought on a three-hour tour of the Forbidden City. It may have been on this day when Cathal and John 'were nearly arrested in Peking when John cast an envious eye on a sample of Chinese calligraphy on a rough board at the entrance to the Forbidden City [and] endeavoured to buy it!!' wrote my father in his diary. 'When we returned it had been removed. He loves the rough, faded or worn.'[31] They were then taken to Chairman Mao's mausoleum, which, understandably, they viewed with a certain amount of reluctance. Lunch was a more pleasant occasion; it was given by John Campbell, in the Dowager Empress Ci Xi's favourite eating place in the nearby palace gardens. Afterwards the ambassador, his wife, John and Cathal walked through the oldest part of Beijing, which sadly was about to be demolished and replaced by apartment blocks.

The concert that evening, which was televised, was a great success. As the following day was Sunday, the orchestra was allowed to spend ten minutes in the Catholic cathedral, which was filling up for Mass. The orchestra was then brought to the famous and beautiful Temple of Heaven, before leaving for the airport and Chengdu.

After a three-hour flight, they arrived to flowers and greetings from members of the Arts Bureau, and professors and students of the Chengdu Music Conservatoire. In the evening they attended a reception, where they met the leading cultural and musical people; none of them had ever seen a harpsichord before.

The following morning Cathal, John, and Betty Sullivan slipped out of the hotel, avoiding the guides and went walking 'in the old part of this most interesting town', Cathal noted. 'We met all the people young and old, took snaps and had our breakfast in a little native restaurant.' John managed to buy the chopsticks with which he had eaten his breakfast. From now on, he and Cathal managed to escape the crippling officialdom and regularly went out on their own in the mornings among the people, much to the consternation of the guides, who reprimanded John for not obeying the rules. John later recollected how, on one evening, he wandered down the side streets while the others were visiting some gardens. He arrived at an ice-cream stall, and as he was so hot and weary, he bought an ice-cream for a trifling sum, sat down on the pavement and ate it while watching the world go by. This, to him, was the essence of pleasure. He said that if he ever returned, he would need more freedom. He cursed the authorities and demanded to know why one was not free to do and see what one liked.[32]

The concert hall in Chengdu held 3200 people and the acoustics were very dry. As there was no air conditioning, electric fans were produced. The orchestra rehearsed in the morning and in the afternoon there was more sightseeing.

Despite the heat and the electric fans 'blowing full blast over great blocks of ice', as Lindsay reported, the concert that evening was a great success.

Cathal and John were up early again the next morning and out walking in the streets. John relished seeing the local people doing their morning exercises under the trees, the children attending to their homework outside their little houses, people eating and men having their hair cut on the street. The first official business of the day was a visit to the zoo, where they saw pandas and a white peacock. Next they were taken to the Chengdu Music Conservatoire, where they met the professors and students. John was 'closeted with no less than nineteen conductors'. He and the various members of the orchestra were suitably impressed by the students' high standard of playing and the excellence of their teachers. In the afternoon they were brought to a Buddhist monastery that housed thirty-two monks. There they were given tea and their questions were answered, though some not very convincingly. At the concert that evening, the orchestra finally agreed to be amplified in order that they might be heard better in the huge hall above the chatter of the audience.

Cathal and John went out the next morning to meet some new friends that John had made: a young man who called himself Martin Mao and who spoke good English, and his girlfriend (whom he later married). John subsequently corresponded with the couple and later Martin's wife visited him in London when she was there. John and Cathal had 'a snack' with them that morning, walked around and returned to the hotel for breakfast. John succeeded in buying a bamboo chair in a shop where he found an elderly man making chairs. This light, practical chair, which was cleverly constructed without nails, was, in John's estimation, the best souvenir that he brought home from China. On flying home, it was tied with string to the stool for the double bass and treated as if it were part of the orchestral equipment. It lasted for the rest of his life and, as John reported, improved with age. 'When it gets my vast weight on it,' he explained, 'it gives a bit of a groan, but actually it keeps it in good condition, you know.'[33]

Later that morning they were taken to the Dujiangyan dam and the two-thousand-year-old irrigation system outside Chengdu. They visited some adjacent temples and were given a 'wonderful lunch with many toasts. We were nearly all tipsy,' Cathal reported.[34] Much to John's chagrin, bamboo chairs identical to the one that he had bought in Chengdu were being sold locally for a few yuan cheaper than for what he had paid. A photograph was taken of John and my father together; in it, John looks happy, though noticeably thin – hardly a figure of 'vast weight'.

As it had been a long day, the orchestra was happy to perform just one third of a concert in the evening; it included Irené Sandford singing 'The Last Rose of Summer' and 'Molly Malone'. Afterwards they were treated to a concert of traditional and classical music given by Chinese musicians: Cathal recorded that two Preludes by Chopin were performed on the piano. Following this came an excerpt from a Chengdu opera, 'clappers and all', during which most of the young people left the hall. Cathal and John relished the performance.

The group left Chengdu on the following morning for an early flight to Xi'an. In the evening they were taken to a three-hour-long classical Xi'an opera, which 'at times was hard going. The costumes were exquisite, the acting fine. We had an interpreter who helped us with the plot.' Lindsay Armstrong noted that there was a lull in the translation for quite some time. He turned around to discover the interpreter lying slumped in his seat fast asleep, 'presumably from linguistic exhaustion'. According to John:

> It went on all evening: a long, complicated story of court intrigue, centuries ago ... I mean, it was absolutely marvellous. And a gang of musicians, traditional instruments, flutes and reed instruments ... and drums – a lot of percussion – in a little kind of caged-in place on the right of the stage, belting away for all they were worth, without any sense of balance at all ... and the noise of the orchestra was tremendous! The hall was absolutely full ... I could really hardly believe I was there – it seemed incredible to be sitting in [the] slums [of] some city in the centre of China, with a crowded audience on a sweltering hot summer night, seeing and listening to this! ... Unforgettable! ... it thrilled me, absolutely.'[35]

On the following morning, the group was brought to see the city walls, a museum and to two pagodas. They rested in the afternoon and then Cathal and John walked through the old parts of the city, where John bought two bowls from a small restaurant. Cathal then brought him to a museum, which he had obviously missed, and showed him the Tang Dynasty glazed pottery figures. There they met a group of students, who promised to bring John to a pottery shop. In the evening, the others were taken to a tea house where they sat on a veranda by a beautiful lake sipping tea and beer in the darkness. By the time they returned to the hotel, John was already there, having bought another six bowls.

The highlight of the tour came on the following morning, when the group was brought to see the excavations at the imperial tomb of Qin Shi Huang, the great emperor and tyrannical founder, in 221 BC, of the Qin Dynasty. Here they saw the buried army of some 6000 terracotta warriors that had become famous throughout the world. The excavation work was far from complete and both Cathal and John saw more figures being unearthed.

In the afternoon, Cathal tuned the harpsichord, and another highly successful concert was given that evening.

The next morning was devoted to a get-together with the musicians from the Art School in Xi'an, who, according to Cathal 'were very appreciative of the help and advice given by members of NICO.'[36] Both he and Lindsay Armstrong recorded the great interest shown in the harpsichord. To demonstrate it, John played the accompaniment of a Tartini violin sonata after the violinist's wife had played it on the piano. Two of the orchestra's violinists, Mary Gallagher and Thérèse Timoney, joined forces with John and Betty Sullivan to play a Bach Trio Sonata, which 'went down very well'.

In the evening the final concert was given; it was a great success. According to Lindsay, Irené Sandford sang better than ever and he added mischievously, 'even a twitch of a smile [was] seen around the corners of John's mouth'.

Cathal's diary for the next day began with a description of being out by seven o'clock with John, Jacques Leydier and Irené Sandford to watch the locals doing 'sword exercises' and walking until breakfast at nine. More sightseeing followed; they rested after lunch and later John and Cathal went ambling around the old part of the city. After they had started to pack for the following morning, they sat down for the official farewell dinner, at the end of which Lindsay made a speech. They then adjourned to John Campbell's suite in the hotel for after-dinner drinks.

Early in the morning of 12 August, the orchestra set off by plane to Beijing. There they hosted a banquet for their guides and friends, and returned to the airport, where they presented gifts to their guides. After an emotional farewell, during which Miss Qing burst into tears (not an uncommon occurrence at that time owing to the harshness of life during and after the Cultural Revolution), they boarded the aircraft and soared off into the darkening sky.[37]

Thirty-Nine
1980–81

Instead of returning to Dublin with everyone else, John made his way to Amsterdam, where he joined Ruth for another holiday in the Netherlands. On their first day in the capital, they stayed overnight with Malcolm Proud and his girlfriend Susan Carolan, who were living in an apartment at the top of a house in a small street named Raamdwarsstraat, overlooking a canal. Before Malcolm and Susan left on the following day for a holiday of their own, John became quite nervous when Malcolm carried his precious collection of bowls down the precipitous stairs to the hall door. Luckily he met with no disaster.[1]

My father had arrived home safely, with the harpsichord and the bamboo chair, which John collected soon after he returned to Dublin at the end of August. During the time he was in China, I had been reading a translation of the Japanese classic *The Pillow Book of Sei Shōnagon*, which he had enthusiastically recommended to my father some time previously. Earlier, he had borrowed James Boswell's *London Journal* from Cathal, which he read and greatly enjoyed; any literature connected with Samuel Johnson interested him immensely.[2]

Vera Škrabánek remembers the enormous impression that the trip to China had made on John. He spoke about it often, brought a highly-treasured bowl to her house, from which they drank tea, and refused to drink anything else but green tea when they ate in a local Chinese restaurant.[3] Everyone learned how he had slipped away from the official guides and mingled with the locals in the back streets, and everyone knew about the bamboo chair.[4]

A person to whom he sent a postcard from China was his former wife, Vera. After they had parted, John had kept in touch with her and had sent her money. She had lived in Galway and Dublin for a while[5] and had continued with her dressmaking and painting.⁵ Examples of her drawings and oil paintings were exhibited along with works by Soonoo Choksey at Lauderdale House, Highgate, in March 1980.⁶ She later moved to France where she lived in Saint-Amour, in the Jura, then Rasiguères, west of Perpignan.⁷

A musical rarity that John conducted for an RTÉ radio programme in August was Schubert's *Grand Duo* in C major, orchestrated by Brahms's friend Joseph Joachim – a work that scholars at the time believed was either a draft or a piano reduction of a lost symphony. This was performed by the RTÉ Symphony Orchestra. The two other works were Igor Stravinsky's *Suites Nos. 1 and 2*.⁸

In the following month the LP issued by Claddagh Records, *Bernadette Greevy sings Bach Arias*, recorded in 1976 and discussed earlier, was released, and John conducted Haydn's Symphony No. 93 in D major and the *Theresienmesse* (Saint Theresa Mass, H. 22/12) at the end of the Kilkenny Arts Festival. This involved the New Irish Chamber Orchestra, the choir of Saint Anne's Cathedral, Belfast, and soloists.⁹

A few days later, John conducted the RTÉ Symphony Orchestra again, this time in the Saint Francis Xavier Hall, Dublin. This 'public studio concert', which was recorded and then broadcast in November, began with Mozart's Symphony No. 34 in C.¹⁰ John used Mozart's Minuet K. 409 between the first and second movements, following the musicologist Alfred Einstein's theory. The other work in the concert was *Four Legends from the Kalevala*, Op. 22 by Sibelius. 'John Beckett has such a reputation for Bach, Purcell and earlier music that it is good to be reminded again of his equal feeling for the romantics', wrote Charles Acton.¹¹ Present at that concert was Honor O Brolchain, who found the performance of these four tone poems by Sibelius 'absolutely staggering'. 'The sound quality is something I remember as being really very, very rich, very unusual and not an actual sound that I had heard before, even though I went to orchestral concerts all the time,' she explained. 'So it was wonderful, wonderful.'¹² David Carmody recollects that the music of Sibelius, along with that of Bach and Mahler, were John's three great passions, and that he 'got terrific sonorities' from the orchestra when he conducted works by Sibelius.¹³

John and Ruth were present at a 'Chinese evening' a couple of days later, hosted by Lindsay Armstrong and Gillian Smith. This was an occasion for members of the New Irish Chamber Orchestra to celebrate the recent tour of China and to look at photographs and ciné films. John looked fed up when some shaky amateurish footage was shown to the accompaniment of Chinese music played on a record, though every time a shot of him or my father appeared, there was a loud cheer from everyone. John and Ruth, along with Irené Sandford, Thérèse and John Kinsella showed more interest in slides that I had taken in Iceland, and which I showed at the end of the evening by way of a change. The two Johns declared that they had wanted to travel to Iceland and now were determined to do so.[14]

The next day, Sunday, John conducted an all-Bach concert in Saint Ann's Church, Dawson Street, in aid of the Christ Church restoration fund. This featured the 'Wedding Cantata', No. 202, sung by Irené Sandford, Cantata No. 82, *Ich habe genug* ('It is enough'), sung by William Young, and John's arrangements of two Trio Sonatas: BWV 529, in C and 525 in E flat (transposed to G for flute and violin). John played the harpsichord realization in the trio sonatas and conducted the two cantatas.[15]

Later in the month I joined Andrew Robinson and friends for an evening of viol music in the Robinsons' house, this time without John. Barra Boydell, now a member of our group, produced some delightful Paduanas, Galliards and Almains by William Brade, several of which we dashed off with great spirit and good humour. We realized that we would not play such music or be so bold with decorations if John had been present.[16] When John did join us at another session the following month, he showed a distinct lack of interest in these pieces and some anonymous dance music, but later launched into some Jenkins pavanes that he gleefully produced from his bag. One piece in particular fascinated him and so we played it again and again, and finally stopped at one o'clock in the morning, exhausted.[17]

When we students assembled for the viol consort class in the Academy in mid November John appeared wearing a pair of black leather clogs, which he had bought in Germany. He had been there with the New Irish Chamber Orchestra and James Galway, who had performed Vivaldi's famous *Four Seasons*, arranged for flute, and probably an arrangement of Bach's violin concerto in A minor, BWV 1041 and the Orchestral Suite No. 2 in B minor, BWV 1067.[18]

If Vivaldi had not been bad enough, John now had to face Handel. Later in the same month he conducted *Alexander's Feast*, performed by the New Irish Chamber Orchestra, Our Lady's Choral Society and soloists in the Augustinian Priory, John's Lane, Dublin. Carol Acton found the performance dull. This, she claimed, was not due to the choir or orchestra, but to the singers, who were 'not so happy'. It seems that John, unsurprisingly, was not happy either, for, as Carol added, 'Ultimate control rests in the conductor and John Beckett's inflexible and four-square beat was the real reason for turning a lovely work into a "worthy" one.'[19]

In mid December John was involved in the Goethe Institute's annual

Christmas concert, which was given in the Examination Hall of Trinity College. This consisted mostly of choral works sung by the Goethe Institute Choir, directed by Cáit Cooper. The concert ended with a performance of Mozart's *Missa Brevis* in C, the 'Sparrow' Mass, conducted by John. 'Altogether this was one of the institute's best Christmas concerts', concluded Acton in his review.[20]

The year ended with John, Ruth and Betty Sullivan coming to our house in Knockmaroon shortly after Christmas to play Mozart piano trios on a newly-completed fortepiano that my father had assembled from a kit. They had not wanted an audience, but were happy to play for us and a friend who lived nearby, David Staines. Typically, there were few preliminaries on arrival; they sat down and immediately launched into Mozart's Piano Trio No. 6 in G, K. 564. For the rest of the evening they worked their way through most of the trios, thoroughly at ease and enjoying themselves. For me, then in my mid twenties, it was a treat to relax before a blazing turf fire and listen to such exquisite music being nonchalantly dashed off by professional musicians. John showed his pleasure by grinning broadly at my father, who turned the pages of his music for him. However, John was not totally satisfied with the sound of the new fortepiano, as the notes buzzed when he played them staccato. Despite this, the others loved the sound. John tried some movements on my father's restored square piano in order to hear the difference.

After a short break for a glass of whiskey, they were off again with renewed vigour. Finally, at ten o'clock, having played themselves to a stop, they joined us for an impromptu supper, during which John drank two cups of hot cocoa that I made him. At half past ten we listened in silence to a Bach cantata on BBC Radio 3 that John had requested to hear and, shortly after it had finished, they left.[21]

The usual three concerts of Bach cantatas in St Ann's Church took place in the new year. The first one, on 1 February, began with Bach's Orchestral Suite No. 4 in D, BWV 1069. The reason for performing this work was that the opening movement of the last cantata to be sung during the third concert was a reworking by Bach of the Suite's first movement with full choral parts added. The second and final work was Cantata No. 78, *Jesu, der du meine Seele* ('Jesus, who hath wrested my soul').[22]

The next concert, on the following Sunday, featured Bach's secular cantata No. 209 in Italian, *Non sa che sia dolore* ('He knows not what sorrow is') and No. 147, *Herz und Mund und Tat und Leben* ('Heart and mouth and deed and life').[23]

The third and final concert took place a week later and began with Cantata No. 12, *Weinen, Klagen, Sorgen, Zagen* ('Weeping, wailing, fretting, fearing'). The second cantata, No. 110, *Unser Mund sei voll Lachens* ('Let our mouths be full of laughter') was the one that incorporated the opening movement of the Orchestral Suite No. 4 plus the four-part choir. 'It certainly was a magnificent sound – how Bach could rejoice!' enthused Acton. He concluded, 'So ends another sequence. What a marvellous service John Beckett performs for us with his friends! May they flourish in our gratitude!' A large and enthusiastic audience attended this last concert. Acton noted that 'Such, again, was the demand for seats that, half an hour before the start, the centre of the church was already full. The popularity of these concerts is extremely heartening, even if it is richly deserved.'[24]

At around this time a review appeared in *The Irish Times* of a record that had been released some two years previously: *Carolan's Favourite – The Music of Carolan Volume 2*. This featured the talented Derek Bell playing music composed by the blind harpist Turlough O'Carolan on a gut-strung neo-Irish harp, sometimes with one or all the members of the traditional Irish group The Chieftains and at other times with the New Irish Chamber Orchestra conducted by John, whose talent, the reviewer believed, was wasted on this occasion.[25]

On a Sunday afternoon towards the end of February, my parents and I collected our friends Professor Tao Kiang and his wife Trudi and drove to John's house in Bray. John had invited us so that we could admire three Chinese scrolls that hung on a wall in his living room. All the scrolls featured elegant calligraphy, written on paper: one had been bought and the other two had been given to John in China by students whom he had met and befriended. Tao had sent them all to Hong Kong to be mounted on silk and now they had been returned.

When we arrived at John's tiny house we were greeted at the gate by him and Ruth. They escorted us into a warm living room, where just inside the door, on a rough white wall, hung the three long vertical scrolls, the strong, black calligraphy standing out boldly against a white background. Pleased as Punch, John bid us sit down in his assorted collection of chairs (including the bamboo one he had brought from China) and asked Tao to translate the texts. One was a poem by the famous Tang dynasty poet Li Bai (Li Po), and the other two, written by the students, were slogans concerning worldwide friendship.

Ruth laid the table with sandwiches, cakes and apple tart, and while we ate and chatted, logs crackled in the fire and John's beloved Black Forest clock ticked loudly on the wall behind him. John talked volubly about the marvellous time that he and Cathal had had in China, asked Tao many questions about the country and its people, and showed us the rough pottery bowls. Although they lacked refinement, they had a certain rustic charm.

Tao was anxious to return home, but John and Ruth begged us to relax and enjoy ourselves, as the 'night was young'. John opened a bottle of fiery Chinese *mao tai* (made from sorghum) which Tao had brought, offered it to us, but when we refused, he poured himself a generous helping and invited us to take some dry Martini, which we accepted.

Despite our protests, John continued to pile more logs on the fire, so that we were obliged to remove layers of clothing. We all had a go at sitting in John's bamboo chair. Having gone through the motions of offering us more *mao tai*, which in normal circumstances is sipped from tiny glasses for formal toasts, John helped himself to another glass and soon became mellow and more talkative. He reminisced about some of his experiences in China and later asked if we would like to hear some good music. Removing a rug from the top of his hi-fi equipment, he treated us to one section of a record, playing it several times in succession: some delightful music by François Couperin played by John's favourite early music group, Musica Antiqua Köln. Taking draughts of his *mao tai*, he rolled his eyes in pleasure, conducted with his arms and expressed his deep appreciation of the music. Obviously uncomfortable, Tao began to fidget again and expressed his wish to go home, despite the fact that everyone else was relaxed and that John was showing him various books containing Japanese calligraphy and art – John was probably unaware that few Chinese people appreciate the Japanese arts. So, reluctantly we made ready to leave and hit the road at about nine o'clock.[26]

John was in great form when I arrived at the Robinsons' house on a wet and windy evening a couple of days later for a session of Fantasias by Jenkins. We laughed and joked a lot, despite the fact that our instruments constantly went out of tune because of the damp weather. We played almost non-stop, only resting briefly to drink a glass of white wine. John would have played all night if Jenny and I had not collapsed from sleepiness, no doubt aided and abetted by the cheap wine.[27]

An event that John and Ruth greatly enjoyed was a reconstruction of a Lutheran service held in the chapel of Trinity College on the first Sunday of March. The original service had taken place in March 1714. The music, which included works by Bach and other composers, was directed by John O'Sullivan. Bach's Cantata No. 182, *Himmelskönig, sei willkommen* ('King of Heaven, be Thou welcome') was performed last. I sat beside John and Ruth, and afterwards went with them to a crowded pub in Pearse Street for a quick drink. John and Ruth then left for home by bus.[28]

On 27 March John faced the biggest challenge in his conducting career: the premiere performance in Ireland of Deryck Cooke's performing version of

Mahler's final symphony, No. 10 in F sharp. Mahler only wrote out the first movement of this mighty work in full; the four remaining movements remained as sketches and drafts. Encouraged by Mahler's widow Alma, the pianist and musicologist Deryck Cooke revised a 1960 version of the work and produced a full performing version in 1964, which was never published. A revision followed in 1972 (which was published in 1976) and another was completed in 1976 (which was not published until 1989).[29] The 1972 revision was therefore the version used by John and the RTÉ Symphony Orchestra, and performed by them in the Saint Francis Xavier Hall in Dublin.[30]

John would have been well acquainted with this music. His main difficulty was to inspire the orchestra to produce an acceptable public performance (which would be recorded) in just three days. At this period the orchestra was not first rate by international standards and had never tackled this long and demanding work before. Gerard Victory, who was then the head of music in RTÉ, must have been very brave to entrust John with this task, considering that his conducting technique was far less sophisticated than most other conductors in Ireland at the time. In order to help him, Victory loaned him a recording of the symphony.[31] Presumably John was chosen because of his knowledge and love of Mahler, though it is quite possible that he had insisted that he conduct the work himself.

Rehearsing this difficult music was frustrating both for the orchestra and for John. Although members of the orchestra were very critical of John's conducting style, there was tremendous respect for his knowledge and musicianship.[32] The trumpeter James Cavanagh, who played on this occasion, points out that as John was a fine example of a person with inbuilt musicianship, his poor conducting technique became secondary owing to the strength of his individuality. The members of the orchestra were irritated by John's habit of stopping after every few bars to correct mistakes and give instructions.[33] Undoubtedly John was frustrated by the poor standard of playing by some of the musicians; David Carmody, who played the horn in the orchestra, remembers how John spent a whole morning, much to the annoyance of the other players, rehearsing just the opening section of the first movement, scored for violas only, in an effort to get them to play in tune. In the end, the hard work paid off and the orchestra gave a reasonably acceptable performance of the work, but it had been diffi-cult for everyone. The live concert was the only occasion when they actually played the work straight through without stopping.[34] Because of this, the music critic Michael Dervan, who attended the concert, opined that it sounded like a rehearsal. However, he qualified this remark by saying that it 'actually sounded a bit like Mahler', which most performances of the composer's music at that time in Ireland did not. 'So, it was astonishingly good, even though it was *very* unpolished,' he added.[35]

Charles Acton expressed a similar view in his review of the public performance, though he was somewhat more circumspect:

> There was no doubt whatever of Mr Beckett's knowledge, understanding, deep love and full sense of Mahlerian style. Not that all the orchestra were as committed to it as he was. For such an undertaking, however, I suspect that rehearsal time had to be on the short side, because in all sections there were imperfections, or evidence of lack of polish as well. May we regard this performance as a try-out for a performance by the orchestra with John Beckett in the National Concert Hall – and, please, soon enough for the results of this occasion's hard work to be still in their minds as they restart rehearsal?[36]

Listening now to an indifferent recording copied for John by RTÉ Radio, it is easy to spot the imperfections.[37] The meandering melody played by the violas at the beginning of the first movement is not quite together and, in general, the ensemble is poor. Acton commented on the rather slow speed that John chose for this movement.[38] The second *scherzo* movement, a sure test for any conductor, sounds rather scrappy; on the whole, it was the least successful of the five movements. From this point on the performance improves; the third *Purgatorio* movement starts confidently but is perhaps a little rushed, in the fourth the differing tempi are handled well, and in the *Finale* the startling drum wallops at the beginning sound a little anaemic; however, the passionate slow sections are quite effective.

The other work in the concert, which was played first, was Schubert's Symphony No. 8 in B minor, D.759 (the 'Unfinished').[39]

A small incident that I noted in my diary shortly afterwards is probably worth mentioning. While playing viol consort music with John in the Robinsons' house, he tore up a handwritten copy of an *In Nomine* by William Byrd, which he had decided he did not like. As John had no qualms about tearing up a work by a composer that he admired so much, he certainly would have had no misgivings about destroying his own music, upon which he set no store.[40]

On Holy Thursday of the following month, John conducted a performance of Bach's *Saint Matthew Passion*, performed in the Ulster Hall, Belfast by the Ulster Orchestra and Singers, with Irené Sandford, Frank Patterson and other soloists. Alfred Burrowes wrote in *The Irish Times*:

> We hear much fine music well performed these days, but very rarely are we brought into contact with the spirit of Bach or the high quality of the music, so

many will be grateful to the Ulster Singers for their foresight in bringing from Dublin Mr John Beckett, along with his genuine feel for the splendour of Bach, one who conveys it straightforwardly and with spacious gesture.

Although he listed some minor faults in the singing and playing, he was happy overall with the performance.[41] In the audience was John's school pal Robin McKinney, who had been in St Columba's College, Dublin with him. The two men were delighted to meet each other once again.[42]

Nicholas Anderson, who had organized the recordings of the Bach cantatas for the BBC, was now engaged in producing a performance of Telemann's four-hour long opera *Der Geduldiger Socrates* ('The Patient Socrates') in English for the 300th anniversary of the composer's birth. The BBC Scottish Symphony Orchestra and fifteen soloists, conducted by Roger Norrington, were to be recorded in Glasgow. A whole week of rehearsals was planned. However, the conductor did not turn up on the first morning. Nicholas rang Roger, who apologized for not being well enough and wondered if Nicholas could find somebody else to take the rehearsal. Nicholas, livid and very nervous, rang the head of his department, Ernest Warburton, and explained his predicament. When Ernest asked him if he had any ideas, he said he had three: he could ask Nicholas Kraemer, John Beckett or 'somebody like Jane Glover' to conduct. As Kraemer was not free, he rang John in Dublin. Nicholas said, 'I've got an orchestra sitting here, a week's work, a Telemann opera and nobody to conduct it.' John's reply was, 'What do you want me to do about it?' When Nicholas asked him if he was free, John said, 'Ring me back in half an hour and I'll give you my answer.'

Nicholas rang him again as planned. 'Nicholas,' said John, 'I'm coming over. Meet me at the airport and make sure you have the score – the whole score – in your hand!' Nicholas had never been so pleased to see John in all his life when he arrived at Glasgow Airport. John seized the score and studied it intently while they travelled by taxi to the studio. Once inside, he took over 'in the most amazing way,' as Nicholas recalls. The orchestra did not like the look of him and when one or two of them 'started playing up', John 'delivered a broadside at them.' As the double-bass player was not performing in the way that John wanted, John said – in front of everybody – 'Can you hear yourself? Can you hear what you're doing?' and tore him apart. 'It's a most *dreadful* noise!' he added, leaning on the word 'dreadful' in his inimitable manner. 'You could almost see steam coming out of his ears,' was Nicholas's description of the double-bass player's reaction. However, by the end of the week all the members of the orchestra genuinely loved John. When several of the musicians approached Nicholas and asked him where he had found John, he replied, 'I found him in Dublin, actually'. John had thrown himself at the whole opera

and it was a huge success. He saved Nicholas's bacon, a great deal of embarrassment and a lot of unnecessary expense. Nicholas felt that he could never thank
him enough for what he had done.[43]

Although modern instruments were used for the production, they were
played in a light manner, in imitation of the Baroque style, and the continuo was
played on a harpsichord. The ensemble is slightly untidy in the Overture, though
all the parts are very clear. The music, composed in 1721, when Telemann was
director of the Opera House, is very fine. The recording was broadcast on BBC
Radio 3 in November.[44]

After the recording, Nicholas and his wife Alison, his sister and her husband,
John, the soprano Patrizia Kwella (who had sung in the opera) and her husband
went out to dinner at an excellent Italian restaurant chosen by Nicholas's sister.
John loved it. After the meal, the waiter asked John if he would like a digestif.
'Yes, I would,' replied John, 'I want a *grappa!*' After a few minutes the manager
appeared and said, '*Grappa* – no *grappa.*' John exploded: 'You call this a bloody
Italian restaurant and there's no *grappa*? Go and find some!' The manager was
obliged to go out and return, about half an hour later, with a bottle of the
requested beverage. Nicholas could hardly believe what had happened. Needless
to say, the manager was very grateful when John gave him a five-pound note for
his troubles.[45]

After John had spent a holiday in Spain with Ruth[46] I next saw him at the
inaugural public concert of the Junior Irish Youth Orchestra in Clongowes
Wood College on 24 July[47] and then, two days later, in the Oscar Theatre in
Ballsbridge, where Imrat and Vilayat Khan performed Indian music on *sitar* and
tabla. The first half consisted of one long *rāg*, divided into several sections. We
greatly admired the musicians' incredible dexterity and ability to extemporise.
The music was both soothing and spontaneous; both the musicians seemed to
read the other's mind and frequently grinned at each other.

In the second half of the concert, three shorter works, introduced by
Imrat Khan, were performed. Afterwards, John and Ruth kindly drove me to
Dundrum, which would have been quite out of their way, so that I could join my
parents in my aunt's house.[48]

The following incident demonstrated – to their friend Vera Škrabánek at
least – how naïve John could be sometimes. One day, when he and Ruth were
visiting Vera and Petr, John said, 'We were walking in the Wicklow Mountains
and came across a little cottage with walls of cut wood arranged around it,
stacked in the continental way.' He and Ruth stopped to talk to the inhabitants,
an elderly couple, and came to the conclusion that they spoke a Slavic language.
When John asked Vera if she would go with them and talk to the people, she said

that she would think about it. She explained to him that people like her, who
had grown up under a Communist regime, needed to be very wary. She then
pointed out that if a couple in their late sixties or seventies lived secluded in
the Wicklow Mountains, they might possibly be hiding and would not welcome
anyone who spoke their language and asked questions. This had not occurred
to John; he just wanted to be friendly and wondered if Vera could act as an
interpreter.[49] Ruth would have been more politically aware, as she had spent
some time in Communist Bulgaria in 1969, researching folk music. As she had
been forced to have an additional vaccination on arrival in Bulgaria, her arm
had become infected and she was sent to hospital under threat of having the
arm amputated – a devastating prospect for a professional musician. While in
Bulgaria, she had written often to her daughter Rose and had posted a ten-page
letter to John.[50]

John and Ruth went on another holiday at around this time, this time to
Germany; we received a picture postcard depicting the cathedral in Bad Aachen
from them with a message scrawled in John's almost unreadable handwriting.
He reported that they were 'Enjoying the trip offaly. No mosquitos!'[51]

In mid September John accompanied Bernadette Greevy in a recital of songs
in the Burke Hall, Trinity College. Charles Acton reported:

> How fortunate Miss Greevy was to have Mr Beckett to work with her! Quite
> apart from his total sympathy and support throughout the evening, his warm
> richness in the Handel was not only a quality of sound that I have not before
> heard from that piano, but created the impression of a full company of strings,
> as it would have been in the opera house. This was undoubtedly one of the best
> of all the recitals I have heard from her. It was a privilege to be there.[52]

Viol sessions now resumed in the Robinsons' house. I played again in John's
viol consort class and, at the end of September, joined his chamber music class
in the Dagg Hall of the Royal Irish Academy of Music to play basso continuo on
my bass viol.[53]

After conducting Vivaldi's *Gloria* and Haydn's *Maria Theresa Mass* in a production featuring the Wicklow Choral Society, the New Irish Chamber Orchestra
and soloists in St Patrick's Church, Wicklow at the end of September,[54] John told
me that he was off for a short visit to London to see the Great Japan Exhibition
in the Royal Academy of Art and to see a Kabuki play. He urged me to go too.
When, shortly afterwards, I discovered that I had a few days off from work over
a bank holiday weekend and told John that I was toying with the idea of going to
London, he simply said, 'Well, *go*! I know you'll enjoy yourself.' I went, visited
the wonderful exhibition, bought the catalogue and saw *The Seven Samurai*, a

film that I believe John had recommended, in the Academy Cinema. A black and white production, it was made in 1954 and directed by Arika Kurosawa.[55]

One day at work in early December I received at least three messages, from three mutual friends, to ring John urgently. It turned out that he had been trying to contact me at home, where our telephone was out of order. When I contacted him, all he wanted to know was if I was free on 19 July in the following year for a recital of viol music in the Dagg Hall! This was a typical example of the way John was inclined to fret about relatively small matters if he could not contact somebody immediately.[56]

In mid December John conducted a Christmas concert presented by the Goethe Institute in the new National Concert Hall. Featuring the Goethe Institute Choir and the New Irish Chamber Orchestra, the programme consisted of German and English Christmas carols, Bach's Brandenburg Concerto No. 4 and Parts 1 and 2 of his *Christmas Oratorio*.[57]

The year ended on a high note for me when I was invited to play basso continuo for a Sonata in F by Telemann for recorder, played by Jenny Robinson, bass viola da gamba, played by Andrew Robinson and harpsichord by David Milne. This was performed, with more chamber music and works sung by the Camerata Singers, in the National Gallery of Ireland. Several of the musicians and singers became anxious when they spotted John and Ruth in the audience. However, when I met John at the reception after the concert, he, mellow after a few drinks, grasped my hand and congratulated me warmly. My parents later told me that he had done likewise with them after we had performed. John then congratulated Andrew and Jenny and mentioned a work by Bach that he wanted us to play. I spent almost the rest of the evening chatting to both him and Ruth in the gallery restaurant, where a reception was in full swing.[58]

Forty

1982

The annual Bach cantata series started on 7 February 1982 with Cantatas Nos. 61, *Nun komm, der Heiden Heiland* ('Come now, saviour of the gentiles') and 71, *Gott ist mein König* ('God is my King'). After a lengthy and informative introductory speech delivered by John, the concert began with No. 71, after which No. 61 was performed, and then No. 71 was repeated in full – a new and innovative feature. When, after the concert, I spoke to John and praised his idea of repeating one cantata, he replied that ideally he would have loved to have performed both, to have had a pint and then to have come back to play them again![1] Charles Acton welcomed John's new idea. 'In general we hear these works only once and for all from Mr Beckett and his friends, therefore virtually only once in a lifetime here. The chance therefore to soak oneself in this glorious music a second time was a cause of real gratitude', he wrote. He described *Gott ist mein König* as a 'splendiferous affair'.[2]

In the second concert, the audience was treated to Cantata No. 60, *O Ewigkeit, du Donnerwort* ('O Eternity, Thou word of thunder'), No. 157, *Ich lasse dich nicht, du segnest mich denn* ('I will not let Thee go, except Thou bless me!') and No. 60 again. John, in his introduction, mentioned that the composer Alban Berg had incorporated the final chorale of the latter cantata, with its extraordinary and complex harmony, into his violin concerto.[3]

My father and I attended the third and last concert of the series. This time we heard Cantata No. 182, *Himmelskönig, sei willkommen* ('King of Heaven, be Thou welcome'), No. 4, *Christ lag in Todesbanden* ('Christ lay in the bonds of death') and No. 182 again, in which Jenny Robinson played the treble recorder obbligato. Once again, Acton was very satisfied with the music, the playing and the singing.[4]

Towards the end of March John went to a concert of Indian music played by Ravi Shankar in the National Concert Hall. He had high praise for this concert when we met in the Robinsons' house for an evening of viol music on the following day and almost ticked me off for not going to hear such a famous Indian musician perform. We conversed while relaxing over a glass of wine, having played through a programme of music that John had drawn up for a proposed recital in Malahide Castle at the end of June.[5]

Bach's *Saint Matthew Passion* was performed for the first time in the new National Concert Hall on Sunday, 4 April; the production, conducted by John, featured the Goethe Institute Choir, the Boys of Saint Patrick's Cathedral, the New Irish Chamber Orchestra and soloists, including Frank Patterson as the Evangelist, Irené Sandford, and William Young as Christus. While Acton praised the performance, he was not happy with the hall's acoustics. This problem would later be rectified.[6]

John's intense love of religious icons was very much in evidence later in the month when I gave him some unwanted Sotheby's catalogues of icons after we had met to rehearse some viol music. He was delighted with these booklets and raved about the icons depicted in them and icons in general. When we relaxed after a subsequent rehearsal, he surprisingly refused to drink any wine with us. We pressed him for an explanation and he reluctantly told us that a friend had given him a present of some excellent poteen and that he had rather overdone it during the afternoon![7]

John was involved in a Haydn 250th anniversary concert that involved Mirette Dowling and her Wicklow Choral Society in May; the choir, soloists and the New Irish Chamber Orchestra performed the composer's Symphony No. 104 (the 'London') and his *Heiligmesse* (the *Missa Sancti Bernadi di Offida* of 1796) in St Patrick's Church, Wicklow.[8]

Before I set off on a holiday around the Greek islands John begged me to bring back an icon for him. As there was no way that I could get my hands on, or even afford, to buy a genuine antique icon in such a touristy region of Greece, I had to settle on a modern and brightly coloured image of the Blessed Virgin, which I purchased in a tourist shop on the island of Santorini for a sum that just about suited my pocket. This, I realized, was a far cry from the type of icon that enthralled John; what he relished were dark, worn, cracked and naively-painted images rescued from obscure Orthodox churches – the cruder the better. John went through the motions of thanking me and admiring the little icon when I presented it to him on my return, but I could see that he was both disappointed and unimpressed.[9]

On 7 June, the first of a series of radio programmes entitled *The Romantic*

Composer, which was presented by John, was broadcast on RTÉ Radio 1. In this first programme, he introduced works by Weber. There were thirteen programmes in all; the rest featured Schumann, Chopin, Mendelssohn, Berlioz, Liszt, Wagner, Brahms, Dvořák, Tchaikovsky, Fauré, Mahler and Richard Strauss.[10] The producer of the programme, Venetia O'Sullivan, reported that the production was 'a bit of a strain', though after they had finished the last programme, John had said to her, 'Thank you very much – you did help.' Venetia remembered that John had agreed to present the programmes as he was short of cash.[11]

In his introduction to the third programme of the series, John O'Donovan wrote in the *RTÉ Guide*'s *Music Notes* that John was 'presenting a Beckettean view of Chopin in his series *The Romantic Composer* at 8.40.' He then took the opportunity to have a go at John:

> An excellent man, John Beckett, if it weren't for the appalling gap in his culture that prevents him from hearing much of any significance in Handel. That mighty man has become an avoided subject between us ever since the day John Beckett, in a carefree moment, made a slighting reference in my presence to George Frideric, receiving in return a stream of invective against his pet Gustav Mahler which seemed to affect him more deeply than I had been by his anti-Handel crack. Incidentally, since his austere shedding of flesh, John Beckett has started to look like Gluck, a development I shall continue to observe with interest.

The article was accompanied by a large impressive photograph of John staring directly into the lens of the camera, wearing his trademark open-necked shirt.[12]

Our concert in Malahide Castle took place on the evening of 27 June. This was the first public recital to be given by our group, which we had decided to call the Dublin Consort of Viols. The consort consisted of John and me on treble viols, Honor O Brolchain and Marion Doherty on tenors and Andrew Robinson on bass. On this occasion we were joined by Jenny Robinson on recorder; unfortunately she was suffering from influenza at the time. We rehearsed in a room upstairs while the seating in the banqueting hall was being arranged. When all was ready, we went down to tune and practise. We retired when members of the audience drifted in and returned when the hall was full. The recital was pleasantly informal and the atmosphere was friendly and relaxed. Despite this, however, one of the pieces – a Fantasy by William Byrd – was rather shaky and even John made a mistake.

During the interval, we relaxed upstairs, drank tea and ate sandwiches. Fifteen minutes later by John's pocket watch, we descended and began the second half with three In Nomines by William Byrd after Andrew had sung the

original plainchant (*In nomine domini*) by way of illustration. After some variations by van Eyck played by Jenny on the recorder, we concluded the concert
with a lively set of dances by Holborne, which was greeted with a hearty round
of applause.

After the concert, we repaired to the kitchen to drink wine and help ourselves
to savouries, mostly supplied by Marion, and to chat to the friends who had
come to hear us. Several glasses of wine later, John had become rather mellow
and, when I casually (and perhaps thoughtlessly) used a cocktail stick as a tooth-
pick, John feigned amazement and pronounced me to be a 'man of the world'.[13]

Two of the loyal supporters who had come to our concert were Anthony
OBrien and his beautiful Indian wife, Najma. Anthony knew that we had been
rehearsing in the Robinsons' house, where the atmosphere, he recollected, 'was
of awed reverence.' He continues:

> One memorable evening having supper at [John's] house, he produced a beau-
> tiful Sawankhalok celadon bowl for my approval. As several bottles of rioja had
> gone the way of all bottles by this stage, John thrust this bowl at me, glared and
> said 'LOOK!' I looked. To a potter the bowl was charming, a lovely soft greeny-
> grey celadon glaze with incised decoration, but not exactly unusual. John was far
> from pleased with my mild response. 'LOOK!!' he repeated and glared harder,
> turning the bowl over to underline the interest of the spiral-marked footring.
> Unwisely I said something along the lines of 'That's just the mark of the turning
> tool. It's quite normal.' 'It's f–ing beautiful!' John bellowed. Some years later he
> stopped by my pottery to watch me throwing and I reminded him of the inci-
> dent, and offered to show him how the spiral mark occurred. He said he would
> love to have been a potter. So I offered then and there to teach him. But he said,
> 'No. It's too late for me now. I'll have to come back and learn in my next life.'
>
> Indian food lay behind another memorable occasion. I used to make a rather
> hot garlic pickle, a version of Kashmiri Masala, of which John was very fond.
> He ate one entire jar with his fingers on the bus back to Bray one evening. Ruth
> complained to me the next day that it was all gone by the time John got home,
> and she'd had none. So I promised I'd make some that even John couldn't devour
> at speed. The extra hot version, consisting of little but ginger, garlic and chil-
> lies in oil, was duly borne off to Bray by a delighted John. It was he who told
> me that he produced it on Christmas Day for Ruth and her visiting family. They
> approached the pickle with caution (having been warned by me that it was very
> hot). But John said, 'Now look, this is how you eat Anto's pickle.' Whereupon
> he got a large teaspoon, dug in deep, and ate the whole lot in one mouthful.
> The effect, he said, was 'seismic'. He said the sweat sprayed out of his face like a
> fountain. He had finally met his match in a pickle.'

Anthony and Najma requested a kitten when they heard that John's cat Murray was yet again pregnant. 'John rang up and said, "We'll have a kitten for you. It will be called Chester. As in Chester-le-Street in England." Chester duly arrived, a black-and-white moggie who became our children's companion, and lived to be twenty. (Murray had lived to be twenty-two.) The last time I saw John in Dublin was a few days after we cremated Chester with due ceremony in our back garden. John came with me as we committed Chester's ashes to the sacred waters of the River Dodder.'[14]

John was involved in a summer school, held in the Royal Irish Academy of Music, beginning on 12 July. During it, a concert took place in the Dagg Hall of early seventeenth-century keyboard music, dances and popular tunes, played by John on harpsichord and the traditional music group KELP, about which John had spoken to us before.[15]

The concert of Haydn music involving the Wicklow Choral Society that had been given in Wicklow back in May was now repeated in September at the end of the Kilkenny Arts Week, this time with the addition of Haydn's madrigal, *The Storm*.[16] A few days later, it was given again in the National Concert Hall in Dublin. This was to celebrate the fact that the choir had been in existence for twenty-one years. Charles Acton reviewed this concert favourably, though he was critical of the choir's bland rendition of *The Storm*.[17]

After a session of viol music in the Robinsons' house one evening in mid October, we fell to talking. Conversation began on an intellectual note but soon became more flippant, until we were telling jokes, working out puzzles and reciting limericks. John took us by surprise by suddenly reciting a limerick that resulted in us collapsing in paroxysms of laughter. It went thus:

> There was a young man who could boast
> Of having received in the post
> A nebulous parcel
> Of the balls and the arsehole
> Of his great-great-great grandfather's ghost.

We went on in this vein, laughing and joking, until finally the party broke up at 1.30 am.[18]

Andrew remembers an incident involving John at around this period. When John was invited to view a private collection of paintings belonging to the chairman of an eminent institution, John loudly denounced one picture as 'the artisitic equivalent of a fart'. 'Ruth fluttered like a hen, trying hopelessly to hush him,' Andrew recollects. 'When a *bon mot* suggested itself, John was powerless to resist uttering it.'[19]

322 PART THREE: DUBLIN 1971–1983

Towards the end of the month, we played at Christ Church Cathedral in a concert shared with the Cathedral Choir, conducted by Eric Sweeney and with John McCann on the organ.[20] It was well attended and the choir sang beautifully. On the previous day, Ruth had come to our rehearsal and had given us advice about balance and performance. We played the music we had performed at Malahide Castle.[21] Apart from some minor quibbles, James Maguire, who reviewed the concert in *The Irish Times*, thought that the performances were 'well studied' and 'thoughtful'.[22]

At the end of October John's student Malcolm Proud gave a seminar in the Royal Irish Academy of Music with the American flautist Nancy Possman and the Japanese viola da gamba player Fumiko Matsui. The trio began the seminar with a performance of a sonata by Geminiani played on modern and then baroque instruments. Afterwards, John, Ruth, Andrew Robinson, Rhoda Draper, Marion Doherty and I were invited to perform and be coached by the professionals. John could not have been amused when he was laughed at and criticized by Nancy.[23]

At the beginning of November John conducted the New Irish Chamber Orchestra in a rather bizarre concert that left Charles Acton quite unimpressed. According to Acton's review, the orchestra was merely used in the second half as a 'backing group' for the traditional Irish music group The Chieftains. In the first half, the group played on their own. When, in the second half, the Chieftains were joined by the orchestra, 'it really seemed ridiculous to have the half dozen of the former so amplified that they overshadowed the unamplified latter', he wrote. If, as Venetia O'Sullivan had reported, John was stuck for cash at this period, he would not have been too fussy about what type of work he did then.[24]

A successful concert of chamber music took place a few days later in the Dagg Hall of the Academy before an audience of just ten people.[25] Shortly afterwards, when we met at the Robinsons' house, John produced a cassette tape of the concert, and played it to us on his little tape recorder. Although the sound was poor, we were able to hear our mistakes and so we spent the rest of the evening making an effort to improve our technique. We worked at speeds and articulation, but John did not seem too comfortable with so much dissecting and correcting. As expected, he played in his usual bland manner, *sempre legato*. Honor made a pointed remark to him, laughingly, that at a certain point he did *not* have to play more legato (in contrast to the rest of us, who did). When we went to the front room in order to relax by the fire, John left. After we had gone, we criticized John's playing, choice of speeds and general stubbornness. It seemed that poor John, who by now was quite set in his ways, was beginning to put his foot in it now and then, and that he was no longer treated with the same awe and respect that he had once commanded.[26]

Our next recital, held in the Douglas Hyde Gallery, Trinity College in mid November, was a disaster. Because of inadequate rehearsal and preparation, we all made serious mistakes, beginning with John, of all people. Thanks to poor publicity, only about twenty people had come to hear us, which perhaps was fortunate.[27]

By the time we met again at the chamber music class in the Academy, John had recovered and was in good form again. Afterwards John treated me to a drink in Kennedy's pub and we settled down to an evening of chatting and laughing. John drank a few whiskeys (to which he probably added cloves of garlic) and left early.[28]

The oddest concert we gave during this period must have been the one in Castleisland, County Kerry, on 12 December. Some bright spark had booked us into the local hall of this small town in the west of Ireland. Marion, Honor, Jenny, Andrew and I travelled to Castleisland in the Robinsons' Volkswagen van and arrived there at five o'clock, just as dusk was falling. I knew that I was definitely in the west of Ireland, for there was an extra bite in the cold, wintry air. We stopped at the Crown Hotel, at one end of the long main street, and suddenly John appeared, smiling and greeting us. We were shown into the sleepy hotel and brought upstairs to our rooms.

After we had eaten our evening meal we walked to the Ivy Leaf Arts Centre, a tiny hall with a quaint, miniscule stage and painted backdrop. Even though the heaters were switched on, it was ghastly cold. We now suddenly realized how ludicrous the situation was. We spent a long time tuning up and thus had little or no time to rehearse. At 8.30 pm when we were due to start, there was no sign of an audience, though we had been told that all the schools and institutions in the neighbourhood had been circularized. We had noticed posters in the town that advertised us performing 'music from the Middle Ages'.

Wondering whether or not we should proceed, Jenny went out to see if anybody had arrived. Five ladies had and were warming themselves at a fire, so we decided to carry on with an edited version of our programme, omitting a Byrd Fantasia and the potentially dreary *In Nomines*.

When three more people arrived (two nuns and one lady) and we prepared to start, John suddenly announced that we would play *all* the items. Dismayed, we proceeded, shivering with the cold. Because of this, we put more energy into our performance and played better than ever. By the end of the recital, the audience had dwindled to four and we received a ragged and short burst of applause.

After we had duly admired the décor of this little 'arts centre' (which admittedly was quite good), we left and ran across to the hotel bar where we huddled around a roaring fire and drank glasses of hot whiskey. Never a hardened drinker, I for once appreciated this warming beverage to the full. When I foolishly expressed my view that buying alcoholic drinks was a waste of money, I was checked by John, who declared, 'I don't mind *spending* money but I hate *wasting* it'. I was amazed to discover how he was able to relax with and chat to the locals and somehow deal with awkward questions such as, 'Who d'you think is goin' to win the match next Sunday?'

Frozen from our ordeal in the near-empty hall, we were disgusted at the waste of so much effort, the long and pointless journey, and the lack of any hospitality from the organizers. However, we soon drowned our sorrows in whiskey – especially John. The bar was crowded and noisy; later, after the official closing time, the barmaids hissed '*ssssh!*' every so often on account of serving after hours and the possible presence of a garda outside. In the end we enjoyed the rest of the evening and began to make plans of how we could drastically change our programme and introduce more variety.[29]

Forty-One
1983

The first major musical event in John's calendar for 1983 was the annual series of Bach cantatas held in Saint Ann's Church in Dublin. At the time, nobody knew that these would be the last cantatas in the series to be conducted by him. Begun in 1973, the series was celebrating its tenth anniversary. 'For a whole decade, John Beckett and his friends have been cheering up the gloom of February by giving three Sunday afternoon concerts of Bach cantatas in St Ann's', wrote Charles Acton in *The Irish Times*:

> With justified pride, they are this year giving us an anthology of their ten years. And they greeted us yesterday with a formidable showcard listing all the 53 that they have already performed, just about a quarter of Bach's extant total. That, let us hope, gives them another thirty years of material.

The first concert, given on 6 February, began with the familiar Sinfonia of Cantata No. 42. We then heard the gentle and very beautiful Cantata No. 82, *Ich habe genug* ('It is enough'), which was once again superbly sung by William Young. The fact that he had sung with hardly any vibrato was commented on by everyone afterwards. The final work was Cantata No. 127, *Herr Jesu Christ, wahr' Mensch und Gott* ('Thou who, a God, as man yet come'). For this, the orchestra was joined by Jenny Robinson and a young David Agnew, who played the 'remarkable length of staccato recorder quavers behind the oboe obbligato in "Die Seele ruht" accompanying Irené Sandford's blissful singing.' Despite the cold and bleak weather, the concert was well attended.[1]

Three days later, John conducted a production of Mozart's opera *The Marriage of Figaro* with an ad hoc orchestra formed from members of the RTÉ Symphony

Orchestra and with student singers. It was performed in the acoustically unsuit-able Gleeson Hall of Kevin Street College in Dublin. Six performances were staged on various dates, finishing on 20 February.[2] The part of Figaro was sung by Nigel Williams. John's friend Sydney Stokes, who attended one of the productions remembered that John was very enthusiastic and encouraging.[3]

Four cantatas were performed in the next concert at St Ann's: No. 150, *Nach dir, Herr, verlanget mich* ('Unto Thee, O Lord, do I lift up my soul'); No. 55, *Ich armer Mensch, ich Sündenknecht* ('I, wretched man, a slave to sin'); No. 54, *Widerstehe doch der Sünde* ('Stand steadfast against transgression') and No. 71, *Gott ist mein König* ('God is my King').[4] My two favourites in the concert were No. 54 and the jubilant No. 71, which had been performed just the previous year.[5]

The two cantatas performed in the very last concert were No. 199, *Mein Herze schwimmt im Blut* ('My heart is bathed in blood') and No. 21, *Ich hatte viel Bekümmernis in meinem Herzen* ('My heart was deeply troubled'). This second cantata concluded appropriately with a great flourish and was loudly applauded. The cantata, wrote Charles Acton, 'is, according to John Beckett, the one that has made the greatest impression upon these performers of all that they have performed, for several reasons. Hence their choice of it for their London Prom concert in 1979.'[6] As this was the last concert in the tenth anniversary series (though there had been no cantatas in 1976) there was a certain sense of occa-sion. Before the applause had finished, William Young bade us be silent and delivered a short speech, thanking John and everyone for everything over the years. He presented John with a book on Chinese art and a book token. John then gave a humble speech of thanks and was rewarded with a standing ovation. It had certainly been a great achievement to produce these popular concerts for ten years.[7]

A few days later I left for Basel for a music course that John had encouraged me to attend; it was given by the Cuban viola da gamba virtuoso José Vázquez.[8] In March John went with the New Irish Chamber Orchestra and James Galway on a month-long tour of Canada and North America. Because the main work was Galway's own transcription for flute of Vivaldi's *The Four Seasons*, which he directed himself, and three other flute concertos by the same composer, John went on the tour very grudgingly in order to play the continuo part.

The tour started in Boston, where everyone was woken from their slumbers during the night by the hotel's fire alarm. Ordered to evacuate their rooms, they had to go down to the lobby in their dressing gowns with their instru-ments, where they waited for the all clear. John was very morose and muttered to Máire Larchet that all this had to be endured just for Vivaldi. Galway and the orchestra were booked into huge halls everywhere, which were filled to capacity – mostly because the locals were expecting the famous flautist to play a programme of popular music, such as *Annie's Song*, which was a big hit at the time. Many people must have been surprised to discover that he was playing 'serious' classical music. Galway and the orchestra then played in the Carnegie Hall, New York. After the concert, the musicians and organizers attended a reception funded by the Irish Industrial Development Authority (IDA).

The following morning they flew to Montreal in Canada, where they gave another concert. They then stayed in Toronto for a few days. During a concert they gave there on Saint Patrick's Day, Galway walked off the stage in a huff, apparently because a draft was blowing the music off his stand. Some people had mistakenly believed that he was drunk. From here they travelled by bus down through Detroit and played again in Minneapolis, where they were met by people, old and young, all dressed in green – some even wearing green wigs – who carried a banner reading 'Welcome to the New Irish Chamber Orchestra'. Naturally the orchestra (and John, especially) were not used to being welcomed in this manner! From here they looped back to Ann Arbor, a university town in Michigan State, where they played in a beautiful concert hall. Afterwards they performed at a big venue in nearby Chicago. This concert was followed by another elaborate reception. The plan was to fly to Los Angeles the next day but they were delayed by heavy snow that had started to fall during the previous evening.

They eventually arrived in sunny Los Angeles, where they stayed a short while and played in Santa Barbara. From here they flew eastwards to Washington DC, where the cherry blossom was in full bloom on the trees and they were able to enjoy fine spring weather. Here they played in a concert that was attended by the Irish Ambassador, Tadhg O'Sullivan, at the John F. Kennedy Center for the Performing Arts. On the following day they returned to New York, where they gave a concert in the Avery Fisher Hall, in the Lincoln Center. After they had given their final concert on Long Island, they flew back to Dublin.[9]

On 1 May our Dublin Consort of Viols gave an evening recital in the Rothe House, Kilkenny to a full house. Although the performance went fairly well, John remained inexplicably glum.[10] A couple of days later, he conducted four Bach cantatas (Nos 199, 55, 54 and 82) in the chapel of his former school, St Columba's.[11]

Towards the end of the month, John conducted two all-Schubert concerts involving the Wicklow Choral Society, the New Irish Chamber Orchestra and soloists. There were just two works: Schubert's Symphony No. 3 and his Mass in A flat, D 678. This programme was performed in St Patrick's Church, Wicklow on 19 May and again, the next day, in the National Concert Hall. The two concerts were promoted in a short piece in *The Irish Times*'s column *Memoranda – an arts notebook*. It concluded, 'Once again they will be conducted by John Beckett, a dedicated Schubertian – not many people heard him start to play the complete Schubert piano sonatas at 5 am and complete them in time for breakfast!'[12]

Performing in the National Concert Hall turned out to be a 'brave and expensive venture', as Charles Acton mentioned in his review.[13] Gillian Smith, who had now taken over running the New Irish Chamber Orchestra after her husband Lindsay Armstrong had ceased to so, recollects that John had insisted on doing this concert with the Wicklow Choral Society and her orchestra. When Gillian had pointed out to him that it would cost the choir a great deal of money, he waved this aside and said, 'Oh, they'll raise the money and they'll have no problem.' He was wrong – they did have a problem, for after the event they were left with an enormous debt. This was another setback for John.[14]

Towards the end of May, the viol player José Vázquez came to Dublin to give a weekend of master classes and a concert on the Saturday evening.[15] Unfortunately I was unable to attend this concert due to illness. My parents went and returned with a glowing report of the event; they were clearly charmed with Vázquez's virtuoso performance.[16] John played the obbligato harpsichord part in Bach's Sonata in G minor for viola da gamba and harpsichord, BWV 1029 and two groups of solo harpsichord music, one by Giles Farnaby and the other by Henry Purcell. Marion Doherty accompanied José in other items by Erlebach, Christopher Simpson, Antoine Forqueray and Jean Marie Leclair. 'The programme turned out to be a little ill-planned,' Acton complained:

> The big disappointment of the evening … was the Bach, which should have been a lovely and equal partnership between these two fine players. Unfortunately, presumably as a matter of registration, Mr Beckett over-powered Mr Vázquez, so that it was only every now and then that I could hear the latter's line through the relentless clangour of the harpsichord. …The joy of the evening was, of course, the gamba playing.[17]

I felt well enough to drive to Willow Park School on the Sunday afternoon to attend the José's master class. After José had announced 'The Dublin Consort of Viols' with an exaggerated flourish, we performed a work selected by John: a Fantasy by John Jenkins. José could make neither head nor tail of the music and expressed his dislike of its one-note theme, which he derided in front of everyone, much to our amusement and to John's doubtless annoyance, though he feigned laughter. José then made us play a Fantazia by William Lawes, which went much better. We all derived great satisfaction from performing this chal-lenging piece of music and greatly benefitted from José's help and suggestions. To this day I often wonder how John felt during that afternoon. Did he feel humiliated and defeated? If he did, he covered it up well, for he later continued to encourage us to avail of José's expert knowledge and tuition.[18]

At a party held in the Robinsons' house on that Sunday evening, John and José aired their views and, in the end, fell out. When John expressed his love of Jenkins, José expressed his view that the composer's Royal Consorts were wonderful but that his Fantasies were not performable because they were too amorphous – he could not tell from reading the score where the theme had come from or where it was going to. John, like most English players, rather liked this unpredictable aspect of Jenkins's music. When they moved on to the subject of Vivaldi and Corelli and how John detested these composers, José was horrified and said to John, 'How can anybody play Baroque music if they don't go along with Corelli? Corelli is the father of Baroque music!' The two men just agreed to differ as they just could not see eye to eye.[19]

After this event I saw John just a few times in the audience at concerts in Dublin. In July I was diagnosed with jaundice (caused by a fault in our supply of drinking water at home) and lost touch with him for a couple of months. As nothing about him appeared in the national press, it seemed as though he was doing little work during the summer.

We were understandably quite astonished when, out of the blue, John telephoned my father in early August to inform us that he had obtained a new job in BBC Radio 3, in London, that the house in Bray and the harpsichord that my father had made him would be sold, and that he and Ruth would be moving to Greenwich. He wanted to know if my father knew anybody who wanted to buy his harpsichord. On the following evening my father drove to his house to fix his instrument and to return music that I had borrowed from him. Cathal enjoyed chatting to John and Ruth about old Dublin and drinking tea with them. He explained a cryptic remark in Joyce's *Ulysses* to John and borrowed a book, *Under the Receding Wave* by C.P. Curran; a marvellous description of Dublin in the late nineteenth century, which I read. Curiously, Ruth was sorry to be leaving, but John apparently was happy. By the end of the month, John had sold his harpsichord to Gerald Sands. He would have been sad to part company with the instrument, as he liked it very much.[20]

Many theories have been advanced to explain why John and Ruth had decided to leave Dublin and return to London, apart from the offer of the new job. It seems that John was just getting fed up with life in Dublin and possibly felt that he was not appreciated that much, which was probably true.[21] His harpsichord student Rosalind Whittaker thought that people just gave him lip service; they praised him for his cantata series and so forth, but 'it was all talk'. He had come to hate working in the Royal Irish Academy of Music, where he found himself teaching indifferent students. He complained to Rosalind that the place was 'like a brothel': people came in to get their 'fix' and then left. He liked to give his lessons and rehearse in the Dagg Hall, but when the hall was needed for other purposes, he was obliged to move out. He now needed money and a 'proper' job that offered a pension – hence his application to the BBC.[22]

Ruth was in a similar position. Although she taught the violin and viola both in the Bray Music Centre and in the Academy,[23] where she had very good pupils, she also was working in institutions that offered no pension. Also, certain aspects of how the Academy was run annoyed her.[24] She was a fine musician but was little appreciated in Ireland and, as a result, was unable to get enough work. In addition to this, she never felt completely at home in Ireland. Although Ruth was greatly liked by some people, others found her difficult to get on with. She had few friends of her own; most of the people she knew were acquaintances of John's.[25] Mary Wheatley, a young violinist in her early twenties, had been interviewed for Ruth's job in Bray early in the year. As she was good, Ruth was convinced that Mary should take her job. However, as Mary had her eye on a vacancy in the RTÉ Symphony Orchestra and very much wanted to play in it (in fact, she did get the job), she burst into tears because of the pressure Ruth put on her.[26] Other issues contributed to the discontent felt by John and Ruth, such as Ruth's relationship with John's sister. Ruth also wanted to return to England to be with her family.

Although RTÉ had given John occasional work, it seems that the relationship between him and the radio producers was not exactly the best; there were rumours towards the end that, in order to make some money, he had been copying music parts for the orchestra, though this is unlikely as his musical hand was highly idiosyncratic. As Michael Dervan has pointed out, just being handed a cheque for conducting music, performing it or presenting a radio programme is not reward enough; one needs to feel accepted, appreciated and understood. John was too challenging a person for many institutions in Ireland to be able to do that for him. Creative performers can only be brought into play in organisations where they can have dialogue with those in charge. Regarding RTÉ, there would have been few people who could have had an intelligent conversation with any conductor or soloist who worked for the organization during this period.

Michael believed that as John was exceptional enough in what he could bring to music making in Ireland in the seventies and early eighties, it always seemed to him a shame that he did not get more opportunities. This would have required institutions to go the extra mile to make it happen. Although Michael was critical about certain aspects of John's performances, conducting abilities and his often rough manner with students, he always had 'fond feelings' for him

– John's heart was in the right place. Michael also believes that he was a loss to the country when he left and that he was not appreciated to the full when he lived and worked in Ireland.[27] An example of how he could be overlooked was the one brief reference to him, contained in half a sentence, in *To Talent Alone*, a 627-page history of the Royal Irish Academy of Music, edited by Richard Pine and Charles Acton.[28] (Richard Pine had upset John once by casually stating that he could not bear Haydn's symphonies and claimed that John never spoke to him afterwards.)[29]

Many people in Ireland were shocked to learn that John was leaving the country. One of these was his friend Vera Škrabánek, who was upset and annoyed that nobody would give him proper work. She felt that although he was doing a fantastic job in Ireland with his concerts and the Bach cantatas, and was bringing a completely different dimension to Irish culture, he was not fully appreciated and did not fit in; according to her, he felt that the country had sent him into exile.[30]

Another person who was deeply affected was Tim Thurston, who sang in the Cantata Singers. When somebody told him that John had gone back to London, he sat down and almost wept, for singing in the Bach cantata concerts under John's direction had been the most wonderful choral experience in his life. For him, John had brought so much fascinating insight into the music.[31] Bernadette Greevy, interviewed for an article in *The Irish Times* published in 2000, said of John, 'He is wonderful. Ireland should never have let him leave'.[32]

Charles and Carol Acton also regretted John's departure; Carol believed that his return to London was a very grave loss for Irish music making.[33] Writing in *The Irish Times* in October, after John had left, Charles had this to say:

> It is a loss to the country that Beckett has left to become a BBC radio producer, with a prospect that he will be making a great contribution to the BBC's celebration in 1985 of the tercentenaries of Bach, Handel and Domenico Scarlatti. England's gain is very much our loss, but we can console ourselves that, during the years since he returned here from London, he has created a school of fine harpsichord players, a school of violinists and an upsurge of baroque music – although he is just as devoted to Schubert and the late romantics as to the baroque and medieval.
>
> One of the things we owe to him is a decade of Bach cantatas on Sundays in February in St. Ann's. What will happen to them? Our musical life would be grossly deprived if Mr Beckett's departure meant the end of them. Considering what Nigel Williams has achieved already with 'Musica Sacra' in TCD, perhaps he will pick up Beckett's mantle. I hope that he will, but he will have to move fast to get resources and finance organised for next February.[34]

In fact the Bach cantatas did continue and were performed again at the beginning of the following year. This time they were conducted by Geoffrey Spratt,
who, as Charles Acton reported, 'conducted with stylishness and enthusiasm,
and introduced the works as skilfully as John Beckett used to do'. The Goethe
Institute Choir replaced the Cantata Singers and the same four soloists sang
(Irené Sandford, Áine Nic Gabhann, Peter Kerr and William Young).[35] Although
the soloists, choir and orchestra were to change, the tradition was kept alive and
would flourish for many more years to come – a true testament to the contribution that John made to music in Dublin.

PART FOUR

London 1983–2007

Forty-Two
1983: London

John's offer of a job in the BBC was due, of course, to the help of his friend Nicholas Anderson, whom he had approached earlier in the year. Nicholas remembers him asking, 'What are the chances of my getting any kind of job in the BBC? I need a job – I just need daily employment – I'm prepared to do anything.' Nicholas explained that that it was not within his power to offer him a job, as he was only a mere producer, but he offered to speak to his head of department, a lady named Christine Hardwick. Christine, who had worked in the BBC since the sixties, knew all about John and the Bach cantatas. Nicholas asked her if there were any vacancies and if there were, if she would be prepared to give him an interview. She hesitated, said that it was not normal to appoint people to jobs when they were on the verge of retirement (John was fifty-six by now), but that she could 'give it a try'. Nicholas replied, 'Well, even if you just saw him for an interview, that would be something.'

As luck would have it, there was a vacancy for a producer in the music department shortly afterwards and Nicholas advised John to apply for it. 'This is it,' he told John; 'I can't do any more.' The interview took place in Broadcasting House.¹ On the interview board were Christine, a personnel officer and Arthur Johnson, who had first met John in the Hampstead studio of Saga Records in 1966 – Arthur had by this stage been working in the BBC for nearly twenty years. The appearance of a 56-year-old candidate was, to say the least, unusual, bearing in mind that the compulsory retirement age in the BBC was sixty. Nevertheless, John impressed them by his depth of knowledge and an unusual sensitivity as regards programme-making. Most of all, he made it clear that, at his age, he considered that he had no chance whatever of getting the job. Despite all of this, and with no more than four years of employment ahead of him, John was offered the post, and, as Arthur put it, 'one of the more unusual appointments in BBC history began to flourish'.[2]

After the interview, Christine went to Nicholas's office and said, 'Well, we've given the job to your friend!' Nicholas was delighted. 'It'll mean a lot to him,' he said. Three months after John had started in October, she came to Nicholas's office again and said, 'The John Beckett thing – it's working really well! You know, he's getting through mountains of work!'

John was in his element. At last he had a good job with regular hours, regular pay, a pension and interesting people to work with, several of whom he already knew. It was obvious to his colleagues that he was very happy.[3] He became close friends with people like Patrick Lambert and Andrew Mussett, and got on quite well with his boss Christine.[4] Arthur Johnson remembers:

> John was always delightful to work with. The fearsome look in the eye that had terrified me all those years ago inevitably softened to a mischievous twinkle whenever the opportunity arose. Respected and admired by all his colleagues, he contributed a great deal to and made the most of his short time working for the BBC, and I know from conversations with him that he always appreciated the brave decision we made in his appointment.[5]

John's friends Frida and Vic Robinson realized how John loved working in the BBC and how lucky his department was to have him.[6]

Lindsay Armstrong visited John in his office in Egton House, an ugly building (now demolished) opposite Broadcasting House, which at one time backed on to the old Queen's Hall. It was a typical BBC office: a small room at the end of a long corridor, packed with a variety of things. John was full of admiration for the system; it was all very efficient and Lindsay imagined that his colleagues paid no attention to the fact that he was Irish – they just wanted good programmes, and that was it.[7]

The first type of work he was given was the job that Nicholas Anderson first had: listening to and reporting on 'foreign' tapes. These were recordings of concerts from European broadcasting associations, which could be broadcast free of charge. Because the introductions were in another language, new ones had to be scripted. After John had written his report, he would hand the programmes over to a scriptwriter such as Adrian Jack[8], who would write new introductions for the BBC broadcast.[9] At this period, the presenters were not personalities, and did not devise their own programmes; instead, this job was done by producers, who used scriptwriters to write all the forward and back announcements for the staff presenters.

At a later stage John attended editing sessions for other people's pro-grammes. When Nicholas took six months off in order to work freelance and write a book, John edited his programmes so that they would be ready for air. As he enjoyed doing this so much, he took to coming in to work an hour before everyone else in the morning, arriving at eight. Nicholas believes that he probably took the over-rail Southern Railway train from Maise Hill to Charing Cross and continued his journey by bus – John never liked using the Tube. He then used to leave punctually at half past four in the afternoon, earlier than his colleagues, so that he would miss the evening rush and arrive home in good time. He and Nicholas sometimes met for lunch, but more often they would go to a Greek restaurant in the evening, where Nicholas's wife Alison would join John and Ruth. Although the whole venture was a great success, Nicholas believes that it would be untrue to say that John was popular in the BBC music department, simply because he did not bother with many of the people.[10]

Patrick Lambert, another Radio 3 producer who shared a suite of offices with John, greatly respected him and claimed that he knew more about music than the other producers as he was a musician himself. Interestingly, Patrick knew almost nothing of John's past and of Musica Reservata – John never spoke about such things to his new colleagues. Patrick wondered if he was shy. He certainly was compartmentalized and although he did not like to talk about certain aspects of his life, Patrick did know about the offhand manner in which Ruth had been treated in Ireland and that she now taught in the Purcell School of Music in Bushey, Hertfordshire, north west of London.

John and Patrick worked together in Egton House. John used to lock himself into his office, where he listened to the foreign tapes and wrote his reports. At the beginning, John's job consisted mostly of 'backroom' work like this – he rarely did much live recording. One of the programmes that John would work on was *This Week's Composer* (later renamed *Composer of the Week*). Patrick recol-lected that when he did write scripts, they were 'a little too literary' and often were returned by the announcers for changes, which was a pity as they were 'written so beautifully'. Patrick had to try to imagine them being read by one of the announcers. John was punctual and reliable, and apart from his formal style of writing, the announcers were always pleased with his results.

One of Patrick's colleagues was a Miss Timmons (or 'Tim' as she was nick-named). She was devoted to the BBC and joined her colleagues when they once went out on strike duty. John's relationship with this lady was a little strange: he was inclined to be rude to her. Both of them often went to the rather stiff parties that members of the staff attended from time to time.

When a special occasion for John was held in Egton House, he insisted on drinking Jameson whiskey, which they were obliged to pour into official BBC plastic or paper cups. John got rather drunk but managed to find his way home somehow. One of his colleagues ended up, literally, under the table.

As Patrick was married to a Czech lady named Jaroslava (known to all as Jarka), he was something of an expert on Czech music. Patrick and John's common love was the music of Dvořák, though not all of it. John once complained that he had to listen to all of Dvořák's oratorio *St Ludmilla* which he did not like; it went on for two and a half hours and he hoped that he would never have to listen to it again. He disliked Janáček, and described him as an 'autistic' composer. Patrick made the mistake of loaning him the memoirs of Janáček's wife (*My Life with Janáček – The Memoirs of Zdenka Janáčková*, edited and translated by John Tyrrell); John was 'disgusted' by it. John of course loved Mahler, but was 'choosy' about the symphonies; like David Lee, Patrick remembered that he did not care much for number two. When discussing modern music, John often shook his head and bemoaned the fact that 'music had finished' or that it 'had come to an end'.

John enjoyed listening to music with Patrick more than anybody else, and loved to play his recordings very loudly indeed. Also, he was enchanted by the sound of Emma Kirkby's voice. He often stayed on late in the office, when the others had all left, listening to early music sung by her. Patrick remembers that he had an old Sugden amplifier at home, which he cherished; when it went wrong he somehow managed to get it fixed free of charge. During the time John worked in the BBC and when he continued working for the company freelance after he had retired, he taught keyboard (piano and harpsichord) at Blackheath Conservatoire.[11]

John's colleague Adrian Jack was also a composer. He had studied piano, composition and organ at the Royal College of Music, and had then studied composition and electronic music in Poland. Back in London he had made his living as a freelancer, writing reviews and teaching. He also gave lectures on the history of music at the Royal College of Music, and during the weekends he painted. He then joined the BBC and worked as a scriptwriter. When Adrian first met John he immediately warmed to him as he was not a 'corporation man' and was totally indifferent to career politics – he had been employed because of what and who he was. Adrian concluded that Christine Hardwick had done him a favour, for if John had not been given the job, he undoubtedly would have had financial worries. Adrian remembers how incredibly conscientious he was at his work and that he was 'altogether selfless as a producer, never allowing his often passionate views to affect his professional judgement.' Although he could be cantankerous at times, he was demonstrative in his likes as well as his dislikes.

Adrian found him a supportive colleague and a generous friend, though not always an easy companion.

Adrian was well aware of John's very definite likes and dislikes, though some of these blew the dust off the cobwebs of conventional opinions. For instance, John thought that the development section in the first movement of Mozart's great C major piano concerto, K. 503, was a very poor example of its type and that it was just a cycle of modulations, a theory that Adrian was inclined to agree with, though it was a very unconventional opinion. Adrian knew that John had recordings of whales singing to each other and that he included them in one of his programmes. John did not like everything that Adrian composed; while he complimented him on some pieces, he was dismissive about a piano trio and pronounced it to be 'fiddle-faddle'.

Adrian also knew that John was fond of reading Joyce. He also remembers him reading a large two-volume biography of Goethe. When John suddenly decided to learn about something or somebody, he would go the whole hog – his reason for reading this biography was simply that he knew nothing about Goethe.

Adrian and John kept in touch after John had left the BBC and the two men and Antony Pitts (a BBC producer) and Stephanie Gush (a senior personal assistant and 'an extremely nice woman') used to meet for lunch now and then, often at a Greek restaurant in Soho. They were sometimes joined by Ruth. Although Stephanie was a devout Roman Catholic and Antony was very religious, it did not stop John from launching into a diatribe about the Roman Catholic Church at one of these lunches. Stephanie silenced him by saying very quietly, 'I'm Roman Catholic'. John was not at all embarrassed; he never had any qualms about trampling on people's feelings if he felt like it.

John was very friendly with the staff in the Greek restaurant and always made a great show of shaking their hands and hugging them on arrival. Although the restaurant was unassuming, had a good atmosphere and nice people, Antony and Adrian did not like the food at all and managed to persuade John to go elsewhere. They moved around the corner to Spaghetti House.

Adrian liked Ruth. It was she who told him that the trouble with John's conducting was that he talked too much. Adrian sometimes visited John and Ruth at their home in Azof Street and once stayed for a weekend. On another occasion he went there for lunch and they were joined by John's colleague Patrick Lambert and his wife Jarka, and his friends Patrick Cuming and wife Melanie.[12] As Patrick and Melanie were then living in Catford, Lewisham, not far from John, they saw each other fairly often. They saw less of him when they moved to Wraysbury, near Staines, some years later.[13] Other regular guests were John's cousins Morris and Deirdre Sinclair. Deirdre remembered that John was meticulously tidy; when he put things in certain places, he liked them to remain there and would get upset if somebody put back one of his treasured possessions in the wrong place.[14]

As the wall between the original two bedrooms of the terraced house in Azof Street had been broken down, John and Ruth had one large bedroom-cum-study upstairs. This was where John kept a harpsichord, his many books and pots, and listened to music on his hi-fi system with, of course, the volume turned up very high. At the back was a small spare bedroom for guests. Downstairs was a small sitting room in which John hung his beloved Black Forest clock, and where he would love to sit by an open fire in the evenings. Behind this was a basic kitchen, which, over a period of time, became decorated with an assortment of photographs and picture postcards stuck directly on to the walls. In the middle of one wall was a photo of the Dalai Lama. At the very back of the house was a bathroom.[15] Over the years, the house was repaired several times; John had a new front door fitted shortly before he died.[16]

Oengus MacNamara noticed that John never turned on the lights when they sat together throughout the afternoon, chatting and listening to music. As daylight faded, the room went dark. Oengus never commented on this or asked if he could turn on a light – he just let it happen. When he stubbed his toe or bumped into something when trying to find his way to the bathroom, a light would finally be switched on in the hallway. John's conversation was inexhaustible – he could talk about anything and everything, and he was extremely well read. Although the two men never discussed politics, Oengus discovered by chance that he hated Margaret Thatcher; her worst crime, in John's view, was that she was an unspeakable woman.

Oengus had also noticed that John loved the company of fellow Irishmen in London and often went to Irish pubs and restaurants, where he chatted to the workmen who came there to drink and eat.

John's taste, Oengus discovered, was impeccable, and his house was full of extraordinary art books: as well as volumes on subjects such as Chinese and Japanese art and calligraphy, there were books on African art, objects from Constantinople, and various types of art from right across history. He shared a vast amount of knowledge concerning the more obscure corners of art with Oengus's father Desmond MacNamara and his former friend, Michael Morrow.[17]

John's one-time student and friend Paul Conway, who had kept in touch with him, came from Dublin to visit him frequently, often staying one or two nights in the house. When John went to Dublin to visit his sister Ann, recorder-playing sessions with John, Ann, Paul, Janet Ashe and Sydney Stokes were regularly organized. These musical sessions continued for many years.[18]

Another visitor to the house in Azof Street was Irené Sandford. On one occasion when she was there, John's cat was due to produce a litter of kittens. As Irené was not fond of animals, she did not pay too much attention. About one hour after they had retired to bed, John called her downstairs to attend to the cat, who was giving birth to the kittens. John, who hadn't bothered dressing, was, as Irené's husband recollected, 'absolutely starkers'![19]

Christopher Nobbs, who had met John briefly in Bruges in 1980, and had met him again through Nicholas Anderson in the BBC, had by now become a good friend. He had been involved professionally with John when Christopher had hired a harpsichord a few times for BBC Radio 3 recordings, two of which John produced. He, his partner Yvonne and his daughter were often invited to the house for 'big, robust Sunday lunches', accompanied with large bottles of Bulgarian red wine. The lunches were excuses for long talks, during which John aired his views on various subjects and expressed his strong prejudices, which Christopher always found thrilling. Christopher felt duty bound to argue with him and fight his case. Although he was well aware of John's despised composers, he once mentioned in passing that he had been to an opera by Donizetti and that he had enjoyed it. John's reaction to this was, 'I think you've misunderstood the whole basis of our friendship!' Another composer John hated was Ravel – he called him 'an interior decorator'. He dismissed Handel as 'just a commercial composer', and, rather bizarrely, pronounced his music to be 'plastic ivy'. Their great shared enthusiasm was Berlioz, and they often discussed the man and his music. John had strong opinions on painting and, as we have noted earlier, was very fond of Paul Klee's works. Christopher was aware that, in literature and the theatre, he regarded his cousin Samuel's works as being on the highest level; as nothing, including the music that he had composed, could compare to them, everything else must be second rate. After he and Christopher had gone to a play by some other playwright, John said that it was very good but 'Sam's plays do spoil you for anything else.'[20] John's friend Frida Robinson felt that Samuel must have been a difficult cousin for him to have, for he worshipped Samuel so much. Every now and then John would talk about his plays, 'but it was almost as if they were so sacred that he could hardly talk about them'. John firmly believed that only Irish actors should take the parts in them – English actors simply would not do.[21]

In short, Samuel was John's hero. In fact, as Christopher discovered, he worshipped heroes to such an extent that he always felt that he could never rise above them or feel proud of his achievements. Another hero of his was Dr Samuel Johnson, whom he often emulated when he had a captive audience; like Dr Johnson, John could 'talk for victory'. Others included Mahler and the poet Emily Dickinson. An odd but delightful enthusiasm was P.G. Wodehouse, whose novels John treasured; he had a copy of every one of them. He even had the text of the broadcasts that Wodehouse had made on German radio and used them to illustrate his defence of the man who most people believed had disgraced himself: John believed that he had just been foolish and had done nothing criminal.

Although Samuel was his hero, John did not approve of his cousin's dislike of Bach – Samuel's favourite composer was Schubert. Also, Samuel loved the paintings of Jack B. Yeats, which John did not; he told Christopher that he could not understand why Samuel was so enthralled by them. John preferred Dutch painters such as Rembrandt and Breughel; he had little sympathy for Italian painting and had not much time for Turner. What he liked was northern realism or twentieth-century expressionism. Of course, his central obsession in literature, after his cousin's works, was James Joyce's *Ulysses* (another shared enthusiasm between him and Christopher), which he boasted he read once every year. They also discussed the novels of Flann O'Brien and Christopher recommended the author Hubert Butler to him, whom he did not know but grew to like. John reciprocated by urging Christopher to read J.M. Synge's *Travels in Wicklow, West Kerry and Connemara*. This short work meant a great deal to John as it was the way in which he would have liked to write about Ireland himself. He thought that Synge was the best of all the straightforward prose stylists, which came as a surprise to Christopher as most people were only acquainted with Synge's plays in the UK, but he realized that John's view was correct.

As Christopher knew that John was interested in folk music, he introduced him to Jewish *klezmer* music. Christopher made him a tape of a recording of *klezmer* bands in America from around the time of World War One and John became very fond of the genre, with its amazing clarinet and xylophone parts.

Like Alison Young and Honor O Brolchain, Christopher noticed John's love of children. On one occasion Christopher and a friend were moving a harpsichord after a concert. As the friend had brought his little daughter along, John held her hand during the procedure and surprised the two men by saying, 'Do you think Bach ever did this?' He was forever thinking about Bach and had suddenly wondered if Johann Sebastian had ever held his children in a similar manner while his instruments were being moved. Although Christopher's daughter had regarded 'this extraordinary character' with a certain amount of awe, she retains intense memories of John and a great fondness for him.[22]

On another occasion, John brought Seán O'Leary's grandson Tristan to see the *Cutty Sark* at Greenwich. When they arrived, the cannon was fired. Because of this, young Tristan nicknamed him 'Bang Bang John Beckett'. Amused at this, John hoped that the name would not be carved on his headstone. Back at home in Azof Street, John produced a stuffed doll for the boy to play with. Seán remembers that he was good at procuring gifts for children.[23]

Roland Morrow, who called to see John now and then, noticed that he was rather lacking in social graces and often said the wrong thing. Once, Roland was sporting a new knitted jumper with an abstract design, which he quite liked. John praised the jumper but later remarked to someone else, 'Normally Roland wears clothes that I wouldn't be seen dead in a ditch in!' When Roland mentioned that he had not read a certain book, John said, 'I envy you,' meaning that he envied him the feeling of reading it for the first time and enjoying it.[24]

From time to time John liked to eat in an Italian restaurant, Pizza Express, in nearby Blackheath, which, because of the good food, he believed was the genuine article; nobody could persuade him that it was one of a chain of restaurants. Although he knew the people there and got on well with them, he was in the habit of clicking his fingers when he wanted to order something. He was forever asking for more garlic – garlic bread never had enough in it – and more *grappa*. Seán O'Leary remembered John asking for a steak, which he had ordered in a restaurant, to be covered in garlic. When the steak arrived at the table with not enough on it, he ordered the waiter to bring it back with more.

When, on one occasion, he sat down at a table in Pizza Express and discovered flowers on it, he said, 'Who put these f–ing flowers here?' He called a waiter and said, 'Take these f–ing flowers away!' Another time he discovered that his chair wasn't the right height, and asked for a cushion. As the Polish waitress was unable to find one, she fetched her coat and rolled it up for him. He was very touched by this gesture and drank to her. He also asked for the muzak to be turned off. He got to know the staff, who put up with his whims. He seemed to like making his presence felt in restaurants; at one time during a meal, he stopped eating and cried 'Christ!' There was silence and everyone turned to look at him. 'It's great to be alive!' he exclaimed.[25]

Mirette Dowling, the director of the Wicklow Choral Society, visited John any time she was staying in London on holidays. She always went to Greenwich and they used to go out for lunch together. Often John would drink a little too much and would say to her, 'I don't think I can stand up!'[26]

In addition to his love of garlic he was very fond of cheese, which he liked 'snotty', as his friend Seán O'Leary remembered: it had to be 'well done' and kept in the airing cupboard. As he had been having trouble with his teeth, he got them all extracted and as a result he had difficulty eating certain things.[27]

John often shared 'rowdy meals' with Judy Jordan, who was distantly related to him through her mother, Freda Beckett, sister of Walter Beckett. She had never met John until he settled down in Greenwich. As she was living nearby, her mother sent her to make herself known and to give family respects. Later, her husband Ray and John would form a bond over shared experiences with heart problems. [28]

Seán O'Leary recollects that John liked jazz, though only certain types, such as New Orleans jazz. A favourite of his was Blind Willie Johnson who sang to the simple accompaniment of a guitar. A.L. Lloyd, who had greatly influenced John, also liked this type of music. John also listened to the singing of an English jazz female singer whose name Seán could not remember; it could have been Cleo Lane, who was born in the same year as John. A song that he liked was 'Don't worry 'bout me', composed in 1938 by Rube Bloom, with lyrics written by Ted Koehler. He would later enjoy the film about Cuban music, *Buena Vista Social Club*, when it was released in 1999. [29]

The first programmes on BBC Radio 3 that John produced was the weekly *Morning Concert* series, broadcast on Mondays, Tuesdays, Thursdays and Fridays between 7.05 and 9 am. John's first programme was broadcast on 14 November 1983. The works played on Monday were by Mozart, Bach, John Dowland, Berlioz, Rimsky-Korsakov, Mendelssohn and Bizet. Other composers featured during the week included Weber, Franz Xaver Mozart, Stravinsky, Haydn, Moeran, Kodály, Bruch, Sibelius and Brahms. All the music in these programmes was played on either gramophone records or tapes and, surprisingly, the programmes were never broadcast live at this period, but were recorded. [30]

Towards the end of December 1983 John and Ruth travelled to Paris to see Samuel, who proposed that they meet in the Hotel PLM Saint Jacques, 17 boulevard Saint Jacques. As Samuel had always paid the bill for meals taken together in restaurants over the years, John 'had the temerity' (as he wrote) to invite him and Suzanne to supper with Ruth and himself. Samuel countermanded this with the words, ''Tis we invite you'. While there, Samuel presented them with an eighteenth-century Chinese vase. [31] Earlier in the year, when John and Ruth had left Ireland and settled in Greenwich, Samuel had sent them a postcard expressing his concern about them moving back to London. 'What I'd like to know,' he wrote, 'is that you don't regret the change. A typed line to that effect would be welcome.' Samuel requested the 'typed line' because, in his message, he regretted that he could not read John's writing. In fact, John had just as much difficulty in deciphering Samuel's difficult hand, and made a note to that effect. [32] Samuel wrote back to say that he was glad to hear what he wanted to hear: that they had not regretted the move. [33]

Forty-Three
1984–89

John again produced the Radio 3 *Morning Concert* series starting on 9 January 1984. The works played during the week were by composers such as Jean Françaix, Beethoven, Haydn, Bach, Sibelius, Brahms and Walton (on Monday), and Louis-Gabriel Guillemain (the music played by John's favourite group, Musica Antiqua Köln), Rachmaninov, Prokofiev, Shostakovich, Strauss, Purcell, Stravinsky, Chopin, Fauré, Weber, Weill, Debussy and others.[1] The inclusion of some of his favourite composers and performers is perfectly understandable, but Debussy, whose music John detested, is proof that John was prepared to put his personal dislikes to one side and be objective when compiling programmes such as these.[2]

At the beginning of the following month John attended a harpsichord recital given by his former pupil Malcolm Proud in the Concert Hall of Broadcasting House, which was relayed live on Radio 3. John met Malcolm afterwards.[3] Soon afterwards, John and Ruth took a short holiday in the Netherlands, from where they sent a card to Samuel. While there, John bought himself a pair of comfortable backless shoes.[4]

John and Ruth were away again in July, this time in the north of Spain, where they stayed for three weeks. We received a postcard from them depicting the very old and weathered portico of the Church of Santa Maria in San Vicente de la Barquera, Santander.[5] John's colleague Patrick Lambert remembers that John and Ruth were quite adventurous when abroad. As well as taking holidays in the northern part of England (where they often visited Ruth's daughter Rose), Norfolk (where they visited Ruth's friends, Frida and Vic Robinson), Yorkshire and the Lake District, they also went to Yugoslavia before the civil war, and stayed in Dubrovnik. They then went up into the mountains and on to Cetinje, the former royal capital of Montenegro. Here they were arrested by the police for some unknown reason and taken to the local police station, where things became difficult because they could not speak the language and the locals had little or no English. Somehow they managed to extricate themselves from the situation and return home safely.[6] Many of John's holidays were pilgrimages to places associated with a favourite composer or writer. As well as these trips, John also visited his cousins Samuel in Paris, Morris Sinclair in Geneva, and the Cusacks in the south of France.[7]

In November my mother received a postcard from John, which depicted the Royal Hospital at Greenwich, painted by Canaletto in about 1755. On the back he wrote, 'Dear Margaret – that was most kind of you to send copies of some of Charles's letters. They're vividly interesting – what a trip! I'd love to see his photos. We were delighted to see Cathal and William here on Wednesday evening – both in great form. Thanks again for the letters – John.' The letters referred to lengthy epistles I had posted home from Japan, where I had spent six eventful weeks on the main island of Honshu. At around the same time, my father and his friend William Stuart had driven around England and had visited John in Azof Street.[8] Another card, undated, but depicting the same Canaletto painting, simply read, 'Warmest greetings to the three of youse – John & Ruth.'[9] ('Youse' is used by some people in Ireland, especially in Dublin, to denote the plural of 'you'.)

John produced more *Morning Concert* programmes in late September and mid-November. Some of the more out-of-the-way composers included Hoffmeister, Arensky, Scott Joplin, Lennox Berkeley, Michel Corette, Machaut, Arthur Benjamin, Alphonse Hasselmann, Silvestre Revueltas and Germaine Tailleferre. He also included music by Saint-Saëns, another composer whom he hated.[10] Between Monday 10 and Friday 14 December John was producer, for the first time, of *This Week's Composer*, which, during that week, was Sibelius, one of John's favourites. As well as some of the more obvious works (such as *Finlandia*, *Pohjola's Daughter* and the *Four Legends*, Op. 22), John chose the *Spring Song*, Op. 16, *Scènes historiques*, Op. 25, *The Dryad*, Op. 45, items from *The Tempest*, Op. 109 and *Funeral Music*, Op. 111 No. 2 for organ.[11]

John was the producer of a programme of Handel's music recorded at the beginning of January 1985. *L'Allegro, Il Pensoroso ed il Moderato*, performed by the Raglan Baroque Players and Raglan Baroque Singers, and conducted by Nicholas Kraemer, was recorded in St John's, Smith Square in honour of the composer's birth three hundred years previously.[12] Nicholas Anderson remembers John being in charge of this anniversary concert; in fact, he had been working on the

European Music Year's Bach and Handel tercentenary project for 1985. Nicholas met John in the church before the concert began and noticed that he was wearing a tie. When Nicholas remarked on this unusual addition to his customary sarto-rial ensemble, John growled, 'Handel and ties seem to go well together'.[13]

The next *This Week's Composer* programmes that John produced were broad-cast in the week beginning 1 April. This time the composer was Max Bruch; an interesting selection of familiar and unfamiliar works was chosen, starting with his Violin Concerto No. 1 in G min, Op. 26.[14] Johann Christian Bach was the subject for a week of programmes in early September, which once again John produced,[15] then Haydn's contemporaries were featured in December.[16]

John's cousin Samuel celebrated his eightieth birthday in April of the following year. In fact, 'celebrated' is hardly the correct word, for Samuel hated all the fuss that was being made about this important birthday. Towards the end of March he had written to John: 'Scarcely know where I am much less where I'll be next month. Look forward to hearing from you when the worst is past.'[17] John continued to produce *This Week's Composer*; and in mid April he worked on a week's series devoted to the composers associated with the Schola Cantorum in Paris, from its foundation in 1894 until the 1970s.[18] John was back on *Morning Concert* by mid May.[19] Mendelssohn, whose music John loved, was the week's composer towards the end of October.[20]

Fauré was the week's composer starting on 26 January 1987. John surely would have loved producing the programmes, which were divided into three periods of the composer's life: the first on Monday, the second on Tuesday and the third on the remaining three days of the week.[21] John, now sixty years of age, formally retired from the BBC in February, but would return to produce and present more programmes. Starting on 6 April, Stravinsky featured in *This Week's Composer*, which John produced; in May he worked on a week of *Morning Concert* programmes, and in early September, Monteverdi was the subject of *This Week's Composer*.[22] John produced a series of six programmes devoted to piano music (mostly by Mozart) played by the Hungarian pianist Lili Kraus, which were broadcast in November and December,[23] and then five programmes of Peter Katin playing piano music by Chopin, which were broadcast in December and January 1988. These had been recorded in November and December of the previous year.[24]

John came to Dublin in April 1987 to conduct a performance of Bach's *Saint John Passion* with the Irish Chamber Orchestra, the Goethe Institute Choir and soloists, and called to our house with his sister Ann a few days before the concert. I recorded in my diary, 'John was in great form and had polished off the remainder of our only bottle of whiskey!'[25]

ˮ I went to the performance of the *Passion*, held at 3 pm on Sunday 12th in the large and reverberant Saint Andrew's Church, Westland Road. The church was quite packed. Although the acoustics were poor, the music was powerful. Afterwards I found John and greeted him. He gave me an extended handshake, holding on to my hand for a while, but had little time to talk to me.[26] Michael Dervan, now the music critic for *The Irish Times*, wrote:

> As far as one could hear within the limitations of the acoustics the Irish Chamber Orchestra played for John Beckett as they play this music for no one else, as if it were in their blood, and the Goethe Institute Choir coped manfully with Bach's demanding music at Beckett's exacting speeds. John Beckett, more than any other conductor working in Ireland at the moment, has the measure of Bach's music and it is a token of his achievement that it is Bach's music, above all, one remembers from this performance.

The soloists included Irené Sandford, Frank Patterson, Nigel Williams, and William Young.[27] The production was recorded by RTÉ Radio and broadcast a year later.[28]

In August, John and Ruth were on holidays in France; we received a post-card depicting a nocturnal view of the Eglise St Nicolas in Civray. Scrawled on the back was, 'Dear Cathal & Margaret – we're rambling around Touraine, seeing church after marvellous church from this period – Charles rang us from Heathrow before we left – in great form – Greetings and love from us both John & Ruth.'[29] I had telephoned them before setting off on a tour of China and Tibet, an adventure that interested John greatly.[30] He and Ruth must have visited Samuel during their time in France, as Samuel later wrote to them and mentioned that it was good to be with them again, though he apologized for being in such poor form.[31]

Samuel sent John a postcard in early December, on which he wrote, 'Bravo for Leigh resuscitation. It made Marion very happy.' This referred to three recordings, made by the BBC, of music by Walter Leigh, which John had conducted. Leigh, a pupil of Paul Hindemith, had shown great promise as a composer, but unfortunately had been killed in North Africa during World War II. Samuel's friend Marion Leigh, who came to the recording sessions, was his widow.[32] The music, performed by the Langham Chamber Orchestra was broadcast on BBC Radio 3 in April, May and July of the following year.[33] John had played a selection of English virginal music on Radio 3 in November;[34] Samuel's comment, on the aforementioned postcard, was, 'I hear you were tinkling the cymbalo on 3rd. That's the spirit.' Samuel's message concluded with the couplet, 'Ochone ochone / dead and not gone'. (The Irish word *ochón* means 'alas'.) This, as John explained, may have been suggested by a photocopy of a piece from the *Fitzwilliam Virginal Book*, entitled *The Irish Ho Hoane*, which John had sent to Samuel.[35]

Max Bruch was again *This Week's Composer* in the first week of January, 1988 and the five programmes were produced by John. One of the works featured on the Wednesday was Bruch's Quintet in A minor, Op. posth., performed by the Hanson String Quartet with Graham Oppenheimer on viola. This was a work that John had unearthed in a library and had edited. It was subsequently published by Albert J. Kunzelmann in Germany, in 1991.[36]

In Dublin, the Bach cantata series of concerts continued, but Michael Dervan was not too impressed with the standards of performance:

> The annual Bach cantata series at St Ann's Church, Dawson Street was so tightly bound up with the musical personality and dedication of John Beckett ... that it has always seemed unlikely that anyone else would successfully manage to perpetuate what was once a rewarding fixture in the musical calendar. And though the current reincarnation by Musica Sacra claims a direct lineage from the original series, yesterday afternoon there was so little in evidence of what John Beckett used to strive for that the claim seemed absurd.

On the following week Michael felt that the performances:

> bore the marks of inadequate rehearsal and lack of musical preparation to such an extent that it would be easy to compile a detailed list of musical and technical faults surprising in a professional presentation. ... it is baffling that the organisers should have the gall to claim kinship with John Beckett's cantata series. Musica Sacra's programme book described the Beckett concerts as a 'major event on the musical and cultural life of the city,' which decidedly the current series was not.[37]

John travelled to Dublin in May to conduct works by Bach, Vaughan Williams, and Mozart in the Royal Hospital, Kilmainham, performed by the RTÉ Concert Orchestra and the RTÉ Singers. Charles Acton, who attended the concert, enjoyed the familiar Orchestral Suite No. 3 by Bach.[38] The programme was broadcast later on RTÉ's new classical music station, FM 3.[39]

After John had produced a week of Boccherini's music on Radio 3's *Composers of the Week* in June,[40] John produced and presented three programmes of folk music, which were broadcast on Radio 3 in August. The first was *Sounds of Transylvania*. This was an interesting though quite straightforward introduction to the music of the region, and John's links were short and to the point. He began by describing the countryside, lush forests and villages of northern Romania, where a local band consisted typically of only one violin and a three-stringed guitar. The music he played included two pairs of wedding dances, two 'dance songs', a song sung by an elderly man, whose technique was learned 'fifty summers ago'– perhaps in the previous century – and a solo on the bagpipes.[41]

The second programme was *Sounds of Sardinia*, which was broadcast on 23 August, and the third was *Sounds of Soviet Georgia*, which was aired on 30 August. John began this last programme with, 'Georgia – that colourful and ebullient land, bordered on the north by the great range of the Caucasus, on the west by the Black Sea, on the south by Turkey and Armenia, and on the east by Azerbaijan.' He played work songs from western Georgia, 'sung mostly in the robust, mostly two, three and four-part polyphony unique to that region.' He described the region as 'an island of polyphony' and warned listeners that one piece was 'loud and harsh'. He added, 'Don't turn down your volume too much – it's meant to be like that!'. One of the recordings was of a solo song, sung by the driver of a wagon pulled by oxen, and recorded in the aisle of an eleventh-century church. John relished out-of-the-way music like this.[42]

Probably the best programme that John produced and presented was one called *Early Birds*, which was broadcast on Radio 3 on 21 September.[43] In the programme, John sounds relaxed and lively, and speaks with his usual excellent diction and choice of words. He started this programme about the pioneers of early music with 'the earliest bird of them all: Arnold Dolmetsch. In delving beneath the surface of the notes on the page, Dolmetsch caught more worms than any of his contemporaries. Scholar, teacher, performer and expert instrument maker, he was lavishly qualified to explore the practices and traditions of the past.' The first musical illustration was Dolmetsch playing a piece by Bach on a clavichord at the age of seventy-three; one can barely hear the tiny sound of the instrument through the sizzle. John then went on to Violet Gordon Woodhouse, 'the first person ever to record harpsichord music' in the 1920s. Under the influence of Dolmetsch, her teacher, she forsook the piano for the harpsichord and clavichord. By way of illustration, John played a recording of her playing the final movement of Bach's *Italian Concerto*, recorded in 1927. Next up was Wanda Landowska playing a Scarlatti Sonata in G on her specially made Pleyel harpsichord. 'As you can hear from the variety of sounds and colours she draws from her "iron-girt" Pleyel, Landowska was no seeker after unattainable authenticity', John commented. He then spoke about Nadia Boulanger and her reluctance to record Monteverdi, and played the famous aria *Chiome d'oro*, sung by two tenors with piano continuo. Mention was made of Thomas Brinkley, who in 1959 established a studio for early music in Munich, and then August Wenzinger of the Schola Cantorum Basiliensis. John then moved on to Michael Tippett and Alfred Deller, whose first recording was made in 1949: Henry Purcell's *Music*

for a While, accompanied on the harpsichord by Walter Bergmann. After music
by Froberger played by Thurston Dart in 1961 on a clavichord made by Tom
Goff, John finished the programme with the famous 1904 recording of the last
castrato, Alessandro Moreschi (who sang in the choir of the Sistine Chapel)
singing Gounod's 'parasitical' *Ave Maria*, superimposed on Bach's piece from the
'Forty-Eight', with a violin part 'thrown in'.[44]

John went to Dublin in March to conduct a performance of Bach's *Saint Matthew
Passion*, played by the Irish Chamber Orchestra, with the Goethe Institute Choir
and the Boys of the Palestrina Choir and soloists, in the Royal Dublin Society
Concert Hall.[45] Kevin Myers, writing in *The Irish Times*'s regular column 'An
Irishman's Diary', described the work as 'one of the triumphs of Western civili-
sation' and mentioned that it would be sung in German for the first time in
Ireland. Myers went so far as to describe John as 'one of the greatest living
exponents of the genius of Bach'. 'When John spoke of a halo of strings which
Bach had written around a five-part harmony,' Myers wrote enthusiastically, 'I
stopped taking notes:

> 'It is music of great density,' said John slowly, measuring each word. 'It is heard
> very, very seldom.' ... 'It is,' said John, again weighing each word like a jeweller
> putting gold dust on a scales, 'extremely difficult music. Sometimes it can be
> distastefully like singing the unsingable – but don't write that. Bach does assume
> that the singer can do anything.' Conducting the 'Passion' requires enormous
> intellectual ability, huge powers of concentration and inexhaustible energy.
> Does he do anything to keep fit? 'Certainly not,' he murmured, appalled. 'The
> choir would walk over broken glass to have him conduct us,' said Cáit Cooper,
> of the Goethe Institute. 'I know John would hate me saying that.' (Though, I
> have to say, John didn't appear to mind). The simple truth is – acknowledged by
> all who know – that John Beckett is the great Bach master.[46]

Michael Dervan's more down-to-earth review of the performance appeared
in print on 20 March:

> John Beckett's vision of Bach's 'St Matthew Passion', as revealed at the RDS
> yesterday afternoon, is an austere one and his rugged handling of the work was
> stronger as a devotional act, a genuflection at the altar of the musical master-
> piece, than as a communication of the narrative of the gospel. Beckett's is an
> almost awe-inspiring vision which presents his audience with a monumental
> musical edifice through which the conductor propels the listeners with a firm
> and inexorable tread.

Dervan then discussed the performances of the other soloists and concluded:

> The members of the Irish Chamber Orchestra were once again inspired by this
> conductor to a mastery of the spirit of the music which transcended the weak-
> nesses of the flesh. But the triumph of the performance as a whole – for which
> credit is due most of all to the conductor – is that what lingers in the memory is
> the music of Bach. And that, I suspect, is how Beckett would want it.[47]

Michael both previewed and reviewed another concert that John conducted
in Dublin on 2 April: a choral and instrumental programme of Bach, Purcell and
Telemann, played by The King's Consort and led by Roy Goodman on baroque
instruments. This was the final event of the second Dublin Festival of Early Music,
held in the Royal Hospital, Kilmainham. John in fact did not conduct all the items
in the programme. Michael Dervan wrote, 'In the Bach cantatas and the excerpts
from Purcell's incidental music to Afra Behn's "Abdelazer" Beckett conducted ...
the King's Consort, and the bright-sounding Cantata Singers in his familiar, taut
fashion.' The Telemann work and excerpts from Purcell's birthday song 'Who
can from joy refrain?' were directed from the harpsichord by Robert King 'with
a more winning grace, a greater expressive latitude and a wider range of colour
and dynamics. ... If Robert King might be regarded, in culinary terms, as an
advocate of nouvelle cuisine, John Beckett could be seen as the creator of a nour-
ishing, chunky broth.'[48] The concert was broadcast on RTÉ FM 3.[49]

In June, John – and presumably Ruth – spent another holiday in the
Netherlands. When he returned on 1 July, he discovered that his passport was
out of date. This meant that he was unable to attend the funeral of Samuel's wife
Suzanne, who died towards the end of July. John wrote to Samuel, who was
now in poor health, to say that he was distressed about this. Samuel's short reply
thanked him for his letter and concluded, 'The end was terrible. The very end.
Before the first rest at last. Much love Samuel'.[50]

Some more programmes featuring John conducting the Langham Chamber
Orchestra were broadcast on Radio 3 at around this period: in June, when they
performed music by Sibelius, and in September and October, when the BBC
repeated two of the Walter Leigh programmes of the previous year.[51] John also
co-produced a programme of the orchestra playing music by Poulenc, Jean
Françaix and John's friend Christopher Bunting, who played his own cello
concerto.[52] Patrick Lambert remembers John arranging the recording of this
concerto, which he thought was worthwhile doing.[53]

A book that was published this year was the first volume of David Cairn's
great biography of Hector Berlioz, *The Making of an Artist*, which John read
avidly. The second volume would not appear for another ten years. David, a

friend of John's, remembers how John used to telephone him from time to time, asking him when the second volume was due to be published. Although John liked Berlioz's music, he did not care for all of it. David remembers that when John was listening to a performance of Berlioz's *L'Enfance du Christ*, he was not exactly impressed by the piece depicting the gathering of the shepherds in the manger, which was written like a fugue, but was not a fugue – it was *fugato*. John, who was rather inebriated at the time, said, 'If he's writing a f–ing fugue, why doesn't he write a f–ing fugue?'[54]

By now Samuel Beckett was critically ill. John went to Paris to be with him and, while there, visited his former harpsichord student Emer Buckley. He told her that he knew that Samuel was dying. He deeply regretted that he could not bring Samuel with him, as he felt that Samuel would have loved her apartment, which was in a former seventeenth-century convent in the rue de Charonne. This street was near the Faubourg Saint-Antoine, a traditional area of joiners, cabinet makers and the many crafts linked to their activities. The building had been used for artisans' workshops in the nineteenth century and the apartment walls had never been redecorated. They were blackened, had patches of old wallpaper here and there, and there were traces of drawings and plans for furniture on them. The fireplace had a black iron 'curtain' (called a *Sorbonne*) which apparently was pulled down when glue was being heated in a pot over the fire. Emer found it easy to imagine a couple of down-and-outs, such as the characters in *Waiting for Godot*, shacking up in the place. Little did she know that this was the last time that she would see John.[55]

John was back in Dublin in December to conduct an all-Bach programme, consisting of the first two parts of the *Christmas Oratorio* and the Magnificat in D. The concert was advertised in *The Irish Times*: 'The Goethe Institute Choir's Christmas concert at the Royal Hospital Kilmainham tomorrow night is conducted by Ireland's leading Bach specialist, John Beckett.'[56] 'The rough-hewn granite of John Beckett's approach to Bach was heard to good effect earlier this year in a performance of the "St Matthew Passion",' wrote Michael Dervan in his review. 'But Beckett and Bach seemed less amenable to each other yesterday at the Royal Hospital'. According to Dervan, most of the faults lay in the orchestral playing. He was happier with the soloists and the choir. 'The quality of the choral singing varied with the difficulty of the music, but even when the flesh was weakest, the celebratory spirit of the works was well communicated.'[57]

Samuel Beckett, who had been in a coma since 11 December (the day after the concert), died peacefully on the 22nd. He was buried privately and secretly with Suzanne in the Cimetière de Montparnasse on the day after Christmas. There was no funeral service.[58] Although John did not attend the funeral, he must have been deeply saddened. He had received the last communication from this much-loved and highly revered cousin in mid October: a picture postcard depicting a black-and-white photo of the Bois de Boulogne, taken in 1900. It bore the simple message:

> *Dear John & Ruth,*
>   *Thanks for yrs. of 8th with good news of health & Xmas Bach. So simply much love [crossed out]. Words fail so simply much love.*
>   *Sam*[59]

This was the first of several emotional blows that would affect John deeply over the coming years.

Forty-Four
1990–95

The new year began with radio broadcasts, the first being *The True Vine* on Radio 3. In this programme John presented recordings that the black American gospel singer and guitarist Flora Molton had made in Paris in her late seventies. Molton, who was born in 1908, would die just four months after John's programme was broadcast. This was another example of John's passion for jazz and earthy, direct music.[1]

Another programme, broadcast on RTÉ FM 3, was Brahms's *Serenade No. 1*, Op. 11 in D, performed by the RTÉ Concert Orchestra, conducted by John.[2] Next was *A Musical Eden*, on BBC Radio 3. According to *The Irish Times*, John presented '1920s recordings of traditional music from Madagascar, the Ukraine, Turkey, Spain and Irish and Welsh settlers in the USA, Cajun music from Louisiana and Jewish prayer for the time of the new moon.'[3] On the same day as this, John was heard conducting more music performed by the RTÉ Concert Orchestra on FM 3: this time Rossini's Overture *Il Signor Bruschino* and two of Schubert's symphonies, Nos 3 and 5.[4]

Towards the end of April, the third Dublin Festival of Early Music got underway with one of the largest undertakings of the Early Music Organisation of Ireland: the launch of the Baroque Orchestra of Ireland. John was to conduct the inaugural concert at the Royal Hospital in Kilmainham, but had to pull out due to ill health; he was replaced by Ivor Bolton. If John had been well enough, he would have conducted an all-Bach programme which included the Brandenburg Concerto No. 5 (with John's friend Christopher Stembridge playing the demanding harpsichord solo) and Cantata No. 82, *Ich habe genug* ('It is enough'), sung by Nigel Williams. The leader of the new baroque orchestra was Marie Leonhardt, wife of the famous Dutch harpsichordist Gustav Leonhardt.[5]

John, in fact, had suffered a heart attack. He was warned by his doctor to do no more conducting, was put on Warfarin and ordered to take it easy. Although he was heard conducting Schumann's Symphony No. 1 (the 'Spring') on RTÉ FM 3 in May,[6] then Sibelius's *Belshazzar* Suite Op. 51 and Fauré's *Masques et Bergamasques* in June,[7] the programmes may well have been recorded before he became indisposed. He appears to have done no more conducting after this. In July he presented two programmes about the music performed during the reigns of King Louis XIV, James II and William of Orange, both entitled *Three Kings* on the same station.[8] He only produced two more series of programmes, entitled *A Dutch Retrospect*, for the BBC: twelve programmes of recordings from the Royal Concertgebouw and Rotterdam Philharmonic's 1990–91 seasons (broadcast later in 1991), and, in 1994, thirteen programmes of recordings of the same two orchestras. Lindsay Armstrong often invited him to come to Dublin in order to conduct, but he turned down all offers – his excuse being that he did not want to 'relive the past'. He even talked Bernadette Greevy out of an engagement that would have involved him.[9]

John was well enough to go on a holiday to France with Ruth in April 1992. He sent a postcard to his friends Seán and Odile O'Leary in Reading from Alsace, which read: 'Dear both – we're leading to the end of a holiday starting in Alsace, then down through the Jura mountains – back to Berne in Switzerland to see the Klee – I'm still in love with him! Enjoying everything – much refreshed – Love as ever – to you both and all – John and Ruth.'[10]

Towards the end of the year, John's ex-wife Vera died. Aidan Higgins's wife Jill had visited her when she was old and in poor health; Vera had been suffering from aphasia, had lost the power of speech and was finding it difficult to walk.[11] Towards the end of her life she lived in assisted accommodation at the back of King's Cross railway station. She had had rooms at the top floor of the building, which faced north, and she had continued to paint. A warden was at hand to attend to her if there was an emergency.[12] Jill recorded her last 'sad visit' to her on Friday, 15 August 1992 and wrote in her diary, 'I closed the door ... and wished her a swift death.'[13] She died, at the age of seventy-eight, in September.[14] Neither her close friend Paddy nor Douglas Slocombe attended her funeral, but John did. It was a quiet affair and John was very upset. He told Roland Morrow, who had been visiting and helping Vera, 'I couldn't live with her and I couldn't live without her.' She left everything to Roland and John;[15] Jill was astonished to discover that she had left John £6000, for she had always behaved as if she had no money.[16] In fact, £25,000 had been found in her bank account when she died. As she had had to pay back taxes, she had sold the house in Rasiguères and had been hard up towards the end.

Roland and his partner cleared her flat after she died and although they were not looking for them, they noticed, when sorting out her underwear, that there were no knickers to be found! Vera had donated many of her clothes to the poor and needy. She had continued to make her own clothes, and they found some garments that she had begun and not finished.[17] Roland also came across the letters that she had written to her mother, describing her flight from Poland. When Roland discovered them, he decided to contact Douglas Slocombe, though he did not know whether he was alive or dead at the time. He looked up the name in the telephone book, found just one Douglas Slocombe, and rang the number. He was lucky – Vera's ex-husband answered the phone and they had a conversation. Before handing over Vera's letters to him, Roland typed their contents into his computer. He still has a copy of Vera's will and the exquisite professionally printed photograph of her mentioned in an earlier chapter.[18]

In February of the following year John came to Dublin again and went with my parents to visit their friends William and June Stuart in Celbridge; my mother was knitting a jumper for their baby daughter Arabella at the time. I was at work that day, but was able to telephone him and chat for about ten minutes. He was in good form.[19] A week later he wrote:

> *Dear Cathal and Margaret – last Sunday was a great day, from first moment to last. It has been far too long since I saw you both, and we spent some time together! What about another trip to China?? I'm glad to have been able to talk to Charles too – hope Margaret got Arabella's jumper finished to her liking – bet she did! We send our love as always – John.*[20]

We received another card from John in mid April, this time from Italy. Depicting a sunlit valley surrounded by rocky mountains, it read: 'Easter Monday. Dear Cathal & Margaret – We're on a 19-day over-Easter trip in North Italy. Staying in this valley at Toblach, where Mahler wrote his last 3 works, 'Das Lied von der Erde' and the 9th and 10th Symphonies. Warm greetings – and to Charles.'[21] Toblach, also known as Dobbiaco, is on the border with Austria. John Sothcott and Seán O'Leary remembered that John and Ruth had spent much of the holiday cleaning up the run-down, flimsy-looking, one-roomed shack or *Komponierhäuschen* some 4000 feet up in the northern Dolomites, where Mahler had composed his music. Although they tried to bring this humble but historic building to the attention of the local authorities, it still is in poor condition.[22] It now lies in private land that has been turned into a wildlife park. In order to visit it, one must buy a ticket for the park and follow the signs to the hut.[23] John and Ruth also travelled around the mountains near the borders with Switzerland and Germany, stopping at the small towns of Gurtis and Landeck, from which John sent a postcard to Patrick Lambert.[24]

Postcard from John Beckett to the Gannon family from Toblach in Italy, 1993.

John came to Dublin for Joe Groocock's eightieth birthday celebration in Trinity College, in November. Jenny Robinson, Joe's daughter, was delighted to meet him again.[25]

On 20 April 1994 Michael Morrow died. Michael had been in poor health and had suddenly deteriorated. While John had ignored him, Seán O'Leary had kept in touch. One day Seán received a very strange telephone call from Michael; as he was making no sense whatever, Seán realized immediately that he was very ill. He was suffering from Hepatitis C, which had affected both his liver and brain. As Seán realized that the man was dying, he went to see him in the Royal Free Hospital in Hampstead, which specialized in haematology; John, however, refused to go.[26]

When Michael died, John showed no inclination to go to his funeral at Golders Green Crematorium. However, he rang Seán a few days beforehand to say that having spoken to Jantina Noorman, he had changed his mind and had decided to go. Desmond MacNamara's son Oengus spoke for his father at the funeral; Heinz Liebrecht, who, with his wife, had looked after Michael, also spoke. John, who was sitting behind Seán, then jumped up and, unannounced and uninvited, made an impromptu speech. He contradicted what Heinz had said, saying that Michael had not been a performer but a musicologist, and went on to praise him.[27] He spoke at length and finally had to be stopped by one of Michael's sons. Although John had given a well-delivered, emotional and truthful speech, in which he stated that he was fond of Michael, most people in the crematorium were embarrassed by the incident – especially members of the Morrow family.[28] Brigid Ferguson, Michael's sister, although a little upset by John's outburst, was at least happy that he had said what a great fellow Michael had been and that he had made his peace with him. Afterwards John went to the family home and spoke with Michael's widow, Hedy.[29] She saw little of him afterwards. She found John 'so complicated' and enormously talented, though in order to get on well with him, one would have to admire him and be respectful to him. She agreed that he was a very private individual.[30]

John lost another friend in 1994. This time it was Vera Škrabánek's husband Petr, who passed away on 21 June. He had contracted a very aggresive form of prostate cancer the year before. When he and Vera received a Christmas card from John and Ruth at the end of 1993 they felt that they could not write and trouble them with more bad news, and so they did not. As a result, when Petr died in the following year, John and Ruth knew nothing about it. When they did find out, they contacted Vera and asked if they could be of any help to her. As Vera had to travel to London to collect a prize on behalf of her late husband in September, she asked if she could stay with them. They collected her from the airport, sat her down in a café and asked her to tell them everything. Vera told them the whole story about Petr's illness and they were extremely touched by it. She went to the special ceremony to receive the prize and they collected her afterwards. From then on, Vera realized that, in the close friendship between them, the focus had now switched from her husband to her. Ruth was especially kind, asking her if she had any financial difficulties and how she would manage to educate her children. She said, 'We have very little, but if you need anything, we'd only be too delighted to help you financially.' John, who had been very fond of Petr, was very sympathetic; she felt that he was one of very few people who could really talk to her about her late husband in such a nice way.[31]

It was probably in August of this year when John and Ruth took a holiday in Yorkshire. John sent a postcard, with a picture of Ribblehead Viaduct, Settle Carlisle Railway, to his friends Seán and Odile O'Leary, which read, 'Dear Seán & Odile, How bizarre yet perfect these viaducts on the Settle to Carlisle Railway look. Our fifth year on holiday in Yorkshire – it never fails. Love to you both – John and Ruth.'[32] They always rented the same house near Dent on the Yorkshire-Cumbria border so that the four grandchildren and their various parents could stay with them.[33]

Although John enjoyed holidays like this and, in general, living in England with Ruth, he was very much torn between his native country and the UK, as Christopher Nobbs was forcibly reminded when they went to an excellent and very realistic production of Synge's *The Playboy of the Western World*, staged in the Almeida Theatre, Islington, during the year. When they entered the theatre, the aroma of burning peat wafting from the stage greeted them. Christopher glanced at John and noticed tears running down his face.[34]

In December John was one of the contributors in a special radio programme, entitled *Lonely Waters*. This was a portrait of the composer E.J. Moeran, who had been born one hundred years ago. The other contributors were Lionel Hill, Vernon Hanley, John Talbot, Stephen Lloyd and Barry Marsh. The presenter was Lyndon Jenkins and the producer was John's colleague and friend Patrick Lambert. John described how Moeran had contacted him when adjudicating the *Feis Ceoil* in Dublin, met him and successfully got him into the Royal College of Music through his connections. The programme, which is illustrated with snippets of music by Moeran, is very interesting and John sounds relaxed and in good spirits.[35]

At around this period Dan Shields, John's friend from Carlow, came to London and visited him and Ruth in Greenwich. John installed him in a nearby Indian B&B, and he was invited to the house for evening meals. Afterwards, they stayed in contact by phone; John would ask, 'Are you still alive?' The phone calls were so long that often Dan had to terminate them. John sent him several gifts: when he revived his interest in Mozart's Italian operas, he sent him a new recording of *Idomeneo*, and he also sent him a copy of Christoph Wolff's biography of Bach.[36]

In April 1995 John and Ruth went to the Esterházy family castle in Eisenstadt, Austria, where Haydn had once lived and worked. A postcard from Fertód found its way to James Plunkett. 'Dear Jimmy,' Ruth wrote, 'we are on a brief trip to Budapest with a string teachers conference. And have [?had] a chance to bus out here to Esterhazy to pay our respects to [Haydn].' John added a footnote: 'Here he lived – here he came – here we went – wonderful to be here!'[37]

In July, John and Ruth went to a 'Colloquium on Early Music in Memory of Michael Morrow'. With the theme *New Thoughts about Old Music*, it was held at 17 Holly Mount, Hampstead (Ruth and Heinz Liebrecht's home, a converted church). Lasting one day, the participants listened to talks given by Margaret Bent, David Fallows, Tess Knighton, Warwick Edwards and Christopher Page. Seán O'Leary, Jantina Noorman and Jill Higgins, who now met Ruth for the first time, were also present.[38]

John regularly played in a viol consort with some friends. As he unwisely practised and played for hours after hardly touching the instrument for some considerable time, he induced a serious circulation problem in one of his arms. Apparently he was warned that he might lose the arm and/or cause further cardiovascular illness by this obsessive urge to practise and play the viol once again. Understandably, Ruth became quite anxious about John's state of health.[39]

The summer of 1995 was particularly hot. On 4 August John and Ruth went to a concert at the Royal Academy of Music, where they heard the Julian quartet, made up of a group of Japanese students, playing Beethoven's String Quartet in F minor, Op. 95.[40] The journey to and from the Royal Academy in the sweltering heat was a gruelling affair; Ruth loathed the Underground and always felt stressed after travelling on the Tube.

The following day when John was out, Ruth went off shopping and returned to the house. As she felt unwell, she lay in bed for a while.[41] There was no way of contacting John, and if she had tried to telephone her daughter Rose and Rose's husband (a medic), they would have been unavailable. Instead, she rang John's friend Patrick Cuming for advice. As Patrick was sufficiently worried about what she told him, he contacted his daughter Tamzin, a hospital doctor, and asked her to phone Ruth. This she did; based on what Ruth told her, she instructed her to get herself to a hospital immediately and not to wait.[42]

When John did come back at lunchtime, they either contacted their local GP or set off for Greenwich Hospital immediately.[43] Apparently John stayed with her for most of the day and learned that she had suffered a mild heart attack. Because of this, Ruth had to remain in hospital. As John could do no more, he returned home. On his arrival, the phone rang and he was told that Ruth had had another heart attack, this time a massive one, and had died.[44] Fate had dealt John another terrible blow; as he had already suffered a heart attack, everyone had assumed that he would go first. As can be imagined, he was devastated by the unexpected news, because apart from being overweight and having some trouble with her knees, Ruth's general health had appeared to be fine.[45]

John's beloved Ruth was cremated at Lewisham Crematorium on 10 August at 3 pm.[46] The ceremony was a simple one. Ruth had asked for no religion and for live music. Fittingly, this was kindly supplied by the Japanese group, who once again played the Beethoven Quartet. John stood up and read a poem by Emily Dickinson twice.[47] After the cremation, the mourners (who included Ruth's immediate family and friends such as Betty Sullivan, Gillian Smith, Lindsay Armstrong, and Vic and Frida Robinson) were invited to join John at home. Understandably, John was very low after Ruth's untimely death. Although he did change the house over the years, some of her personal items, such as her handbag, were left untouched.[48]

Soon after Ruth's death, John, Ruth's daughter Rose and her son Matthew created a bursary in her memory:

> available to students in the Preparatory String Training course of the Junior School of the Guildhall School of Music and Drama, where Ruth taught for the last decade of her life. We are pleased to say that our proposal has the enthusiastic support of the Head of the Junior School, Derek Rodgers. It will be known as the Ruth David Memorial Bursary and its purpose will be to provide financial assistance for parents of talented children who may require it.

This was the wording, penned by John, on a flyer that was posted to those who had known Ruth and who might have wished to contribute some money.[49] Rose had suggested the idea of the bursary to John as it was in keeping with Ruth's lifelong interest in, and passion for, instrumental tuition for children, and as it was something for him to get involved in and to distract him from his huge and traumatic loss. After his death, the name was changed to the Ruth David and John Beckett Memorial Bursary.[50]

In mid September John went to Dublin, where he visited his sister Ann and various friends such as Vera Škrabánek and John O'Sullivan. He also paid a visit to his good friend Janet Ashe, an amateur pianist with whom he liked to play piano duets. He felt quite at ease with Janet and found that he could confide in her. He visited us one afternoon and seemed very pleased to see us all again. He told us about Ruth's death and left around 5 pm after a cup of tea.[51]

John now took to going to Seán O'Leary's house in Reading once a month, armed with a stack of CDs held together with a rubber band. Before beginning the serious business of listening to them, he took the precaution of closing all the doors and windows. When James Knowlson's biography of Samuel Beckett, *Damned to Fame* was published the following year, John joined the the O'Learys and the Knowlsons for dinner. Afterwards, when the Knowlsons had left, John began to weep. 'Ruth was the best thing in my life,' he said. Seán, who could not get him to bed, had to hold his hand for some considerable time.[52]

The place where he was most at peace, and in good company, was at the Mill, Frida and Vic Robinson's restful home by the River Waverley in Suffolk, on the border with Norfolk. As he was with old friends, he was able to relax. Helen Kraemer, a mutual friend, often joined them. When he went to visit the Robinsons, he generally stayed for about four days. At the Mill he could do what he liked:Frida recalls that, when he needed to answer the minor call of nature, he could relieve himself in the bushes or even into the river. She remembers John's love of Thomas Bewick's engravings, which he often photocopied to adorn his homemade Christmas cards. On one occasion they walked along the river towards the nearby weir, carrying bottles of wine. They stopped to watch an angler cast his line. Fascinated, John noted the arc of the line and the bend of the man's body and said, 'Pure Bewick'. Afterwards, John sent them a present of a big book on the artist.

Frida often tried to stop John drinking, but to no avail – he was inclined to get rather drunk. When he began to work his way towards a second bottle of wine, she always promised to say 'no' to him and refuse him more, but when it came to the point, she never could.

As he did when he visited Seán O'Leary in Reading, John brought his CDs to the Robinsons' home and played new discs for them, which they always appreciated as he was so enthusiastic about his latest discoveries.

As well as listening to music, they regularly played music together, with Frida on violin and her husband Vic on the oboe. However, they sometimes disagreed on speeds and phrasing. As John had set ideas on the way they should play, especially when they tackled works by Bach, he rarely allowed his friends to alter his style. Only occasionally, and reluctantly, did he agree to play a piece their way and not his. Vic remembers the advice John gave him when playing Bach: 'You've got to make up your own mind what you're going to do in terms of phrasing, speed and everything else, because Bach never left any indication of what you should do – it's entirely up to the performer.' John never objected to Bach's keyboard music being played on the piano; he could see the merits of such a performance. He also played with professionals and amateurs alike, no matter how good or bad they were; as long as a person was serious about making music, he was happy. Like other people who played music with John, Frida and Vic noticed that he liked to play a favourite piece again and again.

At Christmas time they were joined by another mutual friend, Joyce Rathbone, a fine pianist and teacher who studied at the Royal Academy of Music and the Lausanne Conservatoire, and a couple named Pegeen and Christie. John was at ease with all these people as they posed no threat to him. Frida had noticed that as John tended to be egocentric, he often felt threatened by people, and for that reason, life was hard for him.[53]

When John visited his sister Ann in Dublin he often brought her to Janet Ashe's house in Greystones, where he and Janet played piano duets. It was usual to start at seven in the evening and continue until eleven. Ann would do something else while John and Janet played pieces by Schubert, Mozart, Fauré and (surprisingly) Debussy. According to Janet, John was 'long suffering' about her playing as she was 'nothing like a pianist'. John often sent her volumes of Schubert's music from his home in London. It was a 'great hardship' for her when he no longer came over to play with her and then could no longer play.

Both were very fond of each other. When John was in London, he often rang Janet, generally at meal times, and had long conversations with her. He rang Brigid Ferguson too, also at mealtimes, and kept her for long periods on the phone. Most of the time, she had no idea of what he was talking about.

As John had encouraged Ann to play the recorder, she learned to play the bass. He, Ann, Janet, Sydney Stokes, Brigid Ferguson, a lady named Maureen Cunnane and John's good friend Paul Conway would either meet either in Ann's house or Sydney's in Greystones, and played music by Brade 'by the hour'.[54]

John had produced a BBC Radio 3 programme in 1989 that included his friend Christopher Bunting's Cello Concerto, played by the composer and the Langham Chamber Orchestra.[55] When Christopher became paralysed and confined to a wheelchair during the last ten years of his life, John went to visit him every week, despite the long journey from Greenwich to his home in Hampstead.[56]

John, who had kept in touch with his former BBC colleague Patrick Lambert, often visited him and his wife Jarka at their home in Croftdown Road, Parliament Hill Fields, near Hampstead. He generally arrived bearing a large, one-and-a-half-litre bottle of wine (his favourite was Italian Merlot), most of which he drank himself. Jarka had to hide bottles of liquor, such as whiskey and brandy, for, if John got his hands on them, he probably would have drunk them too.

He loved to eat olives, but would never eat them pitted – they had to have the stones in them. Patrick remembers him savouring the word 'stone' as Krapp did with the word 'spool' in Samuel's play *Krapp's Last Tape*. As John did not like touching the olives, he always asked for a spoon. Meals were always finished with glasses of *grappa*. Patrick and Jarka remember John in their kitchen, attempting to warm up a bottle of red wine by running hot water over it – Jarka thought that he was trying to remove the label.

Once, during a meal with other guests at the Lamberts' house, John suddenly went very quiet; his head had dropped down into his plate and he had fallen asleep. He woke up later. On another occasion he again fell asleep, this time on the couch, after he had drunk too much when visiting them; Patrick recollects that this happened on the day of Yehudi Menuhin's death. Both Jarka and Patrick remember having a party at their house on a summer's day, when John could not bear to sit out in the heat. Instead, he sat at the table by the window overlooking the back garden, surrounded by a group of adoring women. As a lover of the fair sex, one can imagine him relishing the adulation.[57]

Forty-Five
1996–99

In March 1996 John and Seán O'Leary attended a conference at the Blackheath Concert Halls presented by Goldsmiths College in order to mark the ninetieth anniversary of Samuel Beckett. It took place over a period of three days at the end of the month. The event was sponsored by Mary Robinson and Václav Havel, and presided over by the American theatre scholar and leading authority on Samuel Beckett, Ruby Cohn. Quite a number of Japanese people were there. John wished to listen to what was being said, but did not want to get involved with the people. However, he ended up mixing with them as they were all very friendly. When they discovered that John was Samuel's cousin, they wanted to know all about him. The Japanese people, who were very interested in the radio play *Words and Music*, asked John why he had withdrawn the music that he had written for it. Exasperated, he snapped, 'Because it was crap!' Needless to say, they were quite astonished by his reply.

The conference ended with a dinner that John did not wish to attend, but at the last moment he changed his mind and decided to go. He sat beside Ruby Cohn and Seán sat beside a Japanese lady who was a Catholic and whose best friend in Japan was a Father O'Leary. True to form, John drank too much and soon became inebriated. As Seán was worried about him, he ordered a taxi. By the time it arrived, John had dozed off. He suddenly woke up, refused to travel in the taxi and insisted on driving home in his little Fiat. 'This car knows its own way home,' he declared. Although the journey home was 'very shaky' and Seán was extremely nervous, somehow they managed to arrive back in one piece.

Soon after the conference John was stopped by the police for drunken driving and breathalyzed. He rang Seán O'Leary and said, 'Ahem – I have a confession to make: I have to appear in Bow Street Court!' As soon as Seán heard the introductory clearing of the throat, he knew that something was wrong. As he was banned from driving for a year, John decided to sell the car and give up driving for good. From then on he travelled to Seán's home in Reading by train. He would get up very early in the morning and have his breakfast in a café at Waterloo station, where he could get an excellent cup of coffee and chat to a pleasant Italian woman, who always wished him goodbye with a cheery 'Ciao, bello!' He always brought a book with him to read on the journey and arrived on the dot of twelve at the O'Leary household, having travelled from the railway station by bus.

John stayed with Seán and Odile for a couple of days, usually once a month, in order to listen to music. He introduced Seán to an early Serenade by Dvořák, even though he considered him to be an 'uneven' composer. He liked the music of Mendelssohn, although he regarded him as 'variable'. He declared that he 'had started off as a great composer but had got worse as he went on'. When Seán made a disparaging remark about Mendelssohn, John said, 'You never conducted Saint Paul!' When John and Seán got together in Reading, they often listened to eight or nine cantatas by Bach on CD, and frequently played them twice.

He once brought a recording of Mozart's opera Idomeneo, conducted by John Eliot Gardiner, for Seán to hear, as he thought it was marvellous. John's theory was that Mozart had written his other operas to please the public, whereas he wrote this one for himself. Although Seán did not altogether go along with this idea, he could see something in it. He certainly agreed that it was 'a terrific performance'. They had disagreements over Beethoven, whose quartets (especially the late ones) John did not like. He declared that most of Beethoven's music was 'only souped-up Haydn'. One exception was the String Quartet Opus 18, No. 1. Although he was very fond of Sibelius, he did not like his violin concerto; for him it was 'polluted' as it was too showy. Similarly, Handel's music was 'polluted' because Handel always wanted success.

Seán once had an argument with John about a piece of music, which Seán regarded as a work of second rank but marvellous none the less. John did not agree and, after a pause said, 'I'm afraid I'm crucified by my taste'. The implication was that he wanted to like something but could not. He felt that he was bound to judge all music against the high standards of Bach. On another occasion, he said to Seán, 'I have no pause button'. Seán regarded him as a very complex person.

John, who had very strong feelings about all sorts of things, frequently dismissed ideas that were put to him, though he did change his mind from time to time. He would not back down when proved wrong, which was often, and he was provocative when he had drunk too much, although he would usually ring the following day to apologize for what he had said the night before.

Seán remembered that when John spoke about something that he had known about since the year dot (or 'double dot' as he used to say), he 'had a great freshness about it'. He was always willing to explain things patiently to others. The American musicologist H.C. Robbins Landon, who edited Haydn's music, had the same quality. John disagreed strongly with Landon over Haydn's Op. 3 Quartets, which end in a fugue – 'a terrible mistake', according to John. Landon, on the other hand, thought them wonderful.

When he and Seán were listening to Mozart's *Divertimento* in E flat, K. 563, John said, 'The thing you've got to remember is that Mozart made it completely impossible to write a string trio again!' He stopped, thought a moment and continued, 'Jesus Christ – I tried to do that once, *but we won't go into that just now!*' [1]

John was 'nuts' about Jacques Tati and watched all his films. When John discovered that a book about him had been published, he ordered a copy and sent another in the post to Seán with strict instructions to read it immediately. He kept telephoning Seán, who was busy at the time, and badgered him to read it. He was also keen on Woody Allen's films, the Indian Bengali movies directed by Satyajit Ray, such as *The Music Room*, the French films starring Raimu (the stage name of actor Auguste Muraire) and the actors Jack Lemmon and Julie Harris. He spoke French well and, when asked how he was keeping, replied, '*Comme le Pont Neuf*'.[2] When Patrick Lambert telephoned and asked how he was, he often responded with, 'Shuffling up the queue!' Patrick found him quite outspoken at times, and some women were rather frightened of him. He did not like talking about unpleasant things; when the subject of Communism was mentioned, he would say, 'Don't talk about Communists!' Patrick remembers that although John adored Joyce's writings, he would not look at the film that had been made of his short story *The Dead*, even though Frank Patterson had acted and sung in it.[3]

As well as Paul Klee, John's favourite painters included Rembrandt and Pieter Breughel the Elder. His cousin Samuel was very keen on Henri Hayden's paintings, but John was not. He also did not like the work of the two Dutch brothers, Geer and Bram van Velde, which Samuel loved so much.

Seán O'Leary recollects that John often made out that he was an idiot. He used to ask Seán questions about mathematics and before Seán had time to reply, John would interrupt him and say, 'I don't want to know about it – I don't want to know! I haven't got the brains for this kind of thing!' As John had not read many of Shakespeare's works, Seán gave him a book on Shakespeare's language, which he tried to read but found hard going. 'I've a terrible confession to make

– I've no brains!' he moaned. When Seán tried to show him a recording of a BBC television programme about how Andrew Wiles had solved the world's greatest mathematical puzzle, Fermat's Theorem, he fell asleep in his chair. Seán put on the programme again the following morning, when John was fresh and alert. He ended up in tears and said that it was one of the most extraordinary things that he had ever seen and heard.[4] John was similarly affected when he watched a BBC *Timewatch* programme about a twenty-six-year-old model mother, Lilly Wust, who fell in love with a twenty-one-year-old Jewish lesbian, Felice Schragenheim, during the early 1940s in Berlin.[5]

In June 1996 John attended a special concert, followed by a party, to celebrate David Cairns's seventieth birthday. During the party, John (who once again had drunk too much) and David listened to a record of Purcell's Fantasias. David, writing more recently in *The Sunday Times Culture* magazine, recollected how he had been taken through 'this amazing music by that great Purcellian John Beckett, his expression ecstatic, a glass of wine in his left hand, his right hand pointing out crunching dissonances that make Monteverdi seem cautious in comparison.' This little vignette sums up John perfectly – anyone who knew him well can remember him doing this kind of thing, so eager was he to share Purcell's wonderful music with others. Seán O'Leary remembers that he had witnessed scenes like this many times.[6]

David regarded John as a 'wonderful man', though he thought it odd the way John revered Bach and yet hated Handel. David once sent him a photo of an anonymous portrait of Bach that he fancied. As the years went by, he saw less of John as it became increasingly more difficult to get him out of his house in Azof Street, though they did once go to a concert of Mahler's music together. When David did see him, it was generally through Frida Robinson. He noticed that John now tended to be gloomy.[7]

By now, John had sold his harpsichord as he was finding it difficult to play, owing to arthritis in his hands. When his cousin Morris Sinclair came to visit him, they listened to recorded music together and, in this way, John introduced him to a great deal of new music. They kept in touch and regularly complained about their woes over the phone.[8]

Other friends were invited to listen to music. As a neighbour in Azof Street had a son who owned a DVD player, John used to rent DVDs that interested him and went to watch them in the neighbour's house. He listened to the radio regularly and, in his latter years, watched certain programmes on television. He did not read newspapers and expected Seán O'Leary to tell him the latest news.

In general, Seán agreed with John's positive views, but not his negative ones. John had frequent rows with Seán's wife Odile. He lived his life according to certain 'rules' of his own making; if he had decided that he didn't like something in particular, then he would waste no time discussing it. For instance, apart from Joyce, P.G. Wodehouse and certain books by Samuel Beckett and Thomas Mann, he did not like novels and would not read them 'on principle', maintaining that it was not possible to read anything after having read Joyce or Beckett. He did read Samuel's novels, but never re-read them; he preferred the plays and his later short texts.[9]

John announced his intention to give one last harpsichord recital some time in 1997 in Blackheath Conservatoire, where John and Ruth had taught. John used the harpsichord there and invited only a few friends. 'There were only about three or four of us there – it was clearly something he really wanted to do,' recalls Patrick Cuming, who went with his wife Melanie and his brother Michael. John performed several of Bach's Forty-Eight Preludes and Fugues from Book II and played everything twice. Michael was fascinated by his technique.[10]

John still kept in touch with his good friend James Plunkett and wrote to him in mid-March. It appears that James was unwell:

Dear Jimmy –

I have arranged for you to be sent a copy of the Mendelssohn CD – a gift.

It has the String Quintet in A, op. 18, and the Octet, on it. I am very fond of the Quintet, and think that you shared my pleasure in it when we heard it together at the Wigmore Hall.

It should reach you in the course of next week.

Meanwhile take care of yourself, and allow yourself to be taken care of by your dear and loving family.

And when you're confidently on your legs again, come over and take a break with me here in Greenwich and out and about in London.

Spring is at the gates, and St. Patrick's day around the corner –

with my love – as ever – for both – John[11]

In the spring of 1997 Vera Škrabánek and John set off on a holiday to Prague for two weeks. As John was always talking to her about Franz Kafka, Vera said to him: 'John, I'll do something for you. I have a friend who lives in an apartment on the street where Kafka was born, and the back garden of the apartment block is actually a Jewish cemetery – one of the oldest cemeteries in Europe. She has a terrace there and we can actually look into the cemetery. Would you like to come with me?' He said that he would. Vera arranged the trip and they arrived on 30 April. John was absolutely delighted to be in Prague. The apartment was very large and, as Vera's friend's late husband had been an artist, there were pictures and books everywhere.

John had brought a book in which all the details of Kafka's life were listed. He made plans and decided that he was going to see everything associated with Kafka; thus the holiday was turned into a pilgrimage. In fact, they went to so many places that Vera said to John, 'Go on your own because I already know those places!' The house where Kafka was born had been rebuilt along with many others at the turn of the century for 'hygienic reasons'. Not only did they visit this, but all the other apartments where Kafka had lived, for he had often changed his place of dwelling. When they visited Kafka's grave, John noticed a man selling flowers nearby; he bought them all and placed them reverently on the grave. They even went to an old asbestos factory that had belonged to a cousin of Kafka's; John had read that at one time Kafka had been helping his cousin in the capacity of a lawyer. Vera was astounded when John produced the exact name of the street and the number of the building, showed it to her and said, 'Let's go!' Leaving the old quarter of Prague, they walked for half an hour to the working-class area of Žižkov, where they found the factory, which was situated in the yard of an apartment block. They opened the big door and looked around the deserted building. 'It was really an enormous experience,' Vera recalls.

They went to the *Hrad* (the castle), attended concerts in the Rudolfinum and Vera's sister in Prague bought tickets for a performance of Mozart's opera *Don Giovanni* in the Stavovské divadlo or Estates Theatre (formerly the Tyl or Nostitz Theatre), by that time newly reconstructed. John was excited about this and was happy to be in the elegant theatre, ensconced in a box. However, in the middle of the first act, John started to mutter, 'This is dreadful!' and complained about various things that did not meet with his approval. An angry Vera brought him outside after the first act. 'Why is the stage so long?' he asked heatedly. 'All the music disappears and nothing goes into the auditorium! It's all wrong, it's all wrong!' Frustrated, Vera said, 'John, for God's sake – I want to enjoy at least a bit of the opera, you know.' She persuaded him to return to his seat and they stayed for the rest of the production. In the end, John enjoyed it as much as Vera did.

The one thing that John did not like in Prague was the touristy glass and ceramic shops. They annoyed him so much that he said, 'If I had a stone, I would throw it at them and smash everything!' What he enjoyed best of all was sitting on the apartment terrace, which overlooked not only the Jewish cemetery but also the castle, savouring the view. He also liked observing the rooks, which were nesting at the time.

When John started to talk about seeing places associated with Mahler, Vera mentioned this to a friend, who said to her, 'Ask Mrs Smolková next door'. Mrs

Smolková had survived the concentration camps and her husband, who was dead by that time, had also survived the camps and had worked after the war as an archivist. He had discovered documents related to Mahler, and often brought interested tourists to Mahler's birthplace. Because of this, Mrs Smolková knew a person in the area who was an expert on Mahler. 'He's a very nice man – ring him!' she said. Vera did, and relatives of hers kindly arranged everything and drove John and Vera to Kaliště, where Mahler was born. Although the house had been destroyed by fire and rebuilt, it was nice to see the place as it was a beautiful spring day. Leaving the village, they drove along a road that brought them up into the mountains, where they were rewarded with a fine panoramic view of the countryside. They stopped and stood gazing at it for about half an hour, drinking in the view and thinking of Mahler's orchestral song cycle *Das Lied von der Erde* (*The Song of the Earth*).

Vera's relatives also brought them to the Dr Aleš Hrdlička Museum in the town of Humpolec, with its exhibition dedicated to the life and work of Mahler, and to the *Gymnázium* (school), which Mahler had attended as a young boy. John very much enjoyed this.[12] They also visited the nearby town of Jihlava, from which John sent a postcard to Seán and Odile O'Leary: 'Dear both – we went out to Mahler's birthplace and to this town, where the family lived from 1860–75. We were taken on a long roundabout tour of other places and villages [Mahler] would have known – phew! Love – John.'[13] John also wrote to James Plunkett, 'Dear Jimmy – revelling in this beautiful old city [Prague], pursuing my Kafka and Mahler pilgrimages. K. haunts the city. Drove out to M's birthplace in the country yesterday. Love John.'[14]

John also wanted to visit Náchod, a beautiful little provincial town on the Czech-Polish border, where Vera's husband Petr had been born. Náchod had produced a number of eminent people, among them Josef Škvorecký, the writer and publisher who had spent much of his life in Canada. They drove there and stayed with Petr's mother, who cooked for them constantly over a period of three days. John relished the dumplings that she made. She addressed John as '*pan* Beckett' (Mr Beckett) and he addressed her as '*babička*' (granny). He was 'absolutely delighted with the whole thing', Vera recalls. Her relatives also brought them to the nearby forest and mountains.

Another place that John wanted to visit was Nelahozeves, a village to the north of Prague, where the composer Antonín Dvořák was born. It was when they went there that John used his connection to Samuel to good advantage. As they had arrived rather late, the little museum dedicated to Dvořák was about to close. John, who very much wanted to see it, said to Vera, 'Tell them I'm the cousin of Samuel Beckett!' Speaking in Czech, Vera explained to the curator, 'We have here a person who is actually the cousin of the Nobel Prize winner and he's a great musician. Is there any chance that you could let him see inside?' It worked; they were admitted and they had the place to themselves. Afterwards, as the light faded, they lingered on the bank of the River Vltava, where the grass had been cut, and savoured the smell of the Czech countryside. John was enchanted.

John and Vera became closer after this holiday; from time to time he would visit her in Dublin, telephone her from London or post her books, such as Kathi Diamant's *Kafka's Last Love: the Mystery of Dora Diamant* (Basic Books, 2003). (Before the holiday he had recommended *A Hesitation before Birth – The Life of Franz Kafka* by Peter Mailloux, Associated University Press, 1989, to his friend Seán O'Leary.) Vera in turn sent him books to read.

As well as admiring writers such as Kafka, Joyce and his cousin Samuel, John was very taken by the American physicist Richard Feynman, who had won the Nobel prize for physics in 1965. John had all the books written about him. The one he liked best was *Perfectly Reasonable Deviations from the Beaten Track: The Letters of Richard P. Feynman*, edited by Michelle Feynman (Basic Books, 2005). Vera's husband Petr had written about Feynman in *The Lancet*.

Vera was becoming a little worried about John, who was now living on his own and spending most of his time in London. When she asked him what he cooked for himself, he replied, 'Ah, I just boil some celery and that's it'.[15] His friend Janet Ashe recollects that although he still relished good food when it was put in front of him, he was unable to provide himself with a decent meal when on his own. He told her, 'I am a non-cook', and said that he lived on smoked mackerel and cooked beetroot. He ate lots of fruit and squeezed oranges for himself. Naturally, drink was far more important than food.[16] At times he could be harsh – Vera remembers how he had got quite cross with her daughter. She surmised that his sister Ann must have said something to him, for he rang the following day and apologized.[17]

John wrote to James Plunkett in June 1997 about a 'second recording of Frederick May's Quartet', a CD of which, presumably, he had enclosed with his letter. 'Hope you like the performance', he wrote; '– look forward to comparing notes about it when I see you in three weeks or so.'[18] Whether they met in Dublin or London is not known, but John did travel to Dublin for the funeral of his teacher Joe Groocock, who died shortly afterwards, on 13 August. One of people he met was his school pal Adrian Somerfield; Adrian remembers how John had approached him and spoke to him, and how friendly he had been.[19]

John, who was now beginning to think of his own mortality, wrote to Adrian Jack in February 1998 to inform him of the words and music that he wanted for his funeral:

If you will speak it memorably I will be, dare I say, eternally grateful — only wish I could hear you! This part of the proceedings is being organised by a good friend of mine, Patrick Cumin [sic] (pronounced 'come in'). He will be in touch when the time comes — all things being not too unequal, which applies to you too of course.

A two-page document accompanied the letter:

SPEAKER

John himself devised the form of words and music being used this afternoon.

To begin, a poem by the remarkable 19th. Century American poet Emily Dickinson. She was born in 1830 at Amherst, New England, where she lived all her life, and where she died in 1886 — which makes her a contemporary of Brahms. I have read and rejoiced in her work for more than 30 years. She never gave her poems titles.

[Her poem, beginning A Pit — but Heaven over it — is quoted in full.]

The music of Henry Purcell has given me more delight than that of any other composer, and I would like something of his to grace this occasion. I have chosen three Pavans for violins and continuo, early works, but none the worse, indeed all the better, for that — the first and second are for two violins, the last for three.

THE THREE PAVANS ARE HEARD

Those three Pavans by Henry Purcell were played by London Baroque directed by Charles Medlam.

I approach death humbly under the banner of the great American physicist Richard Feynman, who died from cancer in 1988. He once said to a friend: 'You see, one thing is, I can live with doubt and uncertainty and not knowing. I think it's much more interesting to live not knowing than to have answers which might be wrong. I have approximate answers and possible beliefs and different degrees of certainty about different things, but I am absolutely sure of nothing, and there are many things I don't know about, such as whether it means anything to ask why we are here ... I don't have to know an answer. I don't feel frightened by not knowing things, by being lost in a mysterious universe without any purpose, which is the way it really is as far as I can tell. It doesn't frighten me.'

Time for a song: the French chansonier Georges Brassens singing his own setting of François Villon's 'Ballade des dames du temps jadis'.

'BALLADE DES DAME[S] DU TEMPS JADIS' IS HEARD

The voice of Georges Brassens, whose singing, music and the caustic charity of whose poetry, I have long loved.

And so I turn again to Emily Dickinson, my companion for nearly half my lifetime. Here is a short poem, only 14 words long. It was suggested by Saint Paul's reference to an altar in Athens dedicated 'To The Unknown God', and it encapsulates my attitude to the enigma of being.

Lad of Athens, faithful be
To thyself,
And Mystery —
All the rest is perjury —
And so, to end, let the very last words be those of the shortest of all Emily's poems:
Has All —
a codicil?

END OF FUNERAL
    Durations: Speech — 4 minutes
    Music — 15 minutes
    The slot allocated for a cremation 'service' is 30 minutes.
    John Beckett
    February 19th. '98[20]

This was one of several orders of service that John devised. At one point, Ruth's son-in-law, who was to be executor and funeral organiser, received at least two different versions of an all-Bach service. However, it transpired that these roles had been allotted at different times to other people. In addition, the content of the service would change radically over the coming years.[21]

Christopher Nobbs remembers having conversations with John about his funeral. At one time, John wanted Purcell's funeral sentences for the death of Queen Mary performed, but only the first two as there was no mention of God: *Man that is born of a woman hath but a short time to live, and is full of misery. He cometh up and is cut down like a flower; he fleeth as it were a shadow, and never continueth in one stay.* He also recollects that John had begun to take a great interest in the music of Brahms towards the end of his life; it seemed that John felt that he and Brahms had something in common as regards personality.[22]

In early June, John wrote to James Plunkett. 'Dear Jimmy,' he began:

This is to confirm the gathering of family and friends that I have organised, to meet Morris's new partner Anne-Marie Essway, and to see him and each other.

    It is in the form of a lunch at the Killiney Court Hotel, on Saturday, July 25th, at 1 o'clock.

    Ann and I will pick you up from your house, and take you back home afterwards.[23]

John was still in Dublin a month later, staying with his sister Ann. 'Dears – what a marvellously situated city Dublin is!' he enthused when he sent a post-card depicting Dalkey Island to Seán and Odile O'Leary. 'This little harbour (Coliemore Harbour) and this island (Dalkey Island) are just down the road from Ann's house! We're getting out and about into the wilds of Wicklow, and seeing friends. Love to you all. John.'[24] Coliemore Harbour, of course, was where John had lived briefly with his late wife Vera. He called over to us a few days later and came again at the end of the month so that I could interview him for the biography I was writing about my father. Before he left, he made a face and said to me, 'I hope you're not going to use a *word processor* to type your book', with marked emphasis on the term 'word processor', which he detested as it reminded him of processed food. During the interview he unexpectedly threw in some interesting information about his youth.[25]

He was still in Dublin at the end of September and wrote again to Seán and Odile on a postcard showing a view of Killiney Hill in the south of the city. 'This is the great view, looking south into Co. Wicklow, from just up the road – dreadful colour though!! We've been listening to the Purcell and Bach casettes – Ann thanks you warmly for them – Love to you both – and all – John.'[26] It may have been during this holiday with Ann when they went to Belmullet, County Mayo, and Clear Island, off the south-west coast of County Cork. Dan Shields remembers that when they arrived on the island, John hired a bicycle, which Ann used as a walking aid. When John asked the man for a stick, which he could use as a walking aid for himself, he was asked, 'What do you want it for? Is it to bate her with?'[27]

I was able to do a turn for John when a friend and I travelled to the USA on holidays that autumn. When I had told him that we had planned to drive around New England, he asked me if I would be near Amherst, where Emily Dickinson had lived. He had very much wanted to go there when he had toured with the New Irish Chamber Orchestra and James Galway, but there had been no time. He encouraged me to go there, pay a visit to Emily's house, which was open to the public, and 'pluck a leaf from one of the trees' for him.

We did find our way to Amherst and thoroughly enjoyed our tour of the house, thanks to the enthusiasm of the guide. I collected some printed informa-tion, took photographs and we wandered into the back garden, where we picked a few autumnal leaves. Later I posted these to John, who was very grateful for the little gifts.[28] He was back in Dublin again over the Christmas and called to us in the afternoon on Saint Stephen's (Boxing) Day.[29]

At some time during the year, John had telephoned Seán O'Leary to say that he had had an 'extraordinary experience': he had just heard a performance of a Bach cantata that had 'more things right' than any other performance. It had been played by the Bach Collegium Japan, conducted by Masaaki Suzuki. He became hooked on this new series of recordings and bought each new CD when it was issued.[30] Nicholas Anderson believes that his enthusiasm for these recordings became one of the chief reasons for him staying alive. He regularly brought them to Frida and Vic Robinson's home in Suffolk and played them.[31]

John continued to read voraciously and used to telephone Jonathon Gibbs, a book dealer who had become a friend, to order various books. Jonathan remembers that he bought all sorts of books, not just specialist volumes about music, and that he was very well read.[32] He liked the poetry of Philip Larkin, W.H. Auden and John Betjeman. Two of his favourite poems were J.M. Synge's very last poem (quoted earlier) and *The Old Man* at the end of Samuel's novel *Watt*. He was particularly keen on biographies.[33] As well as dealing with Jonathon, he also bought books from John Sandoe (Books) Ltd in Chelsea. (After John died, Jonathon sorted and sold his books, as prescribed in John's will).[34]

The second volume of David Cairns's biography of Berlioz, entitled *Berlioz: Servitude and Greatness* was finally published in 1999. John's ten-year wait was finally over. Cairns had also re-written Volume 1, *The Making of an Artist*, which was also published at around the same time. In the same year, John visited a big exhibition of Rembrandt's self portraits at the National Gallery, *Rembrandt by Himself*, which made a profound impression on him.[35]

In September 1999 BBC Radio 3 broadcast two archival recordings of Samuel Beckett's radio plays, introduced by Martin Esslin: *Words and Music* and *A Piece of Monologue*. The former, of course, featured the music that John had composed. John's opinion of this music was so low that he had withdrawn permission to have it performed again. However, the BBC had every right to broadcast it as often as they wished, for they had commissioned both the play and the music, and it was their property. John, who was very angry, made an attempt to destroy the original recording, which was in the BBC Archives, but at the last moment he chickened out. 'My Protestant upbringing told me that this was the property of the bloody BBC and I had no right to do it, so I left it!' he told Seán O'Leary.[36]

Forty-Six
2000–2007

In August 2000 John set off on a tour of Germany with his friend Paul Conway. In a letter to Patrick and Jarka Lambert, John explained the reason for the tour:

> I'm off on a trip ... with a pal who used to be a student of mine at the Academy of Music in Dublin in the 70s. It will realise a long-held ambition: to meander through Thuringia and Saxony from Eisenach, Bach's birthplace, through all his places of employment – Arnstadt, Mühlhausen, Weimar, Köthen, and so to Leipzig – seeing and hearing as much as possible. We're flying to Frankfurt on August 28th, where a hired car will be waiting for us, and will set off unhurried on our pilgrimage, avoiding motorways and main roads, travelling on country roads and lanes, staying wherever evenings find us – then back to London and Dublin respectively on September 6th.[1]

Fortunately, like Vera Škrabánek, Paul kept a diary during the holiday.

As Paul had flown to Germany from Dublin and John from London, they met in Frankfurt Airport. The car was a light yellow Toyota Yaris, which Paul drove for the entire holiday. They travelled southwards to Eisenach to visit the Georgenkirche, where Bach had been baptized on 23 March 1685. They saw the baptismal font and later drove to nearby Wartsburg to see the castle.

From here they travelled south-eastwards to Arnstadt and found a guest house over a bookshop. Paul recalls that John, who spoke little or no German, had brought a sheet of paper with questions in German typed on it, such as 'Do you have two single rooms, please?' Rather than attempting to read the questions, he proffered them to the owners of the guesthouse.

In Arnstadt they visited the Bachkirche, where Bach had been given his first appointment, aged eighteen; he was organist in the church between 1703 and 1707. John sent a picture postcard of the church to James Plunkett. 'Our Bach pilgrimage is going thrillingly well!' he wrote. 'This is the church in which he got his first appointment as organist at the age of 18. We were there yesterday – with love as ever – John.'¹ They next drove to the small town of Dornheim and stopped at the Church of Saint Bartholomew, where Bach had married Maria Barbara Bach in 1707. When John went up to the organ loft, he found a book of Bach's Choral Preludes; he immediately opened it and began to play some of the Preludes on the historic organ.

The next stop was Erfurt, where they stayed in what Paul described as 'an expensive hotel' that offered free passes for the trams. They saw the organ that Bach had played and visited a big exhibition about Bach. Another highlight there was a meal in the fish market.

From here they made their way north-westwards to Mühlhausen, where Bach had played the organ in the Church of St Blasius. Paul described the church as 'fabulous'. They managed to gain access to the organ loft.

They now drove some 70 km to Nordhausen and stayed in a small family hotel. The following morning, they drove over the mountains to Köthen (Cöthen), where Bach had been employed as a music director by Prince Leopold of Anhalt-Cöthen at his castle, which John and Paul visited. They also saw the Church of St James, where Bach had played the organ. A thunder and lightning storm erupted while they were there.

On 2 September they drove south-eastwards to Leipzig, stopping by chance right beside the St Thomas Church or Thomaskirche, where Bach had been organist between 1723–1750. Here they attended a concert, featuring the choir and organ, at three o'clock in the afternoon and then, after a meal in the Marktplatz, they went to an excellent organ recital in the evening. Having drunk some wine in a restaurant, they repaired to their *pension* for the night. Paul noted that John was tired.

It rained for the whole of the following day, when they went on a long drive northwards to Lüneburg. There they visited the red-bricked Johanneskirche and Michaelikirche, where Bach sang as a boy, having won a scholarship to study there. Paul noticed the Dutch influence in the architecture and the coldness of the weather.

From here they drove to Lübeck on the coast of the Baltic Sea, where they visited the Marienkirche, with its impressive twin steeples, and where Bach's idol and teacher Buxtehude had been organist. However, the church had changed in appearance since Bach's time, as it had been bombed in 1942. They also went to the Jakobikirche, because of its associations with the writer Thomas Mann, and stayed in a *Gasthaus* about four miles south of the city.

On 5 September they set off on a long journey southwards, without having eaten any breakfast, to Weimar, where Bach had written many of his cantatas. On the way they stopped at the Buchenwald Nazi concentration camp, which John did not want to see, so Paul strolled around it on his own. In Weimar they visited the Elephant Hotel, mentioned in one of Thomas Mann's books. They then returned to Eisenach, staying, as at the beginning of their holiday, in the same hotel and eating in the same restaurant. They flew home on the following day. One can imagine John's satisfaction on visiting so many important places associated with the composer that he admired the most.[3]

John's doctor in Dublin had warned him that his hips would give him trouble in the future. They did and John was obliged to undergo surgery at around this time. As John could not tolerate the wait for free comprehensive NHS care, he opted for private treatment.[4] The operation therefore was expensive, and as he did not have enough money, his cousin Morris Sinclair kindly gave him financial help.[5] John was given a pre-operation assessment and an advice session by a therapist, but as he had not realized how important this was and had ignored the advice given to him,[6] he sat in the wrong type of chair: a low one.[7] When Roland Morrow visited him, he got out of the chair the wrong way and dislocated his hip. He was taken off to hospital in considerable pain, and suffered a second heart attack there. As the hospital was in the process of being closed down, John was moved to another one, in Woolwich. Morris, who was crestfallen, flew over from Geneva; he and Roland visited John, who was grumpy but improving. Roland tried to cheer Morris up by bringing him to the *Rembrandt the Printmaker* exhibition in the British Museum.[8] John rang Seán O'Leary from the hospital to say that he was 'at the end of the road'. Although telephoning people from the hospital was a complicated and expensive business, John persisted and had long conversations with his friends.[9] His sister Ann came over to visit him, comfort him and tick him off when he behaved too badly towards the hospital staff.[10] Rose Hilton, Ruth's daughter, remembers that he was behaving so badly that she and Ann were asked to give him an ultimatum by his consultant.[11]

In the following year John had to go over to Dublin to look after Ann, who had been diagnosed with lung cancer. She and John visited Vera Škrabánek and asked her for advice. John wanted Ann to recover but soon realized that there was no chance that she would; he was also worried that she would have so much pain and that he would not be able to look after her. He stayed with her in her home in Sandycove for several months, doing whatever he could. He was with her right until the end, which came on 4 December 2002, after a brief stay in hospital. He rang Vera in the afternoon to tell her that Ann had died.[12] On the following day, a notice that John had written appeared in *The Irish Times*:

> Beckett (Ann) (Sandycove, Co. Dublin) – December 4, 2002, at St. Vincent's
> Private Hospital; after a long, clear-eyed, most courageous struggle with cancer.
> She will be grievously missed by her family, friends and erstwhile colleagues.
> Funeral Service tomorrow (Friday) morning at 11 o'c. in St. Patrick's Church,
> Dalkey. Interment afterwards in Calary Churchyard, Co. Wicklow.[13]

I attended the funeral service at the church in Dalkey, which was packed. Afterwards I approached John, who was busy talking to various people in the church. He saw me, stretched out his hand, and, as he had done before, held on to it for a considerable time while he continued to converse with his friends. This scene has been etched in my memory ever since, and whenever I think of John, I remember it. We eventually had a few moments of private conversation.[14]

I did not attend the burial, but Vera did. She was driven up into the Wicklow Mountains by her daughter, following another car, not knowing exactly where they were going. They eventually arrived at the tiny church in Calary and its cemetery, where Ann was duly buried. When they stood behind John at the graveside, Vera realized that John was now completely on his own: he had neither sister, wife nor partner, and this was the first time in his life when he had no woman to look after him. Later in the day, she rang him at Ann's house and asked him, 'What are you going to do? Where are you going tomorrow?' 'I don't know', he replied. As Vera felt that he was lonely, she asked him if he had any company and he said, 'No, I'm on my own.' She invited him to her house and so he spent the following day with her.

He stayed in Dublin for another three or four weeks, arranging things and visiting Vera when he had time. He also got a stonemason to carve an inscription on Ann's tombstone.[15] Initially he had wanted a long section of verse by Emily Dickinson but his friend Janet Ashe persuaded him to get something simple put on it instead. Afterwards he said to her, 'I'm so glad you stopped me'. The inscription read, 'Ann Beckett 1927–2002 † She gave of herself selflessly for those in need'.[16] Vera went with John to the cemetery to see the tombstone and to photograph it for him, as he was now having difficulty walking and would not be able to come to Dublin regularly. Vera also invited John to stay in an apartment that she was buying in Prague, but he turned down the invitation.[17] Although Ann had left all her money and her house to John, he chose not to live in Dublin. Instead he continued to live in Azof Street and used the money to refurbish the house.[18]

Nicholas Anderson recollects that John became reclusive and from this point onwards he only received homemade Christmas cards from him.[19] This seclusion, followed later by ill health, meant that he all but disappeared and made his name unknown to a generation that might otherwise have revered him.[20] Christopher Nobbs began to see less of him and realized that he was suffering from what he believed was melancholia rather than depression. Christopher found that he had become quite forbidding and now feels slightly ashamed that he did not make more of an effort to make contact with him. On one occasion he hesitated to approach John at Charing Cross Station when he caught sight of him, and walked past. Christopher felt that he was excused because he was in a hurry, but knew that the 'sheer aura of depression about him' had put him off.

A book that John read at this period, and about which he often spoke, was Primo Levi's book *Moments of Reprieve*; he told Christopher, 'I think that *is* life – life is moments of reprieve'. Levi, an Italian Jew and trained chemist, was one of the most famous survivors of Auschwitz. His best-known work is *If This Is a Man*. The first chapter, in which he describes how he and other Italians were taken by train to Auschwitz, is truly terrifying. What seemed to fascinate John was Levi's calm analysis of how people behave in impossible situations. The fact that Levi bore the guilt of the survivor interested him and he recommended his books to everyone.[21]

Although John decided never to go back to Ireland after Ann had died, he did keep in contact with his friends there. He telephoned Janet Ashe frequently at any hour of the day, often at nine o'clock in the morning. They talked about everything, including John's health and the state of his bowels. By now he had phlebitis in his legs and dressed the swellings himself, having been shown how to do it by a nurse. He also wore special medical stockings. He often posted books to Janet, including a couple by Dervla Murphy, the Irish touring cyclist.[22] According to Seán O'Leary, John read Dervla's books over and over again and bought copies for Seán. Apparently he read *Wheels Within Wheels* once a year. 'She should have got the Nobel Prize for literature – not Sam – he didn't want it!' he used to say.[23]

John and Janet once listened to a radio broadcast of Elgar's *Dream of Gerontius* together, with John in London and Janet in Dublin. Immediately afterwards, John telephoned her to discuss the performance. He then posted her a book about Elgar and wrote in it that it was a gift to commemorate the concert that they had enjoyed 'in tandem'.[24]

Although it was a long journey by train for Frida and Vic Robinson, they came to visit him occasionally at Greenwich. The last time that they went, Frida cut his toenails.[25] The loneliness that John was now forced to endure was caused in part by his off-putting behaviour, which made it difficult for most people to spend time with him. However, Ruth's children, loyal old friends of hers, and his cousin Judy remained in regular contact with him. From time to time, members of his own family and various friends called, and an army of neighbours looked out for him and helped in numerous ways.[26]

John's friend Paul Conway managed to persuade John to accompany him on a tour around Switzerland in 2003. They visited various places of interest (including James Joyce's grave in Zurich, where they drank bottles of white wine in honour of him) and scenic spots in the mountains. They drove in a hired car and often stopped in the middle of nowhere, took out collapsible chairs and sat down to admire the scenery. John loved the cows and their cowbells; he always tried to approach them and talk to them. Paul photographed him on one occasion with his shopping bag – the shopping bag went everywhere as he kept his wallet in it.[27]

John visited his cousin Morris Sinclair in Cartigny while they were in Switzerland. However, John and Paul got very drunk and were unable to find the hostelry where they were staying. As they did not have the gumption to ask at the local shop and, as they received no answer when they knocked on the door of Morris's house (Morris was fast asleep), they ended up spending the night in the car. Morris remembered John's fondness for 'a drop of whiskey'. He also liked to drink a certain type of aperitif, but Morris could not remember what it was. Morris declared that John was 'a great friend of *marc*', a drink similar to *grappa*. When John had been in Italy and found a place named 'something something *di Grappa*', he sent Morris a postcard from there as he heartily approved of the name! Now in Switzerland, John and Morris played music together, with Morris on the violin and John on the piano. Morris's sister Deirdre was there too. Morris was one of many people who could not understand John's hatred of Handel, considering that he was a 'composer of some importance'.[28]

One of the highlights of the holiday was to be a visit to a gallery in Bern that housed Paul Klee's paintings. This turned out to be something of a disaster as the gallery was being rebuilt and only ten or fifteen of the paintings were on display. Disappointed, John decided to return the following year and booked flights and accommodation. However, Morris convinced him that it was not worth visiting the new gallery for various reasons – it was too modern and John would not like it – and so John cancelled everything and did not go.

Paul remembers how thorough John was and how paranoid he could be about time and making journeys. He once insisted on a 'dry run' of a trip to Malvern, Worcestershire, which was timed before the actual journey was made. Paul also remembers shopping with John in London. Both were equipped with bags and a shopping list. As the groceries were bought, John ticked them off his list. When they reached the bakery and bought some bread, John suddenly realized that he had not written bread on his list. He therefore took out his pencil, wrote down 'bread' and *then* ticked it off.[29]

In December 2003 John typed a letter to Jantina Barker (née Norman); judging by its tone, they had not communicated for some time.

> <u>Dear</u> *Jantina - I can never forget you, or your unique singing. I think the piece that touched me most was Josquin's Deploration on the death of Ockeghem – I can still hear the wonderful phlegmy (Flemish?) way you pronounced and emphasised his name!. But I cherish so many other musical memories of you also – I even have you in captivity with your smashing performance of the witch in Purcell's (Dido and Aneas) – the only convincing rendering I have heard.*
>
> *Yes, I adore blackberries too. While I was staying with old friends in a remote 18th. Century mill in Norfolk in September I picked a big basket full, which we had after our supper for about three evenings!*
>
> *I am keeping well, at 76, soldiering on expectantly into old age – my life full of music (I have just discovered Stephan [sic] Grapelli – a genius), my books, my pictures, my pots (my beloved cat alas died (in my arms), and much else – and seeing a circle of tried old friends – I'm still glad to be alive.*[30]

Judy Jordan remembers John's passion for Stephane Grapelli. He often brought CDs of Grapelli's music to her house, which reverberated to the music – much to the astonishment of the neighbours – when the volume was turned up full.[31]

When the Sinclairs had a family reunion in Ireland in 2004 John refused to attend it as it took place in Roundwood, County Wicklow, which for him was too close to where Ann was buried.[32] It was also uncomfortably close to The Paddock, where he and Ruth had lived so happily together.[33] When Irené Sandford died of cancer in the following year, John wrote a 'a lovely complimentary letter' to Billy, her husband. After she died, Billy offered John tapes of the Bach cantatas that had been recorded in Dublin, and which the BBC had given him. John did not want to hear them and refused his offer, but then phoned him back to say that he had changed his mind. Billy sent him copies of the tapes and John duly listened to them. Some time later he rang Billy to say that he was quite pleased by what he had heard. The performances were obviously better than what he had imagined.[34]

At around this period, some of the shorter plays by Samuel Beckett, such as *Rough for Theatre* and *Rough for Theatre II*, were staged at the Tricycle Theatre on Kilburn High Road, where Oengus MacNamara performed, and John was invited to attend. He travelled there from Greenwich by bus. As the plays were matinée performances and as there was a discussion about having music between the plays, John was asked for his opinion. His response was, 'What's wrong with *silence?*' When John decided on the sustained, concentrated *shakuhachi* music for his funeral, Oengus wondered if he was thinking of that silence.

When they played *Waiting for Godot* at the Tricycle, at around the same time, John was asked if he would take questions from the audience afterwards. He did not like the idea at first but then agreed to it. In fact, he rose to the challenge and was the 'star turn'. He enjoyed the experience and even produced some of the props featured in the play – white turnips and a radish – from his pockets.

Naturally, John was very familiar with his cousin's work and loved the sucking stones sequence from *Molloy*. Oengus performed that particular section once and found it very difficult to remember.[35]

Paul Conway brought John off for one last holiday in July 2006. As John was very interested in the composer Edward Elgar and the places associated with him, they toured around the Malvern Hills in Worcestershire.[36] John sent a postcard of Elgar's birthplace, a red-bricked house in the village of Lower Broadheath, outside Worcester, to Seán and Odile O'Leary. It read, 'Dear both – the house is kept as it was in Elgar's early years – tiny, pokey rooms, brick floors downstairs boards upstairs – a little upright piano – simple homely furniture. We call on Jonathan [*sic*] Gibbs tomorrow. Love John.'[37] It may have been thanks to Jonathon Gibbs that he discovered the book *Edward Elgar – the record of a friendship* by Rosa Burley and Frank C. Carruthers.[38]

I received a phone call from John out of the blue in early November. Somehow he had heard about the biography that I had written about my father and he wanted to obtain a copy and read it. He also wanted one for his relative Freda Beckett. I volunteered to give a copy to an English friend who was about to travel to Dublin for the book launch, and who would then post it to him when he returned to the UK. John rang me again soon afterwards to report that he had just received the book in the post, that he was delighted to have it, and that he was looking forward to reading it. I also sent him a tape of an interview with my father that had been broadcast on RTÉ Radio some years previously. During one of our conversations, John had said, 'I'm going to be eighty soon – can you believe that?'[39]

In December, just before Christmas, a slightly shaky handwritten letter arrived from John in the post. It read:

I have finished your biography. You say, early on in it, that you were writing of a man you did not know. Nor, of course, did I. In the latter chapters, however, you portray very fully and most interestingly the dear man I did know, and loved. Thank you warmly for the copy.

> *Also for the casette, which has just arrived. I look forward to hearing it. I don't have the little machine that plays it, but a friend has.*
>
> *With best wishes —*
>
> *John*[40]

Vera Škrabánek was in touch with John over Christmas 2006 when he spent some time with Judy Jordan and Freda Beckett. Although Vera was worried about the quantity of red wine that John was drinking, she consoled herself with the thought that at least it gave him pleasure.[41] Another pleasure was listening to the Bach cantatas conducted by Masaaki Suzuki – probably the latest CD, Volume 34, which had been released in January 2007.[42]

Vera, who went to Prague in order to celebrate the new year, bought him a half litre bottle of slivovitz for his birthday on 5 February 2007. Knowing that he adored this drink, she wrapped it up carefully with a nice Filipino handmade card and sent it to him. He received it on Friday 2 February and rang Vera at about eleven in the morning, when she was busy looking after her lively ten-month-old grandson. He was delighted with the present and the card, and thanked her profusely. He was in the humour for a long chat, but Vera had to stop him and say, 'Listen John, I really can't talk very much because I have to look after this little child – I'll give you a ring on Monday.'[43]

Knowing that John got up very early, Janet Ashe rang him at 8 pm to wish him a happy birthday on Monday and got no answer, which she thought was rather strange.[44]

About an hour later Paul Conway arrived at John's house in Azof Street. His journey there had deliberately been kept secret: the plan was for him to take John by surprise and bring him to Judy Jordan's house, where they would join Rose Hilton (Ruth's daughter) and celebrate his birthday. A visit to Theo Wyatt's house had been arranged for the following day. Paul was surprised that there was no answer when he knocked on John's door and assumed that he might have gone out shopping. However, he noticed that the door was ajar and so he opened it. As he could see into the front room and right through into the kitchen, he found nobody in sight. There was no answer when he called out John's name, and so he left, went for a walk and returned.

He knocked on the hall door again but, as before, there was no response. Thinking that John might be upstairs listening to music on his headphones (he preferred this method of listening as it did not disturb the neighbours), Paul gingerly made his way up the staircase and stopped at the return, where he could see John's feet on the floor. He was not wearing his socks and it was obvious that he was sitting down. Not wishing to alarm him, Paul retreated and went out again into the street for another walk.

When he returned to the house for the third time, a neighbour, whom Paul knew, greeted him and asked him if he could help. Paul explained that he had arrived unexpectedly, that John seemed to be upstairs listening to music on his headphones and that he did not wish to alarm him. The neighbour volunteered to go in and tell John that Paul was downstairs and did so. He climbed the staircase, called out, 'John, John' and, after a short pause, came down and said simply, 'I think he's passed away'.

Shocked – and cold by now – Paul went upstairs to John's big bedroom-cum-living room with the neighbour and found John, dressed in his shirt and trousers, sitting in his chair beside an electric fire, slumped to the left. His skin was still warm to the touch, but there was no pulse. They telephoned the medical services and John was taken away.[45]

Paul returned to Dublin in a daze and booked flights for the funeral. Andrew Robinson telephoned me at work in RTÉ on the Monday evening to tell me what had happened and I passed on the details to the newsroom.[46] Vera's daughter heard the news later on RTÉ Lyric FM and rang her mother to tell her that John had died. All Vera could say was, 'That can't be true'.[47]

It transpired that about six weeks beforehand, John had left very detailed instructions regarding what he wanted to happen at his cremation, in a similar manner to the arrangements that he had sent to Adrian Jack. This time he just wanted recorded Japanese Buddhist music played on the *shakuhachi*.

What should have been a pleasant birthday celebration for John, Paul, the Jordans and Rose Hilton turned out to be a very sad occasion: as Paul succinctly expressed it, 'John had other plans'.[48]

Notes

Unless otherwise stated, a person's name followed by a date indicates a conversation or telephone conversation with that person on the date mentioned.
Citations marked with an asterisk [*] are © BBC.
N.B. Some of the websites consulted may no longer exist.

Abbreviations
Files in the BBC Written Archives Centre:
BBC WAC, A: RCONT 1 Composer Beckett, John – File 1 1954–62
BBC WAC, B: RCONT 1 Artists Beckett, John S. – File 1 1954–62
BBC WAC, C: RCONT 1 Copyright Beckett, John S. – File 1 1956–62
BBC WAC, D: John Beckett Composer – File 2 1963–67
BBC WAC, E: RCONT 12 Artists Beckett, John S. – File 2 1963–67
BBC WAC, F: RCONT 18 Copyright John S. Beckett – File 2 1963–69
BBC WAC, G: RCONT 12 Artist John S. Beckett – File 3 1968–72
BBC WAC, H: WAC R83/952/1 Beckett, John
BBC WAC, I: Artists: Musica Reservata File I 1958–1962
BBC WAC, J: Musica Reservata Artists File II 1963–1967
BBC WAC, K: RCONT31/86/1 Musica Reservata Orchestra
BBC WAC, L: RCONT12 Musica Reservata Artists II 1968–1972
BBC WAC, M: RCONT1 Scriptwriter Beckett, Samuel File I 1953–62

Others
KCLCA K/PP93: King's College London, College Archives, GB 0100 K/PP93 *(Morrow, Michael (1929-1994) and Musica Reservata)*
NLI MS: Manuscript in the National Library of Ireland
RTÉ DA: Document in the RTÉ Document Archives
TCD MS: Manuscript in the Trinity College Dublin Manuscript and Archives Research Library
UoR MS 5411: Correspondence from Samuel Beckett to John Beckett, held at the Beckett International Foundation, The University of Reading

Newspapers
Ir. Ind.: Irish Independent
Ir. Times: The Irish Times

One

1. This would later be dubbed 'Statue Corner' on account of a large statue of the Blessed Virgin that was placed at the centre of the junction. (Kathleen Moran, 2007.)

2. Based on descriptions of Sandyford given by Christopher Fitz-Simon, 16 May and 17 September 2008, Irwin Pearson, 11 June 2009, and Alan Geraghty, 13 June and 8 September 2009. Also Christopher Fitz-Simon, *Eleven Houses*, Penguin Ireland, 2007, pp. 44, 47. Although modernized, the Red Cottage still stands and bears the same name. The area, however, has changed considerably; the fields and rural surroundings have gone and in their place are modern houses (notably those in the Mount Eagle estate), a large industrial estate, a noisy motorway, new roads and numerous roundabouts.

3. Superintendent Registrar's District Dublin, Registrar's District No. 4 South City, Births, No. 389. Born 11 October 1922 at 89 Baggot Street, Dublin. (General Register Office, Dublin.)

4. James Knowlson, *Damned to Fame – The Life of Samuel Beckett*, Bloomsbury, London, 1996, p. 6.

5. 552 Superintendent Registrar's District Dublin South, Registrar's District Donnybrook, Births, No. 411 (General Register Office, Dublin).

6. Knowlson, *Damned to Fame*, pp. 6–7. Advertisements for J. and W. Beckett Builders, Ringsend and for James's company, James Beckett Ltd, Building Contractors, Ringsend, regularly appeared in the pages of *The Irish Times* during the 1920s. (Advertisement, *Ir. Times*, 10 August 1922, p. 9.)

7. *Mr. William Beckett*, *Ir. Times*, 22 February 1930, p. 6.

8. James Knowlson, interview with John Beckett, 27 August 1991.

9. Knowlson, *Damned to Fame*, p. 7–8; Knowlson, interview with John Beckett, 27 August 1991; Knowlson, interview with Ann Beckett, 3 August 1992. For the 'infectious disease of matter' quotation, see p. 339 of the Everyman's Library edition of Mann's book, translated by John E. Woods (2005), Everyman's Library, London.

10. Interview with Mirette Dowling, 9 April 2013.

11. Knowlson, interview with Ann Beckett, 3 August 1992; the photographs (with inscriptions on the backs) belonged to the late Deirdre Sinclair.

12. Registrar's District of Rathdrum, 1918. 'Marriage so[le]mnized at Christ Church in the Parish of Taney in the Co. of Dublin. No. 56 When Married: January 15th 1918.' (General Register Office, Dublin). Joseph Collen (b. 1856, d. 25 July 1941) and his wife Hannah Maria Stewart (b. 1850, d. 4 March 1935) were buried in the graveyard of Kilgobbin Church (closed in 1826, now a ruin), near Stepaside. Hannah was James's second wife. According to *The Irish Times* of 13 November 1941, Joseph 'left estate in Eire value £13,577'. See the family tree (p. xiii) and Chapter 1 of *Collen – 200 Years of Building and Civil Engineering in Ireland* by John Walsh, The Lilliput Press, Dublin, 2010.

13. *Irish Wills, Ir.Times*, 13 and 22 November 1941, p. 4/11; Christopher Fitz-Simon, 16 May 2008. Homestead is now a religious institution and belongs to the Pallottine Fathers.

14. Collen Construction Ltd, based in River House, East Wall, Dublin, is nowadays involved in the building of office blocks, residential buildings, colleges, large public facilities, warehouses, airport extensions and so forth. See chapters 1 and 2 of *Collen* by John Walsh (*opus cit.*) and www.collen.com.

15. Superintendent Registrar's District Lurgan, Registrar's District Portadown, Births, No. 14. Born 29 October 1892. (General Register Office, Dublin.)

16. Hannah Sophia Collen was born in 1885 and died in 1960 (see her headstone in Kilgobbin Church graveyard). She lived in the Red Cottage after the Becketts left in 1933. According to Alan Geraghty (13 June 2009), Sophie was a very nice woman, 'short and blocky' in stature and was well liked in the neighbourhood.

17. Christopher Fitz-Simon, 17 September 2008; Irwin and Joyce Pearson, 11 June 2009. At a later stage, Billy would become a friend of Samuel Beckett's; when Samuel was in Dublin, the two men travelled around the countryside together in 1946 and drank regularly in the Brazen Head pub. (Remembered by Hilary Heron Greene: see Deirdre Bair, *Samuel Beckett*, p. 349.)

18. Mary Elizabeth (Molly) Heron, née Collen, was born in 1883 and died in 1959; Hilary Heron, daughter of Molly and James Heron, a bank official, was born on 27 March 1923 and died on 28 April 1977 (see their headstones in Kilgobbin Church graveyard). Molly and Hilary moved into Mount Eagle House in 1937. The house had originally belonged to a Protestant clergyman and, before the Herons, was lived in by the Prendergast family. Paddy Prendergast trained horses for the millionaire Richard Webster ('Boss') Croker (1841–1922), who lived in nearby Glencairn, close to Leopardstown Race Course. Croker's Gallops or Acres feature in several of Samuel Beckett's works. (See *The Beckett Country* by Eoin O'Brien, The Black Cat Press, 1986, pp. 45–50 and notes.) The 35 acres of land around Mount Eagle House (now a housing estate) belonged orginally to 'Boss' Croker; after his death, the land was bought by Tom Murphy for £1800 (Alan Geraghty, 29 June and 8 September 2009). Mount Eagle House was sold in 1955 to the present owners, Irwin and Joyce Pearson. The Pearsons found sections of a limestone statue of a female nude sculpted – and then broken up – by Hilary, which they failed to assemble, and used the feet as a doorstop. The Pearsons also remember that Hilary owned a blue and yellow baby Austin, which she drove very fast. (Theo Snoddy, *Dictionary of Irish Artists, 20th Century*, Wolfhound Press, 1996; Christopher Fitz-Simon, 17 September 2008; Irwin and Joyce Pearson, 11 June 2009; Alan Geraghty, 13 June 2009.)

19. Knowlson, interview with Ann Beckett, 3 August 1992.

20. John Beckett: 'She had terrific feeling, child-nature sort of thing and sexually I think she must have been hot stuff … Sexual object. I remember I was aware of this all the time. She was so childlike.' Knowlson, interview with John Beckett, 27 August 1991. Also Knowlson, interview with Ann Beckett, 3 August 1992.

21. 532 Superintendent Registrar's District Dublin, Registrar's District No 4, Births, Nos. 391 and 392. Born at 87 Lower Baggot Street, Dublin. (General Register Office, Dublin). 'We were christened in a church along the road there.' (Knowlson, interview with John Beckett, 27 August 1991.) The nearest Protestant church is in Kilternan; Kilgobbin Church was closed in 1826.

22. Email from Rose Hilton, 14 February 2014.

23. Knowlson, interview with John Beckett, 8 July 1992, and interview with Ann Beckett, 3 August 1992.

24. Christopher Fitz-Simon, *Eleven Houses*, pp. 45, 47, 49, 52; Alan Geraghty, 8 September 2009.

25. *Funeral of Mr. W. Beckett, Ir. Times*, 14 February 1930, p. 3; William died on the previous day.

26. Knowlson, interview with John Beckett, 27 August 1991.

27. *Funeral of Mr. W. Beckett, Ir. Times*, 14 February 1930, p. 3.

28. *Recent Irish wills: Mr. William Beckett, Ir. Times*, 19 May 1930, p. 8.

29. Knowlson, *Damned to Fame*, pp. 10–13.

30. *Recent Irish wills: Mr. William Beckett, Ir. Times*, 19 May 1930, p. 8.

31. Knowlson, *Damned to Fame*, p. 8–9; Knowlson, interview with John Beckett, 27 August 1991.

32. Knowlson, interview with Ann Beckett, 3 August 1992.

33. Knowlson, interview with John Beckett, 27 August 1991; interview with Ann Beckett, 3 August 1992.

34. *Recent Irish wills: Mr. William Beckett, Ir. Times*, 19 May 1930, p. 8; Knowlson, *Damned to Fame*, pp. 5–6.

35. *Recent Irish wills: Mr. William Beckett, Ir. Times*, 19 May 1930, p. 8; Knowlson, interview with John Beckett, 27 August 1991; Knowlson, *Damned to Fame*, pp. 9–10; Knowlson, interview with Ann Beckett, 3 August 1992.

36. *Recent Irish wills: Mr. William Beckett, Ir. Times*, 19 May 1930, p. 8; Knowlson, *Damned to Fame*, pp. 7–8 and 367; Knowlson, interview with John Beckett, 27 August 1991; information supplied by Morris Sinclair to Deirdre Bair, *Samuel Beckett*, pp. 5, 17, 57–9.

37. Not 'Sonny'. According to Peter Hamilton (May 2008), he was nicknamed 'Sunny' because of his sunny disposition. However, Samuel Beckett referred to him as 'Sonny'.

38. Deirdre Bair, *Samuel Beckett*, pp. 57–9 (from Morris Sinclair).

39. The late Morris Sinclair, 19 May 2007.

40. Knowlson, interview with John Beckett, 8 July 1992; records of the Royal College of Music, London. John remembered that he sometimes joined his father, presumably during the school holidays, on his travels around Wicklow, which often brought them into the remotest parts. (Email from Rose Hilton, 14 February 2014.)

41. Knowlson, interview with Ann Beckett, 3 August 1992. See also Noël Browne's book *Against The Tide*, Gill and Macmillan, Dublin, 1986, which describes the prevalence of TB and the state of sanatoria in Ireland during this period.

42. Seán O'Leary, 31 July 2007; Knowlson, interview with John Beckett, 27 August 1991.
43. Charles Gannon, interview with John Beckett, 31 July 1998.
44. Knowlson, interview with John Beckett, 8 July 1992.

Two

1. Aidan Higgins, *Dog Days – A Sequel to Donkey's Years*, Secker & Warburg, London, 1998, pp. 3, 6, 14, 15, 25.
2. Knowlson, interview with Ann Beckett, 3 August 1992.
3. Thom's Directory, 1943.
4. Christopher Fitz-Simon, *Eleven Houses*, p. 56.
5. Knowlson, interview with John Beckett, 27 August 1991.
6. Letters from Samuel Beckett to John Beckett, Beckett International Foundation, The University of Reading, MS 5411. This correspondence from Samuel Beckett to John, written on plain and picture postcards and sometimes posted in an envelope, was carefully catalogued, annotated and numbered by John. His note for picture postcard No. 25, enclosed in an envelope and dated 14 March 1984, explains Samuel's sentence 'Shamrock card from May and Paddy today': 'Each year they used to send Sam a card for St. Patrick's day – as here', and describes how May looked after him and Ann when they were children at Greystones. John also explains that Paddy used to tend the grave of Samuel's parents in Redford cemetry and Samuel used to send May and Paddy a Christmas card every year.
7. Norman Lush, 14 July 2009.
8. Knowlson, interview with Ann Beckett, 3 August 1992; Knowlson, interview with John Beckett, 27 August 1991.
9. Knowlson, interview with John Beckett, 27 August 1991; letter from Samuel Beckett to John Beckett, 11 May 1975, UoR MS 5411, 6.
10. Deirdre Bair, *Samuel Beckett*, p. 171; Ann Beckett to Deirdre Bair, *ibid*, p. 171.
11. Knowlson, interview with John Beckett, 27 August 1991 and 8 July 1992.
12. David Lee, 18 May 2008.
13. Assorted documents at Aravon School, provided by Thelma Clinton, 2 July 2009; David Sowby, 2 July 2009.
14. Email from Rose Hilton, 14 February 2014.
15. Knowlson, interview with John Beckett, 27 August 1991 and 8 July 1992.
16. Knowlson, interview with John Beckett, 27 August 1991.
17. Charles Mansfield, *The Aravon Story*, Aravon School booklet.
18. David Sowby, 14 July 2009.
19. Author's diary, 27 June 1980.
20. This account of Aravon School is taken from David Sowby's *Memories of Aravon 1936–40*, a privately produced document (2004), and interviews with Thelma Clinton, Rosaleen Cox and David Sowby, 2 July 2009. Two wooden plaques, now

located in the dining room of the present Aravon School, which moved to its spectacular location in Old Connaught, near Bray, in 1985, read: 'P.G.S. Beckett 1932–36' and 'J.S. Beckett 1935–40'.

21. Email from Rose Hilton, 14 February 2014.
22. David Sowby and David Lane, 2 July 2009.
23. *Studio Portrait: John Beckett*, BBC Radio 3, 17 March 1969.
24. Knowlson, interview with John Beckett, 27 August 1991.
25. Christopher Fitz-Simon, *Eleven Houses*, p. 56.
26. Knowlson, interview with John Beckett, 27 August 1991.
27. Email from Rose Hilton, 14 February 2014.
28. Knowlson, interview with John Beckett, 27 August 1991; Knowlson, interview with Ann Beckett, 3 August 1992;
29. Knowlson, *Damned to Fame*, p. 758, note 89; Deirdre Bair, *Samuel Beckett*, p. 279.
30. Knowlson, interview with John Beckett, 27 August 1991; Knowlson, interview with Ann Beckett, 3 August 1992.
31. J.P. Donleavy, *The History of the Ginger Man*, Viking, London, 1994, pp. 89–90. At the time of writing (2009) the hotel was boarded up and in a ruinous state.
32. Knowlson, interview with Ann Beckett, 3 August 1992.
33. Anthony Cronin, *Samuel Beckett – The Last Modernist*, p. 309; Eoin O'Brien, *The Beckett Country*, p. 16.
34. Deirdre Bair, *Samuel Beckett*, p. 300.
35. Knowlson, interview with John Beckett, 27 August 1991; Brigid Ferguson, 3 May 2009.
36. The original manuscript belonged to the late Deirdre Sinclair.
37. Cox, Klein, Taylor (editors), *The Life and Music of Brian Boydell*, p. 73; Oxford Music Online.

Three

1. Letter to Sydney Stokes, 1 June 2006.
2. From the St Columba's College website (www.stcolumbas.ie) and Norman Lush, 2 August 2009.
3. Norman Lush, 14 July 2009; Christopher Fitz-Simon, 17 September 2008; back numbers of *The Columban* for the years 1940–47.
4. *The Columban*, December 1940 and Norman Lush, 2 August 2009.
5. Email from Robin McKinney, 4 July 2009.
6. Norman Lush, 14 and 22 July 2009; Robin McKinney, 4 July 2009; Adrian Somerfield, 22 July 2009 and Norman Lush, 2 August 2009.
7. Anthony Cronin, *Samuel Beckett – The Last Modernist*, p. 309.
8. Adrian Somerfield, 22 July 2009.
9. Norman Lush, 14 July 2009.
10. Adrian Somerfield, 29 July 2009.

11. David Sowby, 2 and 14 July 2009.

12. David Sowby; Andrew Robinson on the BBC's h2g2 website, www.bbc.co.uk/ dna/h2g2/A2116739; Andrew and Jenny Robinson, 2 July 2009.

13. Dioceses of Dublin and Glendalough Church Music Committee, *Soundboard*, May 2005 – contributions from Adrian Somerfield (www.churchmusicdublin.org).

14. Andrew Robinson, h2g2; The Contemporary Music Centre, Ireland (www.cmc. ie/composers).

15. Robin McKinney, 4 July 2009. One photograph is owned by Robin McKinney and the other was owned by Deirdre Sinclair.

16. Andrew and Jenny Robinson, 2 July 2009.

17. David Carmody, 15 March 2013.

18. Robin McKinney, 4 July 2009; Adrian Somerfield, 29 July 2009.

19. Adrian Somerfield, 22 July 2009; Seán O'Leary, 28 April 2007; Robin McKinney, 4 July 2009.

20. Andrew and Jenny Robinson, 2 July 2009.

21. Adrian Somerfield, 22 July 2009.

22. *The Columban*, December 1943.

Four

1. Emails from Philip Shields, Royal Irish Academy of Music, 15 and 16 July 2009; *The Columban*, April 1944.

2. Roland Morrow, 23 October 2007.

3. Aidan Higgins, *Dog Days*, p. 3.

4. James and Elizabeth Knowlson (editors), *Beckett Remembering Remembering Beckett*, Bloomsbury, 2006, pp. 138–9.

5. Knowlson, interview with John Beckett, 8 July 1992.

6. James and Elizabeth Knowlson (editors), *Beckett Remembering Remembering Beckett*, Bloomsbury, 2006, pp. 138–9; Anthony Cronin, *Samuel Beckett – The Last Modernist*, p. 565.

7. Brian Boydell scrapbooks, Trinity College Dublin Manuscript and Archives Research Library, TCD MS 1128/4/1.

8. Gillian Smith and Lindsay Armstrong, 9 July 2009.

9. Email from Barra Boydell, 8 October 2014.

10. Cox, Klein, Taylor, *The Life and Music of Brian Boydell*, pp. 6, 76; Pat O'Kelly, *The National Symphony Orchestra of Ireland 1948–1998: A Selected History*, no page numbers.

11. Brian Boydell scrapbooks, TCD MS 1128/4/1.

12. *An Irishman's Diary, Ir. Times*, 15 May 1944, p. 3.

13. *Jottings, Evening Mail*, 15 May 1944.

14. Adrian Somerfield, 22 July 2009.

15. *Local Composers, Ir. Ind.*, 24 May 1944, p. 3.

16. *Dublin Orchestral Players, Ir. Times*, 24 May 1944, p. 3.

17. *The Columban*, July 1944.

18. Brigid Ferguson, 3 May 2009; Andrew and Jenny Robinson, 2 July 2009.

19. Cox, Klein, Taylor, *The Life and Music of Brian Boydell*, p. 4.

20. *Ibid*, p. 12.

21. Richard Pine, *Music and Broadcasting in Ireland*, p. 83.

22. Seán O'Leary, 24 October 2007.

23. *Lonely Waters: Portrait of E.J. Moeran*, BBC Radio 3, 9 December 1994.

24. Feis Ceoil Association archive.

25. *Lonely Waters: Portrait of E.J. Moeran*, BBC Radio 3, 9 December 1994.

26. Anthony Payne, *Ernest John Moeran, The New Grove Dictionary of Music and Musicians* (1980), Vol. 12, p. 457; www.moeran.com.

27. *Lonely Waters: Portrait of E.J. Moeran*, BBC Radio 3, 9 December 1994.

28. David Lee, 3 August 2007.

29. Morris Sinclair, 19 May 2007.

30. Máire Larchet, 12 July 2009.

31. Email from Philip Shields, RIAM, 15 July 2009.

32. Email from Philip Shields, 15 July 2009; *The Columban*, July 1945; Feis Ceoil Association.

Five

1. *Lonely Waters: Portrait of E.J. Moeran*, BBC Radio 3, 9 December 1994.

2. The Papers of Brian Boydell, TCD MS 11128/2/1/138.

3. *Lonely Waters: Portrait of E.J. Moeran*, BBC Radio 3, 9 December 1994.

4. www.moeran.com.

5. Seán O'Leary, 25 October 2008.

6. *Lonely Waters: Portrait of E.J. Moeran*, BBC Radio 3, 9 December 1994.

7. Email from Christopher Bornet, Royal College of Music, 28 July 2009.

8. Records of the Royal College of Music, London.

9. Hugh Ottaway, *Edmund Rubbra, The New Grove Dictionary of Music and Musicians* (1980), Vol. 16, p. 292; British Library website; Francis Routh, *Contemporary British Music*, 1972 (www.musicweb-international.com/rubbra/index.htm).

10. *Edmund Rubbra: Teacher & guide – as I knew him*, Gary Higginson, 1998 (www.musicweb-international.com/classrev/2000/mar00/higginson.htm).

11. H.C. Colles/Howard Ferguson, *Reginald Owen Morris, The New Grove Dictionary of Music and Musicians* (1980), Vol. 12, p. 591.

12. Stanley Webb, *George Thalben-Ball, The New Grove Dictionary of Music and Musicians* (1980), Vol. 18, p. 723.

13. Frank Howes/Hugh Ottaway, *Gordon Jacob, The New Grove Dictionary of Music and Musicians* (1980), Vol. 9, p. 441.

14. Records of the Royal College of Music, London.

15. William Agnew, obituary for John Yewe Dyer, Royal College of Music Library.

16. Records of the Royal College of Music.

17. *The Columban,* July 1946.

18. Supplement to *The Columban*, July 1946.

19. John Beckett, 31 July 1998.

20. Conversation with John Beckett, noted in author's diary, 10 April 1981.

21. Joan and Ray Stagles: *The Blasket Islands – Next Parish America*, O'Brien Press, Dublin 1984.

22. Seán O'Leary, 28 April 2007.

23. *Song Recital in Dublin*, Ir. Times, 26 October 1946, p. 7.

24. Cox, Klein, Taylor, *The Life and Music of Brian Boydell*, p. 6.

25. Printed programme, TCD MS 1128/4/1.

26. *Conductor and composer is now a singer*, Ir. Ind., 29 October 1946, p. 5.

27. *Brian Boydell's song recital*, Irish Press, 29 October 1946, p. 5.

28. *Brian Boydell's recital*, Ir. Times, 29 October 1946, p. 5.

29. Printed programme, TCD MS 1128/4/1.

30. *An Irishman's Diary*, Ir. Times, 5 July 1947, p. 7; *The Columban*, July 1947.

31. Brigid Ferguson, 3 May 2009.

32. Theo Snoddy, *Dictionary of Irish Artists – 20th Century*, Wolfhound Press, 1996, pp. 420–22.

33. England and Wales, Death Index, 1916–2006 for Vera May K Beckett, Vol. 14, p. 1360; England & Wales, FreeBMD Birth Index, 1837–1915 for Vera K H Stapley, Vol. 1a, p. 783.

34. England and Wales, Marriage Index, 1916–2005 for Vera K Stapley, Vol 1a, p. 757.

35. England and Wales, Marriage Index, 1916–2005 for Vera K L'E, Vol 1a, p. 1844.

36. England and Wales, FreeBMD Birth Index, 1837–1915 for Ralph D V Slocombe, Vol. 1d, p. 1495.

37. England and Wales, Death Index, 1916–2006 for Evelyn May Nielson, Vol. 5h, p. 459.

38. England and Wales, FreeBMD Marriage Index, 1835–1915 for Evelyn M Stapley, Vol. 1b, p. 1212.

39. England and Wales, Marriage Index, 1916–2005 for Evelyn M Stapley, Vol 1a, p. 713.

40. Brigid Ferguson, 3 May 2009; Roland Morrow, 23 October 2007.

41. Knowlson, interview with John Beckett, 27 August 1991.

42. Contemporary Music Centre; David C.F. Wright 1993/1999 (http://www.musicweb-international.com/may/index.htm); Seán O'Leary, 28 April 2007.

43. David C.F. Wright 1993/1999 (http://www.musicweb-international.com/may/index.htm); Michael O'Sullivan: *Brendan Behan – A Life*, pp. 91–3.

44. Morris Sinclair, 19 May 2007.

45. Oengus MacNamara, 28 July 2008.

46. Letter from Aidan Higgins to Arland Ussher, 30 June 1960, TCD MS 9301-41/1538.

47. Aidan Higgins to Arland Ussher, 20 September 1952, TCD MS 9301-41/1471.

48. Seán O'Leary, 18 May 2007.

49. Frida Robinson, 30 April 2009.
50. Michael O'Sullivan: *Brendan Behan – A Life*, pp. 142–3.
51. Walter Moore: *Schrödinger – Life and Thought*, pp. 371–2; 404–14; Seán O'Leary, 26 October 2007.
52. *Eamon de Valera: President of Ireland*, Chelsea House Publishers, USA, 1988.
53. Brendan Lynch, *Desmond MacNamara: Pivotal figure in Bohemian Dublin* (obituary), *The Independent*, 21 January 2008; Kurt Jacobsen, *Desmond MacNamara – Bohemian friend of Irish iconoclasts* (obituary), *The Guardian*, 23 April 2008 (both online).
54. Anthony Cronin, *Dead as Doornails*, p. 9; Michael O'Sullivan: *Brendan Behan – A Life*, pp. 125, 133; Oengus MacNamara, 28 July 2008.

Six

1. Radio Éireann job application form, 1953, RTÉ Document Archives. (Tina Byrne, 26 May 2014.)
2. James Ching, Wikipedia.
3. *Studio Portrait: John Beckett*, BBC Radio 3, 17 March 1969; Patrick Cuming, 28 April 2007.
4. Elaine Andrews, Morley College, 23 May 2007.
5. J.A. Richard, *The Pleyel Harpsichord,* www.harpsichord.org.uk/EH/Vol2/No5/pleyel.pdf; *Early Birds*, BBC Radio 3, 21 September 1988.
6. Letter to Desmond Osland, BBC Music Programme Organiser, BBC Written Archives Centre, RCONT 1 Composer Beckett, John – File 1 1954–62 (A), 20 August 1954.
7. Alfred Deller, Wikipedia; *Classical Collection,* BBC Radio 3, 16 March 2009; *Early Birds,* BBC Radio 3, 21 September 1988.
8. *Music by Contemporary Irish Composers*, Radio, *Ir. Ind.*, 27 October 1947, p. 3.
9. *Entry of the Gladiators – Music Critic Victim of "Solemn Protest"*, *Radio Review, Ireland's National Radio Newspaper*, 16 April 1948, Brian Boydell scrapbooks, TCD MS 11128/4/1.
10. Seán O'Leary, 28 April and 18 May 2007.
11. Records of the Royal College of Music.
12. Craig, Dow Fehsenfeld, Gunn and More Overbeck (editors), *The Letters of Samuel Beckett*, Vol. II, Cambridge University Press, 2011, pp. 95, 99.
13. *Ibid*, footnote 2, p. 99, and email from Edward Beckett, 14 April 2009.
14. Knowlson, interview with John Beckett, 27 August 1991.
15. Knowlson, *Damned to Fame*, pp. 319, 327–9.
16. Email from Edward Beckett, 25 February 2007; Knowlson, interview with John Beckett, 27 August 1991; Knowlson, *Damned to Fame*, p. 288–9.
17. Knowlson, interview with John Beckett, 27 August 1991.
18. Seán O'Leary, 24 October 2007.
19. Knowlson, interview with John Beckett, 27 August 1991.
20. Oengus MacNamara, 28 July 2008; Michael O'Sullivan, *Brendan Behan – A Life*, pp. 146–8.

21. Seán O'Leary, 18 May 2007.
22. Deirdre Bair, *Samuel Beckett*, p. 379–80.
23. Morris Sinclair, 19 May 2007.
24. Oengus MacNamara, 28 July 2008.
25. Anthony Cronin, *Samuel Beckett – The Last Modernist*, p. 497.
26. Knowlson, interview with John Beckett, 27 August 1991.
27. Deirdre Bair, *Samuel Beckett*, p. 379–80; Brendan Lynch, *Desmond MacNamara: Pivotal figure in Bohemian Dublin* (obituary), *The Independent*, 21 January 2008.
28. Email from Virginie Desrante, Conservatoire de Paris, 8 June 2007.
29. Knowlson, interview with John Beckett, 27 August 1991.
30. David Lee, 3 August 2007.
31. Bruno Monsaingeon, *Madamoiselle: Conversations with Nadia Boulanger*, Carcanet Press, 1985, p. 26.
32. Knowlson, interview with John Beckett, 8 July 1992.
33. Bruno Monsaingeon, *Madamoiselle: Conversations with Nadia Boulanger*, pp. 24–25.
34. Harold Lester, 25 November 2007.
35. Morris Sinclair, 19 May 2007; Seán O'Leary, 18 May 2007; Saint Germain-en-Laye, Wikipedia.
36. Adrian Jack, Obituary for John Beckett, *The Independent*, 12 March 2007.
37. Seán O'Leary, 26 July 2007; Christopher Nobbs, 14 April 2013.

Seven

1. Emails from Aleck Crichton and Mary Willis, 30 August and 11 September 2014.
2. Venetia O'Sullivan, 26 February 2007; Morris Sinclair, 19 May 2007.
3. Ray Lynott, *Oenone* (an Appreciation of Venetia O'Sullivan), October 2008.
4. Pat O'Kelly, original material used for *An Appreciation: John O'Sullivan*, Ir. Times, 18 April 2006, p. 15; Kilda Taylor, 15 June 2010.
5. Deirdre Sinclair, 20 April 2008; Charles Acton, *End of season thoughts*, Ir. Times, 20 June 1986, p. 6.
6. Richard Pine, *Charles – The Life and World of Charles Acton, 1914–1999*, The Lilliput Press, Dublin, 2010, p. 212; www.ricorso.net; Anthony Cronin, *Dead as Doornails*, pp. 20–21, 24–27; J.P. Donleavy, *The History of the Ginger Man*, p. 63.
7. Priscilla MacNamara, 17 October 2008; John Calder, Obituary for John Beckett, *The Guardian*, 5 March 2007. It should be noted that the sequence of events concerning John's meeting with Vera is purely conjectural and is based on the limited information available; unfortunately my informants had only hazy memories of when the events occurred. It is quite possible, therefore, that the incident in the car might have happened as early as 1947, when John and Vera were known to be living in the Fitzwilliam Street flat.
8. Morris Sinclair, 19 May 2007 and Roland Morrow, 28 May 2007.
9. Undated photograph belonging to Roland Morrow.

10. Mary Boydell, 27 April 2007.
11. Deirdre Sinclair, 19 May 2007.
12. Morris Sinclair, 19 May 2007.
13. Deirdre Sinclair, 19 May 2007.
14. Roland Morrow, 23 October 2007.
15. Priscilla MacNamara, 28 July 2008.
16. Roland Morrow, 23 October 2007.
17. Patrick Lambert, 25 July 2007.
18. Roland Morrow, 23 October 2007.
19. The letters, written between August and September 1939, were discovered by Roland Morrow when clearing out Vera's flat after she died in 1992 – Roland Morrow, 28 May 2007.
20. Mary Boydell, 27 April 2007.
21. Letter from Fachtna Ó hAnnracháin to John Beckett, 11 January 1950, John Beckett Correspondence, 1950–54, RTÉ Document Archives.
22. John Beckett to Fachtna Ó hAnnracháin, 14 January 1950, John Beckett Corresp., RTÉ DA.
23. John Beckett to Fachtna Ó hAnnracháin, undated, John Beckett Corresp., RTÉ DA.
24. John Beckett to Fachtna Ó hAnnracháin, undated, John Beckett Corresp., RTÉ DA.
25. Fachtna Ó hAnnracháin to John Beckett, 28 February 1950, John Beckett Corresp., RTÉ DA.
26. John Beckett to Fachtna Ó hAnnracháin, undated, John Beckett Corresp., RTÉ DA.
27. Fachtna Ó hAnnracháin to John Beckett, 31 May 1950, John Beckett Corresp., RTÉ DA.
28. John Beckett to Fachtna Ó hAnnracháin, undated, John Beckett Corresp., RTÉ DA.
29. Letter from Fachtna Ó hAnnracháin to John Beckett, letter from Arthur Duff to Mrs W.B. Yeats, letter to Oxford University Press, and letter to Helen Waddell of MacMillan & Co., 3 July 1950, John Beckett Corresp., RTÉ DA.
30. Brigid Ferguson, 3 May 2009.
31. Seán O'Leary, 31 July 2007.
32. Brigid Ferguson, 3 and 20 May, 29 October 2009.
33. Mary Boydell, 27 April 2007.
34. Seán O'Leary, 31 July 2007.
35. David Lee, 3 August 2007.
36. David Lee, 21 April and 3 August 2007, 18 May 2008.
37. Gillian Smith, 9 July 2009; Andrew Robinson, 2 July 2009.
38. *Today's Radio, Sunday Independent*, 23 July 1950, p. 1; *Radio Programmes, Ir. Times*, 22 July 1950, p. 5.
39. Note to Fachtna Ó hAnnracháin, undated, sender's signature unclear, John Beckett Corresp., RTÉ DA.
40. Report on Programmes as Broadcast, for John Beckett's Songs on 23 July 1950, John Beckett Corresp., RTÉ DA.

41. Report on Programmes as Broadcast, for John Beckett (piano) on 23 July 1950, John Beckett Corresp., RTÉ DA.

Eight

1. General Register Office, Deaths Registered in the District of Dublin.
2. *Funeral, Dr. G.P.G. Beckett, Ir. Times*, 6 September 1950, p. 5.
3. Seán O'Leary, 31 July 2007.
4. Knowlson, interview with John Beckett, 27 August 1991; Knowlson, interview with John Beckett, 8 July 1992; Knowlson, interview with Ann Beckett, 3 August 1992.
5. Letter from John Beckett to Arthur Duff, 14 September 1950, John Beckett Corresp., RTÉ DA.
6. Arthur Duff to John Beckett, 21 September 1950, John Beckett Corresp., RTÉ DA.
7. John Beckett to Dr Duff, 22 September 1950, John Beckett Corresp., RTÉ DA.
8. Richard Pine, *Music and Broadcasting in Ireland*, pp. 116, 120 and 133.
9. John Beckett, 31 July 1998.
10. Pat O'Kelly, *The National Symphony Orchestra of Ireland 1948–1998: a selected history*, RTÉ, 1998; TCD MS 11128/4/2.
11. *An Irishman's Diary, Ir. Times*, 21 September 1950, p. 5.
12. Oengus MacNamara, 28 July 2008.
13. Gillian Smith, 9 July 2009.
14. Charles Acton, *Twenty-five years of the M.A.I.*, *Ir. Times*, 30 March 1973, p. 12.
15. *Homage to Bach*, *Ir. Times*, 30 September 1950, p. 9.
16. Letter from John Beckett to Gillian Smith, 1 August 2002.
17. Brian Boydell scrapbooks, TCD MS 11128/4/2.
18. Letter from L.S. Gógan to John Beckett, 6 October 1950, John Beckett Corresp., RTÉ DA.
19. John Beckett to Miss O'Higgins, undated, John Beckett Corresp., RTÉ DA.
20. John Beckett to Fachtna Ó hAnnracháin, 24 October 1950, John Beckett Corresp., RTÉ DA.
21. Fachtna Ó hAnnracháin to John Beckett, 26 October 1950, John Beckett Corresp., RTÉ DA.
22. Fachtna Ó hAnnracháin to John Beckett, 9 November 1950, John Beckett Corresp., RTÉ DA.
23. Internal note for Miss Redmond, 8 November 1950, John Beckett Corresp., RTÉ DA.
24. *Radio, Radio Éireann, Ir. Ind.*, 2 February 1951, p. 5.
25. *Lonely Waters – Portrait of E.J. Moeran*, BBC Radio 3, 9 December 1994.

Nine

1. Letter from John Beckett to Radio Éireann, 4 January 1951, John Beckett Corresp., RTÉ DA.

2. Fachtna Ó hAnnracháin to John Beckett, 6 January 1951, John Beckett Corresp., RTÉ DA.

3. Fachtna Ó hAnnracháin to L.S. Gogan, National Museum of Ireland, 17 January 1950 and undated programme details, John Beckett Corresp., RTÉ DA.

4. John Beckett to Fachtna Ó hAnnracháin, 4 January 1951, John Beckett Corresp., RTÉ DA.

5. Note from Fachtna Ó hAnnracháin to John Beckett, 2 February 1951, John Beckett Corresp., RTÉ DA.

6. Advance Programmes for John Beckett, 4 April 1951, John Beckett Corresp., RTÉ DA.

7. Advertisement, *Ir. Times*, 26 January 1951, p. 5.

8. Brigid Ferguson, 3 May 2009.

9. Carol Acton, 26 March 2008; Richard Pine, *Charles – The Life and World of Charles Acton*, p. 230–38.

10. *Education, Tuitions, Ir. Times*, 17 May 1951, p. 7.

11. Anthony Cronin, *Samuel Beckett – The Last Modernist*, preface.

12. Priscilla MacNamara, 17 September 2008.

13. Seán O'Leary, 24 October 2007.

14. Mary Boydell, 27 April 2007.

15. Typed postcard from The Music Editor, *The Bell*, December 1951, John Beckett Corresp., RTÉ DA.

16. *The Bell*, microfilm reference code OL MICROFILMS 763-770, Ussher Multimedia Area, Trinity College Dublin; Vol. XVII No. 2 May 1951, p. 56–9. Also Index for *The Bell*, Early Printed Books Reading Room, Trinity College Dublin.

17. *The Bell*, Vol. XVII No. 3 June 1951, p. 45–54.

18. *The Bell*, Vol. XVII No. 4 July 1951, p. 46–52.

19. *The Bell*, Vol. XVII No. 12 March 1952, p. 104–9.

20. *The Bell*, Vol. XVIII No. 2 May 1952, p. 103–6.

21. *The Bell*, Vol. XVIII No. 6 November 1952, p. 169–71.

22. Acknowledgment note from Radio Éireann to John Beckett, 23 May 1951, and letter from John Beckett to Fachtna Ó hAnnracháin, 21 May 1951, John Beckett Corresp., RTÉ DA.

23. Letter from John Beckett to Fachtna Ó hAnnracháin, 21 May 1951, John Beckett Corresp., RTÉ DA.

24. Fachtna Ó hAnnracháin to John Beckett, 31 May 1951, John Beckett Corresp., RTÉ DA.

25. Radio Éireann Artistes Engagement Form for broadcast on 2 July 1951, John Beckett Corresp., RTÉ DA, and *Monday Recital, Radio, Radio Éireann, Irish Ind.*, 2 July 1951, p. 5.

26. *Broadcasting Programmes*, Radio Éireann, *Ir.Times*, 25 July 1951, p. 5.
27. *Adults' Summer School at Drogheda, Ir.Ind.*, 5 August 1951.
28. Henry Boylan, *Ussher, (Percy) Arland, A Dictionary of Irish Biography, Third Edition*, Gill and Macmillan Ltd, Dubin, 1998, p. 433.
29. Letter from Aidan Higgins to Arland Ussher, 27 September 1951, TCD MS 9301–41/1465.
30. Aidan Higgins to Arland Ussher, 13 December 1951, TCD MS 9301–41/1466.
31. Letter from John Beckett to Fachtna Ó hAnnracháin, 13 October 1951, John Beckett Corresp., RTÉ DA.
32. Fachtna Ó hAnnracháin to John Beckett, 17 October 1951, John Beckett Corresp., RTÉ DA.
33. Artistes Engagement Form for 11 February 1952 (signed 4 February 1952), John Beckett Corresp., RTÉ DA.
34. Report on Programmes as Broadcast form, for 11 February [1952], John Beckett Corresp., RTÉ DA.
35. *Irish Musical Arts Society concert*, *Ir.Times*, 19 November 1951, p. 3.
36. Emma Kirkby, BBC Radio 3, 22 March 2009.
37. *An Irishman's Diary*, *Ir.Times*, 4 December 1951, p. 5.
38. Joseph O'Neill, *Well balanced singing in oratorio*, *Ir.Ind.*, 8 December 1951, p. 7.

Ten

1. Letter from John Beckett to Fachtna Ó hAnnracháin, 7 January 1952, John Beckett Corresp., RTÉ DA.
2. Fachtna Ó hAnnracháin to Director, Service du Prêt de la Bibliothèque Nationale, 58 Rue de Richelieu, Paris, 8 January 1952, John Beckett Corresp., RTÉ DA.
3. Fachtna Ó hAnnracháin to John Beckett, 9 January 1952, John Beckett Corresp., RTÉ DA.
4. *Radio Orchestral Concert*, *Ir.Times*, 23 January 1952, p. 5.
5. *Music Magazine*, radio listings, *Ir.Ind.*, 23 January and 6 February 1952, pages 3 and 5.
6. Brian Boydell scrapbooks, TCD MS 11128/4/2.
7. Letter from John Beckett to Fachtna Ó hAnnracháin, 21 February 1952, John Beckett Corresp., RTÉ DA.
8. Fachtna Ó hAnnracháin to John Beckett, 1 March 1952, John Beckett Corresp., RTÉ DA.
9. Note from Fachtna Ó hAnnracháin to P.G. O'Raghallaigh, 1 March 1952, John Beckett Corresp., RTÉ DA.
10. Fachtna Ó hAnnracháin to John Beckett, 6 March 1952, John Beckett Corresp., RTÉ DA.
11. Emails from Reginald Gray, 22, 24 November 2010, and 6 May 2011. At a later period, Reginald painted a portrait of John based on the sketch, and in 2010 donated it to St Columba's College, where it now hangs on a wall.

12. Email from Reginald Gray, 24 November 2010. Reginald had the privilege of meeting Schnittke in 1974, and painted him in Moscow.

13. Letter from John Beckett to Fachtna Ó hAnnracháin, 18 May 1952, John Beckett Corresp., RTÉ DA.

14. *The Arts and the State*, Radio Programmes, *Ir. Times*, 30 April 1952, p. 7.

15. *Musical Society to perform work by Bach*, *Ir. Times*, 9 May 1952, p. 7.

16. Joseph O'Neill, *Excellent Performance by Choral Society*, *Ir. Ind.*, 10 May 1952, p. 10.

17. *An Irishman's Diary*, *Ir. Times*, 27 May 1952, p. 7.

18. *College Singers Concert*, *Ir. Times*, 28 May 1952, p. 5.

19. Joseph O'Neill, *Singers Showed Fine Musicianship*, *Ir. Ind.*, 28 May 1952, p. 7. John wrote a review of this concert for *The Bell*: see John Beckett, *Music*, *The Bell*, Vol XVIII No. 4 July 1952, OL MICROFILMS 763-770, Ussher Multimedia Area, TCD.

20. Prof. T.K. Hoppen, Letter, *The Guardian* (online), 16 March 2007; Prof. T.K. Hoppen, 18 April 2007.

21. Priscilla MacNamara, 17 September 2008.

22. Mary Boydell, 27 April 2007.

23. Venetia O'Sullivan, 26 July 2007.

24. Brigid Ferguson, 3 May 2009.

25. Letter from John Beckett to Fachtna Ó hAnnracháin, 15 June 1952, John Beckett Corresp., RTÉ DA.

26. Fachtna Ó hAnnracháin to John Beckett, 18 June 1952, John Beckett Corresp., RTÉ DA.

27. John Beckett to Fachtna Ó hAnnracháin, 13 July 1952, John Beckett Corresp., RTÉ DA.

28. T.K. Hoppen, 18 April 2007; Commentary, on www.amazon.com, on 1952 recording of Wagner's *Die Meistersinger von Nüremberg*, conducted by Hans Knappersbusch.

29. Letters from Werner Schürmann to the author, 8 and 17 February 2002.

30. Brigid Ferguson, 3 May 2009.

31. John Beckett, 31 July 1998; Charles Gannon, *Cathal Gannon – The Life and Times of a Dublin Craftsman*, Lilliput Press, 2006, pp. 203–10.

32. Letter from John Beckett to Fachtna Ó hAnnracháin, 25 August 1952, John Beckett Corresp., RTÉ DA.

33. Fachtna Ó hAnnracháin to John Beckett, 28 August 1952, John Beckett Corresp., RTÉ DA.

34. John Beckett to Fachtna Ó hAnnracháin, 29 August 1952, John Beckett Corresp., RTÉ DA.

35. John Beckett to Fachtna Ó hAnnracháin, 17 September 1952, John Beckett Corresp., RTÉ DA.

36. *Radio, Radio Eireann*, *Ir. Ind*, 22 September 1952, p 5.

37. Mirette Dowling, 9 April 2013.

38. *"Patience" style preserved*, *Ir. Times*, 30 September 1952, p. 5.

39. *Radio, Radio Éireann, Ir. Ind.*, 21 October 1952, p. 5, 28 October, p. 5, and 4 November, p. 5.
40. Carol Acton, 29 March 2008; Cox, Klein, Taylor (editors), *The Life and Music of Brian Boydell*, p. 21.
41. Letter from John Beckett to Fachtna Ó hAnnracháin, 5 December 1952, John Beckett Corresp., RTÉ DA.
42. Fachtna Ó hAnnracháin to John Beckett, 8 December 1952, John Beckett Corresp., RTÉ DA.
43. *A Musical Holiday, Radio, Radio Éireann, Ir. Ind.*, 27 December 1952, p. 3.
44. Richard Pine, *Music and Broadcasting in Ireland*, p. 137.

Eleven

1. Letter from Aidan Higgins to Arland Ussher, 26 January, TCD MS 9301-41/1481.
2. Radio listings, *Ir. Ind.*, 18 February 1953, p. 5, Artistes Engagement Form for John Beckett, signed 4 February 1953, John Beckett Corresp., RTÉ DA. The programme began with *Two Poems of Emily Brontë: Fall leaves, fall* and *In dungeons dark*. Next came *Three Poems of Walter de la Mare: Here today and gone tomorrow, Will o' the wisp* and *Never*. The fifteen-minute programme ended with *Two Poems of Shelley: I went into the deserts of dim sleep* and *Dirge* (the song mentioned by Aidan Higgins).
3. *Musical Society's Choral Concert, Ir. Ind.*, 20 February 1953, p. 8.
4. *Hindemith work at mid-day concert, Ir. Times*, 21 February 1953, p. 4.
5. *An Irishman's Diary, Ir. Times*, 9 November 1955, p. 6.
6. Letter from John Beckett to Fachtna Ó hAnnracháin, 19 February 1953, John Beckett Corresp., RTÉ DA.
7. Radio Éireann job application form, 1953, RTÉ Document Archives.
8. Letter from John Beckett to Fachtna Ó hAnnracháin, 25 May 1953, John Beckett Corresp., RTÉ DA.
9. Handwritten note, 3 June [1953], John Beckett Corresp., RTÉ DA.
10. Typed programme with written date, 17 June [1953], John Beckett Corresp., RTÉ DA.
11. *Broadcasting programmes, Ir. Times*, 14 July 1953, p. 4.
12. Maxwell Sweeney, *Radio Review, Ir. Ind.*, 18 July 1953, p. 5.
13. *Broadcasting Programmes, Ir. Times*, 21 and 28 July, 4 and 11 August 1953, p. 4.
14. Letter from Fachtna Ó hAnnracháin to John Beckett, 2 June 1953, John Beckett Corresp., RTÉ DA.
15. Seán O'Leary, 28 April 2007.
16. Letter from John Beckett to Erskine Childers, 25 July 1953, John Beckett Corresp., RTÉ DA.
17. Secretary for the Minister of State (Erskine Childers) to John Beckett, 30 July 1953, John Beckett Corresp., RTÉ DA.

18. Maurice Gorham to John Beckett, 4 August 1953, John Beckett Corresp., RTÉ DA.
19. *Programmes, Ir. Times*, 11 August 1953, p. 4.
20. Michael O'Sullivan, *Brendan Behan – A Life*, p. 175.
21. Brigid Ferguson, 3 May 2009.
22. *An Irishman's Diary, Ir. Times*, 29 August 1953, p. 7.
23. *Limerick has a backyard theatre, Ir. Times*, 4 September 1953, p. 6; www.irishplayography.com; William Hutchings, *Samuel Beckett's Waiting for Godot – A reference guide*, pp. 82–4.
24. Brigid Ferguson, 3 and 20 May, 29 October 2009.
25. Typed programme for broadcasting on 2 September 1953 and undated note about publishers, John Beckett Corresp., RTÉ DA.
26. *Radio Programmes, Ir. Times*, 26 September 1953, p. 4 (programme on 27th); radio listings, *Connacht Tribune*, 10 October 1953 (programme on 14th), p. 9.
27. Handwritten note, 4 September 1953, John Beckett Corresp., RTÉ DA; *Radio Programmes, Ir. Times*, 19 October 1953, p. 4; radio listings, *Connacht Tribune*, 24 October 1953 (programme on 26th), p. 9; *Radio Programmes, Ir. Times*, 2 November 1953, p. 4; *Connacht Tribune*, 7 November 1953 (programme on 9th), p. 9.
28. Letter from John Beckett to Miss McGreevey of Radio Éireann, 9 October [1953], John Beckett Corresp., RTÉ DA.
29. Letter from Werner Schürmann, 17 February 2002.
30. Priscilla and Oengus MacNamara, 28 July 2008.
31. Aidan Higgins, *Donkey's Years*.
32. Knowlson, interview with John Beckett, 8 July 1992.
33. Letter from John Beckett to Fachtna Ó hAnnracháin, 5 December 1953, John Beckett Corresp., RTÉ DA.
34. Fachtna Ó hAnnracháin to John Beckett, 9 December 1953, John Beckett Corresp., RTÉ DA.
35. John Beckett to Fachtna Ó hAnnracháin, 11 December 1953, John Beckett Corresp., RTÉ DA.
36. Enclosed with letter from Fachtna Ó hAnnracháin to John Beckett, 16 December 1953, John Beckett Corresp., RTÉ DA.
37. Letter from W.T. Davies to Fachtna Ó hAnnracháin, 30 December 1953, John Beckett Corresp., RTÉ DA.
38. Fachtna Ó hAnnracháin to W.T. Davies, 4 January 1954, John Beckett Corresp., RTÉ DA.
39. Brigid Ferguson, 3 May 2009.

Twelve

1. Jill Higgins, 17 April 2008 and 8 September 2009; Aidan Higgins, *Donkey's Years*, p. 222.
2. Letter from John Beckett to Roger Fiske, BBC WAC, B, 20 August 1954.

3. Email from Mimi Waitzman, Deputy Keeper of Musical Instruments, The Horniman Museum and Gardens, 24 May 2010.
4. John Sothcott, *The Recorder Magazine*, 2007, Vol 27, p. 124–5.
5. Programme notes to concert given in l'Eglise Saint-Germain l'Auxerrois, Paris, 3 May 1972.
6. Seán O'Leary, 24 October 2007.
7. Letter from John Beckett to Roger Fiske, BBC WAC, A, 20 August 1954.
8. Seán O'Leary, 24 October 2007.
9. John Sothcott, *The Recorder Magazine*, 2007, Vol 27, p. 124.
10. Harold Lester, 25 November 2007.
11. Desmond MacNamara, *Passionate sound of early music* (Obituary of Michael Morrow), *The Guardian*, 28 April 1994.
12. Brigid Ferguson, 3 May 2009; Mary Boydell, 27 April 2007.
13. Undated short biography of Michael Morrow and Andrew Parrott, King's College London, College Archives, GB 0100 K/PP93 *(Morrow, Michael (1929-1994) and Musica Reservata)*, Box 10.
14. Theo Wyatt, *The Recorder Magazine*, 2007, Vol 27, p. 124.
15. Undated short biography of Michael Morrow and Andrew Parrott, KCLCA K/PP93, Box 10; *Morrow and yesterday's music today,* unidentified newspaper, KCLCA K/PP93, Box 12; Harman and Mellers, *Man and his Music – The story of musical experience in the west*, Barrie and Jenkins, 1971.
16. Letter from John Beckett to Gillian Smith, 1 August 2002.
17. Letter from John Beckett to Fachtna Ó hAnnracháin, 10 February 1954, John Beckett Corresp., RTÉ DA.
18. Fachtna Ó hAnnracháin to John Beckett, 16 February 1954, John Beckett Corresp., RTÉ DA.
19. John Beckett to Fachtna Ó hAnnracháin, 21 February 1954, John Beckett Corresp., RTÉ DA.
20. Fachtna Ó hAnnracháin to John Beckett, 25 February 1954, John Beckett Corresp., RTÉ DA.
21. *time shift: The Third Programme – High Culture for All in Post-War Britain*, BBC Bristol, 2005.
22. Letter from John Beckett to John Davenport, BBC WAC, B, undated.
23. John Beckett to John Davenport, BBC WAC, B, early 1954.
24. Note from John Davenport to Dr Roger Fiske, BBC WAC, B, undated.*
25. Letter to Norman Carrell, BBC WAC, B, 25 May 1954.
26. Poster, BBC WAC, B, 12 June 1954.
27. John Sothcott, The Recorder Magazine, 2007, Vol 27, p. 124.
28. Letter from Norman Carrell to John Beckett, BBC WAC, B, 2 June 1954.
29. BBC audition application form, BBC WAC, B, undated (June 1954).
30. Letter from Roger Fiske to John Beckett, BBC WAC, B, 15 June 1954.*
31. John Beckett to Roger Fiske, BBC WAC, B, 16 June 1954.

32. John Beckett to Desmond Osland, BBC WAC, A, 20 August 1954.

33. Letters to and from Roger Fiske, BBC WAC, B, between 30 August and 1 November 1954.*

34. John Beckett to Roger Fiske, BBC WAC, B, 16 November 1954.

35. Obituaries: John Willett, *The Guardian*, 22 August 2002; Obituaries: John Willett, *The Times*, 22 August, 2002, p. 30.

36. Seán O'Leary, 26 July 2007.

37. Seán O'Leary, 26 July 2007; Fritz Speigl Obituary, *The Independent*, 31 March 2003.

38. Seán O'Leary, 24 October 2007.

39. Letter from Aidan Higgins to Arland Ussher, 20 January [1955], TCD MS 9301-41/1492.

40. Letter from Norman Carrell to John Beckett, and assorted documents, BBC WAC, B, 25 March – April 1955; *John Dowland's Song Books*, BBC Third Programme, *Radio Times*, radio programmes for 14, 18 and 27 April, and 3 May 1955.

41. Letter from Aidan Higgins to Arland Ussher, 30 March 1955, TCD MS 9301-41/1494.

42. The text of these programmes is on microfilm at the BBC Written Archives Centre, Reading.

Thirteen

1. Letter from John Beckett to Roger Fiske, BBC WAC, B, 1 May 1955.

2. Letter from Aidan Higgins to Arland Ussher, 30 March 1955, TCD MS 9301–41/1494.

3. Seán O'Leary, 24 October 2007.

4. Letter from Aidan Higgins to Arland Ussher, 16 July 1955, TCD MS 9301-41/1496.

5. Aidan Higgins, *A Wet Exposed Place*, *Ir. Times*, 5 January 1980, p. 9.

6. Letter from Aidan Higgins to Arland Ussher, 16 July 1955, TCD MS 9301-41/1496; Knowlson, *Damned to Fame*, p. 414.

7. Letter from John Beckett to Roger Fiske, BBC WAC, B, 25 September 1955.

8. Roger Fiske to John Beckett, BBC WAC, B, 2 November 1955.

9. Knowlson, *Damned to Fame*, p. 419.

10. Knowlson, interview with John Beckett, 27 August 1991 and 8 July 1992; Craig, etc, *The Letters of Samuel Beckett 1941–1956*, p. 516 and 561.

11. Letter from Aidan Higgins to Arland Ussher, 10 December 1955, TCD MS 9301-41/1507.

12. *Weddings, Ir. Times*, 2 December 1955, p. 7.

13. Aidan Higgins, *Donkey's Years*, p. 236.

14. *Ibid.*, p. 231.

15. *Ibid.*, p. 222.

16. Brigid Ferguson, 3 May 2009.

17. Aidan Higgins, *Donkey's Years*, p. 222, 231.

18. Knowlson, *Damned to Fame*, pp. 402, 414, 416; Craig, etc, *The Letters of Samuel Beckett 1941–1956*, p. 572.

19. Knowlson, interview with John Beckett, 27 August 1991.

20. Anthony Cronin, *Samuel Beckett – The Last Modernist*, p. 565–6.

21. Letter from Aidan Higgins to Arland Ussher, 10 December 1955, TCD MS 9301-41/1507.

22. Aidan Higgins in *Beckett Remembering Remembering Beckett*, p. 140; Aidan Higgins, *Donkey's Years*, p. 235; Anthony Cronin, *Samuel Beckett – The Last Modernist*, p. 565–6.

23. Letter from John Beckett to Mr Candler, BBC WAC, C, 8 February 1956.

24. Talks Booking Requisition, BBC WAC, B, February 1956; *Franz Xaver Mozart*, Third Programme, *Radio Times*, radio programmes for 15 February 1956.*

25. Microfilm, BBC WAC.

26. *Leopold and Franz Xaver Mozart*, Third Programme, *Radio Times*, radio programmes for 18 February 1956.

27. *Franz Xaver Mozart*, Third Programme, *Radio Times*, radio programmes for 14 June 1968; Patrick Cuming's John Beckett tape recording list, PC 030.

28. Knowlson, interview with John Beckett, 8 July 1992; Samuel Beckett to John Morris, Controller, Third Programme, BBC WAC RCONT1, Scriptwriter, Beckett, Samuel, File I, 1953–1962 (M), 16 February 1956.

29. Harry Croft-Jackson to John Beckett, BBC WAC, A, 29 March 1956.*

30. John Beckett to Roger Fiske, BBC WAC, B, 26 April 1956.

31. John Sothcott, *John Beckett 1927–2007*, *The Recorder Magazine*, Vol. 27, 2007, pp. 124–5.

32. *Musica Reservata*, Early Music, Vol. 4, No. 4, October 1976; Michael Morrow: *Musical Performance and Authenticity*, Early Music, Vol. 6, No. 2, April 1978; David Munrow, *Instruments of the Middle Ages and Renaissance,* Oxford University Press, London, 1976; Seán O'Leary, 24 October 2007.

33. Hedy Morrow, 14 May 2008.

34. *Michael Morrow*, Mining the Archive, BBC Radio 3, 19 May 1995.

Fourteen

1. *Broadcasting Programmes, Ir. Times*, 28 June and 5 September 1956, p. 5.

2. Obituary, *The Guardian*, 5 August 2005; Obituary, *The Independent*, 6 August 2005.

3. Radio listings, *Ir. Ind.*, 29 September 1956, p. 9.

4. Michael Sweeney, *Radio Review, Ir. Ind.,* 6 October 1956, p. 6.

5. *Broadcasting Programmes, Ir. Times*, 31 October 1956, p. 4.

6. *The Bell*, Vol XVIII No. 4, July 1952.

7. James Kelly, 17 May 2014; letter from Ralph Cusack to James Plunkett, 1/2 December 1954, National Library of Ireland MS 40,856 1954–1969.

8. James Plunkett obituaries: *The Independent*, 30 May 2003 and *The Sunday Business Post*, 1 June 2003 (both online).

9. Letter from John Beckett to James Plunkett, 31 October 1956, NLI MS 40,853: 1956–1997.
10. John Beckett to James Plunkett, 10 November 1956, NLI MS 40,853: 1956–1997.
11. Desmond F. Ryan, *A Letter from Paris: The Small Men*, *Ir. Times*, 10 August 1956, p. 5.
12. Knowlson, interview with John Beckett, 8 July 1992; Knowlson, *Damned to Fame*, pp. 431, 433.
13. Knowlson, interviews with John Beckett, 27 August 1991 and 8 July 1992.
14. Letter from Samuel Beckett to Alan Simpson, 14 January 1957, Craig, Dow Fehsenfeld, Gunn and More Overbeck (editors), *The Letters of Samuel Beckett 1957–1965* (Volume III), pp. 14 and 15, note 4 (letter from John Beckett to Alan Simpson, 19 January 1957, TCD MS 10731/46).
15. Craig, etc., *The Letters of Samuel Beckett 1957–1965* (Volume III), p. 3.
16. Knowlson, *Damned to Fame*, pp. 433–4, 436–7; Knowlson, interview with John Beckett, 8 July 1992.
17. *London Letter: Two Plays by Beckett*, *Ir. Times*, 5 April 1957, p. 5.
18. Email from Jeremy Montagu, 20 May 2010.
19. Knowlson, interview with John Beckett, 8 July 1992.
20. Letter from Samuel Beckett to Barney Rosset, 6 April 1957, Craig, etc., *The Letters of Samuel Beckett 1957–1965* (Volume III), p. 40, and letter from Samuel Beckett to Arland Ussher, 14 April 1957, *ibid*, p. 43.
21. Samuel Beckett to Alan Schneider, 16 April 1957: Maurice Harmon (editor), *No Author Better Served – The correspondence of Samuel Beckett and Alan Schneider*, p. 13.
22. Letter from Samuel Beckett to Donald McWhinnie, 7 May 1957, Craig, etc., *The Letters of Samuel Beckett 1957–1965* (Volume III), p. 46.
23. Knowlson, interview with John Beckett, 8 July 1992; email from James Knowlson, 14 July 2010.
24. Letter from John Beckett to James Plunkett, 16 January 1957, NLI MS 40,853: 1956–1997.
25. Talks Booking Requisition, BBC WAC, B, March 1957.
26. Letter from Roger Fiske to John Beckett, BBC WAC, B, 8 February 1957.*
27. Microfilm, BBC WAC.
28. Letter from Samuel Beckett to John Morris, BBC WAC, M, 16 November 1956.
29. Samuel Beckett to Donald McWhinnie, BBC WAC, M, 7 May 1957.
30. Donald McWhinnie to Samuel Beckett, BBC WAC, M, 16 May 1957.*
31. Memorandum from Miss H. Dean, Copyright Dept to Script Editor, Drama (Sound), BBC WAC, M, 19 August 1957.
32. Note from Bernard Keeffe to 'A.H.D.', BBC WAC, A, undated.*
33. Letter from John Beckett to Donald McWhinnie and McWhinnie's reply, BBC WAC, A, undated and 4 September 1957.
34. Donald McWhinnie to Samuel Beckett, BBC WAC, M, 22 November 1957.*
35. Samuel Beckett to Donald McWhinne, BBC WAC, M, 30 June 1957.
36. Letter from Aidan Higgins to Arland Ussher, 20 January 1955, TCD MS

9301-41/1492; *Russian Journey: 1. Slow Boat to Riga* by James Plunkett, NLI MS 40,778/1; email from Rose Hilton, 23 May 2014. Rose has a hazy recollection of John showing her a photograph of all the delegates in Moscow.

37. Author's recollection.

38. Beate Luszeit, Schlosspark Theater, Berlin; Knowlson, interview with John Beckett, 8 July 1992; Email from Jeremy Montagu, 6 July 2010.

39. Letter from Samuel Beckett to Alan Schneider, 21 November 1957, Craig, etc., *The Letters of Samuel Beckett 1957–1965* (Volume III), pp. 73–75. John's handwritten music and words are reproduced on p. 75 (note 21).

40. *Unpublished work by Mr. Beckett, The Times*, 27 November 1957, p. 3; *London Letter, Ir. Times*, 28 November 1957, p. 7.

41. Craig, etc., *The Letters of Samuel Beckett 1957–1965* (Volume III), p. 77, note 6.

42. British Library Sound Archive, tape T5564R.

43. Knowlson, interview with John Beckett, 8 July 1992; Samuel Beckett to Alan Schneider, 29 January 1958: Maurice Harmon (editor), *No Author Better Served*, pp. 33–4.

44. Letter from Samuel Beckett to Donald McWhinnie, 23 December 1957, Craig, etc., *The Letters of Samuel Beckett 1957–1965* (Volume III), pp. 79–80, note 3, and p. 98, note 1.

Fifteen

1. Memorandum from Donald McWhinnie, letter from Donald McWhinnie to Samuel Beckett, and commission request from Donald McWhinnie to Miss Dean, Copyright, BBC WAC, M, 18 February, 20 February and 26 March 1958.*

2. Letter from John Gibson to John Beckett, BBC WAC, A, 2 December 1957.

3. Note from Donald McWhinnie to John Beckett, BBC WAC, A, 6 November 1957; Commission and other documents, BBC WAC RCONT 1 Copywright Beckett, John S. – File 1 1956–62, (C), 9 December to 20 January 1958.

4. Note from John Gibson to Leslie Stokes, Assistant to Controller, and note from Leslie Stokes, 10 March 1958, BBC WAC, A, 5 and 10 March 1958.

5. Knowlson, interview with John Beckett, 8 July 1992.

6. Letter from Samuel Beckett to Donald McWhinnie, 7 March 1958, Craig, etc., *The Letters of Samuel Beckett 1957–1965* (Volume III), p. 115; letter from Samuel Beckett to Donald McWhinnie, 26 February 1958, *ibid*, p. 110, and letter from Samuel Beckett to Barney Rosset, 10 March 1958, *ibid*, p. 116. Sapo is the name of a boy who features in an account that Malone is writing.

7. *St. James's Gate Musical Society in Bach's St. Matthew Passion, Ir. Times*, 24 March 1958, p. 5.

8. Knowlson, interview with John Beckett, 8 July 1992.

9. Interview with Andrew and Jenny Robinson, 2 July 2009.

10. Eithne Clarke, 19 September 2013.

11. Letter from Werner Schürmann to the author, 6 February 2002.

12. Andrew Moore, National Gallery of Ireland, 22 April 2013. The portraits of Samuel Beckett and Gerda Frömel are kept in the National Gallery of Ireland.

13. Eithne Clarke, 19 September 2013. Hilda submitted this work to the annual Royal Hibernian Academy exhibition in 1962, when it was not for sale, and again in 1978, when it was priced at £600 but was not sold. It depicts John in profile and was presumably painted in 1958. (See Ann M. Stewart, *Royal Hibernian Academy of Arts, Index of Exhibitions 1826–1979*, Vol. III, N–Z, Manton Publishing, 1987, pp. 108–9; Theo Snoddy: *Dictionary of Irish Artists – 20th Century*, Wolfhound Press, 1996, p. 428.)

14. Andrew and Jenny Robinson, 2 July 2009.

15. *Malone Dies*, Third Programme, *Radio Times*, radio programmes for 18 and 19 June (repeat) 1958.

16. Letters from Donald McWhinnie to Samuel Beckett, and Donald McWhinnie to Mr Frank Phillips, BBC WAC, M, 1 April 1958 and 16 June 1958.

17. Letter from Aidan Higgins to Arland Ussher, November 1958, TCD MS 9301-41/1527.

18. Letter from Aidan Higgins to Arland Ussher, 14 September 1958, TCD MS 9301-41/1525.

19. Note from Heather Dean, and correspondence about *Pantagleize*, BBC WAC, C, 26 March 1958 and other dates, 1958.

20. *Pantagleize*, Third Programme, *The Times*, radio programmes for 22 April 1958.

21. Commission, BBC WAC, C, 10 July 1958; Miss E.H. Wakeham to David Thomson, and note re fees and recording session, 25 July 1958, BBC WAC, RCONT 18 Copyright John S. Beckett – File 2 1963–69 (F), 21 and 25 July 1958; *Remember Who You Are*, Third Programme, *Radio Times*, radio listings for 23 and 24 July (repeat) 1958.

22. Craig, etc., *Profiles: Leslie Daiken*, *The Letters of Samuel Beckett 1941–1956* (Volume II), p. 701; interview with Patrick and Melanie Cuming, and telephone call with Michael Cuming, 28 April 2007. Melanie married Patrick Cuming in 1980. John became a good friend of theirs and was often invited to their home, where he liked to play piano duets with Melanie. When Melanie found it difficult to play her bass part fast enough, John often scolded her by saying, 'Come on – keep up with me!'

23. Priscilla and Oengus MacNamara, 28 July 2008.

24. Correspondence from John Beckett, then Michael Morrow, to Dr Roger Fiske, BBC WAC, I, 28 and 29 November 1958.

25. Connolly Cole, *A Letter from Oxford: Bloom on the high, Ir. Times*, 3 December 1958, p. 5.

26. Correspondence from Roger Fiske to Michael Morrow, BBC WAC, I, 4 and 31 December 1958.

27. Note from Donald McWhinnie, BBC WAC, A, 9 December 1958; commission, BBC WAC, C, 9 December 1958.

28. BBC Archives.

29. Note from David McWhinnie, 21 January 1959, BBC WAC, C.*

30. *New Beckett Work*, *The Times*, 8 January 1959, p. 5.

31. *London Letter – Legless in Sawdust*, *Ir. Times*, 8 January 1958, p. 5.

32. Letter from Samuel Beckett to Barney Rosset, 20 March 1959, Craig, etc., *The Letters of Samuel Beckett 1957–1965* (Volume III), p. 215.

33. British Library Sound Archive, tape T5562WR BD1.

34. Knowlson, interview with John Beckett, 8 July 1992: Knowlson quotes Samuel Beckett's letter to Aidan Higgins, written on 24 March 1959, which is reproduced in full in *The Letters of Samuel Beckett 1957–1965* (Volume III), pp. 218–220.

35. Letter from Aidan Higgins to Arland Ussher, '11th–12th etc Sept 1959', TCD MS 9301–41/1530.

36. Charles Gannon, *Cathal Gannon*, pp. 232–3.

37. Letter from John Beckett to Gillian Smith, 1 August 2002.

38. *Impressive performance*, *Ir. Times*, 16 March 1959, p. 7; Mary Mac Goris, *Performed Bach's Passion*, *Ir. Ind.*, 16 March 1959, p. 6.

39. Alison Young, 6 June 2013.

40. Roger Fiske's secretary to Ronald Boswell, and change of contract, BBC WAC, I, 7 April 1959 and undated (April 1959); assorted documents, BBC WAC, B and I, April–May 1959; *Claudin de Sermisy and the Paris Chanson*, Third Programme, *Radio Times*, radio programmes for 24 April (cancelled) and 2 May 1959.

41. British Library Sound Archive, 1CDR0005827.

42. Letter from Roger Fiske to Michael Morrow, BBC WAC, I, 5 May 1959.*

43. Commission, and programme details, BBC WAC, C, 8 May 1959 and undated (1959).

44. *Music by Telemann and Beckett*, Third Programme, *Radio Times*, radio programmes for 27 May 1959.

45. Letter from Aidan Higgins to Arland Ussher, 17 June 1959, TCD MS 9301–41/1529.

46. Hedy Morrow, 14 May 2008.

47. Seán O'Leary, 24 October 2007.

48. Hedy Morrow, 14 May 2008.

49. Memos, BBC WAC, C, October–December 1959; Knowlson, *Damned to Fame*, pp. 458–9, 470, 472, 480–1.

50. *First Surrealist Manifesto*, *The Times*, 24 February 1960, p. 15; Third Programme, *Radio Times*, radio programmes for 23 February 1960.

51. Commission, and letter from John Beckett to Miss Wakeham, BBC WAC, C, 2 and 10 December 1959.

52. *Radio and TV Programmes*, *Ir. Times*, 1 January 1960, p. 7.

Sixteen

1. Printed programme, *A concert of mediaeval music given by Musica Reservata*, Fenton House, Hampstead Grove, 30 January 1960, KCLCA K/PP93, Box 7.

2. Assorted recordings including an undated demonstration tape (?) found in John Beckett's attic and supplied by Patrick Cuming, Tape PC003; programme notes from various Musica Reservata concerts.

3. Interview with Nicholas Anderson, 4 March 2010; *Musica Reservata, Early Music*, Vol. 4, No. 4, 4 October 1976, p. 515.

4. *Musica Reservata, Early Music*, Vol. 4, No. 4, 4 October 1976, p. 515; Michael Morrow Papers, Royal Academy of Music. The programme had consisted of works by Obrecht, Dunstable/Bedingham, Dufay, Binchois, de Latins and Ockeghem.

5. *Morrow and yesterday's music today*, unidentified and undated newspaper article, KCLCA K/PP93, Box 12.

6. David Fallows: Musica Reservata, *The New Grove Dictionary of Music and Musicians*, (1980), Vol. 12, p. 827.

7. Interview with Michael Morrow, *Arts Guardian*, 23 June 1975, p. 8, supplied by Seán O'Leary; also KCLCA K/PP93, Box 12.

8. Email from Jeremy Montagu, 20 May 2010.

9. Interviews with Seán O'Leary, 28 April 2007, 26 July 2007, 24 and 25 October 2007.

Seventeen

1. Printed programme, *A concert given by Grayston Burgess*, etc, Hampstead Parish Church, 23 April 1960, KCLCA K/PP93, Box 7.

2. Typewritten programme, *A concert of medieval music*, 17 Holly Mount, Hampstead, 26 May 1960, KCLCA K/PP93, Box 3, Folder 1.

3. Letter from Thurston Dart to John Beckett, May 1960, KCLCA K/PP93, Box 3, Folder 1.

4. Seán O'Leary, 24 October 2007.

5. Chiswickhistory.org.uk.

6. Christina Burstin, 12 April 2007 and 22 August 2014.

7. Clifford Bartlett, *John Beckett, Early Music Review*, April 2007, p. 44.

8. Christina Burstin, 22 August 2014.

9. Seán O'Leary, 28 April 2007; Brigid Ferguson, 3/5/09.

10. Christina Burstin, 22 August 2014.

11. Email from David Fletcher, 17 April 2008.

12. Email from Jeremy Montagu, 20 May 2010.

13. Postcard and printed programme, *Medieval vocal and instrumental music*, Horniman Museum and Library, 2 November 1960, KCLCA K/PP93, Box 3, Folder 1; programme notes for Musica Reservata 'debut' concert, 2 July 1967.

14. Letter from Aidan Higgins to Arland Ussher, 4 May 1961, TCD MS 9301–41/1547.

15. Seán O'Leary, 28 April and 22 July 2007. After Lloyd died in 1982, John used to visit his widow, who was German.

16. Michael Bakewell to Martin Esslin, BBC WAC, M, 20 February 1961; letter from Samuel Beckett to Barbara Bray, 17 February 1961, Craig, etc., *The Letters of Samuel Beckett 1957–1965* (Volume III), p. 399 and 400, note 4. At this point, John was commissioned to write music for a Third Programme production of Harry Craig's

Billy Bud, which was cancelled due to copyright difficulties. (Commission, BBC WAC, C, 8 February 1961; internal document, BBC WAC, B, 23 March 1961.)

17. Knowlson, *Damned to Fame*, p. 483; email from Edward Beckett, March 2007; John Calder, Obituary for John Beckett, *The Guardian*, 5 March 2007; Seán O'Leary, 28 April 2007.

18. Letter from Aidan Higgins to Arland Ussher, 10 March 1961, TCD MS 9301–41/1545.

19. Roland Morrow, 23 October 2007.

20. Adrian Somerfield, 22 July 2009.

21. Knowlson, *Damned to Fame*, p. 483.

22. Brigid Ferguson, 3 May 2009.

23. Venetia O'Sullivan, 26 February 2007.

24. Seán O'Leary, 10 July 2009. More recently, Seán acquired John's copy of Mann's *The Magic Mountain*, translated by H.T. Lowe-Porter. John's name was written inside the cover; he had bought it in a second-hand bookshop for about £4. John became very attached to Mann's literature.

25. Letter from Samuel Beckett to Barbara Bray, 2 April 1961, Craig, etc., *The Letters of Samuel Beckett 1957–1965* (Volume III), pp. 405–6; letter from Samuel Beckett to Barney Rosset, 17 March 1961, *ibid*, p. 406, note 4.

26. Letter from Samuel Beckett to Barbara Bray, 26 April 1961, Craig, etc., *The Letters of Samuel Beckett 1957–1965* (Volume III), p. 409; letter from Samuel Beckett to Donald and Sheila Page, 28 April 1961, *ibid*, p. 410, note 6.

27. Theo Wyatt, *The Recorder Magazine*, 2007, Vol. 27, p. 124.

28. Charles Gannon, *Cathal Gannon*, p. 377.

29. Michael Cuming, 28 April 2007.

30. Printed programme, *Concert of music by Musica Reservata*, Fenton House, Hampstead, 27 April 1961, KCLCA K/PP93, Box 3, Folder 1.

31. *Morrow and yesterday's music today*, unidentified newspaper article in KCLCA K/PP93, Box 12.

32. Typewritten programme, *A programme of 13th and 14th century music given by Musica Reservata*, Chelsea School of Art, 25 May 1961, KCLCA K/PP93, Box 7.

33. Deirdre Bair, *Samuel Beckett*, p. 534; Knowlson, *Damned to Fame*, p. 483; letter from Samuel Beckett to Jacoba van Velde, 20 May 1961, Craig, etc., *The Letters of Samuel Beckett 1957–1965* (Volume III), pp. 414–415.

34. Letter from Aidan Higgins to Arland Ussher, 4 May 1961, TCD MS 9301–41/1547.

35. Note from Michael Bakewell, BBC WAC, A, c. July 1961.

36. P.H. Newby to John Beckett, BBC WAC, A, 28 July 1961.*

37. John Beckett to P.H. Newby, BBC WAC, A, 28 July 1961.

38. Note from Martin Esslin to John Beckett, BBC WAC, A, 14 August 1961.*

39. John Beckett to Michael Bakewell, BBC WAC A, 14 December 1961.

40. Knowlson, *Damned to Fame*, p. 496–7.

41. Knowlson, interviews with John Beckett, 27 August 1991 and 8 July 1992.

42. Knowlson, interview with Ann Beckett, 3 August 1992.
43. John Calder, Obituary for John Beckett, *The Guardian*, 5 March 2007.
44. Brigid Ferguson, 3 May 2009.
45. Roland Morrow, 23 October 2007.
46. Brigid Ferguson, 3 May 2009.
47. Notices, *Ir. Times*, 13 October 1961, p. 13 and 21 October 1961, p. 15.
48. *Social and Personal, Ir. Times*, 31 October 1961, p. 7.
49. Letter from Samuel Beckett to Thomas MacGreevy, 23 October 1961, Craig, etc., *The Letters of Samuel Beckett 1957–1965* (Volume III), p. 438 and p. 439, note 11.
50. Christina Burstin, 22 August 2014.
51. Letter to Michael Bakewell, BBC WAC, A, 30 November 1961.
52. Jill Higgins, 17 April 2008.
53. Harold Lester, 25 November 2007.
54. *Radio and TV Programmes, Ir. Times*, 30 November, 7, 14, 21 December 1961, pp. 6/10/6/6; *RTV Guide*, radio programmes for 14 and 21 December 1961.
55. *R.E.S.O. Concert, Ir. Times*, 23 December 1961, p. 9.

Eighteen

1. Letter from John Beckett to Martin Esslin, BBC WAC, A, 8 February 1962.
2. Maurice Harmon (editor), *No Author Better Served*, pp. 121–2.
3. Email from Mark Windisch, 4 October 2010.
4. Letter from David Thomson, BBC WAC, A, 8 January 1962.*
5. Commission, and details of recorded segments, BBC WAC, C, 22 May 1962 and undated (1962).
6. British Library Sound Archive T8021WR C1.
7. Assorted documents, BBC WAC, A, B and C, July and September 1962; Knowlson, interview with John Beckett, 8 July 1992; memoranda from Michael Bakewell and Martin Esslin to Geoffrey Manuel, Organiser, Production Facilities, BBC WAC, M, 19 June 1962 and 4 September 1962.*
8. Letter from Samuel Beckett to Barbara Bray, 17 September 1962, Craig, etc., *The Letters of Samuel Beckett 1957–1965* (Volume III), p. 501, note 2.
9. Letter from Samuel Beckett to Thomas MacGreevy, 30 September 1962, Craig, etc., *The Letters of Samuel Beckett 1957–1965* (Volume III), p. 502.
10. Email from Theo Wyatt, 31 December 2008.
11. Letter from Samuel Beckett to Thomas MacGreevy, 30 September 1962, Craig, etc., *The Letters of Samuel Beckett 1957–1965* (Volume III), p. 502.
12. Letter from Samuel Beckett to Barbara Bray, 11 October 1962, Craig, etc., *The Letters of Samuel Beckett 1957–1965* (Volume III), pp. 507–8.
13. Knowlson, interview with John Beckett, 8 July 1992; Knowlson, interview with Ann Beckett, 3 August 1992; Knowlson, *Damned to Fame*, pp. 497–503.
14. Commission, BBC WAC, C, 1 June 1962; Assorted documents, BBC WAC, B and

C, June and July 1962; *A Taste of Madeleine*, BBC Third Programme, *Radio Times*, radio programmes for 11 November 1962.

15. *Words and Music*, Third Programme, *Radio Times*, radio programmes for 13 November 1962.

16. British Library Sound Archive, 1CD 0256186D3 BD2; also available commercially in a boxed set of four CDs of Beckett's radio plays from the BBC; Samuel Beckett, *The Complete Dramatic Works*, Faber and Faber, London, 2006, p. 287.

17. *Notes on Broadcasting: Marking Distances and Taking Sights, The Times*, 17 November 1962, p. 4.

18. *Words and Music*, Wikipedia; Interview by Everett C. Frost on www.cnvill.net/mfefrost.htm.

19. Programme details posted to Michael Morrow, BBC WAC, A, 12 November 1962; music details, BBC WAC, A, 18 December 1962; *The Heretic*, Home Service, *Radio Times*, radio programmes for 3 December 1962.

20. *RTV Guide*, radio programmes for 2, 9 and 16 January, 1963.

21. Commission, BBC WAC, RCONT 18 Copyright John S. Beckett – File 2 1963–69 (F), 9 January 1963.

22. Assorted Documents, BBC WAC John Beckett Composer – File 2 1963–67 (D), E and F, January 1963; *Lord Halewyn*, Third Programme, *Radio Times*, radio programmes for 25 January 1963; *Lord Halewyn's Final and Fatal Adventure Retold, The Times*, 26 January 1963, p. 4.

23. Commission, BBC WAC, F, 6 February 1963.

24. Assorted documents, BBC WAC, F, 8 and 9 February 1963; *Spring '71*, Third Programme, *Radio Times*, radio programmes for 8 March 1963.

25. Terence Tiller to A.H.F., BBC WAC, Musica Reservata Artists File II 1963–1967 (J), 20 March 1963; description of *Roman de Fauvel*, BBC WAC Artists: Musica Reservata File I, 1958–1962 (I), undated (1963?).

26. Charles Gannon, *Cathal Gannon*, pp. 254–5; John Beckett, 31 July 1998.

27. *Harpsichord made in 1772 played at Dublin concert, Ir. Times*, 6 May 1963, p. 6. John's *Three pieces* and tempi were: 1. Fanfare. 2. Funeral March – slow and frantic. 3. Wedding March – sprightly and dry. They were performed on the BBC Home Service in July 1963 with music by Telemann. (Home Service, *Radio Times*, radio programmes for 3 July 1963; letter from Mary Bowling (Music Booking Manager) to John Beckett, BBC WAC, E, 4 June 1963.)

28. Michael Cuming, 28 April 2007.

29. Printed concert programme, 26 June 1963, owned by Seán O'Leary; Christina Burstin, 12 April 2007.

30. Printed concert programme, *A programme of Medieval, Renaissance and Contemporary Music*, 26 June 1963, owned by Seán O'Leary; also KCLCA K/PP93, Box 7.

31. David Cairns, *Wigmore Hall – Medieval, Renaissance and Contemporary music, The Financial Times*, 27 June 1963, KCLCA K/PP93, Box 12.

32. Typewritten biography, undated, KCLCA K/PP93, Box 3, Folder 2; Jantina

Noorman, 21 March 2008; FolkWorld article by Eelco Schilder on www.folk-world.de/31/e/dutch.html; Christopher Page, *Mining the Archive*, BBC Radio 3, 19 May 1995; David Fallows, *Spirit of the Age*, BBC Radio 3, 12 March 1994; letter from Jantina Barker to Rhoda Draper, 20 October 2007.

Nineteen

1. Stour Music website (www.stourmusic.org.uk); emails from Mark Deller, 2 November 2009 and 10 July 2010.
2. John Sothcott, *The Recorder Magazine*, Vol. 27, 2007, p. 124.
3. Seán O'Leary, 24 November 2007.
4. J.M. Synge, November 1908. (J.M. Synge: *Collected Works – Poems*, edited by Robin Skelton, Oxford University Press, 1962.)
5. Commission, BBC WAC, F, 20 June 1963.
6. Assorted documents, BBC WAC, E and F, July 1963.
7. *The Lemmings*, British Library Sound Archive, T8023WR C1.
8. Charles Gannon, *Cathal Gannon*, p. 254; John Beckett, 31 July 1998.
9. Commission, BBC WAC, F, 16 August 1963.
10. Letter from John Tydeman to John Beckett, BBC WAC, D, 28 October 1963, and assorted documents in BBC WAC, E and F, October 1963.*
11. *Sound Broadcasting*, Third, *The Times*, 31 October 1963, p. 16 and 16 November 1963, p. 5; John Tydeman, *Fando and Lis*, *Radio Times*, radio programmes for 31 October 1963.
12. Undated document, BBC WAC, E, c. September 1963; Home Service, *Radio Times*, radio programmes for 2 October 1963.
13. Seán O'Leary, 25 October 2007; Patrick Cuming's tape recording list, PC 05.
14. Letter from Charles Acton to John Beckett, 4 October 1963, Charles Acton Papers, National Library of Ireland, Acc 6787, Box 17.
15. Richard Pine, *Charles – The Life and World of Charles Acton, 1914–1999*, The Lilliput Press, Dublin, 2010, p. 300, ff.
16. *RTV Guide*, radio programmes for 14 November 1963; *Music at Night*, BBC Home Service, *Radio Times*, radio programmes for 26 November 1966.
17. Seán O'Leary, 24 October 2007.
18. Letter from Stephen Plaistow to John Beckett, BBC WAC, E, 10 September 1963.*
19. Patrick Cuming's tape recording list, PC 041.
20. *RTV Guide*, radio programmes for 3 December 1963.
21. Stephen Plaistow to the Assistant to the Chief Assistant (MPO), BBC WAC, E, undated, December 1963.*
22. Note with tape, BBC WAC, E, 5 December 1963.
23. Undated report, BBC WAC, E, after 20 December 1963.*
24. Harold Lester, 25 November 2007; Seán O'Leary, 31 July and 24 October 2007.
25. Email from Libby Rice, London Symphony Orchestra archivist, 31 May 2007.

26. *Music at Night*, Home Service, *Radio Times*, radio programmes for 7 January 1964.
27. Printed programme, *Musica Reservata*, Hamilton Room, College of St Mark and St John, Chelsea, 12 February (1964), KCLCA K/PP93, Box 7.
28. Seán O'Leary, 24 and 25 October 2007.
29. Knowlson, interview with John Beckett, 8 July 1992.
30. Letter from Terence Tiller to Michael Morrow, BBC WAC, J, 3 December 1963.
31. Tom Sutcliffe, 17 August and 6 October 2010; Tom Sutcliffe website, operastagecoach.co.uk.
32. *What's On Next Week*, *Ir. Times*, 23 May 1964, p. 16.
33. Printed programme, 25 May 1964.
34. Charles Acton, *John Beckett's harpsichord recital in Dublin*, *Ir. Times*, 26 May 1964, p. 8.
35. M.Y., *Impressive Recital on harpsichord*, cutting from unidentified newspaper, c. 26 May 1964 (author's collection).
36. Bernard Thomas, 10 January 2012. The *crumhorn* and *rauschpfeife* (plural *rauschpfeifen*) are are capped double reed instruments, the latter being much louder than the former. In capped reed instruments, the reeds are covered with a wooden 'cap', into which air is blown forcibly; because of this they are notoriously difficult to play in tune. The rackett is a small double reed instrument, and like the *crumhorn* and *rauschpfeife*, has a distinctive buzzing sound. The shawm, which also has a double reed, is a particularly loud and shrill predecessor of the modern oboe.
37. *RTV Guide*, 29 May 1964, p. 3, and television programmes for 3 June 1964.
38. Author's diary, 26 August 1978.
39. *RTV Guide*, television programmes for 17 June 1964.
40. *Tuesday: R.E.*, *RTV Guide*, 21 July 1964, p. 11 and radio programmes for 21 July 1964.
41. Correspondence, BBC WAC, B, 17, 18, 24 June 1964.
42. Gillian Smith, 9 July 2009; email from Libby Rice, London Symphony Orchestra archivist, 31 May 2007.
43. *Mrs. Shaw would have been pleased*, *Irish Farmers' Journal*, 29 August 1964, p. 24.
44. Email from Theo Wyatt, 29 October 2009, and telephone conversation, 30 October 2009; *The Recorder Magazine*, 2007, Vol. 27, p. 124.
45. Knowlson, *Damned to Fame*, pp. 402, 460, 489–90, 519–20.
46. Charles Acton, *Accomplished and erudite Bach recital*, *Ir. Times*, p. 4.
47. Letter from Charles Acton to John Beckett, 5 November 1964, Charles Acton Papers, NLI, Acc 6787, Box 17.
48. Third Music, *Radio Times*, radio programmes for 8 November 1964 and following issues.
49. Programme details, BBC WAC, J, 27 November 1964.

Twenty

1. Letter from John Beckett to Cathal Gannon, 27 January 1965; Seán O'Leary 25/11/07.

2. Roland Morrow, 23 October 2007.

3. *Amusements, shows and lectures*, Ir. Times, 3 February 1965, p. 7; unidentified newspaper cutting, 6 February 1965, supplied by the late Deirdre Sinclair.

4. Letter from John Beckett to Cathal Gannon, 27 January 1965.

5. Deirdre Bair, *Samuel Beckett*, p. 581.

6. *RTV Guide*, radio programmes for 18 February, 4 and 25 March 1965.

7. *Culwick Society's spring concert*, Ir. Times, 31 March 1965, p. 9. John performed Bach's French Suite No. 5 in G, a group of five sonatas by Scarlatti, and played harpsichord continuo for Bach's Cantata No. 227, *Jesu meine Freude*, conducted by Dr Seoirse Bodley.

8. Author's interview with Cathal Gannon, October 1982.

9. Charles Acton, *Culwick Choral Society spring concert*, Ir. Times, 10 April 1965, p. 14.

10. Articles in *Ir. Times, Ir. Ind., Irish Press* and *Evening Herald*, 13 April 1965.

11. Author's recollection.

12. Letter from John Beckett to Cathal Gannon, 27 January 1965.

13. Typed programme, *Medieval and Early Renaissance Secular Music*, Conway Hall, London, 3 May 1965, KCLCA K/PP93, Box 12.

14. Rose Hilton, 22 July 2014.

15. *Cheerful Medieval Music – From Our Music Critic, The Times*, 4 May 1965, p. 15, KCLCA K/PP93, Box 12.

16. Tom Sutcliffe website, www.operastagecoach.co.uk; Tom Sutcliffe, 17 and 18 August, 6 October 2010.

17. *Music scholar takes two firsts in Paris*, Ir. Times, 8 June 1965, p. 6; Knowlson, interview with John Beckett, 8 July 1992; Deirdre Bair, *Samuel Beckett*, p. 582.

18. *What's On Next Week*, Ir. Times, 12 June 1965, p. 10; Charles Acton, *First of Bach concerts at Rupert Guinness Hall*, Ir. Times, 21 June 1965, p. 8.

19. *What's on next week*, Ir. Times, 19 June 1965, p. 11.

20. Charles Acton, *Richness in concert of Bach's work*, Ir. Times, 23 June 1965, p. 6.

21. David Lee, 3 August 2007.

22. Letter from John Beckett to Cathal Gannon, 7 July 1965.

23. Assorted documents, BBC WAC, F, 23 July to 11 August 1965.

24. Patrick Cuming's tape recording list, PC061.

25. Programme details, 1965, BBC WAC, F, undated (August 1966).

26. Interview with Cathal Gannon, October 1981.

27. Pat O'Kelly, *The National Symphony Orchestra of Ireland, 1948–1998 – a selected history*, (no page numbers).

28. Charles Acton, *Music in candle-light setting*, Ir. Times, 29 September 1965, p. 8.

29. *An Irishman's Diary*, Ir. Times, 30 September 1965, p. 9.

30. Letter from John Beckett to David Owen Williams, 2 October 1965, Cathal Gannon file, GDB/C004.04/0018 (1963–1969), Guinness Archive, Diageo Ireland.

31. Letter from John Beckett to Cathal Gannon, 15 October 1965.

32. Letter from John Beckett to Cathal Gannon, 27 October 1965.

Twenty-One

1. Seán O'Leary 28 April and 24 October 2007.
2. Commission, BBC WAC, F, 6 October 1965
3. Commission, BBC WAC, F, 26 October 1965
4. Letter from John Tydeman to John Beckett, BBC WAC, D, 1 December 1965.*
5. Assorted documents, BBC WAC, F, 10 December 1965.
6. Letter from D.O. Williams to John Beckett, 1 November 1965; appended note to Chief Engineer, 5 November 1965, Cathal Gannon file, GDB/C004.04/0018, Guinness Archive, Diageo Ireland.
7. Letter from John Beckett to Cathal Gannon, 3 November 1965.
8. Letter from John Beckett to Cathal Gannon, 20 November 1965; assorted documents, BBC WAC, F, November and December 1965.
9. Note from D.O. Williams to E.N. Rankin, Chief Engineer, Guinness Brewery, 3 November 1965, Cathal Gannon file, GDB/C004.04/0018, Guinness Archive, Diageo Ireland.
10. Anthony OBrien, 21 April 2010.
11. Photocopy of printed programme, 28 November 1965, supplied by Jantina Noorman.
12. *Sound Broadcasting*, *Third*, *The Times*, 21 December 1965; BBC Archives.
13. Letter from Terence Tiller to A.H.F., BBC WAC, J, 20 March 1963.
14. Terence Tiller, *Le Roman de Fauvel*, *Radio Times*, radio programmes for 24 December 1965.
15. Letter from Terence Tiller to Michael Morrow, BBC WAC, J, 25 March 1965.
16. Recording details, BBC WAC, J, 28 October 1965.
17. *Le Roman de Fauvel*, Third Programme, *Radio Times*, radio programmes for 24 December 1965; typed extract from *Polyphonic Music of the Fourteenth Century*, edited by Leo Schrade, commentary to Vol. 1, BBC WAC, I, undated (?1965).
18. *Mining the Archive*, BBC Radio 3, 19 May 1995.
19. Charles Gannon: *Cathal Gannon*, p. 298.
20. Knowlson, *Damned to Fame*, p. 539; Claddagh Records website (www.claddaghrecords.com).
21. Knowlson, interview with John Beckett, 8 July 1992.
22. Charles Acton, *A unique and memorable musical experience*, *Ir. Times*, 11 February 1966, p. 8.
23. *Electra*, Third Programme, *Radio Times*, radio programmes for 11 February 1966; *Notes on Broadcasting: With It, Within It and Without It*, *The Times*, 5 March 1966, p. 12.
24. Charles Acton, *Bach's St. Matthew Passion at R.D.S.*, *Ir. Times*, 3 March 1966, p. 8.
25. RTÉ Television Archives.
26. Seán O'Leary 28 April 2007.
27. Email from Libby Rice, London Symphony Orchestra Archivist, 31 May 2007.
28. Harold Lester, 25 November 2007.
29. Emails from Arthur Johnson, 4 and 9 May 2008.

30. Author's collection of discs.

31. Email from Arthur Johnson, 20 September 2010.

32. Email from Mark Windisch, 5 October 1010.

33. Michael Dervan, 16 January 2013.

34. Programme details, BBC WAC, J, 24 May 1966.

35. *Early Renaissance Music*, Third Programme, *Radio Times*, radio programmes for 26 July 1966.

36. Recording details, BBC WAC, J, 1 August 1966; programme notes for Musica Reservata concert, 2 July 1967, KCLCA K/PP93, Box 7.

37. PMD., *Music: Lunchtime madrigals made happy ending*, Ir. Times, 20 August 1966, p. 7.

38. Recording details, BBC WAC, J, 10 January 1967.

39. Programme notes for Musica Reservata concert, 2 July 1967, KCLCA K/PP93, Box 7.

40. Email from Rose Hilton, 9 April 2007; England and Wales, Birth Index, 1916–2005 for Ruth C. David, Vol. 2c, p. 235; England and Wales, Marriage Index, 1916–2005 for Ruth C. David, Vol 5d, p. 809; England and Wales, Death Index, 1916–2006 for Ruth Catherine Hilton, Registration No. D64, District & Subdistrict: 2291D, Entry No. 57.

41. Vera Škrabánek, 29 November 2007.

42. Seán O'Leary, 25 November 2007.

Twenty-Two

1. Charles Gannon, *Cathal Gannon*, p. 301.

2. Frank Patterson website: www.frankpatterson.net.

3. David Thomson to John Beckett, BBC WAC, D, 28 September 1966.

4. *Amusements, shows and lectures*, Ir. Times, 30 November, p. 9.

5. Carol Acton, *John Beckett ensemble in T.C.D.*, Ir. Times, 8 December 1966, p. 8. Rosalyn Tureck (1914–2003) was an American pianist and harpsichordist who was particularly associated with the music of J.S. Bach.

6. British Library Sound Archive, T148R; British Library records.

7. Musica Reservata discography: www.medieval.org/emfaq/performers/reservata .html; author's collection of discs.

8. *Music of the Early Renaissance*, The Gramophone, January 1967, pp. 381–2.

9. *Music and Musicians*, May 1967, p. 54.

10. *Records and Recordings*, January 1967, p. 62.

11. Author's collection of discs.

12. *What's On Next Week*, Ir. Times, 18 February 1967, p. 10.

13. Charles Acton, *John Beckett and the RTÉ Quartet*, Ir. Times, 22 February 1967, p. 8.

14. Letter from Werner Schürmann to the author, 6 February 2002, and author's recollections.

15. *The Classical Mandoline: Music by Beethoven and Hummel*, Saga Pan PAN 6200, Saga 5350 (1974) (author's collection).

16. Mark Windisch, 14 October 2010.
17. *The Gramophone: Beethoven's Mandoline Period, The Times*, 25 February 1967, p. 7.
18. Beethoven and Hummel, *The Gramophone*, January 1967 p. 371.
19. BBC Archives; Programme details, BBC WAC, B, undated, c. July 1967.
20. Patrick Cuming's tape recording list, PC 028.
21. Anthony Rooley, *The BBC Archive*, BBC Radio 3, 12 August 1998.
22. Christopher Page, *Mining the Archive*, BBC Radio 3, 19 May 1995.
23. Programme announcer, British Library Sound Archives, 1CDR0005820.
24. *The Musical Times*, May 1968 (KCLCA K/PP93, Box 12).
25. *A Grotto for Miss Maynier*, Radio 3, *Radio Times*, radio programmes for 14 April 1967; letter from John Beckett to Jack Beale, BBC WAC, F, 13 March 1967; *Radio, The Times*, 31 October 1970, p. 18.
26. Recording, RTÉ TV Archives; *RTÉ Guide*, 21 April 1967, pp. 3 and 20.
27. Charles Acton, *Music of Swift's Dublin*, *Ir. Times*, 27 April 1967, p. 10.
28. *Purcell*, Third Network, *Radio Times*, radio programmes for 29 April 1967.
29. Programme notes for Musica Reservata concert, 2 July 1967, supplied by Seán O'Leary; also KCLCA K/PP93, Box 7.

Twenty-Three

1. Tom Sutcliffe, 6 October 2010.
2. Programme notes for Musica Reservata concert, 2 July 1967 (Seán O'Leary); also KCLCA K/PP93, Box 7.
3. *The Daily Telegraph*, 3 July 1967, KCLCA K/PP93 Box 12.
4. Hugo Cole, *Musica Reservata at Queen Elizabeth Hall*, *The Guardian*, 3 July 1967, KCLCA K/PP93, Box 12.
5. *Renaissance top of the pops*, newspaper clipping, KCLCA K/PP93, Box 12. The clipping is clearly labelled '*The Times*, 4 July 1967', but is not to be found in the online digital archive of *The Times*.
6. Nicholas Anderson, 4 March 2010.
7. Tom Sutcliffe, 6 October 2010.
8. David Cairns, *Elizabeth Hall: Musica Reservata*, *The Financial Times*, 4 July 1967, p. 22, KCLCA K/PP93, Box 12.
9. *Recorder and Music Review*, August 1967, KCLCA K/PP93, Box 12.
10. Anthony Rooley, *The BBC Archive*, BBC Radio 3, 12 August 1998.
11. Michael Morrow obituary, *Early Music*, Vol. 22, No. 3, August 1994, pp. 537–9.
12. *The Fitzwilliam Virginal Book: John Beckett, harpsichord*, Third Programme, *Radio Times*, radio programmes for 13 and 21 July 1967.
13. *Music by Robert White*, Third Programme, *Radio Times*, radio programmes for 19 July 1967.
14. Music by William Byrd: *RTÉ Guide*, radio programmes for 5 and 19 July 1967.
15. Recording details, BBC WAC, J, 19 July 1967; BBC Production details for German

422

Music of the Renaissance, KCLCA K/PP93, Box 3, Folder 2.

16. Assorted documents, BBC WAC, D, July–September 1967; *The Good Natur'd Man*, Home Service, *Radio Times*, radio programmes for 27 August 1967.
17. Letter to DavidThomson, letter from DavidThomson, and letter from A. Duncan to John Beckett, BBC WAC, D, 30 August, 4 and 5 September 1967.
18. National Library of Australia website: www.nla.gov.au/collect/prompt/sutherland.html; Theo Wyatt, *The Recorder Magazine*, 2007, Vol 27, p. 124 and email, 30 January 2009.
19. Letters from Francis Grubb to William Glock, BBC WAC, J, 25 September and 1 December 1967.
20. Memo to Glock, and memo from Glock, BBC WAC, J, 18 and 20 December 1967.
21. *Medieval Vocal and Instrumental Works*, The Gramophone, October 1967, p. 224.
22. *Interpretations on Record*, Third Programme, *Radio Times*, radio programmes for 19 October 1967.
23. Seán O'Leary, 18 September 2008.
24. Patrick Cuming's tape recording list PC011. John's typescript can be viewed on microfilm at the BBC Written Archive Centre.
25. Note from John Tydeman (though unsigned), BBC WAC, D, 10 November 1967.*
26. *Oedipus the King*, Radio 3, *Radio, The Times*, 28 March 1968, p. 16.
27. Letter from H.B. Fortuin to John Beckett, BBC WAC, F, 14 November 1967.
28. English Heritage website, viewfinder.english-heritage.org.uk; Seán O'Leary, 25 November 2007.
29. Oengus and Priscilla MacNamara, 28 July 2008.
30. Roland Morrow, 23 October 2007.
31. Vic and Frida Robinson, 30 April 2009.
32. Tom Sutcliffe, 6 October 2010.
33. Letter from John Beckett to D.O. Williams, 16 November 1967, GDB/C004.04/0018, Guinness Archive, Diageo Ireland.
34. John Beckett, 31 July 1998.
35. Letter from John Beckett to James Plunkett, 9 December 1967, NLI MS 40,853: 1956–1997.

Twenty-Four

1. Letter from G. R. Topping to The Rev. J. Sertin, and recording details, 27 November 1967, BBC WAC, J, 22 and 27 November 1968. See Michael Parsons' favourable review, *Last week's broadcast music*, The Listener, 18 January 1968, KCLCA K/PP93, Box 12.
2. Letter from D.G. Martin to John Beckett, BBC WAC RCONT 12 Artist John S. Beckett – File 3 1968–72 (G), 5 January 1968.
3. Details of play, BBC WAC, G, undated (January 1968).*
4. Memo to Assistant to Music Booking Manager, BBC WAC, G, 3 January 1968.

5. Letter from Christopher Holme of the Drama Dept to J. Beale, and letter from J. Beale to John Beckett, BBC WAC, F, 12 and 14 February 1968; document from Christopher Holme, BBC WAC, G, 28 February 1968.

6. *Music at Night*, Radio 4, *Radio Times*, radio programmes for 15 February 1968; www.frankpatterson.net.

7. *Deaths, Ir. Times*, 18 March 1968, p. 18.

8. Knowlson, *Damned to Fame*, p. 556 and 614; Knowlson, interview with John Beckett, 27 August 1991 and 8 July 1992; Knowlson, interview with Ann Beckett, 3 August 1992.

9. Commission, BBC WAC, F, 10 April 1968.

10. Recording details, BBC WAC, G, 10 April 1968.

11. British Library Sound Archive, NP117R C1.

12. Knowlson, *Damned to Fame*, p. 557.

13. Bernard Thomas, 10 January 2012.

14. Musica Reservata discography, www.medieval.org.

15. *A Florentine Festival, The Gramophone*, February 1971, p. 1338. Another favourable review was written by Geoffrey Crankshaw in *Records and Recording*, January 1971, p. 108.

16. *A Florentine Festival* (Argo ZRG 602) and *Early Music Festival* (Decca 289 452 967-2), author's collection of discs.

17. David Cairns, 26 January 2009.

18. Tom Sutcliffe, 18 August 2010.

19. David Cairns, 26 January 2009; Philips CD 432 821-2 (1992), author's collection of discs.

20. *Music from the time of Christopher Columbus, The Gramophone*, March 1969, pp. 1318 and 1321.

21. *Records and Recording*, February 1969, p. 81.

22. *Music of the Court Homes and Cities of England*, Vol. 1, *The Gramophone*, May 1968, p. 602.

23. *Music of the Court Homes and Cities of England*, Vol. 2, *The Gramophone*, June 1968, p. 58.

24. *Records and Recording*, May 1968, p. 64.

25. *Music of the Court Homes and Cities of England*, Vol. 3, *The Gramophone*, June 1968, p. 58.

26. *Music of the Court Homes and Cities of England*, Vol. 4, *The Gramophone*, June 1968, p. 59.

27. *Records and Recording*, July 1968, p. 62.

28. *Music of the Court Homes and Cities of England*, Vol. 6, *The Gramophone*, August 1968, pp. 271–2.

29. Musica Reservata discography, www.medieval.org; *Music to Entertain Henry VIII*, author's collection of discs.

30. *To Entertain a King. Music for Henry VIII and his Court, Gramophone*, June 1968, p. 59.

Twenty-Five

1. Letter from John Beckett to James Plunkett, 26 April 1968, NLI MS 40,853: 1956–1997.

2. Deirdre Sinclair, 19 May 2007.

3. Letter from Ralph Cusack to James Plunkett, Easter Sunday 1969, NLI MS 40,856 1954–1969.

4. Patrick Cuming's tape recording list, PC 014, 021, 015, 016.

5. David Clark, letter to *Early Music Review*, April 2007. The four programmes would be transmitted during the following year. John's arrangement of Bach's Trio Sonata in D minor BWV 527 for two violins and continuo was included in the final programme. *The Golden Age*, *RTÉ Guide*, television programmes for 9 January, 27 February, 13 and 27 March 1969.

6. *Franz Xaver Mozart*, Radio 3, *Radio Times*, radio programmes for 14 June 1968.

7. Commission (note from Martin Esslin to J. Beale), BBC WAC, F, 14 June 1968; recording details, BBC WAC, G, 25 June 1968; memorandum from Martin Esslin to J. Beale, BBC WAC, F, 9 July 1968.

8. *Songs and Dances by Dowland, East and Holborne*, *The Gramophone*, August 1968, p. 271. Reviews were also written by Christopher Grier in *Music and Musicians*, October 1968, p. 62 and Peter Dennison in *Records and Recording*, August 1968, p. 52.

9. *Musical Times*, October 1968, KCLCA K/PP93, Box 12 .

10. Recording details, BBC WAC RCONT12 Musica Reservata Artists II 1968–1972 (L), 4 September 1968.

11. Printed programme for *The Hundred Years War and the Age of Chivalry in France*, 15 September 1968, supplied by Seán O'Leary; also KCLCA K/PP93 Box 7.

12. Bernard Thomas, 10 January 2012.

13. Dominic Gill, *Queen Elizabeth Hall – Musica Reservata, The Financial Times*, 16 September 1968, p. 37, KCLCA K/PP93, Box 12.

14. David Cairns, *Medieval Pop, New Statesman*, 20 September 1968, KCLCA K/PP93, Box 12.

15. Tom Sutcliffe, 6 October 2010.

16. Michael Nyman, *Shawms & rackets*, the *Spectator*, 27 September 1968, KCLCA K/PP93, Box 12.

17. Recording details, BBC WAC, L, 18 September 1968; Edmund Rubbra, *Last week's broadcast music, The Listener*, 17 October 1968, KCLCA K/PP93, Box 12.

18. Seán O'Leary, 24 and 25 October 2007.

19. Bernard Thomas, 10 January 2012.

20. Seán O'Leary, 24 and 25 October 2007.

21. Printed programme, Hexham Abbey Festival, 19 October 1968, KCLCA K/PP93, Box 7.

22. *French Court Music of the Thirteenth Century*, author's collection of discs.

23. *French Court Music of the Thirteenth Century*, *The Gramophone*, November 1968, p. 703.

24. *Records and Recording*, November 1968, p. 89 and March 1973, p. 86.

25. Michael Dervan, 16 January 2013.

26. BBC Archives; programme details, BBC WAC, L, 4 November 1968.

27. Printed programme, *Music by Henry Purcell*, Queen Elizabeth Hall, 8 November 1968, KCLCA K/PP93, Box 7; Stephen Walsh, *Special Kind of Purcell, The Times*, 9

November 1968, p. 19; A.E.P., *Musical Gems by Purcell, Daily Telegraph*, 9 November 1968; Alan Blyth, *Musica Reservata, The Financial Times*, 9 November 1968, p. 6, KCLCA K/PP93, Box 12; British Library Sound Archive, 1CDR0005838.

28. Tom Sutcliffe, 6 October 2010.

29. 'Old Periods Newly Discovered' (typed translation), *De Groene Amsterdammer*, 14 December 1968, KCLCA K/PP93, Box 12; *Music from the time of Christopher Columbus*, author's collection of discs.

30. Certificate, 1969, KCLCA K/PP93, Box 13.

31. Charles Acton, *A 'Messiah' that lacked sparkle, Ir. Times*, 19 December 1968, p. 10.

32. Printed programme, *A Renaissance Christmas*, Queen Elizabeth Hall, 29 December 1968, supplied by Seán O'Leary.

33. Ronald Crichton, *A Renaissance Christmas, The Financial Times*, 31 December 1968, p 3.

34. Printed programme, *Guillaume Dufay*, 29 January 1969, owned by Seán O'Leary.

35. Max Harrison, *Secular Dufay, The Times*, 30 January 1969, p. 7, and Max Harrison, *The Musical Times*, March 1969, KCLCA K/PP93, Box 12.

36. Programme details, BBC WAC, L, 17 January 1969; printed programme, *Music of the time of Boccaccio's Decameron*, 7 February 1969, owned by Seán O'Leary.

37. Anthony Rooley, *The BBC Archive*, BBC Radio 3, 12 August 1998.

38. Record of sessions and times, 19 February 1969, KCLCA K/PP93, Box 3, Folder 2; Musica Reservata discography, www.medieval.org.

39. Note to John Beckett, BBC WAC, G, 20 November 1968; tape of *Studio Portrait* supplied by Seán O'Leary.

Twenty-Six

1. Recording details, (Ruth M. Orpin to Cyril Taylor), BBC WAC RCONT31/86/1 Musica Reservata Orchestra (K), 1 April 1969.

2. Seán O'Leary, 25 October 2007.

3. Recording details, BBC WAC, K, 17 April 1969.

4. Printed programme, *Guillaume Dufay*, Victoria and Albert Museum, 11 May 1969, KCLCA K/PP93, Box 7.

5. Recording details, BBC WAC, G, 16 May 1969.

6. Email from Libby Rice, LSO, 31 May 2007; Clifford Bartlett, Obituary, *Early Music Review*, April 2007, p. 44.

7. *Telefís Scoile, RTÉ Guide*, 30 May 1969, p. 22.

8. *Portrait of a Poet: W.B. Yeats*, videotape copy in RTÉ TV Archives.

10. Letter from John Beckett to James Plunkett, 24 May 1969, NLI MS 40,853: 1956–1997.

11. Letter from James Plunkett to John Beckett, 28 May 1969, NLI MS 40,853: 1956–1997.

12. Email from Rose Hilton, 9 April 2007.

13. Recording details, BBC WAC, G, 7 July 1969; Recording details and memoranda, BBC WAC, K and L, July 1969.

14. Patrick Cuming's tape recording list PC 052.

15. Gillian Smith and Lindsay Armstrong, 9 July 2009.

16. Recording details and memoranda, BBC WAC, K and L, July 1969.

17. JB to Michael Hall, BBC WAC R83/952/1 Beckett, John (H), 5 August 1969.

18. Letter from Francis Grubb to William Glock, 1 December 1967, BBC WAC J.

19. Radio 3, *Radio Times*, radio programmes for 6 August 1969.

20. William Mann: *A daring programme*, The Times, 7 August 1969, p. 5; *Proms Concert*, Arts Guardian, 7 August 1969, KCLCA K/PP93, Box 12.

21. *Musica Reservata, Early Music*, Vol. 4 No. 4, 4 October 1976, p. 515.

22. Recording details, BBC WAC, L, 25 July 1969; radio listings, The Times, 24 September 1969, p. 17.

23. Printed programme, *16th century Dance Music*, Queen Elizabeth Hall, 16 September 1969, Box 7; recording details, BBC WAC, L, 27 August 1969.

24. Alan Blyth, *Musica Reservata*, The Financial Times, 17 September 1969, p. 3; *The Telegraph*, 17 September 1969; *New Season opens with a mixture – Night of Dances*, The Times, 17 September 1969, p. 7, KCLCA K/PP93, Box 12.

25. Philips SAL 3717 (author's collection of discs).

26. David Cairns, 26 January 2009.

27. Charles Acton, *Records: Strange Reluctance, Ir. Times*, 8 October 1969, p. 12. Charles Cudworth wrote a cautious review in *Records and Recording*, October 1969, p. 113, and John O'Donovan wrote about the disc in *Record Review, RTÉ Guide*, 31 November 1969, p. 19.

28. Philips SAL 3717 (author's collection of discs); David Clark, letter to *Early Music Review*, April 2007.

29. John Beckett, 31 July 1998.

30. *The Dancing Master*, details, RTÉ TV Archives.

31. Printed programmes, *French and Italian music*, 15 November (Birmingham) and 16 November 1969 (Durham Castle), KCLCA K/PP93, Box 7. Also in November, reviews of *Music of the Hundred Years War* (Philips SAL 3722) were published; see Denis Arnold, *Music of the Hundred Years War*, The Gramophone, November 1969, p. 799 and Charles Cudworth, *Records and Recording*, November 1969, p. 94.

32. Recording details for programme 5, BBC WAC, G, 5 November 1969; recording details for programme 7, BBC WAC, K, 25 November 1969.

33. Printed programme, *Music by Praetorius and the Gabrielis*, Queen Elizabeth Hall, 16 December 1969, supplied by Seán O'Leary, and KCLCA K/PP93, Box 7; BBC memoranda from Basil Lam, 16 September 1969, Michael Morrow collection, Royal Academy of Music.

34. Gillian Widdicombe, *Elizabeth Hall: Musica Reservata*, The Financial Times, 17 December 1969, p. 3, KCLCA K/PP93, Box 12.

35. Michael Nyman, *Gig of a Lifetime: Daily Telegraph*, 31 August 2006.

36. Letter from Peter Marchbank to Cyril Taylor and subsequent correspondence, BBC WAC, L, 18 November 1969; recording details, BBC WAC, L, 26 November 1969.

37. Letters from John Beckett to James Plunkett, 24 October and 18 December 1969, NLI MS 40,853: 1956–1997.

Twenty-Seven

1. *What's On, Ir. Times*, 2 February 1970, p. 12.

2. Recording details, BBC WAC, L, 6 February 1970; British Library sound archives, P518R C1.

3. Printed programme and notes for *A concert of music by Henry Purcell*, Queen Elizabeth Hall, 10 March 1970, supplied by Seán O'Leary.

4. Stanley Sadie, *The English Orpheus, The Times*, 11 March 1970, p. 14; Gillian Widdicombe, *Musica Reservata, The Financial Times*, 11 March 1970, p. 3, KCLCA K/PP93, Box 12.

5. *Music from the time of Boccaccio's Decameron, The Gramophone*, April 1970, p. 1626/1631.

6. Stephen Walsh, *Music and Musicians*, May 1970, p. 72. See also Edward Greenfield, *Electric Bach, The Guardian*, 20 April 1970, p. 8.

7. Printed programme for *Medieval music of the 13th, 14th and 15th centuries*, 19 May 1970, KCLCA K/PP93, Box 7.

8. Charles Acton, *What's On: Medieval Music, Ir. Times*, 18 May 1970, p. 12.

9. Email from Barra Boydell, 4 July 2008.

10. Charles Acton, *T.C.D. concert of medieval music, Ir. Times*, 25 May 1970, p. 8.

11. Email from Barra Boydell, 4 July 2008.

12. Andrew and Jenny Robinson, 2 July 2009.

13. Email from Anthony OBrien, 31 January 2014.

14. Honor O Brolchain, 23 February 2013.

15. Michael Morrow papers, Royal Academy of Music, London.

16. Details of *Madrigals and Chansons*, BBC WAC, G, 3 June 1970.

17. *Orchestral programme tedious, Ir. Times*, 22 June 1970, p. 8.

18. Letter from John Beckett to Cathal Gannon, 28 November 1971.

19. Email from Rose Hilton, 2 September 2014.

20. Seán O'Leary, 24 and 25 October 2007.

21. Tom Sutcliffe, 6 October 2010.

22. Letter from John Beckett to James Plunkett, 10 July 1970, NLI MS 40,853: 1956–1997.

23. Deirdre Sinclair, 19 May 2007.

24. Seán O'Leary, 24 October 2007.

25. Roland Morrow, 23 October 2007.

26. Printed programmes, *La Chanson Française à la Renaissance* and *La Chanson Française au XVIe siècle*, 15 and 16 July 1970, KCLCA K/PP93, Box 7.

27. Review of concert, in French, 18 July 1970, KCLCA K/PP93, Box 12.

28. Letter from John Beckett to James Plunkett, 28 July 1970, NLI MS 40,853: 1956–1997.

29. Roger Tellart, review in French, 24 August 1970, KCLCA K/PP93, Box 12.

30. Letter from James Plunkett to John Beckett, 4 August 1970, National Library of Ireland MS 40,853: 1956–1997.

31. Letter from K.B. Leverton to James Plunkett, 19 November 1970 and letter from James Plunkett to K.B. Leverton, 21 November 1970, NLI MS 40,853: 1956–1997.

32. Letter from John Beckett to James Plunkett, 17 August 1970, National Library of Ireland MS 40,853: 1956–1997.

33. Letter from Cyril Taylor to Mr Selletrom, 25 July 1970, KCLCA K/PP93, Box 3, Folder 2.

34. Festival programme, notices and reviews in Flemish, August 1970, KCLCA K/PP93, Boxes 10 and 12; printed programme for 24 August 1970 of *Festival van Vlaanderen*, supplied by Jantina Noorman.

35. Letter from John Beckett to James Plunkett, undated, September 1970, NLI MS 40,853: 1956–1997.

36. *An Irishman's Diary: Elegant occasion*, Ir. Times, 1 May 1971, p. 15.

37. Seán O'Leary, 31 July 2007; Frida Robinson, 30 April 2009.

38. Seán O'Leary, 31 July 2007.

39. Letter from John Beckett to James Plunkett, 26 September 1970, National Library of Ireland MS 40,853: 1956–1997.

40. *16th Century Italian & French Dance Music*, Boston Skyline BSD 123, 1994; Musica Reservata Discography on www.medieval.org.

41. Harold Lester, 25 November 2007.

Twenty-Eight

1. Milan Poštolka: Leopold Kozeluch, *The New Grove Dictionary of Music and Musicians*, (1980), Vol. 10, p. 225.

2. *Anthology: A Shade Superior to Monsieur Kozeluch, RTÉ Guide*, television programmes for 7 October 1970. See also the article *A shade superior to Monsieur Kozeluch, RTÉ Guide*, 2 October 1970, p. 19.

3. *Television, Sunday Independent*, 11 October 1970, p. 27.

4. Letter from John Beckett to James Plunkett, 17 October 1970, NLI MS 40,853: 1956–1997.

5. Printed programme, *German and Spanish Music of the Early 16th Century*, 27 October 1970, supplied by Jantina Noorman.

6. Gillian Widdicombe, *Elizabeth Hall: Musica Reservata, The Financial Times*, 28 October 1970, p. 3, KCLCA K/PP93, Box 12.

7. *Anthology: A Shade Superior to Monsieur Kozeluch, RTÉ Guide*, television programmes for 2 December 1970.

8. Recording details, BBC WAC, L, 9 December 1970; printed programme, *Music at Christmas*, 20 December 1970, KCLCA K/PP93, Box 7; *Radio Times*, Radio 3, *A Late Renaissance Entertainment*, programmes for 22 August 1971.

9. Gillian Widdicombe, *Elizabeth Hall: Musica Reservata, The Financial Times*, 21 December 1970, p. 3, KCLCA K/PP93, Box 12.

10. Harold Lester, 25 November 2007.

11. Programme for *15th and 16th century English music* (supplied by Seán O'Leary), 15 February 1971, Queen Elizabeth Hall; Seán O'Leary 26 July 2007; Ian Payne, *New Light on 'New Fashions' by William Cobbold (1560–1639) of Norwich, Journal of the Viola da Gamba Society*, Vol. 30 (2002), p. 11. John's reconstructed version was recorded in 1992 by Circa 1500 with Redbyrd, directed by Nancy Hadden on the CRD label; *'New Fashions': Cries and Ballads of London*; *Queen Elizabeth Hall concert, The Guardian*, 16 February 1971, KCLCA K/PP93, Box 12.

12. Letter from John Beckett to James Plunkett, 17 October 1970, NLI MS 40,853: 1956–1997.

13. *Ireland from the Air*, Television by Ken Gray, *Ir. Times*, 15 March 1971, p. 12. See also James Plunkett, *Bird's-eye over Ireland*, *RTÉ Guide*, 12 March 1971, p. 3 and television programmes for 17 March 1971.

14. *Bird's Eye View: Inis Fáil*, RTÉ Television Archives.

15. *Wexford Festival of Living Music*, *Ir. Times*, 13 March 1971, p. 12; advertisement, *Ir. Times*, 16 March 1971, p. 20; *What's on This Weekend*, *Ir. Times*, 20 March, 1971, p. 20.

16. Letter from James Plunkett to Aidan Higgins, 25 March 1971, NLI MS 40, 859: 1971.

17. Letter from John Beckett to James Plunkett, 14 April 1971, NLI MS 40,853: 1956–1997.

18. Letter from John O'Donovan to James Plunkett, 18 March 1971, NLI MS 40,878: 1940–1980.

19. Letter from John Beckett to Andréas Ó Gallchóir, 8 May 1971, NLI MS 40,853: 1956–1997.

20. Letter from John Beckett to James Plunkett, 8 May 1971, NLI MS 40,853: 1956–1997.

21. Letter from John Beckett to James Plunkett, 13 May 1971, NLI MS 40,853: 1956–1997.

22. Recording details, BBC WAC, L, 15 April 1971; *Radio, Medieval French and English Music, The Times*, 2 December 1971, p. 31; printed programme for *13th and 15th century French and English Music*, 18 May 1971, supplied by Seán O'Leary; review, *The Guardian*, 19 May 1971, KCLCA K/PP93, Box 12.

23. Letter from John Beckett to James and Valerie Plunkett, 30 [May 1971], NLI MS 40,853: 1956–1997.

24. Musica Reservata Discography at www.medieval.org. See favourable reviews by Charles Cudworth, *Records and Recording*, January 1973, p. 67 and Jeremy Noble, *Sixteenth-century French Dance Music, The Gramophone*, January 1973, pp. 1357–8.

25. *16th Century Italian & French Music*, Boston Skyline BSD 123.

Twenty-Nine

1. Charles Acton, *Welcome back to John Beckett, Ir. Times*, 21 July 1971, p. 10.

2. Letters from John Beckett to James Plunkett, 3 July and 6 August 1971, NLI MS 40,853: 1956–1997.

3. Letter from John Beckett to Miss Williams, 26 July 1971, BBC WAC, G.

4. John's explanatory note to letter from Samuel Beckett to him, 15 May 1977, UoR MS 5411, 10.

5. James Kelly, 17 May 2014; Ross and Mary Kelly, 19 August 2014; Billy Reid, 13 April 2015.

6. Irené Sandford's recollection, author's diary, 21 November 1980.

7. Email from Rose Hilton, 2 September 2014.

8. Morris Sinclair, 19 May 2007.

9. Billy Reid, 28 November 2013.

10. James Kelly, 17 May 2014. The lake is now dry.

11. Aleck Crichton, 11 September 2014.

12. Rhoda Draper, 2007.

13. Venetia O'Sullivan, 26 February 2007.

14. Brigid Ferguson, 3 May 2009.

15. Gerry Pullman, 17 July 2009.

16. Gillian Smith, 9 July 2009; email from Rose Hilton, 2 September 2014; author's diary, 19 September 1978.

17. Gillian Smith and Lindsay Armstrong, 9 July 2009.

18. Theo Wyatt, *The Recorder Magazine*, 2007, Vol. 27, p. 124; emails from Theo Wyatt, 31 December 2008 and 29 October 2009, and telephone conversation, 30 October 2009.

19. Janet Ashe, 20 March 2008.

20. Andrew and Jenny Robinson, 2 July and 5 August 2009.

21. Andrew and Jenny Robinson, 2 July 2009; *Celebrating John Beckett*, programme for commemorative concert, 24 November 2007, p. 17.

22. Charles Acton, *Concluding Bach concert*, *Ir. Times*, 20 May 1971, p. 10.

23. Printed programme for concert in St Canice's Cathedral, Kilkenny, 29 August 1971 and *Musica Reservata speelt muziek uit 14e ~ 16e eeuw*, printed programme for Kleine Zaal Concertgebouw, 30 August 1971, KCLCA K/PP93, Box 7.

24. Advertisement, *Ir. Times*, 6 September 1971, p. 11; author's recollection.

25. Letter from John O'Donovan to James Plunkett, 16 October 1971, NLI MS 40,878: 1940–1980.

26. Letter from Michael Morrow to Dick Hill, RTÉ, 3 January 1972, KCLCA K/PP93, Box 3.

27. *What's on in the arts: Television*, *Ir. Times*, 4 October 1971, p. 10; *Television*, *Ir. Times*, 5 October 1971, p. 17; *The age of the Troubadours*, *RTÉ Guide*, 1 October 1971, p. 5 and programmes for 5 October; Michael Morrow papers, Royal Academy of Music.

28. Printed programme, *16th century French and Netherlands Chansons and Dances*, Queen Elizabeth Hall, 20 October 1971, KCLCA K/PP93, Box 7, and reviews, 20 October (*The Financial Times*) and 22 October 1971 (*The Times*), Box 12.

29. Xavier Carty, *Haydn in London*, *RTÉ Guide*, 29 October 1971, page 6.

30. First programme: *Haydn in London*, *RTÉ Guide*, television programmes for 2

November 1971; *What's on in the arts: Music, Ir. Times,* 1 November 1971, p. 12; *Television, Ir. Times,* 2 November 1971, p. 17. Second programme: *Haydn in London, RTÉ Guide,* television programmes for 9 November 1971; *What's on in the arts: Music, Ir. Times,* 8 November 1971, p. 10; *Television, Ir. Times,* 9 November, p. 19.

31. Printed programme, *NOS / Muziek uit middeleeuwen en renaissance,* 6 November 1971, KCLCA K/PP93, Box 7.
32. Review, translated from the Dutch, in *De Gooi,* 8 November 1971, KCLCA K/PP93, Box 12.
33. *Synge and Music,* Radio 3, *Radio, The Times,* 14 November 1971, p. 8.
34. Letter from John Beckett to Cathal Gannon, 28 November 1971.
35. Copies of letters sent from Cathal Gannon to John Beckett, 6 and 28 December 1971, and 17 January 1972.
36. *Anniversary Documentary, RTÉ Guide,* 20 August 1971, p. 4; Aindréas Ó Gallchóir, "The State of the Nation", *RTÉ Guide,* 3 December 1971, p. 3; *The State of the Nation, RTÉ Guide,* programmes for 6 December 1971.
37. *An Irishman's Diary, Ir. Times,* 3 December 1971, p. 13.
38. *The State of the Nation,* LX 4201, RTÉ Television Archives.
39. Printed programme, *Monteverdi and his Contemporaries,* 13 December 1971, KCLCA K/PP93, Box 7.
40. *The Financial Times,* 14 December 1971, p. 3, KCLCA K/PP93, Box 12; Keith Horner, *Musica Reservata, Queen Elizabeth Hall, The Times,* 14 December 1971, p. 10.
41. Recording details, BBC WAC, G, 15 November 1971; BBC production details of both programmes, KCLCA K/PP93, Box 3, folder 2.

Thirty

1. Author's diary, 15 January 1972.
2. Letter from John Beckett to Cathal Gannon, 19 January 1972.
3. Letter from John Beckett to Cathal Gannon, 20 January 1972.
4. Letter from John Beckett to Cathal Gannon, 20 February 1972.
5. Denis Arnold, *Music from the Court of Burgundy, The Gramophone,* January 1972, p. 1252.
6. Kenneth Long, *Music from the Court of Burgundy, Records and Recording,* January 1972, p. 86.
7. Charles Acton, *More about Monteverdi, Ir. Times,* 30 July 1973, p. 10.
8. RTÉ Television and Sound Archives; radio and television listings, *RTÉ Guide,* for 16 and 18 January 1972.
9. Alison Young, 6 June 2013.
10. Charles Acton, *Bicentenary Recital, Ir. Times,* 11 February 1972, p. 8.
11. Email from Malcolm Proud, 21 July 2013.
12. Email from Anthony OBrien, 31 January 2014.
13. Charles Acton, *Bicentenary Recital, Ir. Times,* 11 February 1972, p. 8.

14. Charles Acton, *Bach's St. John Passion at R.D.S.*, *Ir. Times*, 18 February 1972, p. 10.

15. RTÉ Television Archives; *The Light of Other Days* edited by Kieran Hickey, Allen Lane, 1973.

16. Printed programme, John Coffin Memorial Concert, University of London, 16 March 1972, KCLCA K/PP93, Box 7; printed programme, *The Macnaghten Concerts: 40th Anniversary Season 1971–72*, Queen Elizabeth Hall, London, 28 March 1972, KCLCA K/PP93, Box 7.

17. *English Music*, Radio 3, *Radio Times*, radio programmes for 10 April 1972.

18. Recording details, BBC WAC, L, 20 March 1972; BBC production details, KCLCA K/PP93, Box 3, folder 2; *Music by Josquin des Pres*, Radio 3, *Radio Times*, radio programmes for 27 July 1974.

19. Recording details, BBC WAC, L, 2 May 1972; BBC production details, KCLCA K/PP93, Box 3, folder 2.

20. Bernard Thomas, 10 January 2012.

21. Author's diary, 28 April 1972.

22. Charles Acton, *Haydn recital on a contemporary pianoforte*, *Ir. Times*, 2 May 1972, p. 12.

23. Assorted documents, 3–5 May 1972, KCLCA K/PP93, Box 7 and 12.

24. Printed programme, *Sixteenth-century German, Polish and Netherlands chansons and dances*, 24 May 1972, supplied by Seán O'Leary.

25. Seán O'Leary, 24 October 2007. See Stephen Walsh's review, *Concert at the Queen Elizabeth Hall*, *The Times*, 25 May 1972, p. 12, KCLCA K/PP93, Box 12.

26. Musica Reservata Discography, www.medieval.org; *The Instruments of the Middle Ages and Renaissance*, Vanguard Classics, OVC 8093/94 (author's collection of discs).

27. Musica Reservata Discography, www.medieval.org; *A Concert of Early Music*, available as an MP3 download (in author's collection of music).

28. Printed programme, belonging to Jantina Noorman, 1 August 1972; programme notes for forthcoming concert in Queen Elizabeth Hall, 24 May 1972.

29. Patrick Cuming, February 2007.

30. Festival van Vlaanderen Programmes (Jantina Noorman), 7 and 8 August 1972; translated reviews, August 1972, KCLCA K/PP93, Box 12. For a review on the group and the sound that they produced, see unidentified newspaper article, *Becketts visie op de Muziek der Middeleeuwen* (Beckett's vision regarding Medieval Music), KCLCA K/PP93, Box 12.

31. Author's diary, 29 and 31 August 1972; author's recording.

32. Author's diary, 2, 4, 6–8 September 1972.

33. *Music Magazine*, Venetia O'Sullivan, *Music Magazine*, *RTÉ Guide*, 9 February 1973, p. 5 and programmes for 12 February 1973.

34. Venetia O'Sullivan, *Music Magazine*, *RTÉ Guide*, 25 May 1973, p. 15; radio, *RTÉ Guide*, radio programmes for 31 May 1973; RTÉ Sound Archives.

35. Denis Arnold, *An Elizabethan Evening*, *The Gramophone*, December 1972, p. 133.

Most of the music was played by members of the Jaye Consort. See also Charles
Cudworth's favourable review in *Records and Recording*, September 1972, p. 92.

36. Printed programme, belonging to Jantina Noorman for *Berliner Festwochen*, 28
     September 1972.

37. *Die Welt*, 2 October 1972, KCLCA K/PP93, Box 12. See also an unfavourable
     review in *Der Tagesspiegel*, 20 September 1972, KCLCA K/PP93, Box 12.

38. Programme notes for Queen Elizabeth Hall concert, belonging to Seán O'Leary;
     24 May 1972; Bernard Thomas, 10 January 2012; printed programme, belonging
     to Jantina Noorman, for *Musica Antiqua*, 2 October 1972, Vienna.

39. *Salzburger Nachrichten*, 4 October 1972, KCLCA K/PP93, Box 12. Back in London,
     Musica Reservata performed in the Queen Elizabeth Hall. See printed programme,
     Music from 14th century Italy and the Court of Burgundy, 31 October 1972, KCLCA
     K/PP93, Box 7 and Bayan Northcott's review, *Elizabeth Hall, Musica Reservata*,
     The Financial Times, 1 November 1972, p. 3, KCLCA K/PP93, Box 12. See also
     Stephen Walsh, *Musica Reservata, Queen Elizabeth Hall, The Times*, 1 November 1972,
     p. 11, KCLCA K/PP93, Box 12.

40. *Celebrating John Beckett* – programme for special commemorative concert in St
     Ann's Church, Dawson Street, Dublin, 24 November 2007, p. 16.

41. Andrew Robinson, h2g2.

42. Michael Dervan, *Making a Career of the Organ*, *Ir. Times*, 28 April 1987, p. 10.

43. Carmel Harrison, 26 December 2007.

44. Marion Doherty, 19 December 2013.

45. Gerald Barry, 26 May 2015.

46. Andrew Robinson on h2g2 and 1 February 2014.

47. Michael Dervan, 4 and 16 January 2013.

48. Rhoda Draper, February 2007 and 16 January 2013; author's recollection.

49. Email from Siobhán Yeats, 2 May 2008.

50. Andrew Robinson, h2g2 and *Beckett, John [Stewart]*, *The Encyclopaedia of Music in
     Ireland*, Part 1, p. 71.

51. Paul Conway, 10 February 2007.

Thirty-One

1. Author's diary, 11 January 1973.

2. Lindsay Armstrong, 9 July 2009.

3. Charles Acton: *Bach Cantatas on Sunday afternoons*, *Ir. Times*, 31 January 1973, p. 12.

4. Tim Thurston, 16 January 2012.

5. Charles Acton: *Bach Cantatas on Sunday afternoons*, *Ir. Times*, 31 January 1973, p. 12.

6. *Second of Bach Cantata series in St. Ann's*, *Ir. Times*, 6 February 1973, p. 10.

7. *Final concert in series of Bach Cantatas*, *Ir. Times*, 13 February 1973, p. 10; Gillian
    Smith and Lindsay Armstrong, 28 May 2015.

8. Lindsay Armstrong, *A Tribute to John Beckett*: from a speech made at a concert of

Bach cantatas at St Ann's, Dawson Street on 11 February 2007.

9. Colm Tóibín, *In search of ghosts of Dublin, Sunday Independent*, 7 May 2000, p. 21.
10. Jenny and Andrew Robinson, 2 July 2009.
11. Honor O Brolchain, 23 February 2013.
12. Gerald Barry, 26 May 2015.
13. Tim Thurston, 16 January 2012.
14. Gillian Smith and Lindsay Armstrong, 9 July 2009.
15. Alison Young, 6 June 2013.
16. Michael Dervan, *Obituaries: John Beckett – Early music pioneer who created shockwaves, Ir. Times*, 17 February 2007, p. 14.
17. Author's diary, 2 March 1975.
18. Gillian Smith and Lindsay Armstrong, 9 July 2009.
19. Andrew Robinson, h2g2.
20. Gillian Smith and Lindsay Armstrong, 9 July 2009.
21. Tim Thurston, 16 January 2012.
22. Gillian Smith and Lindsay Armstrong, 9 July 2009.
23. Michael Dervan, 16 January 2013.
24. Tim Thurston, 16 January 2012.
25. Gillian Smith and Lindsay Armstrong, 9 July 2009.
26. Printed programme, *The music of 15th century Spain*, 21 February 1973, KCLCA K/PP93, Box 7 and review in *The Musical Times*, April 1973, Box 12.
27. Printed programmes for 9 and 10 May 1973, and reviews, May 1973, KCLCA K/PP93, Box 12. The reviews were favourable.
28. Undated postcard from John Beckett to Seán O'Leary, May 1973.
29. Printed programme, *15th Century Secular Music by Dunstable, Dufay and Josquin*, 22 May 1973, supplied by Seán O'Leary; reviews in *The Times* and *The Financial Times*, 25 May 1973, KCLCA K/PP93, Box 12.
30. Charles Acton, *Harpsichord recital at lunch time, Ir. Times*, 13 July 1973, p. 12.
31. *Bach to Killarney, Sunday Independent*, 28 July 1974, p. 13. See also Charles Acton, *Killarney Bach Festival, Ir. Times*, 1 August 1973, p. 14.
32. Gillian Smith and Lindsay Armstrong, 9 July 2009. 22 stone is 308 lbs or 139 kilos. In September, John conducted Musica Reservata in Belgium, at the Gerechtshof in Mechelen. See printed programme, *Musica Reservata*, Gerechtshof, 14 September 1973 (supplied by Jantina Noorman) and Appendix E.
33. Gillian Smith, 9 July 2009.
34. Jenny Robinson, 2 July 2009.
35. Honor O Brolchain, 23 February 2013.
36. Printed programme, *15th and 16th century English Music*, 24 October 1973, KCLCA K/PP93, Box 7.
37. Printed programme, *Europalia 73 Great-Britain*, 26 October 1973, supplied by Jantina Noorman.
38. Letter from John Beckett to Heinz Liebrecht, 21 November 1973, KCLCA K/

PP93, Box 3, Folder 2.

39. Printed programme, *English and French Music of the 13th, 14th and 15th centuries*, 27 November 1973, supplied by Jantina Noorman; also KCLCA K/PP93, Box 10.

40. Assorted documents, KCLCA K/PP93, Box 3, Folder 2, and Box 13.

41. Seán O'Leary, 25 October 2007.

42. Bernard Thomas, 10 January 2012.

43. Seán O'Leary, 25 October 2007.

44. Hedy Morrow, 14 May 2008.

45. Seán O'Leary, 25 October 2007.

Thirty-Two

1. Charles Acton, *Bach cantatas at St. Ann's*, Ir. Times, 28 January 1974, p. 10; Charles Acton, *More Bach cantatas at St. Ann's*, Ir. Times, 4 February 1974, p. 10; Charles Acton, *Bach cantata concert*, Ir. Times, 12 February 1974, p. 10.

2. Michael Richter, 21 December 2007.

3. Email from Rose Hilton, 30 September 2014; Frida Robinson, 30 April 2009.

4. Card from Samuel Beckett to John Beckett, 7 March 1974, UoR MS 5411, 4.

5. General Register Office entry, 13 February 1974.

6. Card from Samuel Beckett to John Beckett, 18 February 1974, UoR MS 5411, 3.

7. Knowlson, *Damned to Fame*, p. 603.

8. Seán O'Leary, 24 October 2007.

9. Email from Malcolm Proud, 21 July 2013.

10. *Two Thousand Miles of Peril*, RTÉ Guide, television programmes for 4 March 1974; *An Irishman's Diary*, Ir. Times, 4 May 1972, p. 11; *An Irishman's Diary*, Ir. Times, 24 October 1972, p. 11; www.tcd.ie/irishfilm. The film, sponsored by RTÉ Television, was awarded the Military Marine Cup in Milan, 1972.

11. Author's diary, 15 March 1974.

12. *Cinemas*, Ir. Times, 20 May 1974, p. 21. The film was produced in 1973.

13. www.tcd.ie/irishfilm and *George Morrison*, Wikipedia.

14. Patrick Cuming's tape recording list, PC 035.

15. Dublin Arts Festival programme, 1974. See also Charles Acton, *Festival starts with Bach tribute*, Ir. Times, 11 March 1974, p. 10.

16. Charles Gannon, *Cathal Gannon*, p.p. 324–6 (where André Prieur is incorrectly credited with conducting the orchestra).

17. Charles Acton, *James Wilson's "Snark" revived*, Ir. Times, 16 March 1974, p. 12.

18. *Letters to the Editor*, Ir. Times, 16 February 2007, p. 21.

19. Charles Acton, *Hesketh Piano Quartet's welcome debut*, Ir. Times, 4 April 1974, p. 12.

20. Charles Acton, *An exciting amount of public musical life*, Ir. Times, 7 October 1975, p. 13.

21. Author's diary, 20 January, 20, 25 27 April, and 4 May 1974.

22. *Next week in the arts*, Ir. Times, 27 April and 4 May 1974, p. 12; Charles Acton,

Carlow's weekend of Haydn, Ir. Times, 6 May 1974, p. 10.

23. Dan Shields, 16 July 2007.

24. John Honohan, *Bach to Killarney*, Sunday Independent, 28 July 1974, p. 13; Geraldine Neeson, *Ulster Orchestra at Killarney Bach Festival*, Ir. Times, 1 August 1974, p. 10.

25. Charles Acton, *The Kilkenny Arts Week*, Ir. Times, 4 September 1974, p. 10.

26. *Elizabethan Heritage—Volume 1*, Gramophone, August 1974, p. 393 and advertisement, June 1974.

27. *Music Magazine*, RTÉ Guide, 6 September 1974, p. 6 and programmes for 13 September 1974.

28. Venetia O'Sullivan, 26 February 2007.

29. Michael Dervan, 16 January 2013.

30. Charles Acton, *Celebration Concert by B.B.C. in T.C.D.*, Ir. Times, 7 November 1974, p. 11.

31. Lindsay Armstrong, 9 July 2009.

32. Author's diary, 23 November 1974.

33. *Connacht Tribune*, 29 November 1974, p. IX; *Purcell Consort Recital*, Connacht Sentinel, 26 November 1974, p. 4.

Thirty-Three

1. Charles Acton, *St. Matthew Passion at the R.D.S.*, Ir. Times, 27 January 1975, p. 11.

2. Alison Young, 6 June 2013.

3. *Next Week in the Arts*, Ir. Times, 8 February 1975, p. 12.

4. Author's diary, 16 February 1975.

5. Charles Acton, *Bach cantata series at St. Ann's*, Ir. Times, 17 February 1975, p. 10.

6. Billy Reid, 28 November 2013.

7. Author's diary, 23 February and 2 March, 1975; Carol Acton, *Last of Bach cantata series*, Ir. Times, 4 March 1975, p. 10.

8. Author's diary, 9 March 1975.

9. Author's diary, 11 March 1975.

10. Charles Acton, *Festival concert of music by Henry Purcell*, Ir. Times, 12 March 1975, p. 11.

11. Andrew and Jenny Robinson, 2 July 2009.

12. *Music Room*, RTÉ Guide, radio programmes for 11 and 18 March 1975.

13. Charles Acton, *Bach Passion by Our Lady's Choral Society*, Ir. Times, 27 March 1975, p. 11.

14. Billy Reid, 28 November 2013.

15. Charles Acton, *Carlow's Schubertiad*, Ir. Times, 6 May 1975, p. 10.

16. Card from Samuel Beckett to John Beckett, 11 May 1975, UoR MS 5411, 6.

17. Author's diary, 17–24 May 1975; John Beckett, 31 July 1998; *Choral society will perform at Papal audience*, Ir. Times, 19 May 1975, p. 9; Lindsay and Gillian Armstrong, 9 July 2009; Alison Young, 6 June 2013.

18. Author's diary, 14 June 1975.

19. Author's diary, 24 June 1975.

20. Email from Jeremy Timmis, 20 July 2009.

21. Andrew and Jenny Robinson, 2 July 2009; Lindsay and Gillian Armstrong, 9 July 2009; email from Malcolm Proud, 31 July 2013.

22. Andrew and Jenny Robinson, 2 July 2009.

23. Author's diary, 8 August 1975.

24. Killian Schürmann, 19 September 2013.

25. Michael Morrow, *Gerda Frömel – an appreciation*, obituary in unidentified newspaper, KCLCA K/PP93, Box 12.

26. Rhoda Draper, 2007.

27. Author's diary, 22 August 1975.

28. *An Irishman's Diary*, Ir. *Times*, 30 October 1975, p. 11; *RTÉ Guide*, television programmes for 9 November 1976; television programmes, *Sunday Ind.*, 1 January 1978, p. 2; www.tcd.ie/irishfilm. This film won first prize in the Industrial Maritime Documentaries category at the 17th International Review of Maritime Film Documentaries in Milan.

29. Author's diary, 29 November 1975.

30. *Music for the Christmas Season*, *RTÉ Guide*, radio programmes for 1, 8 and 22 December 1975.

31. *Christmas Music*, *RTÉ Guide*, 19 December 1975, p. 16 and television programmes for 23 December 1975; RTÉ Television Archives.

32. Lindsay and Gillian Armstrong, 9 July 2009.

33. Eileen Battersby, *The Diva of Dublin*, Ir. *Times*, 1 June 2000, p. 13.

34. RTÉ Television Archives.

Thirty-Four

1. *Next Week in the Arts*, Ir. *Times*, 3 January 1976, p. 12; author's diary, 15 January 1976.

2. Author's diary, 27 January, 1976.

3. Email from Andrew Robinson, 9 January 2013.

4. Author's diary, 27 January 1976.

5. Author's recollection.

6. Author's diary, 27 January, 5 February and 2 March 1976.

7. Michael Dervan, 4 January 2013.

8. Charles Acton, *Records – Exploring Bach*, Ir. *Times*, 19 July 1976, p. 8.

9. Charles Acton, *Festival concert with NICO*, Ir. *Times*, 8 March 1976, p. 9.

10. Nicholas Anderson, 4 March 2010 and his contribution in *Celebrating John Beckett*, the programme for John's memorial concert, 24 November 2007, p. 15.

11. Author's diary, 16 March 1976; G.D.H., *Peterson and Pass at RDS*, Ir. *Times*, 16 March 1976, p. 6.

12. *Bernadette Greevy sings Bach Arias*, CSM53CD (author's collection of discs).

13. Charles Acton, *The Best of Bach*, Ir. *Times*, 29 September 1980, p. 10.

14. Michael Dervan, *Classical*, Ir. *Times*, 13 January 1995, p. 14.

15. *Afternoon Recital*, *RTÉ Guide,* radio programmes for 7 April 1976; RTÉ Sound Archives.

16. James Cavanagh, 21 March 2013.

17. Alfred Burrowes, *Concert by Ulster Orchestra*, Ir. Times, 17 May 1976, p. 10.

18. Charles Acton, *Our Lady's Choral Society in Bach Mass*, Ir. Times, 18 May 1976, p. 19.
See also Mary Mac Goris, *Brilliant effect in B-minor Mass*, Ir. Ind., 18 May 1976, p. 11.

19. *Next Week in the Arts*, Ir. Times, 15 and 22 May 1976, p. 10.

20. Katherine J. Worth, *Beckett's fine shades* – Play, That time, *and* Footfalls, The English
Department at Florida State University website (www.english.fsu.edu/jobs/
num01/Num1Worth.htm) and John Calder, *Review: The Royal Court Theatre, London:
Beckett's 70th birthday season* (www.english.fsu.edu/jobs/num01/Num1Calder.htm).

21. Card from Samuel Beckett to John Beckett, 27 July 1976, UoR MS 5411, 7.

22. *Studio Concerts*, RTÉ Guide, 4 June 1976, p. 12; Charles Acton, Ó Riada and
Rachmaninoff's 'The Bells', Ir. Times, 5 June 1976, p. 15.

23. Archives of the Contemporary Music Centre, Dublin.

24. Author's diary, 22 and 30 July 1976.

25. Author's diary, 14–20 August 1976.

26. Charles Acton, *Recital by Bernadette Greevy*, Ir. Times, 18 October 1976, p. 11.

27. Author's diary, 22 October 1976; Charles Gannon, unabridged *Cathal Gannon*, p.
331; RTÉ Archives.

28. *Look to the Sea*, RTÉ Guide, television programmes for 9 November 1976.

29. *Orchestral Concert*, RTÉ Guide, radio programmes for 10 December 1976.

30. John O'Donovan, *Music Notes*, RTÉ Guide, 19 September 1980, p. 20.

31. *Orchestra appeals for funds*, Ir. Times, 19 October 1976, p. 11; *Letters to the Editor: New
Dublin orchestra*, Ir. Ind., 22 October 1976, p. 8.

32. Author's diary, 20 December 1976. See also Charles Acton, *Training Orchestra's first
concert*, Ir. Times, 21 December 1976, p. 5.

33. James Cavanagh, 21 March 2013.

Thirty-Five

1. Author's diary, 12 and 19 January 1977.

2. *Next Week in the Arts*, Ir. Times, 5 February 1977, p. 10.

3. Author's diary, 13 and 20 February 1977.

4. Charles Acton, *Series of Bach cantatas resumed*, Ir. Times, 14 February 1977, p. 8.

5. *Next Week in the Arts*, Ir. Times, 19 February 1977, p. 10.

6. *Next Week in the Arts*, Ir. Times, 26 February 1977, p. 10.

7. Email from Malcolm Proud, 21 July 2013.

8. Charles Acton, *Final afternoon of Bach cantatas*, Ir. Times, 1 March 1977, p. 8.

9. Nicholas Anderson, 4 March 2010.

10. Malcolm Proud, 21 July 2013.

11. Nicholas Anderson, 4 March 2010.

12. Alison Young, 6 June 2013.

13. Nicholas Anderson, 4 March 2010.

14. Michael Dervan, 16 January 2013.
15. Author's diary, 2, 9 and 26 March 1977.
16. *Next Week in the Arts*, *Ir. Times*, 2 April 1977, p. 10.
17. Card from Samuel Beckett to John Beckett, 15 May 1977, and John Beckett's explanatory note, UoR MS 5411, 10.
18. Nicholas Anderson, 4 March 2010.
19. *Bernadette Greevy at the National Gallery*, *RTÉ Guide*, television programmes for 12 May 1977; RTÉ Television Archives.
20. Advertisement, *Ir. Times*, 8 April 1977, p. 17.
21. Dan Shields, 16 July 2007.
22. *Next Week in the Arts*, *Ir. Times*, 21 May 1977, p. 10.
23. Mirette Dowling, 9 April 2013.
24. Gillian Smith, 9 July 2009.
25. Charles Acton, *Wicklow Choral Society sings 'St Paul'*, *Ir. Times*, 26 May 1977, p. 13.
26. *Afternoon Recital*, *RTÉ Guide*, radio programmes for 3 August 1977; RTÉ Sound Archives; *John O'Donovan's Music Notes*, *RTÉ Guide*, 14 October 1977, p. 37.
27. *Concerts*, *Ir. Times*, 24 June 1977, p. 27.
28. Author's diary, 19 August 1977.
29. Nicholas Anderson, *Celebrating John Beckett*, programme for John Beckett memorial concert, 14 November 2007, pp. 15–16.
30. *Let's Sing a Song*, *RTÉ Guide*, radio programmes for 5 November and 3 December 1977.
31. Charles Acton, *Christmas Oratorio in the Pro-Cathedral*, *Ir. Times*, 23 November 1977, p. 9.
32. *Next Week in the Arts*, *Ir. Times*, 26 November 1977, p. 14.
33. Charles Acton, *TCD Christmas concert from Goethe Institute*, *Ir. Times*, 19 December 1977, p. 9.
34. Author's diary, 22 December 1977.

Thirty-Six

1. Letter from Samuel Beckett to John Beckett, 19 January 1978, UoR MS 5411, 12.
2. Email from Rose Hilton, 30 September 2014.
3. Mirette Dowling, 9 April 2013.
4. Alison Young, 6 June 2013.
5. Andrew Robinson, 2 July 2009.
6. Alison Young, 6 June 2013. On 23 January, John and Bernadette Greevy gave a recital in the concert hall of the Royal Dublin Society. Included were songs by Haydn, Mahler, Larchet, Schubert and Granados. The performance was repeated at lunchtime on the following day. See *Next Week in the Arts*, *Ir. Times*, 21 January 1978, p. 12; *What's on today*, *Ir. Times*, 24 January 1978, p. 15.
7. Charles Acton, *Bach Cantata series resumed*, *Ir. Times*, 6 February 1978, p. 8.

8. Charles Acton, *Second concert of Bach series*, Ir. Times, 13 February 1978, p. 8.

9. BBC Archives.

10. Charles Acton, *Final Bach cantata concert*, 20 February 1978, p. 10.

11. Nicholas Anderson, 4 March 2010.

12. *Next week in the Arts*, Ir. Times, 4 March 1978, p. 16.

13. John Calder, 11 August 2009; Chris Bastock, Gallery Records, Tate Library and Archive, 22 July 2010.

14. Charles Acton, *Bach concert by N.I.C.O.*, Ir. Times, 2 May 1978, p. 8; author's diary, 29 April 1978.

15. Michael Williams, *Second NICO Bach programme*, Ir. Times, 2 May 1978, p. 8.

16. Author's diary, 30 April 1978.

17. Carol Acton, *DTO at St Catherine's*, Ir. Times, 16 May 1978, p. 8.

18. James Cavanagh, 21 March 2013.

19. Nos. 123, *Liebster Immanuel, Herzog der Frommen* ('Dearest Emmanuel, Lord of the Righteous'), and 164, *Ihr, die ihr euch von Christo nennet* ('Ye who bear the name of Christ'); BBC Archives. These were broadcast in June of the following year.

20. Author's diary, 19 September 1978.

21. Author's diary, 27 September 1978; Dr Anna Lee, March 2015.

22. Author's recollection.

23. Seán O'Leary, 18 May 2007; E. John Tyler, *Black Forest Clocks*, pp. 1–4.

24. Author's recollection.

25. *Schubert's Other Unfinished Symphony*, RTÉ Guide, radio programmes for 11 November 1978; RTÉ Sound Archives.

26. *Schubert*, RTÉ Guide, radio programmes for 18 November 1978; RTÉ Sound Archives. The RTÉ Lyric FM presenter Éamonn Lawlor was very moved by these fine performances and included them in one of his evening programmes, on the second anniversary of Bernadette's death. (Éamonn Lawlor, 14 October 2010.)

27. RTÉ Sound Archives.

28. Author's diary, 22 November 1978.

29. Email from Malcolm Proud, 21 July 2013.

30. Author's diary, 22 November 1978.

31. Author's diary, 7 December 1978.

32. Charles Acton, *Goethe Institute concert*, Ir. Times, 18 December 1978, p. 8.

Thirty-Seven

1. Charles Acton, *O Riada tribute at RTESO concert*, Ir. Times, 15 January 1979, p. 8.

2. *What's on today*, Ir. Times, 31 January 1979, p. 19.

3. Author's diary, 31 January 1979.

4. Patrick Cuming, 28 April 2007.

5. Email from Jeremy Timmis, 20 July 2009.

6. Charles Acton, *Bach Cantata series in St. Ann's*, Ir. Times, 6 February 1979, p. 8.

7. Nicholas Anderson, 4 March 2010.
8. BBC Archives.
9. Nicholas Anderson, 4 March 2010.
10. Charles Acton, *Second Bach cantata concert*, Ir. Times, 13 February 1979, p. 8.
11. Charles Acton, *Last of Bach cantata series*, Ir. Times, 19 February 1979, p. 8; BBC Archives.
12. *Memoranda – an arts notebook: Rare Haydn*, Ir. Times, 3 March 1979, p. 12.
13. *An Irishman's Diary*, Ir. Times, 28 February 1979, p. 11.
14. Charles Acton, *Haydn and the Brothers of St. John of God*, Ir. Times, 13 March 1979, p. 8.
15. *Records by Charles Acton*, Ir. Times, 18 March 1980, p. 10.
16. *Obituaries: Professor Petr Skrabanek*, The Times, 27 June 1994.
17. Vera Škrabánek, 29 November 2007.
18. *Next Week in the Arts*, Ir. Times, 24 March 1979, p. 12.
19. Billy Reid, 28 November 2013.
20. Charles Acton, *Wicklow Choral Society in Pro-Cathedral*, Ir. Times, 9 April 1979, p. 8.
21. *Next Week in the Arts*, Ir. Times, 28 April 1979, p. 16.
22. Charles Acton, *RTECO play Mozart in St. Catherine's*, Ir. Times, 7 May 1979, p. 8.
23. Charles Acton, *RTECO at St Catherine's*, Ir. Times, 14 May 1979, p. 8.
24. *Invitation to Music*, RTÉ Guide, radio programmes for 8 March 1980.
25. *Song Recital*, RTÉ Guide, radio programmes for 17 May 1979; Patrick Cuming's tape recording list, PC 067.
26. Patrick Cuming's recording, tape PC068.
27. Advertisement, Ir. Times, 28 April 1979, p. 27.
28. Charles Acton, *Festival concert at RDS*, Ir. Times, 7 June 1979, p. 10.
29. Email from Jeremy Timmis, 20 July 2009.
30. Charles Acton, *Mozart and Bach at the RDS Festival*, 8 June 1979, p. 10.
31. Carol Acton, *Dublin Festival at the RDS*, Ir. Times, 12 June 1979, p. 8.
32. Letter from Charles Acton to John Beckett, 24 June 1979, Charles Acton Papers, NLI Acc 6787, Box 19.
33. Letter from John Beckett to Charles Acton, 26 June 1979, Charles Acton Papers, NLI Acc 6787, Box 19.
34. Fanny Fehan, *Beautiful playing in concert*, Evening Herald, May 1979, attached to John Beckett's letter to Charles Acton, 26 June 1979, Charles Acton Papers, NLI Acc 6787, Box 19.
35. Letter from Charles Acton to John Beckett, 30 June 1979, Charles Acton Papers, NLI Acc 6787, Box 19.
36. *Prom Talk*, Radio 3, Radio Times, radio programmes for 15 July 1979.
37. *Music Magazine*, RTÉ Guide, radio programmes for 16 July 1979.
38. *Next Week in the Arts*, Ir. Times, 14 July 1979, p. 16.
39. Alison Young, 6 June 2013.
40. Charles Acton, *Preview of Albert Hall Bach*, Ir. Times, 20 July 1979, p. 10.

41. Printed Prom programme; *Prom concert, Royal Albert Hall*, Radio 3, *Radio Times*, radio programmes for 22 July 1979.

42. *The New Irish Chamber Orchestra at the London Proms*, *RTÉ Guide*, radio programmes for 22 July 1979.

43. Nicholas Anderson, 4 March 2010.

44. Charles Acton, *Records*, *Ir. Times*, 30 August 1979, p. 10. See also Harriet Kinsella, *Prom concert at Albert Hall*, *Ir. Times*, 25 July 1979, p. 8.

45. Gillian Smith and Lindsay Armstrong, 9 July 2009.

46. Mozelle Moshansky, *Irish Bach*, *The Guardian*, 23 July 1979.

47. Nicholas Anderson, 4 March 2010.

48. Lindsay Armstrong, 9 July 2009.

49. Advertisement, *Ir. Times*, 28 July 1979, p. 22.

50. *Next Week in the Arts*, *Ir. Times*, 25 August 1979, p. 12.

51. Anthony OBrien, 31 January 2014.

52. RTÉ Archives and Sound Archives; colour film, 1978.

53. Rosalind Whittaker, 11 April 2007.

54. Author's diary, 5 December 1979.

Thirty-Eight

1. Geraldine Neeson, *Harpsichord recital in Cork*, *Ir. Times*, 23 January 1980, p. 8.

2. Charles Acton, *Records – Bach organ series*, *Ir. Times*, 28 January 1980, p 8, and *New series of Bach cantatas in St. Ann's*, *Ir. Times*, 13 February 1980, p. 8.

3. Charles Acton, *Second Bach cantata in St. Ann's*, *Ir. Times*, 18 February 1980, p. 10.

4. Charles Acton, *Final Bach cantata afternoon*, *Ir. Times*, 26 February 1980, p. 8.

5. *Orchestral Concert*, *RTÉ Guide*, 20 February 1980.

6. Charles Acton, *Bach Passion in St Patrick's Cathedral*, *Ir. Times*, 1 April 1980, p. 10.

7. Michael Richter, 21 December 2007.

8. *Early Music Forum*, BBC Radio 3, *Radio Times*, radio programmes for 19 April 1980.

9. Charles Acton, *RTESO back to public studio concerts*, *Ir. Times*, 15 May 1980, p. 10.

10. *Next Week in the Arts*, *Ir. Times*, 2 June 1980, p. 14.

11. Vera Škrabánek, 29 November 2007.

12. Charles Acton, *NICO Concert in TCD*, *Ir. Times*, 26 June 1980, p. 10.

13. Lindsay Armstrong, 9 July 2009.

14. Author's diary, 25 June 1980.

15. Author's diary, 27 June 1980.

16. Honor O Brolchain, 23 February 2013.

17. Author's diary, 27 June 1980.

18. Andrew and Jenny Robinson, 2 July 2009; author's recollection.

19. Charles Acton, *Frank Patterson sings Purcell at Christ Church*, *Ir. Times*, 4 July 1980, p. 8.

20. *Next Week in the Arts*, *Ir. Times*, 19 July 1980, p. 14.

21. Charles Acton, *NICO give preview of Flanders Bach programme*, *Ir. Times*, 22 July 1980, p. 10.

22. Charles Acton, *NICO's second Bach Flanders concert*, *Ir. Times*, 23 July 1980, p. 7.

23. Printed programme for *Festival van Vlaanderen, Brugge 1980*.

24. Email from Malcolm Proud, 23 July 2013.

25. Author's diary, 28 July 1980, 6 January 1978 and 24 June 1980.

26. Lindsay Armstrong, 4 November 2013; Lindsay Armstrong and Gillian Smith, 9 July 2009.

27. Author's diary and recollection.

28. John Beckett, 31 July 1998.

29. Author's diary, 23 December 1980.

30. John Beckett, 31 July 1998.

31. Cathal Gannon's diary of events, 28 July to 12 August 1980.

32. Author's diary, 22 February 1981.

33. John Beckett, 31 July 1998.

34. Cathal Gannon's diary of events, 28 July to 12 August 1980.

35. John Beckett, 31 July 1998.

36. Cathal Gannon's diary of events, 28 July to 12 August 1980.

37. John Beckett, 31 July 1998; Lindsay Armstrong, 4 November 2013 and *Irish Musicians in China*, *Ir. Times*, *Weekend* supplement, 11 October 1980, p. 9; Cathal Gannon's diary of events, 28 July to 12 August 1980.

Thirty-Nine

1. Emails from Malcolm Proud, 21 and 23 July 2013.

2. Author's diary, 13 August and 2 September 1980.

3. Vera Škrabánek, 29 November 2007.

4. Margaret Quigley, 8 March 2013.

5. Roland Morrow, 23 October 2007.

6. Printed invitation sent to Seán O'Leary, March 1980.

7. Roland Morrow, 23 October 2007.

8. *John O'Donovan's Music Notes: The Grand Which?*, *RTÉ Guide*, 22 August 1980 and radio programmes for 24 August 1980.

9. *Next Week in the Arts*, *Ir. Times*, 6 September 1980, p. 14.

10. *Orchestral Concert*, *RTÉ Guide*, RTÉ Radio 1, 13 November 1980.

11. Charles Acton, *RTESO back to studio concerts*, *Ir. Times*, 11 September 1980, p. 10.

12. Honor O Brolchain, 23 February 2013.

13. David Carmody, 15 March 2013.

14. Author's diary, 13 September 1980.

15. Charles Acton, *John Beckett directs Bach*, *Ir. Times*, 16 September 1980, p. 8.

16. Author's diary, 26 September 1980.

17. Author's diary, 24 October 1980.

18. Gillian Smith and Lindsay Armstrong, 9 July 2009.
19. Carol Acton, *St. Cecilia's Day Handel recital*, Ir. Times, 24 November 1980, p. 8.
20. Charles Acton, *Goethe Institute Choir at TCD*, Ir. Times, 15 December 1980, p. 8.
21. Author's diary, 27 December 1980.
22. Charles Acton, *Bach cantatas in St Ann's*, Ir. Times, 3 February 1981, p. 8.
23. Michael Williams, *Bach Cantatas in St. Ann's*, Ir. Times, 9 February 1981, p. 8.
24. Charles Acton, *End of St. Ann's Bach series*, Ir. Times, 17 February 1981, p. 8.
25. Charles Acton, *Records – Studies on Bacon*, Ir. Times, 9 February 1981, p. 8.
26. Author's diary, 22 February 1981.
27. Author's diary, 27 February 1981.
28. Author's diary, 1 March 1981.
29. Michael Quinn, programme note for a performance of Mahler's Symphony No. 10 by the National Symphony Orchestra in the National Concert Hall, Dublin on 8 February 2013, p. 7.
30. *Next Week in the Arts*, Ir. Times, 21 March 1981, p. 14.
31. Lindsay Armstrong, 9 July 2009.
32. David Carmody, 15 March 2013.
33. James Cavanagh, 21 March 2013.
34. David Carmody, 4 February 2007.
35. Michael Dervan, 16 January 2013.
36. Charles Acton, *John Beckett conducts Mahler's Tenth*, Ir. Times, 30 March 1981, p. 10.
37. Patrick Cuming's tape recording list, PC 076, 077 and 078.
38. Charles Acton, *John Beckett conducts Mahler's Tenth*, Ir. Times, 30 March 1981, p. 10.
39. *RTÉ Guide, Radio 1, Programme Variations, VHF*, radio programmes for 20 April 1981.
40. Author's diary, 10 April 1981; Patrick Cuming and Seán O'Leary, 28 April 2007.
41. Alfred Burrowes, *St Matthew Passion at Ulster Hall*, Ir. Times, 20 April 1981, p. 8.
42. Robin McKinney, 4 July 2009.
43. Nicholas Anderson, 4 March 2010.
44. British Library Sound Archives, T4572BW.
45. Nicholas Anderson, 4 March 2010.
46. Picture postcard from Samuel Beckett to John Beckett, 11 July 1981, UoR MS 5411, 16.
47. Author's diary, 24 July 1981.
48. Author's diary, 26 July 1981.
49. Vera Škrabánek, 29 November 2007.
50. Email from Rose Hilton, 20 October 2014; Vera Škrabánek, 29 November 2007.
51. Author's collection.
52. Charles Acton, *Bernadette Greevy and John Beckett in Burke Hall*, Ir. Times, 15 September 1981, p. 8.
53. Author's diary, 17, 23, 25, 29 September 1981.
54. Concerts, Ir. Times, 28 September 1981, p. 16.
55. Author's diary, 15, 20, 24–30 October 1981.

56. Author's diary, 4 December 1981.
57. Concerts, *Ir. Times*, 5 December 1981, p. 15.
58. Author's diary, 22 December 1981.

Forty

1. Author's diary, 7 February 1982.
2. Charles Acton, *New series of Bach cantatas at St Ann's*, *Ir. Times*, 8 February 1982, p. 10.
3. Charles Acton, *Bach Cantatas at St Ann's*, *Ir. Times*, 15 February 1982, p. 10.
4. Charles Acton, *Final Bach cantata concert in St Ann's*, *Ir. Times*, 22 February 1982, p. 16.
5. Author's diary, 27 March 1982.
6. Charles Acton, *St Matthew Passion in National Concert Hall*, *Ir. Times*, 5 April 1982, p. 10.
7. Author's diary, 15 and 16 April 1982.
8. *Next Week in the Arts*, *Ir. Times*, 8 May 1982, p. 14.
9. Author's diary, 25 May 1982.
10. *It's summer on RTÉ Radio 1*, *RTÉ Guide*, 4 June 1982, p. 5.
11. Venetia O'Sullivan, 26 February 2007.
12. John O'Donovan, *Music Notes*, *RTÉ Guide*, 18 June 1982.
13. Author's diary, 27 June 1982.
14. Anthony OBrien, 31 January 2014.
15. *Memoranda – Summer School*, *Ir. Times*, 10 July 1982, p. 14; *Next Week in the Arts*, *Ir. Times*, 17 July 1982, p. 14.
16. *Next Week in the Arts*, *Ir. Times*, 4 September 1982, p. 14.
17. Charles Acton, *Wicklow choir gives Haydn recital*, *Ir. Times*, 11 September 1982, p. 8.
18. Author's diary, 15 October 1982.
19. Andrew Robinson, *Celebrating John Beckett*, programme for commemorative concert, 24 November 2007, p. 17.
20. *Next Week in the Arts*, *Ir. Times*, 23 October 1982, p. 16.
21. Author's diary, 22 and 23 October 1982.
22. James Maguire, *Recital of Viols and choir at Christchurch*, *Ir. Times*, 28 October 1982.
23. Author's diary, 28 and 29 October 1982.
24. Charles Acton, *The Chieftains combine with NICO for Paddy Moloney*, *Ir. Times*, 3 November 1982, p. 10.
25. Author's diary, 6 November 1982.
26. Author's diary, 12 November 1982.
27. Author's diary, 17 November 1982.
28. Author's diary, 23 November 1982.
29. Author's diary, 12 December 1982.

Forty-One

1. Author's diary, 6 February 1983; Charles Acton, *Bach cantatas back in St Ann's*, Ir. *Times*, 7 February 1983, p. 8.

2. Charles Acton, *Opera for singers of the future*, Ir. *Times*, 9 February 1983, p. 10.

3. Sydney Stokes, May 2009. See also Charles Acton, *"The Marriage of Figaro" with music students*, Ir. *Times*, 14 February 1983, p. 8.

4. Charles Acton, *Bach cantatas at St Ann's*, Ir. *Times*, 15 February 1983, p. 8.

5. Author's diary, 13 February 1983.

6. Charles Acton, *Last Bach cantata of season*, Ir. *Times*, 21 February 1983, p. 8.

7. Author's diary, 20 February 1983.

8. Author's diary, 25 February to 7 March 1983.

9. Gillian Smith, 9 July 2009 and 9 March 2013; Margaret Quigley, 8 March 2013.

10. Author's diary, 1 May 1983.

11. *Arts week at St Columba's*, Ir. *Times*, 30 April 1983, p. 5.

12. *Memoranda – an arts notebook*, Ir. *Times*, 14 May 1983, p. 14.

13. Charles Acton, *Wicklow Choral Society's Dublin concert*, Ir. *Times*, 23 May 1983, p. 8.

14. Gillian Smith, 9 July 2009.

15. *Memoranda – an arts notebook: Viol Virtuoso*, Ir. *Times*, 28 May 1983, p. 16.

16. Author's diary, 28 May 1983.

17. Charles Acton, *Viola da gamba virtuoso at St Ann's*, Ir. *Times*, 30 May 1983, p. 8.

18. Author's diary, 29 May 1983.

19. Andrew Robinson, 2 July 2009.

20. Author's diary, 4, 5, 6 and 30 August 1982.

21. Gillian Smith and Lindsay Armstrong, 9 July 2009.

22. Rosalind Whittaker, 11 April 2007.

23. Frida Robinson, 30 April 2009.

24. Andrew and Jenny Robinson, 2 July 2009; Gillian Smith and Lindsay Armstrong, 9 July 2009.

25. Brigid Ferguson, 3 May 2009.

26. Mary Wheatley, 28 May 2008.

27. Michael Dervan, 16 January 2013.

28. *To Talent Alone – The Royal Irish Academy of Music, 1848–1998* (editors Richard Pine and Charles Acton), Gill and Macmillan, Dublin 1998, p. 335.

29. Email from Richard Pine, 16 April 2008.

30. Vera Škrabánek, 29 November 2007.

31. Tim Thurston, 16 January 2012.

32. Eileen Battersby, *The Diva of Dublin*, Ir. *Times*, 1 June 2000, p. 13.

33. Carol Acton, 26 March 2008.

34. Charles Acton, *Music: Generous, how are you! Ireland's loss...*, Ir. *Times*, 2 October 1983, p. 10.

35. Charles Acton, *New Bach Cantata season*, Ir. *Times*, 14 February 1984, p. 10.

Forty-Two

1. Nicholas Anderson, 4 March 2010.
2. Email from Arthur Johnson, 6 May 2008.
3. Seán O'Leary, 25 October 2007; Frida Robinson, 30 April 2009.
4. Nicholas Anderson, 4 March 2010.
5. Email from Arthur Johnson, 6 May 2008.
6. Frida Robinson, 30 April 2009.
7. Lindsay Armstrong, 9 July 2009.
8. Nicholas Anderson, 4 March 2010.
9. Adrian Jack, 30 April 2007.
10. Nicholas Anderson, 4 March 2010.
11. Patrick Lambert, 20 and 25 July 2007.
12. Adrian Jack, 30 April 2007; Adrian Jack, Obituary: *John Beckett – Early music revivalist*, *The Independent*, 12 March 2007.
13. Patrick Cuming, 2007.
14. Morris Sinclair, 19 May 2007; Deirdre Sinclair, 19 May 2007.
15. Author's recollection.
16. Patrick Lambert, 25 July 2007.
17. Oengus MacNamara, 28 July 2008.
18. Paul Conway, 15 February 2007.
19. Billy Reid, 28 November 2013.
20. Christopher Nobbs, 14 April 2013.
21. Nick and Frida Robinson, 30 April 2009.
22. Christopher Nobbs, 14 April 2013.
23. Seán O'Leary, 24 October 2007.
24. Roland Morrow, 23 October 2007.
25. Seán O'Leary, 28 April 2007.
26. Mirette Dowling, 9 April 2013.
27. Seán O'Leary, 24 October 2007.
28. Email from Judy Jordan, 3 March 2007.
29. Seán O'Leary, 25 November 2007.
30. *Morning Concert*, Radio 3, *Radio Times*, radio programmes for 14–18 November 1983; Nicholas Anderson, 4 March 2010.
31. Picture postcards from Samuel Beckett to John Beckett, 16 October and 26 November 1983, UoR MS 5411, 23 and 24.
32. Picture postcard from Samuel Beckett to John Beckett, 30 September 1983, UoR MS 5411, 22.
33. Picture postcard from Samuel Beckett to John Beckett, 16 October 1983, UoR MS 5411, 23.

Forty-Three

1. *Morning Concert*, Radio 3, *Radio Times*, radio programmes for 9–13 January 1984.
2. Nicholas Anderson, 4 March 2010.
3. Author's diary, 1 and 2 February 1984.
4. Picture postcard from Samuel Beckett to John Beckett, 14 March 1984, UoR MS 5411, 25.
5. Picture postcard from John Beckett to Cathal Gannon, 23 July 1984, author's collection.
6. Patrick Lambert, 25 July 2007.
7. Seán O'Leary, 24 October 2007.
8. Postcard from John Beckett to Margaret Gannon, 3 November 1984, and author's recollection.
9. Undated card, author's collection.
10. *Morning Concert*, Radio 3, *Radio Times*, radio programmes for 24–28 September and 12–16 November 1984.
11. *This Week's Composer: Sibelius*, Radio 3, *Radio Times*, radio programmes for 10–14 December 1984.
12. Charles Acton, *Music*, *Ir. Times*, 13 January 1984, p. 10; Handel concert, Radio 3, *Radio Times*, on 7 January 1985.
13. Nicholas Anderson, 24 November 2007.
14. *This Week's Composer: Max Bruch*, Radio 3, *Radio Times*, radio programmes for 1–5 April 1985.
15. *This Week's Composer: Johann Christian Bach*, Radio 3, *Radio Times*, radio programmes for 2–6 September 1985.
16. *This Week's Composer: Haydn's Contemporaries*, Radio 3, *Radio Times*, radio programmes for 2–6 December 1985.
17. Picture postcard from Samuel Beckett to John, 27 March 1986, UoR MS 5411, 29.
18. *This Week's Composers: Schola Cantorum*, Radio 3, *Radio Times*, radio programmes for 21–25 April, 1986.
19. *Morning Concert*, Radio 3, *Radio Times*, radio programmes for 12–16 May 1986.
20. *This Week's Composer: Mendelssohn*, Radio 3, *Radio Times*, radio programmes for 27–31 October 1986.
21. *This Week's Composer: Fauré*, Radio 3, *Radio Times*, radio programmes for 26–30 January 1987.
22. *This Week's Composer: Stravinsky*, Radio 3, *Radio Times*, radio programmes for 6–10 April 1987; *Morning Concert*, Radio 3, *Radio Times*, radio programmes for 29 May–2 June 1987; *This Week's Composer: Monteverdi*, Radio 3, *Radio Times*, radio programmes for 31 August–5 September 1987.
23. *Lili Kraus*, Radio 3, *Radio Times*, radio programmes for 22 and 29 November, and 6, 13, 20 and 27 December 1987. Music by Mozart, Bartók and Schubert. Lili Kraus was born in Budapest in 1903; she settled in the UK after World War II, and died in 1986 in North Carolina, USA.

24. BBC Archives; Radio 3, *Ir.Times*, radio programmes for 28, 29, 30 and 31 December 1987, and 1 January 1988.

25. Author's diary, 6 April 1987.

26. Author's diary, 12 April 1987.

27. Michael Dervan, *John Beckett conducts Bach's 'St John Passion'*, *Ir.Times*, 13 April 1987, p. 12.

28. Radio 1, *RTÉ Guide*, radio programmes for 1 April 1988.

29. Picture postcard from John Beckett to Cathal and Margaret Gannon, 21 August 1987.

30. Author's diary, 21 August 1987.

31. Picture postcard from Samuel Beckett to John Beckett, 23 September 1987, UoR MS 5411, unnumbered.

32. Picture postcard from Samuel Beckett to John Beckett, 5 December 1987, UoR MS 5411, 31.

33. *Langham Chamber Orchestra conducted by John Beckett*, Radio, BBC Radio 3, *Ir. Times*, 15 April 1988, p. 31, 13 May 1988, p. 31, 15 July 1988, p. 29.

34. *English Virginals Music*, Radio, BBC Radio 3, *Ir.Times*, 20 November 1987, p. 31.

35. Postcard from Samuel Beckett to John Beckett, 5 December 1987, UoR MS 5411, 31.

36. *This Week's Composer: Max Bruch*, Radio 3, *Radio Times*, radio programmes for 4–8 January 1988; Seán O'Leary, 26 July 2007; Adrian Jack, 30 April 2007; Bruch, Quintet in A minor, Op. posth., edition Kunzelmann, © 1991, GM 1352.

37. Michael Dervan, *Bach cantatas at St Ann's*, *Ir.Times*, 15 February 1988, p. 12, and 21 February 1988, p. 14.

38. Charles Acton, *Beckett conducts RTECO*, *Ir.Times*, 14 May 1988, p. 12.

39. *RTÉ at the Royal Hospital Kilmainham*, RTÉ FM 3, *RTÉ Guide*, radio programmes for 1 October 1988.

40. *Composers of the Week: Boccherini*, BBC Radio 3, *Radio Times*, radio programmes for 20–24 June 1988.

41. *Sounds of Transylvania*, Radio, BBC Radio 3, *Ir. Times*, 16 August 1988, p. 19; BBC Written Archives; British Library Sound Archive, 1CDR0021821 BD2.

42. *Sounds of Sardinia* (23 August 1988), Monica Thapar, BBC Written Archives; *Sounds of Soviet Georgia*, Radio, BBC Radio 3, *Ir. Times*, 30 August 1988, p. 19; British Library Sound Archive, 1CDR0021855 and 1CDR0021874 BD3.

43. *Early Birds*, Radio, BBC Radio 3, *Ir.Times*, 21 September 1988, p. 23.

44. British Library Sound Archive, 1CDR0022124 BD2[1].

45. Concerts, *Ir.Times*, 18 March 1989, p. 18.

46. Kevin Myers, *An Irishman's Diary*, *Ir.Times*, 18 March 1989, p. 11.

47. Michael Dervan, *'St Matthew Passion' at RDS*, *Ir.Times*, 20 March 1989, p. 14.

48. Michael Dervan, *John Beckett conducts Bach at RHK*, *Ir.Times*, 3 April 1989, p. 10.

49. *The King's Consort*, Radio, FM3, *RTÉ Guide*, radio programmes for 25 June 1989.

50. Card from Samuel Beckett to John and Ruth, 26 July 1989, UoR MS 5411, 34.

51. Radio, BBC Radio 3, *Ir. Times*, 16 June 1989, p. 31; *Langham Chamber Orchestra conducted by John Beckett*, 4 September 1989, p. 17 and 19 October 1989, p. 19.

52. BBC Archives: recorded 2 August 1989, broadcast 6 March 1990; *Langham Chamber Orchestra conducted by Christopher Adey*, Radio, BBC Radio 3, *Ir. Times*, 6 March 1990, p. 23.

53. Patrick Lambert, 20 July 2007.

54. David Cairns, 26 January 2009.

55. Email from Emer Buckley, 3 October 2014.

56. *The Week Ahead: Music*, *Ir. Times*, 9 December 1989, p. 24.

57. Michael Dervan, *John Beckett conducts Bach at RHK*, *Ir. Times*, 11 December 1989, p. 12.

58. Knowlson, *Damned to Fame*, pp. 703–4.

59. Picture postcard from Samuel Beckett to John, 16 October 1989, UoR MS 5411, 35.

Forty-Four

1. *The True Vine*, BBC Radio 3, *Radio Times*, radio programmes for 24 January 1990; www.allmusic.com website.

2. *Music by Brahms*, FM 3 (RTÉ), *Ir. Times*, 27 January 1990, p. 27.

3. *A Musical Eden*, BBC Radio 3, *Ir. Times*, 28 February 1990, p. 29; British Library Sound Archive.

4. *RTÉ Concert Orchestra…*, FM 3 (RTÉ), *Ir. Times*, 28 February 1990, p. 29.

5. Fergus Linehan (editor), *Backdrop: More time for Early Music*, *Ir. Times*, 21 April 1990, p. 29.

6. *Schumann*, FM 3 (RTÉ), *Radio*, *Ir. Times*, 19 May 1990, p. 29.

7. *RTÉ Concert Orchestra*, FM 3 (RTÉ), *Radio*, *Ir. Times*, 30 June 1990, p. 33.

8. *Three Kings*, FM 3 (RTÉ), *Radio*, *Ir. Times*, 19 July 1990, p. 21; *Three Kings*, FM 3 (RTÉ), *RTÉ Guide*, radio programmes for 26 July 1990.

9. *A Dutch Retrospect*, Radio 3, *Radio Times*, radio programmes for 6, 13, 20, 27 October, 3, 10, 17, 24 November, 1, 8, 15, 22 December 1991; *A Dutch Retrospect*, Radio 3, *Radio Times*, radio programmes for 3, 10, 17, 24, 31 January, 7, 14, 21, 28 February, 7, 14, 21, 28 March 1994; Lindsay Armstrong, 27 January 2014.

10. Postcard, April 1992, Seán O'Leary's collection.

11. Jill Higgins, 17 April 2008.

12. Roland Morrow, 23 October 2007.

13. Jill Higgins, 17 April 2008.

14. Vera May K Beckett, England & Wales, Death Index, 1916–2006, Vol. 14, p. 1360.

15. Roland Morrow, 23 October 2007.

16. Jill Higgins, 17 April 2008.

17. Roland Morrow, 23 October 2007.

18. Roland Morrow, 28 May 2007.

19. Author's diary, 7 February 1993.

20. Postcard from John Beckett, 13 February [1993], author's collection.

21. Picture postcard from John Beckett, 13 April 1993, author's collection.
22. John Sothcott, *The Recorder Magazine*, 2007, Vol 27, p. 125; Seán O'Leary, 24 October 2007; Jonathan Carr, *The Real Mahler*, p. 178.
23. YouTube video.
24. Picture postcard from John Beckett to Patrick Lambert from Landeck, Austria, 6 April 1993.
25. Jenny Robinson, 2 July 2009.
26. Seán O'Leary, 26 July 2007.
27. Seán O'Leary, 24 and 25 October 2007.
28. Hedy Morrow, 14 May 2008.
29. Brigid Ferguson, 3 May 2009.
30. Hedy Morrow, 14 May 2008.
31. Vera Škrabánek, 16 July and 29 November, 2007.
32. Postcard to Seán and Odile O'Leary, 16 August [?1994], Seán O'Leary's collection.
33. Email from Rose Hilton, 25 November 2014.
34. Christopher Nobbs, 14 April 2013.
35. *Friday Feature: Lonely Waters*, BBC Radio 3, *Ir. Times*, 9 December 1994, p. 26.
36. Dan Shields, 16 July 2007.
37. Picture postcard from John Beckett and Ruth David to James Plunkett, 8 April 1995, NLI MS 40,853: 1956–1997.
38. Printed programme for *New Thoughts about Old Music*, supplied by Seán O'Leary; Seán O'Leary, 22 July 2007; Jill Higgins, 17 April 2008.
39. Email from Rose Hilton, 25 November 2014.
40. Patrick Cuming, 28 April 2007 and email, 3 May 2009.
41. Email from Rose Hilton, 27 March 2008.
42. Email from Patrick Cuming, 3 May 2009.
43. Email from Rose Hilton, 27 March 2008.
44. Vera Škrabánek, 29 November 2007.
45. Patrick Lambert, 20 July 2007.
46. *Deaths, The Times*, 8 August 1995.
47. Email from Rose Hilton, 27 March 2008.
48. Email from Rose Hilton, 3 February 2014.
49. *Ruth David 1921–1995*, document posted to Seán and Odile O'Leary, Seán O'Leary's collection.
50. Emails from Rose Hilton, 3 February and 25 November 2014.
51. Vera Škrabánek, 16 July 2007, Seán O'Leary, 26 July and 25 November 2007; author's diary, 16 September 1995.
52. Seán O'Leary, 26 July and 24 October 2007.
53. Frida and Vic Robinson, 30 April 2009.
54. Janet Ashe, 20 March 2008; Brigid Ferguson, 3 May 2009.
55. BBC Archives: recorded 2 August 1989, broadcast 6 March 1990; *Langham Chamber Orchestra conducted by Christopher Adey*, BBC Radio 3, *Radio, Ir. Times*, 6 March 1990, p. 23.

56. Seán O'Leary, 26 July 2007.
57. Patrick Lambert, 25 July 2007.

Forty-Five

1. Seán O'Leary, 28 April, 18 May, 26 July, 26 October and 25 November 2007; January and 1 November 2010.
2. Seán O'Leary, 25 November 2007.
3. Patrick Lambert, 25 July 2007.
4. Seán O'Leary, 28 April, 26 October and 25 November 2007; *Horizon: Fermat's Last Theorem*, BBC 2, 15 January 1996, *Ir. Times*, p. 22.
5. *Timewatch: Love Story*, BBC 2, 25 February 1997, *Ir. Times*, p. 28; Monica Thapar, BBC Written Archives.
6. David Cairns, 26 January 2009 and *Purcell: Fantasias for the Viols, Hesperion XX, dir Jordi Savall*, *The Sunday Times Culture* magazine, 16 November 2008; Seán O'Leary, December 2008.
7. David Cairns, 26 January 2009.
8. Morris Sinclair, 19 May 2007.
9. Seán O'Leary, 28 April and 31 July 2007.
10. Patrick and Michael Cuming, 28 April 2007.
11. Letter from John Beckett to James Plunkett, 13 March 1997, National Library of Ireland MS 40,853: 1956–1997.
12. Vera Škrabánek, 16 July and 29 November 2007.
13. Picture postcard to Seán and Odile O'Leary, 4 May 1997.
14. Picture Postcard from John Beckett to James Plunkett, NLI MS 40,853: 1956–1997.
15. Vera Škrabánek, 16 July and 29 November 2007.
16. Janet Ashe, 20 March 2008.
17. Vera Škrabánek 29 November 2007.
18. Letter from John Beckett to James Plunkett, 5 June 1997, NLI MS 40,853: 1956–1997.
19. Jenny Robinson, 2 July 2009; Adrian Somerfield, 22 July 2009.
20. Letter, with document, from John Beckett to Adrian Jack, 19 February 1998.
21. Email from Rose Hilton, 25 November 2014.
22. Christopher Nobbs, 14 April 2013; quotation from the Elizabethan *Book of Common Prayer*, 1559.
23. Letter from John Beckett to James Plunkett, 8 June 1998, NLI MS 40,853: 1956–1997.
24. Postcard from John Beckett to Seán and Odile O'Leary, 10 July 1998, supplied by Seán O'Leary.
25. Author's diary, 19 and 31 July; interview with John Beckett, 31 July 1998.
26. Postcard from John Beckett to Seán and Odile O'Leary, 30 September 1998, supplied by Seán O'Leary.
27. Dan Shields, 16 July 2007.

28. Author's diary, 31 July and 17 October 1998.
29. Author's diary, 26 December 1998.
30. Seán O'Leary, 26 July 2007.
31. Nicholas Anderson, 4 March 2010; Frida Robinson, 30 April 2009.
32. Jonathon Gibbs, 24 November 2007.
33. Seán O'Leary, 26 and 31 July 2007.
34. Email from Rose Hilton, 9 April 2007.
35. David Cairns, 26 January 2009; Christopher Nobbs, 14 April 2013.
36. *Radio* and *Radio Highlights*, *Ir. Times*, 9 September 1999, p. 31; Seán O'Leary, 28 April 2007.

Forty-Six

1. Letter to Patrick and Jarka Lambert, 20 August 2000.
2. Picture postcard from John Beckett to James Plunkett, National Library of Ireland MS 40,853: 1956–1997.
3. Paul Conway, 15 February 2007.
4. Email from Rose Hilton, 25 November 2014.
5. Seán O'Leary, 26 July 2007.
6. Email from Rose Hilton, 25 November 2014.
7. Janet Ashe, 20 March 2008.
8. Roland Morrow, 23 October 2007.
9. Seán O'Leary, 26 July and 26 October 2007.
10. Frida Robinson, 30 April 2009.
11. Email from Rose Hilton, 25 November 2014.
12. Vera Škrabánek, 29 November 2007.
13. *Deaths*, *Ir. Times*, 5 December 2002, p. 33.
14. Author's recollection.
15. Vera Škrabánek, 29 November 2007.
16. Janet Ashe, 20 March 2008.
17. Vera Škrabánek, 29 November 2007.
18. Seán O'Leary, 26 July 2007.
19. Nicholas Anderson, 4 March 2010.
20. John Calder, Obituary, *The Guardian*, 5 March 2007 (online).
21. Christopher Nobbs, 14 April 2013.
22. Janet Ashe, 20 March 2008.
23. Seán O'Leary, 26 and 31 July 2007.
24. Janet Ashe, 20 March 2008.
25. Frida Robinson, 30 April 2009.
26. Email from Rose Hilton, 25 November 2014.
27. Paul Conway, 15 February 2007.
28. Morris and Deirdre Sinclair, 19 May 2007.

29. Paul Conway, 15 February 2007.

30. John Beckett to Jantina Barker, 21 December 2003.

31. Judy Jordan, 3 March 2007.

32. Roland Morrow, 23 October 2007.

33. Email from Rose Hilton, 25 November 2014.

34. Billy Reid, 28 November 2013.

35. Oengus MacNamara, 28 July 2008.

36. Postcard from Paul Conway to Seán and Odile O'Leary, 8 July 2006; Paul Conway, 15 February 2007.

37. Postcard from John Beckett to Seán and Odile O'Leary, undated.

38. Seán O'Leary, 26 July 2007.

39. Author's recollection.

40. Letter from John Beckett to the author, 20 December 2006.

41. Vera Škrabánek, 16 July 2007.

42. Michael Cuming, 28 April 2007.

43. Vera Škrabánek, 16 July and 29 November 2007.

44. Janet Ashe, 20 March 2008.

45. Paul Conway, 15 February 2007.

46. Author's recollection.

47. Vera Škrabánek, 29 November 2007.

48. Paul Conway, 15 February 2007. John was cremated in Lewisham Crematorium on 16 February 2007.

Appendix A
Compositions

Piano piece, 1939, page 19

A Short Overture for Orchestra, c. 1944, p. 27–29

String Quartet, 1944, p. 30

Three Songs: settings of poems by Emily Dickinson, Emily Brontë and Thomas Hardy
   (?), ?1944, p. 30

Three Songs: Had I the Heaven's Embroidered Cloths (W.B.Yeats), *Strike Churl* (G.M.
   Hopkins), *Peace, O my stricken Lute!* (Peter Abelard) for baritone and piano, 1946, ,
   p. 37, 38, 57, 74

Concerto for flute and strings, before 1948, p. 45

Songs: settings of poems by Shelley and William Blake; also by Robert Bridges (?),
   before 1948, p. 45

Two Poems of Shelley for tenor with piano, c. 1950, p. 56, 403 (Eleven, note 2)

Three Fairy Poems of Walter de la Mare for soprano with string quartet, c. 1950, p. 56

Three Poems of Walter de la Mare for tenor with piano, c. 1950, p. 56, 403 (Eleven, n.2)

Four Poems of Emily Brontë for mezzo-soprano with piano, c. 1950, p. 56, 403 (Eleven, n.2)

Grotesques for piano, c. 1953, p. 84

Wedding March for descant recorder and harpsichord, c. 1959, p. 124, 145

Funeral March for descant recorder and harpsichord, c. 1959/?60, p. 145

Fanfare for descant recorder and harpsichord, c. 1963, p. 145

Performed together, May 1963: 1. *Fanfare*; 2. *Funeral March (slow and frantic)*; 3.
   Wedding March (sprightly and dry), p. 145, 415, note 27

Music for radio

Molloy by Samuel Beckett, 1957 (BBC Third Programme; British Library Sound
   Archive), pp. 114–6

Malone Dies by Samuel Beckett, 1958 (Third Programme; not archived), pp. 117–9

The Ballad of the Northern Wastes by Wolfgang Weyrauch, 1958 (Third Programme; not archived), p. 117

Pantagleize by Michel de Ghelderode, 1958 (Third Programme; not archived), pp. 117, 119–20

Remember Who You Are by David Paul, 1958 (Third Programme, not archived), p. 120

The Bow and the Beads by D.S. Savage, 1958 (Third Programme, not archived), p. 122

The Unnamable by Samuel Beckett, 1958–9 (Third Programme, British Library Sound Archive), p. 122

The Voice of Shem: passages from James Joyce's *Finnegans Wake*, 1959 (Third Programme, not archived), p. 123

Ubu Roi by Alfred Jarry, 1959–60 (Third Programme, not archived), p. 124

Come All You Gallant Poachers by H.A.L. Craig and Dominic Behan, 1959 (Third Programme, not archived), pp. 124–5

Billy Bud by Harry Craig, 1961 (written for Third Programme but production cancelled), p. 412, note 16

Words and Music by Samuel Beckett, 1961–2 (Third Programme, British Library Sound Archive and BBC CD set), pp. 135, 137–8, 140–3, 376

Home Sweet Honeycomb by Bernard Kops, 1962 (Third Programme, British Library Sound Archive), pp. 140–1

A Taste of Madeleine by Kay Cicellis (Kaiē Tsitselē), 1962 (Third Programme, not archived), p. 142

Lord Halewyn by Michel de Ghelderode, 1963 (Third Programme, not archived), p. 143

Spring '71 by Arthur Adamov, adapted for radio by John Bakewell, 1963 (Third Programme, not archived), p. 143–4

The Lemmings by Bernard Kops, 1963 (Third Programme, British Library Sound Archive), p. 149

Fando and Lis by Fernando Arrabal, 1963 (Third Programme, not archived), p. 149–50

The Plain Dealer by William Wycherley, 1965 (Third Programme; tape of music in Patrick Cuming's collection, PC061), p. 160–1

Ubu Cocu by Alfred Jarry, 1965 (Third Programme, not archived), pp. 163–5

Electra by Euripides, trans. David Thompson, 1965 (Third Programme, not archived), pp. 163–4, 166

A Grotto for Miss Maynier by F.C. Ball, 1967 (Third Programme, not archived), p. 171

The Good Natur'd Man (Oliver Goldsmith), 1967 (Third Programme, not archived), p. 179

Seventeen Speakies: O! by Sandro Key-Åberg, 1967 (Radio 3, not archived), p. 181

Oedipus the King by Sophocles, 1967–8 (Radio 3, not archived), p. 181

The Chinese Jig by Gerard McLarnon, 1968 (Radio 3, not archived), p. 184

Poor Mrs Machiavelli by David Paul, 1968 (Radio 3, British Library Sound Archive), p. 185

Ubu Enchained by Alfred Jarry, 1968 (Radio 3, not archived), p. 190

Music for the theatre

Music for *Acte sans paroles* (Act without Words) by Samuel Beckett, 1955–6,
    pp. 102–3, 105, 110–13
Arrangements of *God Save the Queen* and the *Marseillaise*, c. 1957, p. 111–12
Bloomsday by Alan McClelland, based on James Joyce's *Ulysses*, 1958, p. 121

Music for film

Irish Rising: 1916, directed by George Morrison, 1966 (RTÉ Television Archives),
    p. 167
Portrait of a Poet: W.B. Yeats, produced by James Plunkett, 1969 (RTÉ Television
    Archives), p. 196
Bird's Eye View: Inis Fáil, produced by Edward Mirzoeff, scripted and presented by
    James Plunkett, 1971 (BBC/RTÉ; RTÉ Television Archives), p. 211
The State of the Nation, produced by Aindréas Ó Gallchóir, written by James Plunkett,
    RTÉ Television, 1971, p. 223
Éamon de Valera, an RTÉ-sponsored documentary directed by George Morrison, 1973,
    pp. 167, 248–9
Two Thousand Miles of Peril, a government-sponsored documentary for the Irish Lifeboat
    Service, directed by George Morrison, 1972; transmitted on RTÉ Television in
    March, 1974, p. 248
Look to the Sea, a Bord Iascaigh Mhara documentary directed by George Morrison,
    1975, pp. 259–60, 267
That Solitary Man, RTÉ Television documentary on J.M. Synge, directed by James
    Plunkett, 1979, p. 293

Arrangements

Chorale Preludes from J.S. Bach's *Orgelbüchlein*, arranged for recorders; Schott, 1959,
    p. 95
First Set of Pieces and *Second Set of Pieces* from *The Fairy Queen* by Henry Purcell,
    arranged for descant, treble, tenor and bass recorders, Recorder Ensemble
    series Nos 23 and 24; Schott, 1961.

Edited music

Max Bruch: Quintet in A minor, Op. posth., published by Albert J. Kunzelmann,
    Germany, 1991, GM 1352, p. 349

Reconstruction

Reconstruction of missing quintus part of William Cobbold's *New Fashions*, c. 1971,
    p. 210

Appendix B
Discography

Sources: various, including original recordings, the medieval.org discography complied by Pierre-F. Roberge and Jon Stringer (www.medieval.org/emfaq/performers/reservata.html) and back numbers of *Gramophone* magazine. Because of the lack of dates on the original LPs, the recordings are listed in approximate chronological order, based on the dates of reviews.

?1960s: Songs by Gustav Mahler, sung by Werner Schürmann and accompanied by John Beckett on piano (recorded in Dublin); p. 149

1963: Music by J.S. Bach (recorded in Dublin on a harpsichord made by Cathal Gannon); LP, p. 149

1963: *Music of Shakespeare's Time*, Vols 1 and 2. Various artists, including Viols of the Schola Cantorum Basiliensis and the Dolmetsch Consort. Includes two songs by Robert Johnson, *Full fathom five* and *Where the bee sucks*, edited by John Beckett. HMV Q CLP 1633–4, Q CSD 1487–8 (set of two LPs).

1966: *Scarlatti Sonatas for Harpsichord*, played by John Beckett on a two-manual harpsichord by Robert Goble: A major, K.268; F minor, K.69; D major, K.278; E flat major, K.193; E minor, K.263; E major, K.264; D minor, K.517; C major, K.513; D major, 492; E major, K.206; E major, K.28. Saga Pan PAN 6205 (LP, UK); p. 168

1966: *MacGowran Speaking Beckett*, Jack MacGowran reads from the works of Samuel Beckett, with John Beckett, harmonioum, Edward Beckett, flute and Samuel Beckett, gong. Slow movement from Schubert's Quartet in D minor, *Death and the Maiden*, D 810. Recorded in Pye Studios, London, January 1966; launched 11 August 1966. Claddagh Records, Ireland, CCT3 (LP and CD); p. 166

1966: *Music of the Early Renaissance: John Dunstable and his contemporaries*, Purcell Consort of Voices and Musica Reservata conducted by Grayston Burgess; John Beckett (treble viol). Music by Anon, de Lantins, Adnemar, Dunstable, Dufay, Frye, Hermannus Contractus. Vox Turnabout TV4058 (LP, mono) / TV34058S (LP, stereo); FSM Turnabout TV 34058 (LP, stereo); KTVC 34058 (cassette); pp. 172–3

1967: *The Classical Mandoline: Music by Beethoven and Hummel*, Hugo D'Alton (mandoline), John Beckett (fortepiano). Saga Pan SPAN 6200, Saga 5350 (1974) (LP); pp. 173–4

1967: *Medieval Vocal and Instrumental Works*, The Jaye Consort of Viols with Gerald English (tenor), Jantina Noorman (mezzo-soprano), Nigel Rogers (tenor), Andrew Brunt (boy soprano), Desmond Dupré (lute) and John Beckett (virginals and organ). Music by various anonymous composers, de la Halle, de Vaqueiras, Richard I. Pye Golden Guinea GGC4092, GGC14092 (LP); p. 180

1968: *Music of the Court Homes and Cities of England*, Vol. 1: *Composers of the Chapel Royal*. Various artists. Includes John Bull: Galliard, *St Thomas Wake*, John Beckett (harpsichord), and Henry Purcell (ed. Beckett): Trio Sonata No. 10 in A major, Ruth David and Roderick Skeaping (violins), Desmond Dupré (viola da gamba), John Beckett (harpsichord). HMV HQS 1140 (LP); p. 187

1968: *To Entertain a King: Music for Henry VIII and his Court* (also *Music to Entertain a King* and *Music to Entertain Henry VIII*), Purcell Consort of Voices and Musica Reservata conducted by Grayston Burgess; John Beckett, harpsichord. Music by Cornish, Barbireau, Henry VIII, Anon, Richafort, Isaac, Busnois, Daggere. Argo RG566 (LP, mono) / ZRG566 (LP, stereo); Argo 905564 (LP, 1977), Argo ZK 24 (LP); p. 188

1968: *Music of the Court Homes and Cities of England*, Vol. 2: *Music at Hampton Court*. Various artists. Includes Henry VIII (ed. J. Stevens): *Consort*, William Cornyshe (ed. J. Stevens): *Fa la Sol*, Albarte (ed. Morrow): *Pavan and Galliard*, Anon (edited by Morrow): *Bransle*, Musica Reservata conducted by Michael Morrow. HMV Q HQS 1141 (LP); p. 187–8

1968: *Music of the Court Homes and Cities of England*, Vol. 3: *Composers of Whitehall Palace and Wilton House*. Various artists. Includes William Lawes (ed. Beckett): Sonata No. 7 in D minor, Ruth David and Roderick Skeaping (violins), Desmond Dupré (viola da gamba) and John Beckett (organ); and Henry Lawes (ed. Beckett): Dance Suite, Ruth David and Roderick Skeaping (violins), Desmond Dupré (viola da gamba) and John Beckett (harpsichord). HMV HQS 1146 (LP); p. 188

1968: *Music of the Court Homes and Cities of England*, Vol. 4: *Composers of Greenwich House and Ingatestone House*. Various artists. Includes William Byrd: *Pavana Bray*, John Beckett (harpsichord), and Coperario (ed. Beckett): Suite, Ruth David and Roderick Skeaping (violins), Desmond Dupré (viola da gamba) and John Beckett (organ). HMV HQS 1147 (LP); p.

1968: *Music of the Court Homes and Cities of England*, Vol. 5: *Hatfield House and Hengrave Hall*. Various artists. Includes William Byrd: *The Queens Almain*, John Beckett (virginals). HMV HQS 1151 (LP); p. 188

1968: *Music of the Court Homes and Cities of England*, Vo. 6: *Composers of Chichester and Worcester*. Various artists. Includes Thomas Tomkins (ed. Fuller Maitland): *Worcester*

Brawls, John Beckett (harpsichord). HMV HQS 1158 (LP); p. 188

1968: *French Court Music of the Thirteenth Century*, Musica Reservata conducted by John Beckett. Music by de Vaqueiras, de la Halle, Anon and Brulles. Delysé ECB 3201 (LP, mono), Delysé DS 3201 (LP, stereo), Everest 3270 (LP), L'Oiseau-Lyre SOL R332 (LP), Musical Heritage Society MHS 4960 (LP); pp. 191–2

1968: *Music from the time of Christopher Columbus*, Musica Reservata conducted by John Beckett. Recorded March 1968. Music by Anon, Cabezón, de Madrid, del Encina, de Mudarra, de la Torre, de Ceballos (Çavallos), Garcimuños and Millán. Philips SAL 3697 (LP); Philips Trésors classiques 839 714 LY (LP), – 831 714 (LP), – 5 839 714 (LP), – 18 249 CAA (Cass.); Philips 412 026-1 PSP (LP), – 412 026-4 PSP (Cass.), – 432 821-2 PM (CD, 1992); pp. 186–7, 193

1968: *Metaphysical Tobacco: Songs and Dances by Dowland, East and Holborne*, Musica Reservata, John Beckett (harpsichord and tenor viol). Argo RG 572 (LP, mono), ZRG 572 (LP, stereo); p. 190

1968: *Music from the 100 Years War*, Musica Reservata conducted by John Beckett. Music by Anon, Machaut, Vaillant, Dufay, Solage, Fontaine, Acourt, Dufay, Alanus, Cooke, Morton. Philips SAL 3722 (LP), Philips Trésors classiques 839 753 LY (LP, Germany), Philips 5 839 753 (LP, France); p. 191

1969: *Henry Purcell: Songs*, Frank Patterson (tenor), John Beckett (harpsichord) and Adam Skeaping (viola da gamba). Revision and thorough bass realization by John Beckett. 'If music be the food of love' (1693); 'Ah, how sweet it is to love'; 'Sweeter than roses'; 'Music for a while'; 'Fly swift, ye hours'; 'I'll sail upon the Dog-Star'; 'Since from my dear Astrea's sight'; 'If music be the food of love' (1695); 'Fairest Isle'; 'On the brow of Richmond Hill'; 'Oh solitude, my sweetest choice'; 'Mystery's song'; 'Cease, anxious world'; 'Not all my torments'; 'What a sad fate is mine'; 'Love, thou canst hear'. Philips SAL 3717, ALP 2728 (LP); pp. 198–9

1970: *Music from the time of Boccaccio's Decameron*, Musica Reservata conducted by John Beckett. Music by Landini, Anon, Giovani da Firenze, Gheradello da Firenze. Recorded in Wembley Town Hall, 21 and 22 February 1969. Philips Trésors classiques 802 904 LY (LP), Philips SAL 3781 (802 904 LY) (LP, UK); pp. 194, 201

1970: *Music from the Court of Burgundy*, Musica Reservata conducted by John Beckett. Music by Anon, Dufay and Morton. Philips Trésors classiques 6500 085 (LP); p. 226

1971: *A Florentine Festival*, Musica Reservata conducted by John Beckett. Music by Monteverdi, Marenzio, Malvezzi, Cavalieri, Festa, Anon, Trombocino, da Nola and Cara. Recorded in Kingsway Hall, London, May and August 1968. Argo ZRG 602 (LP); Decca Serenata 414 325-IDS (LP, 1985); reissued in a double-CD collection, *Early Music Festival*, Decca/London 289 452 967-2 (1998, see below); p. 186

1971: *Sixteenth Century Italian Dance Music*, Musica Reservata conducted by John Beckett. Music by Azzaiolo, Anon, Paccolini, Ruffo, Dalza. Recorded October 1970. Philips 6500 102 (LP); p. 208

1972: *An Elizabethan Evening*, Jaye Consort of Viols with Jantina Noorman (mezzo-soprano), Andrew Brunt (treble), Nigel Rogers (tenor), Desmond Dupré (lute) and John Beckett (virginals and organ). Music by Anon, Byrd, Morley, Farmer, Farnaby, Campian, Bull, Philips, Johnson, Rosseter, Dowland and Ravenscroft. Pye GSGC 14139; LP. Released as *A Bawdy Elizabethan Evening in Merrie Old England*, Legacy International, September 1994. Available as MP3 download, April 2008; pp. 229–30

1972: *Sixteenth Century French Dance Music*, Musica Reservata conducted by John Beckett. Recorded July 1971. Music by Anon, Claudin de Sermisy, Heckel, Pacoloni, Clemens non Papa, Janequin, Passereau, Courtois. Philips Trésors classiques 6500 293 (LP); p. 213

1970, 1979 (?): *Musik der Renaissance*, various artists including (tracks 19–26) Purcell Consort of Voices and Musica Reservata conducted by Grayston Burgess; John Beckett (treble viol). Tracks from *Music of the Early Renaissance: John Dunstable and his contemporaries* (1966). Vox FSM 33030/31 (double LP, Germany).

1972: *The Instruments of the Middle Ages and Renaissance*, Musica Reservata, John Beckett (tambourine, harpsichord, organ). Demonstration of musical instruments. Recorded Conway Hall, London, 1972. Vanguard VSD 7 1 219/20 (two LPs, 1972), Vanguard Classics 08 9095 72 (CD, Europe, 1997), Vanguard Classics (Omega) OVC 8093/94 (CD, USA); p. 228

1973, 1978: *Muziek voor kerk en kroeg. Hof en straat, liefde en lust, krijg en vrede tussen 1350 en 1500 / Musik für Kirche und Keipe / Musique d'église et de taverne du Moyen-âge à la Renaissance*, Musica Reservata conducted by John Beckett (organ, drum). Compilation of tracks from various Philips discs: *Music from the time of Christopher Columbus*, *Music from the 100 Years War*, *Music from the time of Boccaccio's Decameron* and *Music from the Court of Burgundy*. Recorded 1973 in UK. Philips 6833046 (LP, Netherlands, Germany), 6570043 (LP, France).

1974: *Elizabethan Heritage*, Vol. 1 and 2, The Madrigal Singers, conducted by Louis Halsey, Stuart Ward (tenor), Desmond Dupré (lute), John Beckett (harpsichord), English Consort of Viols, conducted by Dennis Nesbitt. Music by Thomas Morley, William Byrd, Francis Pilkington, Robert Jones, Philip Rosseter and Orlando Gibbons (Vol. 1), and Giles Farnaby, Mundy, Harding, Thomas Vautor, John Dowland, John Wilbye, Thomas Tomkins, William Byrd, Thomas Weelkes (Vol. 2). Saga 5347 and 5348; p. 251

1978: *A Concert of Early Music*, Musica Reservata, John Beckett (organ, tambourine). Music by Anon, Morton, Dunstable, Azzaiolo, Senfl, Certon, Dalza, de Vaqueiras, de Sermisy, Othmayr, Frye. Recorded in Conway Hall, London, 1972. Vanguard Classics VSD-71223 (LP, c. 1978), Vanguard (Omega) Classics SVC 96 (CD, 25/8/1998); p. 228–9

1979: *Carolan's Favourite – The Music of Carolan Volume 2*, played by Derek Bell (harp) with the Chieftains and the New Irish Chamber Orchestra, conducted by John Beckett. Claddagh Records CC 28 (LP), later released as a CD; p. 309

c. 1980: *Lieder und Tänze aus dem 13.–16. Jahrhundert*, boxed set of five previously issued Philips LPs: *Musik aus der Zeit Christoph Columbus* (839 714 LY), *Musik aus dem*

Hundertjährigen Krieg (839 753 LY), *Musik aus der Zeit von Boccaccios Decamerone* (802 904 LY), *Musik am Hofe von Burgund* (6500 085), *Italienische Tanzmusik des 16. Jahrhunderts* (6500 102). Philips 6747 004 (five LPs, Germany). UK edition named *The Sounde of Musicke: Songs and Dances from the 13th to the 16th Centuries*; no dates on box or notes.

1980: *Bernadette Greevy sings Bach Arias*, with the New Irish Chamber Orchestra conducted by John Beckett. Recorded in Saint Patrick's Hall, Dublin Castle, 1976. Claddagh Records CSM 53 St.; released as a CD in 1995, CSM53CD; pp. 264, 306

1987: *Derek Bell's Musical Ireland*, played by Derek Bell (harp, oboe, cor anglais) with members of the Chieftains and the New Irish Chamber Orchestra, conducted by John Beckett. Recorded May 1982. Claddagh Records, CC 35 (LP), CC35CD (CD).

1992: *Music from the time of Christopher Columbus*, Re-issue of 1968 recording. Philips 432 821-2 (CD).

1994: *Sixteenth Century Italian and French Dance Music*, Musica Reservata conducted by John Beckett. Compilation of tracks from *Sixteenth Century Italian Dance Music* (1971) and *Sixteenth Century French Dance Music* (1972). Music by Azzaiolo, Anon, Pacoloni, Dalza; Anon, de Sermisy, Pacoloni, Clemens non Papa, Janequin, Passereau. Boston Skyline BSD 123 (CD, USA); pp. 208, 213

1998: *Early Music Festival / Ein Fest mit Alter Musik / Festival de Musique ancienne*. A double CD compilation of two previous releases: 1. *Ecco la primavera – Florentine Music of the 14th century*, The Early Music Consort of London, directed by David Munrow, Argo ZRG 642 (LP), and 2. *A Florentine Festival*, Musica Reservata, conducted by John Beckett Argo ZRG 602 (LP). Decca London 289 452 967-2 (2 CDs).

2006: *Samuel Beckett: Works for Radio*. Set of four CDs issued by the BBC on 13 April. Disc 3: *Words and Music*, music by John Beckett; orchestra conducted by John Beckett. With Patrick Magee (Words) and Felix Felton (Croak). Produced by Michael Bakewell.

Appendix C
Radio Éireann, Telefís Éireann, RTÉ Radio and Television Programmes

Unless otherwise stated, the programmes listed are radio programmes. Radio Éireann and Telefís Éireann (television) became RTÉ Radio and Television in 1966.

Abbreviations for sources: RTVG: *RTV Guide*; RTÉG: *RTÉ Guide*; RTÉ SA: RTÉ Sound Archives; RTÉ DA: RTÉ Document Archives; RTÉ TVA: RTÉ TV Archives; IT: *The Irish Times*; II: *Irish Independent*; SI: *Sunday Independent*; CT: *Connacht Tribune*; TH: *Tuam Herald*; AC: *Anglo-Celt*.

Radio Éireann (and Telefís Éireann)

1944, 23 May, Radio Éireann, 8.00–8.45 pm: Second half of concert in the Metropolitan Hall, Dublin. *A Short Overture for Orchestra*, John Beckett; Symphony No. 4 in C Minor (Tragic), Schubert; Satirical Suite: *The House of Cards*, Op. 18a, Brian Boydell. Dublin Orchestral Players, conductor Brian Boydell. Boydell scrapbooks, Box 10, Printed programme; pp. 27, 28

27 October 1947, Radio Éireann, 9.20–9.50 pm, Music by Contemporary Irish Composers – No. 3, John Beckett. IT.

23 July 1950, Radio Éireann, 9.30–9.50 pm, Tomás Ó Súilleabháin, baritone, in songs by John Beckett. IT, SI; p. 59

29 September 1950, Radio Éireann, 7.15–8.35 pm, Mass in B minor, Bach, Part 1 (John Beckett, harpsichord.) IT; p. 64

30 September 1950, Radio Éireann, 7.00–8.15 pm, Mass in B minor, Bach, Part 2 (John Beckett, harpsichord.) IT; p. 64

2 February 1951, Radio Éireann, 7.30–7.50 pm, Corelli: Sonatas for two violins, cello and harpsichord. François d'Albert (violin), William Shanahan (violin), Betty Sullivan (cello), John Beckett (harpsichord). IT, II; p. 65

7 May 1951, Radio Éireann, 8.25–8.55 pm, *Monday Recital*: Dublin Harpsichord Ensemble, Piano Trio No. 7 in A major and Trio No. 4 in E major by Joseph Haydn. RTÉ DA; p. 67

2 July 1951, Radio Éireann, 7.30–8.10 pm, *Monday Recital*: Doris Cleary (flute), Francois d'Albert (violin), Betty Sullivan (cello), John Beckett (piano). Trio No. 31 in G for flute, cello and piano, Trio No. 26 in C for violin, cello and piano by Joseph Haydn and Adagio in B minor for piano by Mozart. IT, II, RTÉ DA; p. 71

25 July 1951, Radio Éireann, 9.05–9.35 pm, Schubert Piano Duets: John Beckett and Seán Lynch. IT, II; p. 71

23 January 1952, Radio Éireann, 7.30–8.20 pm, *Music Magazine*, including John Beckett on Beethoven's Sketch Books. II; p. 74

6 February 1952, Radio Éireann, 7.15–8.30 pm, *Music Magazine*, including John Beckett on Beethoven's Sketch Books. II; p. 74

11 February 1952, Radio Éireann, 9.15–9.55 pm, music by Couperin. Dublin Harpsichord Ensemble with John Beckett. RTÉ DA

30 April 1952, Radio Éireann, 7.10–7.50 pm, *Wednesday Recital:* Dublin Harpsichord Ensemble. Mollie Reynolds (soprano), François d'Albert (violin), Betty Sullivan (cello), Gilbert Berg (bassoon), John Beckett (harpsichord). Sonata in A by Handel, Toccatas by Frescobaldi and Bach's Cantata No. 160. 7.50–8.35 pm, *The Arts and the State:* a discussion between John Beckett, Seán O Faoláin and Thomas McGreevy, with Edgar M. Deale as Chairman. IT, II, RTÉ DA; p. 76

3 June 1952, Radio Éireann, 8.05–8.35 pm, Viola and harpsichord: Shirley Pollard and John Beckett. Sonata in G major for viola and harpsichord by William Flackton and Sonata in C minor for viola and harpsichord by W.F. Bach. IT, II, RTÉ DA.

16 July 1952, Radio Éireann, 7.45–8.30 pm, Dublin Harpsichord Ensemble: François d'Albert (violin), John Beckett (harpsichord). Violin Sonata in A, two Divertimenti in C and Violin Sonata in G by Joseph Haydn. RTÉ DA, TH; p. 78

5 August 1952, Radio Éireann, 7.20–7.40 pm, music by Purcell (?and Arne), Mary Johnston (soprano) and John Beckett (harpsichord). RTÉ DA.

13 August 1952, Radio Éireann, 9.25–9.40 pm, Buxtehude: *Jubilate Deo*, performed by Alfred Deller, counter-tenor; John Beckett (harpsichord) and Maurice Meulien (cello). CT.

22 September, 1952, Radio Éireann, 7.10–7.25 pm, *Music in Ireland*: A Book Talk by John Beckett. TH; p. 80

21 October 1952, Radio Éireann, 7.25–7.45 pm, *Songs of Gabriel Fauré*: Programme arranged by John Beckett. Singer: Tomás Ó Súilleabháin. II; pp. 78, 80, 81

28 October 1952, Radio Éireann, 6.50–7.10 pm, *Songs of Gabriel Fauré*: Programme arranged by John Beckett. Singer: Tomás Ó Súilleabháin. II; pp. 78, 80, 81

4 November 1952, Radio Éireann, 6.50–7.15 pm, *Songs of Gabriel Fauré*: Programme arranged by John Beckett. Singer: Tomás Ó Súilleabháin. II; pp. 78, 80, 81

8 December 1952, Radio Éireann, 7.05–7.25 pm, Philip Rodgers: recorder (accompanied on the harpsichord by John Beckett). II.

28 December 1952, Radio Éireann, 7.40–8.10 pm, *Music Magazine*, including the contribution *A Musical Holiday* by John Beckett. II; p. 81

19 January 1953, Radio Éireann, 8.15–8.30 pm, *Book Reviews*: John Beckett reviews four recently-published books, including *Notes Without Music* by Darius Milhaud. IT.

18 February 1953, Radio Éireann, 8.20–8.35 pm, *New Songs by Irish Composers (Second Series)*: No. 1, John Beckett. Singer: Arthur Moyse (tenor). II; p. 83, 403 (Eleven, note 2)

27 February 1953, Radio Éireann, 8.30–9.20 pm, *Lute, Harpsichord and Song*, with John Bilton (tenor), John Beckett (harpsichord) and Michael Morrow (lute). IT, II.

22 March 1953, Radio Éireann, 9.35–10.00 pm, *Elizabethan Love Songs* sung by Elizabeth Breen (soprano), with John Beckett (harpsichord). II.

13 April 1953, Radio Éireann, 7.20–7.40 pm, *Recorder and Harpsichord*: Philip Rodgers and John Beckett. (Possibly a repeat of programme on 8 December 1952.) II.

29 April 1953, Radio Éireann, 6.50–7.20 pm, music by Telemann, with Peter Schwarz (recorder), Raymond Flynn (oboe), Betty Sullivan (cello) and John Beckett (harpsichord). RTÉ DA.

17 June 1953, Radio Éireann, 6.45–7.15 pm, popular German songs of the 16th century arranged for organ and lute, Werner Schürmann (baritone), Michael Morrow (lute and recorder), John Beckett (organ and drum). RTÉ DA, II; p. 85

14 July 1953, Radio Éireann, 9.30–9.45 pm, *The Neo-Classicism of Stravinsky*: a talk by John Beckett. IT; p. 85

21 July–11 August 1953, Radio Éireann, 7.00–7.20 pm, *John Dowland's Achievement as a Song Writer*, devised and presented by John Beckett. With John Bilton (tenor) and Michael Morrow (lute and recorder). Programme 1: 21 July; Programme 2: 28 July; Programme 3: 4 August; Programme 4: 11 August. IT, II; p. 86

11 August, 1953, Radio Éireann, 8.00–9.00 pm, *Ravel's L'Enfant et les Sortilèges*: introduced by Brendan Burke, script by John Beckett. IT, II; p. 88

2 September 1953, Radio Éireann, 6.45–7.15 pm, *Wednesday Recital*: music by Bartók, Mozart and Telemann, performed by Musica da Camera, with John Beckett on piano, celeste and harpsichord. RTÉ DA, II; p. 89

9 September 1953, Radio Éireann, 6.45–7.15 pm, *Music of J.S. Bach*: Sonatas in A major and B minor, played by François d'Albert (violin), John Beckett (harpsichord) and Betty Sullivan (cello). RTÉ DA, II, p. 89.

27 September 1953, Radio Éireann, 6.01–6.20 pm, *Voice and Harpsichord*: Alfred Deller and John Beckett. IT; p. 89

14 October 1953, Radio Éireann, 6.50–7.15 pm, *Wednesday Recital*: Alfred Deller and John Beckett, harpsichord. CT; p. 89

19 October 1953, Radio Éireann, 7.15–7.35 pm, *Music of J.S. Bach*: Sonata in G major, played by François d'Albert (violin), John Beckett (harpsichord) and Betty Sullivan (cello). RTÉ DA, II; p. 89

26 October 1953, Radio Éireann, 7.15–7.35 pm, *Music of J.S. Bach*: Sonata in C minor, played by François d'Albert (violin), John Beckett (harpsichord) and Betty Sullivan (cello). RTÉ DA, II; p. 89

2 November 1953, Radio Éireann, 7.15–7.35 pm, *Music of J.S. Bach*; Sonata in E Major, played by François D'Albert (violin), John Beckett (harpsichord), and Betty Sullivan (cello). II; p. 89

9 November 1953, Radio Éireann, 7.15–7.35 pm, *Music of J.S. Bach*; Sonata in F Minor, played by François d'Albert (violin), John Beckett (harpsichord) and Betty Sullivan (cello). II; p. 89

28 June 1956, Radio Éireann, 11.15–11.30 pm, *Cello and Harpsichord*: Christopher Bunting (cello) and John Beckett (harpsichord). IT; p. 108

5 September 1956, Radio Éireann, 6.45–7.30 pm, *Recital*: Piano duets, and music for cello and harpsichord played by Christopher Bunting (cello), John Beckett (piano and harpsichord) and John O'Sullivan (piano). IT, II; p. 108

30 September, 1956, Radio Éireann, 7.30–8.15 pm, *Mozart's Son*: illustrated talk by John Beckett on the life of Franz Xaver Mozart, with Jaroslav Vaneček (violin), Rhona Marshall (piano) and Michael Ledwith (tenor). Repeated 15 January 1957. IT, II; p. 108

31 October 1956, Radio Éireann, 6.45–7.30 pm, *Wednesday Recital*: music by W.A. Mozart's father and son with John Beckett (harpsichord), Jaroslav Vaneček (violin), Maurice Meulien (cello), Rhona Marshall (piano) and Michael Ledwith (tenor). IT; p. 108

26 November 1956, Radio Éireann, 11.15–11.30 pm, *Music for harpsichord and recorder* played by John Beckett and John Sothcott. IT.

12 June 1957, Radio Éireann, 6.45–7.30 pm, *Wednesday Recital*: Jürgen Hess (violin), Betty Sullivan (cello) and John Beckett (piano). IT.

7 July 1958, Radio Éireann, 6.45–7.15 pm, Schubert: Music for piano duo played by John Beckett and Harold Lester. IT.

18 August 1958, Radio Éireann, 10.30–10.45 pm, Music for piano duo played by John Beckett and Harold Lester. IT.

28 January, 1959, Radio Éireann, 6.45–7.30 pm, *Wednesday Recital*: Music by Schubert and Lennox Berkeley played by Harold Lester and John Beckett (piano duo). IT.

3 April 1959, Radio Éireann, 10.45–11.00 pm, Brahms: Harold Lester and John Beckett, piano duo. IT.

10 April 1959, Radio Éireann, 10.45–11.00 pm, Brahms: Harold Lester and John Beckett, piano duo. IT.

29 July 1959, Radio Éireann, 6.45–7.30 pm, *Music Makers*: The Dublin Chamber Orchestra. John Beckett introduces three Mozart compositions. IT.

2 September 1959, Radio Éireann, 7.00–7.45 pm, *Music Makers*: John Beckett introduces music by Wolf and Fauré. IT.

4 January 1960, Radio Éireann, 6.45–7.15 pm, Harold Lester and John Beckett (piano duet). IT.

24 August 1960, Radio Éireann, 6.45–7.30 pm, *Music Makers*: Schubert's *Grand Duo* played by Harold Lester and John Beckett, piano duet. IT.

3 September 1960, Radio Éireann, 10.45–11.00 pm, Mozart: Sonata in D, K. 381, for harpsichord duet, played by Harold Lester and John Beckett. IT.

30 November 1961, Radio Éireann, 9.30–10.00 pm, *Personal Choice*: Some great performances of great music selected and presented by John Beckett. IT; p. 139

7 December 1961, Radio Éireann, 9.30–10.00 pm, *Personal Choice*: Some great performances of great music selected and presented by John Beckett. IT; p. 139

14 December 1961, Radio Éireann, 9.30–10.00 pm, *Personal Choice*: Schubert: Three Songs from *Die Schöne Müllerin*; Chopin: Three Preludes from Op. 28; Mussorgsky: Four Songs. RTVG; p. 139

21 December 1961, Radio Éireann, 9.30–10.00 pm, *Personal Choice*: Schönberg: First scene from *Moses and Aaron*; Haydn: Representation of Chaos from *The Creation*; Stravinsky: Extracts from the ballet *Agon*. RTVG; p. 139

26 May 1962, Radio Éireann, 5.01–5.15 pm, *Piano Duets for Young Listeners* played by John Beckett and John O'Sullivan. CT, RTVG.

25 July 1962, Radio Éireann, 10.45–11.00 pm, Bach Recital: Prelude and Fugue in G sharp minor (Book 2 of the 48); Prelude and Fugue in A flat major (Book 2 of the 48). John Beckett (harpsichord). IT, RTVG.

29 August 1962, Radio Éireann, 10.45–11.00 pm, *Recital*: Movements (*Minuet, Gavotte, Sarabande, Passepied, Courant*) from Bach's English Suites arranged by John Beckett for recorder and harpsichord. John Sothcott, recorder, John Beckett, harpsichord. CT, RTVG.

8, 12, 15, 19, 22 November 1962, Radio Éireann, 5.40–5.55 pm, Piano duets played for young listeners by John Beckett and John O'Sullivan. RTVG.

5 December 1962, Radio Éireann, 10.45–11.00 pm, Henry Purcell: Airs, grounds and dances, played by John Beckett, harpsichord. RTVG.

2, 9, 16 January 1963, Radio Éireann, *Music Can Tell* – John Beckett explains how. Music for children. No. 1: 5.40–5.55 pm; No. 2: 5.15–5.30 pm; No. 3: 5.45–5.55 pm RTVG; p. 143

15 May 1963, Radio Éireann, 10.45–11.00, Recital: Haydn, *Sonatina in F major*, *Sonatina in C major*. John Beckett, harpsichord. RTVG.

14 November 1963, Radio Éireann, 9.15–9.45, Recital: Bach: Partita in B minor. John Beckett, harpsichord. AC, RTVG; p. 150

3 December 1963, Radio Éireann, 9.01–10.00 pm, Orchestral Concert. Haydn: Symphony No. 43 in E flat; Mozart: Motet *Ave Verum*; Mozart: Mass in C, K. 317 ('Coronation'). Radio Éireann Symphony Orchestra Group, St James's Gate Choral Society, soloists, conductor John Beckett. RTVG; p. 151

10 December 1963, Radio Éireann, 9.01–10.00 pm, Orchestral Concert. Mozart: Two Marches in D (K. 249 and K. 335); Haydn: Symphony No. 53 in D (*l'Impériale*); Mozart: Motet *Exultate, Jubilate* (K. 165). Radio Éireann Symphony Orchestra Group, Barbara Elsy (soprano), conductor John Beckett. RTVG.

3 June 1964, Telefís Éireann, 10.50–11.09, *Music Room*: recital of harpsichord music by Henry Purcell. *Trumpet Tune, A New Irish Tune, Minuet, Sefauchi's Farewell, Hornpipe, Ground, A New Ground, A New Scotch Tune, Air*. IT, RTVG; p. 154

17 June 1964, Telefís Éireann, 10.50–11.05, *Music Room*: recital of music by Mozart and Haydn. Mozart: *Andante, Allegro, Menuett* and *Allegro*; Haydn: Sonata No. 1 in C: *Allegro, Andante, Menuett*. IT, RTVG; p. 154

21 July 1964, Radio Éireann, 11.00–11.30, Bach: Partita No. 6 in E minor. John Beckett, harpsichord. RTVG; p. 155

18 February 1965, Radio Éireann, 9.15–9.45, *Masters and Moderns*: Songs by Purcell, sung by Barbara Elsy. Harpsichord: John Beckett. (Also Gunther Bialas: Sinfonia Piccola. The Radio Éireann Symphony Orchestra Group, conductor Hans Waldemar Rosen.) RTVG; p. 158

4 March 1965, Radio Éireann, 10.45–11.00 pm, Recital: French Suite No. 5 in G by Bach. John Beckett, harpsichord. IT; p. 158

25 March 1965, Radio Éireann, 9.15–9.45 pm, *Masters and Moderns*: Bach: Cantata No. 54, *Widerstehe doch der Sünde*; Grayston Burgess (counter-tenor), Radio Éireann Symphony Orchestra Group, conductor John Beckett. (Also Seoirse Bodley: *An Bás is an Bheatha*; Radio Éireann Singers, conductor Hans Waldemar Rosen.) RTVG; p. 158

11 November 1965, Radio Éireann, 9.15–9.45 pm, *Masters and Moderns*: Including three arias by Monteverdi. Grayston Burgess (counter-tenor), John Beckett (harpsichord), Betty Sullivan (cello). RTVG.

12 November 1965, Radio Éireann, 9.01–10.00 pm, Symphony Concert, including J.C. Bach: Sinfonia, Op. 18, No. 4 in D; J.S. Bach: Concerto in E for harpsichord and orchestra. The Radio Éireann Symphony Orchestra, conductor Tibor Paul, soloist John Beckett. RTVG.

25 November 1965, Radio Éireann, 9.15–9.45 pm, *Masters and Moderns*: including Bach's Cantata No. 202, *Weichet nur, betrübte Schatten*; soloist Barbara Elsy. Radio Éireann Symphony Orchestra Group, conductor John Beckett. RTVG.

18 March 1966, Radio Éireann, 9.01–10.00 pm, Symphony Concert, including Bach's Brandenburg Concerto No. 5; David Lillis (violin), André Prieur (flute) and John Beckett (harpsichord). The Radio Éireann Symphony Orchestra, conductor Tibor Paul. RTVG.

13 April 1966, Radio Éireann, 11.15–11.30 pm, Recital: John Beckett introduces and plays harpsichord music from a 16th-century manuscript in Trinity College, Dublin. (The first of two talks). RTVG.

14 April 1966, Radio Éireann, 11.15–11.30 pm, Recital: John Beckett introduces and plays harpsichord music from a 16th-century manuscript in Trinity College, Dublin. (The second of two talks). RTVG.

RTÉ Radio (and Television)

22 September 1966, RTÉ Radio, 9.15–9.45 pm, *Masters and Moderns*: including Fauré's Five Chansons sung by Barbara Elsy (soprano), with John Beckett (piano).

15 December 1966, RTÉ Radio, 9.15–9.45 pm, *Masters and Moderns*: including two cantatas by Telemann, *Ihr Völker hört* and *Ew'ge Quelle, milder Strom*. Frank Patterson (tenor), John Beckett (harpsichord), Edward Beckett (flute) and Betty Sullivan (cello). RTÉG.

8 March 1967, RTÉ Radio, 9.01–9.45 pm, Recital: including ten pieces for harpsichord by Henry Purcell, recorded at Waterford Music Club, performed by John Beckett. RTÉG.

16 March 1967, RTÉ Radio, 9.15–9.45 pm, *Masters and Moderns*: including Bach's Cantata No. 12, *Was ist mir doch das Rühmen nütze?* Frank Patterson (tenor), Edward Beckett (flute), John Beckett (harpsichord) and Betty Sullivan (cello). RTÉG.

30 March 1967, RTÉ Radio, 9.15–9.45 pm, *Masters and Moderns*: including Byrd's Prelude and Fantasia for harpsichord, played by John Beckett, and Telemann's Fantasia No. 8 in C minor for solo flute, played by Edward Beckett. RTÉG.

27 April 1967, RTÉ Television, 10.10–11.35 pm, *The Music of Swift's Dublin*. Concert celebrating the tercentenary of Johathan Swift's birthday, held in Dublin Castle. Written and introduced by Brian Boydell; music arrangements by John Beckett, who also plays the harpsichord. With Hugh Maguire (violin), Iona Brown (violin), Edward Beckett (flute), Betty Sullivan (cello), Nigel Rogers (tenor), Cáit Lanigan (soprano) and Catriona Yeats (harp). RTÉG; p. 175

27 April 1967, RTÉ Radio, 10.45–11.00 pm, Recital: Five pieces from the Anna Magdalena Notebook by Bach, played by John Beckett, harpsichord. RTÉG.

31 May 1967, RTÉ Radio, 9.01–9.45 pm, The RTÉ String Quartet: David Lillis and Audrey Park (violins), Archie Collins (viola) and Coral Bognuda (cello), with John Beckett (harpsichord). Purcell: Sonata in G minor for two violins and continuo; Mozart: Quartet in C major, K. 465 (*The Dissonance*). RTÉG

5 July 1967, RTÉ Radio, 9.01–9.45 pm, Cremona String Quartet: Hugh Maguire and Trevor Connah (violins), Cecil Aronowitz (viola) and Terence Well (cello). With John Beckett (harpsichord). William Byrd: Praeludium and Fantasia. Brahms: Quartet in C Minor Op. 51, No. 1. Recorded at the R.D.S. Concert Hall, Ballsbridge. RTÉG

19 July 1967, RTÉ Radio, 9.01–9.45 pm, The RTÉ String Quartet, with John Beckett, harpsichord. William Byrd: 5 Pieces from the Firzwilliam Virginal Book; Bartók: String Quartet No. 2 Op. 17. RTÉG.

13 September 1967, RTÉ Radio, 9.01–9.45 pm, The RTÉ String Quartet, with John Beckett, harpsichord. Purcell: Trio Sonata in A; Turina: *La Oración del Torero*; Bartók: Quartet No. 1. RTÉG.

25 October 1967, RTÉ Radio, 9.01–9.45 pm, The RTÉ String Quartet, with John Beckett, harpsichord. Purcell: Trio Sonata in G minor; Frederick May: String Quartet. RTÉG.

30 November 1967, RTÉ Radio, 10.35–11.30 pm, Abridged repeat of *The Music of Swift's Dublin*. RTÉG.

14 March 1968, RTÉ Radio, 10.45–11.00 pm, Recital: John Beckett, harpsichord. Henry Purcell: ten pieces for harpsichord. IT, RTÉG.

19 June 1968, RTÉ Radio, 9.01–9.45 pm, The RTÉ String Quartet, with John Beckett, harpsichord. Purcell: Trio Sonata in G minor; Bartók: Quartet No. 1, Opus 7. RTÉG.

30 July 1968, RTÉ Radio, 7.45–8.00 pm, Songs by Purcell: Werner Schürmann (baritone), John Beckett (harpsichord) and Betty Sullivan (cello). RTÉG.

24 December 1968, RTÉ Radio, 9.55–11.20 pm, Highlights from Handel's *Messiah*. Recordings from a performance given at the National Stadium in Dublin on Wednesday, 18 December. Soloists: Mary Sheridan (soprano), Bernadette Greevy (contralto), Patrick Ring (tenor), Paschal Allen (bass), John Beckett (harpsichord), with Our Lady's Choral Society. The RTÉ Symphony Orchestra. Conductor: Aloys Fleischmann. RTÉG.

9 January 1969, RTÉ Television, 10.25–11.00 pm, *The Golden Age*: A series of four fortnightly recitals featuring eighteenth-century instrumental music and Henry Purcell songs. Frank Patterson (tenor), Hugh Maguire and Iona Brown (violins), Edward Beckett (flute), John Beckett (harpsichord), Betty Sullivan (cello). IT, RTÉG.

14 January 1969, RTÉ Radio, 3.30–3.45 pm, *Music Matters*: Chamber music by Purcell, played by the RTE String Quartet with John Beckett, harpsichord. RTÉG.

27 February 1969, RTÉ Television, 10.55–11.25 pm, *The Golden Age*: the second programme in the series. RTÉG; p. 190

13 March 1969, RTÉ Television, 10.55–11.25 pm, *The Golden Age*: the third programme in the series. RTÉG; p. 190

27 March 1969, RTÉ Television, 10.55–11.25 pm, *The Golden Age*: the fourth programme in the series. RTÉG; p. 190

5 June 1969, RTÉ Television, 3.00–3.50 pm, Telefís Scoile (Television for Schools),

English Literature: No. 15, Portrait of a Poet. A biographical account on film of the life of W.B. Yeats. With Niall Tóibín and Ginette Wadell. Narrator: Padraic O Neill. Music composed by John Beckett. Produced by James Plunkett. Repeated 25 May 1970, 11 March 1971, 24 February 1972. RTÉG; p. 196

24 July 1969, RTÉ Radio, 10.20–10.45 pm, *From the Golden Age of the Madrigal.* Brian Boydell conducts the RTÉ Singers in madrigals by Thomas Weelkes. Keyboard music by William Byrd, John Beckett (harpsichord). RTÉG.

7 October 1970, RTÉ Radio, 10.30–11.15 pm, *Anthology: A Shade Superior to Monsieur Kozeluch.* The first of two recitals devised by John Beckett to mark the bicentenary of the birth of Beethoven. Including Frank Patterson singing five of the traditional Irish airs arranged by Beethoven, accompanied by John Beckett (piano), David Lillis (violin), and Betty Sullivan (violincello). RTÉG; p. 209

22 October 1970, RTÉ Radio, 10.20–10.45 pm, *English Music from three centuries.* Ancient and modern madrigals and pieces for harpsichord. John Beckett (harpsichord) and the RTÉ Singers, conducted by Peter Gellhorn. RTÉG.

2 December, 1970, RTÉ Radio, 10.30–11.15 pm, *Anthology: A Shade Superior to Monsieur Kozeluch.* The second of two recitals devised by John Beckett to mark the bicentenary of the birth of Beethoven. Including five Irish traditional airs, arranged by Beethoven and sung by Bernadette Greevy, contralto, accompanied by John Beckett, piano. IT, RTÉG; p. 210

17 March 1971, RTÉ Television, 8.00–9.00 pm, *Bird's Eye View – Inis Fáil.* A journey by helicopter over Ireland, in search of her legends and history, her poetry and music, her tourist attractions, and her way of thinking and living. A BBC/RTÉ Production. Scripted and presented by James Plunkett. Music specially composed and conducted by John Beckett. The RTÉ Symphony Orchestra; Frank Patterson (tenor). Repeated 8 May 1972. RTÉG; p. 211

5 October 1971, RTÉ Television, 10.20–11.00 pm, *The age of the Troubadours*, Musica Reservata, conducted by John Beckett. French and Englsih music and songs of the 13th century. RTÉG; pp. 203, 221

2 November 1971, RTÉ Television, 10.20–11.15 pm, *Haydn in London.* The first of two programmes presented by John Beckett, in which he evokes the flavour of Joseph Haydn's day-to-day life in London during his two visits there towards the end of his long career. Including songs sung by Frank Patterson, the Trio in C for two flutes and cello (with Edward Beckett, Patricia Dunkerly, flutes and Betty Sullivan, cello), and the Trio in D played by John Beckett (piano), Margaret Hayes (violin) and Betty Sullivan (cello). Recorded in the National Gallery, Dublin. RTÉG; pp. 210, 213, 222

9 November 1971, RTÉ Television, 10.20–11.15 pm, *Haydn in London.* The second of two programmes presented by John Beckett. Including Scottish and English songs sung by Frank Patterson and the Trio in E flat played by John Beckett (piano), Margaret Hayes (violin) and Betty Sullivan (cello). RTÉG; pp. 210, 213, 222

6 December 1971, RTÉ Television, 7.50–9.30 pm, *The State of the Nation*. The story of the political development of the State from the signing of the Anglo-Irish *Articles of Agreement for a Treaty* in December 1921 up to the beginning of the Second World War, compiled from actuality film of the period. Written by James Plunkett. Music composed and conducted by John Beckett. Repeated 17 April 1972. RTÉ Light Orchestra. RTÉG; p. 223

16 January 1972, RTÉ Radio, 9.05–10.05 pm, *Ceolchoirm Chuimhneacha Sheán Uí Riada*: Part 2 of a Seán Ó Riada Memorial Concert from the Gaiety Theatre, Dublin. Ó Riada: *Nomos*, No. 2. The RTÉ Symphony Orchestra, conducted by Albert Rosen. William Young (baritone), John Beckett (harpsichord). With the RTÉ Singers, the RTÉ Choral Society and the Choir of the German Institute. RTÉG; p. 226

18 January 1972, RTÉ Television, 10.20–11.10 pm, *Music on Tuesday*: Part 2 of the Seán Ó Riada Memorial Concert from the Gaiety Theatre, Dublin. Ó Riada: *Nomos*, No. 2. (Televised production of the concert on 16 January.) RTÉG; p. 226

22 March 1972, RTÉ Radio, 10.30–10.45 pm, *Music Room*: The first of two recitals of 14th and 15th century keyboard music introduced and played by John Beckett. RTÉG.

29 March 1972, RTÉ Radio, 10.30–10.45 pm, *Music Room*: The second of two recitals of 14th and 15th century keyboard music introduced and played by John Beckett. RTÉG.

12 February 1973, RTÉ Radio, 10.00–10.35 pm, *Music Room*: Music by Haydn, introduced by John Beckett. *Variations in F minor* for piano; Piano Trio No. 45 in E flat. Margaret Hayes (violin), Betty Sullivan (cello), John Beckett (piano). Recorded at Knockmaroon House, Co. Dublin. RTÉG; p. 229

24 May 1973, RTÉ Radio, 10.20–10.45 pm, Songs by Haydn. The first of two programmes. Frank Patterson (tenor), John Beckett (square piano); the RTÉ Singers, conductor, Hans Waldemar Rosen. Recorded in Knockmaroon House. RTÉG; p. 229

31 May 1973, RTÉ Radio, 10.20–10.45 pm, Songs by Haydn. The second of two programmes. Frank Patterson (tenor), John Beckett (square piano); the RTÉ Singers, conductor, Hans Waldemar Rosen. Recorded in Knockmaroon House. RTÉG; p. 229

25 June 1973, RTÉ Radio, 10.00–10.35, *Music Room*: Music by Bach. Sonata in G for flute, violin and continuo (arranged from the Organ Sonata in E flat by John Beckett); three songs from the Schemelli Song Book; Sonata in E minor for two violins and continuo (arranged from the Organ Sonata in D minor by John Beckett). Edward Beckett (flute), Mary Gallagher and Thérèse Timoney (violins), Frank Patterson (tenor), John Beckett (harpsichord) and Betty Sullivan (cello). RTÉG.

8 August, 1973, RTÉ Radio, 10.30–11.00 pm, *Music Room*. The first of two recitals given by Helmut Seeber (oboe), John Beckett (harpsichord) and Betty Sullivan (cello). Telemann: Sonata in G minor. Fiocco: Arioso. Repeated 14 November 1973. IT, II. (Different programme in RTÉ Guide; repeat correct.)

15 August 1973, RTÉ Radio, 10.30–10.45 pm, *Music Room*. The second of two recitals given by Helmut Seeber (oboe), John Beckett (harpsichord) and Betty Sullivan (cello).

Telemann: Sonata in A minor; Handel: Sonata in G minor. Repeated 21 November 1973. IT, II. (Different programme in RTÉ Guide; repeat correct.)

24 September 1973, RTÉ Radio, 10.00–10.35 pm, *Music Room*. Bach: Sonata No. 1 in G minor for unaccompanied violin; Trio Sonata in G for two flutes and continuo. Brian McNamara (violin), Edward Beckett and James Galway (flutes), John Beckett (harpsichord) and Betty Sullivan (cello). RTÉG.

25 October 1973, RTÉ Television, 10.30–11.25 pm, *Scope*: Killarney Bach Festival, filmed in July 1973. With Katharine Hansel (soprano), Ruth Maher (contralto), Frank Patterson (tenor), Patricia Dunkerley (flute), John Beckett (harpsichord) and Gerard Gillen (organ). The Guinness Choir and the New Irish Chamber Orchestra. Musical director: George Manos. RTÉG; p. 243

25 February 1974, RTÉ Radio, 10.00–10.35 pm, *Music Room*: Music by Fauré. *Elégie*, Opus 24 and *Sicilienne*, Opus 78 for cello and piano. Song Cycle, *La chanson d'Eve*, Opus 95. Anne Woodworth (mezzo-soprano), John Beckett (piano), Betty Sullivan (cello). Introduced by John Beckett. RTÉG.

4 March 1974, RTÉ Television, 7.20–7.55 pm, *Two Thousand Miles of Peril*, a George Morrison Production for The Lifeboat Service of Ireland, music by John Beckett. RTÉG; p. 248

12 June 1974, RTÉ Radio, 10.25–10.40 pm, *Music Room*. The first of two programmes given by the Henry Purcell Consort. Five dances from the Fitzwilliam Virginal Book; William Lawes: Five Court Ayres for violin and continuo. Thérèse Timoney (violin), Betty Sullivan (viola da gamba) and John Beckett (harpsichord). Introduced by John Beckett. RTÉG.

19 June 1974, RTÉ Radio, 10.25–10.40 pm, *Music Room*. The second of two programmes given by the Henry Purcell Consort. Purcell: Four pieces for harpsichord; Violin Sonata in G minor. Thérèse Timoney (violin), John Beckett (harpsichord) and Betty Sullivan (viola da gamba). Introduced by John Beckett. RTÉG.

13 September 1974, RTÉ Radio, 10.00–11.00 pm, *Orchestral Concert*. Haydn: Symphony No. 67 in F, conductor: John Beckett. The RTÉ Symphony Orchestra, leader: Joseph Maher. RTÉG; p. 251

11 March 1975, RTÉ Radio, 9.45–10.00 pm, *Music Room*. John Beckett introduces the first of two harpsichord recitals in which he plays pieces from the Dublin Virginals Manuscript. RTÉG; p. 255

17 March 1975, RTÉ Television, 8.00–9.00 pm, *The Light of Other Days*. Irish life at the turn of the century in the photographs of Robert French, from the Lawrence Collection. Made by B.A.C. Films, directed by Kieran Hickey. *Oft in the Stilly Night* sung by Frank Patterson, accompanied by John Beckett. Flute solos performed by Edward Beckett. Repeated 17 March 1980. RTÉ TVA, RTÉG; p. 227

18 March 1975, RTÉ Radio, 8.45–9.00 pm, *Music Room*. John Beckett introduces the second of two harpsichord recitals in which he plays pieces from the Dublin Virginals Manuscript. IT; p. 255

24 April 1975, RTÉ Radio, 8.45–9.00 pm, *Music Room*. Anne Woodworth (mezzo-soprano), Mary Gallagher (violin), Ruth David (viola) and John Beckett (piano). Fauré: Berceuse Op. 16. Brahms: Two songs, Op. 91. RTÉG.

30 June 1975, 4.01–4.30 pm, *Music Magazine*. John Beckett talks about Schubert and Seoirse Bodley discusses recent records. IT, RTÉG.

13 July 1975, RTÉ Radio, 11.00–11.20 pm, *Oboe Virtuoso*. Lothar Faber, oboe, with John Beckett (harpsichord) and Betty Sullivan (cello), plays sonatas by Handel and Vivaldi. RTÉG.

29 July, 1975, RTÉ Radio, 8.00–8.45 pm, *Music Room*. Bach-Busoni: Chaconne in D. Hanae Nakajima (piano). Bach: Cantata No. 199, *Mein Herze schwimmt in Blut*, Nora Ring (soprano), New Irish Chamber Orchestra, conductor John Beckett. IT, RTÉG.

4 September 1975, RTÉ Radio, 4.01–4.30 pm, *Afternoon Recital*. Songs by Schubert, introduced by John Beckett and sung by Bernadette Greevy (contralto), with John Beckett (piano). RTÉG.

21 October 1975, RTÉ Radio, 8.01–8.45 pm, *Music Room*. Songs by Henry Purcell, performed by the Henry Purcell Consort: Irené Sandford (soprano), Frank Patterson (tenor), Arthur McIvor (violin), John Beckett (harpsichord) and Betty Sullivan (viola da gamba). RTÉG.

10 November 1975, RTÉ Radio, 9.20–10.00, The RTÉ Singers, conductor Proinsias Ó Duinn. Music by Monteverdi and Telemann. Soloists: James Galway and Edward Beckett (flutes) and John Beckett (piano). Repeated 12 July 1976. RTÉ Sound Archives, RTÉG.

1 December 1975, RTÉ Radio, 9.20–10.00 pm, *Music for the Christmas season*. John Beckett (piano); the RTÉ Singers, conducted by Proinnsias Ó Duinn. RTÉG, p. 260

8 December 1975, RTÉ Radio, 9.20–10.00 pm, *Music for the Christmas season*. John Beckett (piano and celeste), Andrew Robinson (guitar), Alfred Barry and John Fennessy (percussion); the RTÉ Singers, conducted by Proinnsias Ó Duinn. RTÉG, p. 260

22 December 1975, RTÉ Radio, 9.15–10.00 pm, *Music for the Christmas season*. John Beckett (harpsichord); the RTÉ Singers, conducted by Proinnsias Ó Duinn. RTÉG, p. 260

23 December 1975, RTÉ Television, 9.50–10.20 pm, *Bernadette sings Johann Sebastian Bach*. A recital in the National Gallery, Dublin, given by Bernadette Greevy, with the New Irish Chamber Orchestra, conducted by John Beckett. Bach: Cantata No. 53, *Schlage doch, gewünschte Stunde*; Aria from Cantata No. 30, *Freue dich, erlöste Schar*; song from the Anna Magdalena Book; aria from the *Saint Matthew Passion*. (One of a series of six programmes recorded in the National Gallery, two of which featured John.) RTÉG, RTÉ TVA; p. 260, 264

29 December 1975, RTÉ Radio, 9.20–10.00 pm, *Portrait of Winter*. John Beckett (harpsichord). Áine Moynihan and Conor Farrington, readers. The RTÉ Singers, conductor, Prionnsias Ó Duinn. RTÉG.

23 February 1976, RTÉ Radio, 9.15–10.00 pm, Palestrina: *Tantum Ergo, Sicut Cervus*; Galuppi: Cello Sonata in D; Zimmermann: Vespers. RTÉ Singers, conducted by Proinnsias Ó Duinn with John Beckett (harpsichord), Philomena Madden (double bass), John Fennessy (vibraphone), Vincenzo Caminiti (cello), Veronica McSwiney (piano). Repeated 26 July 1976. IT.

7 April 1976, RTÉ Radio, 4.01–4.30 pm, *Afternoon Recital*. Songs by Brahms sung by Bernadette Greevy with Ruth David (viola) and John Beckett (piano). Introduced by John Beckett. RTÉG; p. 264

12 April 1976, RTÉ Radio, 9.15–10.00 pm, The RTÉ Singers, conductor Proinnsias Ó Duinn, with Gerard Gillen (organ), John Beckett (harpsichord) and Brighid Mooney (cello). Organ music by Bach and *Stabat Mater* by Domenico Scarlatti. RTÉG.

9 November 1976, RTÉ Television, 9.00–9.30 pm, *Look to the Sea*. Five thousand years of fishing in the West of Ireland, encapsulated in a film directed by George Morrison. Music by John Beckett. Repeated 1 January 1978. IT, RTÉG; pp. 259–60, 267

9 November 1976, RTÉ Television, 9.50–11.30 pm, *Bernadette Greevy – a musical profile*. A filmed portrait of soprano Bernadette Greevy, in which she talks to Andy O'Mahony about her career and sings the music of those composers most closely linked with her name – Bach, Schubert, Berlioz, Mahler and Elgar. Featuring, among others, the New Irish Chamber Orchestra conducted by John Beckett. RTÉG

10 December 1976, RTÉ Radio, 8.01–9.00 pm, *Orchestral Concert*. Including John Kinsella: *A Selected Life*, in memory of Seán Ó Riada. A setting of the poem by Thomas Kinsella. With Patrick Ring (tenor), Peter McBrien (speaker), John Beckett (harpsichord), David Carmody (bodhrán) and the RTÉ Choral Society. RTÉG; p. 267

14 December 1976, RTÉ Radio, 8.01–8.30 pm, *The RTÉ Singers*. The fourth in a series of programmes in which the RTÉ Singers are joined by a guest conductor. This week: John Poole with John Beckett (piano and organ). Music by Monteverdi, Haydn, Schubert and Brahms. RTÉG.

12 May 1977, RTÉ Television, 9.00–9.30 pm, *Bernadette Greevy at the National Gallery*. Mahler: *Blumine*; *Lieder: Wer hat dies Liedlein erdacht?*, *Liebst du um Schönheit*, *Ich atmet' einen Linden Duft*, *Blicke mir nicht in die Lieder*, *Ich bin der Welt abhanden gekommen*. The New Irish Chamber Orchestra, conductor John Beckett. (Another of the series of six programmes recorded in the National Gallery, two of which featured John.) RTÉG; p. 272–3

7 June 1977, RTÉ Radio, 8.01–8.30 pm, The RTÉ Singers, conducted by Eric Sweeney. Music by Schütz, Hassler and Buxtehude. With Mary Gallagher and Thérèse Timoney (violins), Andrew Robinson (viola da gamba) and John Beckett (organ). RTÉG.

21 June 1977, RTÉ Radio, 8.01–8.30 pm, The RTÉ Singers, conducted by Eric Sweeney. Monteverdi: *Ond'ei, di morte*; Bach: *Lobet den Herrn, alle Heiden*; Ina Boyle: Five Gaelic Hymns. With John Beckett (harpsichord) and Brighid Mooney (cello). RTÉG.

23 June 1977, RTÉ Radio, 8.45–9.00 pm, *Music Room*. Geminiani: Sonata in E minor,

Telemann: Sonata in A minor. The first of two recitals given by Helmut Seeber (oboe), John Beckett (harpsichord) and Betty Sullivan (cello). RTÉG.

28 June 1977, RTÉ Radio, 8.01–8.30 pm, The RTÉ Singers, conducted by John Murphy with John Beckett (harpsichord). Music by Weelkes, Tomkins, Gretchaninov, Ó Laoghaire, Kodály and Hindemith. RTÉG.

30 June 1977, RTÉ Radio, 8.45–9.00 pm, *Music Room.* The second of two recitals given by Helmut Seeber (oboe), John Beckett (harpsichord) and Betty Sullivan (cello). Rameau: *Gavotte;* Telemann: Partita No. 2 in G. RTÉG.

3 August 1977, RTÉ Radio, 4.01–4.30 pm, *Afternoon Recital.* Songs by Gustav Mahler. Bernadette Greevy and John Beckett; introduced by John Beckett. Repeated 16 October 1977, 18 January 1978. RTÉ Sound Archives, RTÉG, IT; pp. 273

3 September 1977, RTÉ Television, 7.00–7.45 pm, *Portrait of a Library.* A filmed account of the work and history of the National Library of Ireland, with tributes from Edna O'Brien, Seán Ó Faoláin, Mary Lavin and Terence de Vere White. Script by Maurice J. Craig. Commentary spoken by Cyril Cusack. Music selected and played by John Beckett (harpsichord). Directed by Kieran Hickey. RTÉ TVA. RTÉG; pp. 266–7

23 October 1977, RTÉ Radio, 11.45 am–12.15 pm, Programme Variations: VHF only, Recital. Cima: Sonata in G for oboe and continuo; Maderna: Two fragments for cor anglais; Boguslawski: *Musica Notturna* for musette, oboe and piano; Lapis: Sonata in A for oboe and continuo. Lothar Faber (oboe), Betty Sullivan (cello), John Beckett (harpsichord and piano). RTÉG.

5 November 1977, RTÉ Radio, 10.45–11.00 am, Programme Variations: MW and VHF, *Let's Sing a Song.* Bernadette Greevy sings and gives some hints on performance and interpretation. This week: Songs by Herbert Hughes. Accompanist: John Beckett. RTÉG; p. 274

27 November 1977, RTÉ Radio, 3.00–4.00 pm, Programme Variations: MW and VHF, *Invitation to Music.* Light classical music played by the RTÉ Concert Orchestra, leader Audrey Park, conducted by John Beckett with Frank Patterson (tenor) and Darina Gibson (piano). (Repeat.) RTÉG.

3 December 1977, RTÉ Radio, 10.45–11.00 am, Programme Variations: MW and VHF, *Let's Sing a Song.* Bernadette Greevy sings and gives some hints on performance and interpretation. This week: *Tonadillas* by Granados. Accompanist: John Beckett. RTÉG; p. 274

15 June 1978, RTÉ Radio, 10.30–11.00 pm, RTÉ Singers, conducted by Eric Sweeney. Monteverdi: *Lamento d'Ariana;* Bryan Kelly: *Three London Songs.* Accompanied by Betty Sullivan (cello) and John Beckett (harpsichord). IT, RTÉG.

11 November 1978, RTÉ Radio, 7.30–8.30 pm, *Schubert's Other Unfinished Symphony.* A recording of the first part of a studio concert given before an invited audience to mark the 150th anniversary of Franz Schubert. The RTÉ Concert Orchestra, with Bernadette Greevy (contralto) and John Beckett (conductor and accompanist). *Overture in the*

Italian Style, D591; *Lieder*; Symphony No. 7 in E, D729. Introduced by John Beckett. RTÉ SA. RTÉG; p. 281

18 November 1978, RTÉ Radio, 7.30–8.30 pm, *Schubert*. A recording of the second part of a studio concert given before an invited audience to mark the 150th anniversary of Franz Schubert. The RTÉ Concert Orchestra, with Bernadette Greevy (contralto) and John Beckett (conductor and accompanist). *Entr'acte* from incidental music to *Rosamunde*; *Lieder*; Symphony No. 8 in B minor (unfinished). RTÉ SA, RTÉG; pp. 281–2

19 November 1978, RTÉ Radio, 3.00–4.00 pm, Programme Variations. *Schubert*. The RTÉ Concert Orchestra, leader Audrey Park with Bernadette Greevy (contralto) and John Beckett (conductor and accompanist). SI; pp. 281–2

17 May 1979, RTÉ Radio, 10.30–11.00 pm, *Song Recital*, Linda Howie, soprano and Frank Patterson, tenor, accompanied by John Beckett, harpsichord, sing solos and duets by Purcell. Introduced by John Beckett. RTÉG; p. 286

16 July 1979, RTÉ Radio 1, 4.01–4.30 pm, *Music Magazine*. Including Venetia O'Sullivan talking to John Beckett about the New Irish Chamber Orchestra's forthcoming Promenade Concert in the Royal Albert Hall. RTÉG; p. 290

22 July 1979, RTÉ Radio 1, 8.35–9.50 pm, The New Irish Chamber Orchestra at the London Proms. Part 2 of a concert being given at The Royal Albert Hall. Irené Sandford (soprano), Bernadette Greevy (contralto), Frank Patterson (tenor), William Young (bass). The Cantata Singers and The New Irish Chamber Orchestra, leader Mary Gallagher. Conductor: John Beckett. J.S. Bach: *Sinfonia from Cantata No. 42*; *Cantata No. 30 "Freue dich, erlöste Schar"*. RTÉG; p. 290–1

9 October 1979, RTÉ 1 Television, 9.20–10.25 pm, *Insight: Wits and Dreamers – No. 3: That Solitary Man*. A film on the life and work of J.M. Synge, written and directed by James Plunkett. Incidental music by John Beckett. RTÉG; pp. 293

29 November, 1979, RTÉ Radio 1, 10.30–11.00 pm, The RTÉ Singers, conducted by Alan Cutts. With Betty Sullivan (cello) and John Beckett (piano and harpsichord). Bach: *Motet: Lobet den Herrn, alle Heiden*. Elgar: *Two songs for ladies' voices*. Tippett: *Two songs*. RTÉG.

19 January 1980, RTÉ Radio 1, 1.45–2.00 pm, Programme Variations. Song Recital: Violet Twomey, accompanied by John Beckett. IT, RTÉG.

23 January 1980, RTÉ Radio 1, 8.45–9.45 pm, Orchestral Concert. The RTÉ Symphony Orchestra. Including Mozart: Symphony No. 33 in B flat, conducted by John Beckett. RTÉG.

20 February 1980, RTÉ Radio 1, 8.45–9.45 pm, Orchestral Concert. Including Sibelius: *Rakastava*. The RTÉ Symphony Orchestra, conductor John Beckett. RTÉG; p. 295

8 March, 1980, RTÉ Radio 1, 7.30–8.30 pm, *Invitation to Music*. A concert of light classical music given by the RTÉ Concert Orchestra conducted by John Beckett, with guest artist Violet Twomey (soprano). Including Overture to *Idomeneo*, K. 366; *Ah! lo previdi*, K. 272; Minuet in D, K. 409; *Nehmt meinen Dank*, K. 383; Serenade No 9 in D *(Posthorn)*

K. 320. Recorded concert in St Catherine's Church, Thomas Street, Dublin, during the 1979 Liberties Festival. RTÉG; p. 286

29 May 1980, RTÉ Radio 1, 10.30–11.00 pm, The RTÉ Singers, conductor Eric Sweeney. John Beckett (piano). Part songs by Mendelssohn and Brahms. RTÉG.

23 July 1980, RTÉ Radio 1, 8.40–9.45 pm, Orchestral Concert. The RTÉ Symphony Orchestra, conductor Pierre Colombo. Including Frank Martin: *Petite Symphonie Concertante*, with Denise Kelly (harp), John Beckett (harpsichord) and Lynda Byrne (piano). RTÉG; p. 295

24 August 1980, RTÉ Radio 1, 9.00–10.00 pm, Programme Variations: *Sunday Concert*. Stravinsky: Suites Nos. 1 and 2; Schubert/Joachim: Symphony Opus 140 *(Grand Duo)*. The RTÉ Symphony Orchestra, conducted by John Beckett. RTÉG; p. 306

24 September 1980, RTÉ Radio 1, 8.40–9.45 pm, Orchestral Concert. The RTÉ Symphony Orchestra, conductor Colman Pearce. Including John Kinsella: *A Selected Life in memory of Seán O Riada*. Frank Patterson (tenor), Aiden Grennell (speaker), John Beckett (harpsichord) and David Carmody (bodhrán). RTÉG; p. 283

13 November 1980, RTÉ Radio 1, 8.45–10.00 pm, Orchestral Concert. The RTÉ Symphony Orchestra, conductor John Beckett. Mozart: Symphony No. 34 in C, K. 338, with minuet K. 409; Sibelius: *Four legends from the Kalevala,* Op. 22. Recorded 10 September 1980 at the Saint Francis Xavier Hall, Dublin. RTÉG; p. 306

20 April 1981, RTÉ Radio 1, 1.35–3.30/?4.00 pm, Programme Variations. RTÉ Symphony Orchestra, conductor John Beckett. Schubert: Symphony No. 8 *(Unfinished)*; Mahler: Symphony No. 10 (performing version by Deryck Cooke). Recorded in Saint Francis Xavier Hall, 27 March 1981. IT, RTÉG; pp. 310–2

19 November 1981, RTÉ Radio 1, 8.45–10.00 pm, Orchestral Concert. The RTÉ Symphony Orchestra, conductor John Beckett. Stravinsky: Suite No. 2 for small orchestra; Mahler-Cooke: Symphony No. 10. RTÉG; pp. 310–2

17 January 1982, RTÉ Radio 1, 9.05–9.50 am, Programme Variations, VHF, The New Irish Chamber Orchestra, conductor John Beckett. Bach: Cantata No. 202, Wedding Cantata. Irené Sandford (soprano), Patricia Harrison (oboe obligato). Bach: Suite No. 4 in D. RTÉG.

7 June 1982, RTÉ Radio 1, 8.35–9.30 pm, *The Romantic Composer:* Carl Maria von Weber. Introduced by John Beckett. Series of 13 programmes. RTÉG; p. 318–9

14 June: Schumann

21 June: Chopin

28 June: Mendelssohn

5 July: Berlioz

12 July: Liszt [8.35 pm]

19 July: Wagner [8.40 pm]

26 July: Brahms

2 Aug: Dvořák

9 Aug: Tchaikovsky

16 Aug: Fauré [8.40 pm]

23 Aug: Mahler

30 Aug.: Richard Strauss

17 November 1983, RTÉ Radio 1, 9.00–9.15 pm, Song Recital: Áine Nic Gabhann (alto), sings Cantata No. 54, *Widerstehe doch der Sünde*, by J.S. Bach, with string ensemble directed by John Beckett. Recorded in St Columba's College, Rathfarnham, on 3 May 1983. IT, RTÉG.

29 April 1984, RTÉ Radio 1, Programme Variations, VHF, Song Recital. William Young (bass), with instrumental ensemble, conducted by John Beckett, sings Cantata No. 82, *Ich habe genug*, by Bach. Recorded in St. Columba's College on 3 May 1983. RTÉG.

1 April 1988, RTÉ Radio 1, 8.00–10.00 pm, Bach: *St John Passion*. Frank Patterson (tenor – Evangelist), William Young, (bass – Christus), Irené Sandford (soprano), Alison Browner (alto), Peter Kerr (tenor), Nigel Williams (bass) and Conor Biggs (bass – Pontius Pilate); Goethe Institute Choir; Gillian Smith (harpsichord continuo), John O'Sullivan (organ continuo), Irish Chamber Orchestra, conductor John Beckett. Recorded in St Andrew's Church, Westland Row, Dublin on 12 April, 1987. RTÉG; p. 347–8

1 October 1988, RTÉ Radio 1, 8.30–10.11 pm, RTÉ at the Royal Hospital Kilmainham. The RTÉ Chorus, the RTÉ Concert Orchestra, conductor John Beckett. Speaker: Barry McGovern. Bach: Suite No. 3 in D, BWV 1068; Vaughan Williams: *An Oxford Elergy*. Mozart: *Thamos King of Egypt*. Repeated 5 May 1990. RTÉG; p. 349

25 June 1989, RTÉ FM 3, 8.00–10.00 pm, The King's Consort. Gillian Fisher (soprano), Charles Brett (counter-tenor), Andrew King (tenor), Michael George (baritone), Catherine Latham (recorder), Rachel Brown (flute); The Cantata Singers. Bach: Cantata No. 33 *Allein zu dir Herr Jesu Christ*; Purcell: Incidental music from *Abdelazer*; Bach: Cantata No. 151, *Süsser Trost, mein Jesus Kömmt*; Telemann: Concerto in E minor for recorder, flute, strings and continuo; Purcell: Instrumental numbers from the *Birthday Song for the Duke of Gloucester*; Bach: Cantata No. 187, *Es wartet alles auf dich*. Chamber organ: Robert King (director). Conductor: John Beckett. Part of the second Dublin Festival of Early Music at the Royal Hospital, Kilmainham, on 2 April, 1989. RTÉG; p. 352

9 January 1990, RTÉ FM 3, 8.00–9.20 pm, *International Irish Artists*. Including Bach: Sinfonia from Cantata No. 42. New Irish Chamber Orchestra, conductor John Beckett. IT.

27 January 1990, RTÉ FM 3, 9.15–10.00 pm, Music by Brahms. RTÉ Concert Orchestra, conductor John Beckett. Brahms: Serenade No. 1, Op. 11, in D. IT; p. 355

28 February 1990, RTÉ FM 3, 8.00–9.30 pm, RTÉ Concert Orchestra, conductor John Beckett. Rossini: Overture *Il Signor Bruschino*; Schubert: Symphony No. 3 in D; Mozart: Minuet in C, K. 409; Schubert: Symphony No. 5 in B flat. IT; p. 355

19 May 1990, RTÉ FM 3, 9.25–10.00 pm, *Schumann*, The National Symphony Orchestra, leader Audrey Collins. Conductor, John Beckett. Symphony No. 1 in B flat ('Spring'). IT; p. 356

30 June 1990, RTÉ FM 3, 8.40–9.10 pm, RTÉ Concert Orchestra, conductor John Beckett. Sibelius: *Belshazzar Suite*, Op 51; Fauré: *Masques et Bergamasques*. IT; p. 356

19 July 1990, RTÉ FM 3, 8.00–9.00 pm, *Three Kings*. John Beckett introduces some of the music made during the reigns of Louis XIV, James II and William of Orange. First of two programmes. RTÉG; p. 356

26 July 1990, RTÉ FM 3, 8.00–9.00 pm, *Three Kings*. John Beckett introduces some of the music made during the reigns of Louis XIV, James II and William of Orange. Second of two programmes. RTÉG; p. 356

10 April 1992, RTÉ FM 3, 8.00–9.35 pm, *International Irish Artists*. Bach: two arias: *Wo zwei und drei versammlet sind*; *Vergnugte Ruh, beliebte Seelenlust*. Bernadette Greevy, New Irish Chamber Orchestra, conductor John Beckett. IT.

13 April 1995, RTÉ FM 3, 8.15–10.15 pm, *Classical and Romantic*. Jane Carty presents her personal choice, including J.S. Bach: Sinfonia and arias from Cantatas and the *St Matthew Passion*. Bernadette Greevy with the New Irish Chamber Orchestra, conductor John Beckett. RTÉG.

Appendix D
BBC Radio and Television Broadcasts

Sources: BBC A: BBC Archives; BBC WAC: BBC Written Archive Centre; BLSA: British Library Sound Archive; RT: Radio Times; T: *The Times*; IT: *The Irish Times*; KCLCA K/ PP93: King's College London.

14 April 1955, Third Programme, 10.30–10.50 pm, first of four programmes devised and introduced by John Beckett: John Dowland's Song Books (recorded 31 March 1955). Musical illustrations by Alfred Deller and Desmond Dupré, producer Roger Fiske. The First Book of Airs: *If my complaints could passions move*; *Dear, if you change*; *Sleep, wayward thoughts*; *Away with these self-loving lads*. BBC WAC, RT; pp. 96–7, 99

18 April 1955, Third Programme, 10.05–10.30 pm, second of four programmes in the series John Dowland's Song Books (recorded 31 March 1955). The Second Book of Airs: *A shepherd in a shade*; *Lachrimae*; *Shall I sue*; *Sorrow, stay*. BBC WAC, RT; pp. 96–7, 99

27 April 1955, Third Programme, 7.30–7.50 pm, third of four programmes in the series John Dowland's Song Books (recorded 2 April 1955). The Third Book of Airs: *I must complain*; *Me, me, and none but me*; *Weep you no more, sad fountains*; *It was a time when silly bees*. BBC WAC, RT; pp. 96–7, 99

3 May 1955, Third Programme, 10.30–11.00 pm, fourth of four programmes in the series John Dowland's Song Books (recorded 2 April 1955). The Fourth Book of Airs, 'A Pilgrimes Solace': *If that a sinner's sighs*; *Stay, Time, awhile thy flying*; *In this trembling shadow cast*; *Go nightly cares*; *In darkness let me dwell*. BBC WAC, RT; pp. 96–7, 99

14 July 1955, Home Service, 9.00–9.30 am, recital of music by Dowland, Robert Johnson, Loeillet and Telemann, performed by Maurice Bevan (baritone), Josephine Lee (piano), John Sothcott (recorder) and John Beckett (harpsichord). Recorded 13 July 1955, Studio II, Maida Vale, Delaware Road. BBC WAC, IT, T, RT.

1 5 February 1956, Third Programme, 7. 1 5–8.05 pm, *Franz Xaver Mozart (1791-1844)*, *a programme of music by Mozart's son*, devised and introduced by John Beckett. Musical illustrations played by David Martin (violin) and Iris Loveridge (piano), and sung by Wilfrid Brown (tenor), accompanied by Charles Spinks (piano). Recorded on 1 4 February 1956, producer Roger Fiske. BBC WAC, T, RT; pp. 102, 105

1 8 February 1956, Third Programme, 10.10–10.55 pm, recital of music by Leopold and Franz Xaver Mozart, devised by John Beckett. Wilfrid Brown (tenor), David Martin (violin), Iris Loveridge (piano), Florence Hoorton (cello), Charles Spinks (harpsichord and piano). BBC WAC, T, RT; pp. 102, 105

6 March 1957, Third Programme, 7.15–8.00 pm, *My Ophelia*, *programme about Harriet Smithson, the Irish actress who married Berlioz*, written and narrated by John Beckett, with actors Hugh Mannin, Sheila Raynor and Raymond Nemorin. Recorded 2 March 1957, producer Roger Fiske. BBC WAC, T; pp. 98, 106, 109, 113–14

1 0 September 1957, 7.15–7.55 pm; 20 September 1957, 6.00–6.45 pm; 27 September 1957, 10.45–11.30 pm, Third Programme, music by Telemann and Haydn: John Beckett, harpsichord and John Sothcott, recorder; with the St Ceclia Trio (10 September), the Judy Hill Trio (20 September) and the Reizinstein Trio (27 September). Producer A. Giles. BBC WAC, T, RT.

1 0 December 1957, Third Programme, 9.45–10.45 pm, extract from Samuel Beckett's *Molloy* read by Patrick Magee, with incidental music composed by John Beckett and conducted by Berthold Goldschmidt. Music recorded 1 and 2 December 1957, producer Donald McWhinnie. Repeated 13 December 1957. BBC WAC, BBC A, T, RT; pp. 114–16

5 February 1958, Third Programme, 10.05–11.05 pm, Nigel Stock, June Tobin and Carleton Hobbs in *The Ballad of the Northern Wastes,* a radio play by Wolfgang Weyrauch, translated from the German by Charlotte and A.L. Lloyd, with incidental music composed for eight instruments by John Beckett, conducted by Bernard Keeffe. Music recorded 1 February 1958, producer John Gibson. BBC WAC, T, RT; p. 117

22 April 1958, Third Programme, 9.00–10.30 pm, *Pantagleize*, a farce by Michel de Ghelderode, translated by George Hauger, with incidental music for seven instruments (2 violins, 1 trumpet, 1 trombone, 1 piano and 2 percussionists) by John Beckett, conducted by Bernard Keeffe. With Donald Pleasence. Recorded 11 April 1958 in Studio 2, Maida Vale, Delaware Road, producer John Gibson. Repeated 25 April 1958. BBC WAC, T; pp. 117, 119–20

1 8 June 1958, Third Programme, 8.00–9.15; 9.30–10.45 pm, extract from Samuel Beckett's *Malone Dies* read by Patrick Magee, with incidental music composed by John Beckett, conducted by Bernard Keeffe. Repeated 19 June and 15 October 1958. Producer Donald McWhinnie. BBC WAC, T, RT; pp. 117–19

23 July 1958, Third Programme, 9.50–10.40 pm, Gladys Young and Donald Pleasence in *Remember Who You Are*, a cautionary comedy by David Paul with incidental music for seven instruments (recorder, 2 violins, 1 trombone, 2 percussionists, 1 piano) by John

Beckett. Producer David Thomson. Repeated 24 July 1958 and 4 February 1959. BBC WAC, T, RT; p. 120

9 January 1959, Third Programme, 8.00–9.00 pm, Michael Bryant and Eric Francis in *The Bow and the Beads*, a comparison by D.S. Savage of two ways towards mystical enlightenment, with incidental music for 11 instruments (6 viols, 2 piccolos, 1 lute, 2 percussionists) by John Beckett. Producer David Thomson. Repeat 27 January 1959. BBC WAC, T, RT; p. 122

19 January 1959, Third Programme, 8.35–9.35 pm, extracts from Samuel Beckett's *The Unnamable* read by Patrick Magee, with incidental music by John Beckett, conducted by Bernard Keeffe. Music recorded 17 January 1959; producer Donald McWhinnie. Repeated 10 February. BBC WAC, BBC A, T, RT; p. 122

27 April 1959, Third Programme, 10.25–11.05 pm (as advertised; broadcast deferred to 2 May 1959, 10.25–11.05 pm), *Claudin de Sermisy and the Paris Chanson*, devised and introduced by Michael Morrow. With Alfred Deller (counter-tenor), Demond Dupré (lute and cittern), Julian Bream (lute), Eric Halfpenny (cross flute), John Beckett (harpsichord), and the London Consort of Viols. Music recorded 2 April 1959 in Studio 3, Maida Vale, Delaware Road; Michael Morrow's talk recorded 21 April 1959. Producer Roger Fiske. BBC WAC, RT, BLSA, KCL, T; pp. 121–3

27 May 1959, Home Service, 9.25–9.55 am, music by Telemann and Beckett. Telemann: *Die kleine Kammermusik*, for descant recorder and harpsichord; Telemann: Sonata in D minor, for treble recorder and harpsichord; John Beckett: *Wedding March*, for descant recorder and harpsichord. Performed by John Sothcott (recorder) and John Beckett (harpsichord). Recorded 24 May 1959. Producer Bernard Keeffe. BBC WAC, T, RT; p. 124

27 May 1959, Third Programme, 8.00–9.30 pm, *The Voice of Shem,* passages from James Joyce's *Finnegans Wake*, freely adapted by Mary Manning, with incidental music composed by John Beckett, conducted by Bernard Keeffe. Cast includes Cyril Cusack and Patrick Magee. Recorded 14 and 22 May 1959, producer Michael Bakewell. Repeated 20 June 1959. BBC WAC, BBC A, T; p. 123

23 August 1959, Third Programme, 5.20–5.55 pm, music by Telemann and Loeillet. Telemann: Cantata: *Hemmet den eifer, verbannet die Rache*; Loeillet: Sonata in G major; Telemann: Cantata: *In gering- und rauhen Schalen*. Performed by Margaret Ritchie (soprano), John Sothcott (recorder), Desmond Dupré (viola da gamba), John Beckett (harpsichord). Producer Bernard Keeffe. BBC WAC, T, RT.

17 October 1959, Home Service, 9.25–10.00 am, *Music for Wind Instruments*. John Sothcott (descant and treble recorders), John Beckett (harpsichord), Stephen Waters, Archie Jacob and Basil Tchaikov (clarinets). Music by Alan Frank, Telemann, C.P.E. Bach, Loeillet and Arnold Cooke. Live from Studio 2, Maida Vale, Delaware Road. BBC WAC, T, RT.

28 November 1959, Third Programme, 10.45–11.00 pm, Sonata in D minor by Telemann, performed by John Sothcott (recorder) and John Beckett (harpsichord). Part of programme originally broadcast on 10 September 1957 (see above). BBC WAC, T.

1 January 1960, Third Programme, 8.00–9.30 pm, *Come All You Gallant Poachers*, a ballad opera by H.A.L. Craig and Dominic Behan about transportations to Australia and Tasmania, with incidental music and arrangements of traditional ballads by John Beckett. Repeated 7 February and 28 August 1960. Producer Francis Dillon. BBC WAC, T, RT; pp. 124–5

23 February 1960, Third Programme, 9.45–10.45 pm, Art–Anti Art: Maurice Denham and Betty Herdy in *Ubu Roi*, play by Alfred Jarry, translated by Barbara Wright, with incidental music for eight instruments composed by John Beckett, conducted by Bernard Keeffe. Singer: John Frost. Produced by Barbara Bray. Repeated 13 March 1960. BBC WAC, T, RT; p. 124

7 May 1960, Third Programme, 6.00–6.30 pm, Telemann: Church Cantatas (*Der harmonische Gottesdienst*): *Durchsuche dich, o stolzer Geist* and *Lauter Wonne, lauter Freude*. Margaret Ritchie (soprano); John Sothcott (treble recorder), John Beckett (harpsichord) and Desmond Dupré (bass viol). Recorded 16 April 1960, Studio 3, Maida Vale, Delaware Road, producer H. Middlemiss. BBC WAC, IT, T.

3 September 1960, Home Service, 9.25–10.00 am, music by Telemann, Corelli, Purcell and John Beckett (Two pieces for descant recorder and harpsichord: *Funeral March* and *Wedding March*), performed by John Sothcott (recorder), John Beckett (harpsichord) and Daphne Webb (cello). Recorded 21 August 1960. BBC WAC, T.

27 November 1960, Home Service, 2.30–3.25 pm, Sunday Symphony Concert, with BBC Symphony Orchestra, conductor Lorin Maazel. Paul Beard (violin), Arthur Leavins (violin), Harry Danks (viola) and Alexander Kok (cello). Music by Brahms and Geminiani: Concerto Grosso, op. 3 No. 2, continuo played by John Beckett. Live from Maida Vale, Delaware Road. BBC WAC, T, RT.

24 July 1962, Third Programme, 8.00–9.30 pm, *Home Sweet Honeycomb*, radio play by Bernard Kops with incidental music by John Beckett for 11 musicians (2 flutes/piccolos, 2 clarinets, 2 trumpets, 1 bass tuba, 3 percussionists and 1 double bass). Recorded 13 and 19 June 1962 at Farringdon Memorial Hall, producer Michael Bakewell. Repeated 15 August 1962 and 22 February 1963. BBC WAC, BBC A, T; p. 140–1

5 November 1962, Home Service, 10.30–10.45 pm Recital: music by Telemann and Purcell. John Sothcott (recorder) and John Beckett (harpsichord). T, RT.

11 November 1962, Third Programme, 8.10–9.35 pm, *A Taste of Madeleine*, radio play by Kay Cicellis with incidental music for piano solo composed and performed by John Beckett. Recorded 14 July 1962, producer David Thomson. Repeated 3 May 1963. BBC WAC, T; p. 142

13 November 1962, Third Programme, 9.35–10.05 pm, *Words and Music*, radio play by Samuel Beckett, with incidental music for ad hoc orchestra of 12 players, composed and conducted by John Beckett. Actors: Patrick Magee and Felix Felton. Recorded 5 July and 10 September 1962, produced by Michael Bakewell. Repeated 7 December 1962 and 7 May 1963. BBC WAC, BBC A, T; pp. 135, 137–8, 140–3

3 December 1962, Home Service, 8.30–10.00 pm, *The Heretic*, play by Jean Morris with incidental music chosen and arranged by John Beckett and Michael Morrow, and played by Musica Reservata. Recorded 26 November 1962, Studio 6A, Broadcasting House, producer Michael Bakewell. Repeated 14 March 1965. BBC WAC, T, RT; p. 143

25 January 1963, Third Programme, 8.40–9.40 pm, *Lord Halewyn*, play by Michel de Ghelderode with incidental music for 8 musicians and singers composed by John Beckett. Recorded 17 January 1963, Studio 6A, Broadcasting House, producer H. B. Fortuin. Repeated 10 February 1963. BBC WAC, T, RT; p. 143

8 March 1963, Third Programme, 8.20–10.05 pm, *Spring '71*, play by Arthur Adamov, translated by Peter Meyer, with incidental music for orchestra of 10 players, composed and conducted by John Beckett. Recorded 23 February 1963, producer Michael Bakewell. Repeated 24 March 1963. BBC WAC, T, RT; p. 143–4

16 May 1963, Home Service, 10.30–10.45 pm, harpsichord music by Purcell played by John Beckett. Recorded 13 May 1963 in Studio 2, Maida Vale, Delaware Road. BBC WAC, T, RT.

3 July 1963, Home Service, 9.25–9.55 am, music by Anon (17th century), Telemann, Haydn and John Beckett, performed by John Sothcott (recorder) and John Beckett (harpsichord). Three pieces for descant recorder and harpsichord by John Beckett: 1. *Fanfare*. 2. *Funeral March* – slow and frantic. 3. *Wedding March* – sprightly and dry. Recorded 28 June 1963. BBC WAC, T, RT; p. 415, note 27

31 July 1963, Home Service, 9.25–9.45 am, music by Sweelinck and Loeillet played by John Sothcott (recorder) and John Beckett (harpsichord). RT, T.

11 August 1964, BBC Two Television, 7.30–8.45 pm, *The Artist in Society: 1: The Middle Ages*. Contributors include Brian Trowell on 'Medieval Music in France and Italy' with Musica Reservata: Grayston Burgess and John Whitworth (counter-tenors), Daphne Webb (rebec), John Sothcott (recorder) and Michael Morrow (lute). RT, T.

16 August 1963, Third Programme, 9.05–10.10 pm, *The Lemmings*, radio play by Bernard Kops with incidental music for ad hoc orchestra (1 flute, 1 piccolo, 2 vibraphones, 1 violin, 1 viola, 1 double bass, 1 percussionist) composed and conducted by John Beckett. Music recorded 12 July 1963, production recorded 6 August 1963; producer Michael Bakewell. Repeated 1 September 1963. BBC WAC, BBC A, T; p. 149

2 October 1963, Home Service, 9.20–9.55 am, harpsichord music by Bach (Partita No. 4 in D major) performed by John Beckett. Recorded 6 September 1963. Repeated 6 May 1967 on the Home Service and 16 March 1970 on Radio 4. BBC WAC, T, RT; p. 150

31 October 1963, Third Programme, 9.25–10.25 pm, *Fando and Lis,* play by Fernando Arrabel with incidental music composed by John Beckett. Recorded 10 September 1963, Studio 4, Maida Vale, Delaware Road, producer John Tydeman. Repeated 16 November 1963. BBC WAC, T; pp. 149–50

7 January 1964, Home Service, 11.15–11.45 pm, *Music at Night:* music by Telemann and Haydn performed by John Sothcott (recorder), John Beckett (harpsichord) and Daphne Webb (cello). Repeated 3 April 1964. BBC WAC, T, RT; p. 152

23 February 1964, Home Service, 2.30–3.00 pm, *Laureate of the Lowly*, play by Robert Service with incidental ragtime and classical piano music chosen and performed by John Beckett. Recorded 20 May in Studio 3, Maida Vale, Delaware Road, producer David Thomson. Repeated 24 August 1964. BBC WAC, T, RT.

13 March 1964, Third Programme, 10.30–11.00 pm, *Music at the Court of Henry VIII*: music by Henry VIII, Cornyshe, Prioris, Anon, performed by the Deller Consort – Honor Sheppard (soprano), Alfred Deller (counter-tenor), Max Worthley (tenor), Maurice Bevan (baritone), and John Sothcott, John Beckett and Theo Wyatt (recorders); Desmond Dupré (lute and bass viol). Directed, arranged and introduced by John Stevens. RT.

20 September 1964, Home Service, 11.02–11.45 pm, *Music at Night*. BBC Chorus, conductor, Peter Gellhorn; John Beckett, harpsichord. Frescobaldi: Six Madrigals for five voices; Bach: Four duets for harpsichord (BWV 802–805); Pizzetti: *Due composizioni corali* (1961); Pizzetti: *Due canzoni corali* (1913). RT.

8 November 1964, Third Music Programme, 4.30–4.45, Bach: French Suite No. 5 in G major, played by John Beckett (harpsichord). RT; p. 156

31 March 1965, Network Three, 9.04–9.45 am, *This Week's Composer: Purcell*, harpsichord pieces played by John Beckett. RT.

17 April 1965, Third, 7.25–8.30 pm, *A Breath of Fresh Air*, adaptation of a story by F.C. Ball with incidental music composed by John Beckett. Producer David Thomson. Repeated 25 December 1965, 27 February 1967 and 1 June 1973. BBC WAC, T, RT.

1 May 1965, Third, 7.05–7.45 pm, *Mediaeval Music*, music by Machaut, Binchois performed by Musica Reservata, with Jantina Noorman, Grayston Burgess, John Whitworth, Ian Partridge, John Sothcott, Don Smithers and John Beckett. First of four programmes of medieval music. RT.

20 June 1965, Network Three, 4.35–5.00 pm, Scarlatti sonatas played by John Beckett (harpsichord). RT.

25 July 1965, Network Three, 4.20–5.00 pm, Scarlatti sonatas played by John Beckett (harpsichord). RT.

7 August 1965, Third, 8.35–9.35 pm, *The Composer Conducts*, Amaryllis Fleming (cello), English Chamber Orchestra, leader Emanuel Hurwitz, John Beckett (harpsichord continuo), conducted by Sir Arthur Bliss. RT.

14 August 1965, Home Service, 8.30–10.00 pm, Saturday Night Theatre: *Mrs Thompson* by Mollie Hardwick, with Mollie Wolfit and William Eedle. Other parts played by members of the BBC Drama Repetory Company. Singers: Betty Huntley-Wright and Gordon Faith; John Beckett (harpsichord). Produced by Betty Davies. RT.

28 September 1965, Third, 7.55–10.05 pm, *The Plain Dealer,* play by William Wycherley with incidental music composed and played on harpsichord by John Beckett. Producer John Tydeman. Repeated 22 October 1965, 22 August 1966. BBC WAC, T, RT; pp. 160–1

21 December 1965, Third Programme, 7.30–8.30 pm, *Ubu Cocu (Ubu Cuckolded): a 'paraphysical' extravaganza,* play by Alfred Jarry, translated by Cyril Connolly, with incidental music for eight musicians (2 piccolos, 2 trumpets, 2 tubas and 2 percussionists) composed and conducted by John Beckett. Producer Martin Esslin. Repeated 10 January 1966. BBC WAC, BBC A, T; pp. 163–5

24 December 1965, Third Programme, 8.15–9.20 pm, *Le Roman de Fauvel* (c. 1310–20) by Gervais du Bus. A verse-translation of selected passages, written and produced by Terence Tiller with associated music by Philippe de Vitry and others. Transcribed and arranged by Michael Morrow. Played by members of Musica Reservata, conducted by John Beckett. Narrator: Denis Goacher; Fauvel: Victor Lucas. Recorded 2 November 1965, Studio 3, Maida Vale, Delaware Road, producer Terence Tiller. Repeated 15 January 1966. BBC WAC, T, RT; pp. 144, 153, 165

11 January 1966, Home Service, 11.15–11.45 pm, *Music at Night.* Music by Bach played by Andrew McGee (violin) and John Beckett (harpsichord). Sonata in G major, for violin and continuo, BWV 1021 [1023 in *Radio Times*] and Sonata in C minor for violin and harpsichord BWV 1017. RT, T.

1 February 1966, Home Service, 11.15–11.45 pm, *Music at Night.* Byrd: *John come kisse me now*; *The Mayden's Songe*; *Pavana: Bray*; *Prelude* and *Fantasia*; *Walsingham Variations*. John Beckett (harpsichord). RT, T.

11 February 1966, Third Programme, 8.35–10.00 pm, *Electra,* play by Euripedes translated by David Thompson, with incidental music composed and conducted by John Beckett. Recorded 26 and 29 November 1965, producer John Tydeman. Repeated 27 February 1966, 23 April 1967 and 23 September 1968. BBC WAC, BBC A, T, RT; pp. 163–4

18 February 1966, Network Three, 11.00–12.15 pm, *Music Making.* Bach: music including the Trio Sonata in C minor (*The Musical Offering*) performed by Ralph Holmes (violin), John Beckett (harpsichord) and members of the English Chamber Orchestra, directed by Arnold Goldsbrough. RT, T.

6 March 1966, Network Three, 4.15–4.30 pm, *From the Fitzwilliam Virginal Book.* John Beckett (harpsichord). Possibly a repeat of programme on 1 February 1966. RT, T.

11 May 1966, Network Three, 3.30–4.00 pm, *English Song.* Songs by John Stanley and Pepusch. Patricia Clark (soprano), Mary Thomas (soprano), Nona Liddell (violin), John Sothcott (recorder), John Beckett (harpsichord) and Dennis Nesbitt (viola da gamba). RT, T.

8 June 1966, Third, 7.30–7.55 pm, *Music for Trumpet and Harpsichord,* Don Smithers (trumpet), John Beckett (harpsichord) and Daphne Webb (cello continuo). Music by Purcell and Viviani. Repeated 31 March and 4 July 1968. RT, T.

16 June 1966, Third, 8.50–9.40 pm, *Music in Venice: sixteenth-century vocal and instrumental dance music,* performed by Musica Reservata, conducted by John Beckett. Recorded 13 June 1966, Studio 1, Maida Vale, Delaware Road and 14 June 1966, Studio 1, Egton

House, All Souls Place, producer Basil Lam. Repeated 29 September 1972. BBC WAC, T, RT; p. 169

23 June 1966, Home Service, 8.00–8.45; 9.05–10.00 pm, Isaac Stern in four concertos with Roger Lord (oboe), John Beckett (harpsichord continuo), a section of the London Symphony Orchestra led by Andrew McGee, directed by Isaac Stern. From the Royal Festival Hall, London. Music by Bach, Haydn and Mozart. RT, T.

26 July 1966, Third, 10.05–11.00 pm, *Early Renaissance Music:* Spanish, German, French and Italian music performed by Musica Reservata, conducted by John Beckett and introduced by Michael Morrow. Music recorded 5 May 1965, Studio 1, Maida Vale, Delaware Road, producer Basil Lam. BBC WAC, T, RT; p. 169

1 September 1966, Network Three, 11.00–12.15 am, *Music Making*, Hyman Bress (violin), John Beckett (harpsichord), Arne Skjold Rasmussen (piano). Music by Beethoven. RT.

26 November 1966, Home Service, 11.10–11.42 pm, *Music at Night*, Partita No. 6 in E minor, BWV 830, John Beckett (harpsichord). RT, T; p. 150

24 January 1967, Third, 9.35–10.35 pm, *The Scotch songs of J.C. Bach*, illustrated talk by Roger Fiske, with Margaret Kingsley (soprano), Duncan Robertson (tenor), James Galway (flute), Christopher Hyde-Smith (flute), Tess Miller (oboe), the Amici Quartet and John Beckett, square piano and harpsichord. Repeated 5 May 1968. BLSA, T, RT; p. 172

14 April 1967, Network Three, 8.30–9.30 pm, *A Grotto for Miss Maynier*, adaptation, by F.C. Ball, of the novel by F.C. Ball with incidental music composed by John Beckett. Recorded 8 March 1967, Studio 1, Picadilly, producer David Thomson. Repeated 30 April 1967, 26 December 1967 and 6 November 1970 (on Radio 4). BBC WAC, T; pp. 171, 174–5

29 April 1967, Network Three, 6.00–6.45 pm, *Purcell*, Frank Patterson (tenor), John Beckett (harpsichord), Daphne Webb (cello continuo). Songs: 'If love's a sweet passion'; 'Pious Celinda goes to pray'rs'; 'Cease, anxious world, your fruitless pain'; 'Hark! how all things with one sound rejoice'; 'If music be the food of love'; 'Love, thou can'st hear, tho' thou art blind'; harpsichord pieces: Trumpet tune; A new Irish tune; Minuet; Sefauchi's farewell; Round O; A new ground; Ground; Air; A new Scotch tune; Air; songs: 'Solitude'; 'Fairest isle'; 'Ah! how sweet it is to love'; 'Mystery's song'. RT; p. 175

26 May 1967, Network Three, 9.45–10.30 pm, music by Monteverdi performed by the Purcell Consort of Voices with John Beckett (harpsichord), Desmond Dupré (viola da gamba), Francis Baines (double bass). Repeated in *This Week's Composer*, Radio 3, 5 March 1968, 4 February and 29 July 1969. RT, T.

27 June 1967, Network Three, 8.30–9.30 pm, music by Obrecht (*Missa Fortuna desperata*) and Busnois performed by members of Musica Reservata, conducted by John Beckett (organ). Introduced by Michael Morrow. Recorded 28 July 1966, Studio 1, Maida Vale, Delaware Road. BBC WAC, T, RT; p. 169

28 June 1967, Network Three, 3.35–5.25 pm, *Bach's Instrumental Music*. Included: Partita No. 6 in E minor, BWV 830, played by John Beckett, harpsichord (second broadcast). RT, T.

2 July 1967, Network Three, 7.15–7.55; 8.15–8.55 pm, *A concert of Renaissance and Medieval Music*, live from the Queen Elizabeth Hall, London. (South Bank 'debut' concert.) Conductor, John Beckett. RT, T; pp. 176–9

9 July 1967, Network Three, 9.04–9.35 am, *Purcell*, sacred songs sung by the Purcell Consort of Voices, with John Beckett (chamber organ continuo) and Daphne Webb (cello continuo). 'O Lord our Governor'; 'O happy man'; 'Early, O Lord, my fainting soul'; 'Great God and just'; 'Lord I can suffer'; 'O all ye people, clap your hands'. Repeated 28 April 1968. RT, T.

13 July 1967, Network Three, 10.25–11.00 pm, *The Fitzwilliam Virginal Book*: music by Tomkins, Dowland, Bull, Anon, Farnaby. John Beckett (harpsichord). RT, T; p. 179

19 July 1967, Network Three, 7.30–8.05 pm, music by Robert White performed by Musica Reservata, conducted by John Beckett. *O praise God in his holiness*; *Lord who shall dwell in Thy tabernacle*; *The Lamentations of Jeremiah*. Recorded 5 April 1967, St George the Martyr, Queen Square, producer Basil Lam. Repeated 7 January 1969. BBC WAC, BBC A, RT, T; pp. 174, 179

21 July 1967, Network Three, 7.30–8.00 pm, *The Fitzwilliam Virginal Book:* music by William Byrd. John Beckett (harpsichord). RT, T; p. 179

28 July 1967, Network Three, 10.10–10.50 pm, *Spanish Music* performed by Musica Reservata: Jantina Noorman, Grayston Burgess, Tom Sutcliffe (counter-tenor), John Dudley (tenor); John Sothcott, Don Smithers (cornett and crumhorn), Tony Moore (trombone), Alan Lumsden (trombone), Ruth David (rebec), Daphne Webb (rebec), Desmond Dupré (lute and viol), John Beckett (harpsichord and viol), Jeremy Montagu (percussion); director Michael Morrow (lute and crumhorn). Repeated 1 August 1968. RT, T; p. 169

6 August 1967, Home Service, 11.02–11.45 pm, *Music at Night*, John Beckett (harpsichord). Second broadcast of sonatas [?]. RT, T.

27 August 1967, Home Service, 10.10–10.50 pm, *The Good Natur'd Man*, the story of Oliver Goldsmith by Felix Felton, with incidental music for flute and harp by John Beckett. With Jack MacGowran. Recorded 27 July 1967, producer David Thomson. BBC WAC, RT, T; p. 179

12 October 1967, Radio 3 (Study Session), 7.00–7.30 pm, *Music and Dancing, part 2: Dances of the Middle Ages*, Further Education Study Session programme; talk by Michael Morrow with music performed by Musica Reservata, conducted by John Beckett. Recorded 23 September 1967, Concert Hall, Broadcasting House, producer Peter Dodd. BBC WAC, T, RT.

14 October 1967, Radio 4, 11.10–11.42 pm, *Music at Night*, Scarlatti sonatas played by John Beckett. RT, T.

19 October 1967, Radio 3 (Study Session), 7.00–7.30 pm, *Music and Dancing, part 3: Dances of the Renaissance*. Further Education Study Session programme; talk by Michael Morrow with music performed by Musica Reservata, conducted by John Beckett (harpsichord and organ). BBC WAC, RT, T.

19 October 1967, Radio 3, 9.50–10.50 pm, *Interpretations on Record: illustrated talk*. Mahler's Ninth Symphony, speaker John Beckett, with recorded musical illustrations. Repeated 21 September 1968. BBC WAC, RT, T; p. 181

31 October 1967, Radio 3, 8.30–9.15; 9.35–10.25 pm, *Tuesday Invitation Concert*: music performed by Musica Reservata, conducted by John Beckett (harpsichord); Alan Hacker (clarinet), Stephen Pruslin (piano), Thomas Hemsley (baritone), Miguel Zanetti (piano). First half: Spanish secular music of the early Renaissance (Musica Reservata); music by John Cage and Peter Maxwell Davies. Second half: music by Schubert and Schumann. Recorded 21 September 1967, Middleton Hall, University of Hull, producer Tim Souster. BBC WAC, RT, T.

18 November 1967, Radio 3, 6.00–6.50 pm, *Bach cantatas*, Nos 25, 118 and 96. Margaret Price (soprano), Delia Woolford (contralto), Ian Partridge (tenor), John Noble (baritone); London Bach Society; Richard Taylor (recorder), Stanley Taylor (recorder), John Beckett (recorder), Richard Adeney (flute); English Chamber Orchestra, conducted by Paul Steinitz. Repeated 15 September 1968. RT, T.

10 January 1968, Radio 3, 7.30–8.10 pm, Tallis: Church Music. *Lamentations,* motet *Miserere nostri* and *Missa Salve Intemerata Virgo*, sung by Musica Reservata Choir, conductor John Beckett; Harold Lester, organ. Recorded 4 January 1968, St George the Martyr Church, Queen Square, producer Basil Lam. BBC WAC, BLSA, RT, T; p. 184

12 January 1968, Radio 3, 8.25–9.35 pm, *Seventeen Speakies: O! – translation with music*, play by Sandro Key-Åberg, translated from the Swedish by Rian Rothwell, with incidental music for 6 players (2 piccolos, E flat / bass clarinet, trumpet, piano accordion, percussionist) composed by John Beckett. Recorded 5 January 1968, producer H. B. Fortuin. Repeated 28 January 1968. BBC WAC, RT, T; pp. 181, 184

11 February 1968, Radio 3, 6.20–7.10 pm, German music of the renaissance performed by Musica Reservata, conducted by John Beckett (organ). Recorded 25 July 1967, Farringdon, London, producer Basil Lam. Repeated 17 October 1973. BBC WAC, RT, T, KCL; p. 179

15 February 1968, Radio 4, 11.15–11.45 pm, Music at Night: Frank Patterson (tenor), John Beckett (harpsichord), Betty Sullivan (cello). Songs by Purcell. Repeated as part of *Music Making*, Radio 3, on 14 June 1968. BBC WAC, RT; pp. 184–5

28 March 1968, Radio 3, 7.30–8.55 pm, *Oedipus the King*, play by Sophocles, translated by W.B. Yeats and adapted for radio by John Tydeman, with incidental music for 15 musicians (piccolo, 2 oboes/cor anglais, 3 trumpets, 3 trombones, 3 cellos, 1 double bass, 2 percussion) composed and conducted by John Beckett. Recorded 11 and 15 January 1968, producer John Tydeman. Repeated 21 April 1968. BBC WAC, BBC A, RT, T; pp. 181, 184

3 June 1968, Radio 3, 7.30–8.10 pm, *Poor Mrs Machiavelli: a tragic domestic interlude* by David Paul, with incidental music for harpsichord and vibraphone performed by John Beckett and James Blades, composed by John Beckett. With Flora Robson and Hugh Burden. Recorded 18 May 1968, Studio 8A, Broadcasting House, producer David Thomson. Repeated 26 June 1968. BBC WAC, RT, T; p. 185

6 June 1968, Radio 3, 8.55–9.40 pm, *The Chinese Jig*, play by Gerard McLarnon, with incidental music for 5 musicians (piccolo/flute, E flat clarinet/bass clarinet, tuba, piano accordion, percussion) composed and conducted by John Beckett. Music recorded 7 March 1968, Studio 3, Maida Vale, Delaware Road, producer Christopher Holme. Repeated 28 June 1968. BBC WAC, RT, T; p. 184

14 June 1968, Radio 3, 7.30–8.05 pm, Franz Xaver Mozart: six songs and music performed by Hugh Maguire (violin), Viola Tunnard (fortepiano), Frank Patterson (tenor) and John Beckett (fortepiano). Announcements recorded 21 February 1968, producer Alan Walker . BBC WAC, RT, T; pp. 105, 190

9 July 1968, Radio 3, 1.45 –2.30 pm, *Early Renaissance Music* performed by Musica Reservata, directed and with an introduction by Michael Morrow. BBC A.

26 July 1968, Radio 3, 7.40–8.40 pm, *Ubu Enchained*, play by Alfred Jarry with incidental music for 'pub style' piano, bass tuba, clarinet and percussion, composed, performed and directed by John Beckett (piano). Recorded 4 July 1968 in Concert Hall, Broadcasting House, producer Martin Esslin. Repeated 10 August 1968. BBC WAC, T; p. 190

8 October 1968, Radio 3, 9–9.50; 10.10–10.45 pm, *Invitation Concert*, music by Guillaume Dufay performed by Musica Reservata, conducted by John Beckett (chamber organ) – first half; and music by Peter Maxwell Davies (*L'homme armé*) performed by the Pierrot Players conducted by Peter Maxwell Davies – second half. Recorded 3 October 1968 in Studio 1, Maida Vale, Delaware Road. BBC WAC, RT, T; p. 191

21 October 1968, Radio 3, 8.45–9.35; 9.55–10.40, *The Age of Chivalry in France and the Hundred Years War*, performed by Musica Reservata, conducted by John Beckett (organ). Concert at the Queen Elizabeth Hall, recorded 15 September 1968, producer Basil Lam. BBC WAC, KCL, IT, RT, T; pp. 190–1

19 November 1968, Radio 4, 11.15–11.45 pm, *Music at Night*, Scarlatti sonatas performed on harpsichord by John Beckett. Recorded 12 November 1968, Studio 2, Maida Vale, Delaware Road, producer Stephen Plaistow. BBC WAC, RT.

17 March 1969, Radio 3, 4.00–4.30 pm, *Studio Portrait: John Beckett*, presented by John Beckett, with musical illustrations by Dufay, Byrd, Scarlatti, Purcell and Bach played by John Beckett on portative organ and harpsichord. Recorded 2 February 1969 in Studio 2, Maida Vale, Delaware Road, producer Ivor Walsworth. BBC WAC, BBC A, RT, T; pp. 15, 43, 194

2 April 1969, Radio 3, 1.50–3.00 pm, music by Henry Purcell performed by Musica Reservata, conducted by John Beckett: Incidental music to *Abdelazer or The Moor's*

Revenge; Chacony in G minor; Song: *If ever I more riches did desire*; Ode in commemoration of the centenary of Trinity College, Dublin: *Great Parent, Hail!* Concert at the Queen Elizabeth Hall, recorded 8 November 1968, producer Michael Hall. Repeated 3 March 1970 and 28 July 1975. BBC WAC, IT, RT, T; p. 192–3

27 April 1969, Radio 3, 9.05–9.50 am, Bach Cantatas 103, *Ihr werdet weinen und heulen* and 12, *Weinen, Klagen, Sorgen, Zagen* performed by Musica Reservata and Wandsworth School Boys' Choir, conducted by John Beckett. Recorded 15 April 1969, Concert Hall, Broadcasting House, producer Michael Hall. BBC WAC, T; p. 195

13 May 1969, Radio 4, 11.15–11.45 pm, *Music at Night*, John Beckett (harpsichord). RT.

24 June 1969, Radio 3, 10.00–11.00 pm, Bach Cantatas 167, *Ihr Menschen, rühmet Gottes Liebe* and 30, *Freue dich, erlöste Schar* performed by Musica Reservata and Wandsworth School Boys' Choir, conducted by John Beckett. Recorded 17 April 1969, Studio 1, Maida Vale, Delaware Road, producer Michael Hall. BBC WAC, RT, T; p. 195

27 July 1969, Radio 3, 9.15–10.20 pm, Bach Cantatas 10, *Meine Seel' erhebt den Herren* and 147, *Herz und Mund und Tat und Leben* performed by Musica Reservata and Wandsworth School Boys' Choir, conducted by John Beckett. Recorded 23 July 1969, St Andrew's Church, Holburn, producer Michael Hall. Repeated 12 July 1970. BBC WAC, RT, T; p. 198

6 August 1969, Radio 3, 7.30–7.55; 8.15–9.40 pm, Proms concert, Royal Albert Hall. Part one: 15th century French music performed by Musica Reservata, conducted by John Beckett. Anon: 15th century basse danse; Dufay: *Donnés l'aussault*; *Adieu m'amour*; *Adieu ces bons vins de Lannoys*; *Mon cuer me fait*; *Resveilliés vous*; Anon: 15th century basse danse. Part two: Messiaen's Turangalila Symphony performed by the BBC Symphony Orchestra, conducted by Charles Groves. Part one repeated 2 July 1971. BBC WAC, RT, T; p. 198

17 September 1969, Radio 3, 9.45–10.40 pm, Bach Cantata 71, *Gott ist mein König* and 119, *Preise, Jerusalem, den Herrn* performed by Musica Reservata and Wandsworth School Boys' Choir, conducted by John Beckett. Recorded 21 July 1969 at St Andrew's Church, Holburn, producer Michael Hall. Repeated 18 January 1970. BBC WAC, RT, T; p. 197

24 September 1969, Radio 3, 10.20–11.00 pm, *13th century Polytextual Motets* performed by Musica Reservata, conducted by John Beckett. Introduced by Michael Morrow. Recorded 8 August 1969, Studio 8A, Broadcasting House, producer Terence Tiller. BBC WAC, RT, T; p. 198

5 October 1969, Radio 3, 8.10–9.00; 9.20–10.10 pm, *A Renaissance Entertainment*, music from France, the Netherlands, Germany, Poland and Italy performed by Musica Reservata, conducted by John Beckett. Concert at the Queen Elizabeth Hall recorded 16 September 1969, producer Basil Lam. Repeated 26 February 1972. BBC WAC, IT, RT; p. 198

11 October 1969, Radio 3, 8.10–8.55 / 9.15–10.10 pm, *Italian music of the 14th and 15th centuries* performed by Musica Reservata, conducted by John Beckett (organ). Concert in Purcell Room, Royal Festival Hall, recorded 7 February 1969, producer Basil Lam. BBC WAC, BBC A, T, RT; p. 194

30 October 1969, Radio 3, 9.04–9.45 am, *This Week's Composer: Purcell*. Songs sung by Frank Patterson, with John Beckett (harpsichord) and Adam Skeaping (viola da gamba). RT.

9 December 1969, Radio 3, 9.45–11.00 am, *Purcell: Choral concert (Purcell Series, programme 5)*: Birthday Song: *Sound the Trumpet*; Incidental music: *The Double Dealer* and *Yorkshire Feast Song*, performed by Musica Reservata and Wandsworth School Boys' Choir, conducted by John Beckett. Recorded 29 November 1969, Studio 2, Maida Vale, Delaware Road, producer Michael Hall. Repeated 12 April 1970. BBC WAC, RT, T; p. 199

23 December 1969, Radio 3, 9.45–11.00 am, *Purcell (Purcell Series, programme 7)*: Incidental Music: *The Married Beau*; Sacred Songs: *Begin the song and strike the living lyre*; Anthem: *O Lord, grant the King a long life*; Songs: *Thy genius lo! (The Massacre of Paris)*; *Let the dreadful engines of eternal will (Don Quixote)*; Birthday Song for Queen Mary: *Arise my muse*. Performed by Musica Reservata Orchestra and Wandsworth School Boys' Choir, conducted by John Beckett. Recorded 1 December 1969, Studio 1, Maida Vale, Delaware Road, producer Michael Hall. Repeated 26 April 1970. BBC WAC, RT, T; p. 199

18 January 1970, Radio 3, 8.45–9.35; 9.55–10.40 pm, The First Venetian School: music by Praetorius and the Gabrielis performed by Musica Reservata, soloists and Wandsworth School Boys' Choir, conducted by John Beckett. Concert at the Queen Elizabeth Hall recorded on 16 December 1969, producer Basil Lam. BBC WAC, RT, T; p. 200

12 April 1970, Radio 3, 6.40–7.30 pm, *Music by Walter Frye*: Mass, *Flos regalis*; two chansons; *Ave Maria*, performed by Musica Reservata, conducted by John Beckett. Recorded 13 February 1960, Studio 1, Maida Vale, Delaware Road, producer Basil Lam. BBC WAC, RT, T; p. 201

18 April 1970, Radio 3, 10.00–11.30 pm, *Haydn, Mendelssohn, Brahms: symphony concert*, music performed by BBC Welsh Orchestra, conducted by Irwin Hoffman, with John Beckett (harpsichord continuo in Haydn Symphony No. 7). Recorded 20 March 1970 in Studio 1, Broadcasting House, Llandaff, Cardiff, producer Moelfryn Harries. BBC WAC, RT, T.

29 June 1970, Radio 3, 9.05–9.55 pm, *Madrigals and Chansons* – transcribed by Peter Philips in the Fitzwilliam Virginal Book. Performed by the Purcell Consort of Voices and John Beckett, harpsichord. Recorded 8 June 1970 in Studio 1, Maida Vale, Delaware Road, producer Basil Lam. BBC WAC, RT, T; p. 203

17 February 1971, Radio 3, 11.20–11.30 am, interval talk by John Beckett on Bach's *Goldberg Variations*. Main programme: Tamás Vásáry (piano) playing, in part one, Beethoven's Sonata in B flat major, op. 106 ('*Hammerklavier*') and, in part two, Bach's *Goldberg Variations*. Interval talk repeated on 16 July 1972 (see below). RT.

22 April 1971, Radio 3, 7.00– 7.30 pm, *Musical Interpretation: No. 4, Early Enquiries*. John Beckett plays examples of keyboard music from the late 13th to the 18th centuries in which written or improvised ornamentation needs to be introduced, and demonstrates how the performer sets about providing it. Producer David Epps. Repeated 10 March 1972. BBC WAC, RT, T.

22 August 1971, Radio 3, 9.50–10.35; 10.50–11.30, *A Late Renaissance Entertainment:* music by Praetorius, Monteverdi and Scheidt performed by Musica Reservata and Wandsworth School Boys' Choir, conducted by John Beckett. Concert at the Queen Elizabeth Hall recorded 20 December 1970, producer Basil Lam. BBC WAC, RT, T; p. 210

14 November 1971, Radio 3, 9.10–10.15 pm, *Synge and Music*, talk, with musical illustrations, written by John Beckett; section of the Music Group of London, directed by John Beckett, and John Kelly (traditional fiddler). With Denys Hawthorne as J. M. Synge and Olwen Griffiths. Recorded 15 and 16 October 1971 in London and 15 September 1971 in Dublin, producer Terence Tiller. BBC WAC, T, IT, RT; p. 222

2 December 1971, Radio 3, 9.30–10.20; 10.40–11.30 pm, *Medieval French and English Music*, performed by Musica Reservata, conducted by John Beckett. Concert at the Queen Elizabeth Hall recorded 18 May 1971, producer Basil Lam. BBC WAC, T; p. 213

10 April 1972, Radio 3, 10.15–11.00 pm, English music by Nicholson, Byrd, John Johnson, Elway Bevin, William Inglot and William Cobbold, performed by Musica Reservata, conducted by John Beckett (harpsichord). Recorded 9 November 1970, Studio 1, Maida Vale, Delaware Road, producer Basil Lam. BBC WAC, RT, T; p. 227

2 June 1972, Radio 3, 11.35–11.55 pm, Lassus: *Missa super Osculetur Me*, performed by the Choir of Musica Reservata and Trinity Boys' Choir, Croydon conducted by John Beckett. Recorded 21 April 1972 in St George the Martyr Church, Queen Square, producer Basil Lam. BBC WAC, RT, T; p.227

16 July 1972, Radio 3, 12.55–1.10 pm, interval talk with gramophone record illustrations, by John Beckett, on Bach's *Goldberg Variations*. (Main programme: George Malcolm playing Bach's *Goldberg Variations* at the Cheltenham Festival.) Recorded 12 February 1971, producer Alan Walker. BBC A, BBC WAC, RT, T.

17 August 1972, Radio 3, 11.20–11.55 pm, songs and music by Purcell performed by David Thomas, bass, John Beckett, harpsichord, Desmond Dupré, viola da gamba and Adam Skeaping, violone. First of two programmes performed by Musica Reservata. Recorded 16 December 1971 in the concert hall, Broadcasting House, producer Basil Lam. Music includes *Begin the Song (The Resurrection)*, harpsichord solos (including *A New Irish Tune*) and *Let the Dreadful Engines* (from the *Comical History of Don Quixote*). BBC WAC, RT, T; p. 224

23 August 1972, Radio 3, 11.25–11.55 pm, songs and music by Purcell performed by David Thomas, bass, John Beckett, harpsichord, Desmond Dupré, viola da gamba and Adam Skeaping, violone. Second of two programmes performed by Musica Reservata. Recorded 17 December 1971 in the concert hall, Broadcasting House, producer Basil Lam. Music includes the song *Awake, and with Attention hear*, harpsichord solos, and two songs, *Thy Genius, lo, from his sweet bed of Roses* and *Anacreon's Defeat*. BBC WAC, RT, T.

11 May 1973, Radio 3, 11.30–11.55 pm, *French Court Music of the 13th century*. An anthology of mainly anonymous songs and dances. Performed by Musica Reservata, conducted by John Beckett. Gramophone records. RT, T.

5–10 November 1973, Radio 3, 9.05–9.50 am, *This Week's Composers: Dufay and Josquin.* Gramophone records. 6 November – Dufay: Chanson, *Se la face ay pale* (three versions); Musica Reservata, conductor John Beckett. RT.

15 April 1974, Radio 3, 3.10–3.55; 4.10–4.40 pm, *The Public Concert: The origins in 17th and 18th century Italy.* In part one: A Florentine Festival of 1589: excerpts from the second *intermedio.* Musica Reservata, conducted by John Beckett. RT.

27 July 1974, Radio 3, 9.40–10.15 pm, Music by Josquin des Prés, performed by Musica Reservata, conducted by John Beckett (organ). Recorded 20 April 1972 in the concert hall, Broadcasting House, producer Basil Lam. Repeated 19 June 1975. BBC WAC, KCL, RT, T; p. 277

31 July 1974, Radio 3, 10.35–11.15 am, *English and Burgundian music,* performed by Musica Reservata, conducted by John Beckett. Part of a public concert given in the Queen Elizabeth Hall, 28 March 1972. BBC WAC, RT.

23 November 1974, Radio 4 Northern Ireland, 10.15–10.45 pm, Four Centuries of Music in Ireland, Henry Purcell Consort, with John Beckett (Part one of a concert held in Trinity College Dublin. IT); p. 251–2

30 November 1974, Radio 4 Northern Ireland, 10.15–10.45 pm, Four Centuries of Music in Ireland, New Irish Chamber Orchestra, conducted by John Beckett. (Part two of a concert held in Trinity College Dublin. IT); p. 251–2

21 December 1975, Radio 3, 10.05–10.30 pm, Francesco Landini: *Chosi pensoso; Gram piant' agli occhi miei; Questa fanciull', amor; Non avrá ma' pietá; Musicha son.* Musica Reservata, conducted by John Beckett. Records. RT.

17 March 1976, Radio 3, 10.30–11.20 am, Bach Cantatas 167, *Ihr Menschen, ruhmet Gottes Liebe* and 127, *Herr Jesu Christ, wahr' Mensch und Gott.* Irené Sandford (soprano), Bernadette Greevy (contralto), Frank Patterson (tenor), William Young (bass). Guinness Choir, chorus master Victor Leeson, New Irish Chamber Orchestra, leader Mary Gallagher, conducted by John Beckett. Public concert given in St Ann's Church, Dawson Street, Dublin on 16 February 1975, producer Nicholas Anderson. BBC Northern Ireland. RT; pp. 253, 263

4 August 1976, Radio 3, 9.05–9.45 am, *This Week's Composer: Dufay.* Musica Reservata, conducted by John Beckett. *Vergine bella; Resveilliés vous et faites chiere lye; Mon cuer me fait tous dis penser; Bon jour, bon mois; Adieu, ces bons vins de Lannoys.* RT.

17 December 1976, Radio 3, 8.05–9.00 am, *Morning Concert.* Beethoven: Sonatina in C minor, played by Hugo D'Alton (mandoline) and John Beckett (fortepiano). Repeated in *This Week's Composer,* 6 April 1979. RT.

27 February 1977, Radio 3, 10.55–11.25 pm, Bach Cantata 167, *Ihr Menschen, ruhmet Gottes Liebe.* Irené Sandford (soprano), Bernadette Greevy (contralto), Frank Patterson (tenor), William Young (bass). Guinness Choir, New Irish Chamber Orchestra, leader Mary Gallagher, conducted by John Beckett. Public concert given in St Ann's Church,

Dawson Street, Dublin on 16 February 1975, producer Nicholas Anderson. RT; pp. 253, 263

27 March 1977, Radio 3, 5.00–6.00 pm, *Music for Ferdinand and Isabella*, performed by Musica Reservata, conducted by John Beckett, the Early Music Quartet and the Early Music Consort of London, directed by David Munrow. Gramophone records. RT.

28 April 1977, Radio 3, 4.15–5.25 pm, *Concert from the 1976 Dublin Arts Festival*. Purcell: a sequence of songs and orchestral pieces; Handel: Concerto Grosso in B minor, op. 6, No. 3; Bach: Cantata No. 51, *Jauchzet Gott in allen Landen*. Irené Sandford (soprano), Michael Laird (trumpet), Gillian Smith (harpsichord continuo), Betty Sullivan (cello continuo), New Irish Chamber Orchestra, leader Mary Gallagher, conducted by John Beckett. RT.

23 July 1977, Radio 3, 10.00–10.45 pm, Bach Cantata No. 32, *Liebster Jesu, mein Verlangen* and No. 27, *Wer weiss, wie nahe mir mein Ende!*. Performed by soloists, the Cantata Singers and the New Irish Chamber Orchestra conducted by John Beckett. Irené Sandford (soprano), Bernadette Greevy (contralto), Frank Patterson (tenor), William Young (bass). John O'Sullivan, organ continuo. Recorded in St Ann's Church, Dawson St, Dublin, on 13 February 1977, producer Nicholas Anderson. BBC A, IT, RT, T; p. 269

9 August 1977, Radio 3, 10.45–11.25 pm, Bach Cantata No. 84, *Ich bin vergnügt mit meinem Glücke, das mir der liebe Gott beschart* and No. 79, *Gott, der Herr, ist Sonn und Schild*. Irené Sandford (soprano), Áine nic Gabhann (contralto), William Young (bass), the Cantata Singers and the New Irish Chamber Orchestra, conducted by John Beckett. Recorded at a public concert in St Ann's Church, Dawson Street, Dublin on 27 February 1977, producer Dr Edgar Boucher of BBC Northern Ireland. RT; p. 269

6 April 1979, Radio 3, 11.30–11.55 pm, Bach Cantata No. 99, *Was Gott tut, das ist wohlgetan*. Irené Sandford (soprano), Áine nic Gabhann (contralto), Frank Patterson (tenor), William Young (bass), the Cantata Singers and the New Irish Chamber Orchestra, conducted by John Beckett. Recorded in St Ann's Church, Dawson St, Dublin, on 13 February 1978, producer Nicholas Anderson. BBC A, IT; p. 277

23 April 1979, Radio 3, 10.45–11.30 pm, Bach Cantata No. 21, *Ich hatte viel Bekümmernis* by J.S. Bach. Irené Sandford (soprano), Frank Patterson (tenor), William Young (bass), John O'Sullivan (organ), the Cantata Singers and the New Irish Chamber Orchestra conducted by John Beckett. Recorded in St Ann's Church, Dawson St, Dublin, on 12 February 1978, producer Nicholas Anderson. BBC A, IT, RT; p. 277

17 May 1979, Radio 3, 11.00–11.55 pm, Bach: Sinfonia (Cantata No. 42) and Cantata No. 30, *Freue dich, erlöste Schar*. Irené Sandford (soprano), Bernadette Greevy (contralto), Frank Patterson (tenor), William Young (bass), John O'Sullivan (organ), the Cantata Singers and the New Irish Chamber Orchestra, conducted by John Beckett. Recorded in St Ann's Church, Dawson St, Dublin, on 19 February 1978, producer Nicholas Anderson. BBC A, RT; p. 277

31 May 1979, Radio 3, 7.05–8.00 am, *Overture*, part 1: The Greek Connection.

Monteverdi: Toccata (*Orfeo*), played by Musica Reservata, conducted by John Beckett. RT. Repeated on *Morning Concert*, 1 January 1982.

8 June 1979, Radio 3, 11.30–11.55 pm, Bach Cantata No. 163, *Nur jedem das Seine*. Irené Sandford (soprano), Áine Nic Gabhann (contralto), Frank Patterson (tenor), William Young (bass), the Cantata Singers and the New Irish Chamber Orchestra conducted by John Beckett. Recorded in the Masonic Hall, Dublin, on 16 February 1978, producer Nicholas Anderson. BBC A, IT; p. 277

27 June 1979, Radio 3, 9.45–10.25 pm, Bach Cantata No. 123 *Liebster Immanuel, Herzog der Frommen*, and Cantata No. 164, *Ihr, die ihr euch von Christo nennet*. Irené Sandford (soprano), Bernadette Greevy (contralto), Frank Patterson (tenor), William Young (bass), the Cantata Singers and the New Irish Chamber Orchestra conducted by John Beckett. Recorded in St Ann's Church, Dawson St, Dublin, on 12 September 1978, producer Nicholas Anderson. BBC A, IT; p. 279

15 July 1979, Radio 3, 10.30–11.00 am, *Prom Talk:* Interpreting Bach cantatas – a conversation with John Beckett. Presented by Jeremy Siepmann; producer Piers Burton. BBC A, IT; p. 290

19 July 1979, Radio 3, 11.15–11.55 pm, Bach Cantata No. 86, *Wahrlich, wahrlich, ich sage euch* and Cantata No. 138, *Warum betrubst du dich, mein Herz?*. Violet Twomey (soprano), Áine nic Gabhann (contralto), Frank Patterson (tenor), William Young (bass), the Cantata Singers and the New Irish Chamber Orchestra conducted by John Beckett. Recorded in St Ann's Church, Dawson St, Dublin, on 11 February 1979, producer Nicholas Anderson. BBC A, IT; p. 284

22 July 1979, Radio 3, 7.30–8.20 / 8.40–10.00 pm, Prom concert, Royal Albert Hall: Bach Cantatas Nos. 174, 21, (42), 30. Irené Sandford (soprano), Bernadette Greevy (contralto), Frank Patterson (tenor), William Young (bass), the Cantata Singers and the New Irish Chamber Orchestra conducted by John Beckett. Live broadcast. Printed programme, RT; pp. 290–1

9 August 1979, Radio 3, 11.05–11.55 pm, Bach Cantata No. 133, *Ich freue mich in dir* and No. 117, *Sei Lob und Ehr dem höchsten Gut*. Irené Sandford (soprano), Áine nic Gabhann (contralto), Frank Patterson (tenor), William Young (bass), the Cantata Singers and the New Irish Chamber Orchestra conducted by John Beckett. Recorded in St Ann's Church, Dawson St, Dublin, on 4 February 1979, producer Nicholas Anderson. BBC A, IT; p. 283

31 August 1979, Radio 3, 10.55–11.55 pm, Bach Cantata No. 174, *Ich liebe den Höchsten von ganzem Gemüte* and No. 177, *Ich ruf zu dir, Herr Jesu Christ*. Irené Sandford (soprano), Bernadette Greevy (contralto), Frank Patterson (tenor), William Young (bass), the Cantata Singers and the New Irish Chamber Orchestra conducted by John Beckett. Recorded in St Ann's Church, Dawson St, Dublin, on 1 March 1979, producer Nicholas Anderson. BBC A, IT; p. 284

6 September 1979, Radio 3, 11.20–11.55 pm, Bach Cantata No. 144, *Nimm, was dein ist,*

und gehe hin and No. 150, *Nach dir, Herr, varlanget mich*. Violet Twomey (soprano), Áine nic Gabhann (contralto), Frank Patterson (tenor), William Young (bass), the Cantata Singers and the New Irish Chamber Orchestra conducted by John Beckett. Recorded in St Ann's Church, Dawson St, Dublin, on 7 February 1979, producer Nicholas Anderson. BBC A, IT; p. 284

1 November 1979, Radio 4, 8.50–9.30 pm, Bach Cantata No. 208, *Was mir behagt, ist nur die muntre Jagd!* by J.S. Bach. Irené Sandford (soprano), Violet Twomey (soprano), Frank Patterson (tenor), William Young (bass), the Cantata Singers, the New Irish Chamber Orchestra and Gillian Smith, harpsichord, conducted by John Beckett. Recorded in the Masonic Hall, Dublin, on 10 September 1977, producer Nicholas Anderson. Repeated 2 June 1980. BBC A, RT; p. 274

11 February 1980, Radio 3, 7.05–8.00 am, *Overture*. Cavalieri, ed. Malvezzi: *Intermedio No. 6* (1589), played by Musica Reservata, conducted by John Beckett. RT.

19 April 1980, Radio 3, 1.05–2.00 pm: *Early Music Forum*, presented by Nicholas Anderson. Music by Byrd, Munday, Farnaby, and Inglot played on the virginals by John Beckett. Bach Cantata No. 199: 'Mein Herze schwimmt in Blut', Irené Sandford (soprano), New Irish Chamber Orchestra, John O'Sullivan (chamber organ), conducted by John Beckett. T, IT, RT; p. 295

15 August 1980, Radio 3, 2.35–3.10 pm, *English harpsichord music* (Byrd and Purcell) played by John Beckett (harpsichord). Recorded 3 March 1980. Repeated 1 February 1981. BBC A, T, RT.

8 September 1980, Radio 3, 11.05–11.15 pm, *Beethoven*, Adagio in E flat, played by Hugo D'Alton (mandoline) and John Beckett (fortepiano). Gramophone record. RT.

30 October 1980, Radio 3, 11.05–11.15 pm, *Beethoven*, Theme and Variations in D, played by Hugo D'Alton (mandoline) and John Beckett (fortepiano). Gramophone record. RT.

13 December 1980, Radio 3, 1.05–2.00 pm, Early Music Forum, introduced by Nicholas Kenyon. Keyboard music by William Byrd and Johann Froberger, played by John Beckett and Christopher Hogwood. Other contributors: Peter Holman and Howard Brown. Recorded 12 December 1980, producer Clive Bennett. BBC A, T, RT.

7 January 1981, Radio 3, 11.30 am –12.05 pm, *Purcell*. Sacred and secular songs performed by Frank Patterson (tenor), Andrew Robinson (viola da gamba) and John Beckett (harpsichord). RT.

13 August 1981, Radio 3 VHF, 1.05–2.25 pm, *English Arrangements*. John Beckett (harpsichord), the Academy of Ancient Music, leader Catherine Mackintosh, director Christopher Hogwood. Geminiani: Concerto Grosso in E (after Corelli); Scarlatti: Sonatas Kk 13, 4 and 2; Avison: Concerti Grossi, Nos. 2 and 5 (after Scarlatti); Geminiani: Concerto Grosso in A (after Corelli). RT.

15 November 1981, Radio 3, 2.00–3.10 / 3.20–4.35 / 4.55–6.30 pm, *The Patient Socrates (Der Geduldige Socrates)*, opera in three acts by Georg P. Telemann. Sung in Norman Platt's English translation. Performed by soloists and the B.B.C. Scottish

Symphony Orchestra conducted by John Beckett. Recorded 12 June 1981. BBC A, T; pp. 313–4

24 April 1982, Radio 3, 1.05–2.00 pm, *Early Music Forum*. Christopher Hogwood discusses the eighteenth-century English passion for arrangements and why they are useful to today's performers. Scarlatti: Sonata in C minor, Kk 11; Sonatas in D minor, Kk 41 and 5 performed by John Beckett, harpsichord. RT, T.

28 September 1982, Radio 3, 7.05–9.00 am, *Morning Concert*, Hummel: Sonata in C played by Hugo D'Alton (mandoline) and John Beckett (fortepiano). Repeated in *This Week's Composer*, 16 May 1986. RT, T.

14–18 November 1983, Radio 3, Monday–Friday, 7.05–9.00 am, *Morning Concert*. Music by various composers. Producer: John Beckett. RT; p. 344

9–13 January 1984, Radio 3, Monday–Friday, 7.05–9.00 am, *Morning Concert*. Music by various composers. Producer: John Beckett. RT; p. 345

31 January 1984, Radio Ulster, 7.20–8.30 pm, Ulster Orchestra, conducted by John Beckett. Brahms: Serenade No. 2, Sibelius: *Rakastava*. IT.

24–28 September 1984, Radio 3, Monday–Friday, 7.05–9.00 am, *Morning Concert*. Music by various composers. Producer: John Beckett. RT; p. 346

12–16 November 1984, Radio 3, Monday–Friday, 7.05–9.00 am, *Morning Concert*. Music by various composers. Producer: John Beckett. RT; p. 346

10 December 1984, Radio 3, Monday, 9.05–10.00 am, *This Week's Composer:* Sibelius. The Symhonic Poems. *En Saga*, op. 9; *Spring Song*, op. 16; *Scènes historiques*, op. 25; *Finlandia*, op. 26. Producer: John Beckett.

> Tuesday: *Four Legends*, op.22: *Lemminkäinen and the Maidens of Saari*, *The Swan of Tuonela*, *Lemminkäinen in Tuonela*, *Lemminkäinen's Homeward Journey*.
> Wednesday: *Pohjola's Daughter*, op. 49; *The Dryad*, op. 45, No. 1; *Night Ride and Sunrise*, op. 55; *In Memoriam*, op. 59; *Pan and Echo*, op. 53.
> Thursday: *The Bard*, op. 64; *Luonnotar*, op. 70; *The Oceanides*, op. 73; Six Humoresques for violin and orchestra, op. 87, Nos. 1 and 2; op. 89, Nos. 1–4.
> Friday: Items from *The Tempest*, op. 109; *Funeral Music*, op. 111, No. 2 for organ; *Tapiola*, op. 112. RT; p. 346

7 January 1985, Radio 3, 7.30–8.35 pm; 8.55–10.10 pm, Handel: *L'Allegro, Il Pensoroso ed il Moderato*. Raglan Baroque Players and Raglan Baroque singers, conductor Nicholas Kraemer. Recorded in St John's, Smith Square on 5 January 1985; repeated 13 April 1985. Producer: John Beckett [?]. RT; p.346

1 April 1985, Radio 3, Monday 9.05–10.00 am, *This Week's Composer:* Max Bruch – The works for violin and orchestra. Violin Concerto No. 1 in G min, op. 26; Two piano pieces, op. 12, Nos 1 and 2; *Konzertstück*, op. 84 (records). Producer: John Beckett.

> Tuesday: Violin Concerto No. 2 in D min, op. 44; *Romanze*, *Fantasiestück*, op. 14; *In Memoriam*, op. 65 (records).

Wednesday: Romanian Melody, op. 83, No. 5; Three Pieces, op. 83, Nos. 2, 6 and 7; Scottish Fantasy, op. 46 (records).

Thursday: Romance, op. 42; Violin Concerto No. 3 in D min, op. 58.

Friday: Serenade, op. 75; Two Piano Pieces, op. 12, Nos. 4 and 5; Adagio appassionato, op. 57 (records). RT; p. 347

26 July 1985, Radio 3, 7.00– 7.30 pm, *Schubert orchestrated by Liszt and Britten*, Irené Sandford (soprano), Ulster Orchestra led by Maurice Cavanagh, conducted by John Beckett. Orch. Liszt: *Grande marche héroïque*; *Die junge Nonne*; *Gretchen am Spinnrade*; *Lied der Mignon*; orch. Britten: *Die Forelle*. RT.

2 September 1985, Radio 3, Monday, 9.05–10.00 am, *This Week's Composer:* Johann Christian Bach. *Gloria in excelsis* in G (records). Producer: John Beckett.

Tuesday: *Duetto* in A, op. 18; Quintet in E flat, op. 11 No. 4, *Tre canzonette a due*, op. 4, Nos. 1–3; Piano Concerto in D, op. 13, No. 2.

Wednesday: Sinfonia Concertante in C; Scena and Aria from *La Clemenza di Scipione*; Sinfonia Concertante in E flat.

Thursday: Overture: *La cascina*; Quintet in D, op. 22, No. 1; Sonata in C minor, op. 5, No. 6; Symphony in G minor, op. 6 No. 6.

Friday: Quartet in D, op. 19, No. 2; *Amadis des Gaules* (Tragédie lyrique) – Overture and Act 2. RT; p. 347

2 December 1985, Radio 3, Monday, 9.05–10.00 am, *This Week's Composer:* Haydn's Contemporaries. Georg Reutter: *Servicio di tavola*; Nicola Porpora: Recitative and Aria; Gregor Joseph Werner: *Hirtenlied*; C. P. E. Bach: Sonata in E, Wq 48, No. 3; C. P. E. Bach: Symphony in A, Wq 182, No. 4. Producer: John Beckett.

Tuesday: Georg Christoph Wagenseil: Symphony in D; Florian Leopold Gassman: String Quartet No. 3 in E minor; Mozart: String Quartet in D minor, K. 173; Gluck: Ballet: *Don Juan* (finale).

Wednesday: Ignaz Pleyel: *Symphonie concertante* in F, for flute, oboe, bassoon, horn and orchestra; Johann Ladislaus Dussek: Rondo on *O dear, what can the matter be?*; Paul Wranitzky: Symphony in C.

Thursday: Michael Haydn: *Magnificat* in F; Hummel: Mass in E flat.

Friday: F. X. Mozart: Sonata in E; Beethoven: *Sally in our Alley*, op. 108, No. 25; Beethoven: Piano Trio in C minor, op. 1, No. 3. RT; p. 347

21 April 1986, Radio 3, Monday, 9.05–10.00 am, *This Week's Composer:* Composers associated with the Schola Cantorum in Paris, from its foundation in 1894 until the 1970s. Alexandre Guilmont: Sonata No. 2 in D, op. 50, for organ; Charles Bordes: *Promenade matinale*, for baritone and orchestra; D'Indy: *Symphonie sur un chant montagnard français*, op. 25. Producer: John Beckett.

Tuesday: Albéniz: *El Puerto*; *Navarra*; Albéric Magnard: Symphony No. 3 in B flat minor, op. 11.

Wednesday: Déodat de Severac: *Sous les lauriers roses*, for piano; Roussel: Symphony

No. 3 in G minor, op. 42; Satie: *En habit de cheval* (piano duet); Déodat de Severac: *Tantum ergo sacramentum*.

Thursday: Georges Auric: Sonata in F for piano; Louis Durey: *Le printemps au fond de la mer*; Marcel Mihalovici: Sonatina for oboe and piano; Edgard Varèse: *Hyperprism*.

Friday: Daniel-Lesur: *Le cantique des cantiques*; Maurice Ohana: *Tiento*, for guitar; Maurice Ohana: *Lys de madrigaux*. RT; p. 347

12–16 May 1986, Radio 3, Monday–Friday, 7.05–9.00 am, *Morning Concert*. Music by various composers. Producer: John Beckett.

28 July–1 August 1986, Radio 3, Monday–Friday, 7.05–9.00 am, *Morning Concert*. Music by various composers. Producer: John Beckett. RT.

27 October 1986, Radio 3, Monday, 9.05–10.00 am, *This Week's Composer:* Mendelssohn. Apprenticeship. Sonata in G minor, op. 105, for piano; *Hexenlied*, op. 8, No. 8; Symphony No. 1 in C minor, op. 11. Producer: John Beckett.

Tuesday: Precocious Mastery. *Scherzo* (Octet, op. 20); String Quintet in A, op. 18; *Caprice*, op. 16, No. 3, for piano; Overture: *Calm Sea and Prosperous Voyage*, op. 27.

Wednesday: Maturity. Overture: *The Hebrides*, op. 26; Symphony No. 3 in A minor, op. 56 (Scottish).

Thursday: The Neo-Classical Romantic. *St Paul*, op. 36 (Part 1: Overture and Nos. 1–15).

Friday: The Last Year. *Magnificat*, op. 69, No. 3; String Quartet in F minor, op. 80; *Lieder*; *Andante* and *Scherzo*, op. 81. RT; p. 347

22–26 December 1986, Radio 3, Monday–Friday, 7.05–9.00 am, *Morning Concert*. Music by various composers. Producer: John Beckett. RT.

26 January 1987, Radio 3, Monday, 9.05–10.00 am, *This Week's Composer:* Fauré. The First Period: 1860–85. *Puisqu'ici-bas toute âme*; *Barcarolle* No. 1 in A minor, op. 26 (played by the composer, piano roll, 1913); Songs; Nocturne No. 5 in B flat; Violin Sonata in A, op. 13. Producer: John Beckett.

Tuesday: The Second Period: 1885–1906. *La bonne chanson*, op. 61; Piano Quintet in D minor, op. 89.

Wednesday: The Third Period (1): 1906–14. *Le don silencieux*, op. 92; *Chanson*, op. 94; *Vocalise-étude*; Nine Preludes, op. 103, for piano; *Le jardin clos*, op. 106, for soprano and piano; Nocturne No. 11 in F sharp minor, op. 104, No. 1, for piano.

Thursday: The Third Period (2): 1915–18. Sonata in E minor, op. 108, for violin and piano; Nocturne No. 12 in E minor, op. 107, for piano; Cello Sonata in D minor, op. 109.

Friday: The Third Period (3): 1919–24. *Mirages*, op. 113, for baritone and piano; *Barcarolle* No. 13 in C, op. 116, for piano; *L'Horizon chimérique*, op. 118, for baritone and piano; String Quartet in E minor, op. 121. RT; p. 347

6 April 1987, Radio 3, Monday, 9.10–10.10 am, *This Week's Composer:* Igor Stravinsky.

Sonata in F sharp minor; *Scherzo* (Symphony in E flat, op. 1); *The faun and the shepherdess*, op. 2; *Fireworks*, op. 4. Producer: John Beckett.

> Tuesday: *Pribaoutki*; *Three pieces for string quartet*; *Les noces*; *Symphonies of wind instruments* (1920 version).
>
> Wednesday: *Serenade in A*; *Apollo*; *Piano Rag Music* (played by Stravinsky).
>
> Thursday: *Cantata on Old English Texts*; Septet; *Three Shakespeare Songs*; *Epitaphium 'für das Grabmal des Prinzen Max Egon zu Fürstenberg'*.
>
> Friday: *Agon*; *Requiem Canticles*; *Variations for Orchestra*; *The owl and the pussy-cat*. RT; p. 347

29 May–2 June 1987, Radio 3, Monday–Friday, 7.05–9.00 am, *Morning Concert*. Music by various composers. Producer: John Beckett. RT; p. 347

31 August–5 September 1987, Monday, 9.10–10.10 am, *This Week's Composer: Monteverdi*. *La prima prattica:* Mass a 6 (*In illo tempore*); *La seconda prattica: Magnificat* a 7.

> Tuesday: Pieces from the Fourth and Fifth Books of Madrigals.
>
> Wednesday: *Ballo delle ingrate.*
>
> Thursday: Pieces from the Seventh and Eighth Book of Madrigals.
>
> Friday: *Selva morale e spirituale*: *Beatus vir* (1); *Chi vol che m'innamori*; *Confitebor tibi, Domine*; *Adoramus te*; *Gloria* a 7. RT; p. 347

20 November 1987, Radio 3, 1.45–2.25 pm, *English Virginals Music*, John Beckett (virginals). Music by Byrd, John Munday, William Inglot and Giles Farnaby. RT, IT.

22 November 1987, Radio 3, 8.10–9 am, *Lili Kraus* (piano). The first of a series of six programmes. Music by Mozart. Producer John Beckett. RT; p. 347

29 November 1987, Radio 3, 8.10–9 am, *Lili Kraus* (piano). The second of a series of six programmes. Music by Bartók and Mozart. Producer John Beckett. RT; p. 347

6 December 1987, Radio 3, 8.10–9 am, *Lili Kraus* (piano). The third of a series of six programmes. Music by Mozart. Producer John Beckett. RT; p. 347

13 December 1987, Radio 3, 8.10–9 am, *Lili Kraus* (piano). The fourth of a series of six programmes. Music by Mozart. Producer John Beckett. RT; p. 347

20 December 1987, Radio 3, 8.10–9 am, *Lili Kraus* (piano). The fifth of a series of six programmes. Music by Mozart. Producer John Beckett. RT; p. 347

27 December 1987, Radio 3, 8.10–9 am, *Lili Kraus* (piano). The sixth of a series of six programmes. Music by Schubert and Mozart. Producer John Beckett. RT; p. 347

28 December 1987, Radio 3, 10.00–10.30 pm, first of five programmes of Chopin Nocturnes performed by Peter Katin (piano). Recorded 15 November 1986 in Studio 2, Maida Vale, Delaware Road, producer John Beckett. BBC A, IT; p. 347

29 December 1987, Radio 3, 9.00–9.20 pm, second of five programmes of Chopin Nocturnes performed by Peter Katin (piano). Recorded 21 November 1986 in Studio 2, Maida Vale, Delaware Road, producer John Beckett. BBC A, IT; p. 347

30 December 1987, Radio 3, 9.45–10.10 pm, third of five programmes of Chopin

Nocturnes performed by Peter Katin (piano). Recorded 27 November 1986 in Studio 2, Maida Vale, Delaware Road, producer John Beckett. BBC A, IT; p. 347

31 December 1987, Radio 3, 9.55–10.30 pm, fourth of five programmes of Chopin Nocturnes performed by Peter Katin (piano). Recorded 27 November 1986 in Studio 2, Maida Vale, Delaware Road, producer John Beckett. BBC A, IT; p. 347

1 January 1987, Radio 3, 11.25–11.57 pm, fifth of five programmes of Chopin Nocturnes performed by Peter Katin (piano). Recorded 4 December 1986 in Studio 2, Maida Vale, Delaware Road, producer John Beckett. BBC A, IT; p. 347

4 January 1988, Radio 3, Monday, 9.10–10.10 am, *This Week's Composer:* Max Bruch. Six Songs, op. 7; Trio in C minor, op. 5; Seven Songs, op. 6. Producer: John Beckett.

> Tuesday: *Romanze*, op. 14, No. 1; *Fantasiestück*, op. 14, No. 2; Fantasia in D minor, op. 11; String Quartet in C minor, op. 9.
> Wednesday: Quintet in A minor, op. posth. (edited John Beckett); *Adagio* on Celtic Melodies, op. 56 for cello and orchestra; Serenade on Swedish Melodies, op. posth., for strings; *Kol Nidrei*, op. 47, for cello and orchestra.
> Thursday: Seven Part Songs, op. 71; *Scottish Fantasy*, op. 46.
> Friday: Three Pieces, op. 83, Nos. 3, 5 and 6 for clarinet, viola and harp; Five Songs, op. 99; Concerto for clarinet and viola, op. 88. RT; p. 349

15 April 1988, Radio 3, 9.35–10.25, Langham Chamber Orchestra conducted by John Beckett: Mozart (Symphony No. 14), Walter Leigh: *Music for strings*; Hindemith: *Spielmusik*; Leigh: *Interlude for the theatre*. Repeated on 4 September and 19 October 1989. RT, IT; p. 348

13 May 1988, Radio 3, 10.00–10.45 am, Langham Chamber Orchestra conducted by John Beckett: Walter Leigh: Overture: *Jolly Roger*; Hindemith: *Spielmusik*; Mozart: Symphony No 14: Walter Leigh: *Interlude for the Theatre*. RT, IT; p. 348

20 June 1988, Radio 3, 8.35–9.35 am, *Composers of the Week:* Boccherini. Cello Sonatas in A; Trios in F and B flat for two violins and cello. Producer: John Beckett.

> Tuesday: String Quartets in G minor and F, arranged for two harpsichords; String Quartets in C and E minor.
> Wednesday: *Stabat Mater.*
> Thursday: String Quintets in G minor and D major; Guitar Quintet in E.
> Friday: Symphonies in D and A; Cello Concerto in C. RT; p. 349

15 July 1988, Radio 3, 9.35–10.25 am, Langham Chamber Orchestra conducted by John Beckett, with Melvyn Tan (harpsichord). Mozart: Minuet in C K 409; Walter Leigh: Concertino for harpsichord and string orchestra; Suite: *A Midsummer Night's Dream*; Mozart: 6 German Dances K. 509. Repeated 29 November 1989. RT, IT; p. 348

16 August 1988, Radio 3, 6.30–7.00 pm, *Sounds of Transylvania*, presented by John Beckett. BBC WAC, BLSA, RT, IT; pp. 349–50

23 August 1988, Radio 3, 6.30–7.00 pm, *Sounds of Sardinia,* presented by John Beckett. BBC WAC, BLSA, RT, IT; p. 350

27 August 1988, Radio 3, 10.40–11.10 pm, *Bach's English Suites.* No. 1 in A, BWV 806, Melvyn Tan (harpsichord). Series producer: John Beckett. RT.

28 August 1988, Radio 3, 10.00–10.30 pm, *Bach's English Suites.* No. 2 in A minor, BWV 807, Melvyn Tan (harpsichord). Series producer: John Beckett. RT.

29 August 1988, Radio 3, 10.25–11.00 pm, *Bach's English Suites.* No. 3 in G minor, BWV 808, Melvyn Tan (harpsichord). Series producer: John Beckett. RT.

30 August 1988, Radio 3, 6.30–7.00 pm, *Sounds of Soviet Georgia,* presented by John Beckett. Repeated 20 June 1990. BBC WAC, BLSA, RT, IT; p. 350

30 August 1988, Radio 3, 10.25–11.00 pm, *Bach's English Suites.* No. 4 in F, BWV 809, Melvyn Tan (harpsichord). Series producer: John Beckett. RT.

1 September 1988, Radio 3, 10.25–11.00 pm, *Bach's English Suites.* No. 5 in E minor, BWV 810, Melvyn Tan (harpsichord). Series producer: John Beckett. RT.

2 September 1988, Radio 3, 10.25–11.00 pm, *Bach's English Suites*. No. 6 in D minor, BWV 811, Melvyn Tan (harpsichord). Series producer: John Beckett. RT.

13 September 1988, Radio 3, 9.35–10.05 am, *Domenico Scarlatti*, Sonatas in C minor (Kk 158), in E (Kk 206 and 207), in A (Kk 429) and in B minor (Kk 377). Kenneth Gilbert, harpsichord. Series producer: John Beckett. RT.

14 September 1988, Radio 3, 9.35–10.00 am, *Domenico Scarlatti*, Sonatas in G (Kk 241), in D (Kk 288), in A (Kk 322 and 323) and in E (Kk 380 and 381). Kenneth Gilbert, harpsichord. Series producer: John Beckett. RT.

15 September 1988, Radio 3, 9.35–10.10 am, *Domenico Scarlatti*, Sonatas in C (Kk 513), in F (Kk 524 and 525), in D (Kk 490, 491 and 492). Kenneth Gilbert, harpsichord. Series producer: John Beckett. RT.

21 September 1988, Radio 3, 3.10–4.00 pm, *Early Birds,* programme about the performers of early music, beginning with Dolmetsch in the early 1900s. Presented by John Beckett. BLSA, RT, IT; pp. 350–1

17 March 1989, Radio 3, 2.00–2.40 pm, Sibelius. Langham Chamber Orchestra, conducted by John Beckett, with Krysztof Smietana (violin): *Andante festivo*; *Humoresques* Nos 1 and 2, op. 87 and Nos 3–6, op. 89; *Rakastava*. Repeated 8 February 1990. RT, IT; p. 352

16 June 1989, Radio 3, 2.35–3.15 pm, Sibelius. *Rakastava*, op. 14; Serenades, op. 69, Nos 1 and 2; Suite: *Belshazzar's Feast*, op. 51. Krysztof Smietana (violin), Langham Chamber Orchestra, conducted by John Beckett. Repeated 16 May 1990. RT, IT; p. 352

24 January 1990, Radio 3, 5.00–5.30 pm, *The True Vine*. John Beckett presents recordings which the black American gospel singer Flora Molton made in Paris in her late 70s. Records. RT; p. 355

28 February 1990, Radio 3, 5.00–5.30 pm, *A Musical Eden*. John Beckett presents 1920s recordings of traditional music from Madagascar, the Ukraine, Turkey, Spain and Irish

and Welsh settlers in the USA, Cajun music from Louisiana and Jewish prayer for the time of the new moon; mono. Repeated 17 October 1990. IT, RT; p. 355

6 March 1990, Radio 3, 4.00–4.45 pm, Music by Poulenc: *Deux Marches et un inter-mède*, *Mouvements perpetuels*; Jean Françaix: *Sérénade*; and Christopher Bunting: Cello Concerto, performed by the Langham Chamber Orchestra. With Christopher Bunting (cello) and conducted by Christopher Adey. Recorded 2 August 1989, producers John Beckett and H. Warwick. BBC A, RT; pp. 352, 364

6 October 1991, Radio 3, 11.00–12.30 am, *A Dutch Retrospect*. First of twelve record-ings from the Royal Concertgebouw and Rotterdam Philharmonic's 1990/91 seasons. Royal Concertgebouw, conductor Riccardo Chailly. Wagner: *Overture* and *Bacchanale* from *Tannhäuser*; Diepenbrock: *Hymne an die Nacht*; Brahms: Symphony No. 4. Series producer John Beckett. RT; p. 356

13 October 1991, Radio 3, 11.00–12.45 am, *A Dutch Retrospect*. Second programme: Rotterdam Philharmonic, conductor Jacques van Steen. Elgar: *Overture: Cockaigne*; Vaughan Williams: *The Lark Ascending*; Walton: *Capriccio burlesco*; Bax: *Tintagel*; Britten: *The Young Person's Guide to the Orchestra*; Maxwell Davies: *An Orkney Wedding, with Sunrise*. Series producer John Beckett. RT; p. 356

20 October 1991, Radio 3, 11.00–11.40 am, *A Dutch Retrospect*. Third programme: Royal Concertgebouw, conductor Carlo Maria Giulini. Tchaikovsky: Symphony No. 2 in C minor, op. 17. Series producer John Beckett. RT; p. 356

27 October 1991, Radio 3, 11.00–12.30 am, *A Dutch Retrospect*. Fourth programme: Rotterdam Philharmonic, conductor Reinbert de Leeuw. Messiaen: *Turangalila Symphony*. Series producer John Beckett. RT; p. 356

3 November 1991, Radio 3, 11.00–12.45 am, *A Dutch Retrospect*. Fifth programme: Royal Concertgebouw, conductor Wolfgang Sawallisch. Beethoven: Overture: *Fidelio*, op. 72; Piano Concerto No. 4 in G, op. 58; Symphony No. 6 in F, op. 68 (*Pastoral*). Series producer John Beckett. RT; p. 356

10 November 1991, Radio 3, 11.03–12.45 am, *A Dutch Retrospect*. Sixth programme: Rotterdam Philharmonic, conductor Valery Gergiev. Shostakovich: Cello Concerto No. 1 in E flat, op. 107; Symphony No. 11, op. 103. Series producer John Beckett. RT; p. 356

17 November 1991, Radio 3, 11.00–12.25 am, *A Dutch Retrospect*. Seventh programme: Royal Concertgebouw, conductor Mariss Jansons. Berlioz: *Overture: Le Carnaval romain*; Debussy: *La Mer*; Elgar: Cello Concerto in E minor, op. 85; Ravel: *La Valse*. Series producer John Beckett. RT; p. 356

24 November 1991, Radio 3, 11.00–12.30 am, *A Dutch Retrospect*. Eighth programme: Rotterdam Philharmonic, conductor Reinbert de Leeuw. Frank Martin: *The Lay of the Love and Death of Cornet Christoph Rilke*; Charles Ives: *Three Places in New England* (conductor Jürg Wyttenbach). Series producer John Beckett. RT; p. 356

1 December 1991, Radio 3, 10.45–12.45 am, *A Dutch Retrospect*. Ninth programme: Royal

Concertgebouw, conductor Nikolaus Harnoncourt. Mozart – the Apotheosis of His Art as a Symphonist. Symphony No. 39 in E flat (K. 543); Symphony No. 40 in G minor (K. 550); a sequence of aphoristic statements by Busoni on the nature of Mozart's genius; Symphony No. 41 in C (K. 551) (*Jupiter*). Series producer John Beckett. RT; p. 356

8 December 1991, Radio 3, 11.00–12.25 am, *A Dutch Retrospect*. Tenth programme: Rotterdam Philharmonic, conductor Paavo Berglund. Sibelius: Violin Concerto in D minor, op. 47; Walton: Symphony No. 1 (conductor Jeffrey Tate). Series producer John Beckett. RT; p. 356

15 December 1991, Radio 3, 11.00–12.45 am, *A Dutch Retrospect*. Eleventh programme: Royal Concertgebouw, conductor Klaus Tennstedt. Schoenberg: *A Survivor from Warsaw*; Mahler: *Symphony No. 5 in C sharp minor*. Series producer John Beckett. RT; p. 356

22 December 1991, Radio 3, 11.00–12.30 am, *A Dutch Retrospect*. Final programme: Royal Concertgebouw, conductor Riccardo Chailly. Bruckner: Symphony No. 5 in B flat. Series producer John Beckett. RT; p. 356

3 January 1994, Radio 3, 2.00–3.20 pm, *A Dutch Retrospect*. First of 13 concerts recorded during the 1991/92 seasons of the Royal Concertgebouw, Amsterdam, and the Rotterdam Philharmonic. Royal Concertgebouw, conductor Riccardo Chailly. Mosolov: *The Foundry*; Ives: *The Unanswered Question*; Varèse: *Arcana*; Peter Schat: *The Heavens*. Series producer John Beckett. RT; p. 356

10 January 1994, Radio 3, 2.05–3.25 pm, *A Dutch Retrospect*. Second programme: Rotterdam Philharmonic, conductor Jeffrey Tate. Strauss: Symphonic Interlude (Intermezzo); Mozart: Piano Concerto No. 25 in C (K. 503); Tristan Keuris: Capriccio for 12 wind instruments and double bass; Strauss: Symphonic Fantasy. Series producer John Beckett. RT; p. 356

17 January 1994, Radio 3, 2.00–3.30 pm, *A Dutch Retrospect*. Third programme: Royal Concertgebouw, conductor Wolfgang Sawallisch. Beethoven: Overture *The Consecration of the House*; Symphony No. 4 in B flat; Symphony No. 7 in A. Series producer John Beckett. RT; p. 356

24 January 1994, Radio 3, 2.00–3.20 pm, *A Dutch Retrospect*. Fourth programme: Rotterdam Philharmonic, conductory Valery Gergiev. Honegger: *Pastorale d'été*; Rachmaninov: Piano Concerto No. 3 in D minor; Ravel: *Boléro*. Series producer John Beckett. RT; p. 356

31 January 1994, Radio 3, 2.00–3.25 pm, *A Dutch Retrospect*. Fifth programme: Royal Concertgebouw, conductor Nikolaus Harnoncourt. Haydn: Symphony No. 93 in D; Mozart: *Ch'io mi scordi di te*; Beethoven: *Ah, perfido!* Schubert: Symphony No. 2 in B flat. Series producer John Beckett. RT; p. 356

7 February 1994, Radio 3, 2.05–3.45 pm, *A Dutch Retrospect*. Sixth programme: Rotterdam Philharmonic, Valery Gergiev. Stravinsky: *Scherzo fantastique*; Scriabin: Piano Concerto in F sharp minor; Rimsky-Korsakov: *Sheherazade*. Series producer John Beckett. RT; p. 356

14 February 1994, Radio 3, 2.00–3.30 pm, *A Dutch Retrospect*. Seventh programme: Royal Concertgebouw, conductor Riccardo Chailly. Webern: Passacaglia; Bruckner: Symphony No. 2 in C minor. Series producer John Beckett. RT; p. 356

21 February 1994, Radio 3, 2.10–3.20 pm, *A Dutch Retrospect*. Eighth programme: Rotterdam Philharmonic, conductor Frans Brüggen. Mozart: Piano Concerto No. 24 in C minor (K. 491), Deszo Ranki (piano); Symphony No. 41 in C (K. 551) ('Jupiter'). Series producer John Beckett. RT; p. 356

28 February 1994, Radio 3, 2.00–3.25 pm, *A Dutch Retrospect*. Ninth programme: Royal Concertgebouw, conductor Charles Dutoit. Stravinsky: *Symphonies of wind instruments*; Violin Concerto in D; *The Firebird*. Series producer John Beckett. RT; p. 356

7 March 1994, Radio 3, 2.00–3.15 pm, *A Dutch Retrospect*. Tenth programme: Rotterdam Philharmonic, conductor Simon Rattle. Bruckner: Symphony No. 7 in E. Series producer John Beckett. RT; p. 356

14 March 1994, Radio 3, 2.10–3.45 pm, *A Dutch Retrospect*. Eleventh programme: Royal Concertgebouw, conductor André Previn. Brahms: Violin Concerto in D; Elgar: Symphony No. 2 in E flat. Series producer John Beckett. RT; p. 356

21 March 1994, Radio 3, 2.00–3.10 pm, *A Dutch Retrospect*. Twelfth programme: Rotterdam Philharmonic, conductor Hans Vonk. Arr. Stravinsky: *The Star-Spangled Banner*; Varèse: *Amériques*; Dvořák: Symphony No. 9 in E minor (*From the New World*). Series producer John Beckett. RT; p. 356

28 March 1994, Radio 3, 2.05–3.45 pm, *A Dutch Retrospect*. Last programme: Royal Concertgebouw, conductor Riccardo Chailly. Messiaen: Turangalila Symphony. Series producer John Beckett. RT; p. 356

9 December 1994, Radio 3, 10.45–11.30 pm, *Friday Feature: Lonely Waters*. The music of English composer E. J. Moeran, born 100 years ago this month. With contributors including John Beckett. Producer, Patrick Lambert. BBC WAC, IT, Patrick Lambert. Repeated 7 September 1995; p. 360

12 April 1997, Radio 3, 10.30–11.15 pm, *Between the Ears*. Six experimental radiophonic programmes. 2: From the Diary of a Fly. At the centre of Adrian Jack's musical tangled web are the diaries of Margaret Fountaine, linking her fascination with butterflies and her appetite for life. Joining Anna Massey in her travels are the Rev. W.M. Atkins, John Beckett ... Christopher Page and John Steane. Instrumentalists add their scrapings and flutterings to the music of Earth's smallest creatures. RT.

9 September 1999, Radio 3, 10.40–11.30 pm, *Beckett's Radio Plays*. Martin Esslin introduces the last of three programmes dedicated to the radio plays of Samuel Beckett. 3: *Words and Music*. Remastered from the original 1962 BBC production. Music by John Beckett, director Michael Bakewell. *A Piece of Monologue*. Originally broadcast in 1986 and performed by Ronald Pickup. Director Ronald Mason. RT; p. 376

Appendix E
Musica Reservata Concerts
(in which John Beckett was involved)

In concerts when musicians play the same instruments and singers sing in the same vocal ranges, this information is not repeated; only variations are noted. For example, Jeremy Montagu always played percussion and Grayston Burgess always sang counter-tenor.

Date unknown: performance for The Fellowship of the White Boar (The Richard III Society). No details of musicians. Music by Obrecht, Dunstable/Bedingham, Dufay, Binchois, de Lantins and Ockeghem. (*Early Music* magazine; Royal Academy of Music, London.) p. 127

30 January 1960: *A concert of medieval music*, Fenton House. Grayston Burgess (counter-tenor); Eric Halfpenny (early cross flute), John Sothcott (recorder), June Baines (tenor viol), John Beckett (tenor viol and regal), Francis Baines (hurdy-gurdy and bagpipes), Michael Morrow (lute) and Jeremy Montagu (percussion). Music by Dufay, Binchois, Dunstable, Ockeghem, Landini, and de Lantins. (King's College London.) pp. 126–7

23 April 1960: Concert in Hampstead Parish Church. Grayston Burgess; John Sothcott, Daphne Webb (cello), Theo Wyatt (recorder) and John Beckett, harpsichord. Music by Telemann, Bach, Loeillet, Monteverdi, Sweelinck and Purcell. (King's College London.) p. 131

26 May 1960: *A concert of medieval music*, 17 Holly Mount, Hampstead. Grayston Burgess, John Whitworth (counter-tenor); John Sothcott, Eric Halfpenny, John Beckett (treble viol), June Baines, Alan Lumsden (sackbut), Francis Baines, Joan Rimmer (psaltery), Michael Morrow, Guy Oldham (bowed monochord and cymbal), Jeremy Montagu. No details of music performed. (King's College London.) pp. 131

2 November 1960: *Medieval vocal and instrumental music*, Horniman Museum and Library,

London. Grayston Burgess, John Whitworth; John Sothcott, John Beckett (treble viol), Michael Morrow, Jeremy Montagu. Music by Dufay, Dunstable, from the Buxheimer Orgelbuch, Binchois, Landini, de Vaqueiras, de la Halle, Anon (13th and 14th century). (King's College London.) p. 134

27 April 1961: *Concert of music by Musica Reservata*, Fenton House, Hampstead. Grayston Burgess, John Whitworth; John Sothcott, June Baines (tenor viol), Daphne Webb (rebec), Michael Morrow, Guy Oldham (portative organ), Jeremy Montagu. John Beckett, now in hospital after car crash, was to play the rebec, and was replaced by Daphne Webb. Music by Arbeau, Binchois, Dufay, from Buxheimer Orgelbuch, Landini, de Vaqueiras and de la Halle. (King's College London.) pp. 136–7

25 May 1961: *A programme of 13th and 14th century music given by Musica Reservata*, Chelsea School of Art. John Beckett was to be the conductor, but was still in hospital. French and Italian music. (King's College London.) p. 137

4 November 1961: *Musica Reservata*, Dr Challomer's Grammar School, Amersham, Buckinghamshire. Margaret Philpot (contralto), Edgar Fleet (tenor), John Dudley (tenor); Catherine Mackintosh (rebecs), Trevor Jones (tenor rebec and bass viol), Bernard Thomas (recorder, crumhorn and rauschpfeifen), Richard Harvey (recorder, crumhorn, rauschpfeifen and lute), and Jeremy Montagu. John Beckett was to conduct, but was convalescing in Dublin. Music by de la Halle, Ghirardello da Firenze and Anon (French, Italian, Spanish and English music). (King's College London.)

15 and 16 June 1962: *The Raising of Lazarus*, Coventry Cathedral Festival. Thirteenth-centry play produced by Brian Trowell. Subsequently performed at the Bath, City of London and King's Lynn festivals. The group used wide-bore Renaissance-style recorders, believed to be the only ones in the country at the time. (Seán O'Leary; Programme notes for Musica Reservata's 'debut' concert at the Queen Elizabeth Hall, 2 July 1967; Programme for Coventry Cathedral Festival, 1962; Centre for Performance History, Royal College of Music.)

26 June 1963: *A programme of Medieval, Renaissance and Contemporary Music*, Wigmore Hall, London. Jantina Noorman (mezzo-soprano); John Sothcott, Daphne Webb, John Whitworth, John Beckett (treble viol), Michael Morrow. Also Malcolm Williamson (piano) and The Elizabethan Singers, conductor Louis Halsey. Medieval songs and dances by de Vaqueiras, Anon, de la Halle and de Vitry; fourteenth-century French and Italian songs and dances by Landini, Anon and Machaut, and fifteenth- and sixteenth-century French *chansons* by des Prés and Jannequin. (King's College London.) p. 145–6

12 February 1964: *Musica Reservata*, Hamilton Room, College of St Mark and St John, Chelsea. Jantina Noorman, Grayston Burgess, Geoffrey Mitchell (counter-tenor); John Sothcott, John Beckett (treble viol), Daphne Webb, Michael Morrow, Jeremy Montagu. Italian and French music: de la Halle, Landini, Machaut, Binchois, Dufay, Anon. (King's College London.) p. 152

3 May 1965: *Medieval and Early Renaissance Secular Music*, Conway Hall, London. Jantina Noorman, Grayston Burgess, John Whitworth; John Beckett (viol and virginals),

Desmond Dupré (viol and lute), Michael Morrow and Jeremy Montagu. French and Italian music by de la Halle, Landini, Machaut, Binchois, Dufay, Claudin and Senfl. (King's College London.) p. 159

28 November 1965: 1308th Concert at Balliol College Musical Society, Oxford. Jantina Noorman, Grayston Burgess; John Sothcott, Don Smithers (cornett and crumhorn), David Munrow (crumhorn), John Beckett (viol and harpsichord), Daphne Webb, Michael Morrow and Jeremy Montagu. Music by de Contreras, del Encina, de Sermisy (?), Crecquillon, Marco Cara, Tromboncino, de Vaqueiras, de la Halle, de Vitry, Landini, Machaut and Binchois. (Jantina Noorman.) pp. 164–5

2 July 1967: *Musica Reservata*, Queen Elizabeth Hall, London. Jantina Noorman, Grayston Burgess, John Whitworth, Tom Sutcliffe (counter-tenor), Geoffrey Shaw (baritone), John Frost (bass); Ruth David (violin and treble rebec), Roderick Skeaping (tenor viol and lyra-viol), Dietrich Kessler (bass viol), Adam Skeaping (violone); Don Smithers (cornett and crumhorn), Alan Lumsden, Tony Moore and John Pritchard (sackbuts); John Sothcott, John Lawes, Michael Oxenham and Francis Grubb (recorders); David Munrow (crumhorn and shawm), Richard Bethell, David Fallows and Claire Shanks (crumhorns); John O'Sullivan (organ and harpsichord), Harold Lester (harpsichord), Christopher Hogwood (regal and virginals), Desmond Dupré (bass viol, lyra-viol and chitarrone), Michael Morrow (chitarrone and lute), Ian Harwood (cittern), Brian Wilson (harp) and James Blades (percussion). Conducted by John Beckett. Music of the Italian Renaissance (by Monteverdi, Massaino, Giovanni Gabrieli, Marenzio, Malvezzi and Cavalieri); music from thirteenth- and fourteenth-century France and early sixteenth-century Spain (de Vaqueiras, de la Halle, de Vitry, Machaut, del Encina and Cevallos). (Seán O'Leary; King's College London.) pp. 176–9

15 September 1968: *The Hundred Years War and the Age of Chivalry in France*, Queen Elizabeth Hall. Jantina Noorman, Simon Woolf (treble), Grayston Burgess, Nigel Rogers (tenor), Edgar Fleet, Geoffrey Shaw (baritone); Don Smithers (cornett and crumhorn), Alan Lumsden (sackbut), Tony Moore (sackbut), David Munrow (shawm and crumhorn), Bernard Thomas (shawm and crumhorn), John Sothcott (recorder and citole), Ruth David, Daphne Webb, Desmond Dupré (viol and rebec), Brian Wilson (harp), Michael Morrow, Jeremy Montagu, John Beckett (organ and conductor). Music by Adam de la Halle, Machaut, Aleyn, Dufay, Cook, Acourt, Fontaine, Vaillant, Morton and Dufay. (King's College London.) p. 190–1

19 October 1968: *French music of the thirteenth and fourteenth centuries*, Hexham Abbey Festival. Jantina Noorman; Tom Finucane (lutes and flute), Christopher Page (lutes), Daphne Webb, John Beckett (harpsichord and conductor). Music by de la Halle, Machaut, Solage, Jean Vaillant. (King's College London.) p. 191

8 November 1968: *Music by Henry Purcell*, Queen Elizabeth Hall, London. Valerie Hill (soprano), Jantina Noorman, Grayston Burgess, Nigel Rogers, Edgar Fleet, Geoffrey Shaw, Wandsworth School Boys' Choir, John Beckett (conductor). *Abdelazer or The Moor's Revenge*, Chacony in G minor, *If ever I more riches did desire*, Ode in commemoration of

the centenary of Trinity College, Dublin: *Great Parent, Hail!* (King's College London.) pp. 192–3

29 December 1968: *A Renaissance Christmas*, Queen Elizabeth Hall, London. Jantina Noorman, Valerie Hill, Grayston Burgess, Nigel Rogers, Edgar Fleet, Geoffrey Shaw, Choir of Musica Reservata with boys from Wandsworth School; Roderick Skeaping (violin and bass viol), Ruth David (violin and treble viol), Kenneth Skeaping (alto and tenor viols), Daphne Webb, Desmond Dupré (tenor viol), Adam Skeaping (bass viol and violone), John Sothcott, David Munrow (recorder, shawm and crumhorn), Tess Miller (crumhorn), Bernard Thomas (crumhorn), Richard Bethell (crumhorn), Michael Morrow (crumhorn and lute), Tony Moore (sackbut), John Edney (sackbut), Ephraim Segerman (lute), Harold Lester (harpsichord), Christopher Hogwood (organ and regal), Jeremy Montagu, John Beckett (conductor). Music by Smert, Obrecht, Tromboncino, Giovane da Nola, Festa, Clemens non Papa, Praetorius, Scheidt, Marenzio, and de Sermisy. (King's College London.) pp. 193–4

29 January 1969: *Guillaume Dufay*, Purcell Room, London. Jantina Noorman, Grayston Burgess, Nigel Rogers; Ruth David, Daphne Webb, Desmond Dupré (tenor rebec and bass viol), John Sothcott, David Munrow (recorder, shawm and crumhorn), Alan Lumsden (sackbut), Brian Wilson (harp), John Beckett (organ and conductor). Music included the anonymous *basse danse 'La spagna'* ('The Spanish lady'), and *Donnés l'aussault* ('Start the assault'), *Adieu m'amour* ('Goodbye, my love'), *Se la face ay pale* ('If my face is pale'), *Pouray-je avoir vostre merchi* ('Could I have your thanks'), *Bon jour, bon moys* ('Good day, good month'), *Vergene bella* ('Fair Virgin'), *La belle se siet* ('The fair maid sits at the foot of the tower'), and *Adieu, ces bons vins de Lannoy* ('Farewell, the fine wines of Lens') by Dufay. (Seán O'Leary.) p. 194

7 February 1969: *Music from the time of Boccaccio's Decameron*, Purcell Room, London. Jantina Noorman, Grayston Burgess, Nigel Rogers, Edgar Fleet; Ruth David, Daphne Webb, Desmond Dupré (tenor rebec and tenor viol), John Sothcott, David Munrow (shawm and crumhorn), Bernard Thomas (crumhorn), John Leach (psaltery and dulcimer), Michael Morrow, Jeremy Montagu, John Beckett (organ and conductor). Music by Landini, Jacopo da Bologna, Giovanni da Firenze and Ghirardello da Firenze. (Seán O'Leary.) p. 194

11 May 1969: *Guillaume Dufay*, Victoria and Albert Museum, London. Music by Dufay. Jantina Noorman, Grayston Burgess, Nigel Rogers; Ruth David, Daphne Webb, Adam Skeaping (tenor rebe, bass viol), John Sothcott, David Munrow (recorder, shawm, crumhorn), James Tyler (lute), Alan Lumsden (sackbut), Tony Moore (sackbut), Jeremy Montagu and John Beckett (organ and conductor). Music by Dufay, including basse dance *La Spagna*, *Donnés l'aussault*, *Adieu m'amour*, *Se la face ay pale* and *Franc cuer gentil*. (King's College London.) p. 195

6 August 1969: *Early fifteenth-century French music* and Messiaen's Turangalila Symphony performed by the BBC Symphony Orchestra, conducted by Charles Groves, Henry Wood Promenade Concert, Royal Albert Hall. Singers included Jantina Noorman and

Nigel Rogers; musicians included Ruth David, Daphne Webb and Desmond Dupré (all playing rebecs). Music by anonymous composers and Dufay, including his *Donnés l'aussault, Adieu m'amour, Adieu ces bons vins de Lannoys, Mon cuer me fait* ('My heart makes me think of you every day') and *Resveilliés vous* ('Wake up!'). (Radio Times; King's College London.) p. 198

16 September 1969: *16th century Dance Music*, Queen Elizabeth Hall, London. Jantina Noorman, Grayston Burgess, Nigel Rogers, Edgar Fleet, Geoffrey Shaw; large ensemble, conducted by John Beckett. Music from France and the Netherlands by Janequin, de Sermisy, Heckel, Courtois, Certon, Passereau and Hubert Waelrant; from Germany and Poland, and from Italy, by Dalza, Azzaiolo, Pacolini, Hessen and Ruffo. Recorded by the BBC as *A Renaissance Entertainment* and broadcast on Radio 3, 5 October 1969. (King's College London.) p. 198

15 November 1969: *French and Italian music*, St Paul's Church, Birmingham. Conducted by John Beckett. Music by de la Halle, Machaut, Dufay and Landini. (King's College London.) p. 199

16 November 1969: *French and Italian music*, Durham Music Festival, the Great Hall, Durham Castle. Jantina Noorman, Grayston Burgess, Nigel Rogers, Edgar Fleet; Ruth David, John Sothcott, James Tyler (lute, viol), Bernard Thomas (crumhorn), Michael Morrow (crumhorn), Don Smithers (cornett), Tony Moore (sackbut), John Beckett (conductor). Music by de Vaquieras, de la Halle, Anon, Machaut, Dufay and Landini. (King's College London and Royal Academy of Music.) p. 199

16 December 1969: *Music by Praetorius and the Gabrielis*, Queen Elizabeth Hall, London. Valerie Hill, Jantina Noorman, Grayston Burgess, John Whitworth, Ian Hunter (counter-tenor), Nigel Rogers, Edgar Fleet, Geoffrey Shaw, Wandsworth School Boys' Choir, Choir and instrumentalists of Musica Reservata, conducted by John Beckett. Music by Monteverdi, Giovanni Gabrieli, Marenzio, Andrea Gabrieli, Praetorius, Tiburtio Massaino. Recorded by the BBC and broadcast as *The First Venetian School* on Radio 3, 18 January 1970. (King's College London.) p. 200

10 March 1970: *A concert of music by Henry Purcell*, Queen Elizabeth Hall, London. Jantina Noorman, Wyndham Parfitt (bass); Frances Mason (violin), Duncan Druce (violin), Ruth David (violin), Adam Skeaping (bass viol), John Gray (violone), John Beckett (harpsichord), Members (trebles and basses) of Wandsworth School Choir. Trio Sonata in G minor, Z 806, *A Pastoral Elegy on the Death of Mr John Playford*, Z 464, *A Morning Hymn*, Z 198, *An Evening Hymn*, Z 193, *The Blessed Virgin's Expostulation*, Z 196, *Awake, and with Attention Hear, Thou Drowsie World*, Z 181, Trio Sonata in G minor, Z 807; Trio Sonata in C minor, Z 798, *Thy Genius, Lo, from her Sweet Bed of Rest*, Z 604A, *Let the Dreadful Engines of Eternal Will*, Z 578/3, *She that would gain a Faithful Lover*, Z 414, *Olinda in the Shades unseen*, Z 404, *Love's Pow'r in my Heart shall find no Compliance*, Z 395, *From Rosie Bow'rs, where sleeps the God of Love*, Z 578/9, *The Plaint: O Let me Weep*, Z 629/40 and Fantasia: 3 parts upon a ground, Z 731. (Seán O'Leary.) p. 201

19 May 1970: *Medieval music of the 13th, 14th and 15th centuries*, Queen Elizabeth Hall,

London. Conducted by John Beckett. French and Italian music, including works by Landini and Dufay. (King's College London.) p. 201

23 May 1970: *Music from the Court of Burgundy*, Trinity College, Dublin. The same programme as on 19 May 1970 in London. Fifteen performers, including Jantina Noorman, Edgar Fleet, Bernard Thomas (*rauschpfeife* and *crumhorn*) and John Beckett (small drum and conductor). (*Ir. Times.*) p. 201–2

15 July 1970: *La Chanson Française à la Renaissance*, Collégiale Saint-Martin de Trôo (Loir-et-Cher), France. Conducted by John Beckett. No details. (King's College London.) p. 205

16 July 1970: ?*La Chanson Française à la Renaissance* or *La Chanson Française au XVIe siècle*, Abbaye de Fontevrauld (Maine-et-Loire), France. Conducted by John Beckett. No details; probably the same programme as 15 July 1970. (King's College London.) p. 205

18 July 1970: Concert, Festival Vaison-Carpentras, Carpentras, Provence-Alpes-Côte d'Azur region, France. Conducted by John Beckett. Dufay *La Belle se siet*, French and English music of 13th century, 100 Years War, Italian music of 14th century and English and French music of 15th century. (King's College London.) p. 205

4 August 1970: Concert, Festival Estival, La Sainte Chapelle, Paris. Jantina Noorman, Nigel Rogers. Conducted by John Beckett. Music by Machaut, Dufay and Dunstable. (King's College London.) p. 206

20 August 1970: Concert, ?*Music from the time of Elizabeth I*, Noordekerk, Amsterdam. Conducted by John Beckett. Music by Anon, Dunstable and Frye. (King's College London.) p. 207

24 August 1970: *Music of Kings and Queens*, *Festival van Vlaanderen* (Flanders Festival), Memlingmuseum, Bruges, Belgium. Jantina Noorman, Grayston Burgess, Edgar Fleet, Geoffrey Shaw; Ruth David, Daphne Webb, Adam Skeaping (viola da gamba), James Tyler (lute), Anthony Rooley (lute), Michael Morrow (lute) John Beckett (virginal, harpsichord, positive organ and conductor). Music by Anon, John Dunstable, Robert Morton, Walter Frye, John Johnson, Thomas Simpson, Alfonso Ferrabosco, William Byrd, Anthony Holborne, Adrianus Valerius, Richard Nicholson, Elway Bevin and William Cobbold. (Jantina Noorman; King's College London.) p. 207

27 October 1970: *German and Spanish Music of the early 16th century*, Queen Elizabeth Hall, London. Jantina Noorman, Edgar Fleet, John Dudley, Martyn Hill (tenor), Geoffrey Shaw, David Thomas (bass); Ruth David (treble rebec), Catherine Mackintosh (tenor viol), Daphne Webb (tenor rebec and bass viol), James Tyler (bass viol, cittern and lute), Adam Skeaping (bass viol), Anthony Rooley (lute), John Sothcott, Michael Oxenham (recorder and crumhorn), Richard Harvey (crumhorn and shawm), Bernard Thomas (crumhorn and shawm), Philip Pickett (crumhorn and shawm), Roger Brenner (sackbut), John Beckett (organ and conductor). Music by Anon, Bartolomeo Brulo, Ludwig Senfl, Wolf Heckel, Johannes Weck, Hans Buchner; Juan del Enzina, Francisco

de la Torre, Antonio de Cabezón, Luis Milán, Francesco Cevallos and Alonso Mudarra. (Jantina Noorman.) p. 210

20 December 1970: *Music at Christmas*, Queen Elizabeth Hall, London. Jantina Noorman, Valerie Hill (soprano), Poppy Holden (soprano), Grayston Burgess, Edgar Fleet, John Dudley, Geoffrey Shaw, David Thomas (bass), Wandsworth School Boys' Choir, conducted by John Beckett. Music by Monteverdi (Toccata, *Lamento delle ninfe*, *Con che soavita*), Praetorius (*Puer natus est*, 3 dances, *Wachet auf*, 4 dances, *Ach mein Herre*, *In dulce Jubilo*), Scheidt (Canzon: *O nachbar Roland*, Canzon: *Est ce mars*). (King's College London.) p. 210

15 February 1971: *15th and 16th century English music*, Queen Elizabeth Hall, London. Jantina Noorman, Grayston Burgess, Edgar Fleet, Geoffrey Shaw; Ruth David (treble rebec), Catherline Mackintosh (treble viol), Daphne Webb (tenor rebec, tenor viol), Carolyn Sparey (tenor viol), Adam Skeaping (bass viol), James Tyler (tenor viol, lute), Anthony Rooley (lute), Don Smithers (cornett), Michael Laird (cornett), Roger Brenner, Peter Goodwyn and Martin Nicholls (sackbuts), John Beckett (organ and conductor). Music by Frye, Dunstable, Holborn, John Johnson, Byrd, Valerius, Richard Nicholson, William Inglot and William Cobbold. (Seán O'Leary.) p. 210

18 May 1971: *13th and 15th century French and English music*, Queen Elizabeth Hall, London. Jantina Noorman, Margaret Philpot (mezzo-soprano), Grayston Burgess, Edgar Fleet, John Dudley; Ruth David (treble rebec, vielle), Eleanor Sloan (treble rebec), Daphne Webb (tenor rebec), Desmond Dupré (tenor rebec, tenor viol), John Sothcott (recorder, vielle), Bernard Thomas (crumhorn, shawm), Richard Harvey (crumhorn, shawm), Martin Nicholls (sackbut), James Tyler (crumhorn, lute, cittern), Anthony Rooley (lute, cittern), Michael Morrow (lute, bells), Brian Wilson (harp), Jeremy Montagu (nakers, percussion); John Beckett (conductor). Music by de Vitry, Dunstable/Ockeghem, Walter Frye, Dufay. (Seán O'Leary.) p. 212–3

29 August 1971: *Musica Reservata*, St Canice's Cathedral, Kilkenny. Conducted by Howard Williams – John Beckett was not involved. (King's College London.) p. 220–1

30 August 1971: *Musica Reservata speelt muziek uit 14e ~ 16e eeuw*, Kleine zaal Concertgebouw, Amsterdam. Directed by Michael Morrow – John Beckett was not involved. (King's College London.) p. 221

20 October 1971: *16th century French and Netherlands Chansons and Dances*, Queen Elizabeth Hall, London. Jantina Noorman, Margaret Philpot, Grayston Burgess, Edgar Fleet, John Dudley, David Thomas (bass); John Beckett (conductor). Music by Clement Janequin, Claudin de Sermisy, Giovanni Pacoloni, Passereau, Wolff Heckel, Clemens non Papa and Jean Courtois. (King's College London.) p. 221

6 November 1971: *NOS / Muziek uit middeleeuwen en renaissance*, VARA-studio 1, Hilversum. Conducted by John Beckett. No details. (King's College London.) p. 222

13 December 1971: *Monteverdi and his Contemporaries*, Queen Elizabeth Hall, London. Valerie Hill (soprano), Jantina Noorman, Margaret Philpot, Grayston Burgess, Edgar Fleet, John Dudley (tenor), David Thomas; John Beckett (conductor). Music

by Massaino, Monteverdi, Walter Porter, Richard Dering, Samuel Scheidt, Wilbye, Dowland, Alfonso Ferrabosco and Giulio Caccini. (King's College London.) p. 224

16 March 1972: John Coffin Memorial Concert, University of London. Jantina Noorman, Margaret Philpot, Edgar Fleet; Catherine Mackintosh (trebel rebec, viols), Daphne Webb, Adam Skeaping (bass rebec, bass viol), Richard Harvey (crumhorn, recorder), Bernard Thomas (crumhorn, recorder), Brian Gulland (crumhorn). Fifteenth-century music by Walter Frye, John Dunstable/Bedingham, Dufay, Johannes Tinctoris, Johannes Vincenet. (King's College London.) p. 227

28 March 1972: *The Macnaghten Concerts: 40th Anniversary Season 1971–72*, Queen Elizabeth Hall, London. Jantina Noorman, Margaret Philpot, Edgar Fleet; Catherine Mackintosh (treble rebec and viol), Eleanor Sloan (treble rebec and vielle), John Sothcott (vielle and recorder), Daphne Webb, Desmond Dupré (tenor and bass viols), Richard Harvey (shawm, crumhorn and recorder), Bernard Thomas (shawm, crumhorn and recorder), Martin Nicholls (sackbut), Jeremy Montagu, John Beckett (conductor). Thirteenth and fifteenth-century English and Burgundian music (music by Anon, Walter Frye, John Dunstable, Dufay and Vincenet); Anthony Gilbert, *A man who tried to hijack an airliner*. (King's College London.) p. 227

3 May 1972: English and French music, l'Eglise Saint-Germain l'Auxerrois, Paris. Jantina Noorman, Grayston Burgess, Edgar Fleet, John Dudley; Eleanor Sloan (treble rebec and vielle), Daphne Webb, Trevor Jones (tenor rebec), Bernard Thomas (crumhorn, shawm and recorder), Richard Harvey (crumhorn, shawm and recorder), Brian Gulland (crumhorn, shawm and recorder), Roger Brenner (sackbut), Jeremy Montagu, John Beckett (conductor). Music by de la Halle, de Vaqueiras, Landini, Dunstable and Frye. (King's College London.) p. 228

4 May 1972: *Musica Reservata*, Theatre de l'Hotel de Ville, le Havre. No details. (Seán O'Leary.) p. 228

5 May 1972: *Musica Reservata – Concert de musique ancienne*, Eglise Saint-Jacques, Dieppe. 13th-century French and 14th-century Italian music. (King's College London.) p. 228

24 May 1972: *16th century German, Polish and Netherlands chansons and dances*, Queen Elizabeth Hall, London. Eleanor Sloan, Catherine Mackintosh, Daphne Webb, Desmond Dupré and Trevor Jones (rebecs and viols); Adam Skeaping (viol and violone); John Sothcott; Bernard Thomas, Richard Harvey, Brian Gulland and Michael Oxenham (recorders, crumhorns and shawms); James Tyler, Anthony Rooley, Ephraim Segerman (lutes); Michael Laird (cornett); Peter Goodwin, Colin Sheen, Paul Beer, Stephen Saunders (sackbuts); Melanie Daiken (harpsichord and organ); Jeremy Montagu; John Beckett (conductor). Music by Anon, des Prez, Wolf Heckel, Luis de Naváez, Girolamo Cavazzoni, Francesco Spinacino, Ludwig Senfl, Hans Buchner, Thomas Crecquillon, Nicolas de la Grotte/Adrien le Roy and Clemens non Papa. (Seán O'Leary.) p. 228

1 August 1972: *Hommage à Heinrich Schütz*, 7th Festival Estival, Sainte-Chapelle, Paris. Jantina Noorman, Margaret Philpot, David Thomas; Eleanor Sloan (violin), Philip Saudek (violin), Trevor Jones (viola), Penelope Howard (viola), Daphne Webb (cello),

Bernard Thomas (recorder), Richard Harvey (recorder), Brian Gulland (bassoon), Melanie Deakin (harpsichord), John Beckett (conductor). Music by Richard Dering, Anthony Holborne, Henry Lawes, Heinrich Schütz, Johann Hermann Schein and Samuel Scheidt. (Jantina Noorman.) p. 229

7 August 1972: *Medieval French and English church and court music*, International Fortnight of Music 1972, Flanders Festival, Sint-Annakerk, Bruges. Jantina Noorman, Margaret Philpot; Trevor Jones and Daphne Webb (rebec), Bernard Thomas (crumhorn, shawm and recorder), Richard Harvey (crumhorn and recorder), Brian Gulland (crumhorn), Don Smithers (cornett), Martin Nicholls (sackbut), Jeremy Montagu, John Beckett (portative organ and conductor). Music by Anon, de Vaqueiras, Dunstable, Frye and des Prez. (Jantina Noorman.) p. 229

8 August 1972: *Music at the courts of Italy (14th to 16th centuries) and Spain (15th/16th century)*, International Fortnight of Music 1972, Flanders Festival, Memlingmuseum, Bruges. Same musicians as 7 August, with the addition of the singers Edgar Fleet and David Thomas. Music by Anon, Landini, da Firenze, Azzaiola, Muñoz, Milán and de Mudarra. (Jantina Noorman.) p. 229

28 September 1972: *English and German music*, Berliner Festwochen, Orangerie, Schloß Charlottenburg, Berlin. Jantina Noorman, Margaret Philpot, Edgar Fleet, David Thomas; Catherine Mackintosh, Eleanor Sloan, Daphne Webb, Bernard Thomas, Richard Harvey, Brain Gulland, Martin Nichols, Anthony Rooley, Jeremy Montagu. Conducted by John Beckett. No music details. (Jantina Noorman.) p. 230

2 October 1972: *Music from the time of Christopher Columbus*, Brahms-saal, Vienna. Jantina Noorman, Margaret Philpot, John Dudley, David Thomas; Eleanor Sloan (alto rebec, bass viol), Richard Harvey (tenor viol, crumhorn and recorder), Daphne Webb (tenor rebec, bass viol), Christopher Wilson (lute), Bernard Thomas (crumhorn, recorder and shawm), Brian Gulland (crumhorn, recorder), Paul Beer (sackbut), Jeremy Montagu, John Beckett (harpsichord and conductor). Music by Francisco Guerrero, Anon, Luis Milán, del Encina, de Narváez, Juan Vásquez, de Mudarra, Adrian Willaert, de Cabezón, Juan Ponce, Escobar, de Sermisy and de la Torre. (Jantina Noorman.) p. 230

31 October 1972: *Music from 14th century Italy and the Court of Burgundy*, Queen Elizabeth Hall, London. Jantina Noorman, Margaret Philpot, Grayston Burgess, Edgar Fleet, John Dudley; Catherine Mackintosh (treble rebec), Daphne Webb (tenor rebec), Adam Skeaping (bass rebec), Bernard Thomas and Richard Harvey (recorders, crumhorns and shawms), Roger Brenner (sackbut), Jeremy Montagu (nakers, percussion), John Beckett (conductor). Three motets from *Le Roman de Fauvel*, one by de Vitry; music by Machaut, Landini, Giovanni da Firenze, Acourt, Walter Frye and Francesca de la Torre. (Seán O'Leary, King's College London.)

21 February 1973: *The Music of 15th century Spain*, Queen Elizabeth Hall, London. Jantina Noorman, Margaret Philpot, Edgar Fleet, John Dudley, David Thomas, John Beckett (conductor). Music by Luis Milán, Juan del Encina, Luis de Narváez, Juan Vásquez, Alonso Mudarra, Antonio de Cabezón, etc. (King's College London.) p. 242

9 May 1973: *15th century Burgundian music*, Auditório Dois, Gulbenkian Foundation, Lisbon. Conducted by John Beckett. Music by Binchois, Dufay, Ockeghem, Josquin des Prés and their contemporaries (Tromboncino, Ghislin, etc.) (King's College London.) p. 242

10 May 1973: *French and English music of the 13th, 14th and 15th centuries*, Auditório Dois, Gulbenkian Foundation, Lisbon. Conducted by John Beckett. Music by Philippe de Vitry, Dufay and Ockeghem. (King's College London.) p. 242

22 May 1973: *15th century secular music by Dunstable, Dufay, and Josquin*, Queen Elizabeth Hall, London. Jantina Noorman, Margaret Philpot, Edgar Fleet, John Dudley, David Thomas; Catherine Mackintosh (rebec, viol), Trevor Jones (rebec, viol), Daphne Webb (rebec, viol), Desmond Dupré (rebec, viol), Christopher Wilson (lute), Bernard Thomas (crumhorn, recorder), Trevor Herbert (sackbut), Jeremy Montagu (percussion), John Beckett (conductor). Music by Binchois, Dunstable, Dufay, Pierre de la Rue, Ockeghem, Josquin des Prez, Johannes Ghiselin, Hayne van Ghizeghem, Bartolomeo Tromboncino, Nicola Pifaro. (Seán O'Leary.) p. 243

14 September 1973: *Musica Reservata*, Gerechtshof, Mechelen, Belgium. Jantina Noorman, Margaret Philpot, Edgar Fleet, John Dudley, Paul Hillier (bass); Daphne Webb, Ian Gammie, Michael Edwards and Trevor Jones (viols), Bernard Thomas (recorder), Christopher Wilson (lute), Trevor Herbert (sackbut). Conducted by John Beckett. Music by Binchois, Dunstable, Dufay, Ockeghem, Anon, Johannes Ghiselin, Bartolomeo Tromboncino, Nicola Pifaro; Josquin des Prez. (Jantina Noorman.) p. 434, note 32

24 October 1973: *15th and 16th century English Music*, Queen Elizabeth Hall, London. Jantina Noorman, Grayston Burgess, Edgar Fleet, John Dudley, David Thomas. Conducted by John Beckett. Music by Walter Frye, Anon, John Dunstable, Buxheim Manuscript, Anthony Holborne, Azzaiolo, William Byrd, Valeriu, Richard Nicholson, William Inglot and William Cobbold. (King's College London.) p. 244

26 October 1973: *Musica Reservata*, Stadhuis (Hôtel de Ville), Brussels. Jantina Noorman, Grayston Burgess, Edgar Fleet, John Dudley, David Thomas; Catherine Mackintosh (rebec and viol), Trevor Jones (rebec and viol), Daphne Webb (rebec and viol), Adam Skeaping (bass viol), James Tyler (tenor viol and lute), Christopher Wilson (lute), Trevor Herbert (sackbut), John Beckett (conductor and organ). Music by Anon, Walter Frye, Dunstable, Holborne, Byrd, Azzaiolo, Adrianus Valerius, Richard Nicholson, William Inglot, William Cobbold. (Jantina Noorman.) p. 244

27 November 1973: *English and French Music of the 13th, 14th and 15th centuries*, Wearmouth 1300 Festival, St Gabriel's Church, Sunderland. Jantina Noorman, Margaret Philpot, Edgar Fleet, John Dudley; Daphne Webb (rebec and viol), Trevor Jones (rebec and viol), Richard Harvey (viol, crumhorn and recorder), Bernard Thomas (crumhorn, recorder and rauschpfeife), Brian Gulland (crumhorn), Trevor Herbert (sackbut), Jeremy Montagu, John Beckett (conductor). Music by Anon, Philippe de Vitry, Walter Frye, Dunstable/Bedingham, Ockeghem and Dufay. This was the last Musica Reservata concert that John conducted. (Jantina Noorman.) p. 245

Appendix F

Bach Cantata Series, St Ann's Church, Dawson Street, Dublin

Public concerts in the series were held on Sundays at 3.30 pm; 'preview' concerts (listed below) and special BBC recordings (which were not public concerts) were held on other days of the week. For the broadcast dates of the BBC recordings, see Appendix D.

1973

Sunday 28 January

    Cantata No. 82, *Ich habe genug*

    Sinfonia from Cantata No. 42

    Cantata No. 81, *Jesus schläft, was soll ich hoffen?*

    Bernadette Greevy (contralto), Frank Patterson (tenor), William Young (bass).

    The Guinness Choir and the New Irish Chamber Orchestra (NICO), conductor
        John Beckett; p. 237

Sunday 4 February

    Trio Sonata in G, from BWV 525

    Mein Jesu, was für Seelenweh; *Kommt, Seelen, dieser Tag*; *Komm süsser Tod* (from
        Schemelli's *Gesangbuch*)

    Trio Sonata in E minor, from BWV 527

    Cantata No. 55, *Ich armer Mensch, ich Sündenknecht*

    Edward Beckett (flute), Mary Gallagher and Thérèse Timoney (violins), Frank
        Patterson (tenor).

    The Guinness Choir and the NICO, conductor John Beckett; p. 237

Sunday 11 February

    Cantata No. 54, *Widerstehe doch der Sünde*

    Sinfonia from Cantata 42

    Cantata No.154, *Mein liebster Jesu ist verloren*

    Bernadette Greevy (contralto), Frank Patterson (tenor), William Young (bass).

    The Guinness Choir and the NICO, conductor John Beckett; p. 237

1974

Sunday 27 January

    Cantata No. 166, *Wo gehest du hin?*

    Cantata No. 42, *Am Abend aber desselbigen Sabbats*

    Mabel McGrath (soprano), Bernadette Greevy (contralto), Frank Patterson (tenor), William Young (bass).

    The Guinness Choir and the NICO, conductor John Beckett; p. 246

Sunday 3 February

    Cantata No. 53, *Schlage doch, gewünschte Stunde*

    Cantata No. 54, *Widerstehe doch der Sünde*

    Bernadette Greevy (contralto).

    The Guinness Choir and the NICO, conductor John Beckett; p. 246

Sunday 10 February

    Cantata No. 33, *Allein zu dir, Herr Jesu Christ*

    Cantata No. 159, *Sehet, wir geh'n hinauf gen Jerusalem*

    Mabel McGrath (soprano), Bernadette Greevy (contralto), Frank Patterson (tenor), William Young (bass).

    The Guinness Choir and the NICO, conductor John Beckett; p. 246

1975

Sunday 16 February

    Cantata No. 167, *Ihr Menschen, rühmet Gottes Liebe*

    Cantata No. 127, *Herr Jesu Christ, wahr' Mensch und Gott*

    Irené Sandford (soprano), Bernadette Greevy (contralto), Frank Patterson (tenor), William Young (bass).

    The Guinness Choir and the NICO, conductor John Beckett.

    (Recorded by the BBC.) pp. 253, 263

Sunday 23 February

    Cantata No. 151, *Süsser Trost, mein Jesus kömmt*

    Cantata No. 8, *Liebster Gott, wenn werd ich sterben?*

    Irené Sandford (soprano), Bernadette Greevy (contralto), Frank Patterson (tenor), William Young (bass).

The Guinness Choir and the NICO, conductor John Beckett.
(Recorded by the BBC) p. 254

Sunday 2 March
   Cantata No. 199, *Mein Herze schwimmt in Blut*
   Cantata No. 56, *Ich will den Kreuzstab gerne tragen*
   Nora Ring (soprano), William Young (bass).
   The Guinness Choir and the NICO, conductor John Beckett.
   (Recorded by the BBC.) p. 254

1977

Sunday 13 February
   Cantata No. 32: *Liebster Jesu, mein Verlangen*
   Cantata No. 27: *Wer weiss, wie nahe mir mein Ende?*
   Irené Sandford (soprano), Bernadette Greevy (contralto), Frank Patterson (tenor),
       William Young, (bass).
   The Cantata Singers and the NICO, conductor John Beckett.
   (Recorded by the BBC.) p. 269

Sunday 20 February
   Cantata No. 158: *Der Friede sei mit dir*
   Cantata No. 140: *Wachet auf, ruft uns die Stimme*
   Irené Sandford (soprano), Brendan Cavanagh (tenor), William Young (bass)
   The Cantata Singers and the NICO, conductor John Beckett; p. 269

Sunday 27 February
   Cantata No. 84: *Ich bin vergnügt mit meinem Glücke*
   Cantata No. 79: *Gott, der Herr ist Sonn' und Schild*
   Irené Sandford (soprano), Áine Nic Gabhann (contralto), William Young (bass)
   The Cantata Singers and the NICO, conductor John Beckett.
   (Recorded by BBC Northern Ireland.) pp. 269–70

   BBC recording in the Masonic Hall:

Saturday 10 September
   Cantata No. 208: *Was mir behagt, ist nur die muntre Jagd!*
   Irené Sandford (soprano), Violet Twomey (soprano), Frank Patterson (tenor),
       William Young (bass)
   The Cantata Singers and the NICO, conductor John Beckett; p. 274

1978

Sunday 5 February
   Brandenburg Concerto No. 1
   Cantata No. 208: *Was mir behagt, ist nur die muntre Jagd!*

Irené Sandford (soprano), Violet Twomey (soprano), Frank Patterson (tenor), William Young (bass)

The Cantata Singers and the NICO, conductor John Beckett; pp. 276–7

Sunday 12 February

O Jesulein süss, BWV 493; *Komm, süsser Tod*, BWV 478; *Kommt, Seelen*, BWV 479; *Liebster Herr Jesu*, BWV 484 (from Schemelli's *Gesangbuch*)

Cantata No. 21: *Ich hatte viel Bekümmernis in meinem Herzen*

Irené Sandford (soprano), Frank Patterson (tenor), William Young (bass)

The Cantata Singers and the NICO, conductor John Beckett.

(Recorded by the BBC.) p. 277

BBC recordings in St Ann's, Dawson Street or the Masonic Hall:

Monday 13 February

Cantata No. 99: *Was Gott tut, das ist wohlgetan*

Irené Sandford (soprano), Áine Nic Gabhann (contralto), Frank Patterson (tenor), William Young (bass)

The Cantata Singers and the NICO, conductor John Beckett; p. 277

Thursday 16 February

Cantata No. 163: *Nur jedem das Seine*

Irené Sandford (soprano), Áine Nic Gabhann (contralto), Frank Patterson (tenor), William Young (bass)

The Cantata Singers and the NICO, conductor John Beckett; p. 277

Sunday 19 February

Sinfonia from Cantata No. 42

Cantata No. 30: *Freue dich, erlöste Schar*

Irené Sandford (soprano), Bernadette Greevy (contralto), Frank Patterson (tenor), William Young (bass)

The Cantata Singers and the NICO, conductor John Beckett.

(Recorded by the BBC.) p. 277

BBC recording in St Ann's, Dawson Street or the Masonic Hall:

Tuesday 12 September

Cantata No. 123: *Liebster Immanuel, Herzog der Frommen*

Cantata No. 164: *Ihr, die ihr euch von Christo nennet*

Irené Sandford (soprano), Bernadette Greevy (contralto), Frank Patterson (tenor), William Young (bass)

The Cantata Singers and the NICO, conductor John Beckett; p. 279

1979

Sunday 4 February

Cantata No. 133: *Ich freue mich in dir*

Cantata No. 117: *Sei Lob und Ehr' dem höchsten Gut*

Irené Sandford (soprano), Áine Nic Gabhann (contralto), Frank Patterson (tenor),
    William Young (bass)

The Cantata Singers and the NICO, conductor John Beckett; p. 283
(Recorded by the BBC)

BBC recording in St Ann's, Dawson Street:

Wednesday 7 February

Cantata No. 144: *Nimm, was dein ist, und gehe hin*

Cantata No. 150: *Nach dir, Herr, verlanget mich*

Violet Twomey (soprano), Áine Nic Gabhann (contralto), Frank Patterson (tenor),
    William Young (bass)

The Cantata Singers and the NICO, conductor John Beckett; p. 284

Concerts in St Ann's, Dawson Street:

Sunday 11 February

Cantata No. 86: *Wahrlich, wahrlich, ich sage euch*

Cantata No. 138: *Warum betrübst du dich, mein Herz?*

Violet Twomey (soprano), Áine Nic Gabhann (contralto), Frank Patterson (tenor),
    William Young (bass)

The Cantata Singers and the NICO, conductor John Beckett; p. 284

Sunday 18 February

Cantata No. 123: *Liebster Immanuel, Herzog der Frommen*

Cantata No. 177: *Ich ruf' zu dir, Herr Jesu Christ*

Irené Sandford (soprano), Bernadette Greevy (contralto), Frank Patterson (tenor),
    William Young (bass)

The Cantata Singers and the NICO, conductor John Beckett; p. 284

BBC recording in St Ann's, Dawson Street or the Masonic Hall:

Thursday 1 March

Cantata No. 174: *Ich liebe den Höchsten von ganzem Gemüte*

Cantata No. 177: *Ich ruf zu dir, Herr Jesu Christ*

Irené Sandford (soprano), Bernadette Greevy (contralto), Frank Patterson (tenor),
    William Young (bass)

The Cantata Singers and the NICO, conductor John Beckett; p. 284

Preview of concert performed at the BBC Henry Wood Promenade Concert:

Thursday 19 July

Sinfonia from Cantata 174

Cantata No. 21: *Ich hatte viel Bekümmernis in meinem Herzen*

Sinfonia from Cantata No. 42

Cantata No. 30, *Freue dich, erlöste Schar*

Irené Sandford (soprano), Bernadette Greevy (contralto), Frank Patterson (tenor),
    William Young (bass)

The Cantata Singers and the NICO, conductor John Beckett; p. 290

These works were performed in the Royal Albert Hall, London, on 22 July.

1980

Sunday 10 February

Cantata No. 57: *Selig ist der Mann*

Cantata No. 39: *Brich dem Hungrigen dein Brot*

Irené Sandford (soprano), Alison Browner (contralto), William Young (bass)

The Cantata Singers and the NICO, conductor John Beckett; p. 294

Sunday 17 February

Cantata No. 150: *Nach dir, Herr, verlanget mich*

Cantata No. 105: *Herr, gehe nicht ins Gericht mit deinem Knecht*

Irené Sandford (soprano), Alison Browner (contralto), Frank Patterson (tenor),
William Young (bass)

The Cantata Singers and the NICO, conductor John Beckett; p. 294

Sunday 24 February

Brandenburg Concerto No. 3

Cantata No. 174: *Ich liebe den Höchsten von ganzem Gemüte*

Bernadette Greevy (contralto), Frank Patterson (tenor), William Young (bass)

The Cantata Singers and the NICO, conductor John Beckett; p. 294

Previews of two concerts given at the Flanders Festival in Bruges:

Monday 21 July, 8 pm

Brandenburg Concerto No. 3

Cantata No. 174: *Ich liebe den Höchsten von ganzem Gemüte*

Brandenburg Concerto No 1

Cantata No. 79: *Gott der Herr ist Sonn' und Schild*

Irené Sandford (soprano), Violet Twomey (soprano), Áine Nic Gabhann
(contralto), Frank Patterson (tenor), William Young (bass)

The Cantata Singers and the NICO, conductor John Beckett; p. 298

Tuesday 22 July, 8 pm

Cantata No. 150: *Nach dir, Herr, verlanget mich*

Cantata No. 151: *Süsser Trost, mein Jesus kömmt*

Cantata No. 208: *Was mir behagt, ist nur die muntre Jagd!*

Irené Sandford (soprano), Violet Twomey (soprano), Áine Nic Gabhann
(contralto), Frank Patterson (tenor), William Young (bass)

The Cantata Singers and the NICO, conductor John Beckett; p. 298

These works were performed in Bruges on Saturday 26 July and Sunday 27 July.

1981

Sunday 1 February
  Suite No. 4 in D, BWV 1069
  Cantata No. 78: *Jesu, der du meine Seele*
  Irené Sandford (soprano), Áine Nic Gabhann (contralto), Frank Patterson (tenor),
    William Young (bass)
  The Cantata Singers and the NICO, conductor John Beckett; p. 308

Sunday 8 February
  Cantata No. 209: *Non sa che sia dolore*
  Cantata No. 147: *Herz und Mund und Tat und Leben*
  Irené Sandford (soprano), Áine Nic Gabhann (contralto), Frank Patterson (tenor),
    William Young (bass)
  The Cantata Singers and the NICO, conductor John Beckett; p. 308

Sunday 15 February
  Cantata No. 12: *Weinen, Klagen, Sorgen, Zagen*
  Cantata No. 110: *Unser Mund sei voll Lachens*
  Irené Sandford (soprano), Áine Nic Gabhann (contralto), Frank Patterson (tenor),
    William Young (bass)
  The Cantata Singers and the NICO, conductor John Beckett; p. 308–9

1982

Sunday 7 February
  Cantata No. 61: *Nun komm, der Heiden Heiland*
  Cantata No. 71: *Gott ist mein König*
  Irené Sandford (soprano), Áine Nic Gabhann (contralto), Peter Kerr (tenor),
    William Young (bass)
  The Cantata Singers and the NICO, conductor John Beckett; p. 317

Sunday 14 February
  Cantata No. 60: *O Ewigkeit, du Donnerwort*
  Cantata No. 157: *Ich lasse dich nicht, du segnest mich denn*
  Áine Nic Gabhann (contralto), John Brady (tenor), William Young (bass)
  The Cantata Singers and the NICO, conductor John Beckett; p. 317

Sunday 21 February
  Cantata No. 182: *Himmelskönig, sei willkommen*
  Cantata No. 4: *Christ lag in Todesbanden*
  Irené Sandford (soprano), Áine Nic Gabhann (contralto), John Brady (tenor),
    William Young (bass)
  The Cantata Singers and the NICO, conductor John Beckett; p. 317

1983

Sunday 6 February

    Sinfonia from Cantata 42

    Cantata No. 82: *Ich habe genug*

    Cantata No. 127: *Herr Jesu Christ, wahr' Mensch und Gott*

    Irené Sandford (soprano), Áine Nic Gabhann (contralto), Peter Kerr (tenor), William Young (bass)

    The Cantata Singers and the NICO, conductor John Beckett; p. 325

Sunday 13 February

    Cantata No. 150: *Nach dir, Herr, verlanget mich*

    Cantata No. 55: *Ich armer Mensch, ich Sündenknecht*

    Cantata No. 54: *Widerstehe doch der Sünde*

    Cantata No. 71: *Gott ist mein König*

    Irené Sandford (soprano), Áine Nic Gabhann (contralto), Peter Kerr (tenor), William Young (bass)

    The Cantata Singers and the NICO, conductor John Beckett; p. 326

Sunday 20 February

    Cantata No. 199: *Mein Herze schwimmt im Blut*

    Cantata No. 21: *Ich hatte viel Bekümmernis in meinem Herzen*

    Irené Sandford (soprano), Peter Kerr (tenor), William Young (bass)

    The Cantata Singers and the NICO, conductor John Beckett; p. 326

Bibliography

PRIMARY SOURCES
(Published and unpublished)

Armstrong, Lindsay, 'A Tribute to John Beckett', speech written for concert in St
   Ann's Church, Dawson Street, Dublin, on 11 February 2007

Bair, Deirdre, *Samuel Beckett* (London: Jonathan Cape 1978)

Beckett International Foundation, The University of Reading, Letters from Samuel
   Beckett to John Beckett, MS 5411

Beckett, John: interviewed by the author, 31 July 1998, for biography of Cathal
   Gannon (see below)

Beckett, John: musical reviews in *The Bell* journal (editor, Peadar O'Donnell), Vol.
   XVII No. 2–Vol XVIII No. 6 (1951 and 1952), on microfilm, Ussher Multimedia
   Area, Trinity College Dublin

BBC Archives: summaries of radio programmes involving John Beckett as musician,
   conductor and presenter

BBC Written Archives Centre, Caversham, Reading, UK:

> RCONT 1 COMPOSER BECKETT, John – File 1 1954–62
>
> RCONT 1 ARTISTS BECKETT, John S. – File 1 1954–62
>
> RCONT 1 COPYRIGHT BECKETT, John S. – File 1 1956–62
>
> JOHN BECKETT COMPOSER – File 2 1963–67
>
> RCONT 12 ARTISTS BECKETT, John S. – File 2 1963–67
>
> RCONT 18 COPYRIGHT JOHN S. BECKETT – File 2 1963–69
>
> RCONT 12 ARTIST JOHN S. BECKETT – File 3 1968–72
>
> WAC R83/952/1 Beckett, John
>
> ARTISTS: MUSICA RESERVATA FILE I 1958–1962
>
> MUSICA RESERVATA ARTISTS FILE II 1963–1967

RCONT31/86/1 MUSICA RESERVATA ORCHESTRA

RCONT12 MUSICA RESERVATA ARTISTS FILE II 1968–1972

RCONT1 SCRIPTWRITER BECKETT, SAMUEL File I 1953–62

British Library Sound Archive, London: recordings of music and BBC radio
  programmes involving John Beckett as musician, composer and presenter,
  including records and BBC radio programmes of music performed by Musica
  Reservata, summaries of which can be viewed on the online British Library Sound
  Archive catalogue

Cathal Gannon file, GDB/C004.04/0018 (1963–1969), Guinness Archives,
  Diageo Ireland

Connacht Sentinel, 1974, online digital archive

Connacht Tribune, 1952–3, 1974, online digital archive

Cox, Gareth, Klein, Axel, Taylor, Michael (editors), *The Life and Music of Brian Boydell*
  (Dublin: Irish Academic Press 2004)

Craig, Dow Fehsenfeld, Gunn and More Overbeck (editors), *The Letters of Samuel
  Beckett 1941–1956* (Volume II) (Cambridge: Cambridge University Press 2011)

Craig, Dow Fehsenfeld, Gunn and More Overbeck (eds), *The Letters of Samuel Beckett
  1957–1965* (Volume III) (Cambridge: Cambridge University Press 2014)

Cronin, Anthony, *Dead as Doornails* (Dublin: The Lilliput Press 1999)

Cronin, Anthony, *Samuel Beckett – The Last Modernist* (London: HarperCollins
  Publishers 1996)

Daily Telegraph, 1967–9, 2006, King's College London

Early Music magazine: articles on Musica Reservata (Vol. 4, No. 4, October 1976),
  Michael Morrow (Vol. 6, No. 2, April 1978) and Michael Morrow obituary (Vol.
  22, No. 3, August 1994).

Early Music Review, 2007

Evening Herald, 1965, ?1979

Evening Mail, 1944

Fitz-Simon, Christopher, *Eleven Houses – A Memoir of Childhood* (Dublin: Penguin
  Ireland 2007)

Gannon, Charles, Diaries (1970–1999, unpublished)

Gannon, Charles, *Cathal Gannon – The Life and Times of a Dublin Craftsman* (Dublin:
  Lilliput Press 2006)

General Registrar Office, Dublin: records of births, marriages and deaths

Grove, George, *The New Grove Dictionary of Music and Musicians*, Stanley Sadie (ed.)
  (London: Macmillan 1980) (reprinted 1986)

Harmon, Maurice (ed.), *No Author Better Served – The correspondence of Samuel Beckett
  and Alan Schneider* (Cambridge: Harvard University Press 1999)

Higgins, Aidan, *Dog Days – A Sequel to Donkey's Years* (London: Secker & Warburg 1998)

Higgins, Aidan, *Donkey's Years – Memories of a life as story told* (London: Minerva 1996)

Irish Independent, 1946–59, online digital archive

Irish Press, 1946–65, online digital archive

Journal of the Viola da Gamba Society, Vol. 30 (2002), online digital archive

King's College, London College Archives: Morrow, Michael (1929–94) and Musica
   Reservata, GB 0100 KCLCA K/PP93 (13 boxes)
      Box 3: Correspondence re Musica Reservata
      Box 7: Musica Reservata programmes
      Box 10: Advertising leaflets
      Box 12: Press cuttings, etc., re Reservata concerts
      Box 13: Photographs and posters

Knowlson, James, *Damned to Fame – The Life of Samuel Beckett* (London: Bloomsbury 1996)

Knowlson, James and Elizabeth (eds), *Beckett Remembering Remembering Beckett*
   (London: Bloomsbury 2006)

Lynott, Ray, *Oenone* (an Appreciation of Venetia O'Sullivan), October 2008

Mansfield, Charles, *The Aravon Story,* Aravon School booklet

Music and Musicians, 1967–70, bound volumes, British Library, St Pancras, London

Musical Times, 1968–9, 1973, King's College London

Musica Reservata concert programmes belonging to Seán O'Leary and
   Jantina Noorman

National Library of Ireland, Manuscripts Department: Charles Acton Papers, Acc
   6787, Box 17, 19 and 21; Papers of James Plunkett, Acc 4540 and 6156: John
   Beckett MS 40,853: 1956–1997, Ralph Cusack and family MS 40,856: 1954–1969,
   Aidan Higgins MS 40,859: 1971, John O'Donovan MS 40,878: 1940–80

New Statesman, 1968, King's College London

O'Brien, Eoin, *The Beckett Country* (Dublin: The Black Cat Press / Faber and Faber 1986)

O'Kelly, Pat: original material used for *An Appreciation: John O'Sullivan*, *Ir. Times*,
   18 April 2006, p. 15

O'Sullivan, Michael, *Brendan Behan – A Life* (Dublin: Blackwater Press 1997)

Pine, Richard, *Music and Broadcasting in Ireland* (Dublin: Four Courts Press 2005)

Radio Times, 1955–1999, on microfilm, microfiche and in bound volumes at the British
   Library Newspapers Department, Colindale, London; also online digital archive

Records and Recordings, 1967–71, bound volumes, British Library, St Pancras, London

Roberge, Pierre-F. and Stringer, John: *Musica Reservata Discography,* online at http://
   www.medieval.org/emfaq/performers/reservata.html

Royal Academy of Music, London: Michael Morrow papers (uncatalogued)

Royal College of Music, London: assorted records

RTÉ Document Archives, Dublin: Correspondence with John Beckett, 1950–54

RTV / RTÉ Guide, 1961–90, RTÉ in-house digital archive

Schürmann, Werner: letters to the author, 2002

Sowby, David, *Memories of Aravon 1936–40*, privately produced document, 2004

Spectator, 1968, King's College London

Swann, Margaret, *Arts and Society in Britain since the Thirties – Aspect of and reasons for
   the proliferation of "Early Music groups"* (thesis, 1983)

The Columban, 1940–47, Aravon School monthly magazine

The Financial Times, 1967–73, King's College London and online digital archive

The Gramophone, 1967–74, online digital archive

The Guardian, 1965–2008, online digital archive

The Independent, 2003–8, online digital archive

The Irish Times, 1922–2006, online digital archive

The Listener, 1968, King's College London, online digital archive

The Recorder Magazine, 2007, online digital archive

The Telegraph, 1969, King's College London

The Times, 1957–85, online digital archive

Thomson, J.M.; Sothcott, John; Fallows, David; Page, Christopher: Obituaries: Michael Morrow, 1929–94, *Early Music,* Vol. 22, No. 3 (August 1994), pp. 537–539

Trinity College Dublin, Manuscripts Library: Brian Boydell Scrapbooks, TCD 1128/4/1, 2, 3 and 4, and Letters from Aidan Higgins to Arland (Percy) Ussher, TCD MS 9301–41/1465–1584

SECONDARY SOURCES

Anderson, Nicholas, *Baroque Music —From Monteverdi to Handel* (London: Thames and Hudson 1994)

Beckett, Samuel, *The Complete Dramatic Works* (London: Faber and Faber 2006)

Boylan, Henry, *A Dictionary of Irish Biography*, *Third Edition* (Dublin: Gill and Macmillan Ltd 1998)

Browne, Noël, *Against The Tide* (Dublin: Gill and Macmillan 1986)

Carr, Jonathan, *The Real Mahler* (London: Constable 1997)

Cusack, Ralph, *Cadenza* (Illinois: Dalkey Archive Press 1984)

Donleavy, J.P., *The History of the Ginger Man* (London: Viking 1994)

Donleavy, J.P., *The Ginger Man* (London: Abacus 2002)

White, Harry and Boydell, Barra (general eds.), *The Encyclopaedia of Music in Ireland* (Dublin: University College Dublin Press 2013)

Gorham, Maurice, *Forty Years of Irish Broadcasting* (Dublin: The Talbot Press Ltd 1967)

Hilda Roberts HRHA 1901–1982, A Retrospective Exhibition, Bicentenary Committee of Newtown School, Waterford, 1998

Hughes, Rosemary, *The Master Musicians series: Haydn* (London: J.M. Dent & Sons Ltd 1974)

Huizinga, Johan, *The Waning of the Middle Ages* (London: Penguin Books 1976)

Levi, Primo, *If This is a Man / The Truce* (London: Abacus 2004)

Levi, Primo, *Moments of Reprieve* (London: Penguin Books 2002)

Mann, Thomas, *The Magic Mountain*, translated by John E. Woods (London: Everyman's Library 2005)

Mansfield, Charles, *The Aravon Story*, Aravon School booklet

Monsaingeon, Bruno, *Madamoiselle: Conversations with Nadia Boulanger* (Manchester: Carcanet Press 1985)

Moore, Walter, *Schrödinger – Life and Thought* (Cambridge: Cambridge University Press 1993)

Munrow, David, *Instruments of the Middle Ages and Renaissance* (Oxford: Oxford University Press 1976)

O'Brien, Eoin, *The Beckett Country* (Dublin: The Black Cat Press 1986)

O'Kelly, Pat, *The National Symphony Orchestra of Ireland 1948–1998 – a selected history*, Radio Telefís Éireann, 1998

Pine, Richard, *Charles – The Life and World of Charles Acton, 1914–1999* (Dublin: The Lilliput Press 2010)

Pine, Richard and Acton, Charles (eds.), *To Talent Alone – The Royal Irish Academy of Music, 1848–1998* (Dublin: Gill and Macmillan 1998)

Skelton, Robin (ed.), J.M. Synge, *Collected Works – Poems* (Oxford: Oxford University Press 1962)

Snoddy, Theo, *Dictionary of Irish Artists – 20th Century* (Dublin: Wolfhound Press 1996)

Stagles, Joan and Ray, *The Blasket Islands – Next Parish America* (Dublin: O'Brien Press 1984)

Stewart, Ann M. (compiler), *Royal Hibernian Academy of Arts, Index of Exhibitions 1826– 1979*, Vol. III, N–Z (Manton Publishing 1987)

Thom's Directory, 1943

Tyler, John E., *Black Forest Clocks* (London: N.A.G. Press 1977)

Various contributors: *Irish Women Artists – From the Eighteenth Century to the Present Day*, The National Gallery of Ireland, The Douglas Hyde Gallery, 1987

Walsh, John, *Collen – 200 Years of Building and Civil Engineering in Ireland* (Dublin: The Lilliput Press 2010)

Index